Hilliard Branch
15821 CR 108
Hilliard, FL 32046

THIS EDITION WRITTEN AND RESEARCHED BY

**Mark Baker**
Marc Di Duca, Tim Richards

# welcome to Poland

## A Thousand Years

Poland's roots go back to the turn of the first millennium, leaving a thousand years of twists and turns and kings and castles to explore. History buffs of the WWII vintage are well served. Tragically, Poland found itself in the middle of that epic fight, and monuments and museums dedicated to its battles – and to Poland's remarkable survival – can be seen everywhere. There's a growing appreciation, too, of the country's rich Jewish heritage. Beyond the deeply affecting Holocaust memorials, synagogues are being sensitively restored, and former Jewish centres such as Łódź and Lublin have set up heritage trails so you can trace this history at your own pace.

## Castles to Log Cabins

The former royal capital of Kraków is a living lab of architecture over the ages. Its nearly perfectly preserved Gothic core proudly wears overlays of Renaissance, Baroque and Art Nouveau, a record of tastes that evolved over the centuries. Fabulous medieval castles and evocative ruins dot hilltops elsewhere in the country, and the fantastic red-brick fortresses of the Teutonic Knights stand proudly in the north along the Vistula. At the other extreme, simple but finely crafted wooden churches hide amid the Carpathian hills, and the ample skills of the country's highlanders are on display at the region's many skansens (open-air ethnographic museums).

*Chic medieval hot spots like Kraków and Gdańsk vie with energetic Warsaw for your urban attention. Outside the cities, woods, rivers, lakes and hills beckon for some fresh-air fun.*

(left) Kluszkowce, Carpathian Mountains (p185)
(below) Savoury items for sale, Kraków (p112)

## Heart-Warming Food

If you're partial to good home cooking, the way your grandmother used to make it, you've come to the right place. Polish food is based largely on local ingredients like pork, cabbage, mushroom, beetroot and onion, combined simply and honed to perfection. Regional specialities like duck, goose, herring and even bison keep things from getting dull. As for sweets, it's hard to imagine a more accommodating destination. Cream cakes, apple strudel, pancakes, fruit-filled dumplings and a special national mania for *lody* (ice cream) may have you skipping the main course and jumping straight to the main event.

## Fresh-Air Pursuits

Away from the big cities, much of Poland feels remote and unspoiled. While large swathes of the country are flat, the southern border is lined with a chain of low-lying but lovely mountains that invite days if not weeks of splendid solitude. Well-marked hiking paths criss-cross the country, taking you through dense forest, along broad rivers and through mountain passes. Much of the northeast is covered by interlinked lakes and waterways that are ideal for kayaking and canoeing – no experience necessary. Local outfitters are happy to set you up for a couple of hours or weeks.

# ❯ Poland

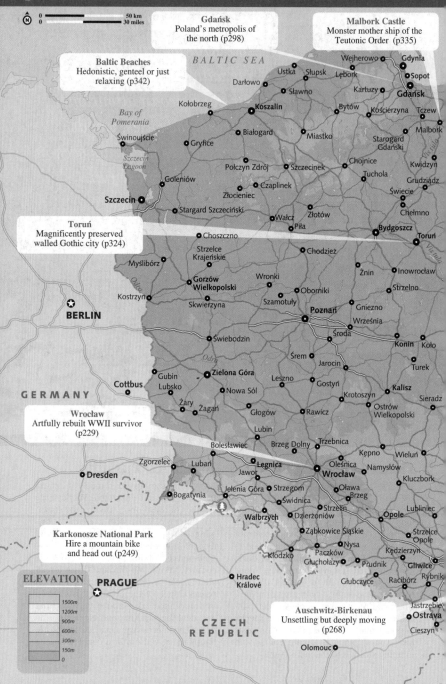

**Gdańsk**
Poland's metropolis of
the north (p298)

**Malbork Castle**
Monster mother ship of the
Teutonic Order (p335)

**Baltic Beaches**
Hedonistic, genteel or just
relaxing (p342)

BALTIC SEA

**Toruń**
Magnificently preserved
walled Gothic city (p324)

**Wrocław**
Artfully rebuilt WWII survivor
(p229)

**Karkonosze National Park**
Hire a mountain bike
and head out (p249)

**Auschwitz-Birkenau**
Unsettling but deeply moving
(p268)

ELEVATION

GERMANY

BERLIN

CZECH
REPUBLIC

PRAGUE

## Map labels

Wejherowo, Gdynia, Sopot, Gdańsk, Ustka, Słupsk, Lębork, Kartuzy, Darłowo, Sławno, Kościerzyna, Tczew, Kołobrzeg, Koszalin, Bytów, Malbork, Białogard, Miastko, Starogard Gdański, Gryfice, Chojnice, Kwidzyn, Świnoujście, Szczecinek, Tuchola, Grudziądz, Goleniów, Połczyn Zdrój, Świecie, Złocieniec, Czaplinek, Chełmno, Szczecin, Wałcz, Złotów, Bydgoszcz, Toruń, Stargard Szczeciński, Piła, Choszczno, Chodzież, Strzelce Krajeńskie, Myślibórz, Żnin, Inowrocław, Gorzów Wielkopolski, Wronki, Oborniki, Strzelno, Kostrzyn, Skwierzyna, Szamotuły, Poznań, Gniezno, Berlin, Września, Świebodzin, Środa, Konin, Koło, Śrem, Jarocin, Turek, Zielona Góra, Leszno, Gostyń, Kalisz, Gubin, Lubsko, Nowa Sól, Krotoszyn, Ostrów Wielkopolski, Sieradz, Cottbus, Żary, Żagań, Głogów, Rawicz, Lubin, Lubin, Brzeg Dolny, Trzebnica, Kępno, Wieluń, Bolesławiec, Oleśnica, Namysłów, Zgorzelec, Lubań, Legnica, Wrocław, Kluczbork, Jawor, Dresden, Jelenia Góra, Strzegom, Oława, Brzeg, Opole, Bogatynia, Świdnica, Strzelin, Lubliniec, Wałbrzych, Dzierżoniów, Strzelce Opole, Ząbkowice Śląskie, Nysa, Kędzierzyn, Gliwice, Kłodzko, Paczków, Rybnik, Głuchołazy, Prudnik, Racibórz, Głubczyce, Jastrzębie, Ostrava, Hradec Králové, Auschwitz-Birkenau, Cieszyn, Olomouc

0 ——— 50 km
0 ——— 30 miles

Bay of
Pomerania

Szczecin
Lagoon

Odra

Warta

Noteć

Wisła

1500m
1200m
900m
600m
300m
150m
0

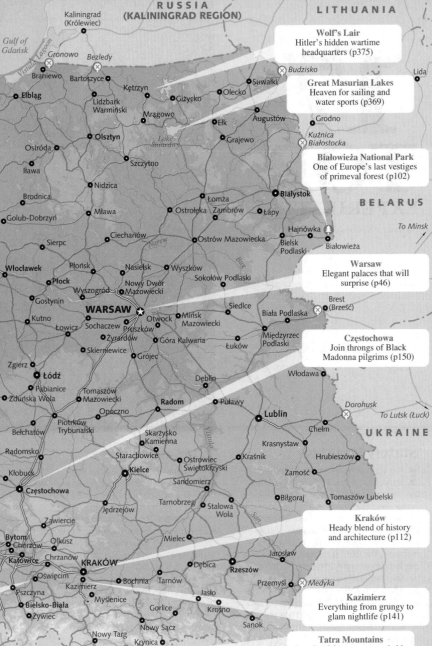

**Wolf's Lair**
Hitler's hidden wartime
headquarters (p375)

**Great Masurian Lakes**
Heaven for sailing and
water sports (p369)

**Białowieża National Park**
One of Europe's last vestiges
of primeval forest (p102)

**Warsaw**
Elegant palaces that will
surprise (p46)

**Częstochowa**
Join throngs of Black
Madonna pilgrims (p150)

**Kraków**
Heady blend of history
and architecture (p112)

**Kazimierz**
Everything from grungy to
glam nightlife (p141)

**Tatra Mountains**
Awe-inspiring yet approachable
peaks for hikers (p187)

# 17 TOP EXPERIENCES

## Stately Kraków

**1** A unique atmosphere wafts through the attractive streets and squares of this former royal capital, with its heady blend of history and harmonious architecture. From the vast Rynek Główny (p118), Europe's largest medieval market square, to the magnificent Wawel Castle (p112) on a hill above the Old Town, every part of the city is fascinating. Add to that the former Jewish district of Kazimierz (p124) and its scintillating nightlife (and then contrast it with the communist-era concrete structures of Nowa Huta) and it's easy to see why Kraków is an unmissable destination.

Rynek Główny, Kraków

## Warsaw's Palaces

**2** Images of elegant palaces don't immediately come to mind when thinking of Poland's capital. After all, the city was flattened by the Germans in WWII. But that's where Warsaw really surprises. From Łazienki Park's lovely 'Palace on the Water' (p59) to stately Wilanów Palace (p60), a veritable Varsovian version of Versailles on the city's outskirts, Warsaw sports an elegant side that people rarely see. And if size really does matter, there's that gargantuan Palace of Culture & Science right in the centre (p55).

Palace on the Water, Warsaw

### Gdańsk

**3** Colossal red-brick churches peer down on slender merchants' town-houses, wedged ornately between palaces that line wide, ancient thoroughfares and crooked medieval lanes. A cosmopolitan residue of art and artefact left behind by a rich maritime and trading past packs whole museums, and tourists from around the world compete with amber stalls and street performers for cobblestone space. This is Gdańsk (p298), a Baltic seaport and Poland's metropolis of the north. It was once part of the Hanseatic League, but now it's in a league of its own.

### Wrocław

**4** Throughout its turbulent history, this city (p229) on the Odra River – the former German city of Breslau – has taken everything invaders could throw at it, and survived. Badly damaged in WWII, it was artfully rebuilt around its beautiful main square, with an intriguing complex of buildings at its centre. Another attraction is the Panorama of Racławice, a vast 19th-century painting hung about the walls of a circular building. Beyond historical gems, however, Wrocław has a vibrant night-life, with plenty of dining and drinking options throughout the narrow streets of its lively Old Town.

### Great Masurian Lakes

**5** Sip a cocktail on the deck of a luxury yacht, take a dip, or don a lifejacket, grab your paddle and slide off into a watery adventure on one of the interconnected lakes (p369) that make up this mecca for Polish sailing and water-sports fans. Away from the water, head for one of the region's buzzing resorts, where the slap and jangle of masts competes with the clinking of glasses and the murmur of boat talk. In winter, when the lakes freeze over, cross-country skis replace water skis on the steel-hard surface.

## Baltic Beaches

**6** The season may be brief and the sea one of Europe's nippiest, but if you're looking for a dose of sand, there are few better destinations than the Baltic's cream-white beaches (p342). Many people come for the strands along one of the many coastal resorts, be it hedonistic Darłówko, genteel Świnoujście or the spa town of Kołobrzeg; others opt to flee the masses and head out instead for the shifting dunes of the Słowiński National Park, where the Baltic's constant bluster sculpts mountains of sifted grains. Świnoujście beach

## Malbork Castle

**7** Medieval monster mother ship of the Teutonic order, Gothic blockbuster Malbork Castle (p335) is a mountain of bricks held together by a lake of mortar. It was home to the all-powerful order's grand master and later to visiting Polish monarchs. They have all now left the stage of history, but not even the shells of WWII could dismantle this baby. If you came to Poland to see castles, this is what you came to see; catch it just before dusk when the slanting sunlight burns the bricks kiln-crimson.

## Wolf's Lair

**8** The Wolf's Lair, Hitler's headquarters during WWII, was so well designed that the Allies had no idea it existed until it was overrun by the Red Army in 1945. They might not have needed to had one of Hitler's own men, Colonel Claus von Stauffenberg, been more successful in his bid to assassinate the Führer here six months earlier. The ramshackle location, rapidly being reclaimed by nature, takes a little imagination to appreciate fully, but it's still one of Poland's most fascinating WWII heritage sites and marks a significant chunk of 20th-century history (see boxed text, p375).

## Gothic Toruń

**9** While many of northern Poland's towns went up in a puff of red-brick dust in WWII's end game, Toruń (p324) miraculously escaped intact, leaving today's visitors a magnificently preserved, walled Gothic city by the swirling Vistula. Wander through the old town crammed with museums, churches, grand mansions and squares, and when you're all in, perk up with a peppery gingerbread cookie, Toruń's signature snack. Another treat is the city's Copernicus connections – Poland's most illustrious astronomer allegedly first saw the light of day in one of Toruń's Gothic townhouses.

## Folk Architecture

**10** If the word 'skansen', referring to an open-air museum of folk architecture, isn't a regular part of your vocabulary yet, it will be after your trip to Poland. These great gardens of log cabins and timbered chalets make for a wonderful ramble and are a testament to centuries of peasant life in Poland. You'll find what's reputed to be the country's biggest skansen in Sanok (p204), in the Carpathians, but there are open-air museums around the country. As well as the museums, you'll find remnants of old wooden churches and other buildings sprinkled throughout the mountains.
Wooden church, Ojców National Park

## Black Madonna Pilgrimage

**11** In many parts of Europe, religious buildings are often little more than historical sights or curiosities. It's refreshing, then, in Poland to find churches and monasteries that still feel lived in, and an integral part of everyday life. Nowhere is this more apparent than at the Jasna Góra monastery in Częstochowa (p151). To see what we mean, pay a visit on 15 August, when the Feast of the Assumption draws hundreds of thousands of pilgrims to this relatively small city.

## Sampling Vodka

**12** For most Poles, the day-to-day tipple of choice is beer. But when it comes time to celebrate, someone's bound to break out the vodka. And once that bottle is on the table, you can put to rest any notion about having a convivial cocktail. No one leaves until the bottle is finished. Poles make some of the world's best versions of the stuff and are not afraid to experiment. Proof of this: Żubrówka ('bison vodka') is flavoured with grass from the Białowieża Forest on which bison feed.

## Białowieża Forest

**13** That bison on the label of a bottle of Żubr beer starts to make a lot more sense once you've visited this little piece of pristine wood on the Belarus border. The Białowieża National Park (p102) holds one of Europe's last vestiges of primeval forest, which you can visit in the company of a guide. Nearby there's a small reserve with another survivor from a bygone era: the once-mighty European bison.

## Auschwitz-Birkenau

**14** This former extermination camp, established by the German military occupiers in 1941, is a grim reminder of a part of history's greatest genocide, the killing of more than a million people here in the pursuit of Nazi ideology. Now it's a museum and memorial to the victims (p268). Beyond the infamous 'Arbeit Macht Frei' sign at the entrance to Auschwitz are surviving prison blocks that house exhibitions as shocking as they are informative. Not far away, the former Birkenau camp holds the remnants of the gas chambers used for mass murder. Visiting the complex is an unsettling but deeply moving experience.

## Cycling in the Karkonosze

**15** Slung between Mt Wielki Szyszak (1509m) to the west, and Mt Śnieżka (1602m) to the east, the Karkonosze National Park (p249) is not only a treat for hikers. Through its leafy expanse are threaded 19 mountain-biking trails, covering some 450km, that are easily accessed from the mountain towns of Szklarska Poręba or Karpacz. Pick up a free bike-trail map from the tourist office, hire a bike and head on out through the trees, passing impressively lofty cliffs carved by ice-age glaciers.

## Nightlife in Kazimierz

**16** Once a lively blend of both Jewish and Christian cultures, the western half of Kazimierz (p141) has in recent years become one of Kraków's nightlife hubs. Hidden among its narrow streets and distressed facades are numerous small bars, ranging from grungy to glamorous. The centre of all this activity is Plac Nowy, a small, atmospheric square dominated by a circular central building that was once the quarter's meat market. If Kraków's Old Town is becoming a bit staid for your taste, a night in Kazimierz will revive your spirits.

## Hiking in the Tatras

**17** In many ways, the Tatras (p187) are the perfect mountain range: awe-inspiring yet approachable, with peaks that even ordinary folks – with a little bit of extra effort – can conquer. That doesn't diminish their impact, especially on a summer day when the clouds part to reveal the mountains' stern rocky visage climbing up over the dwarf pines below. The best approach to the peaks is from the Polish mountain resort of Zakopane.

E CHAMPELOVER/ALAMY ©

GKORDUS/DREAMSTIME ©

# need to know

## When to Go

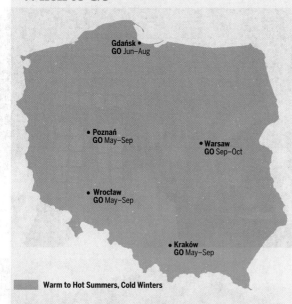

Gdańsk •
GO Jun–Aug

• Poznań
GO May–Sep

• Warsaw
GO Sep–Oct

• Wrocław
GO May–Sep

• Kraków
GO May–Sep

**Warm to Hot Summers, Cold Winters**

### High Season
(May–Sep)

» Expect sunny skies in June and July, but prepare for rain.

» Museums, national parks and other attractions are open for business.

» Prepare for crowds, especially at weekends.

### Shoulder
(Mar & Apr, Oct)

» Some attractions may be closed or have shorter hours.

» April and October are cool, but expect some sunny days.

» Easter weekend can be very crowded; book in advance.

### Low Season
(Nov–Feb)

» Snow in the mountains brings skiers to mountain resorts.

» The week between Christmas and New Year can be crowded.

» Museums and castles in smaller towns may be closed.

## Your Daily Budget

### Budget less than
# 140zł

» Hostel dorm room or low-cost guesthouse: 50zł

» Meals in milk bars and self-catering: 40zł

» Train/bus tickets: 30zł

» Sundries: 10zł

### Midrange
# 200– 240zł

» Room in a midrange hotel or pension: 100–120zł

» Lunch and dinner in decent restaurants: 60zł

» Train/bus tickets: 30zł

» Sundries: 15zł

### Top end over
# 350zł

» Room in the best place in town: 200zł

» Lunch and dinner in the best restaurants: 80zł

» Train/bus/taxi: 50zł

» Sundries: 20zł

## Money

» ATMs widely available. Credit cards accepted in most hotels and restaurants.

## Visas

» Generally not required for stays up to 90 days. Some nationalities will need a Schengen visa.

## Mobile Phones

» Local SIM cards can be used in European, Australian and some American phones. Other phones set to roaming.

## Transport

» Mostly trains for long-distance travel; buses and minibuses within regions.

## Websites

» **Lonely Planet** (www .lonelyplanet.com/ poland) Destination information, hotel bookings, traveller forum and more.

» **Polish National Tourist Office** (www .poland.travel) Official tourist site.

» **Experience Poland** (www.experience poland.com) Wide range of useful info.

» **New Poland Express** (www.newpoland express.pl) Overview of top news.

» **Warsaw Voice** (www .warsawvoice.pl) Covers Polish current affairs.

» **Warsaw Tourist Information** (www .warsawtour.pl) Official Warsaw tourist website.

## Exchange Rates

| Australia | A$1 | 3.12zł |
| --- | --- | --- |
| Canada | C$1 | 2.98zł |
| Europe | €1 | 4.15zł |
| Japan | ¥100 | 3.78zł |
| New Zealand | NZ$1 | 2.47zł |
| UK | £1 | 4.70zł |
| USA | US$1 | 2.90zł |

For current exchange rates, see www.xe.com.

## Important Numbers

When calling between cities, it's no longer necessary to first dial 0.

| Ambulance | ☏999 |
| --- | --- |
| Fire | ☏998 |
| Police | ☏997 |
| Emergency from mobile phone | ☏112 |
| Country code | ☏48 |

## Arriving in Poland

» **Warsaw: Frédéric Chopin Airport**
City bus – 2.80zł; bus 175 to the Old Town
Taxi – about 60zł; 20 minutes to the Old Town

» **Kraków: John Paul II Airport**
Train – 10zł; 18 minutes to Kraków Główny station
Taxi – about 80zł; 20 minutes to the Old Town

» **Gdańsk: Lech Wałęsa Airport**
Airport bus – 10zł; 35 minutes to the centre
City bus – 2.50zł; bus 110 to the suburb of Wrzeszcz
Taxi – about 70zł; 30 minutes to the centre

## Getting Around

While Poland has a decent rail system and a comprehensive bus network, don't underestimate the time you'll need to get from point A to point B. The trains can be agonisingly slow in practice, especially away from the main express lines that link the big cities. The speed of the buses is dependent on the country's highway network, and that remains a work in progress. This is especially true as Poland feverishly prepares to co-host – with Ukraine – the UEFA Euro 2012 football championship. As we were researching this guide, it seemed as if every highway in the country was being dug up, widened or resurfaced, and delays were the rule, not the exception. If you've got your own wheels, budget on two hours of driving time for every 100km.

# first time

*Everyone needs a helping hand when they visit a country for the first time. There are phrases to learn, customs to get used to and etiquette to understand. The following section will help demystify Poland so your first trip goes as smoothly as your fifth.*

## Language

It is perfectly possible to travel in Poland without speaking a word of Polish, particularly if you stick to the tourist spots like Kraków and Warsaw. But life will be a lot easier, particularly in rural areas and small towns, if you take time to master a few basic phrases, even if only 'hello', 'goodbye' and 'thanks'. See the Language section of this book (p432) for the phrases you'll need to get by.

## Booking Ahead

Reserving a room, even if only for the first night, is the best way to ensure a smooth start to your trip. While, admittedly, you're un-likely to have to speak Polish on the phone with a hotel receptionist (particularly if the hotel is used to dealing with foreign visitors), the following phrases should see you through if English isn't spoken.

| Hello. | Cześć. | cheshch |
|---|---|---|
| I would like to book a room. | Chcę zarezerwować pokój. | khtse za·re·zer·vo·vach po·kooy |
| My name is... | Nazywam się... | na·zi·vam shye... |
| from... to... (date) | Od... do... | od... do... |
| How much is it...? | Ile kosztuje...? | ee·le kosh·too·ye... |
| per night | za noc | za nots |
| per person | za osobę | za o·so·be |
| Thank you (very much). | Dziękuję (bardzo). | jyen·koo·ye (bar·dzo) |

## What to Wear

Poland is not a particularly style-conscious destination, though there are some undeniably trendy places in Warsaw, Kraków and Gdańsk. For most occasions, casual dress – shorts, tees and jeans – is sufficient. One exception to this would be visiting churches, where more modesty (trousers for guys and covered shoulders and longer skirts or trousers for women) is called for. For dinner at a table-cloth place or at a more formal concert or opera, a sports coat and trousers (as opposed to jeans) is usually a good choice for men, and a dress or skirt for women. A waterproof coat and sturdy shoes are a good idea in any season.

## What to Pack

» Passport
» Wallet
» Debit/credit card
» Driving licence
» Phrasebook
» Mobile phone charger
» Standard European plug converter (two round pins)
» Prescription drugs
» Sat-nav device (if renting a car)
» Clothes
» Earplugs
» Eye mask
» Mosquito repellent
» Toiletries
» Sunscreen
» Sun hat and shades
» Tissues
» Umbrella
» Padlock
» Pen
» Something to read

## Checklist

» Check the validity of your passport

» Make any necessary bookings (for sights, accommodation and travel)

» Check the airline's baggage restrictions

» Inform your credit/debit card company

» Organise travel insurance (see p418)

» Check if you can use your mobile/cell phone (see p420)

» Find out what you need to hire a car (see p426)

## Etiquette

There's a polite formality built into the Polish language that governs most interactions between people, though the rules are normally suspended for foreigners who *don't* speak Polish.

### » Greetings
It's customary to greet people, including shopkeepers, on entering with a friendly *dzień dobry* (jyen do·bri; good day). On leaving, part with a hearty *do widzenia* (do vee·dze·nya; goodbye).

### » Religion
Treat churches and monasteries with respect and keep conversation to a minimum. It's always best to wear proper attire, including trousers for men and covered shoulders and longer skirts (no short shorts) for women. Refrain from flash photography and remember to leave a small donation in the box by the door.

### » Eating & Drinking
When raising a glass, greet your Polish friends with *na zdrowie* (nah zdroh·vee·ya; cheers)! Before tucking into your food, wish everyone *smacznego* (smach·neh·go; bon appetit)! End the meal by saying *dziękuję* (jyen·koo·ye; thank you).

## Tipping

### » When to tip
Customary in restaurants and at service establishments, such as hairdressers; optional everywhere else.

### » Restaurants
At smaller establishments and for smaller tabs, round the bill to the nearest 5zł or 10zł increment. Otherwise, 10% is standard.

### » Taxis
No need to tip, though you may want to round up the fare to reward good service.

## Money

ATMs are ubiquitous in cities and towns, and even the smallest hamlet is likely to have at least one. The majority accept Visa and MasterCard. Change money at banks or, more commonly, *kantors* (private currency-exchange offices). You can find these in town centres as well as travel agencies, train stations, post offices and department stores. Rates vary, so it's best to shop around. The easiest way to carry money is in the form of a debit card, withdrawing cash as needed from an ATM; check with your home bank about transaction fees and withdrawal limits. Visa and MasterCard are widely accepted for goods and services. The only places you may experience problems are very small establishments. American Express cards are typically accepted at larger hotels and restaurants, though they are not as widely recognised as other cards.

# if you like...

## Castles

If there's a hilltop, you can bet there's a castle. Poland has some humdingers: everything from aristocratic, 19th-century piles to more sombre – and often more elegant – ruins, still standing watch from the Middle Ages.

**Wawel** The granddaddy of them all, the mighty Kraków castle is the symbol of the Polish nation and its continuity (p115)

**Malbork** It took a zillion red bricks to build Europe's biggest medieval fortress, from where the Teutonic Knights lorded it over Poland's north (p335)

**Książ** Silesia's largest castle is a splendid edifice that holds a curious wartime secret beneath its foundations (p244)

**Krzyżtopór** What you get when you cross magic, money and a 17th-century Polish eccentric (p162)

**Krasiczyn** A picture of Renaissance perfection and the turreted castle of your childhood fairy-tale fantasy (p203)

**Lidzbark Warmiński** Follow the red-brick road to this blockbuster castle, built for the all-powerful Warmian bishops (p368)

## Museums

Whether it's art, history, folk architecture or science, Poles are collectors at heart. Warsaw and Kraków in particular have some world-class collections.

**Schindler's Factory** This evocative museum within Oskar Schindler's former wartime factory tells the story of Kraków under German occupation in WWII (p127)

**Rynek Underground** This fascinating new museum lies beneath Kraków's vast market square and uses audiovisual wizardry to illuminate the city's trading history (p118)

**Central Maritime Museum** If maritime flotsam and jetsam float your boat, you'll love this museum in Gdańsk, which lets you walk around a real ship docked on the river (p303)

**Frédéric Chopin Museum** A high-tech, interactive homage to Poland's greatest composer (p54)

**Płock** If too much Baroque is getting you down, check out this stunning collection of Art Nouveau and Art Deco decorative arts and furniture (p91)

**Roads to Freedom Exhibition** If you want to see who knocked over the first domino in the fall of communism, this superb exhibition has the scoop (p309)

## Communist Architecture

From the stern socialist-realist buildings of the 1950s to the wacky retro-futurist '60s and '70s, there's no denying 40 years of communist rule made a mark on the country's built environment.

**Kielce Bus Station** Check out this flash, *Jetsons*-style bus station in a country where a handsome bus station is, admittedly, hard to find (p158)

**Palace of Culture & Science** Stalin's 'gift' to the Polish people continues to shock and awe (p55)

**Nowa Huta** This sprawling 1950s suburb of concrete and blocky buildings makes a startling contrast to Kraków's Old Town (p129)

**Monument to the Victims of June 1956** This dramatic monument to the Poznań workers killed in a brutal crackdown was unveiled in the communist regime's final decade (p275)

**Katowice** Check out the industrial hub's 1970s-style Rynek, then cast your glance northward to the monolithic Hotel Katowice (p263)

WITOLD SKRYPCZAK/LONELY PLANET IMAGES ©

» Książ Castle (p244), near Świdnica

# Hiking

With everything from mountain treks to traversing a farmer's field, Poland is criss-crossed by thousands of kilometres of marked hiking trails. Put on your hiking boots, pick up a map and start walking.

**Zakopane** Just outside the door of your hotel you'll find Poland's highest and most dramatic walks in the Tatras (p187)

**Bieszczady** Green, clean and remote. This little corner wedged between Ukraine and Slovakia is as close to the end of the world as it gets in Poland (p204)

**Karkonosze National Park** Hike the ridge between Mt Szrenica and Mt Śnieżka in this Silesian national park for views of forests and mighty cliffs (p249)

**Góry Stołowe** Explore the strange and fascinating rock formations of this national park within the Sudetes Mountains (p256)

**Wolin National Park** Trails running through here provide hiking happiness for a day or two in the bracing Baltic air (p352)

# Nightlife

Poles love to party. In the summer, town squares across the country are filled with tables and late-night revellers. Big cities offer everything from theatre and classical music to raucous bars and hipster clubs.

**Praga** Warsaw's 'right bank' is where the city goes to let down its hair. We plan out a gritty Praga pub crawl on p71

**Łódź** Poland's post-industrial metropolis boasts a party strip, ul Piotrkowska, that's nearly 5km long (p87)

**Kazimierz** The western half of this Kraków district is home to a plethora of cool, small bars, tucked away behind attractive old facades in narrow streets (p141)

**Poznań** A magnet for both international business people and local students, the city's Old Town is packed with lively pubs, clubs and eateries (p282)

**Sopot** Get down by the Baltic as the fun spills out of Sopot's many nightspots and onto the balmy beach (p317)

# Folk Culture

Interest in folkways is growing. Skansens (open-air ethnographic museums) dot the landscape and the summer calendar is filled with folk-music fests. There's a *karczma* (traditional inn) in every town, even if it's just a few years old.

**Sanok** The open-air folk museum here is the biggest in the country. Tour it in a horse-drawn cart (p204)

**Tarnów** The regional museum here specialises in the folk history of the misunderstood minority Roma people (p194)

**Katowice** This industrial centre isn't the obvious place to find a skansen, but the Upper Silesian Ethnographic Park is spread over 20 hectares of city parkland (p264)

**Kazimierz** The Ethnographic Museum in this Kraków district is a great place to introduce yourself to Poland's folk costume and culture (p124)

**Kashubia** This traditional region of drowsy villages and ethnographic museums provides folksy contrast to the brashness of the coast (p322)

**Olsztynek** Northeast Poland's best open-air museum teleports visitors back to a timber past (p365)

# month by month

## January

January normally starts with a bang at midnight and a weeklong whimper as the country sleeps off its New Year's Eve fun. Don't expect services to be fully restored until after the first week of the year.

### Kraków New Year

New Year's celebrations are held around the country with fireworks and drinking. In Kraków there's that and also a classier alternative: a New Year's concert at the Teatr im J Słowackiego.

### Head for the Hills

Poland's festival pulse is barely beating. A better idea is to head south for a bit of skiing. We've listed Zakopane's best slopes on p189.

## February

The winter ski season reaches its peak in Zakopane and other resorts. The crowds on slopes worsen about mid-month during winter break, when schoolkids get the week off.

### Shanties in Kraków

In case you were wondering, a 'shanty' is a traditional sailor's song. Kraków's held this international shanty fest (www.shanties.pl) since 1981 and it's still going strong – in spite of Kraków's landlocked locale!

## April

After a slow month in March, April begins to pick up with ever-lengthening days, budding trees, and warm, sunny afternoons that promise better days ahead. Easter is a big travel weekend.

### Easter & Beethoven

Easter weekend is celebrated around the country, usually with a big dinner and lots of drinking. The annual Easter Beethoven festival (www.beethoven.org.pl) in Warsaw brings two weeks of concerts over the holiday season.

### Cracovia Marathon

Kraków's marathon (www.cracoviamaraton.pl) has become an increasingly popular running event and now draws more than a thousand runners to its scenic course, which heads out from the Old Town.

## May

May finally brings the return of reliably decent weather, flowers in bloom, and the sound of happy students about to be freed from school. In Kraków, during Juvenalia the students actually take over the city (p133).

### Baltic Music

The Probaltica Music & Art Festival (www.probaltica.art.pl) in Toruń brings together traditional musicians from across the Baltic region.

### Sacral Music

Częstochowa is known as a Catholic pilgrimage site, but each May it shows off its ecumenical side with the 'Gaude Mater' Festival (www.gaudemater.pl), highlighting religious music from Christian, Jewish and Islamic faiths.

# June

**Summer starts to get rolling as the weather warms up and the kids get out of school. Festivals marking Corpus Christi (usually June, but sometimes May) can be raucous. The biggest is in Łowicz.**

 **Theatre in Poznań**

Poznań's Malta Festival (www.malta-festival.pl) is the country's biggest theatre and dramatic arts event. Expect a week of entertaining street theatre – and thousands of people competing for hotel rooms.

 **Jewish Culture Festival**

Kraków's Jewish Culture Festival (www.jewishfestival .pl) is one of the leading events of the year and ends with a grand open-air klezmer concert on ul Szeroka in Kazimierz.

# July

**July can be hot and sunny or cold and rainy, depending on your luck. Resorts are crowded, but not as bad as they will be in August. The festival season kicks into high gear.**

 **Klezmer on the River**

Kazimierz Dolny's Festival of Klezmer Music and Tradition (www.klezmerzy .pl), held in the second week of July to commemorate the town's Jewish heritage, is simply a blast.

 **Warsaw Street Art**

Warsaw's annual street arts festival (www.sztukaulicy.pl) brings five days of theatre, open-air art installations and 'happenings', staged in public places (p62).

# August

**It's the height of summer. Expect big crowds at the seashore as well as lake and mountain resorts, which only worsen at weekends. As compensation, you'll get sunshine, lots of festivals – and a *pierogi* (dumpling) fair in Kraków.**

 **Getting Down With Highlanders**

Zakopane's Festival of Mountain Folklore (www .zakopane.pl) draws high-landers (mountain folk) from around Europe and around the world for a week of music, dance and traditional costume.

 **Dominican Fair**

Gdańsk's biggest bash (www.mtgsa.pl) of the year has been held since 1260. Launched by Dominican monks as a feast day, the fun has spread to streets all around the Main Town (p311).

# September

**The first nip of autumn arrives early in the month as kids return to school and life returns to normal. There's usually a long patch of sunshine in September, perfect to enjoy the crowd-free resorts.**

 **Wratislavia Cantans**

The unforgettably named Wratislavia Cantans (www .wratislaviacantans.pl) is Wrocław's top music and fine arts confab. The focus is on sacral music but given a high-brow twist.

 **Four Cultures**

Each year, Łódź celebrates its historic role as a meeting place of Polish, Jewish, Russian and German cultures with this suitably named festival (www.4kultury.pl). There's theatre, music, film and dialogue.

# October

**The tourist season is officially over, and castles and museums revert to winter hours or fall into a deep slumber. City dwellers turn to jazz festivals to forget the coming winter.**

 **Warsaw Reeling**

The Warsaw International Film Festival (www .wff.pl) highlights the world's best films over 10 days in October. There are screenings of the best Polish films and plenty of retrospectives.

# November

**The first significant snowfalls begin in the mountains, though the ski season doesn't begin in earnest until December. Elsewhere around the country, brisk temps and darkening afternoons herald the coming of winter.**

### ⭐ All Souls' Jazz

Cracovians fight the onset of the winter blues with this week-long jazz festival that commences every year around All Souls' Day (2 November). Look for performances all over town, in clubs, bars and even churches.

### ⭐ Hot Cross Buns

Polish Independence Day falls on 11 November, but in Poznań it's also St Martin's Day, a day of parades and general merriment. The real treat, though, is the baking and eating of special St Martin's Day bread rolls.

# December

**The air turns frosty and ski season in the south begins around the middle of the month. The only thing keeping people going, amid the grey skies, is the coming Christmas and New Year holidays.**

### 🔒 Capital Christmas Market

Christmas markets are found around the country, but arguably the most evocative is in Warsaw's Old Town. A Christmas tree brightens Castle Sq (Plac Zamkowy) and market stalls, filled with mostly tat, spring up all around.

### ◉ Kraków Christmas Cribs

December kicks off an unusual contest to see who can build the most amazing Christmas crèche. The *szopki* (Nativity scenes) are elaborate compositions in astonishing detail fashioned from cardboard, wood and tinfoil (p133).

# itineraries

*Whether you've got six days or 60, these itineraries provide the starting point for the trip of a lifetime. Want more inspiration? Head online to lonelyplanet .com/thorntree to chat with other travellers.*

One Week
## Essential Poland

> Poland's a big country with lots to see, so travellers with limited time will have to choose their destinations carefully. For first-time visitors, especially, the places to start are the capital, Warsaw, and the country's most popular city, Kraków. For a week tour, budget roughly three days in each, and a day for travel.

**Warsaw** is an eye-opener, a scintillating mix of postwar Soviet-style reconstruction and a lovingly restored Old Town, with Baroque and Renaissance architecture.

Leave at least a day for museum-hopping, particularly to the breathtaking **Warsaw Rising Museum** or newer attractions like the **Frédéric Chopin Museum** and the **Museum of the History of Polish Jews**.

From Warsaw, the former royal capital of **Kraków** is a 180-degree turn. If Warsaw is 'old overlaid on new', Kraków is new on top of ancient. Spend a day in the **Old Town** and **Wawel Castle**, a second day around the former Jewish ghetto of **Kazimierz** and the third day with a side trip to the **Wieliczka Salt Mine** (if you have kids in tow) or the **Auschwitz-Birkenau Memorial & Museum**.

# The Big Three: Kraków, Warsaw & Gdańsk

> This tour is similar to the 'Essential Poland' tour, but adds the ravishing Baltic port city of Gdańsk. Though the tour can be done in 10 days, adding extra days allows for more travel time (needed to bridge the long distances) and a chance to tack on some more day trips.

Allow at least four days for **Kraków**, one of the most perfectly preserved medieval cities in Europe. As with the 'Essential Poland' tour, spend the first day meandering around Kraków's delightful **Old Town**. Don't miss the new **Rynek Underground** museum and the chance to see a da Vinci masterpiece, *Lady with an Ermine*, at the **Czartoryski Museum**. The second day will be taken up with the sights of **Wawel Castle**. Spend the third day exploring the former Jewish ghetto of **Kazimierz**. For the last day, plan a side trip to either the **Wieliczka Salt Mine** or **Auschwitz-Birkenau**. If you have an extra day, consider the mountain resort of **Zakopane**, two hours away by bus.

Take the train to **Warsaw** and plan to stay put another three to four days. The extra day leaves more time to see the city's amazing museums, as well as to enjoy the sites of the **Old Town** and stroll down the elegant **ul Nowy Świat**. If you're up for a night of drinking, the gritty dive-bar hood of **Praga** beckons from across the Vistula. A more sedate pleasure involves a walk through lovely **Łazienki Park**. For day trips, consider **Wilanów Palace**, 6km south of the centre, or a full-day journey to the former Nazi-German extermination camp at **Treblinka**.

From Warsaw, take the train to **Gdańsk** and prepare to be dazzled by the stunningly restored **Main Town**, which, like Warsaw, was reduced to ruins in WWII. Proceed down the **Royal Way** and don't miss the **Amber Museum**. Then there's the waterfront district and pretty **ul Mariacka**.

If it's summer and you're lucky enough to get a warm day, spend your last full day on the water, either at the brash but popular beach resort of **Sopot**, or the quieter, more refined strand on the **Hel Peninsula**.

Four Weeks
# Along the Vistula

> The Vistula is Poland's greatest river, winding its way from the foothills of the country's southern mountain range to the Baltic Sea. It's played a key role in the country's very identity, as it passes through – or close to – many of Poland's oldest and most important settlements.

This tour is ideally suited to roaming, for visitors who are not on a strict timetable and are looking for an unusual approach to Poland's core. The four-week schedule assumes that you rely on buses (train services to many of these towns have been cut back in recent years). Naturally, if you have your own wheels, you could cover the terrain in three weeks or even less.

Begin upstream with two or three days at the former royal capital of **Kraków** and take a day tour to **Auschwitz-Birkenau** in Oświęcim. From Kraków, make your way by bus to beautiful **Sandomierz**, one of Poland's undiscovered gems, with its impressive architectural variety and position on a bluff overlooking the river. From here, it's worth taking a detour, again by bus, to the Renaissance masterpiece of **Zamość**, a nearly perfectly preserved 16th-century town.

Back on the path along the Vistula, stop in at the former artists colony – a now popular weekend retreat – of **Kazimierz Dolny**, before hitting **Warsaw** and indulging in its delights for a few days. Next, call in at **Płock**, Poland's art nouveau capital, then follow the river into Pomerania and through the heart of medieval **Toruń**, another nicely preserved Gothic town that also boasts being the birthplace of stargazer Nicolaus Copernicus.

Soon after Toruń, the river heads directly for the sea. In former times, the Vistula's path was guarded by one Teutonic Knight stronghold after another. Today, these Gothic gems silently watch the river pass by. You can see the Knights' handiwork at **Chełmno**, **Kwidzyn** and **Gniew**, but the mightiest example resides at **Malbork**, on the banks of one of the river's side arms. End your journey in the port city of **Gdańsk**, where the river meets the sea.

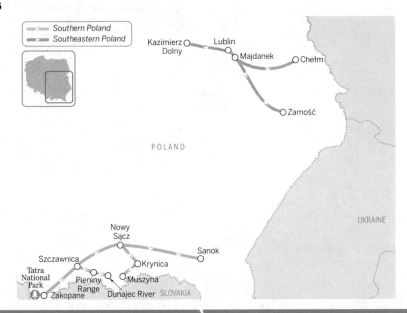

Southern Poland
Southeastern Poland

Kazimierz Dolny ○　Lublin ○
○ Majdanek
○ Chełm
○ Zamość

POLAND

UKRAINE

Nowy Sącz ○
Szczawnica ○　○ Krynica　　Sanok ○
Tatra National Park
Pieniny Range
○ Muszyna
Zakopane ○○　Dunajec River　SLOVAKIA

## One Week
# Southern Poland

Poland's southern border is lined with mountains end to end. This itinerary is ideal for walkers who want to escape the city. Though this trip can be done in a week, bus transport can be spotty in parts.

Start this journey in the mountain resort of **Zakopane**, which is easily reached by bus from Kraków. Reserve at least a day to see the town's historic wooden architecture and the **Museum of Zakopane Style**, and another for a walk into the **Tatras**. Allow more than a day if you want to do a longer trek.

From here you'll have to make some tough choices. We like the **Pieniny** range, east of the Tatras. The spa town of **Szczawnica** makes a good base for hikes, as well as biking and the ever-popular rafting ride down the **Dunajec River**.

From Szczawnica, the medium-sized city of **Nowy Sącz** offers urban comforts, or opt for **Krynica** or **Muszyna**, two popular spa resorts and good jumping off points for more hikes.

A long bus ride from Nowy Sącz brings you to **Sanok**, with its amazing skansen (open-air ethnographic museum) and access to the 70km **Icon Trail** and its wooden churches.

## One Week
# Southeastern Poland

The southeastern corner of the country is seldom explored and a good place to see the country off the beaten path. Begin in **Lublin**, whose Old Town has been much spruced up in recent years, with some great places to see and eat. Don't miss **Lublin Castle** or the chance to clamber up the **Trinitarian Tower** for a commanding view of the countryside. Spend a half-day at the enormous **Majdanek** concentration camp on the outskirts of the city.

Use Lublin as a base to explore nearby **Chełm**, which is best known for its kid-friendly underground **Chalk Tunnels**. It also has one of the best restaurants in the region, **Restauracja Gęsia Szyja**.

Lublin also makes a nice base for visiting the popular riverside artists' retreat at **Kazimierz Dolny**. The town is filled with museums and charming galleries, and the surrounding fields and forests make for a perfect day out on a bike or on foot.

From Lublin, head south to the self-proclaimed (with justification) 'Pearl of the Renaissance': **Zamość**. This is a perfectly preserved Renaissance town from the 16th century, with a lively central square that hosts concerts and music fests throughout the summer.

Map legend:
- Cities of the West
- Eastern Borderlands

## One Week
# Cities of the West

Western Poland is borderland territory, straddling a region hotly contested between Poland and Germany over the centuries. **Wrocław**, with its good transport connections, makes a logical start and merits at least two days. This was the former German city of Breslau, and the architecture retains a Germanic flavour with a Polish pulse. After WWII, Wrocław was repopulated by refugees from Poland's eastern lands lost to the Soviet Union, giving the city an added ethnic dimension.

From here make your way to **Poznań**, a thriving commercial hub with an intoxicating mix of business and pleasure, the latter fortified by a large student population. It was in Poznań that the Polish kingdom got its start a millennium ago.

After Poznań the beautifully preserved Gothic town of **Toruń** is a short bus or train ride away. It boasts enchanting red-brick architecture and gingerbread cookies.

Finish the tour in either **Gdańsk** or **Szczecin**, the latter adding a gritty contrast to the architectural beauty of the other cities.

## Three Weeks
# Eastern Borderlands

Poland's eastern border region feels especially remote. Indeed, this swath of natural splendour is largely cut off from the day-to-day goings on in the rest of Poland. This itinerary will appeal to wanderers who prefer the solitude of nature to the hustle-bustle of the big city.

The trip starts in **Kraków** for convenience sake, but make your way quickly to **Sanok**, with its skansen and icon museum, and then head deeper into the **Bieszczady National Park**. Turn north and take the back roads to the Renaissance town of **Zamość**, via **Przemyśl**. Continue on to **Chełm** to see the underground chalk tunnels and then to the big-city comforts of **Lublin**.

Strike out north through the rural backwaters to the **Białowieża National Park**, and its primeval forest and bison herd. Head north again to the provincial city of **Białystok** and to the tiny hamlet of **Tykocin**, with its unforgettable synagogue.

From here there's a wealth of parklands, including the **Biebrza** and **Wigry** national parks, with their endless hiking and kayaking possibilities. Head west for more boating in the **Great Masurian Lakes**.

# Outdoor Activities

## Best Hiking
Tatra Mountains, Pieniny Mountains, Bieszczady Mountains

## Best Kayaking
Krutynia River, the Drawa Route, the Brda River

## Best Cycling
**Mountain biking** Bieszczady Mountains, Sudetes Mountains
**Road cycling** Almost any rural area

## Best Skiing
Tatra Mountains, Sudetes Mountains

## Best Watersports
Great Masurian Lakes, Augustów Canal and around

## Best Time to Go
**Summer (June to August)** The best time for walking, cycling, kayaking
**Late spring (May) and early autumn (September)** The months either side of summer can be sunny and the trails, lakes and waterways less frequented
**Winter (November to March)** The best time for skiing and snowboarding in the mountain ranges of the south

Poland is not widely known as a haven for adrenalin junkies, but perhaps it should be. What better way could there be to slow down, meet the locals and leave the beaten track far behind? Why experience Poland through the window of a train, pickled in a museum or through the lens of a camera when you can hire a bike, grab a paddle or put on a pair of walking boots and hit some fresh air?

## Then & Now

Poles have a tradition of outdoor fun going back to the 19th century, when the first walking trails were marked out through the mountain ranges in the south. Polish hikers and climbers can always be found in the world's mountaineering hotspots, and the country has financed many expeditions around the world, including to the Himalayas.

Foreign travellers started to get in on the action decades ago, but it's only since the fall of communism that Poland has been discovered as an outdoor destination. Tour operators are increasingly catering to the demands of adventurers from around the world, offering improving facilities and serving up a wider range of adrenalin hits.

## Cycling

Almost every region of Poland now has well-signposted cycling routes, from short and easy circuits to epic international routes.

## SAFE CYCLING

The following advice should see you and your two-wheeler safely through Poland:

» Where possible, stay on marked cycling trails; sharing national roads with Poland's erratic drivers can be a hair-raising experience.

» Motorists in Polish cities are rarely cycle-conscious, so don't expect too much consideration for your space and safety. Ride defensively.

» Even small towns have at least one cycle shop selling spare parts and offering a cheap repair service.

» Poland's roads, especially away from major routes, can be atrocious – watch out for wheel-swallowing potholes and uneven pavement along the road edges.

» Get the best lock you can and always use it, even when storing your bike in buildings and travelling on trains. Better to be safe than cycle-less.

» If in doubt, take your bike with you into your hotel room. Many hotels have specially locked storage rooms that can accommodate bikes, but some don't.

» Check that your accommodation is accessible by bike; some places may not be, owing to street layout, traffic density and road conditions.

» Drinking and cycling don't mix: you could end up in jail if you ride under the influence.

» Check out **Rowery** (www.rowery.org.pl/bicycles.htm) to find out more about the rules of the road for bicycles.

It's possible to restrict yourself to the flatter regions of the country and travel the rest by train, but if you're not deterred by gradients you can cycle some of the more riveting (and relatively unexplored) regions of the country. Maps showing cycling trails can be hard to source outside of Poland but tourist offices can normally supply good cartography. See p424 for practical information about cycling in Poland.

## Where to Cycle

Here's an overview of the best places to cycle in Poland.

### Carpathian Mountains

Some epic bicycle adventures are waiting in the Bieszczady ranges (p204). These tracks will roll you through a montage of deep forest green and rippling meadows, opening up intermittently to postcard-perfect natural and architectural panoramas. Part of the 70km Icon Trail near the town of Sanok is accessible to cyclists and rewards pedalling with views of old timber churches and castles. Sanok also lies astride the **Greenway Bicycle Trail** (Szlak Zielony Rower; www .zielonyrower.pl), a sprawling network of bike-friendly roads and pathways that cover hundreds of kilometres in Poland and extend to neighbouring Slovakia and Ukraine (p206).

The region around the Dunajec River in the Pieniny isn't just for rafting. Szczawnica, in particular, is a great cycling centre. It's the starting point for several rewarding rides and blessed with numerous bike-rental outfits. One of the region's best rides follows the Dunajec River for around 15km all the way to the Slovak town of Červený Kláštor (p223).

### Białowieża Forest

There are some enchanting routes (starting near the village of Białowieża) through the northern part of the Białowieża Forest and the large stretches of undisturbed woods that lie to the north and west of the park proper, including detours into parts of Białowieża National Park itself. Pick up a map from the park's information centre and head off (p104).

### The Northeast

Cycling in the Masuria region is also rewarding and pretty easy as the terrain is as flat as a board. The town of Węgorzewo on Lake Mamry is a convenient base to access 18 marked routes ranging from 25km to 109km circuits. The Augustów Forest and the areas around Suwałki are also great biking territories. You'll find a few bike rental outfits in Augustów (p106).

## CYCLING WEBSITES

The following websites may be useful for anyone planning a cycling holiday in Poland:

**Cycling Poland** (www.cyclingpoland.com) A well-run cycling-tour operator that caters for international tourists.

**Cyklotur** (www.cyklotur.com) Can help with parts and information.

**EuroVelo** (www.ecf.com) European Cyclists' Federation project to establish a 65,000km European Cycle Network throughout the continent. Five of the 12 proposed routes run through Poland.

**Zielony Rower** (www.zielonyrower.pl) Information about ecofriendly bike tours and tracks.

### Sudetes Mountains

The Sudetes are a jackpot for mountain bikers. Stretching to the Czech border, Karkonosze National Park (p249) offers myriad marked mountain-biking trails and is popular with Polish extreme-sports enthusiasts. Some of the trails now cross over into the Czech Republic.

## Cycling Tours

Most cyclists go it alone in Poland, but if you fancy joining an organised group, UK-based **Cycling Poland** (www.cyclingpoland .com) is the leading specialist company to contact. Otherwise you could try **Hooked On Cycling** (www.hookedoncycling.co.uk), which specialises in two-wheeled tours across Europe.

# Walking & Hiking

Poland's mountainous areas are a joy to explore on foot and attract thousands of hikers every year and in every season. There are around 2000km of walking trails sliced through the country's national parks and many are well marked and well equipped with shelters. Nature's repertoire of heights, gradients, climates and terrains is showcased in Poland: hiking options range from week-long treks for the hard-core hiker to hour-long rambles for the ascent-averse.

## Where to Walk & Hike

The southern mountain ranges are best for exhilarating high-altitude hikes, but low-level walks can be found across the country.

### Carpathian Mountains

The Tatra Mountains in the south are the most notable region for hiking Polish-style. The West and the High Tatras offer different scenery; the latter is more challenging and as a result more spectacular. One of the most popular climbs in the Tatras is Mt Giewont (1894m). The cross at the peak attracts many visitors, though the steep slopes deter some. For information on Mt Giewont and various other hikes in the Tatras, see the boxed text, p188.

The valleys around Zakopane (p187) offer walks of varying lengths for walkers of varying fitness levels (some take less than an hour). Similarly, trails around the nearby Pieniny (see boxed text, p225) and the Bieszczady (see the boxed text, p211) in the east offer exciting hiking experiences – even for those who prefer to stroll. Another great option is Beskid Sądecki (p217), which has convenient paths dotted with mountain hostels. Muszyna (p222) or Krynica (p219) are popular bases to access this region.

The lower Beskid Niski mountain range offers less arduous walks and less spectacular views; see the boxed text, p215, for more.

### Sudetes Mountains

The Karkonosze National Park (p249) offers a sterling sample of the Sudetes. The ancient and peculiar 'table top' rock formations of the Góry Stołowe (p256) mountains are among the highlights of the Sudetes. The area is easily accessed from the town of Szklarska Poręba (p249) at the base of Mt Szrenica (1362m), and there is a choice of walking trails from Karpacz (p251) to Mt Śnieżka (1602m). Further south, the village of Międzygórze is another well-kitted base for Sudetes sojourns. Tourist offices in the region stand ready to point you to suitable trails and mountain hostels.

## Other Regions

There are other tracks in the country that certainly deserve a day or two if you are in the vicinity.

The Augustów Forest in the Augustów-Suwałki Region has 55 lakes and many well-paved roads and dirt tracks. Diverse wildlife can be found in various stretches of the forest. There are numerous bays and peninsulas to explore around nearby Lake Wigry in the Wigry National Park (p110) and the 63-sq-km Suwałki Landscape Park (p111) offers drop-dead gorgeous views from its picturesque terrain.

There is also Kampinos National Park (p79) just outside of Warsaw, with its famed sand dunes, Wielkopolska National Park (p286) in Wielkopolska, and the compact Wolin National Park (p352) in northwest Poland.

The lowest mountain range in the country is in the Świętokrzyski National Park (p158) in Małopolska, near Kielce. There's a 17km walk here that takes you past an ancient

## POLAND'S NATIONAL PARKS

Poland has 23 national parks featuring a wide variety of landscapes – here we list the best 10 for outdoor activities. Check national park websites for more information on hiking and cycling routes. Things change, so ask in person before you assume any route is open.

| NATIONAL PARK | FEATURES | ACTIVITIES | BEST TIME TO VISIT | WEBSITE | PAGE |
|---|---|---|---|---|---|
| **Białowieża** | primeval forest; bison, elk, lynx, wolf | wildlife watching, hiking | spring, summer | www.bpn.com.pl | p104 |
| **Biebrza** | river, wetland, forest; elk, great snipe, aquatic warbler | birdwatching, canoeing | spring, autumn | www.biebrza.org.pl | p100 |
| **Kampinos** | forest, sand dunes | hiking, mountain-biking | summer | www.kampinoski-pn.gov.pl | p79 |
| **Karkonosze** | mountains; dwarf pine, alpine flora | hiking, mountain biking | summer, winter | www.kpnmab.pl | p249 |
| **Narew** | river, reed beds; beaver, water-fowl | birdwatching, canoeing | spring, autumn | www.npn.pl | p101 |
| **Ojców** | forest, rock formations, caves; eagles, bats | hiking | autumn | www.opn.pan.krakow.pl | p149 |
| **Roztocze** | forest; elk, wolf, beaver, tarpan | hiking | spring, autumn | www.roztoczanskipn.pl | p183 |
| **Słowiński** | forest, bog, sand dunes; white-tailed eagle, waterfowl | hiking, birdwatching | all year | www.slowinskipn.pl | p343 |
| **Tatra** | alpine mountains; chamois, eagle | hiking, climbing, skiing | all year | www.tpn.pl | p187 |
| **Wolin** | forest, lake, coast; white-tailed eagle, bison | hiking, birdwatching | spring, autumn | www.wolinpn.pl | p352 |

## TREK SAFE

To ensure you enjoy your walk or hike in comfort and safety, put some thought into your preparations before hitting the trail:

» Obtain reliable information about the conditions and characteristics of your intended route from local national park authorities.

» Buy a suitable map from the local bookshop or tourist office.

» If possible, always inform someone of your route and when you expect to be back.

» Always check the weather with the local tourist office or national park authority.

» Weather conditions can be unpredictable in mountainous areas, so pack appropriate clothing and equipment.

» Be sure you are fit enough and feel comfortable for the walk you choose.

» Be aware of the local laws, regulations and etiquette about flora and fauna.

» Always be ready to turn back if things start to go wrong.

hilltop holy site that's now a picturesque monastery.

In addition to these, Roztocze National Park (p183) offers a range of light walks through gentle terrain, and the landscape park surrounding Kazimierz Dolny (p171) offers some easy but worthwhile rambles.

## Walking Tours

Many local companies and individual guides operate along the tracks and trails of Poland's wild side. But if you are looking to organise a guided trek from home, **Venture Poland** (www.venturepoland.eu) specialises in the Carpathian Mountains, while **Walks Worldwide** (www.walksworldwide.com) covers all the southern mountain ranges.

# Canoeing, Kayaking & Rafting

Choices of where to kayak in Poland flow freely: the lowlands of Masuria, Warmia and Kashubia in Poland's north offer literally thousands of lakes and rivers to chose from. Further to the east is the Augustów Canal, and the lakes and rivers connected to it. Just south of Augustów there's a series of seldom-visited national parks that offer more kayaking opportunities in a protected and isolated environment of river tributaries and bogs.

There's no need to haul your kayak through airports either as there are plenty of hire centres, where boats, paddles and lifejackets can be rented for very reasonable rates. Local tourist offices can usually point you in the right direction.

## Where to Get Paddling

The following areas are the top locations for a bit of messing around on the water. Numerous hire centres, tour companies and guides in these areas make hitting the water as easy as it gets.

### Great Masurian Lakes

The town of Olsztyn is a handy base for organising adventures on water, particularly kayaking. **PTTK Mazury** (☑89 527 5156; www.mazurypttk.pl; ul Staromiejska 1) organises trips, equipment and guides; seek advice at the regional tourist office (p365). From Olsztyn it's possible to canoe the Łyna River to the border of Russia's Kaliningrad enclave, or spend a couple of laid-back hours floating closer to the city.

The most popular kayaking route in the Great Masurian Lakes area runs along the Krutynia River (p364), originating at Sorkwity and following the Krutynia River and Lake Bełdany to Ruciane-Nida. Some consider Krutynia the most scenic river in the north and the clearest in Poland. It winds through 100km of forests, bird reserves, meadows and marshes. This

### MOUNTAIN GUIDES

Two commendably practical walking guides for the Tatras are *High Tatras: Slovakia and Poland*, by Colin Saunders and Renáta Nározná, and Sandra Bardwell's *Tatra Mountains of Poland and Slovakia*.

is the queen of the Masuria rivers and arguably the king of kayaking stretches.

Masuren Koch (www.masuren2.de) is a tour company based at Kętrzyn's Hotel Koch that can arrange all kinds of adventures in the Great Masurian Lakes.

## Augustów-Suwałki Region

In the less-visited and arguably far cooler Augustów-Suwałki Region (p105), the lakes are not connected as they are in the Great Masurian Lakes, but the waters are crystal clear. The river to paddle in these parts is the Czarna Hańcza (p107), generally from Augustów along the Augustów Canal, all the way to the northern end of Lake Serwy. This route takes in the 150-year-old Augustów Canal, the Suwałki Lake District and the Augustów Forest. Numerous tour operators cover this loop, but it is also possible to do this and other routes independently.

Close to the city of Suwałki, Lake Wigry in the Wigry National Park (p110) offers surprisingly pristine paddling. In the Augustów-Suwałki region, check in with Szot (www.szot.pl) in Augustów, which offers an excellent selection of short and long trips and English-friendly guides.

South of the Masurian Lakes, the Biebrza River runs through the scenic splendour of the Podlasie region and through Biebrza National Park (p100), with its varied landscape of river sprawls, peat bogs, marshes and damp forests. The principal kayaking route here flows from the town of Lipsk downstream along the Biebrza to the village of Wizna, for a distance of about 140km (seven to nine days). While this is longer than most people will have time for, shorter stretches are also possible and camping sites dot the river along the way to allow for overnight stops.

The Narew National Park, further south, is just as interesting as the Biebrza National Park but not as geared toward visitors. This park protects an unusual stretch of the Narew River that's nicknamed the 'Polish Amazon', where the river splits into dozens of channels. Parts of the Narew can also be kayaked. For adventures in this part of Podlasie, check in with Kaylon (www.kaylon.pl) for canoeing and kayaking adventures.

## Pomerania

The most renowned kayaking river in Pomerania is the Brda, which leads through forested areas of the Bory Tucholskie

### RESCUE SERVICES

Should you be unfortunate enough to need Poland's rescue services, here are the numbers:

» General emergency: ☎112
» Mountain rescue: ☎601 100 300
» Water rescue: ☎601 100 100

National Park and past some 19 lakes. For more information, go to www.park.bory tucholskie.info (website in Polish).

The Drawa Route, which runs through Drawa National Park, is an interesting trip for experienced kayakers. Information on accommodation, kayak hire and routes through Drawa National Park can be found at www.dpn.pl. The Drawa Route is believed to have been a favourite kayaking jaunt of Pope John Paul II when he was a young man.

## Carpathian Mountains

The organised rafting trip to do in Poland is the placid glide through the Dunajec Gorge (p224) in the Pieniny. There's nothing wet and wild about it, but it's a tradition that started in the 1830s, and the scenery hasn't lost a fraction of its splendour since.

# Skiing & Snowboarding

If you haven't skied before, perhaps Poland is the place to start, if only because you'll pay less here for the privilege than elsewhere in Europe. Accommodation in ski-resort areas can range from 50zł for rooms in private homes up to the more luxurious 300zł hotel options. Ski-lift passes cost around 100zł per day.

Southern Poland is well equipped for cross-country and downhill skiers of all abilities and incomes, though there's nothing budget about the scenery.

## Where to Ski

Obviously the mountain ranges of southern Poland are the places to snap on skis, though there's plenty of cross-country skiing in other flatter locations, especially around (and on) the lakes of Masuria.

## Tatra Mountains

The Tatras are the best-equipped skiing area and the country's winter-sports capital of Zakopane is the most popular place to slither (p187). The slopes of this region, which peak at Mt Kasprowy Wierch (1987m), are suitable for all skill levels, and Zakopane has good equipment and facilities. As well as challenging mountains (like Mt Kasprowy Wierch and Mt Gubałówka, with runs of 4300m and 1500m respectively), the varied terrain around Zakopane offers flat land for beginners and plenty of time to learn, with a generous ski season lasting into April some years.

## Sudetes Mountains

Another centre of outdoor action is Szklarska Poręba (p249) in Silesia, at the foot of Mt Szrenica (1362m). The city offers almost 15km of skiing and walking routes, and great cross-country skiing. The nearby town of Karpacz (p251) on the slopes of Mt Śnieżka (1602km) enjoys around 100 days of snow per year, and the town of Międzygórze also hosts ski enthusiasts who venture out to the ski centre (www.czarnagora.pl) at the 'Black Mountain' of Czarna Góra.

## Beskid Śląski

The village of Szczyrk, at the base of the Silesian Beskids, has less severe slopes and far shorter queues than elsewhere in the country. Szczyrk is home to the Polish Winter Olympics training centre and has mild enough mountains for novice skiers and snowboarders. See Szczyrk's official website (www.szczyrk.pl) for information on ski routes, ski schools, equipment hire and tourist services.

# Other Outdoor Activities

## Horse Riding

It's worth spending some time in the saddle in Poland – a country that has enjoyed a long and loyal relationship with the horse. National parks, tourist offices and private equestrian centres have become quite proficient in marking routes and organising horseback holidays along them.

The PTTK (www.pttk.pl) can assist with organising independent horse riding through its Mountaineering and Horse Riding division. There are many state-owned and private stables and riding centres throughout the country, from rustic agrotourism establishments to luxurious stables fit for a Bond film. It's also possible to organise riding tours of a few hours, or a few days, through numerous private operators. The cost of undertaking these experiences varies depending on duration and level of luxury. A down-to-earth horseback ride on a pony for a week can cost around €700, while a weekend at a fine estate with access to steed-studded stables can cost upwards of €400. Shop around until you find something that suits your taste, ability and budget.

For more information on horse riding holidays take a look at the Equine Tourism website (www.equinetourism.co.uk/worldwide horseholidays/poland.htm). Also, the Polish Equestrian Association (www.pzj.pl) has lots of information on every aspect of horse riding across Poland, but it's all in Polish.

---

### WHERE TO RIDE

The following are popular places to jump on a horse in Poland:

Białowieża National Park (p104) Offers the chance to ride (or use horse-drawn carriages and sleighs in winter) on non-designated routes through forests.

The Bieszczady (p209) Several bridle paths cross the Bieszczady range, including within the Bieszczady National Park. The best place to organise a trip is in the town of Ustrzyki Dolne.

Lower Silesia (p240) Offers the 360km Sudety Horse-Riding Route.

Masurian Lake District (p369) Ride horses around the lakes.

Baltic Beaches (p342) The white sand of the Baltic coast is a great place for a romantic gallop.

## Sailing

There's an underexplored seafaring culture in Poland. It's possible to hire yachts or sailing ships complete with their own shanty-singing skipper. The Baltic coast attracts some craft, but the summer crowds testify to the sailing-suitability of the Great Masurian Lakes, which truly live up to their name. This sprawling network of interconnected lakes allows sailors to enjoy a couple of weeks on the water without visiting the same lake twice.

You can hire sailboats in Giżycko (p373), Mikołajki (p376) and several smaller villages.

Boat enthusiasts will get a particular thrill from boat excursions on the Elbląg-Ostróda Canal (p367) in the Olsztyn region. The 159km-long canal, built between 1848 and 1876, has varied water levels (differing by almost 100m). An impressive system of slipways 'carries' boats across the dry land and drops them back into the water on the other side. There are few places in the world where one can travel by boat across 550m of dry land.

Baltic Sea sailing takes place on the bay at Szczecin (p353), shared by Germany and Poland. Sailors can visit Wolin Island and National Park (p352) when sailing this 870-sq-km bay. The bay in Gdańsk (p298) also offers access to sea harbours and quaint fishing towns.

Artificial Soliński Lake in the Bieszczady Mountains (p210) and Czorsztyński Lake in the Pieniny Mountains (p223) are both navigable.

## Windsurfing & Kitesurfing

Windsurfing and kitesurfing are mostly done in the same areas that attract sailors, but the true heartland is Hel (p321) – the Gulf of Gdańsk between Władysławowo and Chałupy along the Baltic coast. The arbitrary dance of wind and currents constantly changes the shape of the enticingly named Hel Peninsula. The Great Masurian Lakes may be popular, but there's no place like Hel. Gdańsk-based **Joytrip** (www.pl.joytrip

### ACTIVELY GREEN

Information about environmentally friendly walking, cycling and horse-riding trails is available at www.greenways.pl and through the **Polish Environmental Partnership Foundation** (www.epce.org.pl), which promotes them.

.eu) is a good tour company to contact for equipment hire etc.

## Hang-Gliding & Paragliding

Hang-gliding and paragliding are taking off in Poland, particularly in the southern mountains. A popular place from which to glide is the Nosal in Zakopane. Enquire at tourist offices and tour operators in Zakopane (p192).

## Climbing & Caving

The Tatras offer climbing opportunities for beginner and advanced climbers. Contact the **Polish Mountain Guides Society** (www.pspw.pl) for further information and a list of qualified guides.

There are more than 1000 caves in the country, but few are ready for serious spelunking. A good one is Bear's Cave in Kletno. There are two caves in the Kraków-Częstochowa Upland (p149). Łokietek Cave stretches over 270m through several passages and can be visited on a 30-minute tour. Nearby Wierzchowska Górna Cave is the longest in the region and goes on for nearly 1km.

## Geocaching

This newish sport/activity, a GPS-based treasure-hunting game, may not be as popular in Poland as it is in other countries such as the UK, but an ever-increasing number of Poles are now finding their way to it. The websites www.opencaching.pl and www.geocaching.pl are good places to start.

# Eat Like a Local

## Best Seasonal Foods

While many Polish staples are served year-round, each season brings something a little special. Watch out for:

## Spring

**Strawberries** Strawberry season arrives in late spring; look for them layered on ice cream, poured over cakes and stuffed inside *pierogi*.

## Summer

**Berries** The Polish summer yields raspberries, blackberries and blueberries. These national treasures are usually poured over pancakes or stuffed inside *pierogi*.

## Autumn

**Mushrooms** Poles are crazy about mushrooms, and the cool damp mornings of early autumn are perfect for picking. Mushrooms are used in soups, as a stuffing for pastries and in sauces.

## Winter

**Beetroot soup** Beets are a staple of Polish cooking and the cold winters bring a renewed appreciation for this oft-overlooked red root. Beetroot soup is a cherished part of the traditional Christmas Eve meal.

Polish food, with its reliance on local ingredients like potatoes, cucumbers, beets, mushrooms, buckwheat and apples, reflects the country's long agrarian tradition. The necessity of making food last the winter means the cuisine is rich in pickles, preserves, smoked fish and meat.

Poles have an opportunistic side too, and have always taken advantage of the wild foods that grow in fields and forests. A favourite pastime is gathering mushrooms and berries, which find their way into dishes in uniquely Polish ways.

## Polish Specialities

### Bread

*Chleb* (bread) has always meant more than sustenance to Poles. It's a symbol of good fortune and is sacred to many; some older people kiss a piece of bread if they drop it on the ground. Traditional Polish bread is made with rye, but bakeries nowadays turn out a bewildering array of loaves, including those flavoured with sunflower, poppy and sesame seeds, and raisins and nuts.

### Soup

Every substantial meal in Poland traditionally begins with *zupa* (soup), and Poland has some good ones. Rye is a staple ingredient in what will likely become a staple order of yours: *żurek*. This soup is made with beef or chicken stock, bacon, onion, mushrooms and sour cream, and given a distinctive tart flavour through the addition of *kwas* (a mixture of rye flour and water that has been left to ferment for several days). It's often accompanied by a hard-boiled egg or *kiełbasa* (Polish sausage) and served inside a hollowed-out loaf of bread.

As Polish as *żurek*, but perhaps not as unique, is *barszcz* (or *barszcz czerwony*), a red beetroot soup known in Russia as borscht that can be served as *barszcz czysty* (clear borscht), *barszcz z uszkami* (borscht with tiny ravioli-type dumplings stuffed with meat) or *barszcz z pasztecikiem* (borscht with a hot meat- or cabbage-filled pastry).

## Pierogi

*Pierogi* (or 'Polish raviolis') are square- or crescent-shaped dumplings made from dough and stuffed with anything from cottage cheese, potato and onion to minced meat, sauerkraut and fruit. They are usually boiled and served doused in melted butter.

*Pierogi* are highly versatile and can be eaten as a snack between meals or as a main course for lunch or dinner. They're a budget traveller's dream. No matter how fancy a restaurant is, the chef will usually be able to whip up an order of *pierogi* for anything from 12zł to 20zł.

They can also be a vegetarian's best friend: many of the more popular versions, especially the ubiquitous *pierogi ruskie* (Russian *pierogi*), stuffed with cottage cheese, potato and onion, are meatless. Just remember to tell the waiter to hold the bacon bits. Popular variations to look for:

» *pierogi z mięsem* – stuffed with spicy minced meat, normally pork

» *pierogi z serem* – with cottage cheese

» *pierogi z kapustą i grzybami* – with cabbage and wild mushrooms

» *z jagodami* – with blueberries

» *z truskawkami* – with strawberries

## Kiełbasa

What would a trip to Poland be without sampling some of the country's signature sausages? *Kiełbasa* is normally eaten as a snack or part of a light lunch or dinner, served with a side of brown bread and mustard. It's usually made with pork, though other meats, like beef, veal and even bison, can be added to lend a distinctive flavour. The sausages are generally seasoned with garlic, caraway and other spices.

The most popular type, *Wiejska kiełbasa*, is a thick cylinder of pork, spiced with garlic and marjoram, that probably comes closest

### DARE TO TRY

In addition to the standard-fare items like beef, chicken and pork, Poland has plenty of options for more adventurous palates:

» *smalec* – fried pork fat topped with crackling and spread on large hunks of bread

» *nóżki w galarecie* – jellied calves' trotters

» *flaki* – seasoned tripe cooked in bouillon with vegetables

» *karp w galarecie* – carp in gelatine

» *czernina* – ducks'-blood broth with vinegar

to the type of *kiełbasa* known outside of Poland. Some other popular varieties:

» *kabanosy* – thin pork sausages that are air-cured and seasoned with caraway seeds

» *krakowska* – as the name implies, these originated in Kraków, though they're found throughout the country; usually thick and seasoned with pepper and garlic

» *biała* – thin white sausages sold uncooked and then boiled in soups like *żurek staropolski* (sour barley soup with white sausage)

## Bigos

If there's one dish more genuinely Polish than any other, it might just be *bigos*. It's made with sauerkraut, chopped cabbage and meat, including one or more of pork, beef, game, sausage and bacon. All the ingredients are mixed together and cooked over a low flame for several hours, then put aside to be reheated a few more times.

As with French cassoulet, this process enhances the flavour. The whole operation takes a couple of days and the result can be nothing short of mouth-watering. Every family has its own well-guarded recipe, and you will never find two identical dishes.

Because it's so time-consuming, *bigos* does not often appear on a restaurant menu and the version served in cheap eateries and cafes is often not worth its name – though you can find worthy variations at Polish festivals and fairs.

## Pork

Polish menus appear to be an egalitarian lot, usually featuring a range of dishes made

## HOW TO DRINK VODKA IN POLAND

Serious vodka drinking normally follows a few standard rules. Vodka is usually drunk from a 50mL shot glass called a *kieliszek*. It's downed in a single gulp – *do dna* (to the bottom), as Poles say. A piece of a snack or a sip of mineral water is consumed just after drinking to give some relief to the throat. Glasses are immediately refilled for the next drink and it goes quickly. Poles say, 'The saddest thing in the world is two people and just one bottle.'

As you may expect, at this rate you won't be able to keep up for long. Go easy and either miss a few turns or sip your drink in stages. Though this will be beyond the comprehension of a 'normal' Polish drinker, you, as a foreigner, will be treated with due indulgence. If you do get tipsy, take comfort in the fact that Poles get drunk too – and sometimes rip-roaringly so. *Na zdrowie!* (Cheers!)

from beef, chicken and pork, as well as other meats like turkey or duck. But don't let that fool you. The main event is almost always *wieprzowina* (pork), and Poles have come up with some delicious ways to prepare it:

» *golonka* – boiled pig's knuckle, usually served with horseradish and sauerkraut

» *kotlet schabowy* – breaded pork chops

» *schab wieprzowy* – succulent roast loin of pork

» *dzik* – means wild boar, a rare treat but one worth trying if you get the chance

### Regional Dishes

There are regional specialities across the country – freshwater fish dishes in the north, aromatic duck preparations in Wielkopolska, large dumplings called *kluski* in Silesia that are often served with bacon (*kluski śląskie ze słoniną*) – but nowhere are specialities so well defined as in the Podhale region at the foot of the Tatras. Among some of the things to try here are *kwaśnica* (sauerkraut soup), *placki po góralsku* (potato pancakes with goulash) and the many types of *oscypki* (smoked sheep's cheese) that come in oblong shapes with distinctive stamps on the rind.

### Vodka

Poles love their *wódka* (vodka) – only the Russians drink more per capita – and make some of the best in the world. While drinking habits are evolving in Poland, and most Poles normally relax over a glass of beer or wine, vodka remains the drink of choice when it comes to holidays, special occasions, or simply times when only vodka will do.

The most popular type of vodka in Poland, as with much of the rest of the world, is *czysta* (clear) vodka, but this is not the only species of the *wódka* family. Look around for some of these varieties:

» *wyborowa* – wheat-based clear vodka

» *żytnia* – rye-based vodka, with a whole spectrum of varieties, from sweet to extra dry

» *myśliwska* – means 'hunter's vodka' and tastes not unlike gin

» *wiśniówka* – flavoured with cherries

» *cytrynówka* – flavoured with lemon

» *pieprzówka* – flavoured with pepper

» *żubrówka* – ('bison vodka') flavoured with grass from the Białowieża Forest on which bison feed (or as local wags have it, 'on which bison peed')

Generally, clear vodka should be served well chilled. Flavoured vodkas don't need as much cooling, and some are best drunk at room temperature. While all vodkas are traditionally drunk neat and – horror of horrors – *never* mixed as cocktails, that too is changing and some experiments have been very successful. *Żubrówka* and apple juice – known as a *tatanka* (buffalo) – is a match made in heaven.

### Beer

There are several brands of locally brewed Polish *piwo* (beer); the best include Żywiec, Tyskie, Okocim and Lech. Beer is readily available in shops, cafes, bars, pubs and restaurants – virtually everywhere – and is almost always lager.

Don't ask us why, but you'll soon see that Poles like to flavour their beer with fruit juice, usually *sok malinowy* (raspberry juice). It's then drunk through a straw.

## How to Eat Like a Local
### When to Eat

Poles tend to be early risers and *śniadanie* (breakfast) is taken between 6am and 8am. Polish breakfasts are similar to their Western counterparts and may include *chleb z masłem* (bread and butter), *ser* (cheese), *szynka* (ham), *jajka* (eggs) and *herbata* (tea) or *kawa* (coffee). Hotels and pensions normally offer a *szwedzki bufet* (Swedish-style buffet), consisting of these items as well as slices of cucumber and tomatoes, pickles and occasionally something warm like a pot of scrambled eggs, *kiełbasa*, *parowki* (frankfurters) or pancakes. Normally, the only coffee available is instant, but some places are starting to offer mini espresso machines (hoorah!).

*Obiad* (lunch) normally kicks off a bit later than you might be used to, around 1pm or 2pm, and can stretch to as late as 4pm or 5pm. It's traditionally the most important and substantial meal of the day.

The evening meal is *kolacja* (supper). The time and menu vary greatly: sometimes it can be nearly as substantial as *obiad*, but more often it's just sliced meats with salad or even lighter – a pastry and a glass of tea.

## Where to Eat

Normally you'll eat in a *restauracja* (restaurant), a catch-all expression referring to any place with table service. They range from unpretentious eateries where you can have a filling meal for as little as 20zł, all the way up to luxurious establishments that may leave a sizeable hole in your wallet. See p418 for price categories used in this book.

The menus of most top-class restaurants are in Polish with English translations, but don't expect foreign-language listings in cheaper eateries (nor waiters speaking anything but Polish).

A cheaper but usually acceptable alternative to a restaurant is a *bar mleczny* (milk bar). This is a no-frills, self-serve cafeteria that offers mostly meat-free dishes at very low prices. The 'milk' part of the name reflects the fact that a good part of the menu is based on dairy products. You can fill up for around 10zł to 15zł. We've listed the best milk bars in Warsaw on p69.

Milk bars open around 8am and close at 6pm (3pm or 4pm on Saturday); only a handful are open on Sunday. The menu is posted on the wall. You tell the cashier what you want, then pay in advance; the cashier gives you a receipt, which you hand to the person dispensing the food. Once you've finished your meal, return your dirty dishes (watch where other diners put theirs). Milk

---

## MEALS OF A LIFETIME

Poland is filled with great restaurants. Big cities like Warsaw and Kraków have the lion's share, but we had some of our very best meals in some of the country's tiniest hamlets.

**Restauracja Tejsza** (p99) The Talmudic house behind the synagogue in the eastern town of Tykocin is home to Poland's best home-cooked kosher – and arguably the best *pierogi* too.

**Stare Sioło** (p211) Open-air dining in the Carpathian village of Wetlina, with grilled fish and great wines.

**Deco Kredens** (p68) King of the capital, this place flaunts an appealingly over-the-top Art Deco dining room and superb roast duck.

**Restauracja Pod Gruszką** (p137) A haunt for writers and artists, luring them with excellent *żurek staropolski*.

**Restauracja Zagłoba** (p262) One of the best in provincial Poland, this cellar eatery serves inspired modern Polish cooking, including 'Casimir's Delight' (pork with wild mushrooms).

**Restauracja JaDka** (p236) This Wrocław treasure presents impeccable modern takes on Polish classics, silver-service table settings and Gothic surrounds.

**Powroty** (p90) This cottage tucked away in the hamlet of Łowicz serves simply cooked but exquisite traditional meals, like *barszcz* flavoured with smoked ham.

**Restauracja Gdańska** (p313) Five salons of antiques and an upper-end menu of herring, white Gdańsk-style *żurek*, duck with apple and cranberry, and slabs of cheesecake as rich as the sumptuous drapery.

## CHEAP TREATS

When it comes to street food, there are some uniquely Polish snacks to sample on the go. While strolling the *ulica*, look for the following:

» *zapiekanki* – The street snack of choice, 'Polish pizza' is an open-faced baguette topped with melted cheese, chopped mushrooms and ketchup, and best (or only) eaten after a heavy night on the town.

» *naleśniki* – Perfect anytime, these are pancakes stuffed with fruit or cottage cheese and topped with a strip of jam, powdered sugar and a dollop of sour cream.

» *obwarzanek* – An irresistible cross between a pretzel and a bagel topped with poppy seeds, sesame or salt. Native to Kraków but occasionally found elsewhere.

» *oscypek* – Smoked highlander sheep's cheese, usually found in mountain areas south of Kraków. Served grilled and served with *żurawiny* (cranberry jam).

» *lody* – The Polish word for ice cream might be the only word you take home with you. OK, so ice cream isn't native to Poland, but it's cheap and a treat and Poles can't get enough of the stuff.

bars are very popular and there are usually queues. No alcoholic beverages are served.

## Menu Advice

Polish menus can be quite extensive and go on for several pages. You'll soon get a general feel, though, for how they're organised, and that doesn't change much from place to place. Menus are normally split into sections, including *zakąski* (hors d'oeuvres), *zupy* (soups), *dania drugie* or *potrawy* (main courses), *dodatki* (side dishes), *desery* (desserts) and *napoje* (drinks). The main courses are often split further into *dania mięsne* (meat dishes), *dania rybne* (fish dishes), *dania z drobiu* (poultry dishes) and *dania jarskie* (vegetarian dishes).

The name of the dish on the menu is accompanied by its price and, in milk bars in particular, by its weight. The price of the main course doesn't normally include side orders such as potatoes, chips and salads; these must be chosen from the *dodatki* section. Only when all these items are listed together is the price that follows for the whole plate of food. Also note that for menu items that do not have a standard portion size – most commonly fish – the price given is often per 100g. When ordering, make sure you know how big a fish (or piece of fish) you're getting.

See the food glossary on p418 for more help deciphering menus.

## Etiquette

Dining out in Poland is fairly straightforward and not much different from eating out anywhere else. Expect slower service,

perhaps, than you might get in other destinations, particularly if it's a crowded place. To speed things up, you're welcome to grab your own menus when you enter a restaurant; there will likely be a stack by the door.

Many places, particularly outdoor cafes, are self-service, so if no one comes to your table right away, it might be a sign you're expected to fetch your own drinks and make food orders at the counter.

Polish restaurants are not particularly kid-friendly. Children are always welcome, of course, and some places even have special children's menus, but you won't find high chairs or even lots of room to push a stroller through in many places.

Service leans towards the officious, rather than the overly friendly. Expect competent and even excellent results from the kitchen. Occasionally, though, your order may be misunderstood by the server or botched in the kitchen. Unless it's a major mistake, though, refrain from sending food back as it inevitably creates ill will and will delay the meal even more. Tip 10% of the tab for good service (slightly more for an extraordinary experience).

## Cook Like a Local

If you'd like to take your appreciation of Polish food to the next level, renowned local chef Kurt Scheller offers a series of cooking courses that feature Polish cuisine. Courses are taught at the **Kurt Scheller Cooking Academy** (☑22 626 8092; www.scheller academy.pl; ul Międzynarodowa 68) in Warsaw. One covering 'Polish Regional Cuisine' lasts about four hours and costs 220zł.

# regions at a glance

Which region of Poland you choose to focus on will depend on whether you prefer an active holiday, centred on hiking, boating and biking, or more urban pursuits, such as museums, cafes and clubs.

For the latter, Poland's trilogy of great cities, Kraków, Warsaw and Gdańsk, offer excellent museums, restaurants and other urban amenities. Kraków, in particular, escaped damage in WWII and is an unmissable mix of modern and medieval.

If sports are on the card, consider the regions of Warmia and Masuria, Mazovia and Podlasie. This is lake country, with abundant kayaking, hiking and biking. The mountains in the south are covered in hiking paths and the place to go to get away from it all.

## Warsaw

**History** ✓✓✓
**Nightlife** ✓✓
**Food** ✓✓

### Modern History
Warsaw is a living, breathing, 3D version of the History channel. The conflicts of WWII are not just the stuff of dusty history tomes, but events that resonate to this day.

### Nightlife
With tens of thousands of students, Warsaw has it all when it comes to whiling away the hours between sundown and sunup, with classic dives, funky coffee shops, trendy cocktail bars and happening clubs.

### Food
Warsaw is the food capital of Poland. Not only are the best Polish restaurants here, but there's a thriving ethnic food scene as well, with Indian, Middle Eastern and the latest craze, Vietnamese, all represented.

**p46**

## Mazovia & Podlasie

**Nature** ✓✓✓
**Water Sports** ✓✓
**Museums** ✓

### Nature
Podlasie is home to three of the best national parks, including Białowieża, which claims a small patch of Europe's last remaining primeval forest. Birders will appreciate the abundant waterfowl at Biebrza National Park.

### Water Sports
The Suwałki region in the extreme northeast is a quieter version of the Masurian Lakes, and home to canals, rivers and lakes that invite hours of kayaking.

### Museums
The city of Łódź may not be much to look at, but there's a lot to see, including two great art museums, a stunning history museum and a quirky museum to the greats of Polish cinema.

**p80**

## Kraków

**Museums** ✓✓✓
**Nightlife** ✓✓✓
**Food** ✓✓

### Museums
Poland's former royal capital has plenty of excellent museums, including several on majestic Wawel Hill. Newer high-tech institutions include the Rynek Underground and Oskar Schindler's former factory.

### Nightlife
Whether you prefer a quiet bar or a pumping nightclub, Kraków has it all. The most distinctive options are its Old Town cellar pubs and the character-packed bars of Kazimierz.

### Food
Kraków has a wide range of dining options, from the humble *obwarzanek* (bread pretzel) sold on every street corner, through traditional Polish dishes to the finest international cuisine.

**p112**

## Małopolska

**History** ✓✓✓
**Heritage** ✓✓
**Architecture** ✓✓

### Sacral History
Częstochowa's Jasna Góra monastery is one of the most important pilgrimage destinations for Catholics, and the monastery retains a feeling of hushed holiness, even to nonbelievers.

### Jewish Heritage
Pre-WWII, the city of Lublin was a leading centre for Jewish scholars, and there is now a fascinating self-guided Jewish heritage trail. Chełm was similarly important. The region was sadly home to three of Nazi Germany's most notorious extermination camps.

### Architecture
Sandomierz is one of Poland's Gothic treasures, with a beautifully preserved town square; the city of Zamość calls itself the 'Pearl of the Renaissance' – with good reason.

**p147**

## Carpathian Mountains

**Hiking** ✓✓✓
**Architecture** ✓✓✓
**Spas** ✓

### Hiking
Walkers are spoiled with choice in the Carpathians. Want drama? Go for the Tatras. Solitude? Head for the Bieszczady. The chance to mix a bit of boating with a hike? The Pieniny.

### Architecture
The Carpathians are sprinkled with the traditional wooden architecture of the country's indigenous highlander population. In Zakopane, this architecture was raised to an art form. Beyond this, old wooden churches dot the countryside.

### Spas
The Carpathian region is blessed with abundant hot springs, and that means spas. Krynica is one of the largest and most popular. Szczawnica, on the Dunajec River, is smaller and quieter.

**p185**

## Silesia

**Hiking** ✓✓✓
**Nightlife** ✓✓
**Architecture** ✓✓

### Hiking
Bordered by the Sudetes Mountains, Silesia is a hiker's dream. The Karkonosze National Park offers hikes among craggy cliffs, while the Góry Stołowe mountains are dotted with strange rock formations.

### Nightlife
Silesia's cultural capital, Wrocław, is a major university town, and thousands of students translate into hundreds of bars, pubs and clubs.

### Architecture
Silesia's tumultuous history has left its mark on the diverse built environment, including the bizarre Chapel of Skulls at Kudowa-Zdrój, the grand facades of Wrocław and the modernist lines of Katowice.

**p227**

## Wielkopolska

**History** ✓✓✓
**Cycling** ✓✓
**Food** ✓

## Gdańsk & Pomerania

**Heritage** ✓✓✓
**Beaches** ✓✓✓
**Folk Culture** ✓✓

## Warmia & Masuria

**Lakes** ✓✓✓
**Sports** ✓✓✓
**Architecture** ✓✓

### History
Wielkopolska's deep history is seen everywhere: from the cathedrals of Poznań and Gniezno, to the plentiful museums across the region that document events from the Middle Ages to the communist era.

### Cycling
One of the flattest parts of Poland, the region is a great place to hire a bike and hit the road, whether it be in Poznań or in the rural countryside.

### Food
Poznań has as sophisticated and varied a dining scene as any big city in Poland and is particularly strong on Asian cuisine.

**p270**

### Gothic Heritage
Medieval Poland's masons must have been busy building the north's hundreds of churches, castles, walls and town halls. Even the Red Army couldn't put a dent in this red-brick wealth, and postwar reconstruction restored many buildings to their former glory.

### Beaches
Poland's Baltic seacoast may be chilly, but when the sun shines and the winds abate, there's no better place for a spot of beach fun than the stretches of white sand along the northern coast.

### Folk Culture
Inland from the coast you'll find the local Kashubian culture thriving at festivals, celebrations and the open-air museum in Wdzydze Kiszewskie.

**p295**

### Lakes
Poland has more lakes than any other country in Europe except Finland – and most are in Masuria. The Great Masurian Lake area boasts Poland's biggest body of water, Lake Śniardwy.

### Water Sports
Where there's water, there's sport, and the Great Masurian Lakes are no exception. This is the best place in Poland to don flippers, grab a paddle or hire a yacht for a bit of waterborne R&R.

### Architecture
Away from watery attractions, the region has some remarkable architecture, starting with the Baroque church at Święta Lipka, followed by the red-brick majesty of Lidzbark Warmiński's castle.

**p360**

Every listing is recommended by our authors, and their favourite places are listed first

Look out for these icons:

 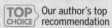 **TOP CHOICE** Our author's top recommendation

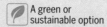 A green or sustainable option

 **FREE** No payment required

# On the Road

# Warsaw

POP 1.72 MILLION

## Best Places to Eat

» Deco Kredens (p68)

» Pierrogeria (p68)

» Cô Tú (p68)

» Bar Nam Sajgon (p68)

» Delikatesy Braci Gessler (p69)

## Best Places to Stay

» Castle Inn (p62)

» Hotel Rialto (p67)

» Le Méridien Bristol Hotel (p63)

» Oki Doki Hostel (p63)

» Krokodyl (p67)

## Why Go?

Kraków may have the beauty and Gdańsk the seashore, but Warsaw has the culture, the energy and the action. Poland's capital was flattened in WWII and, ever since, the city's been racing to replace what was lost. After 1989, that pace accelerated, and central Warsaw today has so many booms, cranes and construction sites, you'd think you'd landed in Beijing.

That energy extends to the city's thriving club and music scene. The annual calendar is filled with funky street fests, edgy art openings, and lots of highbrow, Chopin-inspired music festivals. The best museums are here too. The Warsaw Rising Museum set the standard for a new generation of engaging, interactive exhibitions. Two new museums, one on Chopin and the other on Jewish history, raise the bar even higher.

Sprawling Warsaw may be an acquired taste and your first impressions straight off the train may not be positive. But the vibe and drive of Poland's capital are infectious if you give it time.

## When to Go
### Warsaw

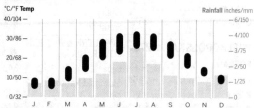

| Mar–May | Jul | Oct |
| --- | --- | --- |
| Watch the trees bud and flowers bloom on a stroll through bucolic Łazienki Park. | Midsummer brings five days of happenings around town during the Street Art Festival. | Film buffs will enjoy 10 days of Polish and international films at the Warsaw Film Festival. |

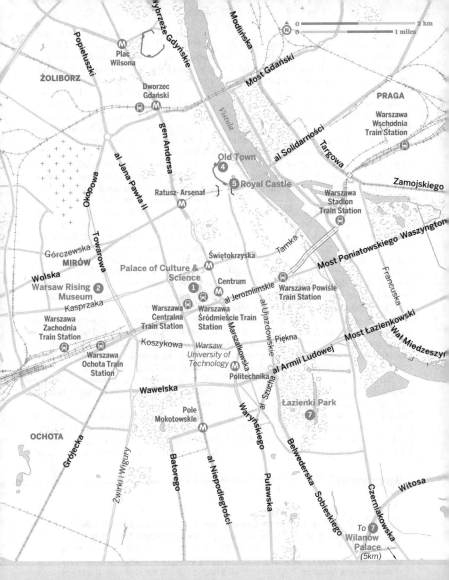

## Warsaw Highlights

**1** Taking in Warsaw and beyond from the top of the **Palace of Culture & Science** (p55)

**2** Listening to first-hand accounts of WWII at the **Warsaw Rising Museum** (p55)

**3** Spending your hard-earned cash on **handmade products** (p75)

**4** Marvelling at the quality of the renovation work in the **Old Town** (p49)

**5** Taking in the regal splendour of the **Royal Castle** (p49)

**6** Tapping into the capital's **nightlife** (p72), whether it be bar-hopping, clubbing, jazz or highbrow entertainment

**7** Admiring Warsaw's palaces at **Łazienki Park** (p59) and **Wilanów Palace** (p60)

## History

Warsaw's history has had more than its share of ups and downs. But like the essence of the Polish character, it has managed to return from the brink of destruction time and time again.

The first semblance of a town sprang up around the beginning of the 14th century, when the dukes of Mazovia built a stronghold on the site of the present Royal Castle. In 1413 the dukes chose Warsaw as their seat of power, and things went swimmingly for over 100 years until, in 1526, the last duke died without an heir. The burgeoning town – and the whole of Mazovia – fell under direct rule of the king in Kraków and was incorporated into royal territory.

Warsaw's fortunes took a turn for the better after the unification of Poland and Lithuania in 1569, when the Sejm (the lower house of parliament) voted to make Warsaw the seat of its debates because of its more central position in the expanded new country. The ultimate ennoblement came in 1596, when King Zygmunt III Waza decided to move his capital from Kraków to Warsaw.

The Swedish invasion from 1655 to 1660 was not kind to Warsaw, but the city recovered and continued to develop. Paradoxically, the 18th century – a period of catastrophic decline for the Polish state – witnessed Warsaw's greatest prosperity. A wealth of palaces and churches was erected, and cultural and artistic life flourished, particularly during the reign of the last Polish king, Stanisław August Poniatowski.

In 1795 the city's prosperity was again shattered. Following the partition of Poland, Warsaw's status was reduced to that of a provincial town. When Napoleon rolled into town in 1806 on his way to defeat in Russia, things started looking up. The warring Frenchman created the Duchy of Warsaw and the city became a capital once more. The celebrations were brief, however, as in 1815 Warsaw, and much of the rest of Poland, fell under Russian rule.

After WWI Warsaw was reinstated as the capital of newly independent Poland and the urban development and industrialisation begun in the late 19th century continued. By 1939 the city had grown to 1.3 million, of whom 380,000 were Jews who had traditionally made up a significant part of Warsaw's community.

German bombs began to fall on 1 September 1939 and a week later the city was besieged; despite brave resistance, Warsaw fell in a month. The conquerors instantly set about terrorising the local population with arrests, executions and deportations, and a Jewish ghetto was built. The city's residents rebelled against the Germans twice; first came an eruption in the Jewish ghetto in April 1943 (see boxed text, p58) and second a general city uprising in August 1944 (see boxed text, p390). Both rebellions were crushed.

At the end of the war, the city of Warsaw lay in ruins and 800,000 people – more than half of the pre-war population – had perished. (By comparison, the total

---

## WARSAW IN...

### One Day

Start a tour of Warsaw at the **Royal Castle**, a former Mazovian stronghold. Spend the rest of the morning exploring the evocative back streets of the **Old Town**, then head to the **New Town** for lunch. Let the food digest while retracing your steps and wandering down **ul Krakowskie Przedmieście** and **ul Nowy Świat** before crossing town to the **Warsaw Rising Museum**. Wait until late afternoon to take in the view from the top of the **Palace of Culture & Science**, then round the day off with dinner at one of the many good restaurants south of **al Jerozolimskie**.

### Two Days

Begin the day with one of the big museums. Depending on your interests, it could be the new **Museum of the History of Polish Jews**, the **Chopin Museum** or the extensive collections of the **National Museum**. Head back toward **ul Nowy Świat** for lunch before embarking south of **al Jerozolimskie** to pass the early afternoon in beautiful **Łazienki Park**. With the rest of the afternoon, explore Warsaw's **markets** or **craft stores** and end the two days with dinner and drinks, and perhaps a jazz concert at **Tygmont** or a pub crawl in **Praga**.

military casualties for US forces in WWII was 400,000, for UK forces 326,000.) A massive rebuilding project was undertaken soon after (see boxed text, p53) and despite over 40 years of Communist rule, the city once again regathered its strength and is now enjoying an unprecedented period of economic growth.

## ◎ Sights

### OLD TOWN

Despite being a mere 50-odd years old, Warsaw's Old Town (Stare Miasto) looks 200 (see p53). It's the first (and sometimes the only) part of the city the tourists hit, and with good reason: this small quarter holds the lion's share of Warsaw's historical monuments, including the Royal Castle and St John's Cathedral. It's also fun just to hang around; Old Town Sq is always buzzing.

**Royal Castle** CASTLE
(Zamek Królewski; Map p56; ☑booking office 22 355 5338; www.zamek-krolewski.com.pl; Castle Sq 4; adult/concession 22/15zł, Sun free, guided tour in English 100zł; ☺10am-6pm Mon-Wed, Fri & Sat, 10am-8pm Thu, 11am-6pm Sun) This massive brick edifice, now a marvellous copy of the original that was blown up by the Germans towards the end of the war, began life as a wooden stronghold of the dukes of Mazovia in the 14th century. Its heyday came in the mid-17th century, when it became one of Europe's most splendid royal residences, and during the reign of Stanisław August Poniatowski (1764–95), when its grand Baroque apartments were created. It then served the tsars and, in 1918, after Poland had regained its independence, it became the residence of the president. Today it is filled with period furniture, works of art, and an army of old ladies watching your every move.

The highlights of the 'Castle Tour' include the **Great Apartment** and its magnificent **Great Assembly Hall**, which has been restored to its 18th-century decor of dazzling gilded stucco and golden columns. The enormous ceiling painting, *The Disentanglement of Chaos,* is a postwar re-creation of a work by Marcello Bacciarelli showing King Stanisław bringing order to the world. The king's face also appears in a marble medallion above the main door, flanked by the allegorical figures of Peace and Justice.

The neighbouring **National Hall** was conceived by the king as a national pantheon; the six huge canvases (surviving originals) depict pivotal scenes from Polish history. A door leads off the hall into the smaller **Marble Room**, decorated in 16th-century style with coloured marble and *trompe l'œil* painting. The room houses 22 portraits of Polish kings, from Bolesław Chrobry to a large gilt-framed image of Stanisław August Poniatowski himself.

Further on from the National Hall is the lavishly decorated **Throne Room**. Connected to the Throne Room by a short corridor is the **King's Apartment**, the highlight of which is the **Canaletto Room** at the far end. An impressive array of 23 paintings by Bernardo Bellotto (1721–80), better known in Poland as Canaletto (he used the name of his more famous uncle), captures Warsaw in great detail from its heyday in the mid-1700s. The works were of immense help in reconstructing the city's historic monuments.

Overlooking Castle Sq from the 1st floor is the **Crown Prince's Apartment**. The lavishness of the rooms here is overshadowed by the collection of historical paintings by Jan Matejko; look for his most famous work, *The Constitution of the 3rd of May 1791,* which shows a triumphant King Stanisław being borne into the castle on the shoulders of a jubilant crowd.

**Old Town Square** SQUARE
(Map p56) The partially walled Old Town (Stare Miasto) is centred on Old Town Sq (Rynek Starego Miasta), which, for those with an eye for historical buildings, is the loveliest in Warsaw. It's lined with tall houses exhibiting a fine blend of Renaissance and Baroque with Gothic and neoclassical elements – aside from the facades at Nos 34 and 36, all were reconstructed after WWII. An 1855 statue of the **Mermaid** (Syrena), the symbol of Warsaw, occupies the square's central position, the site of the city's original town hall, demolished in 1817.

**St John's Cathedral** CHURCH
(Katedra Św Jana; Map p56; ul Świętojańska 8; admission free; ☺10am-1pm & 3-6pm Mon-Sat, 3-6pm Sun) This is considered the oldest of Warsaw's churches; it was built at the beginning of the 15th century on the site of a wooden church, and subsequently remodelled several times. Razed during WWII, it regained its Gothic shape through postwar reconstruction. Look for the red-marble Renaissance tomb of the last dukes of Mazovia in the right-hand aisle, then go downstairs to the **crypt** to see more tombstones,

# Warsaw

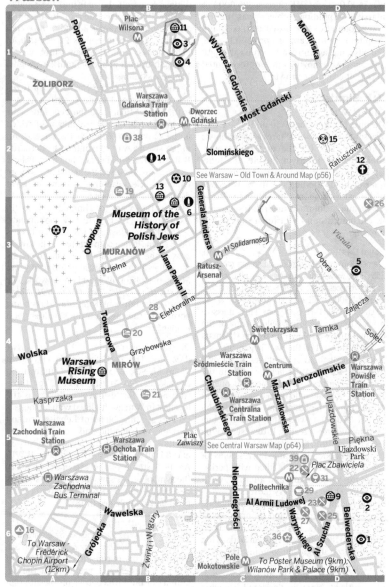

including that of Nobel prize–winning writer Henryk Sienkiewicz.

### NEW TOWN

The New Town (Nowe Miasto) is a bit of a misnomer, considering it was founded at the end of the 14th century and since 1408 has commanded its own jurisdiction and administration. It exudes similar architectural styles to those found in the Old Town, but lacks any defensive walls, probably due to the fact that historically it was inhabited by poor folk.

the work of prominent architect Tylman van Gameren and has a fine Baroque exterior and clean white interior.

### Field Cathedral of the Polish Army CHURCH
(Katedra Polowa Wojska Polskiego; Map p56; www .katedrapolowa.pl, in Polish; ul Długa 13/15) As the name implies, this has been a traditional place of worship for soldiers. There's no homage to the glory of war here; inside the main doors, which feature bas-reliefs of major battles fought by Polish forces, is a gruesome crucifix, with heads protruding from solid metal blocks on all sides of a ruined Jesus. Inside there are numerous plaques to fallen Polish soldiers.

### Monument to the Warsaw Uprising MONUMENT
(Pomnik Powstania Warszawskiego; Map p56) Directly opposite the Cathedral of the Polish Army stands one of Warsaw's most important landmarks. This bronze tableau depicts Armia Krajowa (AK; Home Army) fighters emerging ghostlike from the shattered brickwork of their ruined city, while others descend through a manhole into the network of sewers. The monument was unveiled on 1 August 1989, the 45th anniversary of the uprising (see boxed text, p390).

### Marie Skłodowska-Curie Museum MUSEUM
(Map p56; http://muzeum.if.pw.edu.pl, in Polish; ul Freta 16; adult/concession 11/6zł; ⊙8.30am-4.30pm Tue, 9.30am-5pm Wed-Fri, 10am-5.30pm Sat, 10am-5pm Sun) Marie Curie was born in 1867 along ul Freta, the main street of the New Town, and her former home now houses a museum, that chronicles the life and work of this distinguished scientist.

### CITADEL
North of the New Town, the Citadel (Cytadela; Map p50) is a massive 19th-century fortress overlooking the Vistula that was built by the Russian tsar to intimidate Warsaw following the November Insurrection of 1830. It served as a notorious political prison for years and nowadays is used by the military. The huge gate overlooking the river is known as Brama Straceń (Gate of Execution; Map p50), a spot where political prisoners were executed all too frequently after the 1863 uprising.

### FREE Muzeum Pawilon-X MUSEUM
(Map p50; www.muzeumniepodleglosci.art.pl; ul Skazańców 25; ⊙9am-4pm Wed-Sun) From the

### Nuns of the Holy Sacrament CHURCH
(Kościół Sakramentek; Map p56; New Town Sq 2) Even by Polish standards, the New Town has a lot of churches. Of the six in the immediate vicinity, this church, which dominates New Town Sq, is the most interesting. It's

# Warsaw

gate, a short cobbled road leads to the Block 10 Museum, which preserves a wing of the old political prison. The cells are labelled with the names of the more famous prisoners who were incarcerated here, the best known being Józef Piłsudski, who did time in cell No 25 on the 1st floor. Inside are paintings by Alexander Sochaczewski (1843–1923), a former inmate who, along with 20,000 other anti-Russian insurgents, was transported to the labour camps of Siberia in 1866. The paintings, such as the huge *Pożegnanie Europy* (Farewell to Europe), depict the suffering of his fellow prisoners.

### SOUTH OF THE OLD TOWN

The area running south from Castle Sq to busy al Jerozolimskie is the stomping ground of Warsaw's students, shoppers and socialites. This is nothing new, however; for much of the 19th century it was the commercial and cultural heart of Warsaw.

### UL KRAKOWSKIE PRZEDMIEŚCIE

This wide boulevard, running from Castle Sq to Nowy Świat, marks the start of the Royal Way and a great walk. The boulevard is filled with evocative churches and two **monuments**, one to Polish writer **Adam Mickiewicz** (Map p56), the author of *Pan Tadeusz*, and the other to astronomer **Nicolaus Copernicus** (Pomnik Mikołaja Kopernika; Map p64), who first dared to posit the earth might revolve around the sun. This is also the site of **Warsaw University** (Uniwersytet Warszawski; Map p64; www.uw.edu.pl; ul Krakowskie Przedmieście 26/28), the entrance to which is marked by a decorative gate topped with the Polish eagle.

**Holy Cross Church**      CHURCH
(Kościół Św Krzyża; Map p64; www.swkrzyz.pl; ul Krakowskie Przedmieście 3) This neighbourhood is chock-a-block with sumptuous churches, but the one most visitors will want to see is the Holy Cross, not so much for the fine Baroque altarpieces that miraculously

survived fighting during the Warsaw Rising, but to glimpse a small urn by the second pillar on the left side of the nave. The urn, adorned with an epitaph to Frédéric Chopin, contains what remains of the composer's heart. It was brought here from Paris after Chopin's death in accordance with his will.

**St Anne's Church**                    CHURCH
(Kościół Św Anny; Map p56; ul Krakowskie Przedmieście 68) Marking the start of the Royal Way, this is arguably the most ornate church in the city. It escaped major damage during WWII, which explains why it sports an original *trompe l'œil* ceiling, a Rococo high altar and gorgeous organ. The facade is also Baroque in style, although there are neoclassical touches here and there.

**Carmelite Church**                    CHURCH
(Kościół Karmelitów; Map p56; ul Krakowskie Przedmieście 52/54) This church also escaped the ravages of war and, like St Anne's, has 18th-century fittings, including the high altar designed by Tylman van Gameren.

**Museum of Caricature**             MUSEUM
(Muzeum Karykatury; Map p56; www.muzeum karykatury.pl; ul Kozia 11; adult/concession 5/3zł,

Sat free; ⊘11am-5pm Tue, Wed & Fri-Sun, 11am-6pm Thu) A short detour along ul Kozia leads to this quirky museum holding around 15,000 original works by Polish and foreign caricaturists dating from the 18th century onwards, plus satirical and humorous books, magazines and the like. Displays are rotated on a regular basis.

**Radziwiłł Palace**                    PALACE
(Pałac Radziwiłłów; Map p56; ul Krakowskie Przedmieście 46/48) This neoclassical palace is guarded by four stone lions and an equestrian **Statue of Prince Józef Poniatowski**. The prince was the nephew of the last Polish king, Stanisław August Poniatowski, and commander in chief of the Polish army of the Duchy of Warsaw, created by Napoleon. It was here in 1955 that the Warsaw Pact Treaty was signed, creating the Cold War military alliance to rival NATO. Today the palace is the president's official residence (though not every president chooses to live here) and is not open to the public.

**UL NOWY ŚWIAT**
Running south from the junction of ul Świętokrzyska and ul Krakowskie Przed-mieście to al Jerozolimskie, New World St

## A PHOENIX FROM THE FLAMES

Warsaw's German occupiers did a good job of following Hitler's instructions to raze the city after the Warsaw Rising – at the end of WWII, about 15% of the city was left standing. So complete was the destruction that there were even suggestions that the capital should be moved elsewhere, but instead it was decided that parts of the pre-war urban fabric would be rebuilt.

According to plan, the most valuable historic monuments were restored to their previous appearance based on original drawings and photographs. Between 1949 and 1963 work was concentrated on the Old Town, aiming to return it to its 17th- and 18th-century appearance – today not a single building in the area looks less than 200 years old. So complete was the restoration that Unesco granted the Old Town World Heritage status in 1980.

The Royal Castle took a little longer. It wasn't until 1971 that reconstruction began, and by 1984 the splendid Baroque castle stood again as if nothing had happened. Although the brick structure is a copy, many original architectural fragments have been incorporated into the walls.

The authorities also had to build, from scratch, a whole new city capable of providing housing and services to its inhabitants. This communist legacy is less impressive. The city centre was, until quite recently, a blend of bunker-like Stalinist structures and equally dull edifices of a later era, while the outer suburbs, home to the majority of Warsaw's inhabitants, were composed almost exclusively of anonymous, prefabricated concrete blocks.

The city's skyline is still marred by ugly high-rises, but things have improved markedly since 1989. Newly constructed steel-and-glass towers have begun to break up the monotony, and the city outskirts are steadily filling up with aesthetically pleasing villas and family houses. Warsaw may never regain an architectural landscape that truly appeals, but considering all it's been through, it's doing a great job rectifying things.

is the busiest pedestrian street in Warsaw outside the Old Town. It's long been the city's fashionable shopping street, and is lined with restaurants, shops and cafes. Most of the buildings date from post-WWII, but the restoration was so complete that the predominant style of architecture is 19th-century neoclassical. Aside from shopping, eating and drinking, the best thing to do here (and in its side alleys ul Foksal and ul Chmielna) is find a comfy seat and watch the parade of people.

### Frédéric Chopin Museum    MUSEUM
(Muzeum Fryderyka Chopina; Map p64; ☑22 441 6251; http://chopin.museum; ul Okólnik 1; adult/concession 22/13zł, Tue free; ☉noon-8pm) The Baroque Ostrogski Palace is home to one of the city's newest attractions: a hi-tech, multimedia museum showcasing the works of the country's most famous composer. You're encouraged to take your time through four floors of displays, including stopping by the listening booths in the basement where you can browse Chopin's oeuvre to your heart's content. Visitation is limited each hour, so your best bet is to phone or book your visit in advance over the museum's web page.

### Copernicus Science Centre    MUSEUM
(Centrum Nauki Kopernik; Map p50; www.kopernik.org.pl; Wybrzeże Kościuszkowskie 20; adult/concession 22/16zł; ☉noon-6pm Tue-Fri, 10am-7pm Sat & Sun) One of the city's newest additions to make Warsaw more kid-friendly is this over-the-top, fully interactive, push-the-buttons-and-see-what-happens  science museum. There are too many attractions to list here, but all branches of science are represented. Most exhibits are suited for kids 12 to 18 years of age, though there's plenty on hand to amuse younger – and older – kids. The location is a bit out of the way, several blocks due east of Nowy Świat, but accessible via buses 118, 150, 506, 102, 125, 162, 166, 174 and 185.

### SAXON GARDENS & AROUND
### Saxon Gardens    PARK
(Ogród Saski; Map p64; admission free; ☉24hr) Stretching out a couple of blocks west of Krakowskie Przedmieście, these magnificent gardens date from the early 18th century and were the city's first public park. Modelled on the French gardens at Versailles, the gardens are filled with chestnut trees and Baroque statues (allegories of the Virtues, the Sciences and the Elements), and there's

an ornamental lake overlooked by a 19th-century water tower in the form of a circular Greek temple.

If it looks to you as though the gardens are missing a palace, you'd be right. The 18th-century Saxon Palace (Pałac Saski), which once occupied Plac Piłsudskiego (Piłsudski Sq), was, like so many other buildings, destroyed during WWII. All that survived were three arches of a colonnade, which have sheltered the **Tomb of the Unknown Soldier** (Grób Nieznanego Żołnierza) since 1925. The guard is changed every hour, and groups of soldiers marching back and forth between the tomb and the Radziwiłł Palace are a regular sight, though the big event is the ceremonial changing of the guard that takes place every Sunday at noon.

### Ethnographic Museum    MUSEUM
(Muzeum Etnograficzne; Map p64; www.ethno museum.pl; ul Kredytowa 1; adult/concession 10/5zł, Wed free; ☉9am-4pm Tue, Thu & Fri, 11am-6pm Wed, 10am-5pm Sat & Sun) This museum's top floor provides a good introduction into the country's rural heart, with a small but fine assembly of Polish folk art and crafts, but it's the portrait shots of indigenous people from around the world that steal the show.

### PLAC BANKOWY
Due west of the Old Town, Plac Bankowy (Bank Sq) is too big and busy to be honestly appealing. **City Hall** (Ratusz; Map p56) and the former stock exchange and Bank of Poland building, both grand neoclassical buildings that were designed by Antonio Corazzi in the 1820s, lend the square some architectural heft.

### John Paul II Collection    MUSEUM
(Kolekcja im Jana Pawła II; Map p56; www.muzeummalarstwa.pl; Plac Bankowy 1, enter from ul Elektoralna; adult/concession 12/6zł; ☉10am-5pm Tue-Sun) Housed in the Bank of Poland building, this amazing art collection was donated to the Catholic Church by the Carrol-Porczyński family. It's quite a surprise to find the likes of Dali, Van Gogh, Constable, Rubens, Goya and Renoir gracing the walls of a fairly nondescript museum, and to normally have them all to yourself.

### Jewish Historical Institute    MUSEUM
(Żydowski Instytut Historyczny; Map p56; www.jhi.pl; ul Tłomackie 3/5; adult/concession 10/5zł, Sun free; ☉9am-4pm Mon-Wed & Fri, 11am-6pm Thu, 10am-6pm Sun) Just behind the blue skyscraper, this institute houses a library

and paintings, sculptures, and old religious objects related to Jewish culture. However, it's the exhibition on the Warsaw Ghetto (see boxed text, p58) that sticks with you when you leave. Black-and-white photos and 40 minutes of original film footage from the ghetto hit home – images of the atrocious conditions Jews were forced to endure, with starvation and death part of everyday life, tell a disturbing tale.

**Museum of Independence**                    MUSEUM
(Muzeum Niepodległości; Map p56; www.muzeum niepodleglosci.art.pl; al Solidarności 62; adult/concession 6/4zł, Sun free; ◷10am-5pm Tue-Fri, to 4pm Sat & Sun) Stranded on a traffic island in the middle of al Solidarności, this museum has a small room devoted to the Solidarity movement and stages temporary exhibitions related to Poland's struggle for independence. This was once home to Warsaw's Lenin museum and still has some interesting displays of Socialist Realist artwork.

**FINANCIAL DISTRICT**
The open expanses and tall buildings that are bounded by ul Marszałkowska, al Jerozolimskie, ul Jana Pawła II and al Solidarności collectively constitute Warsaw's financial zone.

FREE **Palace of Culture & Science**            HISTORIC BUILDING
(Pałac Kultury i Nauki, PKiN; Map p64; www.pkin .pl; Plac Defilad 1; ◷9am-8pm) The dominating feature of the Financial District (and that of the city) is the Palace of Culture & Science, which rises high above the newly built skyscrapers that have begun to mark this area in the past 10 years.

Love it or hate it, every visitor to Warsaw should visit the PKiN. This 'gift of friendship' from the Soviet Union was built between 1952 and 1955, and at 231m high still remains the tallest building in Poland. It's never sat well with the locals, who have branded it with one uncomplimentary moniker after another; the Elephant in Lacy Underwear, a reference both to the building's size and to the fussy sculptures that frill the parapets, is a particular favourite.

The massive structure is home to a huge congress hall, three theatres, a multiplex cinema and two museums, as well as hectares of office space. However, the best feature of the building is the view it provides (Poles often joke that this is the best view of the city because it's the only one that

doesn't include the 'palace' itself). Take the high-speed lift (enter via the main entrance, facing ul Marszałkowska) to the 30th-floor (115m) **viewing terrace** (adult/concession 20/15zł; ◷9am-8pm) and take it all in – on a clear day the Mazovian plains are laid out before you.

**Fotoplastikon**                           PHOTOGRAPHY
(Map p64; www.fotoplastikonwarszawski.pl, in Polish; al Jerozolimskie 51; adult/concession 4/2zł, Sun free; ◷10am-6pm Tue-Sun) Photo and film buffs will be intrigued by this late-19th-century forerunner of the cinema. It's reputedly the last working example of its kind in Europe, and consists of a large rotating drum set with individual eyepieces displaying stereoscopic 3D photos, some of them in colour. Each session consists of 48 pictures and takes about 20 minutes.

**FORMER JEWISH GHETTO**
Before WWII, Warsaw was the second-largest Jewish city in the world, behind New York. Much of this thriving community at the time lived in Mirów and Muranów, two districts to the west of al Jana Pawła II. It was here that the Nazis created the Warsaw Ghetto in 1940 (see boxed text, p58), which was razed after the 1943 Ghetto Uprising. Today the area is characterised by cheap, communist-era apartment buildings, but a few remnants of Jewish Warsaw survive.

**Warsaw Rising Museum**              MUSEUM
(Muzeum Powstania Warszawskiego; Map p50; www.1944.pl; ul Przyokopowej 28; adult/concession 10/7zł, audioguide 10zł, Sun free; ◷8am-6pm Mon, Wed & Fri, 8am-8pm Thu, 10am-6pm Sat & Sun) On the southwestern edge of the former ghetto stands this modern museum housed in a beautifully restored redbrick power station. It traces the history of the Rising (see boxed text, p390) through three levels of interactive displays, photographs, film archives and the personal accounts of those who survived.

The sheer volume of material is overwhelming, but the museum does an excellent job of instilling visitors with a sense of the desperation Varsovians faced during the war. The ground floor begins with the division of Poland between Nazi Germany and the Soviet Union in 1939 and moves through the major events of WWII. A lift then whisks you to the 2nd floor and the start of the Rising in 1944. The largest exhibit, a Liberator bomber similar to the planes that used to drop supplies for insurgents during the Rising, fills much of the 1st floor.

# Warsaw – Old Town & Around

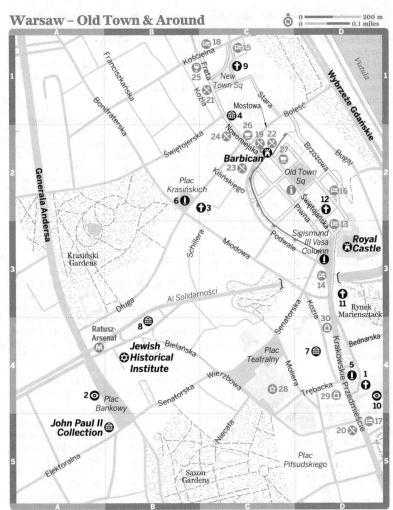

## Museum of the History of Polish Jews

MUSEUM

(Muzeum Historii Żydów Polskich; Map p50; www.jewishmuseum.org.pl; cnr of ul Anielewicza & ul Zamenhofa) When this museum, long in the works, finally opens its doors sometime in 2012, it will form the centrepiece of the city's sights dedicated to Jewish history. Organisers have promised a modern, interactive exhibit about Poland being home to Europe's largest Jewish community until the tragedy of the German invasion in WWII.

## Ghetto Heroes' Monument

MONUMENT

(Map p50; cnr ul Anielewicza & ul Zamenhofa) This stern memorial, in a shady park just behind the Museum of the History of Polish Jews, commemorates the thousands who lost their lives in the ill-fated Ghetto Uprising of 1943. In the northwest corner of the park is **Skwer Willy Brandta** (Willy Brandt Sq), with another memorial marking the visit of German chancellor Willy Brandt to this spot on 7 December 1970. Brandt famously fell to his knees in a gesture of contrition for Germany's crimes against Polish Jews.

# Warsaw – Old Town & Around

Further north on ul Zamenhofa, a short walk past a small garden, is a mound topped by a simple limestone block that forms the **Monument to Mordechaj Anielewicz**, the leader of the Ghetto Uprising, who perished in a bunker on this site in 1943.

**Umschlagplatz**　　　　　　　MONUMENT
(Map p50; ul Stawki near ul Dzika) This moving monument marks the site of the *umschlag-platz,* the railway terminus from which Warsaw's Jews were transported to Treblinka. The rectangular monument's marble walls are carved with more than 3000 Jewish forenames, from Aba to Zygmunt, and the stark message: 'Along this path of suffering and death over 300,000 Jews were driven in 1942–43 from the Warsaw Ghetto to the gas chambers of the Nazi extermination camps'. Its shape is symbolic of the cattle trucks into which the prisoners were herded.

**Jewish Cemetery**　　　　　　CEMETERY
(Cmentarz Żydowski; Map p50; ul Okopowa 49/51; adult/concession 8/4zł; ◷10am-5pm Mon-Thu, 9am-1pm Fri, 11am-4pm Sun) It's a 15-minute walk west along ul Stawki and then south on ul Okopowa to this cemetery. Founded in 1806, it suffered little during the war and still boasts more than 150,000 tombstones, the largest collection of its kind in Europe. A notice near the entrance lists the graves of many eminent Polish Jews, including Ludwik Zamenhof, creator of the international artificial language Esperanto. Look also for the **tomb of Ber Sonnenberg** (1764–1822), one of Europe's finest funerary monuments; take the first paved path on the left beyond the ticket office and when you arrive at a junction on your right, look left: it's the roofed structure over by the wall.

**Ul Próżna**　　　　　　　　STREET
(Map p64) This short street leading off Plac Grzybowski is an eerie and incongruous survivor of WWII. Its crumbling, unrestored redbrick facades, the ornamental stucco long since ripped away by bomb blasts, are still pockmarked with bullet and shrapnel scars. A few blocks to the south, in the courtyard of an apartment building at ul Sienna 55, stands one of the few surviving fragments of the redbrick wall that once surrounded the Warsaw Ghetto.

## THE WARSAW GHETTO

At the outbreak of WWII Warsaw was home to about 380,000 Jews (almost 30% of the city's total population), more than in any other city in the world except New York.

In October 1940 the Germans established a ghetto in the predominantly Jewish districts of Muranów and Mirów, west of the city centre, sealed off by a 3m-high brick wall. In the following months about 450,000 Jews from the city and its surroundings were crammed into the area within the walls, creating the largest and most overcrowded ghetto in Europe. By mid-1942 as many as 100,000 people had died of starvation and epidemic diseases, even before deportation to the concentration camps had begun.

In a massive liquidation campaign in the summer of 1942, about 300,000 Jews were transported from the ghetto to the extermination camp at Treblinka. Then in April 1943, when only 50,000 people were left, the Nazis began the final liquidation of the ghetto. In a desperate act of defiance, the survivors took up arms in a spontaneous uprising, the first in any European ghetto.

From the outbreak of the uprising on 19 April it was clear that the Jews had little chance of victory against the heavily armed Nazis. German planes dropped incendiary bombs, turning the entire district into a chaos of burning ruins. Fierce fighting lasted for almost three weeks until, on 8 May, the Nazis surrounded the Jewish command bunker and tossed in a gas bomb.

Around 7000 Jews were killed in the fighting and another 6000 perished in fires and bombed buildings. The Germans lost 300 men and another 1000 were injured. The ghetto was razed to the ground except for a few scraps of wall, which survive to this day.

A number of personal accounts provide written testament to the brutality of life within the ghetto walls. For further reading pick up a copy of any of the following: *A Square of Sky: A Jewish Childhood in Wartime Poland*, by Janina David; *Beyond These Walls: Escaping the Warsaw Ghetto*, by the late Janina Bauman; and *The Diary of Mary Berg: Growing Up in the Warsaw Ghetto*, by Mary Berg.

**Nożyk Synagogue**                                        SYNAGOGUE
(Map p64; www.warszawa.jewish.org.pl; ul Twarda 6; admission free; ⊙9am-7pm Mon-Fri, 11am-6pm Sun May-Sep, 9am-5pm Mon-Fri, 11am-4pm Sun Oct-Apr) This is the city's only synagogue to survive WWII. Built between 1898 and 1902 in neo-Romanesque style, its interior features heavy metal chandeliers and tall vaulted colonnades. It's still used for religious purposes.

FREE **Pawiak Prison Museum**                    MUSEUM
(Map p50; www.muzeumniepodleglosci.art.pl; ul Dzielna 24/26; ⊙9am-5pm Wed & Fri, 9am-4pm Thu & Sat, 10am-4pm Sun) Pawiak Prison dates from the 19th century and was originally built to incarcerate enemies of the Russian tsar. During WWII it was used by the Gestapo to imprison and torture mostly Polish political prisoners. It's estimated that around 100,000 prisoners passed through these sinister gates from 1939 to 1944, of whom around 37,000 were executed. The prison was blown up by the Germans in 1944, but half of the mangled gateway, complete with rusting, original barbed wire, and three detention cells (which you can visit) survive. Entry is free but poor lighting and lack of English commentary detract from the experience.

### SOUTH OF AL JEROZOLIMSKIE

Al Jerozolimskie is a big, busy thoroughfare that creates a physical east–west border through the city. The area to its south was earmarked by the communists for post-WWII development, and some of the city's boldest socialist-realist architecture can be found here. Ul Marszałkowska, a broad avenue running south from near the financial district, contains the most impressive examples; its stretch between **Plac Konstytucji** (Constitution Sq) and **Plac Zbawciela** is lined with arcades bearing giant reliefs of heroic workers.

**Al Ujazdowskie**, the continuation of the Royal Way as it leaves ul Nowy Świat, is a wide, tree-lined boulevard with many old mansions, now often housing foreign embassies. Near its northern section the road passes through Plac Trzech Krzyży (Three Crosses Sq), a square centred on 19th-century **St Alexander's Church** (Kościół Św Aleksandra; Map p64), which is modelled on the Roman Pantheon.

**National Museum** MUSEUM
(Muzeum Narodowe; Map p64; www.mnw.art.pl; al Jerozolimskie 3; adult/concession 12/7zł, Tue free; ⊙noon-6pm Tue-Thu, Sat & Sun, to 8pm Fri) Containing almost 800,000 items in its permanent galleries, this is the largest museum in the country. It's housed in a massive building, which is wheelchair accessible, at the western end of al Jerozolimskie. Note that as we were researching this guide in summer 2011, the museum was closed for renovation and was expected to re-open sometime in 2012.

The **Faras Collection** is a display of early Christian art originating from a town on the banks of the Nile that was rescued by Polish archaeologists from the rising waters of the Aswan High Dam. Frescoes and architectural fragments, dating from the 8th to 12th centuries, combine ancient Egyptian symbolism with Christian iconography and include beautiful, expressive and often colourful images.

The gallery of **medieval art** features a superb collection of religious painting and sculpture from all over Poland, with many gruesome renditions of the Crucifixion and scenes of grisly martyrdom.

More **Polish art**, this time from the 16th to mid-20th centuries, is housed on the upper floors. Of the many paintings look for works by Jan Matejko, such as his epic *The Battle of Grunwald* (1878).

**Łazienki Park** PARK
(Park Łazienkowski; Map p50; www.lazienki -krolewskie.pl; ul Agrykola 1; admission free; ⊙dawn-sunset) This park – pronounced wah-*zhen*-kee – is a beautiful place of manicured greens and wild patches. Its popularity extends to families, proud peacocks and fans of classical music, who come for the *al fresco* **Chopin concerts** on Sunday afternoons at noon and 4pm from mid-May through September. Once a hunting ground attached to Ujazdów Castle, Łazienki was acquired by King Stanisław August Poniatowski in 1764 and transformed into a splendid park complete with palace, amphitheatre and various follies and other buildings.

*Palace on the Water*
(Pałac na Wyspie; adult/concession 17/12zł; ⊙9am-4pm Tue-Sun) The centrepiece of the park is this neoclassical palace, the former residence of the king. It straddles an ornamental lake and, like most other Łazienki buildings, was designed by the court architect Domenico Merlini. Renovated and refurbished, the palace is open to guided tours – highlights include the 17th-century marble reliefs depicting scenes from Ovid's *Metamorphoses* gracing the original bathhouse (*łazienki* in Polish, hence the name) and the ornate ballroom.

*Island Amphitheatre*
(Amfiteatr na Wyspie) Near the palace, this amphitheatre was built in 1790 and is based on the appearance of the Roman theatre at Herculaneum, Italy. It is set on an islet in the lake, allowing part of the action to take place on the water.

*White House*
(Biały Dom; adult/concession 6/4zł; ⊙9am-4pm Tue-Sun) The 'White House' was erected in 1774 as a temporary residence for the king until the palace was finished. It's incredibly small for a royal home and has managed to retain most of its original 18th-century interior.

*Belvedere Palace*
(Pałac Belweder; ul Belwederska 52) This 18th-century palace at the southern limit of al Ujazdowskie served as the official residence of Marshal Józef Piłsudski (from 1926 to 1935) and Polish presidents from 1945 to 1952 and 1989 to 1994.

**Ujazdów Castle** CASTLE
(Zamek Ujazdowski) Erected in the 1620s for King Zygmunt III Waza as his summer residence, the castle was burned down by the Germans in 1944, blown up by the communists in 1954 and eventually rebuilt in the 1970s. Now it houses changing exhibitions of modern art from the **Centre for Contemporary Art** (Centrum Sztuki Współczesnej; www.csw.art.pl; Al Ujazdowskie 6; adult/concession 12/6zł, Thu free; ⊙noon-7pm Tue-Thu, Sat & Sun, to 9pm Fri).

South of the castle are the **Botanical Gardens** (Ogród Botaniczny; Map p50; www .ogrod.uw.edu.pl; Al Ujazdowskie 4; adult/concession 6/3zł; ⊙9am-8pm Mon-Fri, 10am-8pm Sat & Sun Apr-Aug, 10am-7pm Sep, 10am-6pm Oct).

FREE **Mausoleum of Struggle & Martyrdom** MUSEUM
(Mauzoleum Walki i Męczeństwa; Map p50; www .muzeumniepodleglosci.art.pl; al Szucha 25; ⊙9am-5pm Wed, 9am-4pm Thu & Sat, 10am-5pm Fri, 10am-4pm Sun) This building was used by the Gestapo for interrogation, torture and murder, and now stands as a memorial to the thousands of Poles who passed through its

## GAY & LESBIAN WARSAW

Attitudes toward gays and lesbians are evolving slowly, and Warsaw even hosted a highly successful EuroPride march in 2010. That said, many Poles still do not fully accept a gay lifestyle. Given the prevailing attitude, Warsaw does not have the kind of well-developed scene you might expect for a city its size. For an up-to-date listing of clubs, check out www.warsaw.gayguide.net, www.gay.pl or www.innastrona.pl (a Polish-language gay and lesbian personals site).

Fantom (Map p64; www.fantomwarsaw.com; ul Bracka 20a; ⊘2pm-3am) is Poland's longest-running gay club and has been on the scene since 1994. It's more than just a bar and a club, offering a sauna, a Jacuzzi, a sex shop and a video lounge. The inconspicuous entrance is in the courtyard behind Między Nami.

Galeria (www.clubgaleria.pl; Plac Mirowski 1; ⊘8pm-5am Tue-Sun) is a popular late-night club offering midweek karaoke and DJs at the weekend. Ring the bell at the mirrored door to get get inside.

doors. With its depressing basement holding cells and Gestapo officer's interrogation room (complete with original bullwhips, coshes, knuckledusters etc), it's a hard place to visit.

### PRAGA

Crossing the Vistula from the Old Town into Praga, Warsaw's eastern suburb, is like entering another city. Clean, level streets and renovated buildings are replaced by broken roads and crumbling facades, and much of the populace is working class and poor.

Despite the grit, Praga is *the* place to be. The area is slowly being gentrified as artists, musicians and entrepreneurs move in, attracted by its pre-WWII buildings (as it was not directly involved in the battles of 1944, Praga didn't suffer much damage) and cheaper rent. For a Praga pub crawl see the boxed text, p71.

Zoological Gardens                    ZOO
(Ogród Zoologiczny; Map p50; www.zoo.waw.pl; ul Ratuszowa 1/3; adult/concession 17/12zł; ⊘9am-6pm) Established in 1928, it has some 3000 animals representing 280 species from around the world. Kids will enjoy seeing the zoo's four elephants.

Orthodox Church                    CHURCH
(Cerkiew Prawosławna; Map p50; al Solidarności 52) Close by the zoo, rising from behind a clump of trees just off Praga's main thoroughfare, al Solidarności, are the five onion-shaped domes of this church. Built in the 1860s in Russo-Byzantine style, its small nave still retains original Byzantine portraits and gold upon gold.

Koneser Vodka Factory                    GALLERIES
(Map p50; ul Ząbkowska 27/31) Further into the neighbourhood is this disused redbrick factory dating from the early 20th century. It houses two progressive galleries, Luksfera (www.luksfera.pl; ⊘2-7pm Wed-Fri, 11am-5pm Sat & Sun) and Klimy Bocheńskiej (www.bochenska gallery.pl; ⊘noon-6pm Tue-Fri, to 4pm Sat), the first of which specialises in photography and the second in contemporary art from a wide range of media.

### OUTSIDE THE CENTRE

Wilanów Palace                    PALACE
(off Map p50; www.wilanow-palac.art.pl; ul Wiertnicza 1; adult/concession 20/15zł, Sun free, Polish or foreign-language guide 100zł, advanced booking required; ⊘9am-6pm Sun, Mon & Wed, 9am-4pm Tue, Thu & Fri, 10am-4pm Sat May–mid-Sep, 9am-4pm Wed-Mon mid-Sep–Apr) Warsaw's crowning glory in the park-palace arena is Wilanów (vee-*lah*-noof), some 6km south of Łazienki. Its origins date back to 1677, when King Jan III Sobieski bought the land and set about turning the existing manor house into an Italian Baroque villa (calling it in Italian '*villa nuova*' from which the Polish name is derived) fit for a royal summer residence. Wilanów changed hands several times over the ensuing centuries, and with every new owner it acquired a bit of Baroque here and a touch of neoclassical there. Miraculously, it survived WWII almost unscathed and most of its furnishings and art were retrieved after the war.

The highlights of a visit here include the two-storey Grand Entrance Hall, the Grand Dining Room, and the Gallery of Polish Portraits, featuring a collection of paintings from the 16th to 19th centuries. The exterior of the palace is adorned with impressive murals, including a 17th-century sundial with a bas-relief of Chronos, god of time. As guides are expensive, you might be better off picking up an audioguide (10zł). Note that the free tickets on Sundays tend to run out by noon, so best get there early.

The side gate next to the northern wing of the palace leads to the **gardens and parks** (adult/concession 5/3zł, Thu free; ⊙9.30am-sunset), which, like the palace itself, display a variety of styles. The central part comprises a manicured, two-level Baroque Italian garden, which extends from the palace down to the **lake** (boat trips adult/concession 8/5zł); the south is Anglo-Chinese in design; the northern section is an English landscape park.

*Poster Museum*
(Muzeum Plakatu; www.postermuseum.pl; ul Kostki Potockiego 10/16; adult/concession 10/7zł, Mon free; ⊙noon-4pm Mon, 10am-4pm Tue, Thu & Fri, 10am-10pm Wed, 10am-6pm Sat & Sun) Standing separately from the rest of the complex, this museum houses some 55,000 posters – one of the largest collections in the world – but only a fraction of this is shown at any one time. Exhibitions change regularly, making it a museum to visit time and time again.

Get to Wilanów on bus 116 or 180 from any stop on ul Krakowskie Przedmieście, ul Nowy Świat or al Ujazdowskie.

 **Courses**

Many private schools offer Polish language courses. Three-week intensive courses can run from around 1500zł to 2500zł. Personalised lessons cost anything from 40zł to 60zł an hour.

**Academia Polonica**          POLISH LANGUAGE
(Map p64; ☎22 629 9311; www.academiapolonica .com; al Jerozolimskie 55/14) Offers highly rated Polish language courses aimed at students, business people and expats, as well as short 'crash courses' for visitors.

**IKO**          POLISH LANGUAGE
(Map p64; ☎22 826 2259; www.iko.com.pl; ul Kopernika 3) Offers four-day crash courses in Polish at various dates over the summer for 350zł per person.

**Polonicum**          POLISH LANGUAGE
(Centre of Polish Language & Culture for Foreigners at Warsaw University; Map p64; ☎22 552 1530; www.polonicum.uw.edu.pl; ul Krakowskie Przedmieście 26/28) Affiliated with the University of Warsaw and offering full-year and summer classes in Polish language at beginner, intermediate and advanced levels.

 **Tours**

Warsaw is a big city and the sights are spread out over a large area. Ordinarily, we tend to prefer individual sightseeing rather than guided tours, but if you've only got a day or two to spend in the Polish capital, it

---

## WARSAW FOR CHILDREN

Admittedly, Warsaw is not the best travel destination for infants and small children. Distances are vast and transport options such as trams and buses are often packed and not particularly pram- or child-friendly. Exercise caution on public transport, like trams, that can make sudden stops and unexpected turns. On the streets, traffic can be heavy and many corners lack kerb cuts. You'll find escalators in metros and underpasses in the centre, but outside the centre you'll have to negotiate lots of steps.

That said, there are plenty of parents with prams in Warsaw and kids seem to do just fine. As for sights, there are a handful of crowd-pleasers. Topping the list of attractions would be the Copernicus Science Centre (p54), followed by the Zoological Gardens (p60). Older kids might be lost by the history but will enjoy the visual and sound effects of the highly interactive Warsaw Rising Museum (p55).

Parks abound. Łazienki Park (p59) has plenty of space to run, plus egoistic peacocks to spot, hungry ducks to feed, and a boat trip to take, while Saxon Gardens (p54) and Ujazdowski Park have good playgrounds. There are boat trips at Wilanów too.

The view from the Palace of Culture & Science (p55) is impressive for all ages.

The city's tourist information offices can help out. They offer a colourful foldout *Free Map for Young Travellers* aimed primarily at teens and students, but with some hints for younger travellers as well.

may be worthwhile to consider one of these organised options.

**Mazurkas Travel**   BUS

(☑22 389 4183; www.mazurkas.com.pl; al Wojska Polskiego 27; ☺8.30am-4.30pm Mon-Fri) Warsaw's major tour operator offers three-hour bus tours (120zł per person) of the major sights plus trips to Kraków, with the added benefit of pick-up and drop-off at your hotel.

**Warsaw City Tours**   BUS

(☑22 826 7100; www.warsawcitytours.info) Offers three-hour coach sightseeing tours (140zł per person) of the major sights, with hotel pick-up and drop-off. Book over the phone, online or through your hotel reception desk.

**Our Roots**   JEWISH HERITAGE

(☑22 620 0556; http://our-roots.jewish.org.pl; ☺9am-4pm Mon-Fri) Specialises in tours of Jewish sites; the Jewish Warsaw tour lasts five hours and costs around 500zł. Other tours, including to Auschwitz-Birkenau and Treblinka, can be organised on request.

## Festivals & Events

Warsaw has an active social calendar and you'll find fests and concerts at nearly any time of year. Autumn is the high point, both for classical music and for film. The following list is by no means exhaustive. Check the official website for **Warsaw Tourist Information** (www.warsawtour.pl) for a more extensive list.

**Mozart Festival**   CLASSICAL MUSIC

(www.operakameralna.pl) Staged annually from mid-June to the end of July and organised by the Warsaw Opera Kameralna. Features performances of all 26 of Mozart's stage productions plus a selection of his other works.

**Street Art Festival**   STREET ART

(Festiwal Sztuka Ulicy; www.sztukaulicy.pl) Held in early July, this five-day festival features street theatre, open-air art installations and 'happenings' staged unpredictably in public places such as Old Town Sq, the Royal Way, public parks and even bus stops.

**Warsaw Summer Jazz Days**   JAZZ

(www.adamiakjazz.pl) This series of concerts, from the middle of June and running some years into July, brings leading international jazz stars to town, mixed in with performances by local talent. Major gigs are held in Congress Hall at the Palace of Culture & Science.

**Warsaw Autumn Festival of Contemporary Music**   AVANT-GARDE

(www.warsaw-autumn.art.pl) This 50-year-old festival, held over 10 days in September, is the city's pride and joy, and offers a chance to hear the world's best avant-garde music, including new works by major Polish composers.

**Chopin and His Europe**   CLASSICAL MUSIC

(http://en.chopin.nifc.pl/festival) Two-week festival of orchestral and chamber music held in August and September, and usually devoted to the works of one or two other European composers as well.

**Warsaw International Film Festival**   FILM

(www.wff.pl) Screening of the year's best international films over 10 days in October, plus highlights of the best Polish film and plenty of retrospectives.

## Sleeping

An overnight stay in Warsaw can bust a tight budget. Forget about those tidy 200zł-a-night hotels that Poland seems to have in abundance elsewhere. Many Warsaw hotels are geared toward business travellers and are priced accordingly.

That's not to say things aren't getting better. The number of independent and 'boutique' hostels that close the gap between traditional hostels and hotels is growing. Prices have tended to stabilise in the past couple of years, and the sticker shock is not quite as jarring as it used to be.

Try to time your visit for a weekend as many hotels discount rates. Also, don't neglect the internet; hotels are scrambling to build out their sites and often offer attractive rates for online booking.

The tourist information offices can help find and book accommodation.

### OLD TOWN & AROUND

**TOP CHOICE** **Castle Inn**   HOTEL €€

(Map p56; ☑22 425 0100; www.castleinn.pl; ul Świętojańska 2; s/d 290/400zł; ✳@🛜) Owned and run by Oki Doki Hostel, this nicely done-up 'art hotel' is housed in a 17th-century townhouse. All rooms overlook either Castle Sq or St John's Cathedral, and come in a range of playful styles. Our favourite would be No 121, 'Viktor', named for a reclusive street artist, complete with tasteful graffiti and a gorgeous castle view.

### MaMaison Le Régina
HOTEL €€€
(Map p56; ☎22 531 6000; www.leregina.com; ul Kościelna 12; rm from 1000zł; P@🖥) Housed in a lovely arcaded 18th-century-style palace just a few minutes' walk from the Old Town, the Regina manages a successful combination of traditional architecture and contemporary design. Rooms are light and airy, decorated in shades of chocolate and vanilla, with lots of polished walnut, gleaming chrome and marble in the more expensive rooms.

### Dom Literatury
HOTEL €€
(House of Literature; Map p56; ☎22 828 3920; www.fundacjadl.com, in Polish; ul Krakowskie Przedmieście 87/89; s/d from 220/370zł; P) Dom Literatury is a plush hotel with a wonderful location and far too many stairs. It's also the headquarters of the Polish PEN Club, a writers' organisation. If you're happy enough to lug your bags to the 3rd floor, you'll enjoy views over the Old Town and rooms with formal decor, deep sofas and wooden beams on the ceiling.

### Hostel Kanonia
HOSTEL €
(Map p56; ☎22 635 0676; www.kanonia.pl; ul Jezuicka 2; dm/d 50/180zł; @🖥) Kanonia is a well-run private hostel offering dorm accommodation as well as private singles and doubles at very reasonable prices, given the romantic Old Town location. The simple, functional rooms won't win a beauty contest, but the friendly reception and bar go a long way toward fulfilling most backpackers' needs.

### Dom Przy Rynku Hostel
HOSTEL €
(Map p56; ☎22 831 5033; www.cityhostel.net; Rynek Nowego Miasto 4; dm 50zł; ☺Jul-Sep; @🖥) Located in a quiet corner of the busy New Town, Przy Rynku is a neat, clean and friendly hostel occupying a 19th-century house. Its rooms sleep two to five persons and there's a big kitchen and laundry facilities for guest use.

## SOUTH OF THE OLD TOWN

### Le Méridien Bristol Hotel
HOTEL €€€
(Map p56; ☎22 551 1000; www.lemeridien.pl; ul Krakowskie Przedmieście 42/44; s/d from 900zł; P✱@🖥) If you've got it, flaunt it. Established in 1899 and restored to its former glory after a massive renovation, the Bristol is touted as Poland's most luxurious hotel. Its neoclassical facade conceals a feast of original Art Nouveau features, and huge rooms that are both traditional and homey. Attentive staff cater to every whim, and the

Old Town is only a few minutes' walk away. Book three nights and save 30%.

### Oki Doki Hostel
HOSTEL €
(Map p64; ☎22 828 0122; www.okidoki.pl; Plac Dąbrowskiego 3; dm 45-55zł, s/d from 130/180zł; @🖥) This is arguably Warsaw's most popular hostel and one of the best. Each of its bright, large rooms is individually named and decorated (for David Lynch fans, there's a 'Wild at Heart' room). The owners are well travelled and know the needs of backpackers, providing a late-opening bar (where you can buy breakfast in the morning), a self-service laundry and bike rental.

### Hotel Harenda
HOTEL €€
(Map p64; ☎22 826 0071; www.hotelharenda .com.pl; ul Krakowskie Przedmieście 4/6; s/d/ste 340/380/490zł; P🖥) Housed in an elegant neoclassical building, the Harenda boasts a quiet location close to the Old Town and an appealingly old-fashioned ambience. The single rooms are on the small side but the bathrooms are spotless; you're paying for the location here.

### Hostel Helvetia
HOSTEL €
(Map p64; ☎22 826 7108; www.hostel-helvetia .pl; ul Kopernika 36/40, enter at ul Sewerynow 7; dm from 58zł, d with/without bathroom 220/180zł; @🖥) Another of Warsaw's quality hostels, Helvetia has spick-and-span rooms painted in warm, bright colours with wooden floors and a good amount of space. Bicycles and scooters are available for rent, laundry and kitchen facilities are in top order, and with a limited number of beds, it's best to book ahead in summer.

### Sofitel Victoria
HOTEL €€€
(Map p64; ☎022 657 8011; www.sofitel.com; ul Królewska 11; r from 500zł; P@🖥) Conveniently located midway between the Old Town and the Palace of Culture & Science, the Sofitel offers real luxury at rates that are usually a bit lower than competing five-star properties. With all the bits and bobs you'd expect from a top hotel (great concierge service, full wellness centre, the occasional celebrity overnighting), it's a fine choice, and an even better one if you can secure a discount from the website.

## FINANCIAL DISTRICT
The Financial District is home to some of the city's swankiest five-star hotels, including luxury chains like the **InterContinental** (☎22 328 8888; www.warsaw.intercontinental.com) and

# Central Warsaw

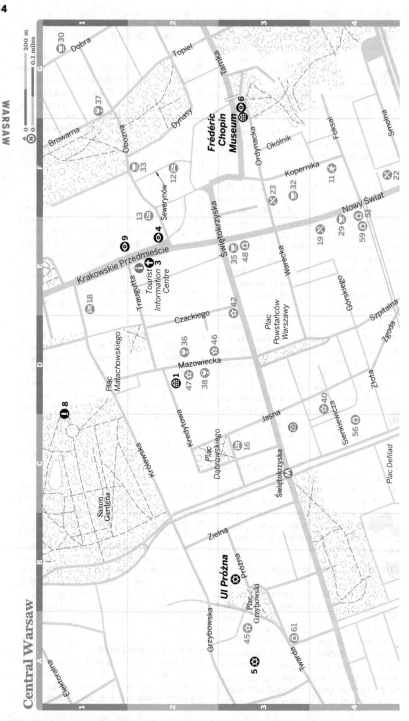

WARSAW

200 m
0.1 miles

Dobra
Topiel
Browarna
Obozna
Dynasy
Tamka
Frédéric
Chopin
Museum
Ordynacka
Okólnik
Foksal
Smolna
Sewerynów
Kopernika
Nowy Świat
Krakowskie Przedmieście
Świętokrzyska
Warecka
Górskiego
Szpitalna
Tourist
Information
Centre
Traugutta
Czackiego
Plac
Powstańców
Warszawy
Zgoda
Złota
Plac
Małachowskiego
Mazowiecka
Jasna
Sienkiewicza
Plac Defilad
Kredytowa
Plac
Dąbrowskiego
Świętokrzyska
Królewska
Saxon
Gardens
Zielna
Ul Próżna
Próżna
Plac
Grzybowski
Grzybowska
Twarda
Elektoralna

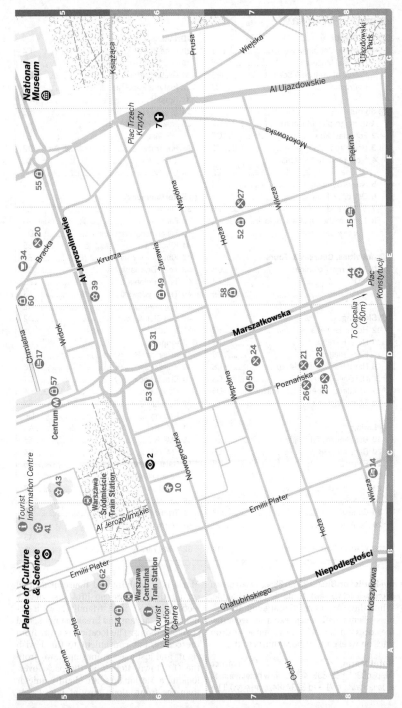

# Central Warsaw

the **RadissonBlu** (☎22 321 8888; www.radisson blu.com/hotel-warsaw), to name but a couple. While these are normally targeted at business clients with deep expense accounts, they occasionally offer deals online or drop rates on weekends. It never hurts to try.

**Hotel Maria**      HOTEL **€€**
(Map p50; ☎22 838 4062; www.hotelmaria.pl; al Jana Pawła II 71; s/d 323/384zł; P❄🛜) The Maria is a rambling old house of a hotel set on three floors (no lifts, just rickety wooden stairs), with friendly staff, a delightful restaurant and breakfast nook, and spacious rooms. The location is away from the centre, but convenient to the Jewish sights and just a few tram stops away from the Old Town. Rooms at the back, overlooking a McDonald's, are slightly quieter than the front, along busy al Jana Pawła

## RENTING YOUR OWN PAD

A short-term rental in a private apartment can be much cheaper than a full-scale hotel, and if you're staying longer than a couple of days, a serious option. Short-term rentals usually have one or two bedrooms (for up to four people), plus a small kitchen with a few handy appliances like a toaster and a coffeemaker. Since there's no reception desk, you'll usually have to phone in advance and set up a meeting place to get the keys. Normally you book online with a credit card or pay in cash on the spot.

**ApartmentsApart** (www.apartmentsapart.com; ☑22 351 2260) offers several attractive apartments in the Old Town area at prices ranging from around 150zł for a tiny studio to 300zł to 500zł per night for larger places. **Warsaw Apartments** (☑22 550 4550; www .warsaw-apartments.com.pl; ul Augustówka 9; 1-/2-person apt 235/265zł; ℗) manages three modern apartment blocks on the outskirts of Warsaw. All are in good order, and the apartments have phones, TVs, cookers and refrigerators, and can be rented by the night; for stays of over a month the nightly rate falls by around half.

**Residence St Andrew's Palace** (Map p64; ☑22 826 4640; www.residencestandrews .pl; ul Chmielna 30; apt from 360zł; ℗@☎) is something a little different. These are exquisitely appointed luxury apartments in a refurbished building on central ul Chmielna. Worth a look and a splurge for something really special.

II. Weekend bookings slice about 100zł off the price.

### Ibis Warszawa Centrum
HOTEL €€

(Map p50; ☑22 520 3000; www.accorhotels.com; al Solidarności 165; s/d 229/289zł; ℗✳@☎) Clean budget chains like Ibis make sense in Warsaw, where reasonably priced hotels with character are in short supply. This one, a little away from the action but well connected by trams, offers tidy, well-appointed rooms, inviting modern baths and a decent breakfast (29zł) to start the day. Book online for an additional 10% discount.

### Premiere Classe
HOTEL €€

(Map p50; ☑22 624 0800; www.premiereclasse .com.pl; ul Towarowa 2; r 189zł; ℗☎) The rooms – and especially the baths – at this modern, purpose-built budget chain are tiny, but standards are relatively high for what you pay. It's also not very handy for the city's attractions, but the walk to the trams that cruise al Jerozolimskie takes only a few minutes and the bus station is just a hundred metres away.

### SOUTH OF AL JEROZOLIMSKIE

TOP CHOICE **Hotel Rialto**
BOUTIQUE HOTEL €€€

(Map p64; ☑22 584 8700; www.rialto.pl; ul Wilcza 73; r from 450zł; ℗@☎) Billed as Poland's first boutique hotel, this converted townhouse is a monument to early-20th-century design and craftsmanship. Each of the hotel's 44 rooms is individually decorated in Art Nouveau or Art Deco style, with antique and reproduction furniture, period light fittings and mosaic-tiled or marbled bathrooms. There are plenty of modern touches where it counts, such as flat-screen TVs, power showers, and a sauna and steam room. The rack rates are scary, but booking over the website brings prices back down to affordable luxury.

### Nathan's Villa Hostel
HOSTEL €

(Map p64; ☑22 622 2946; www.nathansvilla.com; ul Piękna 24/26; dm from 50zł, s/d 174/194zł; @☎) An established hostel set in a quiet courtyard, south of the centre. Like any good hostel, it has a kitchen, a common room and a reading room, but it also provides free laundry and a simple breakfast. Take bus 525, 519, 505 or 131 from Warszawa Centralna train station to the Plac Konstytucji stop.

### Camping 123
CAMPGROUND €

(Map p50; ☑22 823 3748; www.majawa.pl; ul Bitwy Warszawskiej 1920r 15/17; per person/car/tent 15/ 15/15zł; ℗✷) Set in extensive grounds near the Warszawa Zachodnia bus terminal, Camping 123 has well-tended grass, tree-shaded areas and good facilities, including a tennis court and laundry. Wood-panelled, two-person bungalows (160zł) are also available, but beware, the walls are paper-thin.

### PRAGA
### Krokodyl
HOSTEL €

(☑22 810 1118; www.hostelkrokodyl.com; ul Czapelska 24; dm from 50zł, s/d 150/160zł; @☎) Just what a party spot like Praga needed: a decent, private hostel with no lockout and a pleasant setting to crash after a night out. There are lots of pluses here: cheerful rooms, a clean common cooking area, as well as free wireless and free laundry. A short tram ride brings you into the heart of Warsaw.

### Hotel Hit
HOTEL €€

(Map p50; ☑22 618 9470; www.hithotel.pl; ul Kłopotowskiego 33; s/d 190/220zł; P@☎) Pleasing budget option not far from the best bars in Praga. The clean, snug digs are on the bland side, but excellent value for money. In addition to singles and doubles there are a few apartments on hand for rent (from 300zł).

### Hotel Hetman
HOTEL €€

(Map p50; ☑22 511 9800; www.hotelhetman.pl; ul Kłopotowskiego 36; s/d 280/360zł; P@☎) Across the river but only just over a kilometre's walk or bus ride from the Old Town, the Hetman sports English-speaking staff, fresh rooms decked out in soothing neutral tones, gleaming bathrooms, and a fitness room with Jacuzzi. It's in a quiet location, but buses and trams to all parts of the city stop nearby.

## ✗ Eating

Of all the cities in Poland, you'll eat best in Warsaw. It's not just hearty Polish cuisine on offer, either – you'll find a growing selection of European, Southeast Asian, Indian and Japanese restaurants worthy of your hard-earned cash. Naturally prices have risen with the increased variety, but you can still find some good, cheap eats in the centre, particularly in the form of Poland's classic milk bars.

The largest concentration of eateries exists on and around Nowy Świat and south of al Jerozolimskie. The Old Town generally houses expensive tourist traps, but there is a handful of quality spots if you take the time to look.

### OLD TOWN & AROUND

### Fret á Porter
POLISH €€€

(Map p56; ☑22 635 2055; www.fretaporter.pl; ul Freta 37; mains 30-45zł; ☉noon-11pm) One of a number of attractive restaurants on tree-lined New Town Sq. The menu is a mix of Polish and international favourites, so you can start out with an appetiser of *pierogi* (dumplings) and choose something like salmon or steak for a main dish. The terrace is a perfect spot for a meal on a nice evening; there's live entertainment – usually a singer – some nights.

### Pierrogeria
POLISH €€

(Map p56; www.pierrogeria.pl; ul Krzywe Koło 30; mains 20-25zł) The perfect spot for lunch or a light dinner built around an order of *pierogi*, either served in the classical way, boiled, or baked, along with a hearty soup and dessert. The prices are reasonable for this quality of food, and the quaint Old Town setting could not be nicer.

### Restauracja Pod Samsonem
JEWISH €€

(Map p56; www.podsamsonem.pl; ul Freta 3/5; mains 20-35zł) Situated in the New Town, Pod Samsonem is frequented by locals and tourists looking for inexpensive and tasty Polish food infused with a Jewish flavour – marinated herring, gefilte fish and *kawior po żydowsku* ('Jewish caviar' – chopped chicken liver with garlic).

### Podwale 25
POLISH €€

(Map p56; www.podwale25.pl; Podwale 25; mains 25-45zł) The motto here is 'a lot of good food for a reasonable price' and that's what you can expect from this visitor-friendly Bavarian or Czech-style beerhouse, just a few minutes' walk outside the Old Town.

### SOUTH OF THE OLD TOWN

### TOP CHOICE Deco Kredens
POLISH €€€

(Map p64; www.kredens.com.pl; ul Ordynacka 13; mains 35-75zł; ☉10am-11pm Mon-Fri, 11am-11pm Sat & Sun) This place flaunts an appealingly over-the-top Art Deco dining room, which looks for all the world like a 1930s bordello (minus the ladies). Fat armchairs tempt you to linger over a menu of Polish and international cuisine – the crispy roast duck, served on a wooden platter with potato pancakes, beetroot and baked apple, is superb.

### Cô Tú
ASIAN €

(Map p64; Hadlowo-Usługowe 21; mains 12-18zł; ☉10am-9pm Mon-Fri, 11am-7pm Sat & Sun) The wok at this simple Asian diner never rests as hungry Poles can't get enough of the excellent dishes coming from the kitchen. The menu is enormous, covering all the main bases (seafood, vegetable, beef, chicken, pork), and you'll never have to wait more than 10 minutes for your food despite the queues. Hadlowo-Usługowe is accessed through the archway at Nowy Świat 26.

### Bar Nam Sajgon
VIETNAMESE €

(Map p64; Bracka 18; mains 15-24zł; ☉9am-10pm Mon-Thu, 9am-midnight Fri & Sat, 10am-9pm Sun) The line at the counter can stretch pretty

## MORE THAN MILK

Warsaw's booming real estate market has been rough on the city's milk bars (bar mleczny), those dirt-cheap, canteen-like holdovers from communist times where hearty Polish meals – many vegetarian or dairy-based, hence the name – are dished out from steam tables to appreciative, hungry customers. In a town where everyone has their eye on making a złoty, it seems there's not much room for restaurants that still calculate prices in grosze. Don't despair: while the ranks are thinning, there are still several around town, and many in the areas of most interest to visitors.

In the Old Town, just outside the Barbican, look for **Bar Mleczny Pod Barbakanem** (Map p56; ul Mostowa 27/29; mains 5-9zł; ☺8am-5pm Mon-Fri, 9am-5pm Sat & Sun), a staple that's been around for decades. Don't be put off by the faded exterior; this remains a popular place for lunch.

In the swanky part of Warsaw, south of Old Town, **Bar Mleczny Familijny** (Map p64; ul Nowy Świat 39; mains 6-10zł; ☺7am-8pm Mon-Fri, 9am-5pm Sat & Sun) is a sentimental favourite, known around the city for its zupa szczawiowa (sorrel soup) and pierogi z truskawkami (strawberry fruit dumplings).

In the sprawling area south of al Jerozolimskie, stop in for a bite at **Prasowy** (Map p50; ul Marszałkowska 10/16; mains 6-10zł; ☺8am-9pm Mon-Fri, 10am-5pm Sat), with its classy '60s interior so retro it could feature on the cover of Wallpaper magazine.

Praga's favourite milk bar would have to be **Rusałka** (Map p50; ul Floriańska 14; mains 6-10zł; ☺7am-6pm Mon-Fri, 9am-5pm Sat), which attracts a devoted blue-collar clientele and workers from the nearby hospital.

long at lunchtime as nearby office workers line up to get arguably the best pho in this part of the city. Choose from beef or chicken broth, plus a handful of other specialities, take a number and a seat. Your soul-stirring soup will arrive in a few minutes.

**Delikatesy Braci Gessler** POLISH €
(Map p56; www.gessler.pl; ul Krakowskie Przedmieście 13; sandwiches 5zł; ☺8am-11pm Mon-Fri, 9am-11pm Sat, 10am-11pm Sun) If time or money is in short supply, make a beeline for this upscale deli for the city's best over-stuffed, over-sized sandwiches for 5zł each.

### SOUTH OF AL JEROZOLIMSKIE

**Charlotte Chleb i Wino** FRENCH €€
(Map p50; www.bistrocharlotte.com; Plac Zbawiciela; mains 15-30zł; ☺7am-midnight Mon-Fri, 9am-midnight Sat, 9am-10pm Sun; 🛜) Dazzling French bakery and bistro, dishing out tantalising croissants and pastries at the break of dawn, and then transitioning to big salads and crusty sandwiches through the lunch and dinner hours, and finally to wine on the terrace in the evening. Shares the same space as one of the city's favourite beer dives, Plan B, which can make for strange bedfellows some nights when crowds from both places spill out onto the square.

**Dżonka** ASIAN €€
(Map p64; ☏22 621 5015; ul Hoża 54; mains 10-30zł; ☺11am-7pm Mon-Fri, to 6pm Sat & Sun) With only six tables, 'petite' is no over-exaggeration for Dżonka's size. Small it may be, but big it is on Asian cuisine, serving up steaming Thai soups, Mandarin chicken and spicy (by Polish standards) beef Szechwan. Reservations recommended.

**Tomo** JAPANESE €€€
(Map p64; www.tomo.pl; ul Krucza 16/22; mains 50-90zł) You could do worse than spend an hour at Tomo's sushi bar, gazing at the little boats ferrying tiny morsels of sushi and maki in never-ending circles. The likes of tempura and teriyaki are also available, and staff are friendly and English-speaking.

**Ganesh** INDIAN €€
(Map p64; www.ganesh.pl; ul Wilcza 50/52; mains 30-45zł; ☒) This corner restaurant just opposite the Warsaw Tortilla Factory has emerged as the local favourite among a growing number of Indian places in town. The usual selection of tandoori chicken and rogan josh are available, and vegetarians are well catered for too.

**Beirut** MIDDLE EASTERN €
(Map p64; ul Poznańska 12; mains 12-20zł; 🛜☒) Very hip, the small Beirut 'Hummus and Music Bar' brings together two of our

favourite things in life. The limited menu features hummus in a couple of variations, the 'spicy' is surprisingly good, as well as salads, falafel and pita. There are a few tables and some stand-up counters. There's a turntable on hand for later in the evening, when the music part kicks in.

**Tel Aviv** MIDDLE EASTERN €
(Map p64; www.tel-aviv.pl; ul Poznańska 11; mains 10-20zł; 🕾🍴) Just across the street from Beirut, the Tel Aviv offers kosher Middle Eastern and Israeli foods, including lots of vegetarian salads and dips like babaganoush and hummus (though, truth be told, we prefer the hummus at Beirut). Where this place excels (and one-ups Beirut) is in the spacious, light and airy cafe, where you can relax with a book or laptop and enjoy the food.

**Tandoor Palace** INDIAN €€
(Map p50; www.tandoor.com.pl; ul Marszałkowska 21/25; mains 25-50zł; 🍴) A long-time stalwart on Warsaw's Indian food scene and still one of the best in the city. The Palace's food is prepared by experienced North Indian chefs using a genuine tandoor. The extensive menu ranges from classics such as butter chicken, *shahi korma* (chicken or lamb in a mild, creamy sauce with crushed almonds) and *biryani* to Kashmiri *balti* dishes and sizzling platters.

**Warsaw Tortilla Factory** MEXICAN €€
(Map p64; www.warsawtortillafactory.pl; ul Wilcza 46; mains 18-35zł; ⊙noon-1am Sun-Thu, noon-2am Fri & Sat) The rap on this Mexican place is that standards started sliding with a change in ownership, but on our visit in 2011 the burritos were as good as ever, the service friendly and the drinks flowing. Truth be told, this isn't a culinary destination in its own right, but more of a party spot, with decent food thrown into the mix.

**Greenway** VEGETARIAN €
(Map p50; www.greenway.pl; ul Marszałkowska 28; mains 10-15zł; ⊙10am-9pm; 🍴) One branch of a countrywide chain swept to popularity by its healthy food selection. Take your pick from the international menu, which includes Mexican goulash, Warsaw curry, samosas and enchiladas. Portions are hefty, and there's no table service.

## PRAGA

**Mississippi Blues** AMERICAN €€
(Map p50; ☎605 887 857; www.bluesbbq.pl; ul Meksykańska 3; mains 25-30zł; ⊙noon-9pm Sun-Thu, to 10pm Fri & Sat) This tiny restaurant tucked away behind a Carrefour supermarket on the southern end of Praga is no gimmicky chain; it's the real McCoy if you're looking for slow-cooked BBQ, pulled pork, ribs and burgers. The platters are good deals, combining mains with healthy portions of sides like beans, slaw and, naturally, fries. Call ahead to book a table since there're only around 25 chairs and the place fills up fast.

# 🍷 Drinking

Varsovians don't generally distinguish between places that serve coffee and those that serve alcohol. Most places do both, starting out the day pushing caffeine and ending up selling mostly beers and cocktails.

Most drinking establishments open at 11am or noon and close when *ostatni gość* (the last guest) leaves – in practice, any time between midnight and 4am.

Cafe culture is a relatively new phenomenon in Warsaw, but locals adore it. You'll find places across the city, and new ones popping up on a regular basis. In addition to what's listed here, check out the combined coffeehouse-bookstores that have taken the city by storm in recent years (see boxed text, p72).

## OLD TOWN & AROUND

**Polyester** CAFE, BAR
(Map p56; www.polyestercafe.com; ul Freta 49/51; 🕾) Another relative newcomer to the city's drinking scene, Polyester, with its fashionably retro furnishings and vibe, is arguably the hippest cocktail bar in the vicinity of the Old Town. Serves excellent cocktails, as well as a full range of coffee drinks and light food.

**Pożegnanie z Afryką** CAFE
(Map p56; www.pozegnanie.com; ul Freta 4/6; coffees 8-10zł, snacks 8-12zł) 'Out of Africa' is a tiny cafe offering nothing but coffee – but what coffee! Choose from around 50 varieties, served in a little pot, and a range of tempting cakes. This is the original shop in a chain of several branches scattered around Poland's major cities.

**Same Fusy** TEAHOUSE
(Only Tea Leaves; Map p56; www.samefusy.pl, in Polish; ul Nowomiejska 10; tea 12-19zł; snacks 8-12zł; ⊙1-11pm) This place is a superbly designed surprise: an Oriental-style cafe on the 1st floor and a stylish tearoom downstairs. Over a hundred different types of tea, from the accepted norm to the 'out of the ordinary'.

## CONCENTRATED DRINKING

Warsaw's nightlife is as dispersed as it is diverse, but there are a few central points where bar-hopping doesn't require taking the bus.

Arguably, the best grouping of nightspots per square metre can be found along ul Mazowiecka, a couple of blocks west of ul Krakowskie Przedmieście. **U Artystów** (Map p64; www.uartystow.com; ul Mazowiecka 11a) and **Paparazzi** (Map p64; www.paparazzi.com.pl; ul Mazowiecka 12) are both popular drinking and clubbing spots, the former draws an arty crowd, the latter a glamorous one. For dancing, try **Zoo Club & Lounge** (Map p64; www.klubzoo.pl; ul Mazowiecka 13). Nearby, **Tygmont** (Map p64; www.tygmont.com.pl; ul Mazowiecka 6/8) is one of the city's best venues for live acts, including jazz.

If your taste runs to dive bars and holes in the wall, look no further than the happening district of Praga, across the Vistula. There are several bars and clubs within easy walking distance of each other and enough going on that you could easily spend the whole evening – and the wee hours of the morning – on this side of the river. Start a night of carousing at **Po Drugiej Stronie Lustra** (Map p50; www.po2stronielustra.com; ul Ząbkowska 5), with its inviting garden and dozens of different beers, including many hard-to-find microbrews. Across the street there's **W Oparach Absurdu** (Map p50; www.oparyabsurdu.pl; ul Ząbkowska 6), with its eclectic bric-a-brac interior and occasional live bands from countries like Belarus and Ukraine. Just a few steps along Ząbkowska brings you to another classic old-school Praga bar: **Łysy Pingwin** (Map p50; http://lysypingwin.pl; ul Ząbkowska 11). If, after all this drinking, you're in the mood to dance, head a few blocks north to **Sen Pszczoły** (Map p50; www.senpszczoly.pl; ul Inżynierska 3). The name translates loosely as 'The Dream of Bees' – a reference to a Salvador Dali painting. The setting is certainly surreal: an old factory converted to a chilled-out dance club and drinking garden.

### SOUTH OF THE OLD TOWN

**Nowy Wspaniały Świat**          CAFE, BAR
(Map p64; www.nowywspanialyswiat.pl; Nowy Świat 63; 🕾) This bar-cafe-restaurant and cultural centre is a relative newcomer to the Warsaw scene and is already packed day and night. Part of this is simply location, on the sweetest spot on Nowy Świat. The rest is simply the vibe, relaxed and happening at the same time. The little terrace in the back is a popular spot in summer. The restaurant serves mostly snacks, like salads, pancakes and quesadillas.

**Cafe Blikle**          CAFE
(Map p64; www.blikle.pl; ul Nowy Świat 35; coffee from 9zł, donut to go 2.90zł; 🕾9am-7pm Mon-Sat, 10am-6pm Sun; 🕾) The mere fact that Blikle has survived two world wars and the pressure of communism makes it a household name. But what makes this legendary cafe truly famous is its donuts, for which people have been queuing up for generations. Join the back of the line and find out why.

**Między Nami**          COCKTAIL BAR
(Map p64; www.miedzynamicafe.com, in Polish; ul Bracka 20) A mix of bar, restaurant and cafe, 'Between You & Me' attracts a trendy set with its designer furniture, whitewashed walls and excellent vegetarian menu.

### FINANCIAL DISTRICT

**Paparazzi**          COCKTAIL BAR
(Map p64; www.paparazzi.com.pl; ul Mazowiecka 12) Paparazzi is a long-time mainstay on the popular Mazowiecka scene, but it still somehow manages to retain a whiff of fashionable exclusivity. Its speciality is cocktails, and with talented and friendly bar staff, it remains one of the best bars in town.

### SOUTH OF AL JEROZOLIMSKIE

**Plan B**          BAR
(Map p50; www.planbe.pl, in Polish; al Wyzwolenia 18) This phenomenally popular upstairs bar on Plac Zbawiciela draws a mix of students and young office workers. Find some couch space and relax to smooth beats from regular DJs. On warm summer evenings the action spills out onto the street, giving Plac Zbawiciela the feel of a summer block party.

**Coffee Karma**          CAFE
(Map p50; Plac Zbawiciela 3/5; sandwiches & snacks 10-15zł; 🕾7.30am-10pm Mon-Fri, 10am-10pm Sat & Sun; 🕾) This is a laid-back coffeehouse with an enviable perch on Plac

## COFFEE & A GOOD READ

Poles have had a long love affair with literature, but a relatively recent love is coffee. It was therefore only a matter of time before someone came up with the cafe-bookshop, thus providing locals with a practical ménage à trois. These intellectual establishments have sprung up across town, offering racks of books alongside coffee, tea and snacks. They're wonderful places to spend a few hours, dipping into a book or catching a literary event or concert, which are held on a regular basis at many. Some of the more frequented places include the following:

**Kafka** (Map p64; ul Oboźna 3; ⊙9am-10pm; ☎) This quiet cafe serving healthy cakes, quiches and sweet-and-sour pancakes (3zł to 10zł) is our personal favourite. Choose from its big selection of secondhand books and kick back on its low couches or outdoor seating.

**Chłodna 25** (Map p50; http://chlodna25.blog.pl; ul Chłodna 25; ⊙8am-10pm Mon-Thu, 8am-midnight Fri, noon-midnight Sat, noon-10pm Sun; ☎) Bohemian haunt attracting journalists, artists, musicians and anyone else who can fit through the door. Concerts, films, debates and lectures feature regularly; wine, beer and homemade cakes available.

**Instytut Reportażu** (Map p64; www.instytutr.pl; ul Gałczyńskiego 7; ⊙9am-10pm; ☎) Small, peaceful bookstore and coffeehouse that draws journalists and those interested in Polish and world affairs. The location is on a trendy backstreet behind Nowy Świat.

**Czuły Barbarzyńca** (Map p64; ul Dobra 31; ⊙10am-10pm Mon-Thu, 10am-midnight Fri & Sat, noon-10pm Sun; ☎) Stripped-back space where books, discussions and readings come first and coffee (albeit good) is just along for the ride. The 'Gentle Barbarian' was the city's first cafe-bookshop.

**Tarabuk** (Map p64; www.tarabuk.pl; ul Browarna 6; ⊙10am-10pm Mon-Fri, noon-10pm Sat & Sun; ☎) Cosy cafe that not only provides space for books and coffee, but also concerts, readings, lectures and vodka.

Zbawiciela, with comfy couches and light foods and sandwiches. The wireless here is free and reliable, but get here early if you want to snag a spot near an electrical outlet.

**Green Coffee** CAFE
(Map p64; www.greencoffee.pl; ul Marszałkowska 84/92; coffee 9zł, snacks 7-15zł; ⊙7am-11pm; ☎) The rich aroma of coffee pervades your senses as you enter this relaxed cafe on an otherwise nondescript section of Marszałkowska. The coffee is reputedly the best in town, and the food an inviting mix of cakes, quiches, sandwiches and muffins. Service apparently depends on the weather.

## ☆ Entertainment

Warsaw's range of classical and contemporary entertainment options is the best in the country. The city is home to many classical music, opera and theatre venues, and the list of clubs grows longer every year. Film is also well represented in both mainstream and art-house cinemas.

Detailed listings of museums, art galleries, cinemas, theatres, musical events and festivals (in Polish only) can be found in the Friday edition of *Gazeta Wyborcza*. A free what's-on monthly *Aktivist* (www.aktivist.pl in Polish) is distributed through restaurants, bars and clubs, though the listings are only in Polish. Another useful source of listings in Polish (but it can be deciphered with some effort) is the website www.kulturalnie.waw.pl.

As for useful English-language listings, the monthly *Warsaw Insider* (www.warsawinsider.pl) and the entertainment columns of the weekly *Warsaw Voice* (www.warsawvoice.pl) provide some information on cultural events, as well as on bars, pubs and other nightspots.

Tickets for theatre, opera, musical events and visiting shows can be bought from **Eventim** (Map p64; ☎22 590 6915; www.eventim.pl; al Jerozolimskie 25; ⊙9am-7pm Mon-Fri) and some EMPiK stores (see p74).

### Live Music & Clubs

In addition to the clubs mentioned here, check out the places around ul Mazowiecka and in Praga (see boxed text, p71).

**Stodoła**  LIVE MUSIC
(Map p50; www.stodola.pl; ul Batorego 10) Originally the canteen for builders of the Palace of Culture & Science, Stodoła is one of Warsaw's biggest and longest-running student clubs. It hosts events, club nights and touring bands when they're in town.

**Tygmont**  JAZZ
(Map p64; www.tygmont.com.pl; ul Mazowiecka 6/8) Hosting both local and international acts, the live jazz here is both varied and plentiful. Concerts start around 9pm but it fills up early, so either reserve a table or turn up at opening time (6pm). Dinner is also available.

**Fabryka Trzciny**  CLUB
(Map p50; ☑508 365 849; www.fabrykatrzciny.pl; ul Otwocka 14) Located in a revamped factory in the heart of Praga, this art centre hosts a range of events, including well-patronised clubbing nights. Call or check the website before heading out, since this place is only open on event nights.

**Klubokawiarnia**  CLUB
(Map p64; www.klubo.pl, in Polish; ul Czackiego 3/5) Under the steady gaze of communist icons, dance the night away to great music with a chilled party crowd at this basement club. Regular fancy-dress events are held to spice up an already funky night.

## Classical Music & Opera

Warsaw is a great music city, with regular offerings from the symphony orchestras supplemented by lively music fests and church concerts. Buy tickets, which run anywhere from 20zł to 130zł, at venue box offices. Note that many venues take a summer break in July and August.

In addition to the venues listed here, the Chopin Society brings in pianists from around the world for its **free Chopin recitals** in Łazienki Park from mid-May until the end of September at noon and 4pm.

**Filharmonia Narodowa**  CLASSICAL MUSIC
(National Philharmonic; Map p64; ☑22 551 7128; www.filharmonia.pl; ul Jasna 5; ◷10am-2pm & 3-7pm Mon-Sat) Home of the world-famous National Philharmonic Orchestra and Choir of Poland, founded in 1901, this venue has a concert hall (enter from ul Sienkiewicza 10) and a chamber-music hall (enter from ul Moniuszki 5), both of which stage regular concerts. The box office entrance is on ul Sienkiewicza.

**Warszawa Opera Kameralna**  OPERA
(Warsaw Chamber Opera; ☑22 831 2240; www.operakameralna.pl; al Solidarności 76b; ◷box office 9am-6pm Mon-Fri, 3hr before performance Sat & Sun) The Warszawa Opera's repertoire ranges from medieval mystery plays to contemporary works, but it's most famous for its performances of Mozart's operas – the annual Mozart Festival (p62) is staged here.

**Teatr Wielki**  OPERA
(Grand Theatre; Map p56; ☑22 692 0208; www.teatrwielki.pl; Plac Teatralny 1; ◷box office 10am-7pm Mon-Fri) This magnificent neoclassical theatre, dating from 1833 and rebuilt after WWII, is the city's main stage for opera and ballet, with a repertoire of international classics and works by Polish composers, notably Stanisław Moniuszko.

## Cinemas

Most films (except for children's films, which are dubbed into Polish) are screened in their original language with Polish subtitles. Admission prices range from 10zł to 33zł. The best cinemas in Warsaw include the following:

**Kino.Lab**  CINEMA
(www.kinolab.art.pl; Ujadowski Castle; ul Jazdów 2) Art-house fare brought to you by the Centre for Contemporary Art focuses on 'historical and contemporary avant-garde work of both Polish and foreign provenance'.

**Kino Luna**  CINEMA
(www.kinoluna.pl, in Polish; ul Marszałkowska 28) Mainly arthouse films from around the world.

**Kinoteka**  CINEMA
(Map p64; www.kinoteka.pl; Plac Defilad 1) Multiplex housed in the Palace of Culture & Science; entrance faces al Jerozolimskie.

**Muranów Cinema**  CINEMA
(ul Gen Andersa 1) Screens arthouse films.

## Theatre

Polish theatre has long had a high profile and continues to do so. Warsaw has about 20 theatres, including some of the best in the country. Most theatres close in July and August for their annual holidays.

The leading playhouses, all of which lean toward contemporary productions in Polish, include: **Teatr Ateneum** (www.teatrateneum.pl, in Polish; ul Jaracza 2); **Teatr Dramatyczny** (Map p64; www.teatrdramatyczny.pl, in Polish; Palace of Culture & Science, Plac Defilad 1); the

**Teatr Polonia** (Map p64; www.teatrpolonia .pl, in Polish; ul Marszałkowska 56); and **Teatr Powszechny** (Map p50; ul Zamojskiego 20).

The **Teatr Żydowski** (Jewish Theatre; Map p64; ☑22 850 5656; www.teatr-zydowski.art.pl; Plac Grzybowski 12/16; ☺box office 11am-2pm & 3-6pm Mon-Fri, 12.30-7pm Sat, 2.30-6pm Sun) derives its inspiration from Jewish culture and traditions, and some of its productions are performed in Yiddish. Polish and English translations are provided through headphones.

## 🔒 Shopping

Like any modern city, Warsaw has all the brand-name stores and plethora of shopping malls you'd expect in the West. For the most part, prices are a little cheaper here, but things probably won't stay that way for long.

The upshot of all this commercialisation is the slow death of establishments that have existed since the communist era and beyond – a case of goodbye Marx, hello Marks & Spencer. Some still exist, but whether they can weather the shopping storm is anyone's guess.

The main shopping area lies in the maze of streets between the Palace of Culture & Science and ul Nowy Świat, and along the eastern part of al Jerozolimskie and the southern part of ul Marszałkowska.

**Galeria Grafiki i Plakatu** POSTERS
(Map p64; www.galeriagrafikiiplakatu.pl; ul Hoża 40; ☺11am-6pm Mon-Fri, 10am-3pm Sat) This small gallery stocks what is unquestionably the best selection of original prints and graphic art in Poland. It also has a good range of posters.

**Desa Unicum** ANTIQUES
(Map p50; www.desa.pl in Polish; ul Marszałkowska 34/50; ☺11am-7pm Mon-Fri, 11am-4pm Sat) Desa Unicum is an art and antiques dealership that sells a range of old furniture, silverware, watches, paintings, icons and jewellery.

**Traffic Club** BOOKS
(Map p64; www.traffic-club.pl; ul Bracka 25; ☺10am-10pm Mon-Sat, to 7pm Sun) Multilevelled and multicoloured mega store with city maps on the 1st floor and English and German fiction on the 2nd.

**Galeria Art** ART
(Map p56; www.galeriaart.pl; ul Krakowskie Przedmieście 17; ☺11.30am-7pm Mon-Fri, to 5pm Sat) Owned by the Union of Polish Artists, this gallery offers a broad range of contem-porary Polish art for sale, and an English-speaking manager who may – or may not – be of help.

**EMPiK** BOOKS
(www.empik.com, in Polish) ul Marszałkowska (Map p64; ul Marszałkowska 116/122); ul Nowy Świat (Map p64; ul Nowy Świat 15/17); Złote Tarasy (Map p64; ul Złota 59) Has 15 stores Warsaw-wide; stocks a wide selection of British, German, French and US newspapers and magazines.

**Złote Tarasy** MALL
(Map p64; www.zlotetarasy.pl; ul Złota 59; ☺10am-10pm Mon-Sat, to 8pm Sun) A popular, very central mall, with almost every high-street name you can think of. Its distinctive curved glass roof is clearly visible near the Palace of Science & Culture.

**Arkadia** MALL
(Map p50; www.arkadia.com.pl; al Jana Pawła II 82; ☺10am-10pm Mon-Sat, to 9pm Sun) The largest shopping mall in Poland, with almost 200 stores under one roof. It's handy to the Dworzec Gdański metro station.

**American Bookstore** BOOKS
(www.americanbookstore.pl, in Polish) Sadyba Best Mall (ul Powsińska 31); ul Nowy Świat (Map p64; ul Nowy Świat 61; ☺10am-7pm Mon-Sat, to 6pm Sun) Sells English-language publications, including travel guides.

**Cepelia** HANDICRAFTS
(www.cepelia.pl; ☺11am-7pm Mon-Fri, 10am-2pm Sat) Plac Konstytucji (Plac Konstytucji 5); ul Chmielna (Map p64; ul Chmielna 8); ul Krucza (Map p64; ul Krucza 23); ul Marszałkowska (Map p64; ul Marszałkowska 99/101) A long-established organisation dedicated to promoting Polish arts and crafts, Cepelia stocks its shops with woodwork, pottery, sculpture, fabrics, embroidery, lace, paintings and traditional costumes from various Polish regions.

**Atlas** BOOKS
(al Jana Pawła II 26; ☺10am-7pm Mon-Fri, 10am-2pm Sat) Specialises in maps, atlases and travel guides; the best place in town for hiking and national park maps.

**Neptunea** JEWELLERY, CRAFTS
(Map p56; www.neptunea.pl; ul Krakowskie Przedmieście 47/51; ☺11am-7pm Mon-Fri, to 5pm Sat) Talk about a mish-mash of items. Neptunea is a purveyor of Polish jewellery, carved stoneware and crafts, along with furniture, shells and even musical instruments from across the globe.

## TRUE CRAFTSMANSHIP

Forget the shopping malls and generic chain stores. *Real* shoppers should take to the back streets of Warsaw, where the art of handmaking products is still alive, and quality over quantity is paramount. Here are a few of the city's better spots:

**Jan Kielman & Sons** (Map p64; www.kielman.pl; ul Chmielna 6; ⏰11am-7pm Mon-Fri, to 2pm Sat) The Kielman clan has been making shoes since 1883. Their leather footwear starts at 2000zł a pair, but you'll probably have them for life.

**Wyrobów Oświetleniowych** (Map p64; www.oswietlenie.strefa.pl; ul Emilii Plater 36; ⏰9am-5pm Mon-Fri) Need an exquisite chandelier? Pick up a Gothic or fin-de-siécle number here. Most end up in museums and palaces, but there are a few pieces available (wall lamps start at 700zł) for the average Joe.

**Aniela** (Map p64; ul Żurawia 26; ⏰11am-6pm Mon-Fri) Possibly the last corset maker in Warsaw; slim-lined, and tight fitting, since 1896.

**Bracia Łopieńscy** (Map p64; ul Poznańska 24; ⏰9am-5pm Mon-Fri) The oldest bronze-metal foundry in Warsaw has been in business since 1862. Pick up exceptional pieces in the shape of candleholders, mirror and picture frames, wall lamps etc.

### Hala Mirowska    MARKET
(al Jana Pawła II; ⏰dawn-dusk) Despite being converted into a modern supermarket, Hala Mirowska is worth visiting for its architecture alone. The redbrick pavilion of this 19th-century marketplace is in exceptional condition, and there's still a semblance of market atmosphere here; a few stalls selling fresh flowers, fruit and vegetables line its south and west sides.

### Galeria Centrum    SHOPPING CENTRE
(Map p64; ul Marszałkowska 104/122; ⏰9.30am-9pm Mon-Fri, 9.30am-8pm Sat, 11am-5pm Sun) A privatised version of the formerly state-owned chain of Domy Towarowe shops, this department store sells mass-market men's, women's and children's clothing, accessories, shoes, cosmetics and jewellery.

### Sadyba Best Mall    MALL
(www.sadyba.pl; ul Powsińska 31; ⏰10am-9pm Mon-Sat, to 8pm Sun) A modern mall housing a wide range of fashion stores, shoe shops, jewellery and perfume stores, an American Bookstore branch, a multiplex cinema and a dozen different eating places.

### Bazar na Kole    MARKET
(ul Obozowa; ⏰early morning-2pm Sat & Sun) This huge antiques and bric-a-brac market, located in the western suburb of Koło, offers everything from old farm implements and furniture to WWII relics such as rusted German helmets, ammo boxes and shell casings. You will have to pick through the junk to find a bargain, but that's half the fun. Take tram 12, 13 or 24 to the Dalibora stop.

## ℹ Information

### Dangers & Annoyances
Warsaw is no more dangerous than any other European capital city, but you should take precautions while walking at night, and watch your possessions on public transport and in other crowded places. Bikes are particularly at risk; try not to leave your bike out of sight for too long, and always lock it firmly with the strongest lock you can find. Beware also of 'mafia taxis' (see p78).

Praga is getting better but still has a reputation as a rough area at night. Most locals use taxis as transport in and out of the neighbourhood, and so should you.

### Internet Access
Internet cafes in Warsaw come and go. Be forewarned.

**Arena A2** (Plac Konstytucja 5; per hr 6zł; ⏰24h)

**Incognito** (al Jerozolimskie 65/79; per hr 6zł; ⏰24h) In the warren of shops below the Marriott Hotel.

**Verso Internet** (ul Freta 17; per hr 5zł; ⏰8am-8pm Mon-Fri, 9am-5pm Sat, 10am-4pm Sun) Enter off ul Świętojańska.

### Medical Services
For an ambulance call 🕾999, or 🕾112 from a mobile phone. English-speaking dispatchers are rare, however, so you're probably better off phoning the following medical centres. For non-urgent treatment, you can go to one of the city's many *przychodnia* (outpatient clinics). Your hotel or your embassy (see p418) can provide recommendations.

There are plenty of pharmacies in Warsaw where you can get medical advice; look or ask for an *apteka*.

**Apteka 21** (☎22 825 3128; Warszawa Centralna train station, al Jerozolimskie 54; ☺24hr) An all-night pharmacy at the central train station.

**Damian Medical Centre** (☎22 566 2222; www.damian.pl; ul Wałbrzyska 46; ☺7am-9pm Mon-Fri, 8am-8pm Sat, 10am-3pm Sun) A reputable private outpatient clinic with hospital facilities.

**EuroDental** (☎22 627 5888; www.eurodental .pl; ul Śniadeckich 12/16; ☺8am-8pm Mon-Sat, 10am-2pm Sun) Private dental clinic with multilingual staff.

**LIM Medical Center** (☎22 458 7000; www .cmlim.pl; Marriott Hotel Bldg, al Jerozolim-skie 65/79; ☺8am-8pm Mon-Fri, to 4pm Sat) Private clinic with English-speaking specialist doctors and its own ambulance service; carries out laboratory tests and arranges house calls.

### Money

*Kantors* (currency-exchange offices) and ATMs are easy to find around the city centre. There are 24-hour *kantors* at the Warszawa Centralna train station and either side of the immigration counters at the airport, but exchange rates at these places are about 10% lower than in the city centre. Avoid changing money in the Old Town, where rates are poor.

**Bank Pekao** Marriott Hotel (al Jerozolimskie 65/79); Plac Bankowy (Plac Bankowy 2); ul Krakowskie Przedmieście (ul Krakowskie Przedmieście 1); ul Wilcza (ul Wilcza 70) Cashes travellers cheques and has more than a dozen offices in the city centre. Cash advances on Visa and MasterCard.

**Western Union** (Bank Pekao, Plac Bankowy 2; ☺9am-4pm Mon-Fri) Money-transfer service, works through branches of Bank Pekao.

### Post & Telephone

**Main post office** (Poczta Główna; ul Świętokrzyska 31/33; ☺24hr) One of over a hundred post offices in the city. Poste restante is at windows 41 and 42 (address c/o Poste Restante, Poczta Główna, ul Świętokrzyska 31/33, 00-001 Warszawa), and a rack of public phones is close by.

### Tourist Information

Warsaw is blessed with a fantastic network of Tourist Information Centres, with convenient branches all around the city. These centres are invariably staffed with cheerful English speakers with oodles of free brochures on what to do, where to stay, where to eat, and just about everything else. They can help you sort out transport and make accommodation recommendations.

There are several free monthly tourist magazines worth seeking out. Some of the better ones include *Poland: What, Where, When;* *What's Up in Warsaw;* and *Welcome to Warsaw.* All are mines of information about cultural events and provide reviews of new restaurants, bars and nightclubs. They're available in the lobbies of most top-end hotels. The comprehensive monthlies *Warsaw Insider* (10zł) and *Warsaw in Your Pocket* (5zł) are also useful, and are sometimes free for the asking at hotel reception desks.

**Tourist Information Centre** (Centrum Informacji Turystycznej; ☎22 194 31; www .warsawtour.pl) Airport (Arrivals Hall Terminal 2; ☺8am-8pm May-Sep, 8am-6pm Oct-Apr; Financial District (Map p64; Plac Defilad 1; ☺8am-8pm); Old Town (Map p64; ul Krakowskie Przedmieście 15/17; ☺11am-9pm May-Sep, 9am-6pm Oct-Apr); Old Town Square (Map p56; Stary Rynek 19; ☺9am-9pm); Warszawa Centralna train station (Map p64; ☺8am-8pm May-Sep, 8am-6pm Oct-Apr)

### Travel Agencies

**Almatur** (☎22 826 3512; www.almatur.com.pl; ul Kopernika 23; ☺9am-7pm Mon-Fri, 10am-3pm Sat) Handles student travel.

**Kampio** (☎22 823 7070; www.kampio.com .pl; ul Maszynowa 9/2; ☺8am-4.30pm Mon-Fri) Focuses on ecotourism, organising kayaking, biking, walking and birdwatching trips.

**STA Travel** (☎801 401 801; www.sonatatravel .com.pl; ul Krucza 41/43; ☺10am-6pm Mon-Fri, to 2pm Sat) Like Almatur, specialises in student travel.

### Websites

**www.e-warsaw.pl** Official website of the city of Warsaw.

**www.inyourpocket.com/city/warsaw.html** Highly opinionated and often amusing.

**www.warsaw-life.com** Eating, sleeping, drinking and shopping reviews.

**www.warsawtour.pl** Official website of the Warsaw Tourist Information Centre.

**www.warsawvoice.pl** Online version of the English-language magazine.

## ⊙ Getting There & Away

### Air

**Warsaw-Frédéric Chopin Airport** (Port Lotniczy im F Chopina; off Map p50; ☎22 650 4220; www.lotnisko-chopina.pl) lies in the suburb of Okęcie, at the southern end of ul Żwirki i Wigury, 10km south of the city centre; it handles all domestic and international flights.

The airport formally has two terminals, though most flights arrive and depart from the new Terminal 2. Here you'll find a **tourist information desk** (☺8am-8pm May-Sep, to 6pm Oct-Apr), which sells city maps and can help visitors find accommodation. You will also find some **currency-exchange counters** (☺24hr), half a dozen ATMs, and several car-hire agencies. You can buy tickets for public transport from any one of several newsagents.

You'll find information about domestic routes and fares on p424. Tickets can be booked at **LOT** (Polish Airlines; ☑22 222 1000; www.lot.com; Złote Tarasy Mall, ul Złota 59; ⊘9am-9pm Mon-Sat, 10am-8pm Sun) or at most travel agencies. The LOT timetable lists international flights to and from Poland on various airlines, along with LOT's own international and domestic flights.

### Bus

**Warszawa Zachodnia bus terminal** (☑70 340 3330; www.pksbilety.pl; al Jerozolimskie 144), west of the city centre, handles the majority of international and domestic routes in and out of the city. Bus tickets are sold at the terminal.

Various bus operators run regular services to cities throughout Poland. Some sample destinations and fares include: Gdańsk (50zł, five to seven hours), Lublin (41zł, 3½ hours), Częstochowa (40zł, 3½ hours), Kazimierz Dolny (25zł, 2½ hours), Kraków (50zł, 5½ hours), Olsztyn (35zł, 3½ to four hours), Toruń (47zł, four hours), Wrocław (57zł, 6½ hours) and Zakopane (65zł, 7¾ hours).

For information on international bus routes, see p423.

### Car

All the major international car-hire companies have offices in Warsaw (p426), many of which are based at the airport. Polish companies offer cheaper rates, but may have fewer English-speaking staff and rental options. One dependable local operator is **Local Rent-a-Car** (☑22 826 7100; www.lrc.com.pl; ul Marszałkowska 140), which offers a mid-sized Opal in the summer months for around €40 a day, or €220 a week, including tax, collision damage waiver (CDW), theft protection and unlimited mileage.

### Train

Warsaw has several train stations, but the one most travellers use is **Warszawa Centralna train station** (Dworzec Centralny, Warsaw

Central; Map p64; ☑197 57; al Jerozolimskie 54). Refer to the Getting There & Away section in the destination chapters for information about services to/from Warsaw. For details of international trains, see p423).

Centralna was built in the 1970s as a communist-era megaproject but had become pretty seedy by the 2000s. As part of Poland's bid to host the Euro 2012 international football (soccer) tournament, officials embarked on an enormous clean-up, which has restored the main arrival and departure hall to its original gleam (but left the lower-level train platforms and shop arcades still fairly grotty).

You'll find ticket counters, ATMs and snack bars, several newsagents (where you can buy public-transport tickets) and a tourist information desk in the vast main hall. Along the underground passages leading to the tracks and platforms are a dozen *kantors* (one of which is open 24 hours), a **left-luggage office** (⊘7am-9pm; per 24hr 8zł), luggage lockers (9zł per 24 hours), eateries, several other places to buy tickets for local public transport, and bookshops.

The process for buying tickets, both for international and domestic destinations, has eased considerably in recent years. **Ticket counters** (☑197 57; www.intercity.pl; ⊘9am-8pm) line the wall of the main hall and are well marked. Though, in theory, most ticket agents should be able to handle some English, not all do. It's still best to write down your destination, dates and times to be able to communicate with the ticket seller.

Some domestic trains also stop at **Warszawa Zachodnia train station** (Map p50; al Jerozolimskie), next to Warszawa Zachodnia bus terminal, and at Warszawa Wschodnia, in Praga, on the east bank of the Vistula.

## ❶ Getting Around

### To/From the Airport

The cheapest way of getting from the airport to the city (and vice versa) is by city bus 175 (2.80zł, every eight to 15 minutes, 4.50am to 11.10pm), which will take you all the way to the Old Town, passing en route along al Jerozolimskie, ul Nowy Świat and ul Krakowskie Przedmieście. Don't forget to buy a ticket at a newsagent in the arrivals hall, and to validate your ticket in one of the ticket machines when you board the bus.

The taxi stand is right outside the door of the arrivals hall and handles taxis run by Super Taxi, Sawa Taxi and others. They all have desks inside the terminal, so you can ask about the fare to your destination – it should be around 40zł to Centralna station and 60zł to the Old Town.

### Bicycle

Cycling in Warsaw is a double-edged sword. The city is generally flat and easy to navigate, distances aren't too great, and cycle paths are on the increase. However, Warsaw drivers don't give a toss about cyclists and you'll soon be following the locals' lead and sharing the footpath with pedestrians. Bike hire is available from Oki Doki Hostel and Hostel Helvetia.

## Car & Motorcycle

Warsaw's streets are full of potholes – some more dangerous than others – so driving demands constant attention.

The local government has introduced paid parking on central streets. You pay using coins in the nearest ticket machine *(parkomat)* and get a receipt that you display in the windscreen. For security, try to park your car in a guarded car park *(parking strzeżony)*. There are some in central Warsaw, including one on ul Parkingowa, behind the Novotel.

**PZM** (📞196 37 nationwide), the Polish Automobile Association, operates a 24-hour road breakdown service *(pomoc drogowa)*.

## Public Transport

Warsaw's integrated public-transport system is operated by **Zarząd Transportu Miejskiego** (City Transportation Board; 📞24hr info line 22 194 84; www.ztm.waw.pl) and consists of tram, bus and metro lines, all using the same ticketing system. The main routes operate from about 5am to 11pm, and services are frequent and pretty reliable, though it's often crowded during rush hours (7am till 9am and 3.30pm till 6.30pm Monday to Friday). Friday and Saturday nights the metro runs until 2.30am. After 11pm several night-bus routes link major suburbs to the city centre. The night-service 'hub' is at ul Emilii Plater, next to the Palace of Culture & Science, from where buses depart every half-hour.

Buy a ticket before boarding buses, trams and metros. Tickets are sold at Ruch and Relay newsstands, some hotels, post offices, metro stations and various general stores – look for a sign saying 'Sprzedaży Biletów ZTM'.

Tickets, timetables and information are available at ZTM information desks at several underground stations, including the following:
**Punkt informacji ZTM** (Pawilon 09, Ratusz-Arsenal metro station; ⏰7am-8pm Mon-Fri)
**Punkt informacji ZTM** (Pawilon 1002, Plac Wilsona metro station; ⏰7am-8pm Mon-Fri)

Several ticket prices and packages are available depending on your needs. For most trips, a *jednorazowy bilet* (single-journey ticket) is sufficient. It costs 2.80zł (3zł if purchased from the driver; kids under seven ride free). These tickets are not valid for transferring between services.

For several journeys within a short period of time, consider a *90-minutowy bilet* (90-minute

ticket), which costs 6zł, and allows for unlimited transfers.

If you're going to be staying in town for a while, it's more convenient to purchase one-/three-/seven-day unlimited transfer tickets (9/16/32zł). These tickets cover night buses; otherwise a single fare costs 4.80zł. Foreign students under 26 years of age who have an International Student Identity Card (ISIC) get a discount of around 50%.

There are no conductors on board vehicles. Validate your ticket by feeding it (magnetic stripe facing down) into the little yellow machine on the bus or tram or in the metro-station lobby the first time you board; this stamps the time and date on it (or the route number for single-fare tickets). Inspections are common and fines are high (150zł plus 2.80zł for a ticket, payable on the spot). Watch out for pickpockets on crowded buses and trams.

The construction of Warsaw's metro system began in 1983 and so far only a single line is in operation, running from the southern suburb of Ursynów (Kabaty station) to Młociny in the north via the city centre. There are long-term plans to build a second, east–west line. Yellow signs with a big red letter 'M' indicate the entrances to metro stations. Every station has a public toilet and there are lifts for disabled passengers. You use the same tickets as on trams and buses, but you validate the ticket at the gate at the entrance to the platform, not inside the vehicle. Trains run every eight minutes (every four minutes during rush hours).

## Taxi

Taxis in Warsaw are easily available and not too expensive: around 6zł flag fall and 2.40/3.60zł per kilometre during the day/night within the centre. Reliable companies include **MPT Radio Taxi** (📞191 91), which has English-speaking dispatchers, **Super Taxi** (📞196 22), and **Halo Taxi** (📞196 23). All are recognisable by signs on the taxi's roof with the company name and phone number.

Beware of 'pirate' or 'mafia' taxis, which do not display a phone number or company logo – the drivers may try to overcharge you and turn rude and aggressive if you question the fare. They are not as common as in the past, but still haunt tourist spots looking for likely victims.

All official taxis in Warsaw have their meters adjusted to the appropriate tariff, so you just pay what the meter says. When you board a taxi, make sure the meter is turned on in your presence, which ensures you don't have the previous passenger's fare added to yours. Taxis can be waved down on the street, but it is better to order a taxi by phone; there's no extra charge for this service.

# AROUND WARSAW

## Kampinos National Park

Popularly known as the Puszcza Kampinoska, the **Kampinos National Park** (Kampinoski Park Narodowy; http://kampinoski-pn.gov.pl, in Polish) begins just outside Warsaw's north-western administrative boundaries and stretches west for about 40km. It's one of the largest national parks in Poland, with around three-quarters of its area covered by forest, mainly pine and oak.

The park includes Europe's largest area of inland sand dunes, mostly tree-covered and up to 30m high, and it's a strange feeling to have sand between your toes so far from the sea. Other parts of the park are barely accessible peat bogs that shelter much of its animal life.

Kampinos is popular with hikers and cyclists from the capital, who take advantage of its 300km of marked walking and cycling trails. The eastern part of the park, closer to the city, is more favoured by walkers as it's accessible by public transport; the western part is less visited. As well as half- and one-day hikes, there are two long trails that traverse the entire length of the park, both starting from Dziekanów Leśny on the eastern edge of the park. The red trail (54km) ends in Brochów, and the green one (51km) in Żelazowa Wola.

If you plan on hiking in the park, buy a copy of the Compass *Kampinoski Park Narodowy* map (scale 1:30,000), available from bookshops in Warsaw.

Bivouac sites designated for camping are the only accommodation options within the park's boundaries, but there are hotels close by in Czosnów, Laski, Leszno, Tułowice and Zaborów. Warsaw's tourist information centres have a list of places to stay near the park.

### ⓘ Getting There & Away

The most popular jumping-off point for walks in the eastern part of the park is the village of Truskaw. To get there from central Warsaw, take tram 4 or 36 northbound on ul Marszałkowska to Plac Wilsona, then city bus 708 (two or three an hour on weekdays, hourly on Saturday).

PKS buses run from Warszawa Zachodnia bus terminal to Kampinos (around 10zł, one hour, three daily).

## Żelazowa Wola

If it wasn't for Poland's most famous musician, Żelazowa Wola (zheh-lah-*zo*-vah *vo*-lah) wouldn't be on the tourist map. This tiny village 53km west of Warsaw is the birthplace of Frédéric Chopin, and the house where he was born on 22 February 1810 has been restored and furnished in period style to create a **museum** (http://chopin.museum /en; adult/concession museum & park ticket 23/14zł, park only 7/4zł; ☑9am-7pm Tue-Sun May-Sep, 9am-6pm Tue-Sun Oct & Apr, 9am-5pm Tue-Sun Nov-Mar). It's a lovely little country house with beautiful gardens, but there is little in the way of original memorabilia. Nonetheless, the tranquillity and charm of the place make it a pleasant stop.

**Piano recitals**, often performed by top-rank virtuosos, are normally held here each Sunday from the first Sunday in May to the last Sunday in September. There are usually two concerts, up to an hour long, at noon and 3pm; there's no fee other than the park entry ticket. The programme can be found on http://en.chopin.nifc.pl.

### ⓘ Getting There & Away

There are a few PKS buses that run from the Warszawa Zachodnia bus terminal to Żelazowa Wola (10zł, 1¼ hours). The private bus company **Motobus** (www.motobuss.pl; ☑60 473 6522) also runs buses between central Warsaw and Sochaczew that stop in Żelazowa Wola for 7zł each way. As of this writing departures were at 6am, 7.10am and 8.10am, with returns at 2.14pm and 5.54pm. Buses depart from near a shopping centre at ul Marszałkowska 104/122. Call or consult the website for more information.

# Mazovia & Podlasie

POP 6 MILLION

## Includes »

## Best Places to Eat

» Powroty (p90)
» Ato Sushi (p87)
» Restauracja Tejsza (p99)
» Ogródek Pod Jabłoniami (p108)
» Ganesh (p87)

## Best Places to Stay

» Hotel Tumski (p93)
» Andel's (p86)
» Music Hostel (p86)
» Hotel Branicki (p96)
» Jaczno (p111)

## Why Go?

The rolling landscape and rural bliss of Mazovia (Mazowsze in Polish) have a deceptively long history, but the signs are easy to spot if you know where to look. Once a duchy, this province is dotted with castles, cathedrals and palaces, the biggest of which reside in the riverside towns of Płock and Pułtusk. Łódź is Mazovia's reigning capital, with more going for it than meets the eye. It's the country's third-largest metropolis and could easily win 'Poland's Ugliest City' award, but if you take the time to discover its charms, you'll be happy you did.

Podlasie is the verdant green lungs of Poland. Aside from a few patches of urbanisation, this province is a paradise of farmland, forest and lakes. Its four national parks are splendid: Narew and Biebrza for their marshlands; Wigry for its lakes; and Białowieża for its primeval forest and king of Polish fauna, the bison.

## When to Go

### Łódź

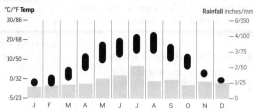

°C/°F Temp                                          Rainfall inches/mm

**May–Jun**
Celebrate spring amid the lush primeval greenery of Białowieża National Park.

**Jul–Aug**
Enjoy the warm weather while kayaking in and around the Augustów Canal.

**Sep**
Łódź celebrates the 'Four Cultures' (Polish, Russian, Jewish, German) festival.

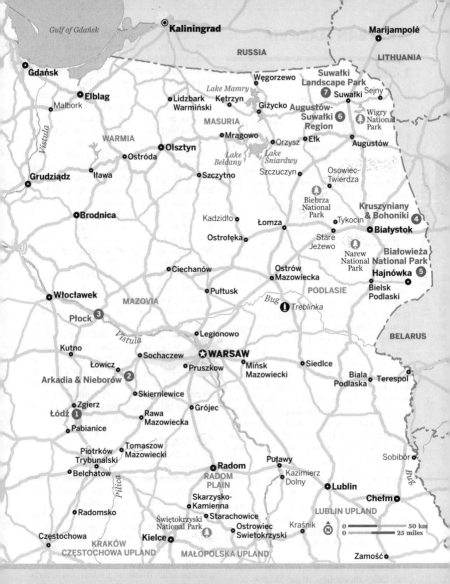

## Mazovia & Podlasie Highlights

① Marvelling at the ugly streets and hidden gems of **Łódź** (p82)

② Harking back to a time when romance was all the rage at **Arkadia & Nieborów** (p91)

③ Wondering how **Płock** (p91) got hold of so many Art Nouveau treasures

④ Exploring the last remnants of Poland's Tatar culture at **Kruszyniany & Bohoniki** (p101)

⑤ Searching primeval forest for a glimpse of the rare European bison at **Białowieża National Park** (p102)

⑥ Relaxing the mind and exercising the body kayaking the Rospuda and Czarna Hańcza in the **Augustów-Suwałki region** (p105)

⑦ Catching your breath as the sun breaks through the clouds to reveal the stunning scenery of the **Suwałki Landscape Park** (p111)

# WESTERN MAZOVIA

## Łódź

POP 737,000

Poland's third-largest city grew fabulously wealthy in the 19th century on the backs of its massive textile mills – and the thousands of workers who toiled inside them. That wealth was shattered in waves: by the Great Depression of the 1930s, the tragic German occupation during WWII, and the inept communist regime that came after. By 1990, the city was an industrial ruin, on par in some ways with present-day Detroit or the former industrial powerhouses in the British Midlands. The future looked bleak.

But Łódź (woodge) is not just a story of decline, but one of rebirth. In recent years, millions of euros have been poured into the city in an effort to spur one of the country's – and continent's – biggest renovation efforts. The investments have led to the rejuvenation of ul Piotrkowska, the main pedestrian thoroughfare, and creation of Manufaktura, Europe's biggest combined shopping, business and amusement centre, carved out of the decaying husks of the old mills.

Łódź has other things going for it as well, including being the centre of the Polish film industry. Polish directorial giants like Andrzej Wajda, Roman Polański and Krzysztof Kieślowski honed their talents here. American film director David Lynch was so smitten by Łódź that he set some of his 2006 film, *Inland Empire,* here. You can even stay in Lynch's suite at the Centrum Hotel.

Travellers interested in Jewish heritage have a special reason to visit. Before WWII, Łódź was Poland's second-largest Jewish city, after Warsaw, with a community numbering some 230,000. During the war, the Germans created Poland's second-biggest Jewish ghetto in a depressed section north of the centre. The area is still impoverished and looks much like it did during those grim years.

### History

Although the first account of its existence dates from 1332, Łódź remained an obscure settlement until the beginning of the 19th century. In the 1820s the government of the Congress Kingdom of Poland – eyeing the town's advantageous position at what was then the border of Russia and Prussia – chose Łódź as a new textile centre.

Enterprising industrialists – primarily Jews, but also Poles, Germans and Russians – rushed in to build textile mills, closely followed by thousands of workers. The wealthy mill owners built opulent palaces (the Historical Museum of Łódź and the Cinematography Museum currently fill two), while workers occupied purpose-built tenements surrounding the factories. By the outbreak of WWI, Łódź had grown a thousandfold, reaching a population of half a million.

Following WWI, the city's growth began to slow. With the newly created independent Poland, the city lost access to the huge Russian market, and then came the Great Depression in 1929. WWII tragically changed the city forever, as the Nazis first incarcerated Łódź' massive Jewish community and then gradually shipped the residents off to extermination camps. More than 200,000 people passed through Łódź' wartime ghetto, and just a few thousand survived.

The communists continued textile production into the modern age, but skimped on investment and the city lost its competitive advantage. The year 1989 saw a city in decline, with a largely impoverished population dependent on an industry that was rapidly disappearing. Around the year 2000, the city's leaders decided to embark on a path of renewal, embracing the city's industrial heritage and carving out today's quirky, likable and historically fascinating destination.

## ◉ Sights

### CITY CENTRE

**Museum of Art**                    MUSEUM

(Muzeum Sztuki; www.msl.org.pl; ul Więckowskiego 36; adult/concession 7/4zł; ◷10am-5pm Tue-Sun) This mostly modern art museum is certainly worth the few blocks' walk west of ul Piotrkowska. On hand is an extensive collection of 20th-century paintings, drawings, sculpture and photography from Poland and abroad. There are also works by Picasso, Chagall and Ernst (though these are not always on display).

**Cinematography Museum**                    MUSEUM

(Muzeum Kinematografii; www.kinomuzeum.pl; Plac Zwycięstwa 1; adult/concession 8/5zł; ◷9am-4pm Tue, 10am-5pm Wed & Fri, 11am-7pm Thu, 11am-6pm Sat & Sun) Housed in the palatial home of 'Cotton King' Karol Scheibler, this attraction is actually two museums in one. The basement and 1st floor are devoted to Polish cinema and contain props, film posters and archaic camera equipment connected to the city's cinematic past. Everything changes, however, once you reach the ground floor – here the wealth of 19th-century Łódź is plain to see. Room after room is filled with extravagant *boiserie* (elaborately carved wood panelling), dreamy ceiling frescoes and elaborate ceramic stoves. The 'Mirror Room' is a particular delight, with three crystal mirrors and angels coated in 24-carat gold.

### Central Museum of Textiles    MUSEUM

(Centralne Muzeum Włókiennictwa; www.muzeum wlokiennictwa.pl; ul Piotrkowska 282; adult/concession 10/6zł; ⊙9am-5pm Tue, Wed & Fri, 11am-7pm Thu, 11am-4pm Sat & Sun) Those wishing to dig a little deeper into Łódź' past should take a gander at this museum. It's appropriately located inside Ludwig Geyer's gorgeous White Factory, the city's oldest textile mill, dating from 1839. The collection consists of textile machinery, early looms and fabrics, clothing and other objects related to the industry.

### Priest's Mill    MUSEUM

(Księży Młyn; www.msl.org.pl; ul Przędzalniana 72; adult/concession 8/5zł; ⊙10am-5pm Tue-Fri, 11am-6pm Sat & Sun) Now a branch of the Museum of Art, the Priest's Mill started life in 1875 as a grand villa of the wealthy Herbst family.

Although the owners fled before WWII, taking all the furnishings and works of art with them, the interior has been restored and furnished like the original, giving an insight into how the barons of industry once lived. The whole area was part of a model 19th-century mill town, now partially restored, the dream of Herbst's father-in-law, Karol Scheibler. The setting is 1.5km east of the Central Museum of Textiles (a 20-minute walk along ul Tymienieckiego).

### JEWISH GHETTO

The rapid industrial expansion of Łódź in the 19th century attracted Jews to the city starting in the 1830s, and as early as the 1840s Jews accounted for around 20% of the population. Many settled in the northern half of the city, in the area around today's Stary Rynek (Old Town Sq), and by the time the Germans invaded in 1939, their numbers had grown to 230,000.

In May 1940 the Germans sealed off the northern part of Łódź to create the second-biggest Jewish ghetto in Poland, after the Warsaw ghetto. Sometimes referred to as the Litzmannstadt ghetto after the German name for Łódź, more than 200,000 Jews passed through its gates between then and August 1944, when the ghetto was liquidated.

## THE 'LITZMANNSTADT' GHETTO

Award-winning films like *Schindler's List* and *The Pianist* in recent years have helped to popularise the plight of Poland's Jews during WWII in Kraków and Warsaw, respectively, but the story of the Łódź – or Litzmannstadt – ghetto remains relatively obscure. Litzmannstadt was the first of the big urban Jewish ghettos to be set up by the Germans, in 1940, and the last of these ghettos to be liquidated, in 1944. At its height, the ghetto held around 200,000 people – mostly local Jews but also sizable groups from Prague, Vienna, Berlin, Hamburg and Luxembourg, as well as 5000 Roma from Austria.

The Litzmannstadt ghetto was not a typical ghetto. It was not used primarily as a holding centre, as in Warsaw, but was more of a forced labour camp harnessed directly to the German war effort. In Łódź, Jews were obliged to barter their labour in exchange for the shred of hope they might survive the war. In the end, only a handful managed.

For four long years, the ghetto survived under the highly controversial leadership of Jewish elder Mordechai Chaim Rumkowski. Rumkowski led a policy of collaboration with the Germans as a way of prolonging the lives of ghetto inhabitants. When in 1942 the Germans demanded more victims to clear space in the ghetto, Rumkowski infamously pleaded with mothers to give up their children. The mothers refused, but in the end 7000 children were rounded up and shipped to the Chełmno extermination camp.

The Łódź ghetto was liquidated in August 1944, just as the Warsaw city uprising was under way and the Soviet Red Army was closing in fast from the east. The Nazis sent 73,000 Jews to Auschwitz-Birkenau in a 20-day period that year from 9 August to 29 August. Rumkowski himself was one of the last to go. He died at Birkenau on 28 August.

After the war, few of the survivors elected to return to Łódź, and the tragic story of the ghetto was eventually buried under a mountain of communist propaganda.

# Łódź

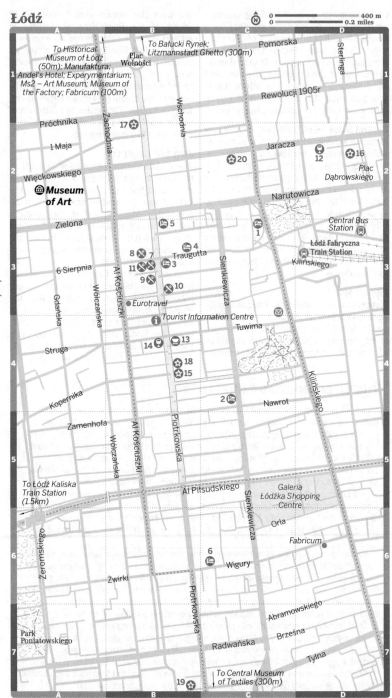

N

0 — 400 m
0 — 0.2 miles

To Historical
Museum of Łódź
(50m); Manufaktura;
Andel's Hotel; Experymentarium;
Ms2 – Art Museum; Museum of
the Factory; Fabricum (100m)

To Bałucki Rynek;
Litzmannstadt Ghetto (300m)

Plac
Wolności

Pomorska

Sterlinga

Próchnika

Zachodnia

17

Wschodnia

Rewolucji 1905r

1 Maja

Jaracza

12

16

Więckowskiego

20

Plac
Dąbrowskiego

Museum
of Art

Narutowicza

Zielona

5

1

Central Bus
Station

8

7

4

Trauggutta

Łódź Fabryczna
Train Station

6 Sierpnia

11

3

Sienkiewicza

Kilińskiego

9

10

Gdańska

Wólczańska

Al Kościuszki

Eurotravel

Tourist Information Centre

Tuwima

Struga

14

13

Kopernika

18

15

Zamenhofa

2

Nawrot

Kilińskiego

To Łódź Kaliska
Train Station
(1.5km)

Al Piłsudskiego

Galeria
Łódzka Shopping
Centre

Żeromskiego

Piotrkowska

Sienkiewicza

Orla

Fabricum

Żwirki

6

Wigury

Piotrkowska

Abramowskiego

Park
Poniatowskiego

Radwańska

Brzeźna

Tylna

19

To Central Museum
of Textiles (300m)

# Łódź

**◉ Top Sights**
Museum of Art .................................. A2

**◉ Sights**
Aleja Gwiazd .............................. (see 3)

**🛏 Sleeping**
1 Centrum Hotel .................................. C3
2 Flamingo Hostel .............................. C4
3 Hotel Grand .................................... B3
4 Hotel Savoy .................................... B3
5 Music Hostel .................................... B3
6 Revelo ............................................ C6

**🍴 Eating**
7 Anatewka .......................................... B3
8 Ato Sushi ........................................ B3
9 Ganesh ............................................ B3
10 Greenway ...................................... B3
11 Presto ............................................ B3

**🍷 Drinking**
12 Bagdad Café .................................. D2
13 Café Kofeina .................................. B4
14 Piotrkowska Klub ............................ B4

**🎭 Entertainment**
15 Cultural Information Centre .............. B4
16 Grand Theatre ................................ D2
17 Jazzga Jazz Club ............................ B2
18 Łódź Kaliska .................................. B4
19 Łódź Philharmonic .......................... B7
20 Teatr Jaracza ................................ C2

The vast majority of these people died from exhaustion, malnutrition or disease, or were dispatched from the **Radegast** rail station to their deaths at extermination camps at Chełmno and Auschwitz-Birkenau (see the boxed text, p83).

The tourist information office hands out a free map called the 'Litzmannstadt Ghetto' as well as a useful free booklet titled 'Jewish Landmarks in Łódź', which traces out a long 10km walking tour of the former ghetto and identifies the main sites, beginning at the **Bałucki Rynek**, the administrative centre of the ghetto, all the way to Radegast station and the **Jewish Cemetery**.

The area today remains remarkably depressed. Many of the buildings where Jews were forced to live are still standing and seemingly little changed from WWII. This is one Holocaust memorial where you can still feel the squalor.

**Radegast Station**          MEMORIAL
(Pomnik Zagłady Litzmannstadt Ghetto; ul Stalowa; admission free; ⊙10am-6pm) Radegast station was the main deportation centre for Jews sent to death camps at Chełmno and Auschwitz-Birkenau. The station, about 3km northeast of Bałucki Rynek, has been preserved and now holds a moving memorial to those lost in the Holocaust. Three original Deutsche Reichsbahn cattle cars used for the deportations stand silently next to the now-defunct station, and original deportation lists (some headed with '*Zur Arbeit*' – 'to work') line a long concrete tunnel nearby. When the Red Army liberated Łódź in 1945, only 880 Jewish survivors remained.

**Jewish Cemetery**          CEMETERY
(Cmentarz Żydowski; ul Bracka, enter from ul Zmienna; admission free; ⊙10am-4pm Sun-Fri) About 1km south of Radegast Station, a 20-minute walk, is the city's Jewish cemetery. Founded in 1892, it is the largest Jewish graveyard in Europe, with around 68,000 surviving tombstones, some of which are very beautiful. It is currently enjoying a partial clean-up, but the further you wander from the entrance off ul Zmienna the more overgrown and wild it becomes.

Both the cemetery and monument are about 3km northeast of the centre. Take tram 1 from ul Kilińskiego or tram 6 from al Kościuszki.

## MANUFAKTURA

The **Manufaktura** (www.manufaktura.com; ul Drewnowska 58; free admission to shops & restaurants; ⊙9am-9pm) shopping, entertainment and office complex deserves to be listed as a tourist attraction in its own right. While most of this enormous (more than 100,000-sq-metre) structure is an ordinary mall, the sheer size and the setting – in a once-abandoned 19th-century textile mill – are extraordinary. In addition to nearly every conceivable retail outlet, there are bowling lanes, a multiplex cinema, a video game arcade and a handful of worthwhile museums. Trams 3 and 11 run from near ul Piotrkowska to Manufaktura.

**TOP CHOICE Historical Museum of Łódź**  MUSEUM
(Muzeum Historii Miasta Łodzi; www.muzeum-lodz.pl; ul Ogrodowa 15; adult/concession 9/5zł; ⊙10am-2pm Mon, 10am-4pm Tue & Thu, 2-6pm Wed, 11am-6pm Sat & Sun) This highly recommended museum is housed in the impressive palace of 19th-century textile

baron Izrael Kalmanowicz Poznański. The museum's opulent interior is a clear indication of the Poznańskis' wealth: it's bedecked with elaborate dark-wood wall panelling, delicate stained-glass windows and a suitably grand ballroom. Despite the exhibitions taking a back seat to the building, they're interesting all the same, covering Łódź' history, the Łódź ghetto, and famous citizens including pianist Artur Rubinstein, writer Jerzy Kosiński and poet Julian Tuwim. All three, of Jewish origin, were born in Łódź.

### Experymentarium MUSEUM
(www.experymentarium.pl; ul Jana Karskiego 5; adult/concession 16/12zł; ☺10am-9pm) Seemingly designed for kids and high school science nerds, this modern, interactive science museum, in fact, is a blast at any age. The exhibits are built around staid subjects like chemistry and astronomy, but the displays encourage visitors to touch and play, and learn in the process. There's a cosmic tunnel, laser games and optical illusions to keep things moving.

### Ms2 – Art Museum MUSEUM
(Ms2 – Muzeum Sztuki; www.msl.org.pl; ul Ogrodowa 19; adult/concession 8/5zł; ☺10am-9pm Tue, noon-8pm Wed-Sun) A worthy adjunct to the city's main art museum, this one focuses on experimental and avant-garde works from the 20th and 21st centuries. The setting, in an abandoned weaving mill, is a treat. There's a good in-house cafe.

### Museum of the Factory MUSEUM
(Muzeum Fabriki; www.muzeum.manufaktura.com; ul Drewnowska 58; adult/concession 4/3zł; ☺9am-7pm Tue-Fri, 11am-7pm Sat & Sun) The Museum of the Factory is not as impressive as other museums in town but is nevertheless a passable rainy-day attraction with some old textile machines, fascinating maps and a short video of the textile king himself, Izrael Kalmanowicz Poznański.

## ★ Festivals & Events

Łódź is blessed with festivals year-round.

### Łódź Ballet Meetings DANCE
A dance and ballet festival that includes both Polish and foreign groups, and runs for two weeks in May every odd-numbered year. Performances are staged in the Grand Theatre.

### Fotofestiwal PHOTOGRAPHY
(www.fotofestiwal.com) Held annually in May, one of the country's leading festivals of photography and visual arts.

### Four Cultures THEATRE
(www.4kultury.pl) Theatre, music and film festival held each year in September celebrating the city's historic role as a meeting place of four cultures: Polish, Jewish, Russian and German.

## 🛏 Sleeping

### TOP CHOICE Andel's HOTEL €€€
(☎42 279 1000; www.andelslodz.com; ul Ogrodowa 17; s/d 400/600zł; P✳@☎☒) The owners of this luxury property could write the book on how to turn a drab, redbrick mill into a fab postmodern palace. The sleek, oversized lobby wows you on entry, then there are the playful throw pillows and beanbag chairs for casual lounging. The rooms are sleek contemporary, with bold colours, flat-screen TVs and stylish bathrooms with big tubs. There are several restaurants on-site and a rooftop pool, and the Manufaktura shopping centre is right on your doorstep.

### Music Hostel HOSTEL €
(☎533 533 263; www.music-hostel.pl; ul Piotrkowska 60; dm 35-50zł; s & d from 120zł; @☎) Enter through the passageway at Piotrkowska 60 and walk all the way to the back of the alley to find this clean and hip hostel on the right-hand side. The theme here is music, with albums and posters of Hendrix, the Beatles and everyone else festooned on the wall. The light, airy rooms feature big wooden bunks and big windows. There's a collective kitchen and computers on hand to surf the web when you're not out on the town.

### Flamingo Hostel HOSTEL €
(☎42 661 1888; http://lodz.flamingo-hostel.com; ul Sienkiewicza 67; dm 40-55zł; s & d from 120zł; @☎) This centrally located chic hostel offers a glamorous shared modern kitchen, handsome room decor – think minimalist boutique rather than youth hostel – and nice extras like free wi-fi, a computer on hand to check email and even bikes to rent. The downside, and it's a deal-breaker if you hate to climb stairs, is that the rooms are a five-floor walk up.

### Revelo BOUTIQUE HOTEL €€
(☎42 636 8686; www.revelo.pl; ul Wigury 4/6; d/apt 250/299zł; P☎) Revelo does an excellent job of mixing old and new in a beautifully preserved villa dating from 1925. Staff greet you dressed in 1920s outfits and lead you up dark wood stairs to immaculate rooms with

period furniture, brass bedsteads, flat-screen TVs and thoroughly modern bathrooms. Downstairs is filled by the boutique hotel's quality restaurant and attached garden. With only six rooms, it's best to book ahead.

### Hotel Grand HOTEL €€
(☑42 633 9920; www.grandlodz.pl; ul Piotrkowska 72; s/d/apt 290/390/590zł; P@⊛) When the luxury hotel group Likus acquired the regal, 19th-century Grand in 2009 the expectation was that they would transform it quickly into a five-star property. For some reason, that renovation has been delayed, leaving this landmark with a slightly faded feeling. The public areas retain a turn-of-the-century atmosphere but the rooms, while comfortable, are modern and bland.

### Hotel Savoy HOTEL €€
(☑42 632 9360; www.centrumhotele.pl; ul Traugutta 6; s/d from 170/240zł; ⊛) One of the city's aging turn-of-the-century hotels offers probably the best trade-off between price and location, just a block from the choicest section of ul Piotrkowska. While the faded exterior and sizable lobby at least hint at some glorious past, the rooms themselves are a plain brown and beige. That said, they are big and clean, and our bed in 2011 was one of the most comfortable we slept in during our research. Austrian writer Joseph Roth used this hotel as the setting for his 1924 novel of the same name.

### Centrum Hotel HOTEL €€
(☑42 632 8640; www.centrumhotele.pl; ul Kilińskiego 59/63; s/d from 240/270zł; P@⊛) The Centrum is a classic rectangular steel and glass monstrosity from the 1970s; nevertheless its brashness is starting to fade and even exude a perverse retro charm with the passage of time. Unfortunately, many of the mod furnishings haven't survived to the present day, with the exception of the groovy ceiling in the lobby. The rooms are corporate correct, with all mod cons at this price point. The 'David Lynch Suite', room 803, is a swanky '70s-era lounge straight out of a blaxploitation film, and can be rented for around 500zł a night.

##  Eating

### Ato Sushi JAPANESE €€
(www.atosushi.pl; ul 6 Sierpnia 1; mains 30-60zł) This is some of the best sushi in this part of Poland, served in a welcoming setting. The menu is a mix of traditional nigiri sushi

and rolls, plus a few inventive, more-modern creations, like the 'Fashion Roll' with fried tofu. The menu is Polish only, but the staff are willing to help translate.

### Ganesh INDIAN €€
(www.ganesh.pl; ul Piotrkowska 69; mains 20-35zł; ☑) One of the country's best Indian restaurants just happens to be inside this passageway at ul Piotrkowska 69. The kitchen is open, allowing you to see the Indian chefs work their way with the chicken tikka masalas and other curries on offer. There's a second branch at Piotrkowska 55, but this original outlet remains our favourite.

### Anatewka JEWISH €€
(☑42 630 3635; www.anatewka.pl; ul 6 Sierpnia 2; mains 25-50zł) This Jewish restaurant just off Piotrkowska is often packed with expats and young Poles eager to sample excellent duck and goose mains. The atmosphere is warm and convivial, and the dining experience is rounded off with live music some nights. It's popular, so you may want to book in advance.

### Greenway VEGETARIAN €
(www.greenway.pl; ul Piotrkowska 80; mains 12-20zł; ⊗9am-9pm; ☑) Part of a Polish vegetarian chain, Greenway is an attractive, modern cafe-bar serving a range of appealing dishes such as Mexican goulash (with beans and sweet corn), Indian vegetable kofta and spinach dumplings. There's also a handy breakfast menu, featuring muesli with yoghurt and fruit. A second Greenway is in the Manufaktura shopping centre.

### Presto ITALIAN €
(www.pizzeriapresto.pl; ul Piotrkowska 67; pizzas 12-30zł) Presto is a simple trattoria with a pizza list almost as long as ul Piotrkowska, and a few pasta dishes thrown in for good measure. What makes it stand out from the crowd? The pizzas are cooked in a wood-fired oven.

## 🍷 Drinking

### Bagdad Café BAR
(www.bagdadcafe.pl; ul Jaracza 45; ⊗9.30am-10pm Mon-Wed, 9.30am-1am Thu, 9.30am-2am Fri, 6pm-2am Sat) Housed in the basement of a crumbling mansion, the Bagdad is the place to head for a cheap, booze-infested night out. The city's top DJs regularly feature on the decks, and a motley crew of students ram the place to overflowing.

## HOLLY-ŁÓDŹ BOULEVARD

Ul Piotrkowska began life in the 19th century as the road to Piotrków Trybunalski (hence its name), then the major town of the region. By the beginning of the 20th century Piotrkowska was an elegant boulevard, lined with Art Nouveau buildings and expensive restaurants, but in the wake of WWII it it became a gloomy, grey street of soot-blackened facades and a handful of half-empty shops. Its revival began in the 1990s, when the Piotrkowska Street Foundation was created by a group of local artists and architects with the aim of turning the derelict street into a lively European avenue. It has also become a sort of homage to locals done good, with statues and stars dedicated to the city's famous sons and daughters.

In front of the Hotel Grand is the **Aleja Gwiazd** (Avenue of the Stars), a series of bronze stars set in the pavement in imitation of Los Angeles' Hollywood Boulevard, each dedicated to a well-known name in Polish film. Nearby, in front of the house (No 78) where the eminent Polish pianist Artur Rubinstein once lived, is **Rubinstein's Piano**, a bronze monument much loved by snap-happy tourists. A few paces down the street is **Tuwim's Bench** (at No 104), another unusual monument, this one created in memory of local poet Julian Tuwim. Touch his nose – it's supposed to bring good luck. The last of the series is **Reymont's Chest** (at No 135), showing the Nobel prize winner for literature, Władysław Reymont, sitting on a large travel trunk.

Although much of ul Piotrkowska is pedestrianised, public transport is provided by a fleet of **bicycle rickshaws** (riksza); for around 6zł they will whisk you from one end to the other.

**Piotrkowska Klub**　　　　　　　　　BAR
(www.97.com.pl; ul Piotrkowska 97; ⊙11am-10pm Sun-Thu, 11am-2am Fri & Sat) Easily recognisable by the two-storey, wrought-iron-and-glass drinking area that stands outside the front door, Piotrkowska Klub has great views up and down its namesake street. Inside it's more sedate, with wood panelling and cosy booths tucked into quiet corners.

**Café Kofeina**　　　　　　　　　CAFE
(ul Piotrkowska 102; ⊙9am-9pm; 🛜) Modern, Starbucks-inspired coffeehouse that nevertheless hits the spot with good espresso-based drinks and a free wireless connection.

## ☆ Entertainment

Both the **Cultural Information Centre** (Centrum Informacji Kulturalnej; ☑42 633 9221; www.cik.lodz.pl, in Polish; ul Piotrkowska 102a; ⊙10am-6pm Mon-Fri, 10am-2pm Sat) and the Tourist Information Centre have information about what's on.

### Clubs

Łódź is well known as Poland's centre for electronic music, but DJs regularly mix it up with hip-hop, house and drum 'n' bass.

**TOP**
**CHOICE/ Łódź Kaliska**　　　　　　　CLUB
(www.klub.lodzkaliska.pl; ul Piotrkowska 102; ⊙noon-2am Mon-Thu & Sun, noon-5am Fri & Sat; 🛜) Łódź Kaliska's reputation as a must-see club extends as far as Warsaw and beyond. With its open-door policy it draws a broad cross-section of Łódź society. The unusual decor – stripped-back walls are covered in fun, semi-erotic photos from the bar's namesake art group – goes well with the dim red lighting and slightly seedy atmosphere. In summer the crowds spill out onto an outdoor terrace above the alleyway.

**Jazzga Jazz Club**　　　　　　LIVE MUSIC
(www.jazzga.info; ul Piotrkowska 17; ⊙11am-1am Mon-Thu, 11pm-5am Fri, 3pm-5am Sat; 🛜) Raucous, student-oriented club and bar that showcases local bands and DJs, but rarely, despite the name, any jazz.

### Opera, Theatre & Classical Music

**Grand Theatre**　　　　　　　　THEATRE
(Teatr Wielki; ☑42 633 9960; www.teatr-wielki .lodz.pl; Plac Dąbrowskiego; ⊙box office noon-7pm Tue-Sat, 3-7pm Sun) The city's main venue for opera and ballet also stages festival events and visiting shows.

**Łódź Philharmonic**　　　　　CLASSICAL MUSIC
(Filharmonia Łódzka; ☑42 664 7979; www .filharmonia.lodz.pl; Narutowicza 20/22; ⊙box office 10am-6pm Mon-Fri) Stages regular concerts of classical music every Friday and occasionally on other days of the week.

## Music Theatre
MUSICALS

(Teatr Muzyczny; ☑42 678 1968; ul Północna 47/51; ⊙box office 11am-6.30pm Tue-Fri, from noon Sat, from 3pm Sun) Stages mostly operettas and musicals. The theatre is located near the northern end of ul Piotrkowska.

## Teatr Jaracza
THEATRE

(☑42 662 3333; www.teatr-jaracza.lodz.pl; ul Jaracza 27; ⊙box office noon-7pm) Among the most respected drama theatres in Poland.

# ❶ Information

### Internet Access
**Jazda Park** (al Piłsudskiego 5; per hr 8zł; ⊙10am-10pm) Situated in the Manufaktura shopping centre.

### Money
**Bank Pekao** (al Kościuszki 47)

### Post
**Main post office** (ul Tuwima 38; ⊙8am-8pm Mon-Fri, 9am-2pm Sat)

### Tourist Information
**Tourist Information Centre** (Centrum Informacji Turystycznej; ☑42 638 5955; www .cityoflodz.pl; ul Piotrkowska 87; ⊙8am-7pm Mon-Fri, 10am-4pm Sat) General tourist information; has a number of worthwhile free booklets in English, including *Jewish Landmarks in Łódź*, *Industrial Architecture* and *Villas and Palaces*. The Tourist Information Centre maintains branches at the Fabryczna train station and the Manufaktura shopping centre.

### Travel Agencies
**Eurotravel** (☑42 630 4488; al Kościuszki 22; ⊙9.30am-5.30pm Mon-Fri, 10am-1pm Sat) Youth travel, domestic and international bus tickets, Eurolines.

**Fabricum** (☑42 636 2825; www.fabricum.pl; ul Drewnowska 58; ⊙9am-5pm Mon-Fri) Offers guided tours of Łódź, its surrounding region and Poland.

**Łódź Airport Travel Centre** (☑42 638 5980; www.airport.lodz.pl; ul Piotrkowska 87; ⊙9am-7pm Mon-Fri, 9am-3pm Sat) Specialises in low-cost air travel inside and outside of Poland. Located in the Tourist Information Centre.

# ❶ Getting There & Away

AIR Łódź' **airport** (☑42 688 8414; www.airport .lodz.pl; ul Gen Stanisława Maczka 35) is small but a potentially useful alternative to Warsaw. It's serviced by a few budget carriers, including Ryanair (www.ryanair.com), and there's regular service to destinations in the UK (London Stansted, Liverpool and East Midlands) and continental Europe (Dortmund, Milan). A **shuttle**

**bus** (☑782 805 202; plustour@plustour.pl) runs from the airport to the centre of town for 5zł. Call or email to arrange a return journey. A taxi to the centre will cost about 45zł.

BUS The **central bus station** (Dworzec Centralny PKS; Plac Sałacińskiego 1) is right outside Łódź Fabryczna train station. There are buses to Warsaw (30zł, three hours, five daily), Płock (25zł, three hours, nine daily) and Łowicz (14zł, 1½ hours, hourly), as well as dozens of other destinations both inside and outside of Poland. Handy timetables for both domestic and international destinations are posted outside where the buses wait.

TRAIN The city has three train stations, though at the time of writing it was unclear which trains would go to which station. For the moment, most trains arriving from and departing for Warsaw (35zł, two hours, hourly) use **Łódź Fabryczna** (Plac Sałacińskiego 1), which lies about 10 minutes by foot east of ul Piotrkowska. Fabryczna also has trains to Kraków (50zł, five hours, two daily), with a stop in Częstochowa. There are plans to redevelop the area around the station and possibly close it altogether, leaving a second station, **Łódź Widzew** (ul Adamieckiego), 5km east of Fabryczna, as the main station. A third station, **Łódź Kaliska** (al Unii Lubelskiej 3/5), to the west of the city centre, handles trains to Wrocław (45zł, four hours, up to five daily) and Poznań (45zł, 4½ hours, four daily).

# ❶ Getting Around

Łódź' public transport system is operated by **Miejskie Przedsiębiorstwo Komunikacyjne** (MPK; www.mpk.lodz.pl) and includes trams and buses, both of which use the same ticket system. A ticket becomes valid for a set length of time after you validate it in the machine on board, and remains valid for unlimited transfers between bus and tramlines. Tickets valid for 30/60 minutes cost 1.70/2.40zł; a 24-hour ticket costs 9.60zł.

Order a taxi through **MPT** (☑191 91) or **Merc Radio** (☑42 650 5050). Bicycle rickshaws ply ul Piotrkowska and cost from 5zł to 10zł per trip (two passengers maximum).

Rent bikes from **Dynamo** (☑42 630 6957; www.dynamo.com.pl; ul Kilińskiego 3).

# Łowicz

POP 30,200

For much of the year Łowicz (*wo-veech*) is close to slipping into a permanent coma, but when Corpus Christi (Boże Ciało) comes around, it's *the* place to be. It can also boast a long and important connection to the Catholic Church – it was for over 600 years the seat of the archbishops of Gniezno, the supreme Church authority in Poland. It's also a regional centre for folk arts and crafts, although you'll see little of this outside Łowicz's museum.

## Sights

### Łowicz Cathedral CHURCH
(Stary Rynek 24/30) Originally Gothic, this vast 15th-century building underwent several renovations and is now a mishmash of styles, including Renaissance, Baroque and Rococo. Twelve archbishops of Gniezno and primates of Poland are buried in the church. The building was undergoing extensive renovations and was closed during our visit here in 2011, but was expected to reopen in 2012. Just near the cathedral, a block south along ul Pijarska, is another grand church, the **Piarists' church** (ul Pijarska), a Baroque marvel that can be viewed during mass times.

### Łowicz Museum MUSEUM
(www.muzeumlowicz.pl; Stary Rynek 5/7; adult/concession 9/5zł; ☻10am-4pm Tue-Sun) On the opposite side of the square, this museum is housed in a 17th-century missionary college designed by Dutch architect Tylman van Gameren. The former priests' chapel, with its fading Baroque frescoes (1695) by Italian artist Michelangelo Palloni and finely carved ivory tusks, is the museum's highlight. The 1st floor comes a close second, with archaeological finds from the region such as Stone Age tools and more tusks, this time from mammoths. In the back garden are two old **farmsteads** from the region, complete with original furnishings, implements and decoration.

## Festivals & Events

### Corpus Christi RELIGIOUS
This feast in honour of the Holy Eucharist falls on a Thursday in May or June, depending on the date for Easter, lasts through the weekend, and is celebrated with gusto in Łowicz. It is marked by a large procession that circles the main square and the cathedral, and most of its participants dress in brightly coloured and embroidered traditional costumes and carry elaborate banners.

## Sleeping & Eating

### Hotel Eco HOTEL €€
(☎46 830 0005; www.hotel-eco.pl; ul Podrzeczna 22; s/d/tr 150/200/270zł; P@) Located 150m west of the Stary Rynek and along one of the main roads, this is easily the nicest hotel

in town. The rooms are plain but spotlessly clean with big comfortable mattresses and modern bathrooms. The restaurant is one of a handful of decent places in town to take a meal.

### Dom Wycieczkowy PENSION €
(☎46 837 3433; promocja@powiat.lowicz.com.pl; Stary Rynek 17; s/d 30/60zł, d with bathroom 80zł; P☎) The Tourist Information Bureau offers around 15 rooms on two floors above the main office. The accommodation, a mix of singles and doubles with and without bathrooms, couldn't be cleaner or cheerier, with simple pinewood beds and desks. Book in advance if you plan on arriving any time near the Corpus Christi holiday. No breakfast.

### TOP CHOICE Powroty POLISH €€
(www.kawiarniapowroty.pl; Stary Rynek 24/30c; mains 15-28zł; ☻noon-8pm) Cosy Polish restaurant and coffeehouse in a comfortable, country-house setting that draws on the region's colourful folk traditions with touches like lilac walls and ceilings. Start off with a simple but delicious white borscht, a sour soup served in a broth of potatoes and smoked ham, then finish off with a Polish favourite (but this one done uncommonly well): potato pancake topped with goulash.

### Café Bordo CAFE €
(Stary Rynek 8; cakes & small sandwiches 10zł; ☻10am-7pm) Surprisingly good coffees and cakes at a family cafe on the Stary Rynek that from the outside, at least, does not look promising in the slightest.

## Information

There are a few banks and ATMs scattered around the Nowy Rynek.

**Tourist Information Bureau** (Biuro Informacji Turystycznej; ☎46 837 3433; www.lowicz.eu; Stary Rynek 17; ☻9am-6pm) The office is filled with brochures and good advice, and even offers clean, reasonably priced accommodation in several rooms above the office.

## Getting There & Away

The bus and train stations are side by side, about a five-minute walk east from the Stary Rynek. There are fast trains to Warsaw's Zachodnia station every two hours (20zł, one hour). For travel to Łódź, you're better off taking the bus (14zł, 1½ hours, hourly). There's regular bus service to many outlying towns and villages,

## THE ROMANCE OF ARKADIA & NIEBORÓW

It's hard to imagine anything of interest in the tiny, rural villages of Arkadia, 4km southeast of Łowicz, and Nieborów (nyeh-bo-roof), about 8km southeast of Łowicz. But hiding among the trees are two perfect backdrops for a Jane Austen novel.

With its overgrown ruins, peeling pavilions, temples and follies, the landscaped garden at **Arkadia** (www.nieborow.art.pl; adult/concession 7/5zł, parking 8zł; ☉10am-dusk) is a romantic pagan enclave in a sea of Catholicism. The park was laid out by Princess Helena Radziwiłł in the 1770s to be an 'idyllic land of peace and happiness', but after the princess' death the park fell into decay. Most of the works of art were taken to Nieborów's palace and can be seen today, and the abandoned buildings fell gradually into ruin. Nowadays, an air of decay only adds to the charm of the place. Tree-shrouded ruins are dotted throughout the park, including a red-brick **Gothic House** (Domek Gotycki) perched above **Sybil's Grotto**, a 'Roman' aqueduct, and the impressive **Archpriest's Sanctuary** (Przybytek Arcykapłana), a fanciful mock ruin dominated by a classical bas-relief of Hope feeding a Chimera. The focus of Arkadia is **Diana's Temple** (Świątynia Diany), which overlooks the lake and houses a display of Roman sculpture and funerary monuments.

Further along the main Łowicz–Skierniewice road (No 70) about 4km brings you to Nieborów and its stunning, late-17th-century **palace**, a classic example of Baroque architecture. The palace was designed by Tylman van Gameren for Cardinal Radziejowski, the archbishop of Gniezno and primate of Poland. In 1774 Prince Michał Hieronim Radziwiłł bought the palace, and he and his wife Helena set about cramming it with as much furniture and works of art as they possibly could.

More than half of the palace rooms are occupied by the **Nieborów Museum** (www.nieborow.art.pl; adult/concession 15/6zł; ☉10am-4pm daily Mar & Apr, 10am-6pm daily May & Jun, 10am-4pm Mon-Fri, 10am-6pm Sat & Sun Jul-Sep, 10am-3.30pm Tue-Sun Oct, closed Nov-Feb). Part of the ground floor features 1st-century Roman sculpture and bas-reliefs collected by Helena, and highly unusual black-oak panelling from the late 19th century. The stairwell leading to the 1st floor, with its ornamental Dutch tiles dating from around 1700, is worth the entry fee alone.

Arkadia is on the Łowicz–Skierniewice road, about 4km southeast of Łowicz; Nieborów is on the same road, 4km beyond Arkadia. Both are reachable by bus from Łowicz.

You can also hike or bike along a specially marked cycling path, known as the 'Prince Bike Trail' (Szlak Książęcy). The blue-marked path runs about 14km and starts at the Stary Rynek in Łowicz, near the entrance to the museum.

including around five buses daily to Nieborów (3zł, 20 minutes). To reach Arkadia by bus, board a coach headed to Nieborów and ask the driver to drop you near the Arkadia museum (2zł, 15 minutes).

## Płock

POP 126,000

Płock (pwotsk), dramatically perched on a cliff high above the Vistula, has a long history and a spruced-up old centre. It also can boast the remnants of a Gothic castle, a glorious cathedral and the finest collection of Art Nouveau in the country.

Płock was a royal residence between 1079 and 1138 and the first Mazovian town to be given a municipal charter (in 1237). Its city walls were built in the 14th century and the town developed as a wealthy trading centre until the 16th century. The flooding of the Vistula in 1532, when half the castle and part of the defensive walls slid into the river, was merely a portent of further disasters to come, and the wars, fires and plagues that struck the town in the following centuries brought its importance to an end.

These days, it's first and foremost a refinery town, with a working-class, blue-collar feel, though there are a few sights to hold a visitor's interest for half a day or so.

### ◉ Sights

Most of the main sights are grouped to the southeast of the Stary Rynek along a picturesque ridge overlooking the Vistula.

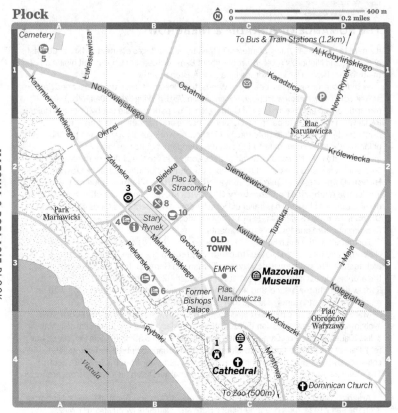

Płock

The dominating features of Płock are two red-brick towers: the **Clock Tower** (Wieża Zegarowa) and the **Noblemen's Tower** (Wieża Szlachecka) – the last vestiges of the original Gothic **castle** that once protected the city. You're free to gaze from the outside, but these are not open to the public.

To the northwest of the castle stretches the Old Town. At the northern end of ul Grodzka is the **Stary Rynek**, formerly the heart of 14th-century Płock; it's dominated by the **town hall** (Ratusz). From atop the town hall, a trumpeter signals the noon hour each day and spectators below are treated to a modest *glockenspiel* spectacle of King Władysław Herman knighting his son Bolesław Krzywousty.

**Mazovian Museum**                    MUSEUM
(Muzeum Mazowieckie; www.muzeumplock.art.pl; ul Tumska 8; adult/concession 8/4zł; ☺10am-5pm Tue-Sun May-Oct, 10am-3pm Tue, 10am-4pm

Wed-Fri, 10am-4.30pm Sat & Sun Nov-Apr) This is a highly worthy collection of Art Nouveau furniture, decorative items, paintings and glassware, with commentary available in English. The holdings show the influences here of both the florid Parisian style of Art Nouveau as well as its sterner, more geometric Viennese cousin, *Secession*. Newer holdings have added an Art Deco room. Among the paintings on the upper floors, our favourite would have to be *Self Portrait With Harpies*.

### Cathedral
CHURCH
(admission free; ⊙10am-5pm Mon-Sat, 2-5.30pm Sun & public holidays) The cathedral dates from the 12th century. The interior, topped with a Renaissance dome in the 16th century, boasts a number of tombstones and altarpieces from various periods, and tasteful Art Nouveau frescoes. The royal chapel (at the back of the north aisle) holds the sarcophagi of two Polish kings, Władysław Herman and his son Bolesław Krzywousty, who lived in Płock during their reigns. Both are in immaculate condition (the tombs, not the kings). Take time to note the bronze doors at the southern end of the cathedral – copies of the original 12th-century doors commissioned by the local bishops. The originals disappeared in mysterious circumstances and reappeared in Novgorod, Russia, where they are today.

### Diocesan Museum
MUSEUM
(Muzeum Diecezjalne; ul Tumska 3a; adult/concession 6/3zł; ⊙10am-3pm Tue-Sat, 11am-4pm Sun May-Sep, 10am-1pm Wed-Sat, 11am-2pm Sun Oct-Apr) Next to the cathedral, this museum houses a large collection of manuscripts, paintings, sculpture, vestments and tapestries. Most of the exhibits are religious in nature, but there are a few secular items, such as the Charter of Płock from 1237, Stone Age archaeological finds, ceramics and coins from across the globe, and medieval weaponry. A few select pieces steal the show though – look for the delicately gilded 12th-century ciborium from Czerwińsk and a first edition of Adam Mickiewicz' *Pan Tadeusz*.

### Zoo
ZOO
(Ogród Zoologiczny; www.zoo.plock.pl, in Polish; ul Norbertańska 2; adult/concession 6/4zł; ⊙9am-7pm May-Aug, 9am-6pm Apr & Sep, 9am-5pm Mar & Oct, 9am-4pm Nov-Feb) Further to the east from the cathedral, beyond the road bridge, is the city zoo. It has a picturesque wooded setting above the river and is reputedly home to the country's biggest collection of reptiles.

## 🛏 Sleeping

### 🔝 Hotel Tumski
HOTEL €€
(☎24 262 9060; www.hoteltumski.pl; ul Piekarska 9; s/d 340/390zł; P✳@🅪) Rooms here at the city's nicest hotel have price tags to match the dramatic riverside views. The Tumski opened in 2009, but everything still feels fresh, from the crisp period styling of the rooms to the elegant dining room. Weekends bring big discounts.

### Hotel Starzyński
HOTEL €€
(☎24 366 0200; www.starzynski.com.pl; ul Piekarska 1; s/d from 210/260zł; P✳🅪) In a bid to keep pace with its nicer neighbour, the Tumski, this communist-era hotel has built a new modern wing and added a health spa and fitness room. The rooms are comfortable and well appointed. Room prices are discounted at weekends.

### Dom Darmstadt
GUESTHOUSE €
(☎24 367 1922; www.dd.pokis.pl; Stary Rynek 8; d 150zł; P@🅪) Ideally situated above the Tourist Information Centre in a historic townhouse, Dom Darmstadt is a quiet, cosy place with three rooms (book in advance) sharing one bathroom and a kitchen.

### Dom Studenta Nr 1
HOSTEL €
(☎24 366 5415; www.pwszplock.pl, in Polish; ul Nowowiejskiego 6; dm 50zł; ⊙Jul & Aug) Płock has three student hostels, including this seasonal option just to the north of the Old Town. The simple, adequate rooms with shared facilities sleep three to four people.

## 🍴 Eating & Drinking

### Browar Tumski
POLISH €€
(www.browartumski.pl; Stary Rynek 13; mains 15-45zł; ⊙11am-8pm Mon-Sat) Arguably the best food on the Old Town Sq, with the added benefit of Browar brewery microbrews on tap. The menu holds few surprises, with the usual items like pork cutlets, duck and fish, but the list of vegetarian meals is longer than usual.

### Restauracja Art Deco
POLISH €€
(www.artdeco.plock.pl; Stary Rynek 17; mains 15-40zł) Set in the middle of the sunny side of the Stary Rynek, this place has the comfiest outdoor tables on the square, and a menu of Polish favourites ranging from *czernina staropolska* (ducks'-blood soup) and a *pierogi* (dumpling) platter to roast duck, roast pork and potato dumplings with pork crackling.

**Czarny Kot**                                    CAFE €

(Stary Rynek 25; ⊘noon-midnight) The musically themed 'Black Cat' lazily occupies one corner of the Old Town's main square and provides comfy sofas and a small terrace for coffee- and beer-drinking guests. Enter on most Friday and Saturday nights and you'll be treated to live jazz and blues.

##  Information

**Bank Pekao** (ul Kwiatka 6)

**Main post office** (ul Bielska 14b)

**Tourist Information Centre** (Centrum Informacji Turystycznej; ☑24 367 1944; www .itplock.pl; Dom Darmstadt, Stary Rynek 8; ⊘9am-6pm Mon-Fri, 10am-4pm Sat, 10am-2pm Sun May-Sep, 9am-4pm Mon-Fri Oct-Apr) Provides a wealth of information on the town and its region, and has free internet access.

## ⓘ Getting There & Away

The train and bus stations are nearly 2km northeast of the Old Town, though passenger train service has been severely curtailed in recent years, and train travel is not a feasible option.

There are frequent PKS buses to Warsaw (22zł, two hours), two a day to Gdańsk and one a day to Toruń, as well as a host of other Polish cities.

# NORTHERN & EASTERN MAZOVIA

## Pułtusk

POP 19,000

A sleepy town with a splendid castle and the longest market square in the country, Pułtusk (*poow*-toosk) is a fine place to stop for a few hours if your travels happen to lead you this way.

Today, Pułtusk is just another dot on the Polish map, but the town's history is long and varied – its roots date back to the 10th century, making it one of Mazovia's oldest towns. It enjoyed its golden age in the 15th and 16th centuries, when it was the residence of the bishops of Płock and an important trade and cultural centre. In 1806 Napoleon's army fought one of its toughest battles in the campaign against Russia here, and in 1944 Pułtusk was on the front line for several months, during which time 80% of its buildings were destroyed.

## ◎ Sights & Activities

The town's historic core, set on an island, is laid out around a 400m-long cobbled **Rynek**. It still operates as a marketplace on Tuesday and Friday, when stallholders selling local farm produce and piles of junk overrun its northern half.

**Regional Museum**                              MUSEUM

(Rynek; adult/concession 4/3zł; ⊘10am-4pm Tue-Sun) In the middle of the square stands the 15th-century brick tower of the town hall, today the Regional Museum. The so-so collection of archaeological finds (many from inside the castle grounds) is rather lame, but the views from the museum's tall tower certainly aren't. Nearby, at **house No 29**, Napoleon recuperated after the Battle of Pułtusk.

**Collegiate Church**                            CHURCH

(Rynek) The northern end of the square is bordered by the collegiate church (*kolegiata*). Erected in the 1440s, the church underwent the usual architectural makeover every few centuries, and contains a dozen Baroque altars, Renaissance stucco decoration on the nave's vault, and aisles with original Gothic features. Note the 16th-century wall paintings in the chapel at the head of the right-hand aisle.

**Castle**                                       CASTLE

(Rynek) At the southern end of the square stands the castle, which was built in the late 14th century as an abode for bishops, and rebuilt several times in later periods. It's now a plush hotel and conference centre.

**Narew River**                                  BOATING

A cobbled road leads around the east side of the castle to a little harbour on the Narew River where you can hire **rowing boats** (per hr 10zł) and **kayaks** (per hr/day 6/60zł) and organise **boat trips** (per 30min/1hr 82/135zł).

## 🛏 Sleeping & Eating

Pułtusk has a weak culinary scene. The best restaurants are inside the castle, but they can be disappointing for what you pay. For lunch, try the castle's riverside self-serve canteen '*Kasztelanka*'.

**Dom Polonii**                                  HOTEL €€

(☑23 692 9000; www.dompolonii.pultusk.pl; ul Szkolna 11; s/d/tr/ste 250/330/390/530zł; P@ 🖗 ) Housed in the restored and much-converted castle, Dom Polonii offers

## REMEMBERING 800,000 AT TREBLINKA

In a peaceful clearing, hidden in a Mazovian pine forest, stands a granite monolith; around it is a field of 17,000 jagged, upright stones, many engraved with the name of a town or village. Beneath the grass, mingled with the sand, lie the ashes of some 800,000 human beings.

Treblinka, the site of the Nazis' second-largest extermination camp after Auschwitz-Birkenau, is another name that will forever be associated with the horror of the Holocaust. Between July 1942 and August 1943, on average more than 2000 people a day, mostly Jews, were gassed in the camp's massive gas chambers and their bodies burnt on huge, open-air cremation pyres.

Following an insurrection by the inmates in August 1943, the extermination camp was demolished and the area ploughed over and abandoned. The site of the camp is now the **Museum of Fighting & Martyrdom** (Muzeum Walki i Męczeństwa; www.treblinka .bho.pl; admission 4zł; ⊙24hr). Access is by a short road that branches off the Małkinia-Sokołów Podlaski road and leads to a car park and a **kiosk** (⊙9am-7pm Apr-Oct, 9am-4pm Nov-Mar) that provides information and sells guidebooks. Across from the kiosk, the ground floor of a white building houses a small **museum** (⊙9am-7pm) with factual yet chilling explanations of the camp (for example, gas chambers could hold up to 5000 people at one time) and a handful of the personal belongings of prisoners found at the site.

It's a 10-minute walk from the car park to the site of the **Treblinka II** extermination camp, alongside a symbolic railway representing the now-vanished line that brought the cattle trucks full of Jews from the Warsaw Ghetto. The huge granite monument, 200m east of the ramp, stands on the site where the gas chambers were located. Around it is a vast symbolic cemetery in the form of a forest of granite stones representing the towns and villages where the camp's victims came from. Unlike Auschwitz-Birkenau, nothing remains of the extermination camp, but the labels on the plan showing the original layout speak volumes.

A further 20-minute walk leads to another clearing and the site of **Treblinka I**, a penal labour camp that was set up before Treblinka II, where remains of the camp, including the concrete foundations of the demolished barracks, have been preserved.

Treblinka is about 100km northeast of Warsaw, a two-hour drive. By train, the nearest station is in Małkinia, about 8km away. There are regular trains from Warszawa Centralna every two hours, and more frequent ones from Warszawa Wileńska station (15zł to 25zł, 1¾ hours). Once in Małkinia, there are no buses to Treblinka so your only option (other than walking) is to take a taxi from the train station; a round trip by taxi will cost from 140zł to 180zł, depending on how long you want the taxi to wait.

atmospheric accommodation in sepia-tinted rooms redolent of past elegance, with creaky parquet flooring and archaic plumbing. There are cheaper rooms in other buildings in and around the castle grounds (singles/doubles from 140/220zł).

**Hotel Baltazar** HOTEL €
(☑23 692 0475; www.hotel-baltazar.com.pl; ul Baltazara 41; s/d/tr 120/150/180zł; P🗺) Hidden away at the end of a minor road, 1km north of the Rynek (signposted), this family-run hotel is an attractive, modern alternative to the Dom Polonii, with bright, spacious rooms and friendly service. Bicycles and kayaks are available for hire, and there's a restaurant on the premises.

### ❶ Getting There & Away

Pułtusk lies on the road from Warsaw to the Great Masurian Lakes. There's no railway in town, but there are regular buses to and from Warsaw (16zł, 1½ hours, half-hourly). Pułtusk's **bus station** (☑23 692 2967; ul Nowy Rynek 3) is just off the main road through town, about 600m southwest of the Rynek.

## SOUTHERN PODLASIE

Southern Podlasie (pod-*lah*-sheh) fills a large swath of northeastern Poland, hogging much of the country's border with Belarus. More than any other region in this vast country, it is here that the influence of foreign cultures can be felt the strongest. The closer you get to the last dictatorship in Europe, the more onion-shaped Orthodox domes you'll see and Belarusian language you'll hear. You'll also be witness to remnants of 17th-century Tatar settlements (see the boxed text, p102). Jews, who once populated the region, have left traces of their presence too.

Despite its rich cultural make-up, the main attraction here is nature. Podlasie literally means 'the land close to the forest', a moniker it has for good reason. This part of the world was once covered in primeval forest, and while much of it has fallen to the wood-cutter's axe, a rich pocket still remains within the Białowieża National Park. Southern Podlasie is also home to unique lowland marshes, which fall under the protection of the Biebrza and Narew National Parks.

# Białystok

POP 292,000

Białystok (byah-*wis*-tok) is Podlasie's metropolis and a large, busy city for these parts. Attractions are few, but its proximity to the region's national parks makes it a good base, and the mix of Polish and Belarusian cultures gives it a special atmosphere found in no other Polish city.

The city may have been founded in the 16th century but it didn't begin to develop until the mid-18th century, when Jan Klemens Branicki, the commander of the Polish armed forces and owner of vast estates – including the town – established his residence here and built a palace. A century later the town received a new impetus from the textile industry, and eventually became Poland's largest textile centre after Łódź. The textile boom attracted an ethnic mix of entrepreneurs, including Poles, Jews, Russians, Belarusians and Germans, and by the outbreak of WWI Białystok had some 80,000 inhabitants and more than 250 textile factories.

During WWII the Nazis practically destroyed the city, murdering half its population, including almost all of the Jews, and razing most of the industrial base and central district. Post-war reconstruction concentrated on tangible issues such as the recovery of industry, infrastructure and state administration. As you can still see today, historic and aesthetic values receded into the background.

## ⊙ Sights

The centre of the city and the locus of evening activity is the triangular Rynek Kościuszki, the former market square, with its 18th-century **town hall** in the middle.

**Podlasie Museum**                                    MUSEUM
(Muzeum Podlaskie; www.muzeum.bialystok.pl; Rynek Kościuszki 10; adult/concession 6/3zł; ⊙10am-5pm Tue-Thu, Sat & Sun, 10am-6pm Fri) The town hall was rebuilt from scratch after the war and now houses this museum, which features a modest collection of Polish paintings on the ground floor, including some important names such as Jacek Malczewski and Stanisław Ignacy Witkiewicz (Witkacy), and archaeological finds from a Viking village unearthed near Elbląg.

**Branicki Palace**                      HISTORIC BUILDING
In Park Pałacowy to the east of the square stands the former residence of Jan Klemens Branicki, Pałac Branickich. Branicki, once a contender for the Polish crown, built the palace as a residence that would rival the king's in importance and luxury after losing to Stanisław August Poniatowski in royal elections. Burned down in 1944 by the retreating Nazis, the palace was restored to its original 18th-century shape, but the interior, which is off limits to the public, was largely modernised. The landscaped gardens are free to wander, however.

**Orthodox Church of the
Holy Spirit**                                            CHURCH
(Cerkiew Św Ducha; ul Antoniuk Fabryczny 13) It's worth making a detour outside the central area to this modern Orthodox church, 3km northwest of the centre (bus 5 from ul Lipowa in the centre will let you off nearby). Begun in the early 1980s, this monumental building is the largest Orthodox church in Poland. The huge central onion-shaped dome is topped with a large cross (weighing 1500kg) symbolising Christ, while 12 smaller crosses around it represent the apostles. The spacious interior boasts a spectacular main iconostasis and two smaller ones on either side, and a fantastic giant chandelier.

## 🛏 Sleeping

**Hotel Branicki**                              HOTEL €€
(☑85 665 2500; www.hotelbranicki.com; ul Zamenhofa 25; s/d/apt 325/375/800zł; P✳🤖) The romantic Branicki is the poshest place in

# Białystok

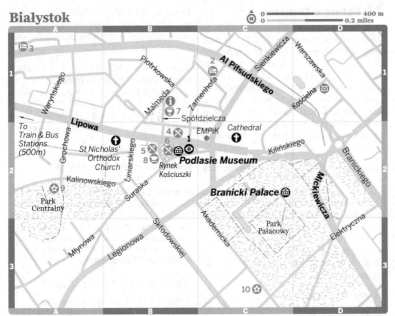

town and a feasible splurge. Each of the 32 rooms has been individually designed and decorated in different colour schemes, but all the rooms offer big comfy beds, thick cotton sheets and all modern conveniences. Most of the rooms have air-conditioning. The in-town location is just a couple of minutes from the Rynek. Prices fall by around a third on weekends.

**Hotel Podlasie** HOTEL €€
(☑85 675 6600; www.hotelpodlasie.pl; ul 27 Lipca 24/1; s/d/apt 158/195/279zł; P🛜) This budget hotel, about 2.5km northeast of the centre, hits all the sweet spots for us. The rooms have been fully renovated and come with little desks and clean bathrooms. The beds have firm mattresses (not easy to find at this price) and the buffet breakfast is one of the best we've seen, including a small self-serve espresso machine. The location is a good 30-minute walk from the centre, though city buses 3, 6 and 18 stop at the hotel's doorstep.

**Youth Hostel** HOSTEL €
(☑85 652 4250; www.hostelpodlasie.pl; al Piłsudskiego 7b; dm 28-38zł; ☉year-round; P) This modern hostel is housed in an old-style villa, incongruously set amid concrete apartment blocks (it's tucked away from the street

## Białystok

### ◉ Top Sights

| | |
|---|---|
| Branicki Palace | C2 |
| Podlasie Museum | B2 |

### ◉ Sights

| | | |
|---|---|---|
| 1 | Town Hall | B2 |

### ⌂ Sleeping

| | | |
|---|---|---|
| 2 | Hotel Branicki | C1 |
| 3 | Youth Hostel | A1 |

### ✘ Eating

| | | |
|---|---|---|
| 4 | Bella Vita | B2 |
| 5 | Chilli Pizza | B2 |
| 6 | Esperanto Café | B2 |

### ☕ Drinking

| | | |
|---|---|---|
| 7 | Castel | B1 |
| 8 | Pijalnia Czekolady | B2 |

### ✦ Entertainment

| | | |
|---|---|---|
| 9 | Białostocki Teatr Lalek | A2 |
| 10 | Odeon Jazz Club | C3 |

behind block No 7). It offers accommodation in pine bunk beds in wood-panelled dorms of six to 16 beds, with kitchen and 24-hour reception.

## ✗ Eating & Drinking

**Chilli Pizza**                    ITALIAN €€
(Rynek Kościuszki 17; pizzas 18-30zł; 🔊) The best pizza (and arguably the best pastas and salads) in town can be found at this popular Rynek venue. On our visit, we broke the mould and opted for pizza 'Perska', with spinach and feta cheese instead of the standard ham and mushrooms. The terrace is popular in summer and affords a wonderful command over Białystok's pretty town square.

**Esperanto Café**         INTERNATIONAL €€
(www.esperanto-cafe.pl; Rynek Kościuszki 10; mains 20-30zł) This popular cafe and restaurant is named in honour of Białystok's own LL Zamenhof, the inventor of Esperanto, who was born here in 1859. The menu is eclectic, with Polish staples sharing space with more inventive international items like baked turkey breast (in this case served with cranberry sauce).

**Pijalnia Czekolady**                CAFE €
(www.wedelpijalnie.pl; Rynek Kościuszki 17; chocolate drinks 11-15zł; 🔊) Serving fabulous chocolate in the form of drinks, cakes and sweets, Pijalnia is a chocolate-lover's dream come true. Willy Wonka would be proud of its chocolate fountain, and there's outdoor seating overlooking the main square.

**Bella Vita**                        CAFE €
(Rynek Kościuszki 22; coffee 8zł, ice-cream sundaes 12-15zł) This is an old-fashioned ice-cream counter. Big booth seating gives it a vaguely diner-style look and provides a comfy seat for coffee and ice cream.

**Castel**                             BAR €
(www.kawiarniacastel.pl; ul Spółdzielcza 10) Castel is an excellent bar with two distinct sections: a romantic, dimly lit interior and an over-the-top garden terrace, with secluded tables, little fountains, and a convivial atmosphere for drinking and chitchat.

## ☆ Entertainment

**Odeon Jazz Club**              LIVE MUSIC
(www.odeonclub.pl; ul Akademicka 10/1; ⊙noon-11pm Sun & Mon, noon-1am Tue-Thu, noon-3am Fri & Sat) Depending on the night, the circular Odeon offers decent live music – jazz and blues – or DJs and karaoke.

**Opera i Filharmonia Podlaska**   CLASSICAL MUSIC
(http://filharmonia.bialystok.pl; ul Podleśna 2; ⊙box office 10am-5pm Tue-Thu, 10am-7pm Fri) Home to the Białystok Symphony Orchestra, with a lively program of classical music and opera. The venue is located about 300m south of the Rynek.

**Białostocki Teatr Lalek**           THEATRE
(www.btl.bialystok.pl; ul Kalinowskiego 1) One of Poland's best puppet theatres, it stages children's shows, such as *Pinocchio* or *Punch and Judy* as well as traditional Polish stories, at least three or four times a week.

## ℹ Information

**Bank PKO** (Rynek Kościuszki 7)
**Main post office** (ul Warszawska 10)
**Piramida Café** (ul Grochowa 2; per hr 5zł; ⊙8am-midnight Mon-Fri, 9am-midnight Sat & Sun) Internet access.
**Tourist Information Point** (Punkt Informacji Turystycznej; ☏85 732 6831; ul Malmeda 6; ⊙8am-5pm Mon-Fri) One of the best tourist information offices in Poland.

## ℹ Getting There & Away

The Dworzec PKS **bus station** (www.pks .bialystok.pl; ul Bohaterów Monte Cassino 10) and Dworzec PKP **train station** (ul Dworcowa 1) are next to each other and connected via a pedestrian overpass, about 1km west of the centre. Walk to the centre in 15 minutes, or take bus 2, 4 or 28 to Rynek Kościuszki.

**BUS** Białystok's bus station is relatively orderly as far as Polish bus stations go, with a helpful information counter and a large publicly posted timetable. PKS Express offers frequent service to and from Warsaw (30zł, 3½ hours, eight daily). Buses to Augustów (20zł, two hours) leave several times a day. Other popular long-haul destinations include to Lublin (51zł, 5½ hours), Rzeszów (65zł, nine hours), Kraków (68zł, 10 hours) and Gdańsk (63zł, nine hours).

Bus service to Belarus is erratic. At the time of writing, only two buses a day were crossing the border to Grodno, departing at 2.20pm and 3.30pm (35zł, two hours).

**TRAIN** The main intercity rail services are to Warsaw (Warszawa Wschodnia station, with a stop at Centralna; 35zł, 2½ hours, every two hours). There are at least four daily trains to Suwałki (22zł, 2½ hours), with a stop in Augustów (20zł, two hours) along the way.

# Tykocin

POP 1900

Like so many of the region's sleepy towns, Tykocin's (ti-*ko*-cheen) importance lies in its past. It started life as a stronghold of the Mazovian dukes, but its real growth didn't begin until the 15th century and was further accelerated after the town became the property of King Zygmunt II August in 1543.

It was during this period that Jews started to settle in Tykocin, and their community grew rapidly to define the town's character for the next four centuries. They also built the town's greatest monument, a 17th-century synagogue that miraculously survived WWII.

The slaughter of the town's Jewish residents in the summer of 1941 is a tragic story and one that gives a visit here special poignancy. On 25 August, shortly after Nazi Germany declared war on the Soviet Union, the Germans called the town's nearly 2000 Jewish residents to the Rynek, from where they were marched (or trucked in the case of women and children) to the Łopuchowo Forest, about 8km west of Tykocin, and shot. They were buried in mass graves.

Though today the village appears relatively prosperous, and was even getting a facelift during our visit in 2011, it's fair to say that Tykocin has never recovered from the massacre. In 1950, owing to the loss of half of its population, it was deprived of its town charter, to become an ordinary village. It recovered its charter in 1994, but otherwise not much has changed.

## ⊙ Sights

Tykocin is relatively compact. The eastern section of town, as you enter from Białystok, was the traditional Catholic part, centred on Plac Czarnieckiego. The Jewish section is 500m to the west, beyond the Rynek. Here you'll find the former synagogue. About 500m further west is the old **Jewish cemetery** (Cmentarz Żydowski), though today it's nothing more than an abandoned field with a couple of headstones popping up through the weeds.

### Former Synagogue                    SYNAGOGUE

The former synagogue, erected in 1642, is considered to be the best-preserved Jewish house of worship in Poland and today is home to the highly worthwhile **Tykocin Museum** (ul Kozia 2; adult/concession 10/5zł; ⊙10am-5pm Tue-Sun). Much of the original interior has been preserved. Adjacent to the former prayer room is a small exhibition containing photos and documents of Tykocin's Jewish community and objects related to religious ritual, such as elaborate brass and silver hanukiahs (candelabras), Talmudic books and liturgical equipment.

*Talmudic House*

The Talmudic House stands just behind and to the right of the synagogue and houses a wing of the museum (tickets are valid for both buildings). The permanent exhibition is a reconstructed old-fashioned pharmacy, but the real treats are the rotating photo and art exhibitions.

## 🛏 Sleeping & Eating

**Villa Regent**                        HOTEL €

(☑85 718 7476; www.villaregent.eu; ul Sokołowksa 3; s/d/tr 90/150/220zł; P🗢) Standing just to the left of the former synagogue, the Villa Regent is a smart-looking, relatively new (opened in 2010) hotel that offers the best accommodation in town. The rooms are ultra-clean and well-appointed – and excellent value at this price. Although we are still partial to Restaurant Tejsza for lunch, the restaurant here (mains 12zł to 20zł) is good, serving a mix of traditional Jewish and Polish cooking.

**Kiermusy Dworek Nad Łąkami**          PENSION, BUNGALOW €€

(☑85 742 1670; www.kiermusy.com.pl; Kiermusy; s/d 180/290zł, house 320-680zł; P🐾) This relatively isolated resort, about 4km west of the synagogue, defies easy description. It's part traditional inn and part bungalow accommodation, though these bungalows border on luxurious. The inn is decorated in traditional Polish style, while the houses have a distinctive rustic look. There's also a wonderful tavern, **Karczma Rzym** (mains 16-30zł), that's worth seeking out even if you're not staying here. The complex is in the village of Kiermusy, west of Tykocin. To find it from the synagogue, walk (or drive) south on ul Kozia for a couple of blocks and turn right (west) at ul Holendry and keep walking straight for 4km.

**TOP CHOICE Restauracja Tejsza**       JEWISH €

(ul Kozia 2; mains 10-20zł; ⊙10am-8pm) In the basement of the Talmudic house (enter from the back), this basic eatery serves excellent and inexpensive home-cooked kosher meals, including some of the best *pierogi* in the country, and a tasty beef goulash stewed in a sauce of carrots and plums. There's also an outdoor seating area.

## ⓘ Getting There & Away

Tykocin is served by hourly buses from Białystok (10zł, one hour); buses stop at the Rynek, 100m from the synagogue.

## POLAND'S STORK VILLAGE

Storks are a common sight in towns and villages across Podlasie, where artificial platforms are carefully constructed for the lanky white birds to build their nests. But **Pentowo**, a collection of farm buildings 2km northwest of Tykocin on the road to Kiermusy, holds the title of Poland's Stork Village. In 1991 a hurricane ripped through the village, snapping many of the trees like twigs, and over the ensuing years storks began to nest in the broken treetops. Storks are notoriously inept at building their homes, so the locals decided to give these bringers of happiness and babies a lending hand, and eight platforms were built.

Today Pentowo can boast 23 nests and at times more than 70 birds. The best time to see nesting storks is between April and August – by the time September comes around they're on their long journey south to Africa.

# Biebrza National Park

The **Biebrza National Park** (Biebrzański Park Narodowy; adult/concession 4/2zł) is Poland's largest and longest, stretching more than 100km from close to the Belarus border to the Narew River near Tykocin. Established in 1993, Biebrza (*byehb*-zhah) is a relatively new park but an important one, protecting the **Biebrza Valley**, Central Europe's largest area of natural bog.

The varied landscape consists of river sprawls, peat bogs, marshes and damp forests. Typical local flora includes numerous species of moss, reed grass and a range of medicinal herbs. The fauna is rich and diverse, and features mammals such as wolves, wild boar, foxes, roe deer, otters and beavers. The king of the park, however, is the elk: about half of the country's population, around 600 animals, live within the park's borders. Birdwatchers flock to Biebrza to glimpse the 270 or so bird species (over half of all species recorded in Poland) that call the park home.

## ○ Sights & Activities

The park can be broadly divided into three areas: the **Northern Basin** (Basen Północny), the smallest and least-visited area of the park; the **Middle Basin** (Basen Środkowy), stretching along the river's broad middle course and featuring a combination of wet forests and boglands; and the equally extensive **Southern Basin** (Basen Południowy), where most of the terrain is taken up by marshes and peat bogs. The showpiece is the **Red Marsh** (Czerwone Bagno) in the Middle Basin, a strictly protected nature reserve encompassing a wet alder forest that is inhabited by about 400 elk.

With over 200km of water trails crisscrossing the length of the valley, the best way to explore the park is by **boat**. The principal water route flows from the town of Lipsk downstream along the Biebrza to the village of Wizna. This 140km stretch can be paddled at a leisurely pace in seven to nine days. Bivouac sites along the river allow for overnight stops and food is available in towns on the way.

The visitor information centre in Osowiec-Twierdza can provide maps and information. You can also hire a kayak for a few hours or a day and cover part of the route; a handy two-hour stretch runs from Goniądz to Osowiec-Twierdza (kayaks can be rented from Goniądz' camping ground). Access to kayak trails costs 6zł for adults and 4zł for students and children per day on top of hire charges.

Despite its overall marshy character, large parts of the park can be explored by **bicycle** and on **foot**. About 250km of signposted trails have been tracked through the most interesting areas, including nearly 50km through the Red Marsh alone. Dikes, boulders and dunes among the bogs provide access to some splendid birdwatching sites.

## 🛏 Sleeping

There are several bivouac sites within the park and more outside its boundaries. The three most strategically located are in Osowiec-Twierdza (2km from the information centre), Grzędy (a gateway to the Red Marsh) and Barwik. All three are accessible by road and have car parks. You'll pay about 6zł per person per night to pitch your tent. There are also five rooms (for up to 16 people) in the **hunting lodge** (per person 35zł) in Grzędy.

The nearest camping grounds and hotels to the park are in Goniądz, Mońki and Rajgród. Youth hostels in the region include those in Goniądz, Grajewo, Osowiec-Twierdza and Wizna; all are open in July and August only. There are also about 70 **agrotourist farms** (d 40-50zł) in the region – the park's information centre can provide details, as can its website (most listings are in the Polish-language section).

## ℹ Information

Park admission can be paid at the **visitor information centre** (☎85 738 3035; www .biebrza.org.pl; Osowiec-Twierdza; ☉8am-7pm daily May-Sep, 8am-3pm Mon-Fri Oct-Apr), just along the road from Osowiec-Twierdza train station. The helpful English-speaking staff will provide information about the park and its facilities. The centre provides information on where to find guides (35zł to 40zł an hour per group), kayaks (per hour/day 6/30zł) and canoes (7/35zł). The office is stocked with maps and brochures on the park. The 1:100,000-scale *Biebrzański Park Narodowy* map (14zł) is among the best, with descriptions of half- and full-day hiking and kayaking trips in several languages.

## ℹ Getting There & Around

Osowiec-Twierdza is 50km northwest of Białystok, and sits on the railway line between Białystok (12zł to 18zł, one hour, five daily) and Ełk (11zł to 15zł, 45 minutes, five daily). The park office is just 200m from Osowiec-Twierdza station, and there are hiking trails and lookout towers within a few kilometres.

Having your own transport is a huge advantage, as you can easily access most of the park's major attractions.

## Narew National Park

The **Narew National Park** (Narwiański Park Narodowy; adult/concession 4/2zł) is just as interesting as Biebrza, but is not as geared towards visitors. Narew (nah-ref) protects an unusual stretch of the Narew River that's nicknamed the 'Polish Amazon', where the river splits into dozens of channels that spread out across a 2km-wide valley, forming a constellation of swampy islets in between. Most of the park's 73 sq km is comprised of rivers, feeder streams and bogs, and much of it is inaccessible to visitors, though you can kayak on stretches of the Narew River and some of its tributaries. There's also a network of paths and dirt and gravel roads that encircle the park and which can be hiked or biked.

The park's **headquarters** (www.npn.pl; ☉7.30am-3.30pm Mon-Fri, 9am-5pm Sat & Sun) is in the tiny hamlet of Kurowo in the northwestern section of the park, where the watery labyrinth of channels is most extensive. The helpful staff here provide maps and can advise on walks and hikes. They also rent out **kayaks** (per hr 6zł) and space to pitch a **tent** (per person 6zł). There's no restaurant, so bring your own food.

Kurowo lies 5km south of the town of Stare Jeżewo, which is 30km west of Białystok along busy highway No 8 to Warsaw. Stare Jeżewo is serviced by frequent buses from Białystok (every two hours), but from there you'll have to hoof it along a 5km dirt track to Kurowo.

The park can also be accessed at its southern end at the village of **Uhowo**, near Łapy. This is the home base of **Kaylon** (☎502 508 050; www.kaylon.pl; ul Kolejowa 8), an agency that organises multiday canoeing expeditions from May to September. Prices start at around 200zł per day for a guide, 30zł for kayak hire, 40zł for a three-person Canadian canoe and 1.60zł per kilometre for transport.

## Kruszyniany & Bohoniki

These two small villages, close to the Belarusian border to the east and northeast of Białystok, are noted for their timber mosques, the only surviving historic mosques in Poland. They were built by the Muslim Tatars who settled here at the end of the 17th century (see the boxed text, p102).

Kruszyniany (kroo-shi-*nya*-ni) is the larger of the two villages and contains the larger of the two mosques. Its green **mosque** (adult/concession 5/3zł; ☉9am-7pm May-Oct, by appointment Nov-Apr) is an 18th-century rustic wooden construction, in many ways similar to old timber Christian churches. You'll find it hidden in a cluster of trees, set back from the main road in the central part of the village.

The mosque's modest interior, made entirely from pine, is divided into two rooms; the smaller one is designed for women, who are not allowed into the main prayer hall (unless they're a tourist). The latter, with carpets covering the floor, has a small recess in the wall, the mihrab, in the direction of Mecca. Next to it is the *minbar,* a pulpit from which the imam says prayers. The painted texts hanging on the walls, the Muhirs, are verses from the Quran.

## THE TATARS OF POLAND

In the 13th century, large parts of Eastern and Central Europe were ravaged by hordes of fierce Mongol horsemen from Central Asia. These savage nomadic warriors (commonly, though confusingly, referred to as the Tatars) came from the great Mongol empire of Genghis Khan, which at its peak stretched from the Black Sea to the Pacific Ocean. They first invaded Poland in 1241 and repeatedly overran and destroyed much of Silesia and Małopolska, including the royal city of Kraków. They withdrew from Europe as fast as they came, leaving few traces other than some folk stories. Not long after, the empire broke up into various independent khanates.

By the end of the 14th century, Poland and Lithuania were facing a different threat, from the Teutonic Knights, who were swiftly expanding southward and eastward. As a measure of protection, Lithuania (which was soon to enter into a political alliance with Poland) began looking for migrants to settle its scarcely inhabited borderlands. To that end, it welcomed refugees and prisoners of war from the Crimean and Volgan khanates, offspring of the once-powerful Golden Horde state ruled by the heirs of Genghis Khan. These new settlers were Muslim Tatars.

The Tatars' military involvement in Polish affairs began in 1410 at the Battle of Grunwald, where King Władysław II Jagiełło defeated the Teutonic Knights; in this battle, a small unit of Tatar horsemen fought alongside Polish-Lithuanian forces. From that time on, the numbers of Tatar settlers grew, and so did their participation in battles to defend their adopted homeland. By the 17th century, they had several cavalry formations to reinforce Polish troops in the many wars of that time.

In 1683, after the victory over the Turks at the Battle of Vienna, Jan III Sobieski granted land in the eastern strip of Poland to those Tatars who had fought under the Polish flag. The Tatars founded new settlements and built their mosques. Of all these villages, only Kruszyniany and Bohoniki have preserved some of their Tatar inheritance, though apart from their mosques and cemeteries not much else remains.

Kruszyniany's **Mizar** (Muslim cemetery) is located in the patch of woodland 100m beyond the mosque. The recent gravestones are Christian in style, showing the extent of cultural assimilation that has taken place, and are on the edge of the graveyard. Go deeper into the wood, where you'll find old tombstones hidden in the undergrowth. Some of them are inscribed in Russian, a legacy of tsarist times.

The **mosque** of **Bohoniki** is similar to Kruszyniany's mosque in its decoration and atmosphere. Bohoniki's **Mizar** is about 1km north of the mosque at the edge of a tree grove; walk to the outskirts of the village then turn left up a tree-lined dirt road.

Kruszyniany offers decent sleeping and eating options. **Dworek Pod Lipami** (☑85 722 7554; www.dworekpodlipami.pl; ul Kruszyniany 51; s/d 70/130zł; 🅿🛜) is a lovely manor house with comfortable rooms and friendly staff. Traditional Tatar food and drink from the region are served, such as *babka ziemniaczana* (potato cakes) and *barszcz* (hot beetroot juice). Only a few doors down is **Tatarska Jurta** (☑85 749 4052; ul Kruszyniany 58; mains 15-25zł), a restaurant that also serves traditional Tatar dishes and wonderful home-made cakes. Take some time to check out the yurt in the backyard.

The two villages are 37km apart, each about 50km from Białystok, and are best reached by car. Visiting by public transport is not feasible.

## Białowieża National Park

The Białowieża (byah-wo-*vyeh*-zhah) National Park (Białowieski Park Narodowy) was established in 1921 and is Poland's oldest national park. It covers an area of about 105 sq km and is part of a bigger forest known as the **Białowieża Forest** (Puszcza Białowieska), which straddles the border between Poland and Belarus.

The national park is famous for two reasons. First, it's the original home of the European bison, the continent's largest land mammal. Though the bison died out in 1919, it's been successfully reintroduced into the wild. The park contains several bison breeding reserves, where animals can be viewed living more or less a natural existence.

Second, much of the park shelters what's considered to be Europe's largest swath of original lowland forest, known in Polish as *puszcza*. It's debatable whether the word 'primeval' can accurately be used to describe this, since there's inevitably been human interaction over the millennia, but much of the park has been undisturbed for centuries, leaving a fascinating mix of old- and new-growth forest, and all of the various flora and fauna that flourish in such a special environment.

The park is divided into three zones: a strictly protected area *(Obręb Ochronny Orłówka)* of old growth that's accessible only under the supervision of a guide; an area of secondary protection *(Obręb Ochronny Hwoźna)* that does not require a guide and has abundant hiking and biking paths; and several small bison reserves *(Ośrodek Hodowli Żubrów)*.

The park owes its existence largely to royalty. It was a private hunting ground for the Polish monarchs and later for Russian tsars and as such was protected for centuries by royal patronage.

These days, Białowieża is a popular weekend destination in summer. People come mainly for the chance to hike, bike and, hopefully, spot a bison (aside from the one on the label of a bottle of Żubr beer).

The starting point for excursions into the national park is the village of Białowieża, 85km southeast of Białystok. It has information points, accommodation, food and several travel agencies that can organise visits to the strictly protected area of the park.

The village straggles along for about 3km on the southern edge of the national park, centred on the rectangular Park Pałacowy (Palace Park), which contains a natural history museum. The helpful PTTK office, which can organise guides, and the Hotel Żubrówka are at the southern entrance to Park Pałacowy; the youth hostel and the national park's own tourist information centre are near the eastern entrance to Park Pałacowy.

If you're arriving by bus, there are three bus stops in Białowieża: one at the entrance to the village, one just after Hotel Żubrówka (closest to the PTTK office), and one at the post office (closest to the youth hostel and museum).

## ◉ Sights

**Strictly Protected Area** FOREST
(Obręb Ochronny Orłówka; www.bpn.com.pl; adult/child 6/3zł) This is the oldest section of the national park and covers an area of around

47.5 sq km hectares, bordered to the north and west by the marshy Hwoźna and Narewka Rivers, and to the east by the Bielawiezskaja Primeval Forest National Park in Belarus.

This part of the park can only be entered in the company of an official guide, who can be hired through the PTTK office or any one of several private tourist agencies (see p105).

Guides typically offer two types of tours. A shorter 'standard' tour takes about three hours and covers about 8km. Prices vary but run about 170zł regardless of the size of the group (note it's perfectly fine to 'share' guides and split the costs with other travellers). A longer tour lasts about six hours, covers around 16km and costs about 330zł.

The terrain is mostly flat, swampy in parts, and covered with mixed forest of oak, hornbeam, spruce and pine. Ancient trees reach spectacular sizes uncommon elsewhere, with spruce 50m high and oak trunks 2m in diameter; some of the oak trees are more than 500 years old. The forest is home to a variety of large mammals, including elk, roe deer, wild boar, lynx, wolves, beavers and the uncontested king of the *puszcza*, the bison. There are about 120 species of birds, including owls, cranes, storks, hazelhens and nine species of woodpecker.

The reserve gets pretty swampy in spring (March to April) and may be closed at times to visitors. Mosquitoes can be a problem throughout the summer, so be sure to cover your arms and legs and bring along some mosquito repellent.

**Park Pałacowy** PARK
(Palace Park; www.bpn.com.pl; admission free; ⊘24hr) The Palace Park was laid out in the 19th century around a splendid palace built for the Russian tsar on the site of an ancient royal hunting lodge once used by Polish kings. The **Russian Orthodox Church**, outside the eastern entrance to the park, was built at the same time. The southern entrance to Park Pałacowy, beside the PTTK office, leads across a pond past a stone **obelisk**, which commemorates a bison hunt led by King August III Saxon in 1752. The royal bag that day was 42 bison, 13 elk and two roe deer.

From the eastern entrance, just past the national park's tourist information centre, the main path leads uphill past a red-brick **gate**, which is all that remains of the tsar's palace – it was burned to the ground by retreating Germans in 1944. The palace site is now occupied by the **Natural History Museum** (Muzeum Przyrodniczo-Leśne; adult/concession 12/8zł, viewing tower & temporary exhibitions 6/3zł; ⊘9am-4.30pm Mon-Fri, 9am-5pm Sat & Sun mid-Apr–mid-Oct, 9am-4pm Tue-Sun mid-Oct–mid-Apr), which features exhibitions relating to the flora and fauna of the park (mostly forest scenes with stuffed animals and a collection of plants), the park's history, and the archaeology and ethnography of the region. The viewing tower provides terrific views over the village, and just north of the museum you will find a grove of 250-year-old oaks.

### European Bison Show Reserve

WILDLIFE RESERVE

(Rezerwat Żubrów; www.bpn.com.pl; adult/concession 6/3zł; ⊘9am-5pm daily May-Sep, 8am-4pm Tue-Sun Oct-Apr) Though there are several smaller bison reserves scattered around the park, this enclosed animal park around 4km west of Park Pałacowy is your best chance to see an actual bison. There are also several other species that are typical of the *puszcza,* including elk, wild boar, wolves and roe deer. You can also see the *żubroń,* a cross between a bison and cow, which has been bred so successfully in Białowieża that it is even larger than the bison itself, reaching up to 1200kg.

Another peculiarity is the tarpan *(Equus caballus gomelini),* a small, stumpy, mouse-coloured horse with a dark stripe running along its back from head to tail. The tarpan is a Polish cousin of the wild horse *(Equus ferus silvestris)* that once populated the Ukrainian steppes but became extinct in the 19th century.

To reach the reserve by car, follow the main road, No 689, in the direction of Hajnówka for about 3km and look for a turn-off to the parking lot. By foot, take the green- or yellow-marked trails, both starting from the PTTK office, or the trail called Żebra Żubra (Bison's Ribs). You can also get here by horse-drawn cart – ask at the PTTK office for details.

### 🏃 Activities

The secondary protected zone of the park that lies largely to the north of the strictly protected area, and the vast *puszcza,* to the west and north of the park proper, do not require a guide to enter and are criss-crossed by hundreds of kilometres of wonderful, well-marked **hiking** and **cycling** paths.

Maps are available for sale at both the PTTK office and the Białowieża National Park Information Centre, as well as at hotels and shops around Białowieża. The 1:50,000 *Puszcza Białowieska* map by Agencja TD has a street plan of Białowieża, and marked cycle and walking paths through the forest. It costs 14zł.

Nearly all hotels and pensions in Białowieża have bikes available for guests. Otherwise, try **Rent a Bike** (☑660 451 540; Ul Olgi Gabiec 11) across the street from Hotel Żubrówka. Prices are 5zł/35zł per hour/day.

### 🛏 Sleeping

Apart from the places listed here, the road approaching Białowieża is lined with dozens of signs advertising *pokoje gościnne* (guest rooms) in private homes (30zł to 40zł per person).

### Hotel Żubrówka

HOTEL €€

(☑85 681 2303; www.hotel-zubrowka.pl; ul Olgi Gabiec 6; s/d 380/420zł, ste 600-1100zł; P@🛜) The Żubrówka, a member of the Best Western hotel chain, is the village's plushest hotel. Rooms are suitably comfortable and modern, and suites have open fireplaces. There's also a spa centre and sauna on-site.

### Wejmutka

PENSION €€

(☑85 681 2117; www.wejmutka.pl; Kolejowa 1a; s/d/q 150/210/600zł; P🛜) This rambling hunting lodge features a beautiful dining and sitting area, plus clean, cosy rooms. The location is ideal, within easy walking distance of both the PTTK office and the National Park Information Centre. The welcome is warm and the breakfast is well above average. Our one complaint: instant coffee at breakfast.

### Hotel Białowieski

HOTEL €€

(☑85 681 2022; www.hotel.bialowieza.pl; ul Waszkiewicza 218b; s/d/ste 210/240/510zł; P@🛜) The rooms at the child-friendly Białowieski are bright and modern and offer the same comfort level as the Żubrówka, but with a little less atmosphere and around a 3km walk to the centre. Many have balconies overlooking the garden. There's a play area at the back and bikes for hire (per hour/day 7/35zł).

### Pensjonat Unikat

PENSION €

(☑85 681 2109; www.unikat.bialowieza.pl; ul Waszkiewicza 39; s/d/q 110/140/240zł; P🛜) Unikat is a good option a few hundred metres east of the National Park Information Centre.

This 60-bed timber guesthouse has clean, functional and sizable rooms, and a fine restaurant.

### Youth Hostel Paprotka HOSTEL €

(☑85 681 2560; www.paprotka.com.pl; ul Waszkiewicza 6; dm 30zł, q/d 35/50zł; P@) This friendly youth hostel is set in an old timber house behind the mustard-coloured school building. There are dormitories that contain between six and 12 beds each, a couple of doubles and quads, a kitchen, and a lovely big common room that has a roaring fire at one end.

## ✖ Eating

There are good restaurants at the Unikat, Białowieski and Żubrówka hotels, and also at the Natural History Museum (Restauracja Parkowa).

### Carska POLISH €€€

(www.restauracjacarska.pl; ul Stacja Towarowa 4; mains 40-60zł) This silver-service restaurant, in the tsar's private railway station 1km south of Białowieża, specialises in game, such as *szynka z sarny* (pickled wild-boar ham).

### Pokusa POLISH €€

(www.restauracja-pokusa.pl; ul Olgi Gabiec 15; mains 20-30zł) One of the better choices in the village, the Pokusa offers decent Polish cooking, including good fried fish, in comfortable digs across the street from the Żubrówka. There's a small garden in the back.

## ❶ Information

### Money

**Hotel Żubrówka** (ul Olgi Gabiec 6) Has an ATM right outside its entrance.

### Tourist Information

**National Park Information Centre** (☑85 681 2901; www.bpn.com.pl; Park Pałacowy; ◷8am-4pm Mon-Fri, 9am-5pm Sat & Sun May-Sep) A small wooden hut at the eastern entrance to Park Pałacowy.

**PTTK Tourist Service** (Biuro Usług Turystycznych PTTK; ☑85 681 2295; www.pttk .bialowieza.pl; ul Kolejowa 17; ◷8am-4pm) At the southern entrance to Park Pałacowy; can help arrange guides and accommodation.

### Travel Agencies

Each of the agencies below offers guides for visiting the strictly protected area of the national park. The major operator is PTTK, which organises English-, German- or Russian-speaking guides (165zł for up to three hours) for visits to the strictly protected area, and trips by *britzka* (horse-drawn cart) or sledge in winter (from 170zł for four people). Weekends are the best times to join English-speaking tours.

Other agencies with English-speaking guides:
**Biuro Turystyki Ryś** (☑85 681 2249; www .turystyka-rys.pl; ul Krzyże 22)
**Nature Tour** (☑669 774 777; http:// bialowiezaforest.net; Park Dyrekcjny 11)
**Puszcza Białowieska** (☑85 681 2898, 85 681 2579; bup@tlen.pl)

## ❶ Getting There & Away

Frequent buses and minibuses (5zł, 30 minutes, up to 12 daily) connect Białowieża to the larger regional city of Hajnówka, from where you can make onward connections. Buses run hourly from Hajnówka to Białystok (10zł, two hours).

# AUGUSTÓW-SUWAŁKI REGION

The northern stretch of Podlasie, known as Suwalszczyzna, is an area of outstanding natural beauty, with large swaths of pristine forest and, towards the north, rugged hills and deep valleys. Its defining feature, though, is water: it is a notable lakeland region, with around 200 lakes, and its rivers and canals are among the most paddled in the entire country.

Like the rest of Poland, the modern population here consists predominantly of Poles, but it was for centuries an ethnic and religious mosaic comprising Poles, Lithuanians, Belarusians, Tatars, Germans, Jews and Russians. Traces of this complex cultural mix can still be found, at least in the local cemeteries.

Despite its natural beauty and historical ethnic make-up, the region attracts few visitors from outside Poland's borders. It is therefore the perfect place to avoid the summer crowds that swamp the Great Masurian Lakes to the west, find your own peaceful pocket and kick back for a couple of days.

## Augustów

POP 30,000

Augustów (aw-*goos*-toof) is a small but appealing town straddling the Netta River as it enters Lake Necko. It's the gateway to the Suwałki region and, with its close proximity to a number of natural wonders, it's a popular base for holidaymakers.

# The Augustów-Suwałki Region

The town itself has retained little historical character due to WWII effectively resetting the clock – during a two-month battle in 1944 the town switched hands several times and 70% of it was destroyed. Its history, however, dates back to the time of King Zygmunt II August, who in 1557 founded the town and modestly named it after himself. Despite the strategic location, its development only really began in the 19th century after the construction of the canal bearing the town's name, and was further boosted when the Warsaw–St Petersburg railway was completed in 1862.

Today, Augustów largely survives on tourism, booming in the summer and effectively dying in the winter. Bear in mind that it's a highly popular Warsaw weekend destination during the summer, so book in advance for Friday and Saturday night accommodation to avoid disappointment.

## Sights

**Regional Museum**                MUSEUM
Augustów's regional museum (Muzeum Ziemi Augustowskiej) is housed in two locations. The most interesting collection is dedicated to the **history of the Augustów Canal** (ul 29 Listopada 5a; adult/concession 3/2zł; 9am-4pm Tue-Sun) and is kept in a quaint, 19th-century wooden cabin a short walk from the pleasure boat wharf. The main section, several blocks from the Rynek, features a small **ethnographic exhibition** (ul Hoża 7; adult/concession 3/2zł; 9am-4pm Tue-Sun). You'll find it on the upper floor of the public library.

## Activities

Augustów is an active destination. The city's perch on Lake Necko and its flat terrain make it ideal for **biking**. One of the most enjoyable, family-friendly pedals is to head out along the shoreline of the lake, where

## AUGUSTÓW CANAL

Built in the 1820s, the Augustów Canal (Kanał Augustowski) is a 102km-long waterway connecting the Biebrza and Niemen Rivers. Linking lakes and stretches of river with artificial channels, it's a picturesque route marked with old locks and floodgates. No longer used commercially, it's experiencing a renaissance as a tourist attraction and kayak route.

The canal was built by the short-lived Congress Kingdom of Poland. It was intended to provide the country with an alternative outlet to the Baltic Sea, since the lower Vistula was in the hands of a hostile Prussia. The project aimed to connect the tributaries of the Vistula with the Niemen River and to reach the Baltic at the port of Ventspils in Latvia.

The Polish part of the waterway was designed by an army engineer, General Ignacy Prądzyński, and built in just seven years (1824–30), though final works continued until 1839. The Russians were meant to build their part from the town of Kaunas up to Ventspils around the same time, but the work was never completed.

The Augustów Canal ended up as a regional waterway, and though it contributed to local development, it never became an international trade route. Its route includes 28km of lakes, 34km of canalised rivers and 40km of canal proper. There are 18 locks along the way (14 in Poland), whose purpose is to bridge the 55m change in water level. The lock in Augustów itself has an extra twist to its history: badly damaged in WWII, it was rebuilt in 1947 in a different place.

The whole Polish stretch of the canal is navigable, but tourist boats from Augustów go only as far east as Lake Studzieniczne – the locks beyond this point are inoperative. By kayak, you can continue to the border.

a bike trail follows the edge for a few kilometres. Most hotels have bikes for guests or try **Jan Wojtuszko** (Nadrzeczna 62; per hr/day 5/25zł), a family-run enterprise with several bikes for hire.

There's also **swimming** – though water temps in summer rarely rise above 20°C – at the **City Beach** (Plaża Miejska), north of the centre along the southern shore of Lake Necko.

### Kayaking

Kayaking is one of the most popular pursuits in Augustów, whether it be a couple of hours of paddling in Lack Necko or a multiday kayaking expedition along the region's lakes and rivers. Numerous local operators, including many hotels and hostels, offer package tours that run anywhere from a day to two weeks, depending on the river and the operator. Alternatively, kayaks can be hired individually (25zł to 30zł per day), to head out on your own.

The **Czarna Hańcza River** is the most popular kayaking destination in the region. The traditional route normally starts at Lake Wigry and follows the river downstream through the Augustów Forest to the Augustów Canal. The trip takes six to eight days, depending on how fast you paddle. Various shorter trips are also available.

Other rivers used for kayaking trips include the Rospuda (four to six days) and the Biebrza (seven to 10 days); some companies also offer trips to rivers in neighbouring Lithuania (seven days).

The tourist information centre has information and brochures on various outfitters.

**Szekla PTTK**　　　　　KAYAKING, RIVER TRIPS
(☑87 643 3850; www.szekla.pl; ul Nadrzeczna 70a) Easier to get to from the centre than Szot, though mainly serves Polish school groups and is less adept at handling walk-ins.

**Szot**　　　　　　　　　KAYAKING, RIVER TRIPS
(☑87 643 4399; www.szot.pl; ul Konwaliowa 2) Has an excellent selection of short and long trips and English-friendly guides, though the offices are a 30-minute walk south of the city centre.

### Pleasure Boat Excursions

**Żegluga Augustowska**　　　RIVER BOAT TRIPS
(☑87 643 2881; www.zeglugaaugustowska.pl; ul 29 Listopada 7) From May to September, pleasure boats operated by Żegluga Augustowska ply the surrounding lakes and a part of the Augustów Canal to the east of town. All trips depart from and return to the **wharf** (ul 29 Listopada). Boats depart around once an hour from 10am to 4.10pm in July and August, and between 10am

and 1.40pm the rest of summer. The shortest trips (30zł, one hour) ply Lake Necko and Lake Białe. More interesting are the cruises further east along the canal system; the longest is a trip to Lake Studzieniczne (40zł, three hours).

If big boating outings are not your thing, take a walk along ul Rybacka on the southern shore of the Netta River (that links the lake to the Augustów Canal) to find several private operators offering smaller trips for two to eight people at prices starting at about 20zł per person.

## ✷ Festivals & Events

**Augustów Theatre Summer** THEATRE
Held in July and August.

**Polish Sailing in Anything Championships** BOATING
The Mistrzostwa Polski w Pływaniu na Byle Czym is a highly bizarre and entertaining open event for homemade vessels, held at the end of July on the Netta River.

## 🛏 Sleeping

**Hotel Szuflada** HOTEL €€
(☏87 644 6315; www.szuflada.augustow.pl; ul Skorupki 2c; s/d/tr 140/170/220zł; 🕸) This is a quality in-town offering, just a couple of steps away from the Rynek, but within easy walking distance of the lake. Rooms are on the ordinary side, but tidy and comfortable. There's a great little cafe on the ground floor, with hands-down the city's best coffee.

**Hotel Warszawa** HOTEL €€€
(☏87 643 8500; www.hotelwarszawa.pl; ul Zdrojowa 1; s/d/ste 285/395/685zł; 🅿@🕸🏊) The most expensive option in town, the Warszawa is a quality luxury hotel with plenty of trimmings such as a restaurant, a bar, a sauna, bikes and boats. Rooms are suitably comfortable and the entire complex is discreetly hidden among trees near the lake. Note that the centre is about 2km away, either by foot along a busy road or following a more looping – and picturesque path – along the perimeter of the lake.

**Hotel Logos** HOTEL €
(☏87 643 2021; www.augustow-logos.pl; ul 29 Listopada 9; s/d/tr 110/130/190zł; 🅿@🕸) Right by the pleasure-boat wharf, the Logos is a neat and reasonable option with high standards. Where it excels is on small details, such as very comfortable beds and low noise levels away from Augustów's busy main road. It has its own restaurant and a travel agency offering all the usual regional activities. Rates do not include breakfast (18zł).

## 🍴 Eating

In summer, head to the semipermanent **beer gardens** (ul Mostowa), by the Netta bridge and strung out along the Netta River, for cheap food and drink in a festive atmosphere.

**TOP CHOICE** **Ogródek Pod Jabłoniami** POLISH €€
(www.miasto.augustow.pl; ul Rybacka 3; mains 10-40zł) The best meal in a town that doesn't offer much in the way of good eating. The draws here are the grilled meats, including pepper steak, pork and chicken, but they also do very good pizza and a whole range of cheap and filling Polish

---

### THE DEEP, DARK AUGUSTÓW FOREST

The Augustów Forest (Puszcza Augustowska) stretches east of Augustów as far as the Lithuanian-Belarusian border. At 1100 sq km, it's Poland's largest continuous forest after the Bory Dolnośląskie in Lower Silesia. It's a remnant of the vast primeval forest that once covered much of eastern Poland and southern Lithuania.

The forest is mainly made up of pine and spruce, with colourful deciduous species such as birch, oak, elm, lime, maple and aspen. The wildlife is rich and diverse, and includes beavers, wild boar, wolves, deer and even some elk. Birds are also well represented and the 55 lakes abound in fish. It was virtually unexplored until the 17th century, but today is criss-crossed by paved roads, dirt tracks, and walking and cycling paths. Despite this, there are large stretches that are almost untouched, and if you want to get firmly off the beaten track in Poland then this is a great swath of nature to do it in.

You can explore part of the forest using private transport; roads will take you along the Augustów Canal to the border. Many of the rough tracks are perfectly OK for bikes and horses, and on foot you can get almost everywhere except the swamps.

treats. The terrace affords a beautiful view of Lake Necko.

### Greek Zorbas
GREEK €€

(ul Kościelna 4; mains 15-35zł; 🛜) This popular restaurant and occasional music club offers an eclectic menu, with Greek dishes like moussaka sharing space with Polish favourites and pizza. Offers daily three-course set menus that are good value.

### ℹ Information

**Bank Pekao** (ul Żabia 3)

**Grota Internet** (ul Żabia 1; per hr 6zł; ⊙10am-9pm) Internet access.

**Main post office** (Rynek 3)

**Tourist Information Centre** (📞87 643 2883; www.augustow.eu; Rynek Zygmunta Augusta 44; ⊙8am-8pm Mon-Fri, 10am-6pm Sat & Sun) Friendly and helpful, with information on the city and its surrounds.

### ℹ Getting There & Away

**BUS** The bus terminal is on the southern side of the Rynek and handles roughly hourly services to Białystok (15zł to 18zł, two hours) and Suwałki (8zł, 45 minutes). There are five buses directly to Warsaw (33zł, 4½ hours); all come through from Suwałki and can be full. Three buses a day run to Sejny (10zł, one hour).

**TRAIN** Augustów has two train stations, but both are a long way from the town centre. Augustów Port train station is convenient for some of the lakeside hotels, but fast trains don't stop there and it doesn't have a ticket office.

There are two fast trains, leaving from the main station, to Warsaw (51zł, 4½ hours) daily, going via Białystok. There are plenty of trains to Suwałki (8zł to 12zł, 30 minutes).

# Suwałki

POP 69,300

Suwałki (soo-*vahw*-kee) is the largest town in the region, but lacks Augustów's charm and immediate proximity to lakes and rivers. There's also little in the way of tourism infrastructure, so if you view it as a gateway to the surrounding countryside, particularly the nearby Wigry National Park, rather than as a destination in itself, you're on the right track.

The town first appeared on the map at the end of the 17th century as one of the villages established by the Camaldolese monks from Wigry. The small multinational community grew slowly; at different times it included Jews, Lithuanians, Tatars,

Russians, Germans and Old Believers, a religious group that split off from the Russian Orthodox Church in the 17th century. Very few members of any of these groups are still present in the town today.

### ◉ Sights

**Cemetery**
CEMETERY

One way to get a flavour of the town's former ethnic mix is to visit the sprawling cemetery about 1km west of the tourist office. It comprises several separate burial grounds for people of different creeds.

Begin your exploration at the doorway to the tiny **Muslim graveyard**, the last remnant of the Tatars. The gate, situated just to the right of ul Zarzecze 12, is locked and the graves are hardly recognisable. The only way you'd know it's a Muslim graveyard is the crescent symbol etched in the wall at the gate.

About 30m along, opposite ul Zarzecze 29, is the entry to the relatively large **Jewish cemetery**, reflecting the one-time size of the community. Their cemetery was destroyed in WWII and only a memorial stands in the middle, assembled out of fragments of old grave slabs. The gate is normally locked, but you can get the key at the Town Hall office at ul Mickiewicza 1.

Opposite ul Zarzecze 19 is the **Orthodox cemetery**, marked by a wooden church, and behind this stands the **Old Believers' graveyard**; both are largely wild and unkempt. The **Catholic cemetery** begins here and stretches for a good long way.

### 🏃 Activities

**PTTK office**
KAYAKING

(📞87 566 5961; http://suwalki.pttk.pl, in Polish; ul Kościuszki 37; ⊙8am-4pm Mon-Fri) Operates kayak trips down the Czarna Hańcza and Rospuda Rivers, and hires out kayaks (around 30zł per day).

### 🛏 Sleeping & Eating

**Hotel Suwalszczyzna**
HOTEL €€

(📞87 566 5922; www.hotelsuwalszczyzna.pl; ul Noniewicza 71a; s/d 160/180zł; 🅿🛜) Tucked away behind an unpromising facade, both the hotel and its ground-floor restaurant offer some of the best standards in town. The collection of framed, signed football shirts on the stairway suggests either an abiding passion for soccer or an unusual preponderance of sporting guests.

MAZOVIA & PODLASIE AROUND SUWAŁKI

### Hotel Dom Nauczyciela       HOTEL €€
(☑87 566 6900; www.domnauczyciela.suwalki.pl; ul Kościuszki 120; s/d/tr 156/190/240zł; ℗⊛) This is a clean, comfortable and well-run hotel across the street from Restauracja Rozmarino and within easy walking distance of the tourist office. The rooms are nothing fancy, but are adequately furnished with beds and desks. The bathrooms are spotless.

### Restauracja Rozmarino       INTERNATIONAL €
(www.rozmarino.pl; ul Kościuszki 75; mains 12-22zł) Never has so much been crammed into so little space with so few negative results. As pizzeria-cum-piano bar-cum-art gallery-cum-restaurants go, this is an amazing place, boasting a two-tiered rainbow-hued summer garden for live music, a menu that looks like a newspaper, and unusual treats such as crab claws and ostrich balls to shake up the usual Italian suspects.

### Einstein       POLISH €€
(www.einstein.suwalki.pl; ul Kościuszki 82; mains 18-31zł) Dine with the great physicist (his portraits and theoretical equations plaster the rich, red walls) at this modern eatery in the heart of town. The menu contains regional cuisine with a few European options thrown in to keep things contemporary. A cheap lunch menu is available during the week.

### ℹ Information
**Bank Pekao** (ul Kościuszki 72)
**Post office** (ul Sejneńska 13)
**Tourist office** (☑87 563 0538; www.cmikt.pl; ul Hamerszmita 16; ⊙9am-6pm Mon-Fri, 9am-5pm Sat, 10am-4pm Sun May-Sep, 8am-4pm Mon-Fri Oct-Apr) Moderately helpful tourist office one block west of ul Kościuszki with an excellent website on the region.

### ℹ Getting There & Away
The train station is 1.5km northeast of the centre; the bus terminal is closer to the central area. Trains are useful mostly for longer journeys, with four daily departures to Białystok (18zł to 31zł, 2½ hours) and two to Warsaw (53zł, five hours).

Frequent buses run to Augustów (10zł, 45 minutes), Sejny (8zł, 45 minutes) and Białystok (26zł, 2¾ hours).

## Around Suwałki
### WIGRY NATIONAL PARK
On the northern fringes of Augustów Forest is arguably the most beautiful lake in Podlasie. At 21 sq km, **Lake Wigry** is also the largest in the region and one of the deepest, reaching 73m at its greatest depth. Its shoreline is richly indented, forming numerous bays and peninsulas, and there are 15 islands on the lake. The lake is the dominating feature of **Wigry National Park** (Wigierski Park Narodowy), a small park to the east of Suwałki whose dense forest belt and plethora of smaller lakes make it a popular destination for kayakers, cyclists and hikers. The Czarna Hańcza River flows through the park, connecting with the Augustów Canal further downstream.

Access is easiest from the Suwałki–Sejny road, which crosses the northern part of the park. The **park headquarters** (☑87 566 6322; www.wigry.win.pl; ⊙7am-3pm Mon-Fri, also 9am-5pm Sat & Sun Jul & Aug) are on this road, in Krzywe, which is 5km from Suwałki.

There are marked trails throughout the park, leading to some truly remote corners. The *Wigierski Park Narodowy* map (available at the park headquarters for 8zł) shows all the necessary detail.

The park's attractions are not restricted to nature. Spectacularly located on a peninsula in the lake, in the village of Wigry, is a former **Camaldolese monastery**, built by the death-obsessed Camaldolese monks soon after they were brought to Wigry by King Jan II Kazimierz Waza in 1667. The whole complex, complete with a church and 17 hermitages, was originally on an island, which was later connected to the shore. It has now been turned into a hotel and restaurant, providing an atmospheric base for exploring the park.

Train lovers can get a fix riding the **narrow-gauge train** (☑87 563 9263; www.augustowska.pl; adult/concession 23/15zł; ⊙10am, 1pm & 4pm Jul & Aug) that skirts the southern fringes of the park from Płociczno-Tartak to Krusznik. The trip takes about 2½ hours, passing through lush forest and providing views of Lake Wigry.

There's also the **Wigier Museum** (www.wigry.win.pl; adult/concession 8/4zł; ⊙10am-3pm) in the village of Stary Folwark, with exhibitions on the flora and fauna to be found in the park and lake.

The little village of Wigry is arguably the most atmospheric place to stay overnight, with the first choice being the former monastery, **Pokamedulski Klasztor w Wigrach** (☑87 566 2499; www.wigry.pro; s/d 120/160zł, apt 300zł; ℗⊛). Outside the monastery there are smaller guesthouses. **U Haliny** (☑87 563

## THE GORGEOUS SUWAŁKI LANDSCAPE PARK

About halfway between Suwałki and the Lithuanian border is a cluster of pristine lakes and rugged hills that certainly merits a detour if you've come this far. The Suwałki Landscape Park (Suwalski Park Krajobrazowy) covers some 63 sq km, and a healthy portion of the park is either lakes (26 in all, totalling 10% of the park's area) or fine forest (another 24%). It's a perfect place for walking or cycling.

The village of **Smolniki**, 20km north of Suwałki, is probably the most convenient base for the park. There are three good viewpoints in the village, which allow you to enjoy some of this landscape. One of the numerous walking options is an hour's walk west to **Lake Hańcza**, the deepest lake in the country. With its steep shores, stony bottom and amazing crystal-clear water, it's like being up in the mountains.

A handful of buses make the 40-minute trip each day (5zł) between Suwałki and Smolniki. For accommodation options, enquire at the Suwałki tourist information office or contact the **park office** (☎87 569 1801; www.spk.org.pl, in Polish; Turtul; ⊙8am-7pm Mon-Fri, 9am-5pm Sat Jul & Aug, 8am-3pm Mon-Fri Sep-Jun) on the southern edge of the park.

One special sleeping option to consider, but only feasible if you've got your own wheels since the location is so remote, is the **Jaczno guest lodge** (☎87 568 3590; www.jaczno.pl; Jaczne 3, Smolniki; s/d/apt 240/320/495zł; P🖥🗱), near the tiny village of Udziejek, about 6km from Smolniki. This is a series of timbered mountain chalets all built around a beautifully restored stone farmhouse.

The 1:50,000 map *Suwalski Park Krajobrazowy* (10zł) is good for exploring the area. It has all the hiking trails marked on it and sightseeing information in English on the reverse.

7042; www.suwalszczyzna.com.pl; r 60zł; P) is a friendly homestay with an on-site camping ground (per person/tent 10/10zł).

The Suwałki–Sejny road is serviced by regular buses. If you want to go directly to the monastery, take the bus to Wigry (four daily buses in summer).

### SEJNY
POP 5000

Sejny, 30km east of Suwałki, is the last Polish town before the Ogrodniki border crossing to Lithuania, 12km beyond. The town grew up around the Dominican monastery, which had been founded in 1602 by monks from Vilnius. The order was expelled by the Prussian authorities in 1804 and never returned, but the proud two-towered silhouette of their **church** still dominates the town from its northern end. It dates from the 1610s, but the facade was thoroughly remodelled 150

years later in the so-called Vilnius Baroque style. Its pastel interior has harmonious Rococo decoration.

At the opposite, southern end of the town is a large **synagogue** built by the sizable local Jewish community in the 1880s. During the German occupation it served as a fire station and after the war as a storage room. Today it's an art gallery operated by the **Borderland Foundation** (Fundacja Pogranicze; ☎87 516 2765; www.pogranicze.sejny .pl; Piłsudskiego 37), focusing on the arts and culture of different ethnic and religious traditions from the region. In summer, the foundation regularly hosts evenings of klezmer music. Concert schedules are normally posted on the door of the synagogue or check the website for details.

Hourly buses run from Sejny to Suwałki (8zł, 45 minutes).

# Kraków

POP 756,000

## Includes »

## Best Places to Eat

» Glonojad (p137)

» Deli Bar (p139)

» Restauracja Pod Gruszką (p137)

» Il Calzone (p137)

» Nostalgia (p137)

## Best Places to Stay

» Dom Polonii (p134)

» AAA Kraków Apartments (p134)

» Hotel Klezmer-Hois (p136)

» Greg & Tom Hostel (p134)

» Wielopole (p134)

## Why Go?

If you believe the legends, Kraków was founded upon the defeat of a dragon, and it's true a mythical atmosphere permeates its attractive streets and squares.

Wawel Castle is a major drawcard, while the Old Town contains soaring churches, impressive museums and the vast Rynek Główny, Europe's largest market square. In the former Jewish quarter, Kazimierz, remnant synagogues reflect the tragedy of the 20th century, just as its lively western quarter symbolises the renewal of the 21st. Here and throughout the Old Town are hundreds of restaurants, bars and clubs.

However, there's more to the former royal capital than history and nightlife. As you walk through the Old Town, you'll sometimes find yourself overwhelmed by the harmony of a quiet back street, the 'just so' nature of the architecture and light. It's at times like these that Kraków reveals its harmonious blend of past and present, an essential part of any visit to Poland.

## When to Go
### Kraków

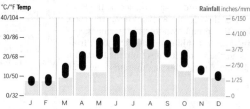

| May or Jun | Aug | Dec |
| --- | --- | --- |
| As spring ends, the Lajkonik Pageant features a parade. | The Pierogi Festival puts paid to summer hunger pangs. | Christmas sees the *szopki* (Nativity scenes) competition. |

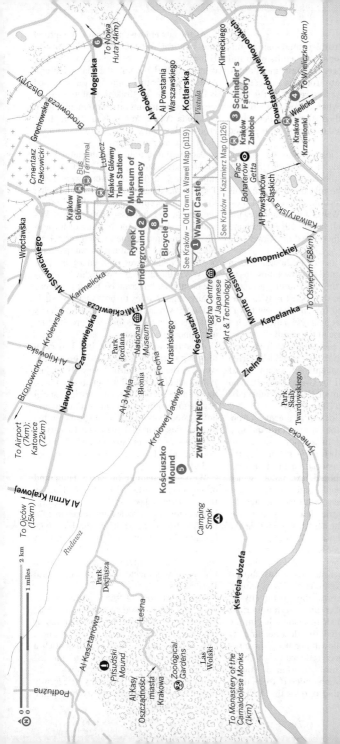

## Kraków Highlights

**1** Immersing yourself in Polish history at the multiple museums within the grand **Wawel Castle** (p115)

**2** Heading beneath the vast Rynek Główny, Europe's largest medieval market square, to experience the multimedia **Rynek Underground** (p118) exhibition

**3** Learning about WWII history in the magnificent museum inside **Schindler's Factory** (p127)

**4** Marvelling at the amazing underground salt sculptures within the **Wieliczka Salt Mine** (p130)

**5** Viewing the city from the heights of the **Kościuszko Mound** (p128)

**6** Absorbing the startling contrasts presented by the communist-era architecture of **Nowa Huta** (p129)

**7** Eyeballing odd elixirs and remedies at the wonderful **Museum of Pharmacy** (p123)

**8** Taking in the sights of the Old Town on a **bicycle tour** (p131)

## History

Poland's former royal capital has a suitably long back story to match its beautiful historic appearance. The first traces of the city's existence date from the 7th century, and the earliest written record of the town dates from 966, when a Jewish merchant from Cordova called Abraham ben Jacob visited and referred to a trade centre called Krakwa.

Greatness was just around the corner; having been made a bishopric in 1000, Kraków became the capital of Poland in 1038, assuming the role from Poznań. This honour was the beginning of a rise in prestige and power. Wawel Castle and several churches were built in the 11th century and the town, originally centred on Wawel Hill, grew in size.

Setbacks were inevitable though, and in 1241 the Tatars burned Kraków almost to the ground. Spotting the silver lining, however, the townsfolk used the opportunity to redefine its layout, and by 1257 the new town's centre had been set on a grid pattern, with a large market square in the middle.

Kraków's long association with the arts and intellectual pursuits was kick-started in 1364 by the enlightened Kazimierz III Wielki (Casimir III the Great; 1333–70), who founded the institution that later came to be called Jagiellonian University.

With its consolidation as a centre of political power and the arts, the 15th and 16th centuries ushered in a golden age of expansion. Kraków became a member of the far-flung trading association the Hanseatic League (see the boxed text, p308), which attracted craftspeople and boosted trade. Nicolaus Copernicus, who would later develop his heliocentric view of the universe, studied here in the 1490s, symbolising the city's status as a centre of learning.

It was a fairytale story of progress and prosperity, and like all such tales had to come to an end. Kraków's status slipped in 1596 when Zygmunt III Waza moved the capital to Warsaw, though the city remained the site of coronations and burials. A series of Swedish invasions, beginning in 1655, accelerated the decline; and by the end of the following century the city's population had been reduced by a third to 10,000. In the Third Partition of Poland (1795), Kraków was sundered from most of Poland, becoming part of the Austrian province of Galicia.

As the city enjoyed a measure of cultural and political freedom within the Austro-Hungarian Empire, by the end of the 19th century it had become the major cultural centre and spiritual capital of the vanished Poland. It was in Kraków that the avant-garde artistic and literary movement known as Młoda Polska (Young Poland) was born around this time, along with a national independence movement.

Back within a united Poland after WWI, Kraków grew to a population of 260,000 inhabitants, 65,000 of whom were Jews. Tragedy was about to doubly strike the city; the German occupation of 1939 led both to the arrest and imprisonment of Kraków's academic elite, and the herding of its Jewish citizens into a ghetto. Transported to Nazi work and extermination camps, most of them would never be seen again. During WWII the city was thoroughly looted by the occupiers, but avoided being the scene of any major battles or bombings. As such, Kraków is virtually the only large Polish city that has retained its pre-war architecture and appearance intact.

After the war, the newly installed communist government established a huge steelworks at the new suburb of Nowa Huta, just 10km east of the Old Town, in an attempt to mould a more working-class city. The social engineering proved less potent than its unanticipated by-product – ecological disaster. Monuments that had managed to survive invasions by Tatars, Swedes and Germans began gradually to be eroded by acid rain and toxic gas.

With the creation of Nowa Huta and other new suburbs after WWII, Kraków tripled in size to become the country's third-largest city, after Warsaw and Łódź. In 1978 the Archbishop of Kraków, Karol Wojtyła, became Pope John Paul II, an elevation which remains a great source of pride for the city's citizens. In the same year, the city's Old Town was included in Unesco's World Heritage list.

The overthrow of the communist regime in 1990 allowed tourism to flourish, and a significant number of technology-related international firms to set up shop. This combination of factors, along with a relatively low unemployment rate, has led to a 21st-century revival of Kraków's medieval confidence and prosperity. It recently became the second-largest city in Poland, surpassing Łódź.

# ◉ Sights

**WAWEL HILL**

This hilltop location is enveloped in the heady atmosphere of Polish history, perhaps more than any other site in the country. Its great castle was the seat of the kings for over 500 years from the early days of the Polish state, and even after the centre of power moved to Warsaw in the late 16th century, it retained much of its symbolic power. Today, Wawel Hill is the silent guardian of a millennium of Polish history, and one of the nation's most popular drawcards for Poles and foreigners alike.

Plan on at least four hours here if you want anything more than just a glance over the place. In summer, it's best to come early as there may be long queues for tickets later in the day.

Buy your tickets at the **visitor centre** (⊙9am-8pm), which also houses a gift shop, post office and cafe. Alternatively, you can prebook your tickets by phoning at least one day ahead or going in person to the **Tourist Service Office** (Map p119; ☑12 422 1697; ⊙9am-2pm Mon, 9am-4pm Tue-Sun). If possible, avoid weekends, when Wawel is besieged by visitors.

⌐TOP⌐
|CHOICE| **Wawel Castle**                      CASTLE
(Zamek Królewski na Wawelu; Map p119; www .wawel.krakow.pl; grounds admission free; ⊙grounds 6am-dusk) As the political and cultural centre of Poland until the end of the 16th century, Wawel Castle is a potent symbol of national identity.

The splendid Renaissance palace you see today was built in the 16th century. The original, rather smaller residence was built in the early 11th century by King Bolesław Chrobry beside the chapel dedicated to the Virgin Mary (known as the Rotunda of SS Felix and Adauctus). Kazimierz III Wielki turned it into a formidable Gothic castle, but when it burned down in 1499, Zygmunt I Stary (Sigismund I the Old; 1506–48) commissioned the new residence. Within 30 years the current palace, designed by Italian architects, was in place. Despite further extensions and alterations, the three-storey structure, complete with a courtyard arcaded on three sides, has been preserved to this day.

Repeatedly sacked and vandalised by the Swedish and Prussian armies, the castle was occupied after the Third Partition by the Austrians, who intended to make Wawel a citadel. They planned to turn the castle into barracks, and the cathedral into a garrison church, while moving the royal tombs elsewhere. They never got that far but they did turn the royal kitchen and coach house into a military hospital and raze two churches standing at the outer courtyard to make room for a parade ground. They also enveloped the whole hill with a new ring of massive brick walls, largely ruining the original Gothic fortifications.

After Kraków was incorporated into the re-established Poland after WWI, restoration work began and continued until the outbreak of WWII. The work was resumed after the war and has been able to recover a good deal of the castle's earlier external form and its interior decoration.

The castle is now a museum containing five separate sections, each requiring a different ticket valid for a specific time. There's a limited daily quota of tickets for some parts, so arrive early if you want to see everything or phone ahead to reserve. You may find you'll have to go on a Polish-language tour if all the English-language tours for the day have been fully booked.

*State Rooms*

(adult/concession 18/11zł; ⊙9.30am-5pm Tue-Fri, 10am-5pm Sat & Sun) The largest and most impressive exhibition in the castle is this apparently never-ending chain of rooms and chambers restored to their original Renaissance and early Baroque style and crammed with period furnishings, paintings, tapestries and works of art.

The two biggest (and the most spectacular) interiors are on the 2nd floor. The **Hall of Senators**, which was originally used for senate sessions, court ceremonies, balls and theatre performances, houses a magnificent series of six 16th-century Arras tapestries following the story of Adam and Eve, Cain and Abel or Noah (they are rotated periodically). The **Hall of Deputies** has a fantastic coffered ceiling with 30 individually carved and painted wooden heads staring back at you. Meant to illustrate the life cycle of man, from birth to death, they are all that have survived from a total of 194 heads, which were carved around 1535 by Sebastian Tauerbach. There's also a tapestry with the Polish insignia dating from 1560.

*Royal Private Apartments*

(adult/concession 25/19zł; ⊙9.30am-5pm Tue-Fri, 10am-5pm Sat & Sun) This tour leads through somewhat more intimate interiors than those of the State Rooms, thus giving an insight into how the monarchs and their families once lived. The dozen or so apartments are visited with a guide, which is included in the ticket price. English-language tours depart at least once an hour.

You'll see plenty of magnificent old tapestries, mostly northern French and Flemish, hanging on the walls. The collection, largely assembled by Zygmunt II August (Sigismund II Augustus; 1548–72), once numbered 360 pieces, but only 138 survive. Even so, this is probably the largest collection of its kind in Europe, and one of Wawel's most precious possessions. Other highlights include the so-called **Hen's Foot**, Jadwiga's gemlike chapel in the northeast tower, and the sumptuous Gdańsk-made furniture in the **Alchemy Room** and annexe. The collection includes a 400kg cupboard.

### Crown Treasury & Armoury

(adult/concession 18/11zł, free Mon Apr-Oct, Sun Nov-Mar; ⊗9.30am-1pm Mon, 9.30am-5pm Tue-Fri, 10am-5pm Sat & Sun) These are housed in vaulted Gothic rooms surviving from the 14th-century castle. The most famous object in the treasury is the Szczerbiec ('Jagged Sword') dating from the mid-13th century, which was used at all Polish coronations from 1320 onwards. The adjacent armoury features a collection of old weapons from various epochs – from crossbows, swords, lances and halberds from the 15th to 17th centuries to muskets, rifles, pistols and cannon from the 18th century onward.

### Oriental Art Exhibition

(adult/concession 8/5zł; ⊗9.30am-5pm Tue-Fri, 10am-5pm Sat & Sun) A collection of 17th-century Turkish banners and weaponry, captured after the Battle of Vienna and displayed along with a variety of old Persian carpets, Chinese and Japanese ceramics, and other Asian antiques.

### Lost Wawel

(adult/concession 8/5zł; ⊗9.30am-1pm Mon, 9.30am-5pm Tue-Fri, 10am-5pm Sat & Sun) Accommodated in the old royal kitchen. Along with the remnants of the late-10th-century Rotunda of SS Felix and Adauctus, which is reputedly the first church in Poland, you can see various archaeological finds (including colourful old ceramic tiles from the castle's stoves), as well as models of the previous Wawel churches, the foundations of which can still be seen in the central courtyard.

TOP
CHOICE **Wawel Cathedral**               CHURCH
(Katedra Wawelska; Map p119; www.katedra-wawel ska.pl; royal tombs, bell tower & museum adult/concession 12/7zł; ⊗9am-5pm Mon-Sat, 12.30-5pm Sun) This cathedral has witnessed most of the coronations, funerals and entombments of Poland's monarchs and strongmen over the centuries. The tradition continued, despite some protest, with the 2010 interment of Lech Kaczyński, the controversial Polish president killed in an air crash that year in Smolensk, Russia.

Wandering around the grandiose funerary monuments and royal sarcophagi is like a fast-forward tour through Polish history. Many outstanding artists have left behind a wealth of magnificent works of art, making the cathedral both an extraordinary artistic achievement and Poland's spiritual sanctuary.

The building you see is the third church on this site, consecrated in 1364. The original cathedral was founded sometime after the turn of the 1st millennium by King Bolesław Chrobry and was replaced with a larger Romanesque construction around 1140. When it burned down in 1305, only the Crypt of St Leonard survived.

The present-day cathedral is basically a Gothic structure, but chapels in different styles were built around it later. Before you enter, note the massive iron door and, hanging on a chain to the left, huge prehistoric animal bones. They are believed to have magical powers; as long as they are here, the cathedral will remain. The bones were excavated on the grounds at the start of the 20th century.

Once inside, you'll get lost in a maze of sarcophagi, tombstones and altarpieces scattered throughout the nave, chancel and ambulatory.

### Holy Cross Chapel

Among a score of chapels, a highlight is the Holy Cross Chapel (Kaplica Świętokrzyska) in the southwestern corner of the church (to the right as you enter). It's distinguished by the 15th-century Byzantine frescoes and the red marble sarcophagus (1492) in the corner by Veit Stoss, the Nuremberg sculptor known to Poles as Wit Stwosz.

## Sigismund Chapel

The showpiece chapel is the Sigismund Chapel (Kaplica Zygmuntowska) up the aisle and on the southern wall. It's often referred to as 'the most beautiful Renaissance chapel north of the Alps' and is recognisable from the outside by its gilded dome.

## Tomb of St Queen Hedwig

Diagonally opposite the Sigismund Chapel is the Tomb of St Queen Hedwig (Sarkofag Św Królowej Jadwigi), a much beloved and humble 14th-century monarch whose unpretentious wooden coronation regalia are on display nearby.

## Shrine of St Stanislaus

In the centre of the cathedral stands the flamboyant Baroque Shrine of St Stanislaus (Konfesja Św Stanisława), dedicated to the bishop of Kraków, who was canonised in 1253 and is now the patron saint of Poland. The silver sarcophagus, adorned with 12 relief scenes from the saint's life, was made in Gdańsk between 1663 and 1691; note the engravings on the inside of the ornamented canopy erected about 40 years later.

## Sigismund Bell

Ascend the tower accessible through the sacristy via 70 steps to see the Sigismund Bell (Dzwon Zygmunta). Cast in 1520, it's 2m high and 2.5m in diameter, and weighs 11 tonnes, making it the largest historic bell in Poland. Its clapper weighs 350kg, and eight strong men are needed to ring the bell, which happens only on the most important church holidays and for significant state events. The views from here are worth the climb.

## Crypt of St Leonard and Royal Crypts

Back down in the nave, descend from the left-hand aisle to the Crypt of St Leonard, the only remnant of the 12th-century Romanesque cathedral extant. Follow through and you will get to the Royal Crypts (Groby Królewskie) where, along with kings such as Jan III Sobieski, many national heroes and leaders, including Tadeusz Kościuszko, Józef Piłsudski and WWII General Władysław Sikorski, are buried in a half-dozen chambers.

**Wawel Cathedral Museum**  MUSEUM

(Map p119; ⊙9am-5pm Mon-Sat) Diagonally opposite the cathedral is this treasury of historical and religious objects from the cathedral. There are plenty of exhibits, including church plate and royal funerary regalia, but not a single crown. They were all stolen from the treasury by the Prussians in 1795 and reputedly melted down.

**Dragon's Den**  CAVE

(Map p119; Smocza Jama; admission 3zł; ⊙10am-5pm) If you've had enough of high art and Baroque furnishings, complete your Wawel trip with a visit to the cheesy Dragon's Den, former home of the legendary Wawel Dragon and an easy way to get down from the hill. The entrance to the cave is next to the Thieves' Tower (Baszta Złodziejska) at the southwestern end of the complex. From here you'll have a good panorama over the Vistula River and the suburbs further west, including the Manggha Centre of Japanese Art & Technology on the opposite bank of the river, and the Kościuszko Mound far off on the horizon.

After you buy your ticket from a coin-operated machine at the entrance, you descend 130 steps into the cave, then stumble some 70m through its damp interior and emerge onto the bank of the Vistula next to a distinctive fire-spitting bronze dragon, the work of contemporary sculptor Bronisław Chromy.

## OLD TOWN

Curiously, the disastrous Tatar invasions of the 13th century were also a gift to Kraków, allowing the city to implement a harmonious street layout in the aftermath of the devastation. It took almost two centuries to envelop the town with a powerful, 3km-long chain of double defensive walls complete with 47 towers and eight main entrance gates, as well as a wide moat.

The major alteration to this set-up took place at the beginning of the 19th century, when the obsolete walls were demolished, except for a small section to the north. The moat was filled up and a ring-shaped park called the Planty was laid out on the site, surrounding the footprint-shaped Old Town with the parkland that is still one of the city's most attractive features.

The Old Town is packed with historical buildings and monuments, including several museums and many churches. It's been included on Unesco's World Heritage List since 1978, and is largely car-free. A tramline crosses it only once (along ul Dominikańska and ul Franciszkańska 150m south of Rynek Główny), so you can stroll largely undisturbed by traffic noise and pollution.

KRAKÓW SIGHTS

Measuring 200m by 200m, Rynek Główny is the largest medieval town square in Europe and one of the finest urban designs of its kind. Its layout, based on that of a *castrum* (Roman military camp), was drawn up in 1257 and has been retained to this day, though the buildings have changed substantially over the centuries. Most of them now look neoclassical, but don't let the facades confuse you – the basic structures are much older, as can be seen by their doorways, architectural details and interiors. Of particular note are the sloping buttresses you'll spot outside many of the square's older buildings; these were an early way of adding extra support to a building's foundations. The cellars beneath date from medieval times. The Rynek is home to a number of interesting attractions.

### Cloth Hall
HISTORIC BUILDING

(Sukiennice; Map p119; Rynek Główny 1) Dominating the middle of the square, this building was once the centre of Kraków's medieval clothing trade. It was created in the early 14th century when a roof was put over two rows of stalls, then extended into a 108m-long Gothic structure. The hall was rebuilt in Renaissance style after a fire in 1555; the arcades were added in the late 19th century.

The ground floor is now a busy trading centre for crafts and souvenirs, while the upper floor is occupied by the recently renovated Gallery of 19th-Century Polish Painting (www.muzeum.krakow.pl; adult/concession 12/6zł, free Sun; ⊙10am-8pm Tue-Sat, 10am-6pm Sun). Its collection features works by Józef Chełmoński, Jacek Malczewski, Aleksander Gierymski and the leader of monumental historic painting, Jan Matejko.

### TOP CHOICE Rynek Underground
EXHIBITION

(www.podziemiarynku.com; adult/concession 13/10zł, free Mon; ⊙10am-8pm Wed-Mon, 10am-4pm Tue) From the northern end of the Cloth Hall you can enter this fascinating new attraction beneath the market square. It consists of an underground route through medieval market stalls and other long-forgotten chambers. The 'Middle Ages meets 21st century' experience is enhanced by a multitude of holograms and other audiovisual wizardry. There's always a scrum at the door, so prebook an entry time at one of the tourist offices.

### St Mary's Church
CHURCH

(Bazylika Wniebowzięcia Najświętszej Marii Panny; Map p119; www.mariacki.com in Polish; Rynek Główny 4; adult/concession 6/4zł; ⊙11.30am-6pm Mon-Sat, 2-6pm Sun) Overlooking the Rynek from the northeast is this striking brick church. Formally titled the Basilica of the Assumption of Our Lady, it's better known in these parts as the Mariacki, or St Mary's. The first church on this site was built in the 1220s and, typically for the period, was oriented eastward. Following its destruction during the Tatar raids, the construction of a mighty basilica began, using the foundations of the previous church.

The facade is dominated by two **towers** of different heights. The lower one, 69m high and topped by a Renaissance dome, serves as a bell tower and holds five bells, while the taller one, which is 81m high, has traditionally been the city's property and functioned as a watchtower. It's topped with a spire surrounded by turrets – a good example of medieval craftsmanship – and in 1666 was given a 350kg gilded crown that's about 2.5m in diameter. The gilded ball higher up contains Kraków's written history. It's from this tower that the *hejnał* (bugle call; see the boxed text, p122) is sounded hourly. In summer you can climb the **tower** (adult/concession 5/3zł; ⊙9-11.30am & 1-5.30pm Tue, Thu & Sat May-Aug) for excellent city views.

The main church entrance, through a Baroque porch added to the southwest facade in the 1750s, is used by worshippers and the faithful; tourists must enter through the side door to the southeast, which leads into the chancel. This is illuminated by the magnificent stained-glass windows dating from the late 14th century; the blue star vaulting of the nave is breathtaking. On the opposite side of the church, above the organ loft, is a fine Art Nouveau stained-glass window by Stanisław Wyspiański and Józef Mehoffer. The colourful wall paintings, designed by Jan Matejko, harmonise beautifully with the medieval architecture and are an appropriate background for the high altar, which is acclaimed as the greatest masterpiece of Gothic art in Poland and allegedly designated the eighth wonder of the world by Pablo Picasso.

The **altarpiece** is a pentaptych (an altarpiece consisting of a central panel and two pairs of side wings), intricately carved

# Kraków – Old Town & Wawel

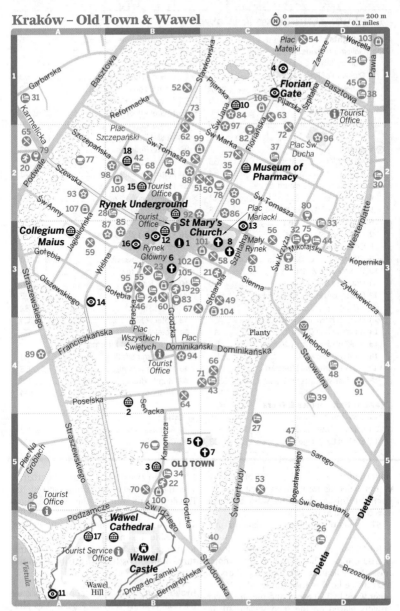

in lime wood, then painted and gilded. The main scene, visible when the pentaptych is open, represents the Dormition (or Assumption) of the Virgin surrounded by the Apostles. The outside has a dozen sections portraying scenes from the life of Christ and the Virgin. The altarpiece is topped with the Coronation of the Virgin in Heaven and, on both sides, the statues of the patron saints of Poland, St Stanislaus and St Adalbert.

Measuring about 13m high and 11m wide, the pentaptych is the largest and most

# Kraków – Old Town & Wawel

important piece of medieval art of its kind. It took a decade for its maker, Veit Stoss, to complete this monumental work before it was consecrated in 1489.

The pentaptych is opened daily at precisely 11.50am and closed at 6pm, except for Saturday when it's left open for the Sunday morning Mass. The altarpiece apart, don't miss the delicate crucifix on the Baroque altar in the head of the right-hand aisle, another work by Veit Stoss, and the still larger crucifix placed on the rood screen, attributed to pupils of the master.

### Church of St Barbara CHURCH

(Kościół Św Barbary; Map p119; Plac Mariacki) South of St Mary's is this sombre 14th-century church sited on the small, charming **Plac Mariacki**, which until the early

19th century was a churchyard. St Barbara's was the cemetery chapel and served the Polish faithful during the Middle Ages (the Mariacki was for Germans). Note the skull and crossbones on the north exterior; just inside the entrance is an open chapel featuring stone sculptures of Christ and three of the Apostles, also attributed to the Stoss school.

### Kraków City History Museum MUSEUM

(Muzeum Historyczne Miasta Krakowa; Map p119; www.mhk.pl; Rynek Główny 35; adult/concession 8/6zł, free Wed; ⊙10am-5.30pm) At the northern corner of the square, the collection within the 17th-century Krzysztofory Palace relates the story of Kraków from 1257 to WWII. The museum features a bit of everything related to the city's past, including old clocks, armour, paintings, Kraków's celebrated *szopki* (Nativity scenes), and the costume of the Lajkonik (see the boxed text, p134).

### Church of St Adalbert
CHURCH

(Kościół Św Wojciecha; Map p119) In the southern corner of the square is this small domed building. It's one of the oldest churches in the Old Town, dating from the 11th century. You can see the original foundations in the basement, where in summer a small exhibition (⊘10am-4pm Mon-Sat Jun-Sep) also presents archaeological finds excavated from the Rynek.

### Hipolit House
MUSEUM

(Kamienica Hipolitów; Map p119; www.mhk.pl; Plac Mariacki 3; adult/concession 7/5zł; free Wed; ⊘10am-5.30pm Wed-Sun) Next to St Mary's

Church, this branch of the Kraków City History Museum contains faithful recreations of townhouse interiors from the 17th to early 19th centuries.

### Town Hall Tower
HISTORIC BUILDING

(Wieża Ratuszowa; Map p119; www.mhk.pl; adult/concession 7/5zł; ⊘10.30am-6pm May-Oct) Southwest of the Cloth Hall, this soaring tower is all that is left of the 15th-century town hall which was dismantled in the 1820s. The 70m-tall tower can be climbed in the warmer months.

### Adam Mickiewicz Statue
MONUMENT

(Map p119) East of the Cloth Hall, Poland's great poet is surrounded by four allegorical figures representing the Motherland, Learning, Poetry and Valour.

## FIRE COMPANY BUGLE BOYS

Every hour on the hour the *hejnał* (bugle call) is sounded four times on a trumpet from the higher tower of St Mary's Church. Today a musical symbol of the city, this simple melody, based on only five notes, was played in medieval times as a warning call. Intriguingly, it breaks off abruptly in midbar. Legend links it to the Tatar invasions; when the watchman on duty spotted the enemy and sounded the alarm, a Tatar arrow pierced his throat midphrase. Because the town was awakened from its collective slumber and defended itself successfully, the tune has stayed that way ever since. The job is now done by a handful of firemen in costume – at least from the waist up. The *hejnał* is also broadcast on Polish Radio every day at noon.

### NORTH OF THE RYNEK

**Collegium Maius**                    HISTORIC BUILDING
(Map p119; ☎12 663 1521; www.maius.uj.edu.pl; ul Jagiellońska 15; adult/concession 12/6zł, free Tue after 3pm; ☺10am-3pm Mon, Wed & Fri, 10am-6pm Tue & Thu, 10am-2pm Sat) The Collegium Maius, built as part of the Kraków Academy (now the Jagiellonian University), is the oldest surviving university building in Poland, and one of the best examples of 15th-century Gothic architecture in the city. It has a magnificent arcaded **courtyard** (☺7am-dusk) and a fascinating university collection.

On the compulsory tour within you'll be shown half a dozen historic interiors, featuring rare 16th-century astronomic instruments used by star pupil **Copernicus** as well as some of his manuscripts; a fascinating alchemy room; old rectors' sceptres; and, the highlight of the show, the oldest existing globe (c 1510) depicting the American continent. You'll also visit an impressive **Aula**, a hall with an original Renaissance ceiling, and crammed with portraits of kings, benefactors and rectors of the university (five of whom were sent to Sachsenhausen concentration camp in 1939). The treasury contains everything from copies of the 1364 university foundation papers and Jan III Sobieski's hammered silver table to film awards (including an Oscar) given to director Andrzej Wajda.

All visits are guided in groups; tours begin every half-hour and there are usually a couple of daily tours at 11am and 1pm in English. In summer it's advisable to reserve in advance, either personally or by phone. The courtyard can be entered free of charge. Try to visit at 11am or 1pm, when the 14th-century replica clock on the south side chimes and its cast of characters go through their paces.

Also here is an exhibition called **World of Senses** (Świat Zmysłów; adult/concession 7/5zł; ☺9am-1.30pm Mon-Sat), which has 40 interactive models that teach visitors how the five senses function (and can be deceived).

**Florian Gate**                    GATE
(Brama Floriańska; Map p119; www.mhk.pl; adult/concession 7/5zł; ☺10.30am-6pm May-Oct) This attractive stone gateway is the only one of the city's original eight gates that was not dismantled during the 19th-century modernisation. It was built around 1300, although the top is a later addition. The adjoining walls, together with two towers, have also been left standing.

To the north of the gate and included in the entry fee is the **Barbican**. The most intriguing remnant of the medieval fortifications, this powerful, circular brick bastion is adorned with seven turrets. There are 130 loopholes in its 3m-thick walls. This striking piece of defensive art was built around 1498 as an additional protection of the Florian Gate, and was once connected to it by a narrow passage running over a moat. It's one of the very few surviving structures of its kind in Europe, and also the largest and perhaps the most beautiful.

**Czartoryski Museum**                    MUSEUM
(Muzeum Książąt Czartoryskich; Map p119; www .muzeum.krakow.pl; ul Św Jana 19) Established in 1800 in Puławy by Princess Izabela Czartoryska as the first historical museum in Poland, this is one of the richest collections in town and has its own exciting history. Secretly moved to Paris after the November Insurrection of 1830 (in which the family was implicated), the collection shifted to Kraków in the 1870s. Another unwelcome move took place during WWII when the occupiers seized it and took it to Germany.

Though not all the works were recovered from this brazen act of theft, there's still a lot to see, including a fascinating collection of European painting, mainly Italian, Dutch and Flemish. The stars of the show are Leonardo da Vinci's masterpiece *Lady with an Ermine* (c 1482), one of only three da Vinci oil paintings extant, and Rembrandt's *Landscape with the Good Samaritan*, also known as *Landscape before a Storm* (1638). Other exhibitions include Greek, Roman, Egyptian and Etruscan art and Turkish weapons and artefacts, such as carpets, saddles and a campaign tent, recovered after the 1683 Battle of Vienna.

At the time of research the museum was undergoing a major renovation, but should have reopened by the time you read this – check with the tourist office for opening hours and entry fees.

### Wyspiański Museum     MUSEUM

(Muzeum Wyspiańskiego; Map p119; www.muzeum .krakow.pl; ul Szczepańska 11; adult/concession 8/4zł, free Sun; ⊙10am-6pm Wed-Sat, 10am-4pm Sun) One of Kraków's most beloved and talented sons is the focus of this museum. A key figure of the Młoda Polska (Young Poland) movement, Stanisław Wyspiański was an impressively multitalented creative type who explored many branches of art. A painter, poet and playwright, he was also a designer renowned for his stained-glass designs, some of which are in the exhibition. Among his never-realised projects was Acropolis, a political, religious and cultural centre to be built on Wawel Hill. There's a model made according to his design – an amazing mix of epochs and styles, including a Greek amphitheatre and a Roman circus.

### Museum of Pharmacy     MUSEUM

(Muzeum Farmacji; Map p119; www.muzeum farmacji.pl; ul Floriańska 25; adult/concession 9/6zł; ⊙noon-6.30pm Tue, 10am-2.30pm Wed-Sun) The name of this museum doesn't sound that exciting, but the Jagiellonian University Medical School's Museum of Pharmacy is one of the largest museums of its kind in Europe and arguably the best. Accommodated in a beautiful historic townhouse worth the visit alone, it features a 22,000-piece collection, which includes old laboratory equipment, rare pharmaceutical instruments, heaps of glassware, stoneware, mortars, jars, barrels, medical books and documents. Several pharmacies dating back to the 19th and early 20th centuries, including one from Lesko, have been painstakingly recreated here, and the garret is crammed with elixirs and panaceas, including vile vials or dried mummy powder. Much attention is given to the 'righteous gentile' Tadeusz Pankiewicz and the Pharmacy Under the Eagle he courageously

kept in operation in the Jewish ghetto during the German occupation (see the boxed text, p128).

### SOUTH OF THE RYNEK

### Archaeological Museum     MUSEUM

(Muzeum Archeologiczne; Map p119; www.ma .krakow.pl, in Polish; ul Poselska 3; adult/concession 7/5zł, free Sun; ⊙9am-2pm Mon, Wed & Fri, 2-6pm Thu, 10am-2pm Sun) You can learn about Małopolska's history from the Palaeolithic period up until the early Middle Ages here, but you'll probably be most enthralled by the collection of ancient Egyptian artefacts, including both human and animal mummies. There are also more than 4000 iron coins from the 9th century. The gardens, laid out with rose bushes, magnolia trees and contemporary sculptures, are a lovely place for a stroll afterwards.

### Church of SS Peter & Paul     CHURCH

(Kościół Św Piotra i Pawła; Map p119; ul Grodzka 54) The Jesuits erected this church, the first Baroque building in Kraków, after they had been brought to the city in 1583 to do battle with supporters of the Reformation. Designed on the Latin cross layout and topped with a large skylit dome, the church has a refreshingly sober interior, apart from some fine stucco decoration on the vault. The figures of the 12 Apostles standing on columns in front of the church are copies of the statues from 1723.

### Church of St Andrew     CHURCH

(Kościół Św Andrzeja; Map p119; ul Grodzka 54) Breathtakingly, this church is almost a thousand years old. Built towards the end of the 11th century, much of its austere Romanesque stone exterior has been preserved. As soon as you enter, though, you're in a totally different world; its small interior was subjected to a radical Baroque overhaul in the 18th century.

### Archdiocesan Museum     MUSEUM

(Muzeum Archidiecezjalne; Map p119; www .muzeumkra.diecezja.pl, in Polish; ul Kanonicza 21; adult/concession 5/3zł; ⊙10am-4pm Tue-Fri, 10am-3pm Sat & Sun) Collection of religious sculpture and paintings, dating from the 13th to 16th centuries and located in a 14th-century townhouse. Also on display is the room where Karol Wojtyła (the late Pope John Paul II) lived from 1958 to 1967, complete with his furniture and belongings – including his skis. There's a treasury of gifts he received here too.

KRAKÓW SIGHTS

## WEST OF THE OLD TOWN

There are a couple of important sights worth the easy walk west from the Old Town.

### Mangagha Centre of Japanese Art & Technology
MUSEUM

(☎12 267 2703; Map p113; www.manggha.krakow.pl; ul Konopnickiej 26; adult/concession 15/10zł, free Tue; ☉10am-6pm Tue-Sun) Lying on the right bank of the Vistula diagonally opposite Wawel Hill, this art museum was the brainchild of the Polish film director Andrzej Wajda. He donated the US$340,000 Kyoto Prize money he received in 1987 for his artistic achievements to fund a permanent home for the National Museum in Kraków's extensive collection of Japanese art, ceramics, weapons, fabrics, scrolls, woodcuts and comic books. The striking modern building, which opened in 1994, was designed by the Japanese architect Arata Isozaki. The bulk of the collection is made up of the 7000 or so pieces assembled by Feliks Jasieński (1861–1929), an avid traveller, art collector, literary critic and essayist, known by his pen name of Manggha. The centre regularly sponsors events relating to Japanese culture, including film, theatre and traditional music.

### National Museum
MUSEUM

(Muzeum Narodowe w Krakowie; Map p113; www.muzeum.krakow.pl; Al 3 Maja 1; adult/concession 18/9zł, free Sun; ☉10am-6pm Tue-Sat, 10am-4pm Sun) Three permanent exhibitions – the Gallery of 20th-Century Polish Painting, the Gallery of Decorative Art, and Polish Arms and National Colours – are housed in this main branch of the National Museum in Kraków, 500m west of the Old Town down ul Piłsudskiego. The painting gallery houses an extensive collection of Polish painting (and some sculpture) covering the period from 1890 until the present day. There are several stained-glass designs (including the ones for Wawel Cathedral) by Stanisław Wyspiański, and an impressive selection of paintings by Witkacy (Stanisław Ignacy Witkiewicz). Jacek Malczewski and Olga Boznańska are also well represented. Of the postwar artists, take particular note of the works by Tadeusz Kantor, Jerzy Nowosielski and Władysław Hasior.

## KAZIMIERZ

For much of its early history, Kazimierz was an independent town with its own municipal charter and laws. Its mixed Jewish and Christian population created a pair of dis-

tinctive communities side by side. Though the ethnic make-up of Kazimierz is now wholly different, the architecture gives hints of the past, with clearly distinguishable elements of what were Christian and Jewish quarters. Today one of Kraków's inner suburbs and located within walking distance of Wawel Hill and the Old Town, the suburb is home to many important tourist sights, including churches, synagogues and museums.

### WESTERN KAZIMIERZ

The western part of Kazimierz was traditionally Catholic, and although many Jews settled here from the early 19th century until WWII – for example, the main Jewish hospital was on ul Skawińska – the quarter preserves much of its original character, complete with its churches.

### Ethnographic Museum
MUSEUM

(Muzeum Etnograficzne; Map p126; www.etnomuzeum.eu; Plac Wolnica 1; adult/concession 9/5zł; ☉11am-7pm Tue-Sat, 11am-3pm Sun) This interesting museum is housed within the former town hall of Kazimierz. It was built in the late 14th century then significantly extended in the 16th century, at which time it acquired its Renaissance appearance. The permanent exhibition features the reconstructed interiors of traditional Polish peasant cottages and workshops, folk costumes, craft and trade exhibits, extraordinary nativity scenes, and folk and religious painting and woodcarving.

### Church of St Catherine
CHURCH

(Kościół Św Katarzyny; Map p126; ul Augustiańska 7) One of the most monumental churches in the city, and possibly the one that has best retained its original Gothic shape, St Catherine's was founded in 1363 and completed 35 years later, though its planned towers have never been built. The church was once on the corner of Kazimierz's market square but the area was built up in the 19th century. The lofty and spacious whitewashed interior boasts the imposing, richly gilded Baroque high altar from 1634 and some very flamboyant choir stalls.

### Corpus Christi Church
CHURCH

(Kościół Bożego Ciała; Map p126; ul Bożego Ciała 26) In the northeastern corner of Plac Wolnica and founded in 1340, this was the first church in Kazimierz and for a long time the town's parish church. Its interior has been almost totally fitted out with Baroque

# THE RISE & FALL (AND RISE) OF KAZIMIERZ

Kazimierz was founded in 1335 by Kazimierz III Wielki on the southern fringe of Kraków. Thanks to privileges granted by the king, the town developed swiftly and soon had its own town hall, a market square almost as large as Kraków's, and two huge churches. The town was encircled with defensive walls and by the end of the 14th century was Małopolska's most important and wealthiest city after Kraków.

The first Jews settled in Kazimierz soon after its foundation, but it wasn't until 1494, when they were expelled from within the walls of Kraków by King Jan Olbracht, that their numbers rapidly rose. They settled in a prescribed area of Kazimierz, northeast of the Christian quarter, with the two sectors separated by a wall.

The subsequent history of Kazimierz was punctuated by fires, floods and plagues, with both communities living side by side, though confined to their own sectors. The Jewish quarter became home to Jews fleeing persecution from all corners of Europe, and it grew particularly quickly, gradually determining the character of the whole town. It became the most important Jewish centre of all Poland.

At the end of the 18th century Kazimierz was administratively incorporated into Kraków, and in the 1820s the walls were pulled down. At the outbreak of WWII Kazimierz was a predominantly Jewish suburb, with a distinct culture and atmosphere. But most Jews were murdered by the Nazi regime in its extermination camps. Of the 65,000 Jews living in Kraków (most of whom lived in Kazimierz) in 1939, only about 6000 survived the war.

During communist rule, Kazimierz was largely a forgotten district of Kraków, partly because the government didn't want to touch the sensitive Jewish question. Then in the early 1990s along came Steven Spielberg to shoot *Schindler's List* and everything changed overnight.

Kazimierz was actually not the setting of the movie's plot – most of the events portrayed in the film took place in the Podgórze ghetto, Oskar Schindler's factory and the Płaszów extermination camp, all of which were further southeast beyond the Vistula. Though Kazimierz is a fascinating place, it's worth crossing the river to grittier Podgórze to get a feel for the whole story.

furnishings, including the huge high altar, extraordinary massive carved stalls in the chancel and a boat-shaped pulpit. Note the surviving early-15th-century stained-glass window in the sanctuary and the crucifix hanging above the chancel.

**JEWISH QUARTER**

The eastern part of Kazimierz became, over the centuries, a centre of Jewish culture equal to no other in the country. However, with the mass deportation and extermination of the Jewish people of Kraków by the German occupiers during WWII, the folklore, life and atmosphere of the quarter was tragically extinguished. Kazimierz became a run-down area after WWII, but in recent years this area has regained some of its Jewish character via the establishment of kosher restaurants complete with live klezmer music, along with museums devoted to Jewish culture. Miraculously, seven synagogues survived the war, and most are available to visit.

The heart of the Jewish quarter is ul Szeroka. Short and wide, it looks more like an elongated square than a street, and is often packed with tourists and coaches.

**TOP CHOICE** **Galicia Jewish Museum** MUSEUM
(Żydowskie Muzeum Galicja; Map p126; www .galiciajewishmuseum.org; ul Dajwór 18; adult/ child 15/8zł; ☺10am-6pm) This museum both commemorates Jewish victims of the Holocaust and celebrates the Jewish culture and history of the former Austro-Hungarian region of Galicia. It features an impressive photographic exhibition depicting modern-day remnants of southeastern Poland's once thriving Jewish community called 'Traces of Memory', along with video testimony of survivors and regular temporary exhibits.

**Jewish Museum** MUSEUM
(Map p126; www.mhk.pl; ul Szeroka 24; adult/ concession 8/6zł, free Mon; ☺10am-2pm Mon, 9am-5pm Tue-Sun) At the southern end of

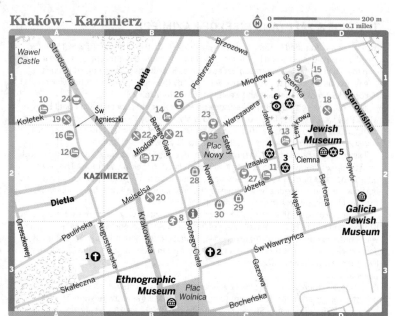

# Kraków – Kazimierz

ul Szeroka is this museum within the fine **Old Synagogue**, which dates back to the end of the 15th century. It's the oldest Jewish house of worship in the country. Damaged by fire in 1557, it was reconstructed in Renaissance style by the Italian architect Matteo Gucci. It was plundered and partly destroyed by the Nazis but later restored. The prayer hall, complete with a reconstructed *bimah* (raised platform at the centre of the synagogue where the Torah is read) and the original *aron kodesh* (the niche in the eastern wall where Torah scrolls are kept), houses an exhibition of liturgical objects; adjacent rooms are dedicated to Jewish traditions and art. Upstairs there's a photographic exhibit focusing on Jewish Kraków and the Holocaust.

### Remuh Synagogue                       SYNAGOGUE
(Synagoga Remuh; Map p126; www.krakow
.jewish.org.pl; ul Szeroka 40; adult/concession 5/2zł; ⊙9am-6pm Sun-Fri) Near the northern end of ul Szeroka is the district's smallest synagogue and the only one regularly used for religious services. The synagogue was established in 1558 by a rich merchant, Israel Isserles, and is also associated with his son Rabbi Moses Isserles, a philosopher and scholar.

### Remuh Cemetery                        CEMETERY
(Cmentarz Remuh; Map p126; ⊙9am-4pm Sun-Fri) Just behind the Remuh Synagogue and founded in the mid-16th century, this cemetery was closed for burials in the late 18th century, when a new and larger graveyard was established. During WWII the German occupiers vandalised and razed the tombstones, but during postwar conservation work some 700 gravestones, many of them outstanding Renaissance examples and dating back four centuries, were uncovered. It seems that the Jewish faithful themselves had buried the stones to avoid their desecration by the foreign armies which repeatedly invaded Kraków in the 18th century. The tombstones have been meticulously restored, making the place one of the best-preserved Renaissance Jewish cemeteries anywhere in Europe.

### Isaac's Synagogue                     SYNAGOGUE
(Synagoga Izaaka; Map p126; ul Jakuba 25, enter from ul Kupa 18; adult/concession 5/3zł; ⊙9am-7pm Sun-Thu, 9am-3pm Fri) Near the southwestern edge of the Remuh Cemetery is Kraków's largest synagogue. Completed in 1644, it was returned to the Jewish community in 1989. Inside you can see the remains of the original stuccowork and wall-painting decoration. Restoration efforts are ongoing,

# Kraków – Kazimierz

so feel free to leave a donation in addition to the entry fee.

**High Synagogue**                          SYNAGOGUE
(Synagoga Wysoka; Map p126; ☏12 426 7520; ul Józefa 38; adult/concession 7/5zł; ⊗9am-7pm) This place of worship was built around 1560, and is the third-oldest synagogue after the Old and the Remuh Synagogues. It contains a photographic exhibition on the 1st floor and Kraków's best Jewish bookshop, Austeria, on the ground floor.

**PODGÓRZE**

This working-class suburb would pique few travellers' curiosities if it wasn't for the notorious role it played during WWII. It was here that the Nazis herded some 15,000 Jews into a ghetto and gradually emptied it via deportations to the concentration camps, including one located a short distance to the southwest in Płaszów. Both ghetto and camp were chillingly recreated in the movie *Schindler's List*.

The centre of the ghetto was Plac Zgody, the ironically named 'Peace Square' which is today known as **Plac Bohaterów Getta** (Heroes of the Ghetto Sq; Map p113). This is where the process of selecting who would stay and who would be placed on the wait-

ing train to one of the camps was completed. Today it's marked by a **memorial** by Kraków architects Piotr Lewicki and Kazimierz Latak consisting of 70 empty chairs, half of which are illuminated. They are meant to represent furniture and other remnants discarded on that very spot by the deportees.

**TOP CHOICE** ⟩ **Schindler's Factory**          MUSEUM
(Fabryka Schindlera; Map p113; www.mhk.pl; ul Lipowa 4; adult/concession 15/13zł, free Mon; ⊗10am-2pm Mon, 10am-6pm Tue-Sun) The highlight of Podgórze is this impressive new museum covering the Nazi occupation of Kraków in WWII. It's housed in the former enamel factory of Oskar Schindler, immortalised in *Schindler's List*. Well-organised, innovative exhibits tell the moving story of the city from 1939 to 1945, recreating urban elements such as a tram carriage, a train station underpass and a crowded ghetto apartment within the factory's walls. It's an experience that shouldn't be missed. From the main post office in the Old Town, catch any tram down ul Starowiślna and alight at the first stop over the river at Plac Bohaterów Getta. From here, follow the signs east along ul Kącik, under the railway line to the museum.

## DARKNESS & LIGHT WITHIN THE GHETTO

At Jerusalem's Yad Vashem, a museum dedicated to the Holocaust, there's a row of trees called the 'Ave of the Righteous Among the Nations'. They represent some of the 21,000-odd Gentiles (non-Jews) who either saved Jews during the Holocaust or came to their defence by putting their own lives at risk. Among those so honoured is Oskar Schindler, probably the best known of the so-called 'Righteous Gentiles' thanks to author Thomas Keneally's book *Schindler's Ark* (1982), made into the award-winning film *Schindler's List* (1993) by Steven Spielberg.

But Schindler is just one of some 6000 Poles – almost one-third of the worldwide total – named in this roll of honour. He was something of an antihero, a heavy-drinking profiteer who originally saved the lives of Jews only because he needed their cheap labour at his enamelware factory in Podgórze (now a museum).

Much more altruistic was the pharmacist Tadeusz Pankiewicz, who cajoled the authorities into letting him keep his business, the Pharmacy Under the Eagle, open in the ghetto until the final deportation. He dispensed medicines (often without charge), carried news from the 'outside world', and even allowed use of the establishment as a safe house on occasion.

His harrowing memoir, *The Cracow Ghetto Pharmacy*, describes many of these deeds in measured detail without bravado or boast, and provides an eyewitness account of the short and tragic history of the Kraków ghetto from beginning to liquidation. It's a remarkable story from a Kraków resident who acted according to the most noble principles of humanity during the city's darkest days.

### Museum of Contemporary Art in Kraków
GALLERY

(Muzeum Sztuki Współczesnej w Krakowie; www.mocak.com.pl; ul Lipowa 4; adult/concession 10/5zł, free Tue; ◉noon-8pm Tue-Sun) Opened in 2011, MOCAK (as it's known for short) is a major museum of modern art, and the first such building in Poland to be constructed from scratch. As it's right next to Schindler's Factory, the two attractions could be combined for an absorbing day out.

### Pharmacy Under the Eagle
MUSEUM

(Apteka Pod Orłem; www.mhk.pl; Plac Bohaterów Getta 18; adult/concession 6/5zł, free Mon; ◉10am-2pm Mon, 9.30am-5pm Tue-Sun) On the south side of Plac Bohaterów Getta is this museum in a former pharmacy, which was run by the non-Jew Tadeusz Pankiewicz during the Nazi occupation. The interior has been restored to its wartime appearance and tells the story of the ghetto and the role of the pharmacy in its daily life.

### Ghetto Wall
MONUMENT

(ul Lwowska 25-29) Just south of Plac Bohaterów Getta are the remains of the Jewish Ghetto wall from WWII, with a plaque marking the site.

### OUTER KRAKÓW

These sights outside central Kraków are worth a half- or full-day excursion.

### ZWIERZYNIEC

### Kościuszko Mound
MONUMENT

(Kopiec Kościuszki; Map p113; www.kopiec kosciuszki.pl; Al Waszyngtona; adult/concession 6/4zł; ◉9am-dusk) A heroic figure who embodied the dreams of independent Poland in times of foreign occupation is the subject of this unusual and impressive memorial in the suburb called Zwierzyniec, just under 3km west of the Old Town. The mound, dedicated to Tadeusz Kościuszko, was erected between 1820 and 1823, soon after the great man's death. The mound stands 34m high, and soil from the Polish and American battlefields where Kościuszko fought was placed here. The views over the city are spectacular.

The entrance is through a small neo-Gothic chapel, which holds an exhibition of memorabilia related to Kościuszko; there's also a separate waxworks exhibition (adult/concession 8/6zł) featuring Polish heroes across the ages. The large brick fortification at the mound's foothill is a fortress built by the Austrians in the 1840s.

To reach the mound by public transport, take tram 1, 2 or 6 southwest to the end of the line at Salwator; then board bus 100, which will take you (every hour or so) directly to the entrance.

## LAS WOLSKI

The 485-hectare Laṣ Wolski (Wolski Forest), west of Zwierzyniec, is the largest forested area within the city limits and a popular weekend destination for city dwellers. It's possible to walk between the three attractions listed below via forest trails.

### Monastery of the Camaldolese Monks
MONASTERY

(Klasztor Kamedułów; Map p113; www.fundacjaka meduli.pl; Al Wędrowników) The order of the Camaldolese Monks, part of the Benedictine family of monastic communities, was brought to Poland from Italy in 1603 and in time founded a dozen monasteries throughout the country. Today there are just two in Poland, including another in Masuria.

The order, with its very strict rules and Memento Mori ('remember you must die') motto, attracts curiosity regarding its members' ascetic way of life. The monks live in seclusion in hermitages and contact each other only during prayers; some have no contact with the outside world at all. They are vegetarian and have solitary meals in their 'homes', with only five common meals a year. The hermits don't sleep in coffins as rumoured, but they do keep the skulls of their predecessors in the hermitages.

Kraków was the first of the Camaldolese seats in Poland; a church and 20 hermitages were established here between 1603 and 1642, and the whole complex was walled in. Not much has changed since. The place is spectacularly located and can be visited, though note the gender-related restrictions laid out below.

You approach it through a long walled alley that leads to the main gate, the ceiling of which is covered in naive frescoes. Once you are let in, you walk to the massive white limestone facade of the **monastery church** (50m high and 40m wide). A spacious, single-nave interior is covered by a barrel-shaped vault and lined on both sides with eight ornate Baroque chapels. The Baroque main altar is impressive.

Underneath the chancel of the church is a large **chapel** used for prayers and, to its right, the **crypt** of the hermits. Bodies are placed into niches without coffins and then sealed. Latin inscriptions state the age of the deceased and the period spent in the hermitage. The niches are opened after 80 years and most of the remains moved to a place of permanent rest. It's then that the hermits take the skulls to keep in their shelters.

In the garden behind the church are 14 surviving hermitages where several monks live (others live in the building next to the church), but the area is off limits to tourists. You may occasionally see hermits in the church, sporting long bushy beards and fine white cassocks.

Men can visit the church and crypt any day from 8am to 11am and 3pm to 4.30pm; guests are allowed in every half-hour. Women can enter the complex only on certain feast days, of which there are a dozen: Easter, Easter Monday, 3 May, Pentecost (two days), Sunday after 19 June, second and fourth Sundays in July, second Sunday in August, Assumption of Mary (15 August), Mary's Birthday (8 September) and Christmas.

The hermitage is 7km west of the city centre. Take tram 1, 2 or 6 to the end of the line at Salwator and change for any westbound bus except the 100. The bus will let you off at the foot of Srebrna Góra (Silver Mountain), then it's a 200m walk up the hill to the church.

### FREE Piłsudski Mound
MONUMENT

(Kopiec Piłsudskiego; Map p113; ⊘24hr) Another mound-based memorial, this time erected in honour of Marshal Józef Piłsudski after his death in 1935; it was formed from soil taken from WWI Polish battle sites. Bus 134, which terminates at the zoo, is the nearest public transport. You can also reach the mound from the Kościuszko Mound on foot via a well-marked trail, taking about 2½ hours.

### Zoological Gardens
ZOO

(Ogród Zoologiczny; Map p113; www.zoo-krakow.pl; Al Kasy Oszczędności Miasta Krakowa 14; adult/concession 18/10zł; ⊘9am-6pm) These 20-hectare zoological gardens are home to thousands of animals. Bus 134 heads to the zoo from its terminus near the National Museum.

#### NOWA HUTA

The youngest and largest of Kraków's suburbs, Nowa Huta (New Steelworks) is a result of the postwar rush towards industrialisation. In the early 1950s a gigantic steelworks was built about 10km east of the centre of Kraków, along with a new town to serve as a dormitory community for its workforce. The steel mill accounted for nearly half the national iron and steel output, and the suburb became a vast urban sprawl populated by over 200,000 people. The steelworks' operations have been scaled back since the fall of communism, and it's now owned by the giant Arcelor-Mittal steel company.

The steelworks can't be visited, but you may want to have a peek at the suburb's austere socialist realist lines (certainly a shock after the Old Town's medieval streets). Tram 4 or 15 from Kraków Główny train station will drop you at **Plac Centralny**, the suburb's central square. Drop into the **tourist office** (☏12 643 0303; www.en.infokrakow .pl; Os Słoneczne 16; ☺10am-2pm Tue-Sat) about 200m north for a free map and to inspect the **Nowa Huta Museum** (www.mhk.pl; adult/ concession 5/4zł, free Wed; ☺9.30am-5pm Tue-Sun) within.

Most of the area is an indistinguishable grey concrete sea of Stalinist-style architecture, but fortunately there are a few interesting sights to pick out.

### Church of Our Lady
### Queen of Poland                        CHURCH

(Kościół Najświętszej Marii Panny Królowej Polski; www.arkapana.pl, in Polish; ul Obrońców Krzyża) In the northwestern part of the suburb is the Church of Our Lady Queen of Poland, otherwise known as the Arka Pana (Lord's Ark). This interesting, though rather heavy, ark-shaped construction was the first new church permitted in Nowa Huta after WWII, and was completed in 1977 entirely by volunteer labourers.

### Church of St Bartholomew          CHURCH

(Kościół Św Bartłomieja; ul Klasztorna) Until the completion of the Church of Our Lady

Queen of Poland Nowa Hutans used the two historic churches that had somehow managed to escape the avalanche of concrete. They are both on the southeastern outskirts of Nowa Huta, in the Mogiła suburb about 1km east of Plac Centralny (tram 15), and are worth a visit if you are in the area.

The small, shingled Church of St Bartholomew dates from the mid-15th century, which makes it Poland's oldest surviving three-nave timber church. If it's locked, enquire at the house at the back, and a nun may open it for you.

### Cistercian Abbey          CHURCH, MONASTERY

(Opactwo Cystersów; ul Klasztorna) Across the street is the Cistercian Abbey, which consists of a church and monastery with a large garden-park behind it. The Cistercians came to Poland in 1140 and founded abbeys around the country, including this one in 1222. The church, open most of the day, has a large three-nave interior with a balanced mix of Gothic, Renaissance and Baroque furnishings and decoration. Have a look at the Chapel of the Crucified Christ (in the left transept), the polyptych in the high altar and the beautiful stained-glass windows behind it.

#### WIELICZKA

### Wieliczka Salt Mine          MINE

(Kopalnia Soli; www.kopalnia.pl; ul Daniłowicza 10; adult/concession 49/35zł; ☺7.30am-7.30pm) Some 14km southeast of Kraków's city centre, Wieliczka (vyeh-*leech*-kah) is famous

---

## NOWA HUTA: SOCIALIST DREAM TURNED NIGHTMARE

The postwar communist regime deliberately built the Nowa Huta steelworks in Kraków to administer a 'healthy' injection of industrial workers as an antidote to the strong aristocratic, cultural and religious traditions of the city. It was of no interest to city planners that Kraków had neither ore nor coal deposits and that virtually all raw materials had to be transported from great distances. The project also did not take into account that the site had one of the most fertile soils in the region, nor that construction of the complex would destroy villages that could trace their histories back to the early Middle Ages.

Perhaps not surprisingly, the communist dream didn't materialise as planned. Rather than threatening the traditional roots of Kraków, it actually became a threat to its creators. Strikes broke out here as frequently as anywhere else, paving the way for the eventual fall of communism. The steelworks also caused catastrophic environmental pollution that threatened its citizens' health, the natural environment and the city's historical monuments.

Nowadays Nowa Huta has been fully integrated into Kraków, and the steelworks operate to higher environmental standards. The greatest indications of change, however, are Nowa Huta's street signs, now divested of communist notables and bearing such names as Pope John Paul II and Ronald Reagan.

for its ultra-deep salt mine, which has been in continuous operation for 700 years. It's an eerie world of pits and chambers, and everything within its depths has been carved by hand from salt blocks. The mine was included on Unesco's World Heritage List in 1978.

The Wieliczka mine is renowned for the preservative qualities of its microclimate, as well as for its health-giving properties. An underground sanatorium has been established at a depth of 135m, where chronic allergic diseases are treated by overnight stays.

The mine has a labyrinth of tunnels, about 300km distributed over nine levels, the deepest being 327m underground. A section of the mine, some 22 chambers connected by galleries, is open to the public as a museum, and it's a fascinating trip.

You visit three upper levels of the mine, from 64m to 135m below the ground, walking through an eerie world of pits and chambers, all hewn by hand from solid salt. Some have been made into chapels, with altarpieces and figures, others are adorned with statues and monuments – all carved out of salt – and there are even underground lakes.

The showpiece is the ornamented **Chapel of St Kinga** (Kaplica Św Kingi), which is actually a fair-sized church measuring 54m by 18m, and 12m high. Every single element here, from chandeliers to altarpieces, is of salt. It took over 30 years (1895) for one man and then his brother to complete this underground temple, and about 20,000 tonnes of rock salt had to be removed. Occasional masses and concerts are held here. Other highlights are the salt lake in the **Eram Barącz Chamber**, whose water contains 320g of salt per litre, and the 36m-high **Stanisław Staszic Chamber**, with its panoramic lift.

Included in the entry price is a visit to the **Kraków Saltworks Museum**, accommodated in 14 worked-out chambers on the third level of the mine, where the tour ends, but most visitors appear to be 'over-salted' by then. From here a fast mining lift takes you back up to the real world.

Visitors are guided in groups and the tour takes about two hours. You walk about 2km through the mine, so wear comfortable shoes. The temperature in the mine is 14°C. In July and August English-language tours depart every half-hour from 8.30am to 6pm. During the rest of the year there are between six and eight daily tours in English.

Minibuses to Wieliczka (2.50zł, look for the 'Salt Mine' sign on the windscreen), depart Kraków frequently between 6am and 8pm from ul Pawia near the Galeria Krakowska shopping mall next to Kraków Główny train station. Alternatively, bus 304 travels to the salt mine from a stop just west of the minibus stands and requires a suburban ticket (3zł), which you can obtain from ticket vending machines at the stop and on the bus itself. Get off at the 'Wieliczka Kopalnia Soli' stop.

To avoid the tremendously long queues at Wieliczka, especially in the high season, you are strongly advised to buy your ticket in advance from the **Kopalnia Soli office** (Map p119; ul Wiślna 12; ⊙9am-5pm Mon-Fri) in Kraków before setting out. Note that the office only has a limited quota of tickets available for each day, so be prepared to be flexible about dates.

## 🏊 Activities

**Bicycle Hire**  CYCLING
You can hire bicycles from several outfits in Kraków including **Cool Tour Company** (Map p119; ☑12 430 2034; www.cooltourcompany.com; ul Grodzka 2; per hr/5hr/day 10/40/50zł; ⊙10am-8pm) in the Old Town and **Dwa Koła** (Map p126; ☑12 421 5785; ul Józefa 5; per 3hr/5hr/day 15/20/30zł; ⊙10am-6pm Mon-Fri, 10am-2pm Sat) in Kazimierz.

**English Language Club**  SOCIAL GROUP
(Map p119; englishclubkrakow@gmail.com; ul Sienna 5; admission 2zł; ⊙6-8pm Wed) Just south of St Mary's, this social group has met weekly since the dying days of communism, when local students wanted to make contact with foreign visitors. Its chatty social gatherings are a fun way to meet a mixed bunch of Poles, expats and tourists in a relaxed setting.

## 👉 Tours

Explore the Old Town and parts of Kazimierz in the little five-seat carts run by **Omega City Tour** (☑12 422 9304; www.incracow.eu) and **Krak Tour** (☑886 664 999; www.kraktour.pl). Expect to pay from 120zł to 280zł per person, depending on distance and attractions visited, for a tour with taped commentary.

**Horse-Drawn Carriages**  CARRIAGE
(half/full hr 100/200zł) The most romantic way to tour Kraków is in one of the many horse-drawn carriages, which line up at the northern end of Rynek Główny and on ul Grodzka

## FOLLOW YOUR NOSE

Kraków is a wonderful city to explore on your own. The streets are well marked, the buses and trams easy to negotiate, and the locals friendly. This book is designed to whet your appetite and to guide you when you arrive; and all the attractions listed in this chapter are great elements of the Kraków package. But we'd like to remind you that this is a guidebook and not a handbook. Leave it in your room or backpack from time to time, and wander outside to make your own discoveries. Want to see a grungier Kazimierz with everyday residents? Head south over the bridge to working-class Podgórze. Street fashion in action? Jump on tram 1, 14 or 22 heading east to **Kraków Plaza** (al Pokoju 44), a popular suburban shopping mall. Or just go blindly into that great maze of streets and rail lines beyond the Old Town, poking your head into little shops, joining in a game of *piłka nożna* (football) in a park or having a beer in a local *piwnica* (pub).

opposite the Church of St Andrew. You decide which route you want to take, or leave it up to the driver to take you for a trot round the sights of the Old Town or even down to Kazimierz.

**Marco der Pole** WALKING
(Map p119; ☑12 430 2131; www.marcoderpole .com.pl; ul Kanonicza 15) A tour of the Old Town departs at 10am and a tour of Kazimierz at 1.30pm daily between April and early November. Both start from near St Mary's Church (look for the guide holding a sign), last three hours and cost 50zł.

**Cool Tour Company** BICYCLE
(Map p119; ☑12 430 2034; www.krakowbiketour .com; ul Grodzka 2) The best bicycle tour in town is the Kraków Bike Tour, a four-hour spin on wheels around town (80zł) that departs daily at 1pm and will take you to everything from the old city walls and Wawel Hill to Oskar Schindler's factory in Podgórze. It has excellent guides and commentary. Its two-hour Kraków by Night Tours (49zł) also run May to September, departing at 7pm.

**Sobieski** RIVER CRUISE
(☑601 560 250; www.ster.net.pl; adult/concession 45/25zł) You can enjoy a cruise on the Vistula River as far as Tyniec Abbey aboard the *Sobieski,* berthed between Wawel Castle and the Dębnicki Bridge below the Sheraton Kraków and accessed from ul Zwierzyniecka. The trip allows a one-hour stop at the abbey before turning around. The company also offers shorter cruises to other locations along the river – ask at the ticket office for the current list.

**Crazy Guides** HISTORY
(☑500 091 200; www.crazyguides.com) Offers entertaining tours of the city's communist-era

suburbs, including a 2½-hour tour to Nowa Huta (129zł), in a restored East German Trabant car.

**Jarden Tourist Agency** JEWISH HERITAGE
(Map p126; ☑12 421 7166; www.jarden.pl; ul Szeroka 2) Specialises in Jewish-heritage tours. The most popular one, Retracing Schindler's List (two hours by car), costs 60zł per person for groups of four or more. Enquire at the office for rates for smaller groups or individuals.

**Cracow on Tour** BUS
(☑12 656 3246; www.cracowontour.pl; day ticket 45zł) A 'jump-on, jump-off' bus.

**Cracow Tours** BUS
(Map p119; ☑12 430 0726; www.cracowtours.pl; ul Krupnicza 3) Offers a four-hour bus tour of the city (adult/concession 120/60zł).

## ★★ Festivals & Events

Kraków has one of the richest cycles of annual events in Poland. Ask any tourist office branch for more details, or check the website www.krakow-info.com.

**New Year's Concert** MUSIC
Kraków ushers in the New Year with classical music at the Teatr im J Słowackiego, while plebs make do with fireworks and rock bands in the Rynek.

**Shanties International Festival of Sailors' Songs** FOLK MUSIC
(www.shanties.pl) Going strong since 1981, despite Kraków's inland location. Held in February.

**Bach Days** CLASSICAL MUSIC
Baroque fugues presented at the Academy of Music in late March.

**Cracovia Marathon**   RUNNING
(www.cracoviamaraton.pl) Increasingly popular international running event, in April.

**Juvenalia**   YOUTH
(www.juwenalia.krakow.pl, in Polish) During this student carnival, students receive symbolic keys to the town's gates and take over the city for four days and three nights. There's live music, street dancing, fancy-dress parades, masquerades and lots of fun. Held in May.

**Krakow Film Festival**   FILM
(www.kff.com.pl) Film festival that's been going for more than half a century screens hundreds of movies from various countries, in May.

**Lajkonik Pageant**   HISTORIC PAGEANT
(www.mhk.pl) Takes place seven days after Corpus Christi (usually in June, but possibly in late May). This colourful pageant is headed by the Lajkonik, a comical figure disguised as a bearded Tatar.

**Music in Old Kraków International Festival**   MUSIC
(www.capellacracoviensis.pl, in Polish) This important musical event goes on for two weeks, spans five centuries of musical tradition from medieval to contemporary, and is presented in concert halls, churches and other historic interiors. From May to July.

**Jewish Culture Festival**   JEWISH CULTURE
(www.jewishfestival.pl) Features a variety of cultural events including theatre, film, music and art exhibitions, and concludes with a grand open-air klezmer concert on ul Szeroka. Held in June/July.

**International Festival of Street Theatre**   THEATRE
Takes place on the Rynek in July.

**Summer Jazz Festival**   JAZZ MUSIC
(www.cracjazz.com) Featuring the best of Polish modern jazz, in July.

**Organ Music Festival**   ORGAN MUSIC
Organ recitals, taking place in several city churches from July to August.

**Pierogi Festival**   FOOD
Three-day celebration of the mighty dumpling, held in Mały Rynek (Small Market Sq) east of St Mary's Church in August.

**Sacrum Profanum**   CLASSICAL MUSIC
(www.sacrumprofanum.pl) Classical music festival dedicated to the composers of a different nominated country each year. Held in September.

**Zaduszki Jazz Festival**   JAZZ MUSIC
This popular festival is held in a range of venues around the city in October and November.

**Kraków Christmas Crib Competition**   CRAFT
Held on the Rynek beside the statue of Adam Mickiewicz on the first Thursday of December, this contest attracts crowds of spectators. A sort of Nativity scene, but very different from those elsewhere in the world, Kraków's *szopki* are elaborate compositions built in an architectural, usually churchlike form, and made in astonishing detail from cardboard, wood, tinfoil and the like – some are even mechanised. The prize-winners are put on display until mid-February at a special exhibition in the Kraków City History Museum on Rynek Główny. You can see gold medallists from previous years at the Ethnographic Museum in Kazimierz.

## 🛏 Sleeping

Kraków is Poland's premier tourist destination so it has plenty of accommodation options. However, advance booking during the busy summer season is recommended for anywhere central.

The Old Town has a selection of accommodation across all budget ranges. Kazimierz also has a number of hostels and atmospheric hotels, in a relatively quiet location. Note that the more expensive hotels sometimes quote prices in euros.

Modern hostels, geared towards the needs and expectations of Western backpackers, have sprung up everywhere. While mainly serving the budget traveller market, nearly all of them also have private rooms in the midrange price bracket.

Private rooms and apartments can also be a good option if you're intending to stay a bit longer. **Jordan Tourist Information & Accommodation Centre** (☑12 422 6091; www.it.jordan.pl; ul Pawia 8; ☺8am-6pm Mon-Fri, 9am-2pm Sat) arranges accommodation in hotels and even private residences (singles/doubles from 150/250zł per person) across the city (so check the location carefully first). Also offers self-contained apartments from 200zł.

## ICONIC LAJKONIK: KRAKÓW'S COLOURFUL HORSEMAN

Another symbol of Kraków is the Lajkonik, a bearded man dressed in richly embroidered garments and a tall pointed hat, riding a hobbyhorse. He comes to life on the Thursday after Corpus Christi (late May or June) and heads a joyful pageant from the **Premonstratensian Convent** (ul Kościuszki 88) in Zwierzyniec to the Old Town's Rynek Główny.

Exact details of the Lajkonik's origins are hard to pin down, but one story involves a Tatar assault on Kraków in 1287. A group of raftsmen discovered the tent of the commanding khan on a foray outside the city walls and dispatched the unsuspecting Tatar leader and his generals in a lightning raid. The raftsmen's leader then wore the khan's richly decorated outfit back to the city.

The pageant, accompanied by a musical band, takes at least six hours to complete the trip, while the Lajkonik takes to dancing, jumping and running, greeting passers-by, popping into cafes en route, collecting donations and striking people with his mace, which is said to bring them good luck. Once the pageant reaches the main square, the Lajkonik is greeted by the mayor and presented with a symbolic ransom and a goblet of wine.

The Lajkonik's garb and his hobbyhorse were designed by Stanisław Wyspiański; the original design is kept in the Kraków City History Museum. It consists of a wooden frame covered with leather and embroidered with nearly a thousand pearls and coral beads. The whole outfit weighs about 40kg.

### OLD TOWN & SURROUNDS

The Old Town has a plentiful supply of budget places, typically bright, clean, modern hostels with multilingual staff and extras such as washing machines and dryers. They also offer private rooms at midrange rates.

There are a decent number of midrange hotels within walking distance of Rynek Główny and other major sights, and no shortage of places for a top-end splurge.

**Dom Polonii**  ROOM €€
(Map p119; ☑12 422 4355; www.wspolnota-polska .krakow.pl; Rynek Główny 14; s/d 200/238zł, ste 270-351zł; @) You couldn't ask for a more central location than this. The Dom has just two high-ceilinged double rooms (overlooking the Rynek) and one double suite, all on the top floor. Needless to say, they get booked out far in advance. Breakfast is 18zł extra per person.

**AAA Kraków Apartments**  APARTMENT €€
(☑12 346 4670; www.krakow-apartments.biz; apt from 235zł; ☎) Company renting out its own renovated apartments in the vicinity of the Old Town; most contain washing machines and wi-fi internet access. The selection in Venetian House, just off the Rynek, is particularly well located. Cheaper rates are available for longer stays.

**Greg & Tom Hostel**  HOSTEL €
(Map p119; ☑12 422 4100; www.gregtomhostel .com; ul Pawia 12; dm 55-70zł, d 170-200zł, apt 200zł; ☎) This well-run hostel is spread over three locations, though all check-in is handled at the main branch. The staff are friendly, the rooms are clean, and laundry facilities are included. On Tuesday and Saturday evenings, hot Polish dishes are served.

**Wielopole**  HOTEL €€€
(Map p119; ☑12 422 1475; www.wielopole.pl; ul Wielopole 3; s 318zł, d 438-480zł; P☎) Wielopole's selection of bright, modern rooms – all of them with spotless bathrooms – is housed in a renovated block with a great courtyard on the eastern edge of the Old Town. The breakfast spread here is impressive.

**Mama's Hostel**  HOSTEL €
(Map p119; ☑12 429 5940; www.mamashostel .com.pl; ul Bracka 4; dm 50-60zł, d 180zł; @) Centrally located red-and-orange lodgings. The beautiful sunlit lounge overlooks a courtyard, with the aroma of freshly roasted coffee drifting up from a cafe below in the mornings. There's a washing machine on-site.

**Hotel Pugetów**  BOUTIQUE HOTEL €€€
(Map p119; ☑12 432 4950; www.donimirski.com; ul Starowiślna 15a; s/d 280/490zł; P☀☎) Charming boutique hotel standing proudly next to the 19th-century neo-Renaissance palace of the same name. It offers just seven rooms with distinctive names (Conrad, Bonaparte) and identities. Think embroidered bathrobes, black-marble baths and a fabulous breakfast room in the basement.

## Hotel Saski
HOTEL €€

(Map p119; ☏12 421 4222; www.hotelsaski.com.pl; ul Sławkowska 3; s 210-295zł, d 280-395zł, tr 450zł; ☎) If you're in the mood for a touch of *belle époque* Central European style, but without the hefty price tag, the Saski may be the place for you. This grand old establishment occupies a historic mansion just off Rynek Główny. The uniformed doorman, rattling century-old lift and ornate furnishings lend the place a certain glamour, and though the rooms themselves are comparatively plain, most have modern bathrooms. The cheaper singles and doubles share a bathroom.

## Hostel Flamingo
HOSTEL €

(Map p119; ☏12 422 0000; www.flamingo-hostel .com; ul Szewska 4; dm 40-80zł, d 180-220zł; ☎) Any place that bills itself as 'run by flamingos for flamingos' gets our custom. We love the pink and lilac decor, the cheeky attitude and the great location just steps west of the Rynek. Dorms have four to 10 beds.

## Mundo Hostel
HOSTEL €

(Map p119; ☏12 422 6113; www.mundohostel .eu; ul Sarego 10; dm 50-55zł, d 160zł; ☎) Attractive, well-maintained hostel in a quiet courtyard location neatly placed between the Old Town and Kazimierz. Each room is decorated for a different country; for example, the Tibet room is decked out with colourful prayer flags. Barbecues take place in summer.

## Hotel Copernicus
HOTEL €€€

(Map p119; ☏12 424 3400; www.hotel.com.pl/copernicus/; ul Kanonicza 16; s 800zł, d 900-980zł; ✳☎☰) Nestled in two beautifully restored buildings in one of Kraków's most picturesque and atmospheric streets, the Copernicus is one of the city's finest and most luxurious hotels. The rooftop terrace, with spectacular views over Wawel, and the swimming pool, accommodated in a medieval vaulted brick cellar, add to the hotel's allure.

## Hotel Stary
HOTEL €€€

(Map p119; ☏12 424 3400; www.stary.hotel.com .pl; ul Szczepańska 5; s/d 800/900zł; ✳☎☰) Setting a high standard, the Stary is housed in an 18th-century aristocratic residence that exudes charm. But the only thing 'old' about this place is its name and the building it's in. The fabrics are all natural, the bathroom surfaces are Italian marble, and the internet service is fast.

## Hotel Pod Różą
HOTEL €€€

(Map p119; ☏12 424 3300; www.lhr.com.pl; ul Floriańska 14; s 650zł, d 650-720zł; ✳☎) A hotel that has never closed, even in the dark, dreary days of communism, 'Under the Rose' offers antiques, Oriental carpets, a wonderful glassed-in courtyard restaurant and state-of-the-art facilities.

## Hotel Campanile
HOTEL €€

(Map p119; ☏12 424 2600; www.campanile.com.pl; ul Św Tomasza 34; r 309zł; ✳☎) Part of a French chain, this modern hotel has somehow succeeded in nestling in the Old Town, just a few blocks from the Rynek. Its attractive, bright rooms are done out with an unremarkable corporate decor. Breakfast is an extra 35zł.

## Hotel Amadeus
HOTEL €€€

(Map p119; ☏12 429 6070; www.hotel-amadeus.pl; ul Mikołajska 20; s/d €145/155; ℙ✳☎) Amadeus, with its Mozartian flair, is one of Kraków's most refined hotels. Its rooms are tastefully furnished (if somewhat small) and service is of a high standard. There's a sauna and a small fitness centre, and a well-regarded gourmet restaurant. Check out the photos of famous guests in the lobby.

## Cracow Hostel
HOSTEL €

(Map p119; ☏12 429 1106; www.cracowhostel.com; Rynek Główny 18; dm 40-85zł; ☎) Location, location, location. This all-dormitory hostel on three floors may not be the best in town, with somewhat cramped rooms of between four and 18 beds. But it's perched high above Rynek Główny, with an amazing view from the comfortable lounge.

## Hotel Pod Wawelem
HOTEL €€

(Map p119; ☏12 426 2626; www.hotelpod wawelem.pl; Plac Na Groblach 22; s 320zł, d 360-420zł, ste 460zł; ℙ✳@) This hotel, at the foot of Wawel and overlooking the river, has a crisp and up-to-date feel to it. The rooms are generously proportioned and look either onto the river or the castle. The view from the rooftop cafe is stunning.

## Hotel Wit Stwosz
HOTEL €€

(Map p119; ☏12 429 6026; www.wit-stwosz.com.pl; ul Mikołajska 28; s/d/tr/ste 295/390/485/550zł; @) Wit Stwosz occupies a renovated 16th-century townhouse east of the Rynek. Its rooms are fully modernised, though some are a bit plain. Overall it's comfortable and stylish.

### Hostel Renesans
HOSTEL €

(Map p119; ☏12 432 9132; www.renesanshostel
.pl; Rynek Główny 9; dm 45-55zł, s/d 110/150zł; ☏)
Placed just off the Rynek within the Pasaż
Bielaka arcade, this hostel couldn't be more
central. Its big tiled lounge area contains an
all-day cafe-bar. Note that all private rooms
have shared bathrooms.

### Hostel Zodiakus
HOSTEL €

(Map p119; ☏12 431 1676; www.zodiakus
hostelkrakow.orangespace.pl; ul Westerplatte 8;
dm/d 45/170zł; ☏) Well-located hostel in a
great location overlooking the Planty, with
a big lounge space. Dorms contain between
four and 12 beds; they're a bit cramped, but
the high ceilings help relieve the sensation.
The decor features soothing tones and
the doors are quirkily covered in zodiac
symbols.

### Hotel Pollera
HOTEL €€

(Map p119; ☏12 422 1044; www.pollera.com.pl; ul
Szpitalna 30; s/d/tr 299/399/480zł; ▣☏) The
Pollera is a classy place dating from 1834,
containing 42 large rooms crammed with
elegant furniture. The singles are unexciting, but the doubles are far nicer, and it's
central and quiet.

### Hotel Wawel
HOTEL €€€

(Map p119; ☏12 424 1300; www.hotelwawel.pl; ul
Poselska 22; s/d 330/460zł; ❋☏☏) Ideally located just off busy ul Grodzka, this hotel contains large, comfortable and stylish rooms.
It's set far enough back from the main drag
to avoid most of the Old Town noise.

### Hotel Royal
HOTEL €€

(Map p119; ☏12 421 3500; hotelewam.pl; ul Św
Gertrudy 26; s 179-249zł, d 279-369zł; ▣☏) This
large and impressive Art Nouveau edifice is
one of the surprisingly few hotels close to
Wawel Hill. It's split into two sections; the
higher-priced two-star rooms are cosy and
far preferable to the fairly drab one-star
ones at the back.

### Hotel Alexander
HOTEL €€€

(Map p119; ☏12 422 9660; www.alexhotel.pl; ul
Garbarska 18; s/d 340/420zł; ▣❋☏) The Alexander is a modern, if slightly anonymous
hotel, offering the usual perks of three-star
comfort. It's on a shabby but quiet street,
just west of the Old Town.

### Hotel Polonia
HOTEL €€

(Map p119; ☏12 422 1233; www.hotel-polonia.com
.pl; ul Basztowa 25; s 136-295zł, d 166-360zł; ☏)
The Polonia occupies a grand old building
near the train station. Though many rooms
overlook the noisy main road, they are light
and modern and the suites are particularly
spacious and attractive. Rooms without en
suite are not so nice, but the price is right
for the location.

### Camping Smok
CAMPGROUND €

(Map p119; ☏12 429 8300; www.smok.krakow.pl; ul
Kamedulska 18; per person/tent 25/15zł, bungalows
d/tr 180/240zł; ▣) This quiet camping ground
is around 4km west of the Old Town in leafy
Zwierzyniec. To get here from the train
station, take tram 2 to the end of the line
at Salwator and change for any westbound
bus (except bus 100).

### Hostel Atlantis
HOSTEL €

(Map p119; ☏12 421 0861; www.atlantishostel.pl; ul
Dietla 58; dm 45-55zł, d/tr 150/195zł; ☏) Hostel
neatly placed for visits to both Kazimierz
and Wawel Hill. Rooms and bathrooms have
been recently renovated.

### Hostel Centrum Kraków
HOSTEL €

(Map p119; ☏12 429 1157; www.centrumkrakow.pl;
ul Św Gertrudy; dm 50-70zł, d 160-176zł; @) Quiet
hostel on three floors, convenient to both
the Old Town and Kazimierz.

## KAZIMIERZ

In addition to some hostels in the vicinity
of busy ul Dietla, Kazimierz has a small
selection of interesting midrange hotels,
some with a distinctive Jewish flavour.
It's a pleasant and peaceful area in which
to stay.

### Hotel Klezmer-Hois
HOTEL €€

(Map p126; ☏12 411 1245; www.klezmer.pl; ul
Szeroka 6; s €52-60, d €65-74, ste €123) This
uniquely stylish little hotel has been restored to its pre-war character. Its airy
rooms are each decorated differently,
though the cheaper rooms don't have
private bathrooms. There's a good-quality
Jewish restaurant on-site, as well as an art
gallery, and live music at 8pm nightly.

### Nathan's Villa Hostel
HOSTEL €

(Map p126; ☏12 422 3545; www.nathansvilla.com;
ul Św Agnieszki 1; dm 47-67zł, d 164-184zł; ▣☏)
One of the best modern hostels in Kraków,
Nathan's is located between the Old Town
and Kazimierz. Comfy rooms, sparkling
bathrooms, a laundry service, a cellar bar,
a back garden with barbecue, and friendly,
professional staff make this place a big hit
with budget travellers.

**Hotel Eden** HOTEL €€

(Map p126; ☑12 430 6565; www.hoteleden.pl; ul Ciemna 15; s/d 250/330zł; ☎) Located within three meticulously restored 15th-century townhouses, the Eden has comfortable rooms and comes complete with a sauna and the only *mikvah* (traditional Jewish bath) in Kraków. Kosher meals are available on request.

**Good Bye Lenin Hostel** HOSTEL €

(☑12 421 2030; www.goodbyelenin.pl; ul Joselewiczka 23; dm 40-55zł, d 140zł; P☎) One of the most distinctive hostels in Kraków, this place has a cheeky communist theme with absurd paintings mocking the imagery of the era. Most dorm rooms have four to six beds and the spacious downstairs lounge is popular for its bar and pool table. It's located down a drab but quiet street off ul Starowiślna.

**Hotel Abel** HOTEL €€

(Map p126; ☑12 411 8736; www.hotelabel.pl; ul Józefa 30; s/d 150/200zł; ☎) Reflecting the character of Kazimierz, this hotel has a distinctive personality, evident in its polished wooden staircase, arched brickwork and age-worn tiles. The comfortable rooms make a good base for exploring the historic Jewish neighbourhood.

**Tournet Pokoje Gościnne** HOTEL €€

(Map p126; ☑12 292 0088; www.nocleg.krakow .pl; ul Miodowa 7; s 110-150zł, d 160-200zł, tr 250zł) This is an attractive and excellent-value pension in the centre of Kazimierz, offering simple but comfortable and quiet rooms. The bathrooms, however, are tiny. Check-in time is 7am to 10pm. There's a restaurant downstairs serving Polish dishes at reasonable prices.

**Hotel Alef** HOTEL €€

(Map p126; 012 424 3131; www.alef.pl; ul Św Agnieszki 5; s/d 160/240zł; P☎) This affordable hotel within the shadow of Wawel Hill has large, charming rooms, furnished with antiques and paintings.

**Hotel Kazimierz** HOTEL €€

(Map p126; ☑12 421 6629; www.hk.com.pl; ul Miodowa 16; s/d 320/380zł; P@) Friendly accommodation offering a number of modern, comfortable rooms above a popular restaurant.

**Ars Hostel** HOSTEL €

(Map p126; ☑12 422 3659; www.arshostel.pl; ul Koletek 7; dm 45-55zł, d200zł; P@) This unfortunately named hostel is famed as much for its moniker (it means 'art' in Latin) as its handy location below Wawel.

## ✖ Eating

By Polish standards, Kraków is a food paradise. The Old Town is tightly packed with gastronomic venues, serving a wide range of international cuisines and catering for every pocket. Kazimierz also has a number of restaurants, some of which offer Jewish-style cuisine and are worth a visit.

Self-caterers can stock up at the supermarket within the Galeria Krakowska shopping mall next to the main train station.

### OLD TOWN & SURROUNDS

**TOP CHOICE ⟩ Glonojad** VEGETARIAN €

(Map p119; Plac Matejki 2; mains 7-13zł; ☺9am-10pm; ☎☑) Attractive modern vegetarian restaurant with a great view onto Plac Matejki, just north of the Barbican. The diverse menu has a variety of tasty dishes including samosas, curries, potato pancakes, burritos, gnocchi and soups. There's also an all-day breakfast menu, so there's no need to jump out of that hotel bed too early.

**Restauracja Pod Gruszką** POLISH €€

(Map p119; ul Szczepańska 1; mains 12-33zł) A favourite haunt of writers and artists, this upstairs establishment is the eatery that time forgot, with its elaborate old-fashioned decor featuring chandeliers, lace tablecloths, age-worn carpets and sepia portraits. The menu covers a range of Polish dishes, including the excellent *żurek staropolski* (sour barley soup with white sausage and cottage cheese).

**Il Calzone** ITALIAN €€

(Map p119; ul Starowiślna 15a; mains 16-44zł) This pleasant slice of Italy is a well-kept secret, tucked away in a quiet nook set back from the street next to the Hotel Pugetów. Pleasant whitewashed decor, charming outdoor terrace, and the food is excellent value.

**Nostalgia** POLISH €€

(Map p119; ul Karmelicka 10; mains 17-76zł) A refined version of the traditional Polish eatery, Nostalgia features a fireplace, overhead timber beams, uncrowded tables and courteous service. Wrap yourself around Russian dumplings, pork loin in green pepper sauce, or veggie options such as potato dumplings in a wild mushroom sauce. In warm weather there's an outdoor dining area.

**Diego & Bohumil**　　　CZECH, ARGENTINE €€
(Map p119; ul Św Sebastiana 6; mains 12-60zł) It's an unusual match made in foodie heaven – the owners of this eatery have drawn on their diverse cultural backgrounds to present both Czech *and* Argentine cuisine on the same menu. Wander towards its quiet side-street location and ponder your options. Stew with dumplings, or a hefty steak?

**Paese**　　　CORSICAN €€€
(Map p119; ul Poselska 24; mains 18-68zł; ⏱1-11pm; ✏) Serving one of the more unusual cuisines available in Kraków is this Corsican restaurant. The thatched-cottage decor is comfortable and the dishes – baked sea bream, veal with grapes, beef fondue – well prepared. Fish and vegetarian options are also on the menu.

**Wentzl**　　　FRENCH, POLISH €€€
(Map p119; www.wentzl.pl; Rynek Główny 21; mains 58-68zł; ⏱1-11pm) Historic eatery dating back to 1792 and perched high above the Rynek, with timbered ceilings, Oriental carpets and fine oil paintings all around. The food is sublime – cognac-flavoured foie gras, duck fillet glazed with honey, monkfish with saffron sauce – and the service of a high standard.

**U Babci Maliny**　　　POLISH €
ul Szpitalna (Map p119; ul Szpitalna 38; mains 8-25zł; ⏱11am-9pm Mon-Fri, noon-9pm Sat & Sun); ul Sławkowska (Map p119; ul Sławkowska 17) 'At Granny Raspberry's' is a godsend for travellers on a budget, with hearty Polish staples at great prices served in an overwrought boudoirlike basement eatery. Duck your head under those wooden beams.

**Il Forno**　　　ITALIAN €€
(Map p119; Mały Rynek 2; mains 17-56zł) An amenable and unpretentious place away from the bulk of the tourist traffic. It has a very long menu of pizza and pasta dishes, along with weightier meat and fish selections. Eat outdoors on the lovely terrace with a view of Mały Rynek. The downstairs bar section is the Arabian-styled Shisha Club, serving Middle Eastern food.

**Ambasada Śledzia**　　　POLISH €
(Map p119; ul Stolarska 6; mains 4-10zł; ⏱7am-late Sun-Thu, 24hr Fri & Sat) The 'Herring Embassy' sits neatly, if cheekily, on this street lined with consulates. It's pioneered an unlikely but successful concept – Polish tapas. Sit at the bar and order tasty snack-sized servings of *śledź* (herring), *kiełbasa* (sausage) or

*golonka* (pork knuckle) to go with your vodka. It's a good place to chow down if you're out late clubbing.

**Pimiento**　　　ARGENTINE €€€
(Map p119; ul Stolarska 13; mains 26-260zł) This upmarket grill serves a dizzying array of steaks to suit both appetite and budget, and offers some reasonable vegetarian alternatives for the meat-averse. Factor the South American wine list into your calculations, and you have a classy night out.

**Cherubino**　　　ITALIAN €€
(Map p119; ul Św Tomasza 15; mains 21-64zł) Cherubino bills itself as a restaurant and winery, and offers lovely Italian dishes amid a charming, artsy interior. The antique carriages filling up the room are wonderful, and there's a pleasant terrace with colourful seating outside.

**Metropolitan**　　　INTERNATIONAL €€
(Map p119; ul Sławkowska 3; mains 21-64zł; ⏱7.30am-midnight Mon-Sat, 7.30am-10pm Sun; 🛜) Attached to the Hotel Saski, the Metropolitan is a snazzy restaurant with a distressed Mediterranean look, serving international cuisine. It has nostalgic B&W photos of international locales plastering the walls and is a great place for breakfast. It also serves pasta, grills and steaks, including luxurious items such as beef tenderloin in a truffle sauce.

**Sakana Sushi Bar**　　　JAPANESE €
(Map p119; ul Sławkowska 5/7; mains 11-90zł; ⏱noon-11pm Mon-Sat, 1-10pm Sun) With sushi and sashimi floating around in little boats which loop around a 'canal' encircling a curvy communal table, the Sakana is different from the usual Kraków offerings. There's also tempura and some unusual soups.

**Taco Mexicano**　　　MEXICAN €€
(Map p119; ul Poselska 20; mains 21-40zł) If you hanker after something from 'south of the border' and Slovakian bread dumplings are not what you had in mind, this cantina is for you. It's popular with locals and visitors alike, and serves fairly authentic enchiladas, burritos and tacos. There's also a tapas menu, with all dishes priced at 9zł.

**Smak Ukraiński**　　　UKRAINIAN €€
(Map p119; ul Kanonicza 15; mains 14-30zł) Hidden away below one of Kraków's most attractive streets, this little place presents authentic Ukrainian dishes in a cosy little cellar decorated with predictably folksy flair. Expect

lots of dumplings, borscht (the Ukrainian variety) and waiters in waistcoats.

### Gruzińskie Chaczapuri          GEORGIAN €
(mains 14-29zł; ⊗9am-11pm Sun-Thu, noon-midnight Fri & Sat; ☑) ul Floriańska (Map p119; ul Floriańska 26); ul Sienna (Map p119; ul Sienna 4); ul Grodzka (Map p119; ul Grodzka 3); ul Św Anny (Map p119; ul Św Anny 4) If you have a hankering for something a little different, this cheap and cheerful chain of Georgian restaurants with four branches in central Kraków serves up grills, salads and steaks and the house speciality: cheese pie. There's also a good range of vegetarian dishes on the menu.

### Cyrano de Bergerac          FRENCH €€€
(Map p119; ul Sławkowska 26; mains 50-90zł; ⊗noon-midnight Mon-Sat) One of Kraków's top eateries, this restaurant serves fine, authentic French cuisine in one of the most beautiful cellars in the city. Artwork and tapestries add to the romance and in warmer months there's seating in a covered courtyard.

### Miód Malina          POLISH €€
(Map p119; ul Grodzka 40; mains 18-68zł) The charmingly named 'Honey Raspberry' serves Polish dishes in colourful surrounds. Grab a window seat and order the wild mushrooms in cream, and any of the duck or veal dishes. There's a variety of beef steaks on the menu as well.

### Indus Tandoori          INDIAN €€
(Map p119; ul Sławkowska 13/15; mains 11-35zł; ⊗10am-10pm Sun-Thu, 10am-midnight Fri & Sat) Reputed to be the best Indian restaurant in town, the Indus serves curries, tandoori dishes and classics such as chicken tikka, in a long narrow dining room with gilded decor.

### Jama Michalika          POLISH €€
(Map p119; ul Floriańska 45; mains 11-47zł; ⊗9am-10pm) Established in 1895, this cavernous place was a hang-out for writers, painters, actors and other artistic types, and the birthplace of the Młoda Polska movement. Today it's a grand, Art Nouveau restaurant with a very green interior and lots of theatrical etchings adorning the walls. The traditional Polish food is reasonable value.

### Greenway          VEGETARIAN €
(Map p119; ul Mikołajska 14; mains 9-22zł; ⊗10am-10pm Mon-Fri, 11am-9pm Sat & Sun; ☑) Some of Kraków's best-value vegetarian and vegan fare is on offer at this branch of the nation-wide veggie chain, with meat-free burgers, enchiladas and salads on the menu.

### Gospoda CK Dezerter          POLISH €€
(Map p119; ul Bracka 6; mains 15-33zł; ⊗9am-11pm) Dezerter is a pleasantly decorated place which focuses on traditional, meaty Galician specialities, and also serves some Austrian and Hungarian choices.

## KAZIMIERZ
### Deli Bar          HUNGARIAN €€
(Map p126; ul Meiselsa 5; mains 10-53zł) A Hungarian guy called László told us this was the best Magyar restaurant in Kraków, and he was right on the money. Its Hungarian owners turn out tasty paprika-laced classics such as goulash, *palacsinta* (crepes) and 'Budapest pork'.

### Momo Bar          VEGETARIAN €
(Map p126; ul Dietla 49; mains 12-17zł; ⊗11am-8pm; ☑) Vegans will cross the doorstep of this restaurant with relief – the majority of the menu is completely animal-free. The space is decorated with Indian craft pieces, and serves up subcontinental soups, stuffed pancakes and rice dishes, with a great range of cakes. The *momo* (Tibetan dumplings; 15zł) are a treat worth ordering.

### Chłopskie Jadło          POLISH €€
Kazimierz (Map p126; ul Św Agnieszki 1); Old Town (Map p119; ul Św Jana 3; mains 16-38zł; ⊗noon-10pm Sun-Thu, noon-midnight Fri & Sat) These eateries look like rustic country inns somewhere at the crossroads in medieval Poland, and serve up traditional Polish 'peasant food' (as the name suggests). Try the *żurek* (sour rye) soup, served in a bread loaf.

### Ariel          JEWISH €€
(Map p126; ul Szeroka 18; mains 17-75zł) One of a number of Jewish restaurants in and around ul Szeroka, this atmospheric joint is packed with old-fashioned timber furniture and portraits, and serves a range of kosher dishes. Try the Berdytchov soup (beef, honey and cinnamon) for a tasty starter. There's often live klezmer music here at night.

### Manzana          MEXICAN €€
(Map p126; ul Miodowa 11; mains 19-49zł; ⊗7.30am-1am) Long opening hours, a breakfast menu and some impressively authentic dishes make this a compelling dining choice. The interior is done out in soothing burnt orange tones, with only a minimum of sombreros as decoration.

## THE KING OF PRETZELS

One of the unmistakable signs that you've arrived in Kraków are the stalls placed seemingly at every street corner selling the *obwarzanek* (ob-va-zhan-ek), a hefty pretzel. This street snack resembles its German cousins, though is somewhat larger and denser than the average Germanic bread-based snack and is created by entwining two strands of dough before baking.

This popular ring of baked bread, traditionally encrusted with poppy seeds, sesame seeds or salt, gives daily employment to myriad men and women while ensuring them a dose of fresh outdoor air (though selling it in winter must, admittedly, be less fun).

It's also a historic curiosity that has outlived numerous kings, republics and military occupiers. There's evidence of *obwarzanki* (the plural) being baked as far back as the 14th century, and Cracovians still happily purchase them in large numbers as a quick bite on the way to work or study – in fact 150,000 are baked every day. Feel free to join in the pretzel celebration, though note that they're definitely much better in the morning than the afternoon, a promising sign perhaps that they contain little in the way of artificial preservatives.

While munching, you'll be enjoying an officially unique Kraków experience – for in 2010, the European Union agreed to register the humble *obwarzanek* on its list of protected regional products, barring anyone but the city's bakers from producing a pretzel and calling it by that name.

 **Drinking**

You'll be spoiled for choice when heading out for a drink in Kraków. The Old Town contains hundreds of bars and pubs. Kazimierz also has a lively bar scene, centred on Plac Nowy and its surrounding streets.

Some bars offer snacks or meals, but most are just watering holes, with many in vaulted medieval cellars. For teetotallers and/or those in search of something hot, there are plenty of cafes too.

### Pubs & Bars
**OLD TOWN**

**Nic Nowego**                     CAFE, BAR
(Map p119; ul Św Krzyża 15; ⊙7am-late Mon-Fri, 10am-late Sat & Sun; 🔊) 'Nothing New', run by a genuine Irishman, is a modern Irish cafe-bar and a popular fixture on the city's drinking scene. It's a bright, modern place with a long bar, a great atmosphere and good food.

**CK Browar**                PUB, BREWERY
(Map p119; ul Podwale 6/7; ⊙9am-2pm Sun-Thu, 9am-4pm Fri & Sat) Serious tipplers will head for this below-ground microbrewery with its own cavernous drinking hall. The amber fluid is brewed on the spot to an old Austro-Hungarian recipe, then poured straight from the tanks into patrons' glasses. Beware the CK Dunkel brew, which is 7% alcohol.

**Paparazzi**                          BAR
(Map p119; ul Mikołajska 9; ⊙4pm-late Mon-Fri, noon-late Sat & Sun) Bright, modern place, with B&W press photos of celebrities covering the walls. The drinks menu includes cocktails such as the Polish martini, built around bison grass vodka. There's also inexpensive bar food.

**Piwnica Pod Złotą Pipą**             PUB
(Map p119; ul Floriańska 30; ⊙noon-midnight) The 'Pub under the Golden Pipes' is another inviting cellar bar. It's more sedate than most such places, better suited to conversation than listening to music, though it does occasionally host classical music recitals.

**Black Gallery**                      PUB
(Map p119; ul Mikołajska 24; ⊙noon-late Mon-Sat, 2pm-late Sun) Underground pub-cum-nightclub with a modern aspect: split levels, exposed steel frame lighting and a metallic bar. It really gets going after midnight.

**U Louisa**                           PUB
(Map p119; Rynek Główny 13; ⊙11am-late; 🔊) This stylish pub is conveniently located below the Rynek as you enter from ul Grodzka. It has big screens on which to watch sports, and wi-fi throughout. There's karaoke on Monday nights from 9pm.

**Ciemnia Club**                       GAY
(www.ciemnia.com.pl; ul Krowoderska 8; ⊙6pm-2am Sun-Thu, 6pm-5am Fri & Sat) This is Kraków's premier gay 'cruising bar' with facilities intended for those seriously OFB (out for business), 300m north of the

Planty. Check out the website for details of upcoming parties and other events.

**KAZIMIERZ**

**TOP CHOICE** Alchemia                                      BAR
(Map p126; ul Estery 5; ⊗9am-late) This Kazimierz venue exudes a shabby-is-the-new-cool look with rough-hewn wooden benches, candlelit tables and a companionable gloom. It hosts regular live music gigs and theatrical events through the week.

**Singer Café**                                  CAFE, BAR
(Map p126; ul Estery 20; ⊗9am-late) Laidback hang-out of the Kazimierz cognoscenti, this relaxed cafe-bar's moody candlelit interior is full of character. Alternatively, sit outside and converse over a sewing machine affixed to the table.

**Le Scandale**                                          BAR
(Map p126; Plac Nowy 9; ⊗8am-late; 🐕) Smooth drinking hole with low black leather couches, ambient lighting and a gleaming well-stocked bar. Join the mellowed-out drinkers in sampling the extensive cocktail list.

**Propaganda**                                          BAR
(Map p126; ul Miodowa 20; ⊗11am-late) This is another one of those places full of communist nostalgia, but so real are the banners and mementoes here that we almost started singing the *Internationale*. Killer cocktails.

**Cafes**

**Café Camelot**                                      CAFE
(Map p119; ul Św Tomasza 17; ⊗9am-midnight) For coffee and cake, try this genteel haven hidden around an obscure street corner in the Old Town. Its cosy rooms are cluttered with lace-covered candle-lit tables, and a quirky collection of wooden figurines featuring spiritual or folkloric scenes.

**Bona**                                          CAFE
(Map p119; ul Kanonicza 11; ⊗10am-8pm Mon-Sat, 11am-8pm Sun; 🐕) Pleasant combination of cafe and bookshop, with its bookshelves sandwiched between the interior and outdoor seating. Buy a book and sip a coffee with a view of the Church of SS Peter & Paul across the way.

**Café Bunkier**                                      CAFE
(Map p119; Plac Szczepański 3a, ⊗9am-late) The 'Bunker' is a wonderful cafe with a positively enormous glassed-in terrace tacked onto the Bunkier Sztuki (Art Bunker), a cutting-edge gallery northwest of the Rynek. It's one of the few modern buildings in the Old Town and looks just like its name suggests. Enter from the Planty.

**Ciasteczka z Krakowa**                              CAFE
(Map p126; ul Stradomska 19; ⊗9am-7pm Mon-Sat, 10am-7pm Sun) This bakery-cum-cafe serves some of the best cakes and pastries in Poland.

# ☆ Entertainment

Kraków has a lively cultural life, particularly in theatre, music and visual arts, and there are numerous annual festivals. The comprehensive Polish and English monthly magazine *Karnet* (www.karnet.krakow.pl; 4zł), available at any branch of the tourist office, lists almost every event in the city. The tourist office at ul Św Jana 2 also specialises in cultural events, and can book tickets to many of them.

The bimonthly *Kraków In Your Pocket* (www.inyourpocket.com), which has a cover price of 5zł but is often free at tourist-information offices, hotels and bars, also has excellent coverage of entertainment, including bars, pubs and clubs.

In addition to the websites Cracow Life (www.cracow-life.com) and Krakow Post (www.krakowpost.com), excellent online sources of information are www.krakow nightlife.com and, for club events and parties, www.where2b.org.

**Nightclubs**

You'll find the majority of nightclubs in the Old Town, particularly along ul Szewska and ul Floriańska.

**TOP CHOICE** Łódź Kaliska                              CLUB
(Map p119; ul Floriańska 15; ⊗6pm-late) Set up by a cutting-edge art collective from Łódź, this club has a wild decor composed of mirrors, antiques, shiny surfaces and crazy lights. A mix of DJs and live performers provide the sounds.

**Stalowe Magnolie**                                  CLUB
(Map p119; ul Św Jana 15; ⊗7pm-late) 'Steel Magnolias' is a brightly decorated venue with an emphasis on live music, presenting pop, rock and jazz. It's a party inside every night of the week.

**Łubu-Dubu**                                          CLUB
(Map p119; ul Wielopole 15; ⊗4pm-2am Sun-Thu, 6pm-4am Fri & Sat) This wackily named club (*woo*boo-*doo*boo) is an echo of the past, from the garish colours to the collection of

objects from 1970s Poland. If you get bored here, there are several other clubs in the same building.

### Prozak
CLUB

(Map p119; Plac Dominikański 6; ☾8pm-late) A legend in its own lifetime, this nightlife giant entices revellers into its labyrinth of passageways, nooks and crannies. It specialises in presenting international DJs.

### Cień
CLUB

(Map p119; ul Św Jana 15; ☾8pm-5am Tue-Thu, 8pm-7am Fri & Sat) The enormous 'Shadow' attracts a perfect (as in fake tans) crowd with house sounds produced by DJs fresh in from Ibiza and great decor.

### Rdza
CLUB

(Map p119; ul Bracka 3/5; ☾9pm-late) This basement club with exposed brick walls and comfy sofas attracts some of Kraków's more sophisticated clubbers with its Polish house music.

## Jazz

Kraków has a lively jazz scene and a number of clubs present live music year-round.

### Piano Rouge
JAZZ

(Map p119; Rynek Główny 46; ☾10am-late) This sumptuous cellar jazz club and restaurant is decked out with classic sofas, louche lampshades and billowing lengths of colourful silk. Live jazz every night at 10pm.

### Jazz Club U Muniaka
JAZZ

(Map p119; ul Floriańska 3; ☾7pm-late) Housed in a fine cellar, this is one of the best-known jazz outlets in Poland, the brainchild of saxophonist Janusz Muniak. There are concerts most nights from 9.30pm.

### Harris Piano Jazz Bar
JAZZ

(Map p119; Rynek Główny 28; ☾9am-late May-Oct, 1pm-late Nov-Apr) Another active jazz haunt, Harris hosts jazz and blues bands most days of the week from 9pm.

### Piec Art
JAZZ

(Map p119; ul Szewska 12; ☾5pm-late) This cosy cellar club tends to stage acoustic jazz on Wednesdays and irregular gigs on other days. Gigs start at 8.30pm.

## Classical Music & Opera

Classical music concerts are staged in various venues throughout Kraków in the summer months, including the Church of SS Peter & Paul south of the Rynek.

**Opera Krakowska** (☏12 296 6260; www.opera.krakow.pl) performs at the Słowackiego Theatre, as there's no designated opera house in the city.

### Kraków Philharmonic Hall
CLASSICAL MUSIC

(Filharmonia Krakowska; Map p119; ☏12 422 4312; www.filharmonia.krakow.pl; ul Zwierzyniecka 1; ☾box office 11am-2pm & 3-7pm Tue-Fri, 1hr before performance Sat & Sun) Home to one of the best orchestras in the country.

### Academy of Music
CLASSICAL MUSIC

(Akademia Muzyczna w Krakowie; ☏12 422 5173; www.amuz.krakow.pl; ul Basztowa 8) Music recitals are held at the Academy of Music near the Barbican, particularly during the Bach Days event in March.

## Cinemas

Two convenient cinemas are **Kino Sztuka** (Map p119; cnr ul Św Tomasza & ul Św Jana) and **Kino Pod Baranami** (Map p119; Rynek Główny 27), the latter located within a courtyard off Rynek Główny.

## Theatre

### Stary Teatr
THEATRE

(Map p119; ☏12 422 4040; www.stary.pl, in Polish; ul Jagiellońska 1; ☾box office 9am-5pm Mon-Fri, 9am-1pm Sat) This is the city's best-known theatre company and has attracted the cream of its actors. To overcome the language barrier, pick a Shakespeare play you know well from the repertoire, and take in the distinctive Polish interpretation. The box office is off Plac Szczepański.

### Słowackiego Theatre
THEATRE

(Teatr im J Słowackiego; Map p119; ☏12 424 4526; www.slowacki.krakow.pl; Plac Św Ducha 4; ☾box office 10am-6pm Mon-Fri, 9am-7pm Sat) This important theatre focuses on Polish classics and large-scale productions. It's in a large and opulent building (1893) that's patterned on the Paris Opera, and is northeast of Rynek Główny.

### Teatr Groteska
THEATRE

(☏12 633 3762; www.groteska.pl; ul Skarbowa 2; ☾box office 8am-noon & 3-5pm Mon-Fri) The 'Grotesque Theatre' stages mostly puppet shows and is well worth a visit. It's 450m west of the Planty along ul Krupnicza.

#  Shopping

Kraków's Old Town has a vast array of shops, selling everything from tacky T-shirts to exquisite crystal glassware, and all within a short walk from Rynek Główny. The obvious place to start (or perhaps end) your Kraków shopping is at the large souvenir market within the Cloth Hall in the centre of Rynek Główny, selling everything from fine amber jewellery to tacky plush dragons. If you're in a mall mood, **Galeria Krakowska** (Map p119; ul Pawia 5; ⊙9am-10pm Mon-Sat, 10am-9pm Sun), next to the train station, has hundreds of shops.

### Antiques

For everything from rusty war relics to attractive collectables, check out the flea market held each Saturday morning in Plac Nowy in Kazimierz.

**Antykwariat na Kazimierzu** ANTIQUES
(Map p126; ul Meiselsa 17) In the basement of the Judaica Foundation in Kazimierz, this Aladdin's cave is a jumble of antique china, glass, paintings, books and other assorted goodies.

**Salon Antyków Pasja** ANTIQUES
(Map p119; ul Jagiellońska 9; ⊙11am-7pm Mon-Fri, 10am-3pm Sat) This is one of the most established antique salons in the Old Town, with clocks, maps and bric-a-brac.

### Art

**Galeria Plakatu** POSTER ART
(Map p119; ul Stolarska 8; ⊙11am-6pm Mon-Fri, 11am-2pm Sat) Poland has always excelled in the art of poster making and this has the city's largest and best choice of posters, created by Poland's most prominent poster makers.

**Labirynt** ARTS & CRAFTS
(Map p119; ul Floriańska 36; ⊙10am-7pm Mon-Fri, 10am-3pm Sat) Labyrinth is an affordable place to buy art, and shows a decent mix of both painting and sculpture.

**Galerie d'Art Naïf** ARTS & CRAFTS
(Gallery of Naive Art; Map p126; ul Józefa 11; ⊙noon-5pm Mon-Fri, noon-3pm Sat) This Kazimierz gallery exhibits and sells the work of some of Poland's most celebrated Naive painters and sculptors, and folk artists.

**Andrzej Mleczko Gallery** ART
(Map p119; ul Św Jana 14; ⊙11am-6pm Mon-Fri, 10am-3pm Sat) The gallery displays and sells comic drawings and other articles by popular satirical cartoonist Andrzej Mleczko.

### Books

**TOP CHOICE** **Massolit Books & Cafe** BOOKS
(ul Felicjanek 4; ⊙10am-8pm Sun-Thu, 10am-9pm Fri & Sat; ☎) Highly atmospheric book emporium selling English-language fiction and nonfiction, both new and secondhand. There's a cafe area with loads of character, starting among the bookshelves and extending into a moody back room. Follow ul Zwierzyniecka west for 300m, then turn right onto ul Felicjanek.

**Księgarnia Hetmańska** BOOKS
(Map p119; Rynek Główny 17; ⊙9am-9pm Mon-Sat, 11am-9pm Sun) Impressive selection of English-language books on Polish history and culture.

**Austeria** BOOKS
(Map p126; ul Józefa 38; ⊙9am-7pm) Best collection of Jewish-themed books and Judaica in Kraków.

**EMPiK** BOOKS
(Map p119; Rynek Główny 5; ⊙9am-10pm) Big chain bookshop, also good for maps, newspapers and magazines.

**Sklep Podróżnika** BOOKS
(Map p119; ul Jagiellońska 6; ⊙11am-7pm Mon-Fri, 10am-3pm Sat) Sells a wide selection of regional and city maps, as well as Lonely Planet titles.

### Gifts

**Boruni** JEWELLERY
(Map p119; ul Kanonicza 22; ⊙9.30am-8.30pm) Shop selling amber, otherwise known as 'Baltic gold', Poland's most treasured semiprecious material. Unlike some amber shops, Boruni includes a certificate of quality with each purchase.

**Galeria Bukowski** GIFTS
(Map p119; ul Sienna 1; ⊙10am-7pm Tue-Sat, 10am-6pm Sun-Mon) This unbearably cute shop specialises in *miś pluszowy* (teddy bears) of all shapes, sizes, hues and descriptions.

**Blazko Jewellery Art Gallery** JEWELLERY
(Map p126; ul Józefa 11; ⊙11am-7pm Mon-Fri, 11am-3pm Sat) Exceptionally well-designed and crafted baubles from a Kazimierz-based jeweller.

## ℹ Information

### Dangers & Annoyances

Kraków is generally a safe city for travellers, although as a major tourist hot spot it has its fair share of pickpockets; be vigilant in crowded public areas.

If you're staying in the centre of the Old Town, especially near the main square, you may experience late-night noise from the area's many restaurants, bars and clubs; ask for a room at the back if this is going to be an issue. In summer, the large numbers of tourists in town can be a little overwhelming and mean long queues for top sights such as Wawel Castle and scarce seating in the more popular restaurants. Keep a wary eye out for the many horse-driven carriages that cart tourists around the Old Town, including along the pedestrianised streets.

Be aware that if carrying a large suitcase or backpack on a Kraków city bus you must buy an extra ticket (2.50zł).

## Internet Access

**Greenland Internet Café** (ul Floriańska 30; per hr 5zł; ⊙9am-midnight)

**Internet Café Hetmańska** (ul Bracka 4; per hr 8zł; ⊙24hr)

**Internet Klub Garinet** (ul Floriańska 18; per hr 4zł; ⊙9am-10pm)

**Klub Internetowy Pl@net** (1st fl, Rynek Główny 24; 4zł; ⊙10am-10pm)

## Kraków Card

The excellent-value **Kraków Card** (www.krakow card.com; 2-/3-day 50/65zł) is available from tourist offices, travel agencies and hotels. It offers free entry to dozens of museums (though not those on Wawel Hill), unlimited travel on public transport including the Wieliczka bus, and discounts on organised tours and at certain restaurants.

## Maps

The free map from the tourist offices should be sufficient for a short visit. If you want something more detailed, one of the best is the 1:10,000 scale *Kraków Plan Miasta* (6.90zł) published by Demart, which usefully includes all tram and bus routes along with their stops.

## Medical Services

**Apteka 24** (☑12 411 0126; ul Mogilska 21; ⊙8am-11pm) This late-hours pharmacy is east of the Old Town.

**Dent America** (☑12 421 8948; www.dent america.pl; Plac Szczepański 3) Dental clinic.

**Falck** (☑1 9675; www.falck.pl) Attends house calls and has its own ambulance service.

**Medicina** (☑600 062 107; www.medicina.pl; ul Barska 12) Private healthcare provider.

**Medicover** (☑500 900 500; www.medicover .pl; ul Rakowicka 7) Has English-speaking specialist doctors and does lab tests.

## Laundry

Most hostels have washing machines (and sometimes even dryers) that you can use, though they may charge a fee.

**Betty Clean** (☑12 423 0848; ul Zwierzyniecka 6; ⊙7.30am-7.30pm Mon-Fri, 8am-3.30pm Sat) Branch of a chain of drycleaners near the southwest edge of the Old Town, which will also accept general laundry.

## Money

*Kantors* (private currency-exchange offices), banks and ATMs can be found around the centre. It's worth noting that many *kantors* close on Sunday, and areas near Rynek Główny and the main train station offer poor exchange rates. Make a point of comparing rates and check whether a commission is being charged.

## Post

**Main post office** (Map p119; ul Westerplatte 20; ⊙8am-8pm Mon-Fri, 8am-2pm Sat)

**Post office** (Map p119; ul Lubicz 4; ⊙24hr)

## Telephone

The best place to pick up a Polish SIM card for your mobile phone is at the Galeria Krakowska shopping mall next to the train station. All the telecommunications companies have outlets here, right next to each other, so you can easily compare rates and offers.

## Tourist Information

**Tourist offices** (www.en.infokrakow.pl) ul Św Jana (Map p119; ☑12 421 7787; ul Św Jana 2; ⊙9am-7pm); Cloth Hall (Map p119; ☑12 433 7310; Rynek Główny 1; ⊙9am-7pm May-Sep, 9am-5pm Oct-Apr); northeastern Old Town (Map p119; ☑12 432 0110; ul Szpitalna 25; ⊙9am-7pm May-Sep, 9am-5pm Oct-Apr); southern Old Town (Map p126; ☑12 616 1886; Plac Wszystkich Świętych 2; ⊙9am-7pm May-Sep, 9am-5pm Oct-Apr); Wawel Hill (Map p119; ul Powiśle 11; ⊙9am-7pm); Kazimierz (Map p126; ☑12 422 0471; ul Józefa 7; ⊙9am-5pm); Nowa Huta (☑12 643 0303; Os Słoneczne 16; ⊙10am-2pm Tue-Sat); airport (☑12 285 5431; John Paul II International Airport, Balice; ⊙9am-7pm) Helpful city-run service.

## Travel Agencies

**Bocho Travel** (☑12 421 8500; ul Stolarska 8) Sells air tickets and intercity train tickets.

**Polish Travel Adventure** (☑693 648 528; www.krakow.tourism.pl; ul Miodowa 26) Well-regarded agency organises excursions and adventure travel within and beyond Kraków.

## Websites

**City of Kraków** (www.krakow.pl) Good general information direct from city hall.

## WANT MORE?

For in-depth information, reviews and recommendations at your fingertips, head to the Apple App Store to purchase Lonely Planet's *Kraków City Guide* iPhone app.

Alternatively, head to **Lonely Planet** (www.lonelyplanet.com/poland/malopol ska/krakow) for planning advice, author recommendations, traveller reviews and insider tips.

**Cracow Life** (www.cracow-life.com) Heaps of information on eating, drinking and entertainment.

**In Your Pocket** (www.inyourpocket.com /poland/krakow) Irreverent reviews of accommodation, sights and entertainment.

**Krakow Info** (www.krakow-info.com) An excellent source for news and events.

**Krakow Post** (www.krakowpost.com) English-language resource with local news, interviews, features and listings.

## ⓘ Getting There & Away

### Air

**John Paul II International Airport** (☎12 295 5800; www.krakowairport.pl) is in Balice, about 15km west of the city. The airport terminal hosts several car-hire desks, along with currency exchanges offering unappealing rates.

LOT flies between Kraków and Warsaw several times a day, and offers direct connections from Kraków to Frankfurt, Paris and Rome, with flights to New York and Chicago during the summer months. Bookings for all flights can be made at the **LOT office** (☎801 703 703; www.lot.com; ul Basztowa 15).

A range of other airlines, including several budget operators, connect Kraków to cities in Europe, including an array of destinations across Britain and Ireland. There are direct flights daily to and from London via EasyJet and Ryanair. Dublin is serviced by Ryanair and Aer Lingus.

### Bus

The modern bus terminal is behind the city's main train station, Kraków Główny, just north-east of the Old Town. Travel by bus is particularly advisable to places like Zakopane (18zł, 2½ hours) as it's considerably shorter and faster than by train. You can buy tickets to Zakopane from the bus driver.

There are 12 daily PKS departures to Częstochowa (30zł, two hours), 11 to Oświęcim (12zł, 1½ hours), five to Lublin (42zł, 4½ hours),

two to Zamość (46zł, six hours) and five to Cieszyn (19zł, three hours) at the Czech border. Other destinations are better served by train.

There are plenty of international buses run by **Eurolines** (www.eurolinespolska.com.pl), including those to Amsterdam (259zł, 19 hours), Budapest (79zł, seven hours), London (360zł, 27 hours), Munich (229zł, 17 hours), Paris (349zł, 21 hours), Prague (139zł, 10 hours), Rome (363zł, 27 hours), Vienna (158zł, eight hours) and Vilnius (186zł, 14 hours). Information and tickets are available from **Jordan** (☎12 393 5266; www.jordan.pl; ☺9am-6pm Mon-Fri, 9am-3pm Sat) in the bus terminal. Check the website www.eurolines-polska.com.pl for the latest prices and timetable information.

### Train

Kraków Główny train station, on the north-eastern outskirts of the Old Town, handles all international and most domestic trains. The only other station of any significance is Kraków Płaszów, 4km southeast of the city centre, which operates a few trains that don't call at Kraków Główny. Local trains between the two stations run every 15 to 30 minutes. All trains listed here depart from the main station. Advance tickets for international and domestic trains can be booked directly at the station or by cash only from Bocho Travel (p144).

Each day from Kraków, 16 trains head for Warsaw; half of these are cheaper TLK trains (54zł, three hours) and the other half are more comfortable ExpressInterCity (EIC) services (116zł, three hours). See p429 for a description of TLK and EIC trains.

There are also 17 trains to Wrocław (50zł, five hours), 11 trains to Poznań (63zł, 7½ hours), two to Lublin (56zł, five hours) and seven services to Gdynia via Gdańsk (135zł, 9½ hours).

There are five services to Częstochowa (26zł, 2½ hours), while trains to Katowice (21zł, two hours) run every half-hour to an hour. There are twice-hourly services to Tarnów (16zł, 1½ hours), and hourly services to Rzeszów (37zł, 2¾ hours). To Oświęcim (14zł, 1½ hours) there are hourly trains.

Internationally, there are daily direct trains to Berlin, Bratislava, Budapest, Lvov, Odesa, Prague and Vienna.

## ⓘ Getting Around

### To/From the Airport

To get to the Old Town by public transport, step aboard the free shuttle bus from the airport to the nearby train station, or walk the 300m to the station. Buy tickets on board the train from a vending machine or the conductor (10zł) for the 18-minute journey to Kraków Główny station. Trains depart once or twice an hour between 4am and 11.30pm.

A taxi between the airport and the city centre should cost about 80zł.

If you need to transfer between Kraków and Katowice airport, the most efficient way to do so is via the seven daily shuttle services offered by **Matuszek** (☑32 236 1111; www.matuszek.com .pl; single/return 44/88zł) to/from the Kraków bus terminal (two hours). Buying on the bus rather than booking online incurs an extra 6zł fee each way.

### Bicycle

See p131 for details of bicycle hire.

### Car & Motorcycle

With limited parking, and much of the Old Town a car-free zone, driving in Kraków will be more of a hindrance than a help. If you are travelling by car, the major route into the city is the A4; note that an 8zł toll is paid when you enter and exit it. The Old Town is closed to traffic, except for access to a guarded car park on Plac Św Ducha if you can find a space. If not, use one of the guarded car parks in the surrounding area, including those along ul Karmelicka northwest of the Old Town, and ul Powiślenortheast of Wawel Hill. Street parking in the area outside the Old Town, known as 'Zone C', requires special tickets (*karta postojowa*), which you buy from ticket machines and then display on your windscreen. They cost 3.50zł for one hour and must be displayed from 10am to 6pm Monday to Friday.

Many of the big international car-rental firms have offices in Kraków including **Hertz** (☑12 429 6262; www.hertz.com.pl; Hotel Cracovia, Al Focha 1; ☺8am-4pm Mon-Fri, 8am-noon Sat). However, you should get a better deal at one of the local firms that distribute their leaflets around town, including **Joka Rent a Car** (☑12 429 6630; www.joka .com.pl; ul Starowiślna 13) next door to the Hotel Pugetów.

### Public Transport

Kraków is served by an efficient network of buses and trams which run between 5am and 11pm. Some night buses (which begin with a '6') run later.

Single-journey (2.50zł), one-hour (3.10zł) and one-/two-/three-day (10.40/18.20/25zł) tickets can be bought at street kiosks, and must be validated as soon as you board. Note that an extra ticket is also required for bulky luggage. Tickets for night buses are 5zł. Most tourist attractions are in the Old Town or within easy walking distance, so you probably won't need buses or trams unless you're staying outside the centre.

### Taxi

If you need a cab, these are some of the better-known companies:

**Barbakan Taxi** (☑12 19661)
**Euro Taxi** (☑12 19664)
**Lajkonik Taxi** (☑12 19628)
**Mega Taxi** (☑12 19625)
**Radio Taxi** (☑12 19191)

# Małopolska

POP 5 MILLION

## Best Places to Eat

» Twierdza (p153)

» Olivio (p163)

» Pireus (p154)

» Restauracja Gęsia Szyja (p177)

» Mandragora (p169)

## Best Places to Stay

» Vanilla Hotel (p169)

» Hotel Śródmiejski (p156)

» Hotel Basztowy (p160)

» Dom Architekta (p174)

» Hotel Senator (p182)

## Why Go?

Małopolska, known in English as Lesser Poland, is the sprawling region surrounding Kraków, running from Częstochowa in the west to Lublin in the east. It's played an outsized role in Polish history, forming the core of the ancient Polish kingdom. These days, though, it's mostly passed over by travellers, who make a beeline for Kraków and then move on.

That's a pity. While Małopolska lacks truly world-class sights, the region is rich in natural beauty, with rolling hills and several national parks. Sandomierz, an ancient Gothic town on a bluff overlooking the Vistula, is one of Poland's prettiest places.

The region is also rich in cultural diversity. The Jasna Góra monastery in Częstochowa is a major pilgrimage site for Roman Catholics. To the east, cities like Lublin and Chełm were once home to large Jewish communities, and moving traces of that centuries-long existence can still be found.

## When to Go

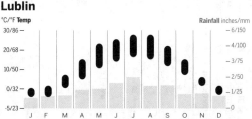

**Lublin**

**May-Jun**
The Corpus Christi holiday is marked by massive weekend festivals.

**Aug**
Thousands of pilgrims gather at the Jasna Góra monastery.

**Aug-Sep**
September brings the International Meeting of Jazz Singers to Zamość.

# Małopolska Highlights

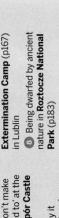

**1** Joining throngs of **Black Madonna** (p154) pilgrims in Częstochowa

**2** Appreciating the perfection of 16th-century town planning in **Zamość** (p178)

**3** Blushing as portraits peer down at you in Kielce's **Palace of the Kraków Bishops** (p155)

**4** Revelling in the grandeur of **Pieskowa Skała Castle** (p149) in Ojców National Park

**5** Chatting to a ghost in the **Chełm Chalk Tunnels** (p177)

**6** Saying 'they don't make them like they used to' at the fairy-tale **Krzyżtopór Castle** (p162) in Ujazd

**7** Wondering why it happened at **Majdanek**

**Extermination Camp** (p167) in Lublin

**8** Being dwarfed by ancient nature in **Roztocze National Park** (p183)

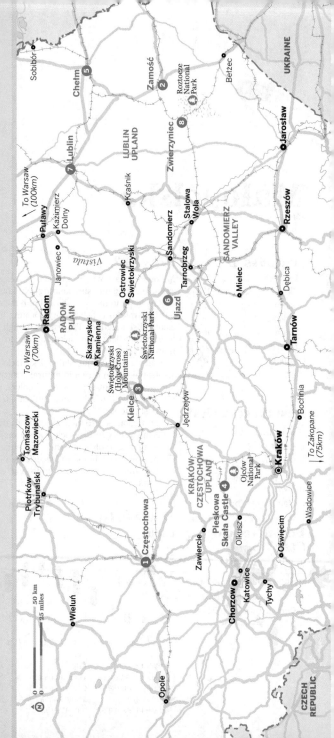

# THE KRAKÓW–CZĘSTOCHOWA UPLAND

When Silesia fell to Bohemia in the 14th century, King Kazimierz III Wielki (Casimir III the Great, 1333–70) fortified the frontier by building a chain of castles from Kraków to Częstochowa. This 100km stretch comprises the Kraków–Częstochowa Upland (Wyżyna Krakowsko–Częstochowska).

The plan worked and the Bohemians were never able to penetrate the wall. Centuries later, in 1655, however, the Swedes invaded and destroyed many castles. More turbulence in the 18th century completed the process, leaving impressive ruins for the 21st-century traveller.

The upland region is also known as the Jura, having been formed from limestone in the Jurassic period some 150 million years ago. Erosion left hundreds of caves and oddly shaped rock formations, which can still be enjoyed in Ojców National Park.

An excellent way to explore the upland is by hiking the Trail of the Eagles' Nest (Szlak Orlich Gniazd), which winds 164km from Kraków to Częstochowa. Tourist offices in Kraków and Częstochowa can provide more information.

## Ojców National Park

Perhaps size doesn't matter after all. Ojców National Park (Ojcowski Park Narodowy) may be the smallest in Poland, but it packs two castles, several caves and countless rock formations into its 21.5 sq km. The flora in the park is beech, fir, oak and hornbeam forest, and the fauna a diverse mix of small mammals, including badgers, ermines and beavers. This postcard-worthy park is one of the most beautiful areas of the Kraków–Częstochowa Upland.

Most tourist attractions line the road running along the Prądnik River between Ojców and Pieskowa Skała. There is no direct bus connecting these villages, but the flat 7km between them is well worth walking. The Trail of the Eagles' Nest also follows this road.

### Sights & Activities

The well-manicured village of Ojców is located in the national park, and is popular with day trippers from Kraków. There are a couple of museums in town, but the true allure of Ojców is its access to the tourist trails running through the national park.

Before you embark on a hike, buy a map of the park in Kraków. There are a couple of versions, but Galileo's *Ojcowski Park Narodowy* (scale 1:20,000, 5.90zł from EMPiK) stands out for detailing every trail, road and rock.

**Pieskowa Skała Castle**          CASTLE

(⌚courtyard 7am-sunset) If you can only do one thing in Ojców National Park, visit this 14th-century castle, one of the best-preserved castles in the upland and one of the brightest feathers in Poland's Renaissance cap. To find the Pieskowa Skała Castle, follow the path up the hill into the national park. The castle was rebuilt in the 16th century in imitation of the royal residence of Wawel and now serves as a branch of the Royal Wawel Castle **museum** (www.wawel.krakow.pl; adult/concession 10/7zł; ⌚10am-4pm Tue-Thu, 9am-1pm Fri, 10am-6pm Sat & Sun May-Aug, 10am-3.30pm Tue-Sun Oct-Apr, closed Mon), with a large collection of art and artefacts from the 15th to the 19th centuries.

From the castle, the red trail along the road towards Ojców takes you to a 25m-tall limestone pillar; it's called **Hercules' Club** (Maczuga Herkulesa), despite obvious temptations to name it after something else.

**Ojców Castle**          CASTLE

(www.ojcow.pl; adult/concession 2.5/1.5zł; ⌚10am-4.45pm Apr-May & Aug-Sep, 10am-5.45pm Jun & Jul, 10am-3.45pm Oct, 10am-2.45pm Nov, closed Mon) Ojców Castle was deserted in 1826, and has since fallen into ruin. The 14th-century entrance gate and octagonal tower are original, but there's little else to explore. The view of the wooden houses scattered across the slopes of Prądnik valley is worth the little money and effort.

**Chapel on the Water**          CHURCH

(Kaplica na Wodzie) About 200m north of Ojców Castle is the frequently photographed Chapel on the Water, which was fashioned in 1901 from the bathhouse that originally stood in its place. In keeping with its exterior simplicity, the three altars inside are shaped as peasants' cottages. You may sneak a peek inside when the doors open for religious service.

**Łokietek Cave**          CAVE

(Grota Łokietka; www.grotalokietka.pl in Polish; adult/concession 7/5zł; ⌚9am-3.30pm Apr, 9am-6.30pm May-Sep, 9am-5.30pm Oct, 9am-4.30pm

Sat & Sun Nov-Mar) Stretching over 270m through several passages, Łokietek Cave is accessible from the black trail heading south from Ojców Castle and can be visited on a 30-minute tour. Legend has it that before he became king in the 14th century, Władysław Łokietek hid from Czech King Vaclav II in the cave. Chambers are named for the various uses made of them by Łokietek. The temperature of the cave remains between 7°C and 8°C all year.

**Wierzchowska Górna Cave** CAVE
(www.gacek.pl; adult/concession 14/12zł; ⊗9am-4pm Apr, Sep & Oct, 9am-5pm May-Aug, 9am-3pm Nov) Just outside the park boundaries, Wierzchowska Górna Cave is in the village of Wierzchowie, 5km southwest of Ojców. At 950m long, Wierzchowska is the largest cave in the Kraków–Częstochowa highlands. Artefacts from the late Stone Age and pottery from the middle Neolithic period were uncovered here during excavations after WWII.

## 🛌 Sleeping & Eating

There are several sleeping and eating options near the Pieskowa Skała Castle and Ojców, and more along the road between them. Ask about private rooms (40zł to 60zł per person) at the **PTTK** (⊘12 389 1466; www.ojcow.pttk.pl; Ojców 15) or contact the **Ecotravel tour operator** (⊘12 648 9977; www.ojcow.pl) in Kraków before you travel. Alternatively, wander along the road between Ojców and Pieskowa Skała and look for 'noclegi' (accommodation) signs.

**Dom Wycieczkowy PTTK Zosia** HOSTEL €
(⊘12 389 2008; Ojców-Złota Góra 4; per person without/with bathroom 25/35zł) You can't beat the value or the vibe at this casual place, just 1km west up the hill from Ojców castle. It offers well-kept rooms, facilities and friendly common areas.

**Zajazd Zazamcze** GUESTHOUSE €€
(⊘12 389 2083; www.zajazdzazamcze.ojcow .pl; Ojców 1b; s/d/tr 100/160/200zł; @🖙) An easy walk from the Ojców turn-off, Zajazd Zazamcze offers bland but airy rooms. The restaurant turns out hearty and wholesome fare in its cosy dining room and boasts a lovely garden.

**Agroturystyka Glanowski** GUESTHOUSE €
(⊘12 389 6212; http://agroglanowski.tur.pl/ in Polish; Pieskowa Skała, Podzamcze 2; per person 30-40zł) Half a kilometre from Pieskowa Skała Castle, with a range of clean, rustic rooms, a simple restaurant and camping facilities.

**Camping Złota Góra** CAMPGROUND €
(⊘12 389 2014; Złota Góra; per adult/under 10yr 5/3.5zł, tent/car/trailer/caravan/motorbike/power connection 4/5/8/10/3/7zł; ⊗19 Apr-15 Oct) A few hundred metres from Dom Wycieczkowy PTTK Zosia, this camping ground has a bonfire at its heart and trees all around. The expanding dining area lures passers-by with its snug seating and fast-flowing beer. It's BYO tent only.

**Pieskowa Skała Castle** RESTAURANT €€
(mains 12-25zł; ⊗10am-8pm) The restaurant-cafe at Pieskowa Skała Castle is accessible without a museum ticket; the restaurant interior is castle-kitsch but the upstairs terrace affords regal views.

## ℹ Information

The small **PTTK office** (⊘12 389 1466; www .ojcow.pttk.pl in Polish; Ojców 15; ⊗9am-3pm May-Oct) is in the car park at the foot of Ojców castle.

## ℹ Getting There & Away

A sporadic minibus service links Kraków and Ojców (5zł, 45 minutes). Buses depart from a small stop at Ogrodowa 4 (next to Galeria Krakowska) and arrive near the PTTK office at the base of Ojców castle. At the time of writing, five minibuses departed from Kraków each weekday from 6am to 7.05pm, and four returned from Ojców between 9.35am and 6.20pm. Weekend timetables are nearly the same, with the first bus leaving Kraków at 8am.

# Częstochowa

POP 246,225

Every year, Częstochowa (chen-sto-ho-vah) attracts four to five million visitors from 80 countries who come to fall at the feet of the *Black Madonna*. Some walk for 20 days over hundreds of kilometres with offerings for the Virgin. Others take a bus from Kraków.

Poland's spiritual heartland is not just for the faithful. The Monastery of Jasna Góra is the country's national shrine and one of the highlights of the region. Since an influx of resources from the EU, renovations are working their way up the main thoroughfare towards the monastery, adding new pride to ancient reverence.

During pilgrimage times – particularly the day of Assumption on 15 August – hordes of devotees become a main attraction for people-watchers, and a deterrent for crowd-weary wanderers.

## History

The first known mention of Częstochowa dates to 1220. Częstochowa's emergence as Poland's spiritual capital began with the arrival of the Paulite order from Hungary in 1382, who named the 293m hill in the western part of the city 'Jasna Góra' (Bright Hill) and erected a monastery on top. Believers were drawn to the site for the miracles credited to the *Black Madonna* painting. The fact that Jasna Góra was one of the few places in the country to survive Swedish aggression (1655–66) was attributed to the miraculous Virgin (despite her having being safely stowed in Silesia at the time).

The town's foundational charter was granted in the 14th century under German law by King Kazimierz III Wielki, placing Częstochowa on an important trade route from Russia. Agricultural and industrial development, aided by the Warsaw–Vienna railway line, saw Częstochowa evolve into an established industrial centre by the end of the 19th century. By the outbreak of WWII, the city had some 140,000 inhabitants.

As with many Polish cities of its size, Częstochowa had a sizable Jewish community until the German occupation during WWII. Most of the Jews were clustered in the neighbourhood around the Stary Rynek (the town's old market square) at the eastern end of al Najświętszej Marii Panny (NMP), which was also where the Nazis built their wartime ghetto. At its peak it held nearly 50,000 Jews. The ghetto was liquidated in September and October of 1942, when around 40,000 Jews were deported to the death camp at Treblinka.

Under communism, the authorities attempted to destabilise the town's religious spirit with a bout of intense industrialisation. Today, much of the original splendour has been restored, and Jasna Góra proudly towers over the city.

## ◉ Sights

**Monastery of Jasna Góra**  MONASTERY
(www.jasnagora.pl; ul Kordeckiego 2; admission by donation; ⊙5am-9.45pm). Impressive though it is, the exterior of Jasna Góra gives little indication of the grandeur layered behind its walls. Exploring this functioning monastery gives a fascinating insight into its history, and a deep appreciation for its present-day relevance. Arrive early and take your time.

You are free to wander around the complex at your own leisure (crowds permitting) and most of the attractions only ask for a small donation to enter. At the time of research, for some inexplicable reason the monastery had discontinued offering audio guides to help navigate the interiors, and it wasn't clear when they would be reintroduced.

To arrange a guided tour in English, contact the information centre **Jasnogórskie Centrum Informacji** (☑34 365 3888; jci@jasnagora.pl; guided tours available for 100zł; ⊙8am-7pm May–mid-Oct, 8am-5pm mid-Oct–Apr).

*Chapel of Our Lady*
(Kaplica Cudownego Obrazu; ⊙5am-9.45pm) The oldest part of the complex contains the revered *Black Madonna* (see boxed text, p154). The picture is unveiled at 6am and 1.30pm (2pm Saturday and Sunday) and covered again at noon and 9.20pm (1pm and 9.20pm Saturday and Sunday). Be sure to note the walls displaying votive offerings brought by pilgrims. Adjoining the chapel is the impressive **basilica** *(bazylika)*. Its present shape dates to the 17th century and the interior has opulent baroque furnishings.

On the northern side of the chapel, paintings in the **Knights' Hall** (sala Rycerska) depict key events from the monastery's history; there's also an exact copy of the *Black Madonna*. Upstairs, the **Golghota Gallery** contains a series of unique paintings by celebrated local painter and cartoonist Jerzy Duda Gracz (1941–2004) whose evocative works are indicative of the monastery's ability to preserve its historical heritage while maintaining modern relevance.

*600th Anniversary Museum*
(Muzeum Sześćsetlecia; ⊙9am-5pm summer, 9am-4pm winter) This museum contains fascinating artefacts, including the founding documents of Jasna Góra from 1382 and a cross made from the steel of the destroyed World Trade Center in New York. Particularly moving are rosaries made from breadcrumbs by concentration camp prisoners. Lech Wałęsa's 1983 Nobel Peace Prize, donated by its recipient, can be found beyond the Father Kordecki Conference Room.

**MAŁOPOLSKA** CZĘSTOCHOWA

# Częstochowa

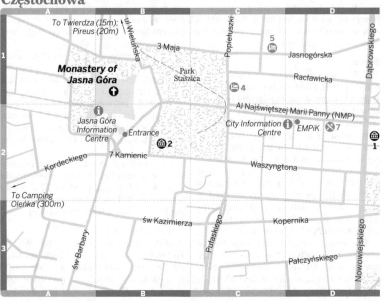

*Belltower*

(admission by donation; ☺9am-4pm Apr-Nov) At 106m this is the tallest historic church tower in Poland and offers views over the monastery complex and the expanse of al NMP. After falling many times over history, the current tower dates to 1906.

*Arsenal*

The arsenal contains various military mementos, including spoils of battle, offerings from soldiers and an impressive collection of Turkish weapons from the 1683 Battle of Vienna.

*Treasury*

(Skarbiec) The 17th-century treasury contains votive offerings dating to the 15th century. Since the 17th century, records have been kept of gifts given to the Madonna.

**Częstochowa Museum**                    MUSEUM
(Muzeum Częstochowskie; www.muzeumczesto chowa.pl; al NMP 45a; adult/concession 8/4zł; ☺11am-5pm Tue-Fri, 11am-6pm Sat & Sun) In the neoclassical town hall on al NMP, this museum contains paintings of Polish artists as well as extensive documentation detailing the history of Częstochowa and the region. Some of the collection is housed in the **Częstochowa Museum outlet** (Park Staszica; ☺11am-5pm Tue-Thu, 11am-5.30pm Wed, Fri, Sat & Sun), close to the monastery.

**Jewish Memorial**                    MONUMENT
(Umschlagplatz; ul Strażacka) A small landmark near the Stary Rynek marks the deportation zone, the *Umschlagplatz*, from where tens of thousands of Jews were transported to their deaths at Treblinka in 1942. The memorial includes a copy of a hauntingly precise train timetable showing trains

departing Częstochowa at 12.29pm and arriving at Treblinka at 5.25am the next morning.

## ✪ Festivals & Events

**Gaude Mater Festival of Religious Music**　　SACRAL MUSIC
(www.gaudemater.pl) Focuses on religious music from Christian, Jewish and Islamic traditions. Held annually in May.

**Marian feasts**　　RELIGIOUS FESTIVALS
(www.jasnagora.pl; 3 May, 16 Jul, 15 August, 26 August, 12 September & 8 December) Draws believers in the tens of thousands.

**Assumption**　　PILGRIMAGE
(www.jasnagora.pl; 15 August) Pilgrims have been travelling by foot to Jasna Góra for Assumption since 1711.

## 🛏 Sleeping

During pilgrimage periods (such as the Marian feast days) book well ahead, or stay elsewhere and make a day trip into Częstochowa.

**Hotel Wenecki**　　HOTEL €
(☏34 324 3303; www.hotelwenecki.pl; Berka Joselewicza 12; s/d/tr 120/150/180zł; P@🎧) The Wenecki is the nicest hotel at its price point in town, with the only possible drawback being the hotel's location, about 20 minutes' walk from the monastery (though only about 10 minutes by foot from the train and bus stations). The rooms are slightly frayed, but clean and quiet. The beds are firm and the baths have nice touches, like hair dryers. Breakfast is a decent spread for 20zł and they'll cook an omelette on the spot on request.

**Mercure**　　HOTEL €€
(☏34 360 3100; www.accorhotels.com; ul Popiełuszki 2; s/d/apt 301/366/570zł; P❄@🎧) The local member of the Mercure upmarket hotel chain offers clean, smartly appointed rooms with all modern conveniences. It also has one of the best locations in town, straddling the monastery to the west and the town centre to the east. Breakfast costs 44zł and parking adds another 40zł a night (though street parking nearby is free).

**Hotel Polonia**　　HOTEL €
(☏34 324 2388; www.polonia-czest.pl; ul Piłsudskiego 9; s/d/tr/q 80/100/130/160zł; 🎧) The aging Polonia is for nostalgia buffs only. Many of Poland's landmark 19th-century hotels have been given expensive makeovers, but this dilapidated grande dame is still awaiting a suitor. From the outside, it's hard to tell whether it's still open. The rooms are plain but clean, and the price and location, near the train and bus stations, can't be beat.

**Youth Hostel**　　HOSTEL €
(☏34 324 3121; ul Jasnogórska 84/90; dm 28-40zł; 🕙Jul & Aug) In summer, you can also try the youth hostel, two blocks parallel to al NMP (look for small green triangular sign). Nothing fancy, but clean and relatively secure. Phone ahead to make sure someone is manning the reception desk.

**Camping Oleńka**　　CAMPGROUND €
(☏34 360 6066; camping@mosir.pl; ul Oleńki 22; car/tent 15/20zł, 4-person bungalow with bath 140zł) This camping ground behind the monastery has space for around 400 people. Those who forget to bring tents can enjoy great value in the self-contained bungalows. The campground is located about 300m southwest of the monastery complex.

## 🍴 Eating & Drinking

**TOP CHOICE Twierdza**　　POLISH €€
(☏34 361 2828; www.twierdza.czest.pl; ul Wieluńska 10; mains 30-50zł) Twierdza is the best of a

## THE BLACK MADONNA OF CZĘSTOCHOWA

Unlike other pilgrimage sites, Jasna Góra has never claimed the appearance of apparitions. Its fame is attributed to the presence of the *Black Madonna*, a 122cm by 82cm painting of the Virgin Mary with the Christ Child on a panel of cypress timber, which was crowned 'Queen of Poland' in 1717.

It is not known for sure when or where the *Black Madonna* was created, but some say she was painted by St Luke the Evangelist on a table in the house of the Holy Family and was brought to Częstochowa from Jerusalem via Constantinople. It arrived in Częstochowa in 1382.

In 1430, the face of the Madonna was slashed by Hussite warriors, battling against what they saw as papal abuses in Rome. The painting still bears the scars, either because they were left as a reminder of the sacrilegious attack or, as legend has it, because they continually reappeared despite attempts to repair them.

Legends about the *Black Madonna's* role in saving Jasna Góra from the Swedish Deluge in 1655 and in keeping the Russians at bay in 1920 are still extolled today. The widespread belief in the legends is evident from the votive offerings – from crutches and walking canes to jewellery and medals – which are still presented to the Virgin by devoted pilgrims today.

**MAŁOPOLSKA** CZĘSTOCHOWA

slim range of good Polish restaurants in town. It has an ambitious menu of traditional specialties, some featuring harder to find items like venison and quail. Our favourite is the beef roulade, which comes grilled and stuffed with chickpeas and caramelised beets. This place is popular, so reserve in advance.

**Pireus**                    GREEK €€

(34 368 0680; www.restauracja-pireus.com.pl; ul Wieluńska 12; mains 25-50zł; ) Pireus is a welcome oasis of excellent, simple Greek food, like tzatziki and fried calamari, in a refined but still relaxed setting. The restaurant is within easy walking distance of the Jasna Góra monastery. Book ahead.

**Café 29**                    CAFE €

(al NMP 29; mains 10-25zł; 10am-10pm Mon-Thu, 10am-11pm Fri & Sat, noon-10pm Sun; ) Walk through the passageway at al NMP 29 to find Café 29, a popular student cafe with smoothies (8zł) and pizzas (from 14zł), as well as the usual coffee and beer. Café 29 shares garden space with the Flash Pub next door and the Galeria Café and Carpe Diem club across the yard, so this is the place to head after sundown for drinks and more.

**Caffe del Corso**            CAFE €

(al NMP 53; coffee 8 zł, ice cream 20zł; 8am-11pm; ) *The* place on al NMP for excellent coffees and extravagant ice cream concoctions and cakes, with a handsome terrace for people watching. Also has a nice range of salads,

toasted sandwiches and pancakes for a light meal.

## ⓘ Information

There are a number of *kantors* (private currency-exchange offices) and ATMs on al NMP.

**Bank Pekao** (ul Kopernika 19) Gives cash advances on Visa and MasterCard.

**City Information Centre** (Miejskie Centrum Informacji; 34 368 2250; www .czestochowa.pl; al NMP 65; 9am-5pm Mon-Sat) Maps and sights information.

**Jasna Gora Information Centre** (Jasnagórskie Centrum Informacji; 34 365 3888; www.jasnagora.pl; ul Kordeckiego 2; 7.30am-7pm May–mid-Oct, 8am-5pm mid-Oct–Apr) Information centre inside Jasna Góra Monastery.

**Multibank** (ul Szymanowskiego 1) Conveniently located 24-hour ATM.

## ⓘ Getting There & Away

**BUS** The **bus terminal** (34 379 11 49; www .pks-czestochowa.pl; information counter 7am-8pm) is close to the central train station and serves many towns in the region including Jędrzejów (12zł, two hours) and Opole (14zł, two hours).

From Kraków (133km away), there are many buses to Częstochowa (18zł, three hours, eight per day, between 6.30am and 9.20pm).

Buses leave for Kielce (24zł, three hours) at two-hour intervals throughout the day.

**TRAIN** The **train station** (al Wolności) handles half a dozen daily fast trains to Warsaw (40zł,

3½ hours) and about four trains to Kraków (34zł, three hours).

There are about eight trains to Kielce (19zł, two hours 20 minutes) throughout the day. Several trains run to Katowice (18zł, 1½ hours) between 3am and 9pm, from where there are connections to Kraków. To Zakopane, there are only a few trains, and these often depart in the inconvenient wee hours (30zł, seven hours).

# THE MAŁOPOLSKA UPLAND

The Małopolska Upland is skirted by the Vistula and Pilica Rivers, but the centrepiece of this beautiful expanse is the Holy Cross Mountains (Góry Świętokrzyskie), a repository of abundant natural beauty, witness to harrowing episodes in the country's history, and object of religious reverence. The main urban centre of Kielce, which sits at the foot of the mountains, is a convenient base to access this varied cultural landscape and the surrounding mountain ranges.

## Kielce

POP 203,800

First impressions of Kielce (*kyel*-tseh) are not likely to be positive. The town is ringed by post-war housing projects that on a rainy day, or any day, can look downright dispiriting. But dig a little deeper and you'll find a lively city with a surprisingly elegant core, centred on the cathedral, the remarkable Palace of the Kraków Bishops, and a pretty expanse of parkland surrounding both of them.

Kielce is not resting on its laurels. During our visit, many of the city's main arteries were being dug up as part of a multiyear renovation project expected to last into 2013 and beyond. The main thoroughfare, ul Sienkiewicza, had already been spruced up and stretches as far as the eye can see with cafes, shops and bars.

In addition to its own attractions, Kielce is a convenient base for seeing the nearby Świętokrzyski National Park.

### ◎ Sights

**TOP** CHOICE **Palace of the Kraków**
**Bishops** MUSEUM
(Pałac Biskupów Krakówskich; www.muzeumkielce
.net; Plac Zamkowy 1; adult/concession 10/5zł;
◎10am-6pm Tue-Sun) Kielce was the property

of the Kraków bishops from the 12th century through to 1789. This palace was built (from 1637 onwards) as one of their seats and remains a testament to the richness of that era.

The highlight of a palace visit is the **National Museum**, where the restored 17th- and 18th-century interiors are so alive you feel like you're trespassing in a bishop's boudoir. The centrepiece of the permanent exhibition is the former dining hall, where the whole brood of bishops stare down from their 56 portraits. The upper and lower portraits of this evocative historical montage were painted two centuries apart. The rest of this captivatingly cavernous multilevel museum leads through collections of porcelain, historical armour and various centuries and genres of Polish painting. The only drawback is a shortfall of English-language information on hand. It's best to take a look at the museum's excellent website, with a good English-language section, beforehand for a thorough description of what awaits.

**TOP** CHOICE *Cathedral*

The cathedral opposite the main entrance to the palace looks nothing like the Romanesque church first erected here in 1171. It was rebuilt in the 17th century and later dressed in baroque decorations. Pope John Paul II celebrated Mass here in 1999. Note that, as with everything else in Kielce these days, during the time of research, the palace and cathedral complex were in the throes of a multiyear renovation, though all of the sights were expected to remain open.

**Museum of Toys and Play** MUSEUM
(Muzeum Zabawek i Zabawy; www.muzeum
zabawek.eu; Plac Wolności 2; adult/concession
8/4zł; ◎10am-5pm Tue-Sun) This delightful museum offers the chance to reminisce about toys you forgot you wanted. The room full of frogs somehow makes sense when you're there.

**Jewish Pogrom Memorial** MEMORIAL
(Planty 7) Kielce was the site of a tragic post-WWII pogrom in 1946 committed by Poles against Jews who had survived the brutalities of the war. The origins of the pogrom are unclear – some believe it was instigated by communist authorities to discredit nationalist Poles – but the violence ended with around 40 Jewish deaths. Nine Poles were executed for taking part. The pogrom is often cited as the reason so few surviving

# Kielce

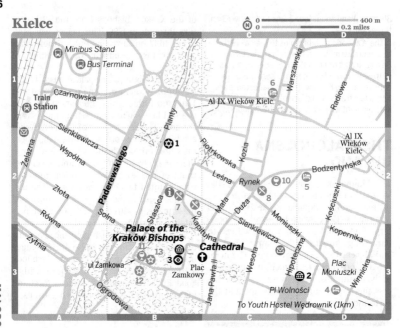

Jews decided to remain in Poland after the war. Today, a small plaque signed by former president Lech Wałęsa identifies the house where the killings took place.

### Open-Air Museum of the
### Kielce Village                          MUSEUM
(Muzeum Wsi Kieleckiej; www.mwk.com.pl in Polish; adult/concession 10/7zł; ⊗10am-6pm Tue-Sun Apr-Oct, 9am-4pm Mon-Fri Nov-Mar) This 80-hectare skansen is located in the village of Tokarnia, about 20km from Kielce. It's a pleasant half-day outing, particularly for kids.

Several minibuses from Kielce pass Tokarnia on their way to other destinations, as do five normal buses (3zł, 30 minutes) between 10.40am and 8.40pm on their way to destinations such as Jędrzejów. Get off at the village of Tokarnia and continue in the same direction on foot for around 1km to the entrance of the skansen.

## ✯ Festivals & Events

Kielce has an active social calendar year-round, but the best fest by far is the annual **Days of Kielce**, which takes place every year in late May or June over the weekend of the Corpus Christi holiday. The whole town shuts down for four days of street food, live music and general merriment.

## 🛏 Sleeping

Budget accommodation is hard to come by in Kielce, but there are abundant midrange options.

**TOP CHOICE** **Hotel Śródmiejski**          HOTEL €
(☑41 344 1507; www.hotelsrodmiejski.pl; ul Wesoła 5; s/d 130/150zł; ℗@🛜) Every town should be so lucky as to have a small, family-run hotel so close to the action, yet still reasonably priced. Don't be put off by the rundown street, the hotel is clean and secure. The rooms are large and tastefully furnished; some have balconies out over the street. Our only (minor) quibble is the rock-hard mattresses.

**Ibis Hotel**                              HOTEL €
(☑41 340 6900; www.ibishotel.com; ul Warszawska 19; s/d 141/161zł; ℗@🛜) Kielce has the distinction of being home to Poland's cheapest Ibis hotel. This paired with the fact the hotel opened only in 2010 means excellent value in what still feels like a brand-new hotel. The rooms are small and boxy, but clean and well appointed. The only drawbacks, as with any Ibis, are the extras like breakfast and parking, which can jack up prices quickly. Breakfast costs 30zł; parking is another 15zł.

# Kielce

Check the website for further discounts on the rack rate.

**Hotel Pod Złotą Różą**      HOTEL €€
(✆41 341 5002; www.zlotaroza.pl; Plac Moniuszki 7; s/d 200/280zł, ste 400-600zł; P@📶) The small but meticulously refurbished rooms shine with a rich brown finish and are good value for money. There's no unnecessary ostentation here; it's just a compact, stylish place with an elegant restaurant.

**Hotel Leśny Dwór**      HOTEL €€
(✆41 362 1088; www.lesnydwor.com.pl; ul Szczepaniaka 40; s/d/ste 160/220/300zł; P@📶🅿) Roughly 3km southwest of the centre but a world away in every other respect, Leśny Dwór is a quaint hotel opposite Park Baranowski. It offers charming rooms and a restaurant capable of anything from roasting a pig for a party to serving vegetarian meals for a couple of travellers. Special Lux rooms cost about 60zł extra and have balconies and forest views.

**Youth Hostel Wędrownik**      HOSTEL €
(✆41 342 3735; ul Szymanowskiego 5; dm 35zł) Uninspiring but adequate; 1.5km east of the centre and a long walk all the way down ul Sienkiewicza from the train station.

## ✗ Eating

Finding good food in Kielce is surprisingly hard for such a large city. The main drag, ul Sienkiewicza, is lined with kebab joints and pizza places, but little of any substance. The nearby Rynek (old town square) is also worth a look. If all else fails, the Ibis and Pod Złotą Różą hotels have good restaurants.

**Moltobene**      ITALIAN €€
(Rynek 12; mains 20zł) This little pizza and ice cream joint on the Rynek is as good a place as any in a city with few decent dining options. Better-than-average pizzas are served comically in giant wooden bowls. Our favourite is the Queen Margarita, just tomato sauce and mozzarella, topped with fresh basil.

**Roy Ben**      STEAKHOUSE €€
(ul Sienkiewicza 21; mains 20-30zł) A faux English pub that nevertheless represents arguably the best central dining option along ul Sienkiewicza. Roy Ben advertises itself as a steakhouse, but the menu is a mish-mash of roast meats, fish, salads and pasta. The 'bekon' cheeseburger is passably close to the real deal.

**A Blikle**      CAFE €
(www.blikle.pl; ul Sienkiewicza 29; mains 12zł; ⊙9am-8pm) A welcome addition to newly sophisticated Kielce, this bakery-cafe is pleasant for a high-calorie break and low-energy people-watching.

## 🍷 Drinking & Entertainment

**CKM**      BAR
(www.ckm.kielce.com; ul Bodzentyńska 2; ⊙10am-late; 📶) CKM is something between a club, a pub, a lounge and a cafe. It draws a mostly student-aged crowd for a night of foosball, pool, drinking and chit-chat.

**Galery Café**      BEER GARDEN
(ul Zamkowa; ⊙10am-late) Popular beer garden located at the tail end of Zamkowa toward the park. Fetch a Lech at the bar and then find a picnic table outside.

**Klub Zamkowa**      CLUB
(www.zamkowa.pl; ul Zamkowa 2; ⊙11am-1am) One of the better dance clubs in town just a couple doors down from the Palace of the Kraków Bishops. The eclectic interior is a mix of Middle Ages-meets-modern-excess.

**Dom Środowisk Twórczych** LIVE MUSIC
(41 368 2054; ul Zamkowa 5) One of the best music venues in town offers temporary exhibitions and live music (depending on the night, from classic to rock and jazz) in a resplendent but relaxed open-air space at the foot of the palace.

## ℹ Information

There are plenty of *kantors* on ul Sienkiewicza. The main post office is next to the train station, and there's another on Sienkiewicza.

**Bank Pekao** (ul Sienkiewicza 18; ☺8am-6pm Mon-Fri, 10am-2pm Sun) Advances on Visa and MasterCard.

**Raiffeisen Bank** (ul Sienkiewicza 60A; ☺10am-6pm Mon-Fri)

**Regional Tourist Information Centre** (ROT Świętokrzyskie; 41 348 0060; www.swietokrzyskie.travel; ul Sienkiewicza 29; ☺9am-5pm Mon-Fri, 10am-5pm Sat & Sun) Impressively helpful tourist office in a newly remodelled space in the centre of town.

## ℹ Getting There & Away

**BUS** Kielce's very cool UFO-shaped bus terminal is well organised and conveniently close to the train station.

Buses to Święty Krzyż (4zł, one hour, four daily) leave between 6.45am and 3.40pm; for Łódź (30zł, 3½ hours, around 10 daily) between 6am and 8.20pm; for Sandomierz (20zł, two hours, 10 daily), between 7am and 7.40pm; and for Kraków (25zł, 2½ hours, 13 daily) between 2am and 5.35pm. Check other destinations at the busy **information desk** (☺6am-8pm).

The minibus stand (opposite the bus terminal) clearly displays schedules. Minibuses to nearby destinations such as Chęciny (4zł, 20 minutes, every half-hour or so) are more constant and convenient than PKS (Państwowa Komunikacja Samochodowa, the main bus operator in Poland) buses. However, minibuses to Kraków (24zł, two hours, every half-hour from 5am to 8.10pm) can fill up fast – a normal bus can often be a better bet for this trip.

**TRAIN** The train station (the key landmark at the western end of ul Sienkiewicza) services many destinations. There are around 15 trains per day to Radom (25zł, two hours), which continue on to Warsaw (40zł, 3½ hours); 14 trains to Kraków (35zł, three hours); four to Lublin (40zł, three hours); and five to Częstochowa (30zł, 1½ hours).

# Świętokrzyski National Park

The 60 sq km **Świętokrzyski National Park** (Świętokrzyski Park Narodowy; adult/concession 5/2.5zł) covers a stretch of low-lying hills known as the Świętokrzyski Mountains. It offers the perfect full-day, back-to-nature respite from urban Kielce. This is Poland's oldest mountainous geological formation (and lowest, due to erosion over more than 300 million years). Unusual piles of broken *gołoborza* (quartzite rock) on the northern slopes hint at how ancient this mountain range is.

The most popular activity is **hiking** and ambitious visitors usually opt to follow the ancient pilgrimage route from the town of Nowa Słupia to a Benedictine monastery high in the hills at Święty Krzyż (Holy Cross) and then continue onward to the hamlet of Święta Katarzyna. The trail, of moderate difficulty, runs about 18km and takes from six to seven hours to complete.

## ◎ Sights

**Benedictine Monastery of Holy Cross** MONASTERY
(Święty Krzyż) This hilltop monastery got its name from the segment of Jesus' cross that was supposedly kept here. The abbey is at the top of Łysa Góra (595m) – the second-highest peak in the range after Łysica (612m).

The Święty Krzyż abbey has a fascinating history. Most sources estimate it was built in the 11th century on an 8th- and 9th-century pagan worship site. With the abolition of the Benedictine Order by the Russians in 1819, the abbey was converted into a prison. After a brief period of restoration, under Nazi Germany the buildings were reconverted into prisons. The Gestapo tortured many monks here before transporting them to Auschwitz-Birkenau, and many Soviet prisoners of war were executed and buried in mass graves near the peak. Under communism, the abbey was transferred to the national park and renovations commenced.

The abbey's **Holy Cross Church** (☺9am-5pm Mon-Sat, noon-5pm Sun & holidays) was rebuilt several times over the years. The present-day church and its mainly neoclassical interior date to the late 18th century. In addition to the church, you can also take a peek at the **crypts** (adult/concession 2/1zł; ☺9am-5pm Mon-Sat, 12:15-5pm Sun & holidays), where you'll see the mummified remains of a very forlorn-looking nobleman, Jeremi Michal Korybut, who died in 1651 at the ripe old age of 39.

### Museum of the Holy Cross Ancient Metallurgy
MUSEUM

(Muzeum Starożytnego Hutnictwa Świętokrzyskiego; ☑41 317 7018; ul Świętokrzyska 59, Nowa Słupia; adult/concession 6/3zł; ⊙9am-4pm) Although it may not look like it, the surrounding region is home to the largest ancient metallurgical centre discovered in Europe to date. The museum was established on the site where primitive 2nd-century smelting furnaces (*dymarki*) were discovered in 1955. The entrance to the museum is about 300m from the national park gate, just outside the village of Nowa Słupia.

### 🛏 Sleeping and Eating

The tourist office in Nowa Słupia can help find agroturist accommodation.

**Jodłowy Dwór**
HOTEL €€

(☑41 302 5028; www.jodlowydwor.com.pl in Polish; Huta Szklana 34; d/tr 170/200zł) Though the exterior looks more like a modern housing estate, this faux rustic lodge in a village along the road between Święty Krzyż and Święta Katarzyna offers arguably the nicest digs in the immediate area. There's a garden with a playground and a decent in-house restaurant.

**Youth Hostel**
HOSTEL €

(☑41 317 7016; ul Świętokrzyska 61, Nowa Słupia; dm per person 20zł; d 30-40zł) This hostel in Nowa Słupia is well tended and has 60 beds in double and dorm rooms. The location is convenient for entering the national park.

### ❶ Information

There is a small **tourist information centre** (Informacja Turystyczna; ☑41 317 7626; ul Świętokrzyska 18; ⊙9am-4pm) in Nowa Słupia, about 500m from the entrance to the national park, which has hiking maps and can offer advice and brochures on places to stay.

### ❶ Getting There & Away

The park is 25km east of Kielce. Buses leave every hour or so from Kielce to Święta Katarzyna (7zł, 30 minutes) roughly between 5am and 7pm, some stopping at Święty Krzyż on the way. To get to Nowa Słupia (7zł, one hour), take a bus bound for either Jeziórko or Rudki (around 10 per day until 6pm or so).

There are frequent buses from both Nowa Słupia (7zł, one hour) and Święta Katarzyna (7zł, 30 minutes) back to Kielce, but from Święty Krzyż there are only buses every few hours.

# THE SANDOMIERZ VALLEY

The Sandomierz Valley (Kotlina Sandomierska) covers an extensive area in and around the fork of the Vistula and San Rivers. In the heart of the valley is the hilltop town of Sandomierz – an underrated gem of Gothic splendour. Nearby are the fantastic fairy-tale ruins of Ujazd castle.

## Sandomierz
POP 24,778

Tourists really should be rolling down the sloping Rynek of Sandomierz and piling up at the town hall. But the grandeur of the Old Town, with the impressive Gothic town hall propped upright in its centre, remains relatively undiscovered. Immaculate buildings painted warming hues of brown, orange and yellow, many festooned with elegant wrought-iron balconies, line the laneways as locals nonchalantly wander by, apparently oblivious to their good fortune in not being overrun by hordes of visitors.

### History

No one is certain of precisely when Sandomierz came to life, but as far back as the 11th century the town was classified (by chronicler Gall Anonim) as a major settlement of the Polish kingdom, along with Kraków and Wrocław.

In the 13th century, repeated assaults by Tatar raiders meant that Sandomierz had to be resurrected several times, most significantly in 1260 when it was rebuilt uphill at the site it occupies today. During the reign of Kazimierz III Wielki (1333–70), Sandomierz became a significant trade hub and saw the construction of the Royal Castle, Opatów Gate and the town hall. The town prospered until the mid-17th century, the same era that saw the arrival of the Jesuits and the invasion of the Swedes – an onslaught from which it never completely recovered.

After having survived WWII with its historic architecture relatively unscathed, the next threat came in the 1960s when its most significant buildings started sliding into the river. The soft silt on which Sandomierz is built (and from which its underground cellars were carved) began to give way, necessitating a large-scale rescue operation. The injection of concrete and steel into the slippery soil stabilised the city and securely tethered its architectural assets.

## ◉ Sights & Activities

**Rynek and Town Hall**  SQUARE, MUSEUM
The Rynek, distinctive for its slope, is ringed with houses from different stylistic periods. Today, only numbers 10 and 27 have the arcades typical of 16th-century houses. The red rectangular **town hall**, erected in the 14th century, is the oldest building on the Rynek; the white clock tower was added in the 17th century and the sundial on the southern wall (the work of Tadeusz Przypkowski) in 1958. The ground floor houses the **Regional Museum – Town Hall** (Muzeum Okręgowe – Ratusz; http://sandomierz.travel in Polish; Rynek; adult/concession 5/4zł; ☺10am-5pm Tue-Sun May-Sep, 9am-4pm Tue-Fri & 10am-3pm Sat & Sun Oct-Apr), focusing on the town's history.

**Underground Tourist Route**  UNDERGROUND
(Podziemna Trasa Turystyczna; ☏15 832 3088; ul Oleśnickich; adult/concession 8/5zł; ☺10am-6.30pm May-Sep, 10am-4pm Oct-Apr) A 40-minute guided tour (in Polish) leads through a chain of 30-odd cellars tidily connected over 500m beneath the Old Town. The cellars – originally used for storage and sometimes for shelter during times of conflict – were built between the 13th and 17th centuries. The deepest point is about 12m below ground, but feels like more, because of disorienting twists, turns and Escher-esque staircases.

**Cathedral**  CHURCH
(www.katedra.sandomierz.opoka.org.pl in Polish; ul Mariacka; ☺10am-5pm Tue-Sat, 11.30am-3.30pm Sun Apr-Oct, 10am-2pm Tue-Sat, 11.30am-1pm Sun Nov-Mar) From the Rynek, take ul Mariacka to the cathedral. Built between 1360 and 1382, this massive church has preserved much of its Gothic exterior, apart from the baroque facade added in the 17th century. The Russo-Byzantine frescoes in the chancel were painted in the 1420s but later white-washed. They were only revealed again at the beginning of the 20th century. Also note the impressive baroque organ gallery of the late 17th century and the marble altar dating to the 18th century.

**Diocesan Museum**  MUSEUM
(Muzeum Diecezjalne; www.domdlugosza.sandomierz.org in Polish; ul Długosza 9; adult/concession 6/3zł; ☺9am-4.30pm Tue-Sat & 1.30-4.30pm Sun Apr-Oct, 9am-3.30pm Tue-Sat & 1.30-3.30pm Sun Nov-Mar) *The* quintessential example of Sandomierz's underrated assets, the medieval **Długosz House** (Dom Długosza) was built in 1476 for Poland's first historian, Jan Długosz. Today it houses the Diocesan Museum, with a rich collection of medieval artwork, sculpture, tapestries, clothing, coins and ceramics.

**Royal Castle and Regional Museum**  CASTLE, MUSEUM
(Muzeum Okręgowe – Zamek; http://sandomierz.travel in Polish; ul Zamkowa 14; adult/concession 8/6zł; ☺10am-5pm Tue-Fri & 10am-6pm Sat & Sun May-Sep, 9am-4pm Tue-Fri & 10am-3pm Sat & Sun Oct-Apr) The Royal Castle was built in the 14th century on the site of a previous wooden stronghold and was gradually extended during the next three centuries. It now accommodates the regional museum, which contains modest ethnographic, archaeological and art collections.

**Opatów Gate**  GATE
(Brama Opatowska; http://sandomierz.travel in Polish; ul Opatowska; adult/concession 4/3zł; ☺9am-6.30pm summer) The main entrance to the Old Town, and the only surviving gate of the four originally built, is 14th-century Opatów Gate. You can climb to the viewing platform at the top for a pleasant (though by no means bird's-eye) view of surrounding terrain.

## 🛏 Sleeping

In addition to the properties noted below, several houses on side streets around the Rynek offer private rooms. Two of the best are on pretty ul Forteczna, a cobblestoned lane just behind the Rynek. Try **Zielone Wzgórze** (☏15 832 3725; www.lasvegas4you.pl; Forteczna 6) or **Willa na Skarpie** (☏665 445 180; Forteczna 8).

**TOP CHOICE ⟩ Hotel Basztowy**  HOTEL €€
(☏15 833 3450; www.hotelbasztowy.pl; Pl Ks J Poniatowskiego 2; s/d/ste 200/240/450 zł; 🅿@☎) The refined Basztowy is prime splurge material. The hotel manages to cater both to business types and holidaymakers, with added touches like a spa and billiard room. The lobby feels fresh and welcoming; the rooms are simple but filled with elegant touches like early modernist ceiling lamps. The breakfast buffet has seldom-seen extras like mozzarella cheese served with tomato slices. The hotel is a two-minute walk southwest of the Rynek, following ul Zamkowa.

**Hotel Pod Ciżemką**  HOTEL €€
(☏15 832 0550; www.hotelcizemka.pl; Rynek 27; s/d/ste 250/270/350zł; 🅿☎) Pod Ciżemką is the

### 365 REASONS NOT TO BE MARTYRED

The interiors of Sandomierz Cathedral give a pleasant first impression, but focus on the details beyond the initial ostentation and you discover the macabre side of Sandomierz.

The paintings on the walls of the cathedral are by 18th-century artist Karol de Prevot (1708–37), who was apparently not of a cheery disposition. The four paintings on the back wall under the organ depict historic scenes such as the 1656 destruction of Sandomierz castle by the Swedes. But it is the series of 12 paintings on the side walls that are a real argument for checking ID at the door of this cathedral.

The series, *Martyrologium Romanum*, depicts the martyrdom of the Dominican Fathers and other people of Sandomierz at the hands of the Tatars between 1259 and 1260. The unfortunate subjects are being sawn, burned, hanged, whipped, quartered, sliced, diced and otherwise discourteously treated.

The 12 paintings are supposed to symbolise the 12 months of the year; next to each image of torture a number represents the day of the month. Legend has it that if you find the day and month on which you were born, you'll discover how you're going to die. Let's hope not.

grandest place in the Old Town and has been extensively refurbished. Set in a 400-year-old house, the stylish rooms are commendable renditions of old-world elegance, as is the onsite restaurant. Note there's no elevator, making this a hard slog if you're physically impaired or carrying lots of luggage.

**Jutrzenka** PENSION €
(☎15 832 2219; ul Zamkowa 1; s/d/tr 60/100/120zł; P) You'll find the cheapest rooms in town at the back of this small, private home, just up from the castle and about five minutes' walk southwest of the Rynek following ul Zamkowa. There are few facilities, but the rooms themselves are freshly painted, clean, and filled with country bric-a-brac.

## Eating & Drinking

The Rynek is lined with places to eat and drink, so walk around and see what looks good.

TOP CHOICE **Café Mała** CREPERIE €
(ul Sokolnickiego 3; mains 10-20zł; ) This cosy, French Provincial style cafe just around the corner from the Rynek is perfect for a cup of coffee or a small meal like a salad or savoury crepe. Even if you don't eat here, stop by for arguably the only real cup of coffee in town and a scrumptious dessert like strawberry shortcake.

**Restauracja Trzydziestka '30'** POLISH €€
(Rynek 30; mains 20-30zł) This Rynek favourite offers a welcome, simple menu of grilled meats, chicken, pork, or beef, with sides of rice, potatoes or buckwheat groats. The elevated terrace in summer offers a sweeping panorama of the square below.

**Café Bar Kordegarda** INTERNATIONAL €€
(Rynek 12; mains 15-30zł; ) This trendy cafe and restaurant offers drinks on the terrace overlooking the Rynek, plus a mix of salads and light food options. Service can be hit or miss, so feel free to grab your own menu or take your food or drinks order to the bar.

## Information

The **Tourist Information Centre** (Centrum Informacja Turystycznej; ☎15 644 6105; http://sandomierz.travel in Polish; Rynek 20; 9am-6pm Mon-Fri, 10am-4pm Sat, Sun May-Sep, 9am-4pm Mon-Fri Oct-Apr) is a gold mine of helpful information and offers a free simple map of the Old Town.

There is a *kantor* in the **post office** (Rynek 10). The **Kredyt Bank** (Rynek 5) a few doors south also changes cash. There are also *kantors* on ul Mickiewicza close to the corner of ul 11 Listopada, about 1km northwest of the Old Town.

## Getting There & Away

BUS The **PKS bus terminal** (☎15 832 2302; ul Listopada 22) is 1.5km northwest of the Old Town; frequent city buses go there from Opatów Gate.

There are a dozen fast buses to Warsaw (50zł, three hours), which cost roughly the same as the train, and four buses per day to Kielce (18zł, two hours).

There are buses to Tarnobrzeg (4zł, 30 minutes, every half-hour). For Ujazd, change at Opatów (7zł, 45 minutes, 30km) or Klimontów.

WORTH A TRIP

## CRAZY KRZYŻTOPÓR CASTLE

The small village of Ujazd (oo-yahst), around 30km from Sandomierz, is home to arguably Poland's most bizarre building. **Krzyżtopór Castle** (www.krzyztopor.org.pl; adult/concession 7/5zł; ☺8am-8pm Apr-Oct, 8am-4pm Nov-Mar) was commissioned by eccentric governor Krzysztof Ossoliński and built according to his fantastic imagination, incorporating his love of magic and astrology, among other things.

The architect commissioned to create Ossoliński's dream was Italian Lorenzo Muretto (known in Poland as Wawrzyniec Senes), who worked on the mammoth project between 1631 and 1644.

History and legend offer zany accounts of the castle. It was designed to embody a calendar, with four towers representing the four seasons, 12 halls for the 12 months of the year, 52 rooms for the 52 weeks, and 365 windows for 365 days – plus one to be used only during leap years. Some cellars were used as stables for Ossoliński's 370 white stallions, and are adorned with mirrors and black marble. The crystal ceiling of the great dining hall is believed to have been the base of an enormous aquarium.

Perhaps the most enchanting report is the one concerning the tunnel that ran under it, linking to the castle of Ossoliński's brother. The 15km tunnel to Ossolin was believed to have been covered with sugar so the two brothers could visit each other on horse-drawn sledges, pretending they were travelling on snow.

Sadly, Ossoliński was barely able to enjoy a full calendar year in his playground; he died in 1645 – only a year after the castle was completed.

After damage done by the Swedes in the 1650s and the abandonment of the castle by its subsequent owners in 1770, this dreamland fell to ruin. Since WWII, talk of converting the castle into a military school or hotel has petered out, leaving Krzyżtopór Castle as a landscape for the daydreams of its visitors.

# THE RADOM PLAIN

The Radom Plain (Równina Radomska) extends between Małopolska to the south and Mazovia in the north. This gentle area is seldom visited by tourists, but Radom is a pleasant enough place to decamp for the night and one of the most expansive skansens in Małopolska is just outside the city.

## Radom

POP 222,500

Radom is a large industrial city that offers few traditional attractions for most visitors. That said, its main pedestrian thoroughfare, ul Żeromskiego, is unexpectedly charming and a nice place for a lunch and a stroll. Radom lies astride one of the country's most important rail connections, linking Kraków and Warsaw, and as such is a convenient stopover point.

### ☉ Sights

Most of the sights are clustered along ul Żeromskiego, which runs uphill for about 3km from the city's rundown Rynek through its lively shopping and leisure core all the way up to an inviting park.

**Historic Churches**　　　CHURCHES

The most significant relic of Radom's earliest years is **St Wenceslaus church** (Kościół Świętego Wacława, Plac Stare Miasto 13) in the Old Town Square. Built originally in the 13th century from wood, it was the first parish church of Old Radom. It was used for various purposes (such as a military hospital and psychiatric ward) and completely restored in the 1970s. The main parish **Church of St John the Baptist** (Kościół Świętego Jana Chrzciciela; www.fara.radom.pl in Polish; Rwańska 6) was founded by Kazimierz III Wielki in 1360 and altered by numerous people up to the present. The church is located just near the Rynek.

**Jewish Radom**　　　HISTORIC SITE

Radom was a significant Jewish settlement and the Jewish community here numbered around 30,000 (over a quarter of the population) just before WWII. Unfortunately, few Jews survived the war and little of that heritage remains. Most Jews lived in the area around the Rynek. Near here, you'll find four stones and a small memorial that mark where the **main synagogue** (cnr ul Bóźnicza & ul Podwalna) once stood.

About 4km east of the city centre is what remains of the former **Jewish cemetery** (Ul Towarowa). The Germans destroyed the cemetery and used the grave markers as paving stones, but in the past decade some of the tombstones have been returned. The gate is usually locked and there's not much to see, but the tourist office may be able to arrange a viewing. To reach the cemetery, take city bus 17 to the Zółkiewskiego stop and walk 100m down the gravel road, ul Towarowa.

**Radom Village Museum**              MUSEUM
(Muzeum Wsi Radomskiej; www.muzeum-radom .pl in Polish; ul Szydłowiecka 30; adult/concession 8/5zł; ☺9am-5pm Tue-Fri, 10am-8pm Sat & Sun) One of the most popular outings is the short hop to this outdoor folklore museum about 8km from the centre. Furnished interiors showcase styles from the whole region. City bus 17 will get you within a few hundred metres of the entrance. Returning to Radom, turn left back onto the highway; the bus stop is in a small side street 20m or so past a turn-off.

## 🛏 Sleeping

There's not much in the way of budget accommodation in Radom, but there are ample moderately priced hotels not far from the train and bus stations.

**Hotel Iskra**                    HOTEL **€**
(☎48 383 8745; www.hoteliskra.radom.pl in Polish; ul Planty 4; s/d 120/170zł; 🅿🛜) Just a couple of minutes' walk from the train station, the Iskra is a revitalised former-communist-era structure that offers bright, well-maintained rooms big enough to stretch out in.

**Hotel Glass**                    HOTEL **€**
(☎48 340 2585; www.hotelglass.radom.pl; ul Prażmowskiego 17; s/d 120/160zł; 🅿✳🛜) This friendly hotel is named for its glass exterior (it could have also been called Hotel Pink). Standard rooms are unremarkable, but apartments offer distinct sleeping and sitting areas. The location, across from the bus station, is excellent.

**Hotel Gromada**                 HOTEL **€€**
(☎48 368 9100; www.gromada.pl; ul Narutowicza 9; s/d 200/220zł, apt 300-400zł; 🅿@🛜) This generic business hotel has spacious rooms and an onsite restaurant and bar. Apartments are reasonable value given their terrace and

kitchen annex. Another branch is located 2.5km west of the town centre.

## 🍴 Eating & Drinking

Pleasant eateries line ul Żeromskiego. For a late afternoon beer, try the cafe in Park Tadeusz Kościuszki at the eastern end of the pedestrian strip.

**TOP CHOICE** Olivio              ITALIAN **€€**
(☎48 363 6300; www.restauracjaolivio.pl; ul Żeromskiego 17; mains 20-35zł; 🍴) This ambitious Italian cafe/restaurant on the main drag offers what is arguably the city's best cooking in a casual yet elegant setting. Start with spicy rolls of grilled eggplant wrapped around goat cheese and salami and then move on to pasta or beefsteak. Eat on the streetside terrace in summer.

**Teatralna**                      ITALIAN **€€**
(☎48 363 7763; www.teatralna.radom.pl; ul Żeromskiego 55; mains 20-40zł) This handsome restaurant has something for everyone. The cooking leans toward Mediterranean, but in addition to the usual offerings of pizza and pasta, you'll find fish, duck, and our favourite: braised pork loin served in mushroom sauce with a side of spinach and pine nuts.

## ℹ Information

There are plenty of *kantors* and ATMs along ul Żeromskiego.

**Post office** (ul Jacka Malczewskiego 5 ☺8am-8pm Mon-Fri)

**Tourist office** (☎48 360 0610; www.informacjaturystyczna.radom.pl in Polish; ul Traugutta 3; ☺10am-5pm Mon-Fri, 11am-1pm Sat) Situated in a kiosk, three minutes by foot from the train station. Look for the free booklet 'A Walk Around Radom' in English.

## ℹ Getting There & Away

The train and bus stations are next to each other, 2km south of ul Żeromskiego.

**BUS** There's a small minibus lot in front of the train station, with frequent minibus service to Warsaw (20zł, 2½ hours). Most big buses bound for Warsaw and Kraków (175km) depart in the afternoon. There are five buses leaving for Łódź (135km) between 6am and 6.30pm, as well as a couple of daily buses to Lublin (15zł, 2½ hours) and Puławy (10zł, 1½ hours).

**TRAIN** Radom lies on a major north-south train line. Around a dozen trains go to Warsaw daily (25zł, 2½ hours, 100km), and six or so to Kraków daily (35zł, 3½ hours, 175km). Kraków-bound trains stop in Kielce (25zł, 1½ hours,

85km). Two trains head to Lublin daily (1½ hours), and at least one train goes to Wrocław (4 hours) daily. For more information, ask at the **information counter** (⊘6am-10pm) in the train station.

# THE LUBLIN UPLAND

Stretching east of the Vistula and San Rivers up to the Ukrainian border is the Lublin Upland (Wyżyna Lubelska). Lublin, its biggest city, still bears the scars of WWII but carries itself with dignity these days. The area also boasts (though not loudly enough) Kazimierz Dolny, a quaint town on the banks of the Vistula that attracts weekenders looking to escape the city – and the 21st century. Also worth visiting is the town of Zamość and the nearby village of Zwierzyniec, both built on the Renaissance dreams of nobleman Jan Zamoyski.

## Lublin

POP 348,400

Lublin is the largest city in southeastern Poland, with a thriving cultural and academic scene. It offers the usual amenities of any city this size, including decent hotels, restaurants, and nightlife. It's also a main transport hub, with excellent road and rail connections to all parts of Poland.

That said, it's not a looker. Lublin was ravaged during WWII and the forced industrialization of the communist period only added insult to injury. Nevertheless, the city's historic core, the Rynek, is slowly being gentrified and trendy clubs and restaurants are giving new lustre to the centre's impressive stock of Renaissance and baroque townhouses.

Lublin is of special interest to travellers seeking Poland's Jewish past. For centuries, the city was a leading centre of Jewish scholarship, giving rise to the Lublin's nickname as the 'Jewish Oxford'. That heritage came to a brutal end in WWII, but here and there you can still find traces.

### History

Though Lublin feels a little marginalized these days, for centuries it played a central role in Polish history. On three separate occasions it was Poland's de facto capital, at least temporarily.

In 1569, it was here in Lublin that the union between the Polish and Lithuania

kingdoms was signed, creating at the time the largest state in Europe. In 1918, at the end of WWI, Lublin was the site of the first government of newly independent Poland. In 1944, at the end of WWII, it was in Lublin that the first provisional communist government installed by the Soviets was housed.

On a more sombre note, during WWII Lublin was chosen by the Germans as their headquarters for 'Operation Reinhard', the name of their secret plan to exterminate the Jewish population of German-occupied Poland. Two of the most infamous Operation Reinhard extermination camps, Sobibór and Bełżec, lie within an hour's drive of Lublin (see boxed text, p168).

## ◎ Sights

### CASTLE AREA
**Lublin Castle**                                   CASTLE
(☑81 532 5001; www.zamek.lublin.pl; ul Zamkowa 9; adult/concession 8.50/6.50zł, free Sat; ⊘9am-4pm Wed-Sat, 9am-5pm Sun) The earliest remnants of Lublin's castle date from the 12th and 13th centuries, and it was here in 1569 where the union with Lithuania was signed. The castle also holds the Chapel of the Holy Trinity, which dates from the 14th century and is acclaimed as an important surviving piece of Gothic architecture.

The castle fell into ruin in the 17th century and was rebuilt in the 19th century by the occupying Russians as a prison to hold political prisoners: mostly Poles opposed to tsarist Russia. During WWII the occupying German army took up the prison theme with a vengeance, holding as many as 40,000 inmates here. The darkest day of the war came in July 1944, just ahead of the prison's liberation by the Soviet Red Army, when the Germans executed 300 prisoners on the spot.

These days the castle has been spruced up and holds both a historical museum dedicated to the city of Lublin and a chapel. Each requires a separate entry ticket.

**Lublin Museum**                                   MUSEUM
(☑81 532 5001; www.zamek.lublin.pl; ul Zamkowa 9; adult/concession 8.50/6.50zł, free Sat; ⊘9am-4pm Wed-Sat, 9am-5pm Sun) Since 1957, the castle has housed the Lublin Museum, with a collection ranging from silverware and porcelain to woodcarvings and weaponry. The particularly impressive art includes big names (such as Jacek Malczewski) and big

pictures, such as the detail-rich *Lublin Union of 1569,* depicting the merging of Poland and Lithuania.

Also worth seeing in the foyer of the castle is the curious **Devil's Paw**, imprinted on the 17th-century table of the Royal Tribunal. The legend explaining its existence relates to a widow who was avenged by a team of devils after being unjustly treated by the Royal Tribunal. The Devil's Paw costs an additional 3zł to view.

### Chapel of the Holy Trinity CHURCH
(☑81 532 5001; www.zamek.lublin.pl; ul Zamkowa 9; adult/concession 8.50/6.50zł; ☺10am-5pm Tue-Sat, 10am-6pm Sun) At the eastern end of the castle is its most prized asset – the exquisite 14th-century chapel, which is featured on many postcards (the photographers must have snuck in a flash and a wide angle lens). The chapel is covered from floor to ceiling with polychrome Russo-Byzantine frescoes. Painted in 1418, only to be later plastered over, they were rediscovered in 1897 and painstakingly restored over a hundred-year period. These are possibly the finest examples of medieval wall paintings in the country.

### OLD TOWN
The winding streets of the Old Town are full of life, with new cafes and restaurants opening. At the Rynek's centre is the 1781 neoclassical Old Town Hall.

### Dominican Priory CHURCH
(Kościół Dominikanów; www.domikikanie.lub.pl in Polish; ul Złota 9; free admission; ☺9am-4pm) Originally a Gothic complex founded by King Kazimierz III Wielki in 1342, the Dominican Priority was rebuilt in Renaissance style after it was ravaged by fire in 1575. Two historic highlights inside the church are the Chapel of the Firlej Family (1615), containing family members' tombstones; and the Tyszkiewicz Chapel (1645–59), with impressive Renaissance stuccowork. For an insight into 18th-century Lublin, note the large historical painting *The Fire of Lublin,* which depicts the 1719 fire (in the Szaniawski family chapel to your right as you enter the church).

### Trinitarian Tower TOWER, MUSEUM
(www.kuria.lublin.pl/muzeum in Polish; Plac Katedralny; adult/concession 7/5zł; ☺10am-5pm Apr-Oct) For an expansive view of the Old Town, climb to the top of Trinitarian Tower (1819), which houses the underrated **Archdiocesan**

**Museum**. The chaotic layout of artworks in hidden nooks and crannies, combined with the lack of English explanations, means that you can discover ancient artefacts in the haphazard manner of Indiana Jones.

### Cathedral CHURCH
(Plac Katedralny; ☺dawn-sunset) Next to the tower is the 16th-century cathedral, formerly a Jesuit church. There are many impressive details to behold, including the baroque trompe l'œil frescoes (the work of Moravian artist Józef Majer) and the 17th-century altar made from a black Lebanese pear tree. The painting of the Black Madonna is said to have shed tears in 1945, making it a source of much reverence for local devotees. The acoustic vestry (so called for its ability to project whispers) and the **treasury** (skarbiec; ☺10am-2pm & 3-5pm Tue-Sun) behind the chapel are also worth some attention.

### Krakowska Gate TOWER
(Brama Krakowska) The only significant remnant of the fortified walls that once surrounded the Old Town is the 14th-century Gothic-style Krakowska Gate. It received its octagonal Renaissance superstructure in the 16th century, and its baroque crown in 1782.

### Historical Museum of Lublin MUSEUM
(Muzeum Historii Miasta Lublina; www.zamek-lublin.pl; Plac Łokietka 3; adult/concession 5/2.50zł; ☺10am-4pm Tue-Sun) Inside the gate (accessed from its eastern wall) is a small museum, which displays documents and photographs relating to the town's civic history.

### JEWISH RELICS
For centuries Lublin served as a centre of European Jewish culture. The first census in 1550 shows that 840 Jews lived in Lublin; 200 years later Lublin had the third-largest Jewish population in Poland. Before WWII around 40,000 of the city's 120,000 residents were Jewish.

Most of the city's Jews lived in a large ghetto surrounding the castle. These days the area has been flattened into an enormous parking lot stretching all the way to the bus station. It's hard to imagine that before the German occupation this was a densely populated community filled with streets, shops and houses. The **Grodzka Gate** (Brama Grodzka) that links the Old Town and the Castle area was once called the 'Jewish Gate', as it effectively marked the

MAŁOPOLSKA LUBLIN

# Lublin

200 m
0.1 miles

Main Bus Terminal

Minibus Station

Al Tysiąclecia

Plac Zamkowy

Zamkowa

**Lublin Castle** 6

**Chapel of the Holy Trinity**

Unii Lubelskiej

Podwale

Podwale po Farze

**Dominican Priory**

Podwale

Furmańska

Kowalska

Grodzka

Bramowa

9

3

Archidiakońska

15

Rybna

7

Złota

12

18

Jezuicka

Rynek

**Trinitarian Tower** 2

1

Plac Katedralny

Lubartowska

Ku Farze

Olejna

Szambelańska

5   4

Plac Łokietka

Kozia

Świętoduska

Plac Ofiar Getta

Wodopojna

Przechodnia

10

17

16

14

Staszica

Narutowicza

EMPiK

Kapucyńska

Niecała

Radziwiłłowska

Plac Litewski

To Buses to Lublin Village Museum (200m); Lublin Village Museum (5km)

Krakowskie Przedmieście

Kościuszki

11

13

Peowiaków

3 Maja

Chmielna

Kołłątaja

8

# Lublin

end of 'Christian' Lublin and the start of the Jewish quarter.

This centuries-old division came to an end with the Nazi occupation of the city on 18 September 1939. The Germans initially moved the Jews into a restricted ghetto made up of part of the traditional Jewish quarter and a relatively small piece of territory marked by today's ul Kowalska and ul Lubartowska. The old Jewish quarter was flattened. The ghetto was liquidated in 1942, with most of the town's Jews sent to their deaths at the extermination camps at Bełżec and Sobibór, and the Majdanek labour camp. Of the approximately 40,000 Jewish Lubliners, only a few hundred survived the Holocaust.

Memories of the Holocaust languished during the communist period, but since 1989, the city has made strides in recognizing the contributions of the city's Jews. The tourist office has marked out an extensive tourist route, 'The Heritage Trail of the Lublin Jews.' The Grodzka Gate – Theatre NN (Brama Grodzka – Teatr NN; http://teatrnn.pl; ul Grodzka 21) is dedicated to preserving Jewish history and frequently holds exhibitions. The theatre's website has a rich section on Jewish Lublin in English (you have to search for it).

Old Jewish Cemetery                    CEMETERY
The old Jewish cemetery, established in 1541, has 30-odd readable tombstones, including the oldest Jewish tombstone in Poland in its original location. The graveyard is on a hill

between ul Sienna and ul Kalinowszczyzna, about 500 metres to the east and north of the main bus terminal. It is surrounded by a high brick wall and the gate is locked. Contact the Sages of Lublin Synagogue (Chachmej Lublin Yeshiva; ☏81 747 0992, ul Lubartowska 85), which may be able to lend the key or arrange a visit.

New Jewish Cemetery                    CEMETERY
(ul Walecznych) The new Jewish Cemetery, founded in 1829, is the resting place of 52,000 Jews buried here until 1942. The cemetery was destroyed by the Nazis during WWII (who used tombstones in the construction of parts of Majdanek extermination camp) and is still in the process of being restored. Broken tombstones form a wall around the cemetery. The graveyard and the small museum can be visited during daylight hours. There is a 24-hour guard on duty. The cemetery is situated about 500 metres north of the Old Jewish Cemetery and about 1km north of the main bus terminal.

**OUTSIDE THE CENTRE**

Majdanek                    CONCENTRATION CAMP
(Państwowe Muzeum na Majdanku; www.majdanek .pl; Droga Męczenników Majdanka 67; admission free; ☉8am-6pm Apr-Oct, 8am-3pm Nov-Mar) Some 4km southeast of Lublin's centre is the German-Nazi Majdanek extermination camp, where tens of thousands of people were murdered. The site is now the Majdanek State Museum, founded only four months after the camp's liberation – the first

**WORTH A TRIP**

## FORGOTTEN HOLOCAUST: SOBIBÓR AND BEŁŻEC

When it comes to the Holocaust, much of the world's attention has gone to the atrocities of the Auschwitz-Birkenau extermination camp. Here, near Lublin, are two death camps – **Sobibór** and **Bełżec** – that are less well known, but that certainly merit a visit in order to better understand the breadth of the Nazis' extermination policy. At these camps, there was no 'selection' process, no chance for the prisoners to work, and crucially no chance for them to survive. The victims were simply transported to the camps, off-loaded, undressed and gassed.

Both camps were formed under the Germans' 'Operation Reinhard', their secret plan to murder the Jewish population of occupied Poland, and both operated from around mid-1942 to 1943. It was at these camps that the Germans perfected their mass-killing techniques, like using gas, that they would later apply at other extermination centres, including Auschwitz-Birkenau. Though the exact numbers of casualties are impossible to verify, the consensus is that around 250,000 people were murdered at Sobibór and 400,000 to 600,000 at Bełżec. There were only two known survivors from Bełżec.

Though these camps attract a tiny fraction of the number of visitors to Auschwitz-Birkenau, both Sobibór and Bełżec have small, thoughtful memorials (Bełżec has a small museum) where you can learn more about these lesser-known killing camps. Sobibór, which lies about 80km east of Lublin (60km north of Chełm), and 10km south of the modern Polish village of Sobibór, is the harder of the two to reach. There's no public transportation that will take you anywhere near the camp. Instead, inquire at the LOIT offices in Lublin about arranging a tour with a guide (p170). As we were researching this guide, the small museum at Sobibór was closed, but the grounds of the former camp were open to the public and signposted in English.

Bełżec, which lies about 100km south of Lublin, is accessible by regular minibus from Zamość or inquire at the LOIT offices in Lublin for tour information. At Bełżec there's a small **museum** (Ul Ofiar obozu 4; www.belzec.org.pl; free admission; ⊙9am-5pm May-Oct) with photos and text.

of its kind in the world. Unlike other extermination camps, the Nazis went to no effort to conceal Majdanek. Coming from the main road, the sudden appearance of time-frozen guard towers and barbed-wire fences interrupting the sprawl of suburbia is disquieting. The details are even more confronting; gas chambers are open to visitors, and many of the prisoners' possessions are on display. The 5km walk through the museum starts at the Visitor's Centre, passes the foreboding Monument of Fight & Martyrdom, through parts of the barracks and finishes at the guarded mausoleum containing the ashes of many victims. Children under 14 are not permitted to visit the museum.

Trolleybuses 23 and 156 (2zł) along ul Królewska, slightly south of Plac Łokietka, go to the entrance of Majdanek.

**Lublin Village Museum**  MUSEUM
(Muzeum Wsi Lubelskiej; www.skansen.lublin.pl; ul Warszawska 96; adult/concession 8/4zł; ⊙9am-6pm) The well-designed skansen, 5km west of the centre on the Warsaw road, covers an undulating terrain of 25 hectares. Appearing as a traditional village of numerous buildings with fully equipped interiors, there is a fine manor house, a windmill, an Orthodox church and a carved timber gate (1903) designed by Stanisław Witkiewicz. The skansen hosts various temporary displays and cultural events.

To get there from the centre, take bus 18, 20 or 5 from al Racławickie.

 **Activities**

If you're challenged for time in Lublin, a good way to get a quick feel for the city's history is to follow one or more of the five self-guided **walking routes**, including the Jewish heritage tour, outlined in free brochures available from the tourist office.

**✯✯ Festivals & Events**

As the largest city in this part of Poland, Lublin has an active cultural calendar, with something big (usually related to music or theatre) nearly every month of the year. Check in with the tourist information office.

**Codes Festival of Traditional and Avant-Garde Music**  ALTERNATIVE MUSIC
(http://codes-festival.com) Dedicated to fusing archaic and new strains in music. Held annually in May.

**Festival of European Neighbours**  THEATRE
(Festiwal Teatrów Europy Środkowej Sąsiedzi; www
.festiwal-sasiedzi.pl) Popular theatre fest involving troupes from neighbouring countries. Takes place in June.

**International Dance Festival**  DANCE
(Międzynarodowe Spotkania Teatrów Tańca; http://
dancefestival.lublin.pl) Held in November.

**International Folk Music Festival**  FOLK MUSIC
(Mikołajki Folkowe; www.mikolajki.folk.pl) Draws folk musicians from around the world in December.

## 🛏 Sleeping

TOP CHOICE **Vanilla Hotel**  BOUTIQUE HOTEL €€
(🖉81 536 6720; www.vanilla-hotel.pl; ul Krakowskie Przedmieście 12; s/d 300/370zł, ste 410zł; P✳@🛜) The name must be tongue-in-cheek. This beautiful boutique, just off the main pedestrian corso, is anything but vanilla. The rooms are filled with inspired, even bold styling, with vibrant colours, big headboards behind the beds and stylish, retro lamps and furniture. Lots of attention to detail here that continues into the stylish Jazz Age restaurant and coffee bar. The terrace, overlooking ul Krakowskie Przedmieście, makes the best ice-cream concoctions in town.

**Grand Hotel Lublinianka**  HOTEL €€€
(🖉81 446 6100; www.lublinianka.com; ul Krakowskie Przedmieście 56; s/d economy 300/360zł, standard 480/540zł, ste 600/800zł; P✳@🛜) What was the Commercial Chamber of Lublin 100 years ago is now the grandest place to stay in Lublin. The classic foyer of this four-star hotel isn't at all overbearing and the same stylish minimalism translates to the calming pastel rooms. Marble bathrooms in suites include bathtubs, but even the economy guest is entitled to use the Turkish bath and sauna.

**Hotel Waksman**  PENSION €€
(🖉81 532 5454; www.waksman.pl; ul Grodzka 19; s/d 210/230zł, s/d apt 270/290zł; P@🛜) Hotel Waksman deserves a blue ribbon for many reasons, not least of which is its location at the historic juncture of Grodzka Gate. Each

standard room (named 'yellow', 'blue', 'green' or 'red' for its decor) has its own individual character; there's even a waterbed in the red room. The two apartments occupying the top floor are very special; they offer ample space for lounging or working, and views over both the Old Town from the front of the building, and the castle from the back.

**Hotel Campanile**  HOTEL €€
(🖉81 531 8400; www.campanile.com; ul Lubomelska 14; s/d 189/249zł; P✳@🛜) The clean, quiet rooms at this business-oriented chain are on the dull side, but good value for money, with niceties like air-conditioning and a reliable wi-fi connection tossed in at no extra cost. The location, about 1.5km west of the Old Town and a good 15 minute walk away, is a potential drawback. Breakfast costs 35zł. Rates drop on the weekend and big discounts can be found on the hotel website.

**Motel PZM**  HOTEL €€
(🖉81 533 4232; www.hotelpzm.pl in Polish; ul Prusa 8; s/d/tr/apt 135/180/249/350zł; P@) The carpeted corridors and dowdy exteriors of the PZM thankfully don't reflect the clean, bright and vigilantly maintained room interiors. The PZM is an easy walk to the bus station and the Old Town. The motel is located 1km due west of the main bus terminal, following the main highway.

**PTSM Youth Hostel**  HOSTEL €
(🖉81 533 0628; ul Długosza 6; dm/tr 30/40zł) A well-run, all-year hostel 2km west of the Old Town (accessible by trolleybus 150 from the train station, and buses 5, 10, 18 and 57 from the bus terminal). Enter the driveway at ul Długosza 8, walk about 30m back to see a low-slung mint green building to your left.

## 🍴 Eating

For fine dining in the Old Town, see what's cooking around the Rynek. If you're in a more modern mood, take a walk along ul Krakowskie Przedmieście.

TOP CHOICE **Mandragora**  JEWISH €€€
(🖉81 536 2020; www.mandragora.lublin.pl; Rynek 9; mains 35-45zł) There's good kitsch and there's bad kitsch, and at Mandragora, it's all good. Sure they're going for the *Fiddler on the Roof* effect here with the lace tablecloths, knick-knacks, and photos of old Lublin on the walls, but the romantic Rynek locale works wonderfully. The food is a hearty mix of Polish and Jewish, with mains like goose and duck playing a prominent role.

**Kobi**  JAPANESE €€€
(www.kobi-sushi.pl; ul Kościuszki 7; mains 30-50zł)
Just across the street from Oregano, this
slick sushi joint serves a creative mix of big
sushi rolls, including a pleasing mix of non-
traditional fusion rolls that incorporate tofu,
barbecue sauce, orange zest, cooked salmon
and other oddities to excellent effect. Sit upstairs at the bar or at the tables downstairs
in an old cellar that's been tricked out to
look like a club lounge.

**Oregano**  INTERNATIONAL €€
(ul Kościuszki 7; mains 30-45zł) This pleasant,
upmarket restaurant specialises in Mediterranean cuisine, pasta, paella and seafood.
There is a well-organised English menu, and
the chefs aren't scared of spice. The downside is the cooking can be uneven, but when
the chefs are on form, it's very good.

## Drinking

**U Szewca Irish Pub**  PUB
(www.uszewca.pl; Rynek 18; mains 19-42zł; 🛜)
Fun, faux-Irish pub that's right on the Rynek
and popular with local Lubliners and visitors alike. Most people come for the extensive beer list, but there's also a decent list of
pub food like pizzas, salads and snacks, and
Irish-sounding things like beef stew, Angus
steaks, and beefburgers.

**Czarna Owca**  PUB
(www.czarnaowca.lublin.pl; ul Narutowicza 9; mains
19-42zł). The 'Black Sheep' serves up a pleasing mix of good pub food, pizzas, toasts
and pork knuckle to a usually full house of
enthusiastic beer drinkers.

## ☆ Entertainment

**Club Koyot**  CLUB
(www.clubkoyot.com; ul Krakowskie Przedmieście
26; ☺noon-late) This popular club is down a
small courtyard off ul Narutowicza; features
live music some nights.

**Klub Czekolada**  CLUB
(www.klubczekolada.pl; ul Krakowskie Przedmieście
19; ☺noon-late) This is a conventional lounge
and dance club that attracts well-groomed
night owls.

**Filharmonia Lubelska**  CLASSICAL MUSIC
(☎81 531 5112; www.filharmonialubelska.pl in
Polish; ul Skłodowskiej-Curie 5) This is a large
auditorium that stages classical and contemporary music concerts. It's located about
2km west of the Old Town, following ul
Krakowskie Przedmieście.

**Teatr im H Ch Andersena**  PUPPET THEATRE
(☎81 532 1628; www.teatrandersena.pl; ul
Dominikańska 1; tickets around 20zł) Performances are in Polish, but the puppets of Hans
Christian Andersen can be enjoyed in any
language. Check the website for show times.

## ℹ Information

Plenty of *kantors* and ATMs line ul Krakowskie
Przedmieście and adjacent streets.
**Bank Pekao** ul Krakowskie Przedmieście (ul
Krakowskie Przedmieście 64; ☺8am- 6pm
Mon-Fri, 10am-2pm Sat); ul Królewska (ul
Królewska 1).
**LOIT Tourist Information Centre** (☎81 532
4412; www.loitik.eu; ul Jezuicka 1/3; ☺9am-
6pm Mon-Fri, 10am-4pm Sat, 10am-3pm Sun
May-Sep, 10am-5pm Mon-Fri, 10am-3pm Sat
Oct-Apr) Extremely helpful English-speaking
staff, souvenirs for sale and lots of brochures,
including handy maps of the most popular
walking tours in Lublin.
**Main post office** (ul Krakowskie Przedmieście
50; ☺9am-5pm)
**Net Box** (ul Krakowskie Przedmieście 52;
per hr 6zł; ☺9am-9pm Mon-Fri, 10am-9pm
Sat, 2-9pm Sun) Internet access, behind the
post office.
**Post office** (ul Grodzka; ☺9am-4pm)

## ℹ Getting There & Away

Numerous transport links make Lublin a
convenient transport hub.
**BUS** Lublin's seedy main **bus terminal** (www
.pks.lublin.pl) is just north of the Old Town,
across from the castle. Slightly west behind
the main bus terminal on ul Ruska is the well-
organised minibus station, which dispatches
buses all over the region and slightly beyond.

Normal buses go to Warsaw (22zł to 40zł,
3½ hours, every hour) between 3am and 10pm.
Minibuses are faster and often cheaper (30zł,
three hours, every 30 minutes).

Minibuses to Kazimierz Dolny (8zł, one hour,
every 30 minutes, 60km) are more efficient than
normal buses (20zł, 2½ hours, every
30 minutes). Normal buses to Puławy pass
through Kazimierz Dolny. Minibuses also service
Zamość (20zł, two hours, every 30 minutes
or so).

**TRAIN** The main **train station** (ul Gazowa 4) is
around 2km from the centre and linked to the
Old Town by trolleybus 160 and several buses
including 13 and 17.

There are around 10 trains per day to
Warsaw (32zł, 3½ hours) and a couple to
Kraków (77zł, six hours). Buy tickets at the train
station.

# Kazimierz Dolny

POP 3600

For more than a century, the ancient river port of Kazimierz Dolny has been an artist colony and a haven for free thinkers. In more recent times, it's evolved into a popular weekend getaway for Warsaw and Lublin residents.

Once you arrive, you'll see why. Kazimierz Dolny is picturesquely perched along the banks of the Vistula. Its ramshackle Rynek, lined with historical buildings, is charming. The little lanes that radiate from the square are filled with quaint artists' galleries, shops, and, naturally, endless places to grab a beer or ice cream cone.

One caveat: because of its popularity, this is one place you'll need to plan your arrival carefully. Avoid turning up in town on a Friday afternoon, when the traffic jams can stretch back kilometres and Kazimierz Dolny-bound buses are filled to bursting. This is doubly true on holiday weekends. Instead, aim for an early weekday arrival. Museums are closed on Mondays, but on the bright side, you'll have this lovely place all to yourself.

## History

Earliest accounts of settlement in the region refer to a wooden cloister along the Vistula in 1181. The town was formally founded in the 14th century by King Kazimierz III Wielki, who built a castle and gave the town its municipal charter. The town was called Dolny (lower), to distinguish it from the town of Kazimierz, upriver, which is today part of Kraków.

Kazimierz Dolny became a thriving trade centre, with grain, salt, wood and oxen being shipped to Gdańsk and further on for export. The 16th and 17th centuries were particularly prosperous, and a number of splendid mansions and granaries were constructed. By 1630, Kazimierz Dolny's population had risen above 2500.

The high times came to an end with the Swedish wars, various epidemics and the slow displacement of the Vistula bed toward the west, which allowed Puławy to overshadow it in the 19th century as the trade and cultural centre of the region.

At the end of the 19th century attempts were made to revive Kazimierz Dolny as a tourist centre, but the two world wars caused serious damage to the town. WWII was particularly tragic. Before the war, the Jews comprised around 50% of the population; by the end of 1942 Nazi Germany had systematically rounded up and deported the entire community to the death camp at Bełżec (see boxed text, p168).

Since the end of WWII, preservation efforts have gone a long way to restore the historical character of Kazimierz Dolny, and it's probably fair to say the town has never looked better.

## ◉ Sights

Most of the main sights, galleries and attractions are on or near the town's postcard-perfect Rynek. At the centre of the town square is a wooden well (it still works, by the way). Fine buildings line the square on all sides, a testament to the town's former prosperity. From an architectural standpoint, the best are probably the two connecting **Houses of the Przybyła Brothers** (Kamienice Przybyłów; Rynek 12), built in 1615 by brothers Mikołaj and Krzysztof, with rich Renaissance mannerist facades. Decorations depict the brothers' patron saints, St Nicholas (guardian of traders) and St Christopher (guardian of travellers). Also on the Rynek are the baroque-style **Gdańsk House** (Kamienica Gdańska; Rynek 16) from 1795 and several characteristic arcaded houses with wooden-tiled roofs from the 18th and 19th centuries.

**House of the Celej Family**          MUSEUM
(Kamienica Celejowska; www.muzeumnadwislanskie.pl in Polish; ul Senatorska 11; adult/concession 8/5zł; ⊙10am-3pm Mon, 10am-5pm Tue-Thu, Sun, 10am-6pm Fri, Sat) The town's main museum is housed in a glorious 17th-century townhouse (built around 1635) for the Celej Family (hence the name). Though it's billed as a general museum, it's actually an art museum, with several rooms on the upper floor dedicated to the considerable output over the decades of the artists who have called Kazimierz Dolny home. Some of the works are fantastic, some merely interesting, but the collection amply demonstrates the town's role in Poland's artistic history. This is one of the few attractions in town open on Mondays.

**Museum of Goldsmithery**          MUSEUM
(Muzeum Sztuki Złotniczej; www.muzeumnadwislanskie.pl; ul Zamkowa 2; adult/concession 8/5zł; ⊙10am-5pm Tue-Sun May-Sep, 10am-3pm Tue-Sun Oct-Apr) While the admission price may seem steep for the tiny size of the museum,

# Kazimierz Dolny

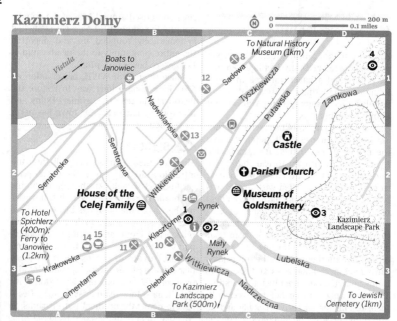

the gold and silverwork collection is captivating. Jewellery lovers will be particularly enraptured with the unique modern designs upstairs.

### Parish Church CHURCH

The Gothic parish church presiding over the Rynek was built in the mid-14th century but remodelled when Renaissance taste swept through Poland. The ornate wooden organ from 1620 sounds as lavish as it looks; organ recitals are often held here. Note the Renaissance stalls in the chancel and the stucco decoration of the nave's vault, a classic example of Lublin-Renaissance style and typical of the region. Be sure to raise an eyebrow at the stag-antler chandelier.

### Castle CASTLE

Above the parish church along ul Zamkowa is what is left of Kazimierz Dolny's castle. Originally built in 1341 as a stronghold against the Tatar incursion, the castle was extended in the 16th century and embellished further during the Renaissance. The castle fell into ruin after its partial destruction by the Swedes; the remaining fragments offer a pleasant view over the town and the Vistula. The **watchtower**, 200m uphill, was built a century before the castle and over

the years served as a fortress, watchtower, lighthouse and prison. Note that as we were researching this guide, the castle was closed for long-term renovation. It was unclear when it would reopen, and admission prices and opening hours were not available.

### Three Crosses' Mountain MOUNTAIN

(Góra Trzech Krzyży) Slightly uphill from the parish church, a path to the right leads to the Three Crosses' Mountain. There is some historical debate about the relationship between the crosses and a cholera epidemic, which decimated the population of the town in 1708. It's doubtful whether human remains found at the site when the crosses were erected in 1852 belong to victims. Some historians believe that the site was referred to as 'cross mountain' long before the epidemic. Whatever the origins of its name, the mountain affords sensational views.

### Natural History Museum MUSEUM

(Muzeum Przyrodnicze; ul Puławska 54; adult/concession 8/5zł; ◷11am-5pm Tue-Sun May-Sep, 10am-3pm Tue-Sun Oct-Apr, closed public holidays & day following) On the opposite side of town on the Puławy road, the natural history museum is housed in a large, finely restored granary from 1591. Though there is little information in English, kids will enjoy

# Kazimierz Dolny

seeing the range of birds, animals and insects (albeit stuffed).

**Jewish Cemetery**  CEMETERY
(Cmentarz Żydowski) Over the centuries, Kazimierz Dolny had a significant Jewish population and in the decades leading up to WWII as much as half the population was Jewish. While few traces of this community can be seen in town, the Jewish Cemetery, outside of the centre, is moving and highly recommended. At the front of the cemetery is a monument to the community assembled in 1984 from several hundred tombstone fragments. The cemetery itself occupies a beautiful forested glen, lending the chipped, forlorn-looking grave markers an even greater poignancy. The cemetery is located about 2km from the Rynek on the road to Opole Lubelskie.

## 🏃 Activities

In 1979, the area around Kazimierz was decreed the **Kazimierz Landscape Park** (Kazimierski Park Krajobrazowy). Many **walking** trails have been traced in its 15,000 hectares, winding through the distinct gorges of the region.

There are three easy short trails known as *szlaki spacerowe* (walking routes) signposted in yellow, green and red, and three significantly longer treks called *szlaki turystyczne* (tourist routes) marked in blue, green and red. Almost all these routes originate in the Rynek. The tourist office sells maps of the park and its trails.

Many of these same trails are also suited to **cycling**. Most area hiking maps also show bike trails. Bicycles can be hired at several places around town, including at **Kawiarnia Rynkowa** (Rynek 7) for 5zł per hour.

## 🎊 Festivals & Events

The highly acclaimed **Festival of Folk Bands & Singers** (www.kazimierz-dolny.pl) takes place in the last week of June. For more than 30 years, performers from the region have gathered at Mały Rynek in traditional garb to perform folk music from eras (and tastes) gone by.

The **Festival of Klezmer Music and Tradition** (Festiwal Muzyki i Tradycji Klezmerskiej; www.klezmerzy.pl) is held annually during the second week of July and is meant to remember the town's important Jewish heritage.

The less raucous **Film & Art Festival** (Festiwal Dwa Brzegi; www.dwabrzegi.pl) in late July and early August lasts around a week and consists of musical concerts, art exhibitions and indoor and outdoor screenings of foreign and national films.

## 🛏 Sleeping

There are options aplenty in Kazimierz, but advanced bookings are essential on weekends in spring and summer. The most common accommodation is rooms in private houses (40zł to 80zł), some of which are run like small hotels. The PTTK office on the Rynek can help with this, or just wander through town looking for '*pokoje*' (rooms) or '*noclegi*' (accommodation) signs. Two good streets to hunt for rooms include ul Krakowska and ul Sadowa.

MAŁOPOLSKA KAZIMIERZ DOLNY

## COCK-A-DOODLE-DOUGH

Spend any time in Kazimierz Dolny and you will soon wonder why its townspeople have such a proclivity for rooster-shaped bread. After seeing enough signs around for *koguty* (roosters), you will find yourself wanting to try some. When you do, you will discover that bread tastes like bread no matter how it's shaped, and promptly return to your initial question: why?

Though its taste may be as bland as, well, bread, the rooster has an interesting history in Kazimierz. In the middle of the last century, a rooster is believed to have averted certain disaster by warning the townsfolk of an approaching devil. This, combined with local bread-weaving traditions, resulted in the rooster's heroic portrayal in dough.

After a golden era in the 1950s, when rooster-shaped bread was baked all over town, tensions suddenly surfaced. In 1996, Piekarnia Sarzyński bakery, convinced that its many awards promoting the product and winning awards for its rooster renditions entitled it to exclusive rights, registered the rooster as its company trademark. The other bakers in town were outraged and demanded that the courts reinstate the rooster's status as the cultural (culinary?) property of the Kazimierz public.

Eight years later, the court released the rooster back into the public domain. But patent or not, no one can bake a bird like Sarzyński's (p175).

### Dom Architekta
HOTEL €€

(☑81 883 5544; sarp@dom-architekta.com.pl; Rynek 20; d from 220zł; P🖥) We like the 'House of Architects'. This refurbished 17th-century townhouse occupies prime real estate on the Rynek, but despite the history and location – and the beautifully tiled and arcaded lobby, the hardwood floors, and the mock Renaissance garden out back – it remains delightfully relaxed and unstuffy. The rooms are on the plain side and not all the furniture fits or works, but it somehow all comes together. Ask for a room with a balcony, overlooking the back garden.

### Hotel Dwa Księżyce
HOTEL €€

(☑81 881 0833; www.dwaksiezyce.com.pl; ul Sadowa 15; s/d/ste 240/280/420zł; P🖥) The 'Two Moons' is a popular place on a quiet street where you can immerse yourself in the pace of Kazimierz Dolny. Some rooms are bigger than others in the same price category (with separate sitting areas), while apartment rooms in the main building have private balconies.

### Willa Agnieszka
PENSION €€

(☑81 882 0411; www.willaagnieszka.pl in Polish; ul Krakowska 41a; d 160-220zł, tr 210-270zł; P) The intimate Willa Agnieszka is crisp and shiny. This place books out quickly on weekends; call ahead. The lower rates apply on weekdays, while the higher rates are charged on Friday and Saturday nights. There's also an onsite restaurant.

### Hotel Spichlerz
HOTEL €€

(☑81 881 0036; ul Krakowska 59/61; s/d 160/270zł; P🖥) Though the Spichlerz is run by the PTTK, it's actually a huge step up from the spartan accommodation this organisation normally offers. The hotel occupies a beautifully converted granary from 1636. The rooms are plain, but clean and comfortable. The location is convenient to the river and the ferry to Janowiec, but it's a 1km trek to the Rynek. Sometimes (depending on weather and mood) campers are allowed to stay in the grounds.

### Youth Hostel pod Wianuszkami
HOSTEL €

(☑81 881 0327; ul Puławska 80; dm/d 40/120zł) Large and relatively pretty for a Polish youth hostel, but 1.5km northeast of town; located in an old granary.

## ✗ Eating

Kazimierz certainly has no shortage of cafes and restaurants; most are around the centre but not all are at the Rynek.

### Knajpa U Fryzjera
JEWISH €€

(www.ufryzjera.pl; ul Witkiewicza 2; mains 18-38zł; ⊙9am-midnight) Knajpa u Fryzjera gets a knock sometimes for serving 'pseudojudaica' food – food that looks Jewish but really isn't. That's not entirely fair. What you get here is filling and well-prepared meals that taste a lot like home cooking. Mains include veal tongue, goose, beef brisket, and stuffed peppers. They open early for breakfast.

### Restauracja Kwadrans
POLISH €€

(http://kwadrans.kazimierzdolny.pl; ul Sadowa 7a; mains 20-40zł; ⊙10am-last customer) In a solid wooden building with a high-ceilinged terrace, Kwadrans demonstrates a love of clocks and heavy food. There are slim pickings for vegetarians but those more inclined towards venison will be very pleased. There are some hearty breakfasts on offer.

### Pod Wietrzną Górą
POLISH €€

(☎081 881 0640; www.wietrznagora.pl in Polish; ul Krakowska 1; mains 15-40zł; ⊗breakfast, lunch & dinner) Right on the junction of ul Krakowska and ul Cmentarna, Pod Wietrzną can be expensive; meal price is calculated by weight and the slices of meat are generous. Otherwise, the quality is excellent, and the adjoining beer garden is a popular place in summer.

### Bar Galeria
POLISH €

(ul Plebanka 7a; mains 10-15zł) This little hole-in-the-wall away from the tourist throng promises *'pierogi domowe'* (homemade dumplings) and that's exactly what you get. They come seven pieces to an order in five varieties, including the usual meat and cabbage, all served by the same woman who cooked them.

### Zielona Tawerna
POLISH €€€

(ul Nadwiślańska 4; mains 30-50zł) This is a rustic old house that's been converted into a stylish – and expensive – restaurant. There are many dining rooms to choose from and smooth tunes add a country-chic vibe. Meals, from the meaty mains to the vegetable platter, are lovingly prepared. Ingeniously, half-sized dishes can be ordered at 70% of the full price.

### Piekarnia Sarzyński
BAKERY €€

(www.sarzynski.com.pl in Polish; ul Nadrzeczna 6; mains from 10zł; ⊗breakfast, lunch & dinner) This bakery institution releases freshly baked aromas and trademark bread-dough roosters into Kazimierz Dolny each day. From breakfast right through to dessert, Sarzyński bakery offers an epic range of pastries, breads, cakes and simple, hearty Polish meals.

## 🍸 Drinking

Most of the drinking in Kazimierz Dolny happens around the Rynek, particularly on the southern side of the square, which is lined with generic cafes that morph magically into bars around the cocktail hour. Two worth seeking out are on picturesque ul Krakowska, not far from the Rynek.

### Galeria Herbaciarnia U Dziwisza
TEAROOM

(http://herbaciarniaudziwisza.pl; ul Krakowska 6; teas from 5zł; ⊗11am-9pm) A civilised taste of an era when tea was a pastime; it boasts more than 100 varieties of tea leaf and an appealing range of calorie-rich accompaniments. Note this place doesn't open until 11am.

### Café Faktoria
CAFE

(www.cafefaktoria.pl; ul Krakowska 6b; coffee 6zł; ⊗10am-9pm) Café Faktoria is a veritable temple to coffee and its loyal companion, chocolate; thrilling concoctions of both are brewing in various pots on the stove.

## ℹ️ Information

Useful amenities are at or near the Rynek. There's a *kantor* in the **post office** (ul Tyszkiewicza 2) and an ATM in the back wall of the same building. There is also an ATM diagonally opposite the PTTK Office (at the Houses of the Przybyła Brothers) and another on the wall of Piekarnia Sarzyński.

**Kawiarnia Rynkowa** (Rynek 7; per hr 5zł or free with coffee purchase; ⊗9am-10pm) Internet access. Also rents bikes for 5zł per hour.

**PTTK office** (☎81 881 0046; pttk_kazimierz _dolny@poczta.onet.pl; Rynek 27; ⊗8am-5.30pm Mon-Fri & 10am-5.30pm Sat May-Sep, 8am-4pm Mon-Fri & 10am-2.30pm Sat Oct-Apr) Can assist with private rooms (40zł to 80zł), maps and brochures.

## ℹ️ Getting There & Around

Kazimierz can be conveniently visited as a stop on your Lublin–Warsaw route, or as a day trip from Lublin. There's no railway in Kazimierz but there's a decent bus service.

Cyclists can acquire a map of bike routes in the area from the PTTK office and some small shops.

**BOAT** In summer, pleasure boats run to Janowiec (one in the style of a Viking ship, minus oars and whips) on the opposite side of the Vistula – ask at the wharf at the end of ul Nadwiślańska.

There's also a **car and passenger ferry** (☎602 858 898; adult/concession/car 5/3/8zł; ⊗8am-8pm Mon-Fri & 8am-9pm Sat & Sun May-Sep), which takes five minutes to cross over to Janowiec and departs from a small landing at the very end of ul Krakowska, 1km west of Hotel Spichlerz.

**BUS** The PKS bus and minibus terminal is about 100m north of the Rynek. There are normal buses to Puławy (4zł, 45 minutes, every half-hour) and urban bus 12 can take you directly to the Puławy train station.

There are around 14 minibuses per day to Lublin (8zł, 1½ hours, roughly every hour) between 6.20am and 5pm; and some to Zamość (12zł, 1¼ hours).

There are five or so daily fast buses to Warsaw (25zł, 3½ hours), or change for the train in Puławy. Check times through the PTTK Office.

# Chełm

POP 67,300

Chełm (pronounced khelm) isn't experiencing the same sort of facelift that other towns in the region are undergoing. While there are a couple of decent places to stay, Chełm is best explored as a day trip from Zamość. Visitors come to experience its proudest asset – the chalk tunnels. The centre is compact and easy to explore on foot.

Chełm is about 70km east of Lublin, 25km from the Ukrainian border. Interestingly, the town sits on an 800m-thick layer of almost pure chalk, a natural phenomenon that has both wreaked havoc and been the source of the town's economic development. It has since been tamed into a tourist attraction. There is also a cathedral sanctuary, which is a pleasant place for a stroll.

Though Chełm's Jewish population was lost during WWII, the Jewish community has left its legacy in various ways. Curiously, the people of Chełm once played the role of the good-natured hick in the rich tradition of Eastern European Jewish humour. Back in the day, many a joke would start out 'there once was a rabbi from Chełm…' that was sure to end in lots of laughter.

## History

Chełm was founded in the 10th century and, like most towns along the eastern border, shifted between the Polish Piast crown and the Kyivan duchy on various occasions. King Kazimierz III Wielki eventually got hold of the area in 1366 and King Władysław Jagiełło established a bishopric here some 50 years later.

Around this time Jews began to settle in the town, and swiftly grew in numbers. By the end of the 18th century, 60% of the town's population was Jewish.

As happened elsewhere in the country, Chełm's golden era ended in the turbulent 17th century. Later came the Polish Partitions, and the town fell under Austrian and later Russian occupation. It wasn't until WWI that Chełm began to recover as part

---

**WORTH A TRIP**

## THE CASTLE AT JANOWIEC

The village of Janowiec (yah-no-vyets) and its **castle** make for a popular day trip from Kazimierz Dolny. You can get there by bus, but a more scenic journey involves taking a ferry and combining that with either a bike ride or a short hike.

The castle was built in the first half of the 16th century by Italian architect Santi Gucci Fiorentino at the request of Mikołaj Firlej. Through many years and owners (including the Tarło, Lubomirski and Osławski families), the castle grew to more than 100 rooms and became one of the most splendid in Poland. The Swedes began the process of ruination and two world wars completed the castle's demise. Under communism, it was the only private castle in Poland; it was finally handed over to the state in 1975 by its last owner, Leon Kozłowski.

The castle is still in ruins, but intense renovations have restored some rooms and revived external painted decorations. Upon entering the castle, note the red-and-white striped walls. This is not the work of a prankster graffiti artist; it is, apparently, how the castle was originally dressed.

The castle houses the **Janowiec Museum** (www.muzeumnadwislanskie.pl in Polish; ul Lubelska 20; adult/concession 12/8zł; ⊙10am-5pm Tue-Sun). Inside the grounds, visitors can climb a few levels to viewing platforms offering a wide perspective of the castle and the surrounding countryside. Various rooms show exhibitions and contemporary art. In the park beside the castle is a **manor house** from the 1760s (another part of the museum), which offers insights into how Polish nobility lived.

It's also worth going down to Janowiec village at the foot of the castle to see its mid-14th-century Gothic **parish church**, extensively rebuilt in Renaissance style in the 1530s. Inside is the tomb of the Firlej family, carved in the workshop of Santi Gucci from 1586 to 1587.

For ferry information on getting to Janowiec from Kazimierz Dolny see p175, and for bike rental information see p173.

From the ferry on the Janowiec side, the most straightforward way to the castle is to walk the flat 2.5km to the Rynek. Return the same way, following the signs to the 'Prom'.

of independent Poland, only to be cast down again by the horrors of WWII two decades later. This included the mass execution of the town's 17,000 Jews by the Germans.

## ◉ Sights

**Chełm Chalk Tunnels**                    UNDERGROUND
(Chełmskie Podziemia Kredowe; ul Lubelska 55a; adult/concession 10/7zł; ◷9am-5pm Mon-Fri, 10am-6pm Sat & Sun) The city's star attraction is an array of chalk passages hewn out by hand about 12m below ground level. The chalk mine began in medieval times. By the 16th century, the chalk extracted here was renowned throughout the country. Over the years, the tunnels expanded in size and complexity, and by 1939 a multilevel labyrinth of corridors had grown to 15km. During WWII some of the shafts served as a shelter for the town's Jews, but these places were eventually discovered and destroyed by the Nazis.

All visits are guided (in Polish only) in groups; tours depart at 11am, 1pm and 4pm daily and take less than an hour. The temperature in the tunnels is 9°C year-round, so come prepared. A friendly and endearingly matter-of-fact ghost haunts the tunnels (in Polish only) and is a quirky highlight of the tour.

**St Mary's Basilica**                    CHURCH
(Bazylika Mariacka; ul Lubelska 2) The hill in the middle of Chełm (once the location of the first settlement and stronghold) is today crowned with the white St Mary's Basilica and a complex of religious buildings that were once a bishop's palace and a monastery. The late-baroque basilica was remodelled in the mid-18th century on the site of the 13th-century church that originally stood here. The sober interior lacks much decoration, except for the silver antependium at the high altar depicting Polish knights paying homage to Our Lady of Chełm. The icon of the Madonna overlooking the altar is a replica; the original was removed by the Russians during WWI and is now in Ukraine. The freestanding 40m-high **belfry**, originally built in the 19th century in the Orthodox style, was later given a partial neoclassical makeover.

**Chełm Museum**                    MUSEUM
(Muzeum Chełmskie; www.mzch.pl in Polish; ul Lubelska 55; adult/concession 6/3zł; ◷10am-4pm Tue-Fri, noon-4pm Sat & Sun) The former monastery houses a museum containing modern Polish painting, natural history displays and

temporary exhibitions. Other outlets of the museum open during the same hours and charge the same admission. The **ethnography and archaeology branch** (ul Lubelska 56a) displays the museum's collection of archaeological finds dating from the Stone Age and stages ethnography and temporary exhibitions. The **Department of History branch** (ul Lubelska 57) houses documents and photographs relating to Chełm's past. The third one, **St Nicholas' Chapel branch** (ul Św Mikołaja 4), showcases religious art from the 18th to the 20th centuries. Concerts of classical music are occasionally held here.

**Former Synagogue**                    SYNAGOGUE
(ul Kopernika 8) Of the scarce Jewish relics to have survived is the easy-to-miss former synagogue, on the corner of ul Kopernika and ul Krzywa. There once was a larger synagogue in addition to this one, but it was destroyed in WWII. This remaining synagogue, built between 1912 and 1914, houses offices and is not open to the public.

## ⊨ Sleeping

Chełm's accommodation options provide a strong argument for not staying overnight. It's better to day-trip from Lublin or Zamość. But if you do decide to stay, here are a couple of decent options.

**Hotel Kamena**                    HOTEL €€
(☑82 565 6401; www.hotelkamena.pl; ul Armii Krajowej 50; s 130-150zł, d 170-190zł, apt 300zł; ᴘ🕏) The Kamena recently got a facelift, and many of the rooms a needed makeover, transforming what was once a drab '60s-style communist pile into an acceptable overnight option. Rooms are divided into economy and lux, with the only difference being the latter have updated baths. Breakfast is not included and costs 15zł.

**PTSM Youth Hostel**                    HOSTEL €
(☑82 564 0022; ul Czarnieckiego 8; dm 40zł) This hostel has seen better days, but is pleasantly situated in a welcome patch of greenery. It's well signed by the green triangle symbol, but not well staffed. Outside 5pm to 10pm, Chełmski Ośrodek Informacji Turystycznej (the Tourist Information Centre) may be able to contact someone to welcome you.

## ✕ Eating & Drinking

TOP CHOICE **Restauracja Gęsia Szyja**          POLISH €€
(ul Lubelska 27; mains 20-30zł) This is the only spot in town for excellent Polish food and

MAŁOPOLSKA CHEŁM

home cooking in the best sense of the term. *Golonka,* or pork knee, is a house favourite, served here with sides of mustard and horseradish and a big plate of pickles. The cellar location is comfortable and romantic, with the jukebox belting out a string of French *chansons* on our visit.

**McKenzee Saloon**                    POLISH €€
(ul Mikołaja Kopernika 8; mains 15-25zł) Popular and fun Western-style saloon, with ample bar food, decent Polish cooking, and lots of beer, all served under the tarp of a wagon.

## ❶ Information

*Kantors* and ATMs are in reasonable supply; try along ul Lwowska and Lubelska. The **main post office** (ul Sienkiewicza 3; ☺10am-5pm Mon-Fri, 9.30am-2pm Sat) is north of Plac Łuczkowskiego. There is a smaller branch on the square itself.

**Bank Pekao** (Al I Armii Wojska Polskiego 41) South of the centre.

**Chełm Tourist Information Centre** (Chełmski Ośrodek Informacji Turystycznej; ☎82 565 3667; www.itchelm.pl; ul Lubelska 63; ☺8am-4pm Mon-Fri, 9am-2pm Sat & Sun) Excellent source of local information, offering a number of very useful brochures.

**Internet Caffe** (☎82 564 0980; ul Szkolna 5a; per hr 4zł; ☺8am-9pm Mon-Fri, 8am-3pm Sat) Centrally located internet.

## ❶ Getting There & Away

**BUS** The bus terminal is on ul Lwowska, 300m south of Plac Łuczkowskiego. There are PKS buses to Lublin (12zł, 1½ hours, every 1½hours), and more frequent private minibuses (13zł, one hour, every hour) departing from just outside the terminal. Half a dozen buses a day run to Zamość (11zł, 1½ hours), plus several private minibuses (12zł, 70 minutes). From Zamość there are regular minibuses to Chełm (12zł, 70 minutes) from 8am onwards. The last minibus back to Zamość leaves Chełm at around 6pm.

There are a couple of daily fast buses to Warsaw (35zł, four hours, 229km).

**TRAIN** The town has two train stations: Chełm Miasto 1km west of the Old Town, and Chełm Główny 2km to the northeast. Most trains stop at both stations, and both are served by the municipal buses. Trains to Lublin (15zł, 1½ hours, 70km) run every hour or two.

## Zamość

POP 66.200

The town of Zamość (*zah*-moshch) is unique in Poland as a nearly perfectly preserved example of Renaissance town planning as

practiced in the 16th century. While it's still a little rough around the edges, the town's pride and joy, its rectilinear Rynek, has been spruced up and pulses with life.

The town owes its origins to a wealthy Polish nobleman, Jan Zamoyski (1542–1605), who came up with the idea to put a town here in the first place, and the Paduan architect he hired to realize his dream, Bernando Morando. Zamość wears its Renaissance roots on its sleeve, embracing not one, but two grandiose nicknames: the 'Pearl of the Renaissance' and the 'Padua of the North'. Take your pick.

An exaggerated sense of civic pride notwithstanding, this Renaissance town has earned its accolades; it has escorted more than 100 architectural monuments through the ages relatively unharmed, it refused to surrender to Swedish invaders in the 17th century, it resisted being renamed 'Himmlerstadt' under the German occupation, and it earned a place on the Unesco World Heritage List in 1992.

### History

Zamość began as something of a Renaissance-era housing estate. When Zamoyski, the country's chancellor and commander-in-chief at the time, decided to build his 'perfect' city, he looked to Italy rather than neighbouring Russia for artistic inspiration. Morando was hired to build Zamoyski's dream, and in doing so created a model city showcasing leading Italian theories of urban design. The project began in 1580, and within 11 years, some 217 houses had been built, with public buildings following soon afterwards.

By the end of the 16th century, the town's beauty – and its location on the crossroads of the Lublin–Lviv and Kraków–Kyiv trading routes – attracted international settlers, including Armenians, Jews, Hungarians, Greeks, Germans, Scots and Italians. Many of the original Jewish settlers here were descendants of Sephardic Jews, fleeing persecution in Spain at the end of the 15th century.

The fortifications built to protect the city and its inhabitants were tested many times. The Cossack raid of 1648 proved little match for the strength of Zamość. Its impregnability was confirmed again in 1656, when Zamość, along with Częstochowa and Gdańsk, boldly withstood the Swedish siege.

Following the Polish partition at the end of the 18th century, Zamość eventually fell under the domain of tsarist Russia. It was during this time that the city took its heaviest aesthetic beating. The Russians adapted many of the town's most splendid buildings for military purposes and almost entirely demolished the fortress walls in 1866, leaving only the ruined fragments that remain today.

Zamość was a key target of Hitler's plan for eastward expansion; German occupiers intended that some 60,000 ethnic Germans would be resettled here before the end of 1943 (former German president Horst Köhler was born near Zamość). Due to fierce resistance by the Polish Underground, the determination of the people of Zamość, and eventually the arrival of the Red Army, the number of Germans to relocate into the town barely reached 10,000. However, the Jewish population was brutally expelled from the town and its surrounds.

After Poland's admission to the EU in 2004, funds poured in and are being invested to enhance Zamość's appeal and ensure its longevity.

## ◎ Sights

### RYNEK WIELKI
The Old Town is 600m long, 400m wide and surrounds a main square of exactly 100m by 100m. Look out for plaques on key buildings around Rynek Wielki, which offer succinct information about the buildings' former use. The Italianate Renaissance Rynek is lined with arcaded burghers' houses (arcades were made compulsory by Jan Zamoyski himself). Each side of the Rynek (bar the northern side dominated by the lofty pink town hall) has eight houses bisected by two main axes of town; one runs west–east from the palace to the bastion, and the other joins the three market squares north to south.

### Town Hall                    HISTORIC BUILDING
The town hall was built between 1639 and 1651, and features were added and extended in the mid-17th century: its curving stairway came in 1768. Zamoyski didn't want the town hall to overshadow the palace or interrupt the view, and so unusually placed it on the northern side of the square rather than the centre. In summer, a bugle is played at noon from the 52m-high clock tower.

### Zamość Museum                    MUSEUM
(Muzeum Zamojskie; http://muzeum-zamojskie .pl in Polish; ul Ormiańska 30, on the Rynek; adult/ concession 8/4zł; ☺9am-5pm Tue-Sun) Originally, all the houses in the square were topped with decorative parapets, but these were removed in the 1820s; only those on the northern side have been (and still are being) restored. As these houses once belonged to Armenian merchants, you will find some distinct motifs on their facades. Two Armenian houses now shelter the Zamość Museum, with intriguing displays like a scale model of the 16th-century town and a letter to Jan Zamoyski from his architect, Bernardo Morando, with a hand-drawn plan of the square and names of the first occupants of each building. Also on display are archaeological finds, such as Gothic treasures found in cemeteries in the Hrubieszów Valley.

### AROUND THE RYNEK
### Cathedral                    CHURCH
The cathedral was built by Morando (from 1587 to 1598) as a votive offering and mausoleum for the Zamoyskis. The exterior of the building changed dramatically in the 19th century, but the interior maintained many original features. Note the authentic Lublin Renaissance–style vault, the stone and stuccowork, and the unusual arcaded organ loft. In the high altar is the rococo silver tabernacle of 1745. Jan Zamoyski's tomb is under the black marble in the chapel at the head of the right-hand aisle. The stairs next to the chapel lead to the family crypt. Note that as this book goes to press, the exterior of the Cathedral is covered in scaffolding and may be obscured during your visit. The interior, however, remains open to the public.

### Sacral Museum                    MUSEUM
(Muzeum Sakralne; ul Kolegiacka 2; admission 4zł; ☺10am-4pm Mon-Fri, 10am-1pm Sat & Sun May-Sep, 10am-1pm Sat & Sun only Oct-Apr) Behind the church is the former vicarage from the 1610s with its splendid ornate doorway. The Sacral Museum features a collection of religious art accumulated by the church. During our visit, the museum was closed because of work being done on the exterior of the adjoining Cathedral.

### Bell Tower                    TOWER
(admission 2zł; ☺10am-4pm Mon-Sat May-Sep) Back outside the church, you can climb the freestanding bell tower, though the terrace is not high enough to offer a bird's-eye view of the Old Town. The present tower was built from 1755 to 1775 after the original timber tower went up in flames. It contains

# Zamość

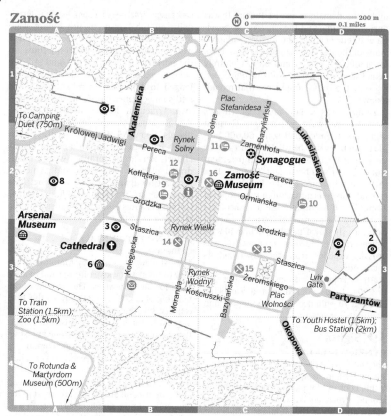

three bells: Wawrzyniec (170kg), Tomasz (1200kg) and the largest, Jan (4300kg).

### Arsenal Museum
MUSEUM

(Muzeum Arsenał; ul Zamkowa 2) This museum displays a modest collection of cannons, swords, muskets and other military hardware. At the time of research, it was closed for repairs and was not expected to reopen until the end of 2012. In the 1830s, the nearby **Zamoyski Palace** (Pałac Zamoyskich) became a military hospital, but now houses government offices and is closed to the public.

### Old Lublin Gate
HISTORIC SITE

(Stara Brama Lubelska) This former gate into the Old Town is a partly ruined brick structure. Just after its construction in 1588 it was walled up in 1604 to commemorate a victorious event. Austrian Archduke Maximilian (a claimant to the Polish throne) was taken prisoner by Jan Zamoyski in

the battle of Byczyna and triumphantly 'escorted' into the town through the gate. He is the last person to have walked through it. To the east of the gate is the **Academy** (Akademia), recognised for making Zamość once a thriving academic centre. The Academy was opened in 1595 with an impassioned appeal by Jan Zamoyski for young Poles to educate themselves. The baroque structure retained little character after tsarist times.

### Hala Targowa
HISTORIC SITE

(Łukasińskiego 2; guided tour 7zł; ⊙tours at 9am, 10am, 11am, noon, 1pm, 2pm, 3pm, 4pm, 5pm May-Sep, noon Oct-Apr) The former Market Hall is built into the surviving fragments of the original town walls. The market itself is not very interesting, merely a string of modern clothing shops and kiosks. The real attraction here is the chance to peek inside the walls and see remnants of the casements

# Zamość

and defence towers. The market is adjacent to the best surviving piece of the wall, **Bastion no 7**. Walking tours of the walls and casements are available daily in summer on the hour from 9am to 5pm, though tours are offered in Polish only. Buy tickets from kiosk number 19.

#### THE JEWISH QUARTER
The area around the Rynek Solny and ul Zamenhofa was once the heart of the Jewish quarter. Jews were granted permission to settle in Zamość in 1588, and by the mid-19th century they accounted for 60% of the town's 4000 people. By the eve of WWII their numbers had grown to 12,000 (45% of the total population). In 1941, they were forcibly removed by the occupying Germans to a ghetto formed to the west of the Old Town, and by the following year most had been murdered in extermination camps.

**Synagogue**                                     SYNAGOGUE
(www.zamosc.fodz.pl; ul Pereca 14; admission 6zł; ⊙10am-6pm Tue-Sun) The city's fascinating synagogue was recently reopened to the public after a long renovation. It was built around 1620 and served as the Jewish community's main house of worship until WWII, when it was shuttered by the Germans. The ceilings and design elements in the small main prayer room have been restored to their former opulence. The highlight of the exhibition is a gripping computer presentation on the history of the town's Jewish community, including its roots in Sephardic Judaism, its diversification over the centuries, and its eventual destruction at the hands of the Germans.

#### BEYOND THE OLD TOWN
**Rotunda & Martyrdom Museum**    MUSEUM
(http://muzeum-zamojskie.pl in Polish; Droga Męczenników Rotundy; adult/concession 6/3zł; ⊙7am-7pm May-Sep, 7am-3pm Mon-Fri Nov-Apr) Roughly 450m southwest of the Old Town is the Rotunda – a ring-shaped fort 54m in diameter surrounding a circular yard. The rotunda was built in the 1820s as part of the defensive infrastructure of the town, but during WWII the German SS converted it into an interrogation centre. Some 8000 people from the Zamość area are believed to have been murdered here and their bodies burnt in the courtyard. The graveyard surrounding the rotunda is the resting place of people who were killed here, including Polish soldiers and members of the Polish underground. Walking through the various cells (particularly by yourself) can be a disturbing and desolate experience.

**Zoo**                                                    ZOO
(Ogród Zoologiczny; ul Szczebrzeska 12; adult/concession 5/3zł; ⊙9am-6pm Apr-Sep, 7am-3pm Oct-Mar) There's a small zoo here that might entertain kids who need a break from all the history.

## ✸ Festivals & Events
The **Zamość Theatre Summer**, organised by **Zamojski Dom Kultury** (www.zdk.zamosc .pl in Polish), takes place from mid-June to mid-August with dramatic open-air performances on the Rynek in front of the town hall.

The town is rich in jazz and blues festivals, including the **International Meeting of Jazz Singers** in August and September (with performances and competitions between jazz singers from the region and far beyond) and **Jazz on the Borderlands** in May.

Every August brings the **Summer Film Festival**, with screenings on the Rynek and at the town's art cinema, **Kino 'Stylowy'** (www.stylowy.net in Polish; ul Odrodzenia 9).

## 🛏 Sleeping

Though accommodation in Zamość caters for most budgets, the range isn't what you would expect from a town of this aesthetic fame. Nevertheless, there are some solid accommodation options available.

### Hotel Senator
HOTEL €€

(☑84 638 9990; www.senatorhotel.pl; ul Rynek Solny 4; s/d/ste 220/250/360zł; P❀@🛜) The Senator offers impressive value and more charm than its chain-hotel competition. Rooms have a tasteful aesthetic and even standard rooms offer impressive space. The onsite restaurant, with its own fireplace, aims for medieval mellow (and looks just a bit like a medieval theatre set). Weekend discounts add to the ambience.

### Hotel Renesans
HOTEL €€

(☑84 677 5930; www.hotelrenesans.pl in Polish; ul Grecka 6; s/d/apt 160/200/230zł; P❀@🛜) Okay, Jan Zamoyski would not be a fan of the scruffy '60s exterior, but the rooms themselves have had a major makeover, complete with big comfy beds, thick carpets, and large, stylish baths. In short, it's excellent value for money, and just a block from the Rynek. Skip the restaurant, though, there's better food to be found elsewhere.

### Hotel Arkadia
HOTEL €

(☑84 638 6507; Rynek Wielki 9; s/d/apt 140/150/200zł; P) With super prices and a superlative location on the Rynek, the Arkadia fills up fast. The scruffiness of this tiny seven-room establishment only lends it charm – and keeps the prices reasonable. The apartment features a view out over the square.

### Orbis Hotel Zamojski
HOTEL €€

(☑84 639 2516; zamojski@orbis.pl; ul Kołłątaja 2/4/6; s/d/ste 230/285/400zł; P@🛜) Occupying three interconnected houses, the Orbis is a reliable choice that offers conventional professionalism. Some rooms are bigger than others, some have more reliable internet access, and some offer better views. The downfall of the Orbis is that the old-world charm of the hotel's exterior has not been matched with modernised interiors. There is an onsite fitness club.

### Camping Duet
CAMPGROUND €

(☑84 639 2499; www.duet.virgo.com.pl in Polish; ul Królowej Jadwigi 14; s/d/tr/q 75/90/130/160zł; P🛏) This conveniently located camping ground, about 1.5km west of the Old Town, has bungalows for up to six people, tennis courts, a restaurant, a sauna and a Jacuzzi. In summer it can be crowded with families.

### Youth Hostel
HOSTEL €

(☑84 638 9500; ul Zamoyskiego 4; dm 25zł; ⊙Jul & Aug) Simple but functional; in a school about 20 minutes' walk from the bus terminal and 1.5km east of the Old Town. It's not easy to find. Walk along Zamoyskiego and turn right just before a pedestrian overpass.

## 🍴 Eating & Drinking

For drinking in summer, a table on the Rynek is the place to be from early afternoon until the wee hours of the morning.

### 🔺TOP CHOICE Corner Pub
POLISH €€

(www.cnr.boo.pl; ul Żeromskiego 6; mains 22-50zł; 🛜) This cosy Irish pub is the place to head in the evening for excellent regional Polish cooking, plus treats like Irish sausages and fish and chips. After dinner, walk downstairs for some live music in the cellar club. There are a few garden tables in summer.

### Restauracja Muzealna
POLISH €€

(www.muzealna.com.pl; ul Ormiańska 30; mains 20-50zł) This is a cut above the typical Rynek offerings in terms of style and presentation, lending the impression they take their food seriously here, and they do. There's an elegant cellar restaurant, or eat upstairs on the Rynek in summer.

### Bohema
POLISH €€

(www.klubbohema.pl; ul Staszica 29; mains 19-50zł; 🛜) The Rynek is brimming with choice when it comes to pizzas, coffees and square-side dining. Bohema is one of the better options, with good home-cooked Polish food (try the 'mixed pierogi' set, with 12 dumplings, including sauces). Poetry could be written about the unsurpassable hot chocolate with chilli (possibly the best 9zł you'll spend in Poland).

### Bar Asia
POLISH €

(ul Staszica 10; mains from 10zł; ⊙8am-5pm Mon-Fri, 8am-3.30pm Sat) For fast and filling soup/

dumplings/cabbage-style food, head to this old-style, self-serve milk bar.

## ℹ Information

Most banks and internet facilities are located around the Rynek or not far from it.

**Bank Pekao** (ul Grodzka 2) Changes cash and advances on Visa and MasterCard.

**Ela Travel** (☑84 639 3001; elatravel_jw@op.pl; ul Grodzka 18; ☺9am-5pm Mon-Fri, 10am-1pm Sat) Can organise international bus, train and air tickets.

**Usługi Ksero + Internet** (Rynek Wielki 10; per hr 3zł; ☺9am-5pm Mon-Fri, 10am-2pm Sat) Internet access.

**Zamość Tourist Information Centre** (Zamojski Ośrodek Informacji Turystycznej; ☑84 639 2292; Rynek Wielki 13; ☺8am-6pm Mon-Fri, 10am-4pm Sat, 10am-3pm Sun May-Sep, 8am-4pm Mon-Fri Oct-Apr) Helpful tourist service in the town hall with maps, brochures and souvenirs. Staff can arrange walking tours of the town in various languages. There is also a computer for respectful gratis internet use and a handy timetable of travel options in and out of town on the wall.

## ℹ Getting There & Away

BUS The **bus terminal** (☑84 638 4986; ul Hrubieszowska 11) is 2km east of the Old Town but well serviced by city bus 3. The tourist information office maintains up-to-date timetables for buses, minibuses, and trains to popular destinations.

Private minibuses are often faster and cheaper than larger buses. They leave from a stand right opposite the main bus terminal; check the timetable for details of departures.

Buses to Lublin (12zł, two hours, every half-hour) run roughly between 5am and 6pm. There are also plenty of minibuses (11zł, two hours, every half-hour). There is an afternoon bus to Puławy (18zł, 2½ hours, 1.15pm) via Lublin. There is sporadic daily service to Kraków (35zł, four to five hours), and there are four buses daily to Warsaw (32zł, five hours).

There are frequent normal buses and minibuses to Zwierzyniec (5zł, 40 minutes, 32km), the entry point for Roztocze National Park.

Several minibuses daily travel to Bełżec, dropping you not far from the former Nazi extermination camp and museum. Contact the tourist information office or call the Tomaszów minibus line (☑84 664 1539).

TRAIN The **train station** (ul Szczebrzeska 11) is about 1km southwest of the Old Town; walk or take the city bus. Note that train service to Zamość has been scaled back in recent years and service to Lublin has been discontinued

altogether. Trains are still useful for Warsaw. Several trains make the trip daily, via Puławy, in around 5 hours (48zł, 293km).

# Zwierzyniec & Roztocze National Park

POP 3800

The town of Zwierzyniec (zvyeh-*zhi*-nyets), 32km southwest of Zamość, is another Jan Zamoyski creation, but on a more modest scale than Zamość. In the 16th century, the Polish nobleman built a summer palace and residential complex here and tossed in an enormous game reserve for his recreational enjoyment. While the family's once-grand summer palace was pulled down in the 19th century (all that's left is a tiny chapel), the game reserve survives to this day and forms the core of the modern-day Roztocze National Park.

Zwierzyniec itself is no great shakes. It's little more than a forlorn-looking square surrounded by a few shops selling cheap clothing. Still, it's the gateway to an enchanting national park, with hundreds of kilometres of unspoiled hiking and biking trails.

## ⊙ Sights & Activities

**Roztocze National Park**                                                    PARK
(Roztoczański Park Narodowy; www.roztoczanskipn.pl; ul Plażowa 2, Zwierzyniec) The park covers an area of 79 sq km to the south and east of Zwierzyniec. It was a nature reserve for more than 350 years as part of the Zamoyski family estate and today it's home to a diverse range of flora and fauna. Elk, wolves and lynxes have been known to visit from time to time.

In 1982 the Polish pony – descendent of a wild horse known as tarpan and now the symbol of the park – was reintroduced to the park. There is a Polish pony refuge near Echo Ponds. The world's last specimens of tarpan were kept here in the 19th century until they were given away when the estate fell into disarray under tsarist rule.

The normal starting point for walks is the Education and Museum Centre (p184), where you can buy booklets and park maps. A particularly nice Roztocze sampler is the **Bukowa Mount didactic path** (2.6km) going south from the museum to the top of Bukowa Góra (Beech Mountain, 306m) along a former palace park lane. If you want to visit the pony reserve near Echo Ponds, there is a short route (1.2km) from the museum.

Longer walks generally weave from Zwierzyniec through forest terrain to neighbouring villages (such as Florianka, also known for its tarpan breeding). Intersecting paths enable you to return by a different route or cut to another path. Note that some of the longer walks require a 4zł admission ticket, which you can buy at the parking lot in front of the Education Museum Centre.

Cycling routes of different durations and difficulty are also marked on tourist maps available from the centre. You can rent bikes at **Rowery na Roztoczu** (☏601 507 306; www.przemko.info/rowery in Polish; ul 1-go Maja 22) not far from the Education and Museum Centre. Rates are 10zł per hour; 25zł for the day.

**Education and Museum Centre**    MUSEUM
(Ośrodek Edukacyjno-Muzealny; ☏84 687 2066; www.roztoczanskipn.pl; ul Plażowa 3; adult/concession 10/6zł; ☉9am-5pm Tue-Sun May-Oct, 9am-4pm Tue-Sun Nov-Apr) Located near the park entrance. It has interesting displays of area flora and fauna, but the primary interest here is the small bookstore, where you can pick up maps and other hiking info. There's a small car park onsite and many of the best hikes set out from around here.

**Chapel on the Water**    CHAPEL
(Kaplica na Wodzie) Just down the road from the Educational and Museum Centre is this small chapel, the only significant structure remaining from the Zamoyski's residential complex. The small baroque church sits on one of four tiny islets on the small lake of Staw Kościelny (Church Pond), which was allegedly dug by Turkish and Tatar prisoners in the 1740s.

**Zwierzyniec Brewery**    BREWERY
Across the road from the chapel, the local brewery is still going strong after more than 200 years. The brewery is not open to visitors, but there's a small bar at the entrance.

## 🛏 Sleeping & Eating

The tourist office can help find agroturist accommodation, well-equipped holiday centres and local rooms in and around town. In most, longer stays bring the rates down.

**Relaks**    PENSION €
(☏607 938 211; www.noclegizwierzyniec.pl; ul 2 Lutego 12a; s/d 60/100zł; P ☎) This well-mannered stucco chalet is a little hard to find, hidden along a small street behind the main square, but it's worth the effort. Inside you'll find eight spotless rooms done out in cheerful colours. Some have full baths, others only showers. One has a balcony and several overlook a grilling gazebo in the back garden.

**Karczma Młyn**    PENSION €
(☏84 687 2527; www.karczma-mlyn.pl in Polish; ul Wachniewskiej 1A; s/d 80/100zł; P) This cheery inn with a postcard-perfect view of the Chapel on the Water offers clean accommodation at reasonable prices, as well as the best meals in town. Eat in the back garden.

**Camping Echo**    CAMPGROUND €
(☏84 687 2314; ul Biłgorajska 3; camp sites per person 12zł, cabins with bathrooms per person 30zł, cabins with basin per person 25zł, cars 2zł; ☉May-Sep; P). This is a pleasant family-oriented camping ground not far from the bus station. Offers spots to pitch a tent as well as comfy bungalows for three to six people.

## ❶ Information

There is a small **tourist office** (☏84 687 2660; zokir@o2.pl; ul Słowackiego 2; ☉8am-4pm) outside the centre of town that sells hiking maps and advises on places to stay. Alternatively, ask at the tourist office in Zamość (p183). To find tourist information, go right instead of left from the bus station to a busy roundabout and then make a left. The tiny office is just behind a small shopping centre. Buses to Zamość (4zł, 40 minutes, 32km) pass every half-hour.

## ❶ Getting There & Away

The bus stop is on ul Zamojska, just north of the lake (if you're facing the road with your back to the bus station, follow the road left to the lake).

# Carpathian Mountains

POP 3.8 MILLION

## Best Places to Eat

» Stare Sioło (p211)

» Bar Rubin (p203)

» Café Helenka (p224)

## Best Places to Stay

» Hotel Zamkowy (p203)

» Grand Hotel (p198)

» Małopolanka (p220)

» Zespół Zamkowy (p226)

## Why Go?

When thinking about Poland, mountains are not usually the first thing to spring to mind. In fact, the country's southern border is defined by the beautiful and dramatic Carpathian (Karpaty) chain, the highest mountain range in Central Europe.

The wooded hills and peaks here are a beacon for hikers, cyclists and skiers in season. And because of the region's remoteness, this 'forgotten corner' has been able to preserve its traditional folkways better than other parts of the country.

The centre of the action is the resort of Zakopane in the heart of the Tatra Mountains (Tatry), the highest section of the Polish Carpathians, but the prettiest hills are arguably in the Pieniny or Bieszczady ranges. Elsewhere, a mosaic of modest towns provide jumping-off points for a half dozen national parks. Historic regional towns such as Przemyśl, Tarnów and Sanok offer insights into the past.

## When to Go
### Zakopane

**Jan–Mar**
Zakopane is *the* place for skiing and snowboarding in a season that lasts through March.

**Apr–Jun**
Welcome the arrival of spring in the Bieszczady, Poland's remotest mountain range.

**Jul–Aug**
There's no better place on a sunny summer afternoon than on a raft on the Dunajec River.

# Carpathian Mountains Highlights

1 Viewing the natural beauty of the Bieszczady up close in **Ustrzyki Górne** (p209)

2 Enjoying a papal cream cake in **Wadowice** (p193), the happy town where Pope John Paul II was born.

3 Marvelling at the colours and patterns of the painted houses of **Zalipie** (p196)

4 Following the **Icon Trail** (p205) from Sanok and visiting the region's charming timber churches

5 Hiking or skiing in the Tatra Mountains above the fashionable resort of **Zakopane** (p187)

6 Relaxing on a raft down the **Dunajec Gorge** (p224)

7 Taking to the waters and having a treatment in peaceful **Krynica** (p219)

8 Hitting the town after dark in lively, studenty **Rzeszów** (p197)

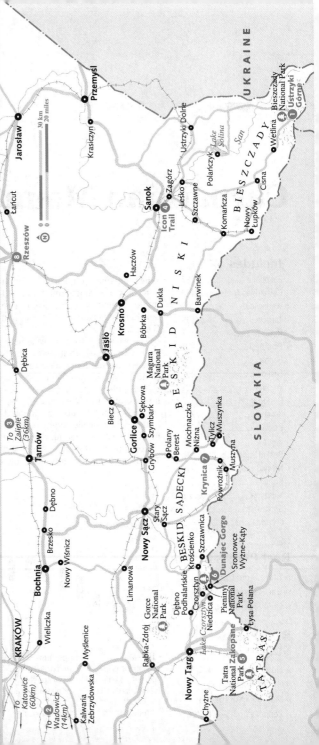

# TATRAS

The Tatras form the highest range of the Carpathians and the only alpine type, with towering peaks and steep rocky sides dropping hundreds of metres to icy lakes. There are no glaciers in the Tatras, but patches of snow remain all year. Winters are long, summers short and the weather unpredictable.

Not surprisingly, this is prime hiking terrain in summer and skiing in winter, with most of the action centred around Poland's leading mountain resort, Zakopane. The region is easily accessible via a two-hour bus ride from Kraków.

The Tatra range, roughly 900 sq km, stretches for 60km across the Polish–Slovakian border and is 15km at its widest point. About a quarter of it is Polish territory and forms the Tatra National Park (Tatrzański Park Narodowy), encompassing 211 sq km and headquartered in Zakopane. The Polish Tatras boast two dozen peaks exceeding 2000m, the highest of which is Mt Rysy (2499m).

The vegetation changes with the altitude, from mixed forest in the lower parts (below 1200m) to spruce woods higher up (to 1500m), then to dwarf mountain shrubs (to 1800m) and highland pastures (to 2300m).

At the northern foot of the Tatras lies the Podhale region, which extends from Zakopane to the city of Nowy Targ. Dotted with small villages populated by *górale* (literally 'highlanders'), the Podhale is one of the few Polish regions where old folk traditions still form a part of everyday life.

## Zakopane

POP 27,300

Nestled in the foothills of the Tatras, Zakopane is Poland's most fashionable mountain resort. It's an excellent base for hiking in summer and skiing in winter, though in high season it can get positively overrun with visitors.

In addition to outdoor pursuits, Zakopane is known throughout Poland for the size and beauty of its wooden mountain villas, dating from the late 19th and early 20th centuries. Some of these now house museums, while others have been converted into hotels or pensions, or remain in private hands. Some remain inexplicably abandoned, apparently awaiting suitors with deep enough pockets to restore them to their original splendour.

The father of this craze for all things wooden was the architect Stanisław Witkiewicz (1851–1915), and the first of several magnificent wooden villas that he built in the area, the Willa Koliba, now houses the Museum of Zakopane Style.

Witkiewicz's creations in the early decades of the 20th century helped to establish Zakopane as a haven for painters, poets, writers and composers. Two of the town's most famous former residents include Witkiewicz's son, the writer and painter Stanisław Ignacy Witkiewicz, better known as Witkacy, and the composer Karol Szymanowski.

Zakopane grew at a faster pace in the interwar period, and shortly before the outbreak of WWII two of the town's leading attractions – the cableway and funicular railway – were built. Development continued after the war but it's still reasonably small. Overall, Zakopane feels more like an overgrown village than a town, its mainly villa-type houses set informally in their own gardens.

## ☉ Sights

### IN THE CENTRE
Most of Zakopane's traditional sights draw on the town's unique wooden architecture and its cultural history as an artistic haven in the late 19th and early 20th centuries.

TOP CHOICE **Museum of Zakopane Style** MUSEUM (Muzeum Stylu Zakopiańskiego; www.muzeum tatrzanskie.pl; ul Kościeliska 18; adult/concession 7/5.50zł; ⊙9am-5pm Wed-Sat, to 3pm Sun) Not far from the northern (lower) end of ul Krupówki stands the remarkable Willa Koliba, the first of several wooden villas designed by Witkiewicz in his 'Zakopane Style'. The museum is a must for architecture fans, particularly admirers of the Arts and Crafts movement, which swept through the US and Britain at the turn of the 20th century. Note the fine details, such as the furnishings and textiles, which were all designed for the house.

**Museum of Zakopane Style – Inspirations** MUSEUM (Muzeum Stylu Zakopiańskiego – Inspiracje; www.muzeumtatrzanskie.pl; ul Droga do Rojów 6; adult/concession 6/4.50zł; ⊙9am-5pm Wed-Sat, to 3pm Sun) This companion museum to the main Zakopane Style museum is more of an ethnographic exhibition, highlighting the highlander folk roots and styles that inspired Witkiewicz in the first place.

## HIKING IN THE TATRA MOUNTAINS

With a huge variety of trails, totalling around 300km, the Tatras are ideal for walking. No other area of Poland is so densely criss-crossed with hiking paths, and nowhere else will you find such a diversity of landscapes.

Although marked trails go all across the region, the most popular area for hiking is **Tatra National Park**, which begins just south of Zakopane. Geographically, the Tatras are divided into three parts: the West Tatras (Tatry Zachodnie), the High Tatras (Tatry Wysokie) to the east, and the adjoining Belianse Tatras (Tatry Bielskie). All the areas are attractive, though they offer quite different scenery. In general the West Tatras are lower and gentler, easier to walk and safer. The High Tatras and Belianske Tatras are completely different: a land of bare granite peaks with alpine lakes at their bases. Hikers will face more challenges here, but will also enjoy much more dramatic scenery.

If you just want to go for a short walk, there are several picturesque and densely forested valleys south of Zakopane, of which **Dolina Strążyska** is arguably the most attractive. It's long been a popular walking and picnic area for locals, and for reasonably fit walkers it should take no longer than 50 minutes to walk all of it by the red trail up to Polana Strążyska. From there you can come back the same way or transfer by the black trail to either of the neighbouring valleys, the **Dolina Białego** to the east being the usual way. It takes around an hour to get to this charming valley and another hour to go all the way down to Zakopane.

The most popular mountaintop climbed in the Tatras is **Mt Giewont** (1894m), the very symbol of Zakopane. You can reach it via the red trail in about 3½ hours from Zakopane. A reasonable level of fitness is required to attempt this climb.

Before you do any walking or climbing, you should get hold of the 1:25,000-scale *Tatrzański Park Narodowy* map (15zł), published by Sygnatura. It shows all the trails in the area, complete with walking times both uphill and downhill. Another option is the 1:20,000-scale *Tatry Polskie* (Polish Tatras) map (10zł), which is divided into two sheets.

Camping is not allowed in the park, but there are several basic PTTK mountain hostels dotted around the slopes and mountaintops. The tourist office in Zakopane has a list and details.

**Old Church and Cemetery** CHURCH
(Stary Kościół; ul Kościeliska) Just a couple of blocks from the Museum of Zakopane Style, along ul Kościeliska, is this small wooden church and adjoining cemetery dating from the mid-19th century. The Old Church was christened in 1851 and has charming carved wooden decorations and pews, and Stations of the Cross painted on glass on the windows. The **stone chapel** standing beside the Old Church is about 30 years older and is in fact the oldest extant structure in Zakopane. Just behind it is the **old cemetery**, with a number of amazing wooden tombs, some dating back to the mid-19th century and resembling giant chess pieces. Witkiewicz himself is buried here beneath a modest wooden grave marker.

**Tatra Museum** MUSEUM
(Muzeum Tatrzańskie; www.muzeumtatrzanskie.pl; ul Krupówki 10; adult/concession 7/5.50zł, free Sun; ⊙9am-5pm Wed-Sat, to 3pm Sun, to 5pm Tue May-Sep) This is the main branch of the Tatra Museum, with sections on regional and natural history, ethnography and geology. It's a good introduction to the region. Though the address is listed as ul Krupówki, it's set back away from the main street.

**Karol Szymanowski Museum** MUSEUM
(Museum Karola Szymanowskiego; www.muzeum.krakow.pl; ul Kasprusie 19; adult/concession 6/3zł, free Sun; ⊙10am-4pm Tue-Sun) About 500m to the southeast of the Museum of Zakopane Style is **Willa Atma**, the home of Polish composer Karol Szymanowski from 1930 to 1935. Though he's practically unknown outside of Poland, Szymanowski is considered the country's second-greatest composer after Chopin.

### OUTSIDE THE CENTRE

TOP CHOICE ⟩ **Morskie Oko** MOUNTAIN LAKE
The emerald-green lake Morskie Oko (Eye of the Sea), about 12km southeast of Zakopane, is a popular day trip. Buses and minibuses regularly depart from ul Kościuszki, across

from the main bus station, for Polana Palenica (30 minutes), from where a 9km-long road continues uphill to the lake. Cars, bikes and buses are not allowed up this road, so you'll have to walk (allow about two hours each way). Alternatively, take a horse-drawn carriage (about 40zł per person) to within 2km of the lake. The last minibus to Zakopane returns between 5pm and 6pm. Most travel agencies organise day trips here (from 150zł).

### Wooden Architecture ARCHITECTURE

About 2km south of the centre are two more prime examples of the Zakopane Style. The **Villa Pod Jedlami** was built in 1897 for the Pawlikowski family, though the interior these days is closed to the public. **Jaszczurówka Chapel** (Kaplica w Jaszczurówka) is considered Witkiewicz's greatest achievement. It was built in 1907 and the folk interior alone is worth the trip.

## 🏃 Activities

In addition to numerous **hiking** possibilities (p188), there are lots of other things to do.

### Skiing

Zakopane is Poland's capital of winter sports. The town's environs have a number of ski areas, ranging from flat surfaces for cross-country touring to steep slopes – suitable for everyone from beginners to advanced – served by 50 ski lifts and tows in all.

**Mt Kasprowy Wierch** (1985m) offers some of the most challenging ski slopes in the area, as well as the best conditions, with the spring skiing season sometimes extending as late as early May. You can get to the top in 20 minutes by **cable car** (return adult/concession 37/32zł; ☺7am-9pm Jul-Aug, to 5pm Mar-Jun & Sep-Oct, 8am-4pm Nov-Feb), then stay in the mountains and use the two chairlifts, in the Goryczkowa and Gąsienicowa Valleys, on both sides of Mt Kasprowy. The view from the top is spectacular (clouds permitting) and you can stand with one foot in Poland and the other in Slovakia.

**Mt Gubałówka** is another popular skiing area and it, too, offers some pistes and good conditions. It's easily accessible from central Zakopane by **funicular** (up & back adult/concession 16/13zł, one way adult/concession 11/9zł; ☺8am-10pm Jul & Aug, 8.30am-7.30pm Sep, 8.30am-6pm Apr, May & Oct-Dec, 7.30am-10pm Jan-Mar, 9am-8pm Jun), covering the 1298m-long route in 3½ minutes and climbing 300m from the lower station just north of ul Krupówki.

Some 2km to the west is **Mt Butorowski Wierch**, with its 1.6km-long chairlift making it yet another good skiing area.

One more major ski area is at the slopes of **Mt Nosal**, on the southeastern outskirts of Zakopane. Facilities include a chairlift and a dozen T-bars.

Ski-equipment hire is available from outlets throughout Zakopane. Try **Sukces Ski Rental** (☑18 200 0231; www.ski-sukces.zakopane .pl; ul Nowotarska 39). Complete kits for skiing/snowboarding average 40/50zł a day.

### Other Activities

A half-hour whirl around Zakopane in a **horse-drawn carriage** (or, in winter, a sleigh) seating four people will set you back around 60zł. They gather near Tatry Sport on ul Piłsudskiego.

An excellent place to cool off on a warm summer's day is **Aqua Park** (www.aquapark .zakopane.pl; ul Jagiellońska 31; per hr/day adult 18/60zł, child 11/40zł; ☺8am-10pm), with indoor and outdoor pools, slides, various saunas and – incongruously – bowling.

In summer, Mt Nosal is a popular spot for **hang-gliding** and **paragliding**. For information, stop by one of the tourist offices in town.

## ⭐ Festivals & Events

Held in August, the **International Festival of Mountain Folklore** (Międzynarodowy Festiwal Folkloru Ziem Górskich; www.zakopane .pl) is the town's leading cultural event. In June and July, a series of **piano concerts** (usually 35zł) presenting the music of Karol Szymanowski and other composers is held in the Villa Atma.

## 🛏 Sleeping

Zakopane has no shortage of places to stay and, except for occasional peaks, finding a bed is no problem. Even if the hotels and hostels are full, there will always be private rooms around, which provide some of the most reasonable and best-value accommodation in town. Check at the tourist office

### MOVING ON?

For tips, recommendations and reviews about Slovakia, head to shop.lonely planet.com to purchase a downloadable PDF of the Slovakia chapter from Lonely Planet's *Central Europe* guide.

# Zakopane

for details (rooms should cost around 40zł to 50zł per person) or look for signs reading 'pokoje', 'noclegi' or 'zimmer frei' outside private homes.

As with all seasonal resorts, accommodation prices in Zakopane fluctuate between the high and low seasons, peaking in late December, January and February, and then again in July and August. Prices given here are for the high season.

**Grand Hotel Stamary** HOTEL €€€
(☎18 202 4510; www.stamary.pl; ul Kościuszki 19; s/d/ste 340/440/690zł; P✲@🛜❄) As posh a hotel as you'll find in the Tatras, this massive 54-room gingerbread house was the bee's knees when it opened in 1905 and is just that now after a total makeover. The emphasis here is on style and health; the spa/wellness centre is among the most attractive and best equipped we've seen in Poland.

**Czarny Potok** HOTEL €€
(☎18 202 0255; www.czarnypotok.pl; ul Tetmajera 20; s/d from 220/320zł; P@🛜❄) The 'Black Stream', set upon a pretty brook amid lovely gardens, is a 36-room pension-like hostelry along a quiet street just south of the pedestrian mall. It has a great fitness centre with two saunas.

**Flamingo Hostel** HOSTEL €
(☎18 200 0222; www.zakopane.flamingo-hostel .com; ul Krupówki 22; dm 30-55zł, d 140-150zł; @🛜) This private, well-run hostel is right on the main drag, with a balcony view over the busiest stretch of ul Krupówki. There are dorm beds in 12-, eight- and four-bed rooms, as well as a few private doubles on offer. There's a big common room and a well-stocked kitchen, as well as niceties such as free wi-fi, computers to check email and free breakfast.

**Hotel Litwor** HOTEL €€€
(☎18 202 4200; www.litwor.pl; ul Krupówki 40; s/d 450/600, ste 625-840zł; P@🛜❄) This is a

# Zakopane

## ◎ Top Sights

## ◎ Sights

## ◎ Activities, Courses & Tours

## ◎ Sleeping

## ◎ Eating

## ◎ Drinking

sumptuous four-star place, with large, restful rooms and all the usual top-end facilities, including a gym and sauna. It has an excellent restaurant serving traditional Polish dishes.

### Goodbye Lenin                          HOSTEL €
(☑18 200 1330; http://zakopane.goodbyelenin .pl; ul Chłabówska 44; dm 35-50zł, d/tr 130/150zł; Ⓟ@⧉) A branch of the popular Kraków hostel, this five-room place with 30 beds in a century-old farmhouse is as chilled a place as you'll find. The only downside, or maybe it's an upside if you've come to Zakopane to get away from things, is location. The hostel is about 2.5km southeast of the centre. With prior arrangement, the hostel will pick you up from the bus and train stations or you can take minibus 73 and get off at the 'Jaszczurówka' stop.

### Szarotka Hostel                        HOSTEL €
(☑18 201 3618; www.schroniskomlodziezowe .zakopane.org.pl; ul Nowotarska 45g; dm/d 35/100zł) This cheerful and homely place with 62 beds gets packed in the high season and is on a busy road. But it's friendly and has a kitchen and washing machine on site.

### Camping Nr 97 Pod
### Krokwią                          CAMPING GROUND €
(☑18 201 2256; www.podkrokwia.pl in Polish; ul Żeromskiego 34; camping per person/tent 15/15zł, beds in bungalows 60zł; Ⓟ) The camping ground has large heated bungalows, each containing several double and triple rooms. They are often full in the July–August period. To get here from the bus or train stations, take any bus heading south and get off at the roundabout.

## ✕ Eating

Ul Krupówki is lined end to end with faux highlander-style rustic taverns all featuring pretty much the same *jadło karpackie* (Carpathian cuisine), accompanied by rather hokey mountain music performed by a *kapela góralska* (folk-music ensemble). Still, there are a few diamonds in the rough.

### Pstrąg Górski                          FISH €€
(Krupówki 6a; mains 20-30zł; ☺9am-10pm) This fish restaurant, done up in traditional style and overlooking a narrow stream, serves some of the freshest trout, salmon and sea fish in town. Trout is priced at around 5zł per 100g (whole fish), bringing the price of a standard fish dinner to around 20zł, not including sides.

### Karczma Zbójecka                        POLISH €€
(ul Krupówki 28; mains 15-40zł) An attractive basement eatery, this place offers regional dishes and meats grilled on a huge woodburning rotisserie. There's always a buzzy atmosphere and decent local folk music on some evenings.

### Pierożek Bar Mleczny                    POLISH €
(ul Weteranów Wojny 2; mains 5-9zł; ☺9am-8pm) Set in a little wood cabin with folk decor just off the main pedestrian street, this tiny place serves the best *pierogi* (dumplings) in Zakopane.

### Karczma Czarny Staw                     POLISH €€
(ul Krupówki 2; mains 20-35zł) Though under the same management as Zbójecka, the 'Black Pond' is more upmarket. It offers a tasty range of Polish dishes, including fish,

CARPATHIAN MOUNTAINS ZAKOPANE

**WORTH A TRIP**

## POLAND'S 'JERUSALEM': KALWARIA ZEBRZYDOWSKA

Fourteen kilometres east of Wadowice (35km southwest of Kraków) is Kalwaria Zebrzydowska (kahl-vah-ryah zeb-zhi-dof-skah), Poland's second most important pilgrimage site after Jasna Góra in Częstochowa.

The town owes its existence and fame to the squire of Kraków, Mikołaj Zebrzydowski, who commissioned the church and monastery for the Bernardine order in 1600. Having noticed a resemblance in the area to the topography of Jerusalem, he set about creating a place of worship similar to the Via Dolorosa in the Holy City. By 1617, 24 chapels were built over the surrounding hills, some of which looked as though they'd been brought directly from the mother city. As the place attracted growing numbers of pilgrims, more chapels were erected, eventually totalling 42. In 1999 Kalwaria Zebrzydowska was added to Unesco's list of World Heritage sites.

The original hilltop church north of the centre was gradually enlarged and today is the massive **Basilica of Our Lady of the Angels** (Bazylika Matki Bożej Anielskiej). The holiest image in the church is the icon of Mary in the **Zebrzydowska Chapel** (Kaplica Zebrzydowska) to the left of the high altar. Tradition has it that the eyes shed tears of blood in 1641, and from that time miracles occurred. Pilgrims come to Kalwaria year-round but especially on Marian feast days, when processions along the **Calvary Trails** (Dróżki Kalwaryjskie) linking the chapels take place. The basilica is flanked to the north by the huge **Bernardine Monastery** (Klasztor Bernadynów; ☺7am-7pm), which contains impressive 16th- and 17th-century paintings in its cloister.

Kalwaria is also known for its **Passion plays**, a blend of religious ceremony and popular theatre re-enacting the final days of Christ's life and held here since the 17th century. They are performed by locals, including Bernardine monks, during a two-day procession starting in the early afternoon of Maundy (Holy) Thursday during Holy Week of Easter.

much of it cooked before your very eyes on the central grill. There's a good salad bar, with home-preserved vegetables and mushrooms.

**Karczma Zapiecek**　　　　POLISH €€
(ul Krupówki 43; mains 15-25zł) One of the better choices among a group of very similar highlander-style restaurants along ul Krupówki, with great food, an old stove and a terrace.

 **Drinking & Entertainment**

**Paparazzi**　　　　COCKTAIL BAR
(ul Gen Galicy 8; ☺4pm-1am Mon-Fri, noon-1am Sat & Sun) This branch of the popular chain with a media theme keeps both the après-ski crowd and tourists well lubricated into the wee hours. Great cocktails – try anything mixed with *miód pitny* (mead). They also serve pretty good pizza and quesadillas.

**Café Appendix**　　　　CAFE
(ul Krupówki 6; ☺11am-midnight; 🛜) A mellow venue for an alcoholic or caffeine-laden drink, hidden away above a mineral shop with an ambient old-meets-new decor. It occasionally hosts live jazz.

### ℹ Information

**Internet Access**
**Internet** (ul Gen Galicy 6; per hr 5zł; ☺9am-10pm Mon-Fri, to midnight Sat & Sun)

**Money**
**Bank Pekao** (al 3 Maja 5; ☺8am-6pm Mon-Fri, 9am-1pm Sat)
**Bank Pekao** (ul Krupówki 19; ☺8am-6pm Mon-Fri)

**Post Office**
**Main post office** (ul Krupówki 20; ☺7am-8pm Mon-Fri, 8am-2pm Sat year-round, 8am-6pm Sat Jul–mid-Sep & mid-Jan–Feb)

**Tourist Information**
Zakopane has three city-run tourist offices where you can get free city maps and buy hiking maps of the Tatras.
**Tatra National Park headquarters** (Tatrzański Park Narodowy; ☎18 202 3288; www.tpn.pl in Polish; ul Chałubińskiego 42/44; ☺8am-3pm Mon-Fri)
**Tourist office** Main branch (☎18 201 2211; www.zakopane.pl; ul Kościuszki 17; ☺8am-8pm Mon-Sat, 9am-5pm Sun); ul Krupówki (ul Gen Galicy 8; ☺8am-6pm Mon-Fri); ul Kościelska (ul Kościelska 7; ☺8am-6pm Mon-Fri)

### Travel Agencies

**Tatra Tourist Centre** (Centrum Turystyki Tatry; ☑18 201 3744; www.cttatry.pl; ul Kościuszki 16; ⊘9am-6pm Mon-Fri, to 2pm Sat); ul Krupówki (1st fl, ul Krupówki 50); Strama (☑18 200 1386; www.nosal.pl; ul Krupówki 58; ⊘9am-9pm) Arrange accommodation, sell transport tickets and have tours to popular regional destinations, including Dunajec Gorge.

## ❶ Getting There & Away

Most regional routes are covered by bus. The train is better for long-distance travel (eg to Warsaw).

**BUS Szwagropol** (www.szwagropol.pl) operates regular, hourly bus service to Kraków (18zł, 1¾ hours), departing from the main bus station (ul Kościuszki 23, stand 5 or 6). Here you'll find buses to cities throughout Poland, including at least two daily to Nowy Sącz (20zł, three hours), Przemyśl (40zł, 4½ hours) and Rzeszów (40zł, 4½ hours).

Several private minibuses offer direct service to near Morskie Oko (around 12zł). These depart from a small stand across the road from the bus station.

**TRAIN** A number of trains go to Kraków (20zł, 3½ hours), but buses are faster and more frequent. At least one train (more in the high season) runs daily to Warsaw (around 100zł, 6½ hours).

# CARPATHIAN FOOTHILLS

The Carpathian Foothills (Przedgórze Karpackie) form a green and hilly belt sloping from the Vistula and San River valleys in the north to the true mountains in the south. Except for Wadowice and Kalwaria Zebrzydowska, which are usually visited from Kraków, most sights in the region are located along the Kraków–Tarnów–Rzeszów–Przemyśl road (and are ordered accordingly in this section).

## Wadowice

POP 19,200

The birthplace of one Karol Wojtyła (better known to the world as Pope John Paul II), Wadowice (vah-do-*vee*-tsah) has evolved into a popular pilgrimage destination in its own right.

People come here to walk the town's pretty cobblestones, pay their respects to the Wojtyła family home and, maybe most importantly, have a slice of the town's legendary cream cake, *kremówka*. The pope himself was a big fan.

The **tourist office** (☑33 873 2365; www .it.wadowice.pl; ul Kościelna 4; ⊘9am-5pm Mon-Fri, 10am-4pm Sat & Sun) can provide you with all the information you need, including a free booklet titled *Karol Wojtyła's Foot Trail*, which marks out the 11 most important pope-related sights in town.

Inside the same building you'll find the **Town Museum** (Muzeum Miejskie; www.muzeum .wadowice.pl; ul Kościelna 4; adult/concession 5/3zł; ⊘9am-4.30pm Mon-Fri, 10am-3.30pm Sat & Sun), which features an interactive, multimedia exhibition on the pope's life and Wadowice at the time of his childhood.

Opposite the tourist office is the **Family Home of John Paul II** (Dom Rodzinny Jana Pawła II; www.domrodzinnyjanapawla.pl; ul Kościelna 7), where Karol was born in May 1920. The house was under reconstruction during our visit, but was expected – optimistically – to reopen in 2012. Normally it houses a replica of how the rooms looked during the pope's childhood, but that exhibition has now moved to the **Catholic House** (Dom Katolicki; Plac Jana Pawła II 1; adult/concession 5/3zł; ⊘9am-6pm).

To the north is the 18th-century **Lesser Basilica** (Bazylika Mniejska; Plac Jana Pawła II), where the pope was baptised. Outside the church is a **monument** to Pope John Paul II.

Naturally, you can't miss trying a *kremówka*, the calorific pastry of cream, eggs, sugar and a dash of brandy. Everyone claims to serve the real McCoy, but we think the best is at **Kawiarna Mieszczańska** (ul Kościelna 6; cream cakes 4.50zł; ⊘9am-7pm Apr-Oct, to 5pm Nov-Mar), next to the tourist office.

## ❶ Getting There & Away

There are hourly buses to Kraków (8zł, 1¼ hours), some of which go via Kalwaria Zebrzydowska (4zł, 30 minutes). A half dozen daily buses go to Katowice (14zł, two hours) via Oświęcim (7zł, one hour).

## Tarnów

POP 116,500

Though you probably wouldn't guess it while strolling about its pleasant, finely restored Old Town, Tarnów (*tar*-noof) is an important regional industrial centre and transport hub. With just the right number of attractions and of a manageable size, it's the perfect place to stay put for a while.

# Tarnów

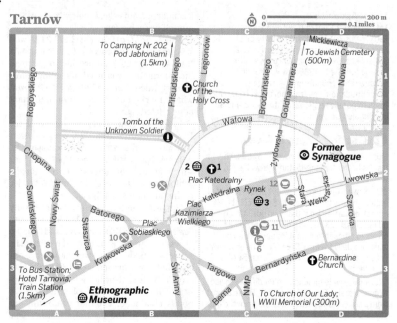

The town layout – an oval centre with a large square in its middle – is unusual, suggesting the town was planned in medieval times. Tarnów is indeed an old city: its municipal charter was granted in 1330. Developing as a trade centre on the busy Kraków–Kyiv route, the town enjoyed good times in the Renaissance period. But a fire in the 15th century completely destroyed the medieval city, which was not rebuilt for almost 200 years.

Tarnów traditionally had a sizable Jewish community, which by the 19th century accounted for half the city's population. Of the 25,000 Jews living here in 1939 (45% of the town's population), only a handful survived WWII. To remind itself and others of its past, Tarnów uses a stylised yellow Star of David in its tourist office logo.

The city is also one of the major centres for Poland's small Roma population and the museum here has one of Europe's few exhibitions of Roma history. The museum includes a small section on the Roma Holocaust, in which hundreds of Roma from around the Tarnów region were rounded up by the Germans and killed.

## ◎ Sights

**Ethnographic Museum**      MUSEUM
(Muzeum Etnograficzne; ul Krakowska 10; adult/concession 5/3zł; ⊙10am-5pm Tue & Thu, 9am-3pm Wed & Fri, 10am-2pm Sat & Sun) This branch of the city's regional museum has Europe's only

permanent collection relating to Roma culture. It's housed in an old inn featuring exterior walls with floral motifs from Zalipie (p196).

### Tarnów Regional Museum    MUSEUM
(Muzeum Okręgowe w Tarnowie; www.museum .tarnow.pl; Rynek 1; adult/concession 5/3zł; ⊙10am-5pm Tue & Thu, 9am-3pm Wed & Fri, 10am-2pm Sat & Sun) This branch of the regional museum is in the Town Hall and has a fine collection of historic paintings, armour, furniture, glass and porcelain, and items relating to the life of Józef Bem (1791–1850), a Polish general born in Tarnów who took part in the Hungarian War of Independence in 1848–49 and is revered as a hero there.

### Basilica    CHURCH
(Plac Katedralny) The basilica dates from the 14th century but was remodelled at the end of the 19th century in neo-Gothic style. The interior shelters several Renaissance and Baroque tombs, of which two in the chancel are among the largest in the country. Also of interest are the 15th-century oaken stalls under the choir loft, a pair of ornately carved pulpits facing one another and two early-16th-century stone portals at the western and southern porches.

### Diocesan Museum    MUSEUM
(Muzeum Diecezjalne; Plac Katedralny 6; admission free; ⊙10am-noon & 1-3pm Tue-Sat, 9am-noon & 1-2pm Sun) This museum has a good collection of Gothic sacred art, including some marvellous Madonnas and altarpieces, and an extensive display of folk and religious painting on glass.

### Jewish Quarter    NEIGHBOURHOOD
The area east of the Rynek was traditionally inhabited by Jews, but little of the original architecture survived the German occupation in WWII. Of the 17th-century former synagogue off ul Żydowska, destroyed by the Germans in 1939, only the brick *bimah* (from where the Torah was read) still stands.

The Jewish cemetery (Cmentarz Żydowski) is about 500m north of ul Żydowska along ul Goldhammera, which was the centre of Jewish life in Tarnów before the war. To reach it, walk north from the Rynek then turn right onto ul Słoneczna. The cemetery dates from the 16th century and has about 4000 tombstones in various states of decay and disarray. The tourist office also has a free brochure called *Jewish*

*Heritage* that will take you by these and other sites of Jewish interest.

### Historic Churches    CHURCHES
Worth a look are two small wooden churches south of the Old Town. The shingled **Church of Our Lady** (Kościół Najświętszej Marii Panny; ul Najświętszej Marii Panny), dating from 1442, has charming folk decorations inside and a fine Rococo high altar. Note the poignant **WWII memorial** on the edge of the Old Cemetery (Cmentarz Stary) opposite.

About 500m south along ul Tuchowska and behind the cemetery is the **Church of the Holy Trinity** (Kościół Św Trójcy; ul Tuchowska 5), built in 1597, with a similar naively charming rustic interior that includes an early Baroque high altar.

## 🛏 Sleeping

### Hotel U Jana    HOTEL €€
(☑14 626 0564; www.hotelujana.pl; Rynek 14; s 210-240zł, d 240-310zł, tr 280-560zł; ☎) This all-suite hotel is the classiest and most central place to stay in the Old Town, conveniently located on the Rynek. The 10 apartments have decent artwork on the walls, the beds are huge and the bathrooms up to date. Breakfast is 15zł extra.

### Tourist Information Centre    HOSTEL €
(☑14 688 9090; www.it.tarnow.pl; Rynek 7; s/d 85/100; ☎) Tarnów's tourist information centre offers one of the best sleeping deals in town, indeed in all of Poland, letting out rooms above its office on the Rynek. Don't expect luxury: this is as basic as it gets – just a clean bed and bath. But you can't beat it for value. No breakfast, but plenty of cafes are nearby.

### Hotel Bristol    HOTEL €€
(☑14 621 2279; www.hotelbristol.com.pl; ul Krakowska 9; s 190-210zł, d 320zł, ste 270-380zł; P✳☎) This survivor of the interwar years, with its 15 sumptuous guestrooms and chilled atmosphere, is one of our favourite places in town, especially the retro restaurant, which is a flashback to the 1970s.

### Hotel Tarnovia    HOTEL €€
(☑14 630 0350; www.hotel.tarnovia.pl; ul Kościuszki 10; s 190-240zł, d 240-310zł, ste 420-510zł; P@☎) The large Tarnovia is a holdover from the communist era (and looks like it), but the location is convenient to the bus and train stations. Fortunately, the interior of the hotel and the rooms are a big improvement over the exterior.

**DON'T MISS**

## PAINTED HOUSES OF ZALIPIE

The village of Zalipie, 36km northwest of Tarnów, has been known as a centre for folk painting for more than a century, since its inhabitants started to decorate both the inside and outside of their houses with colourful floral designs. Today about 20 such houses can be seen in Zalipie, with another dozen or so in the neighbouring villages of Kuzie, Niwka and Kłyż.

The best-known painter was Felicja Curyłowa (1904–74), and since her death her three-room farmhouse has been opened to the public as the **Felicja Curyłowa Farmstead Museum** (Muzeum Zagroda Felicji Curyłowej; www.muzeum.tarnow.pl; adult/concession 3/2zł; Zalipie 135; ☺10am-4pm Tue-Sun). Every flat surface is painted with colourful flowers, and on display are painted dishes, icons and costumes.

In order to help maintain the tradition, the Painted Cottage (Malowana Chata) contest for the best-decorated house has been held annually since 1948, during the weekend after Corpus Christi (late May or June).

At the **House of Painters** (Dom Malarek; Zalipie 128a; ☺8am-6pm Mon-Fri, 11am-6pm Sat & Sun Jun-Aug, 8am-4pm Mon-Fri Sep-May), which serves as a centre for the village's artists, you can watch the women painters at work.

Unfortunately, there are only a few buses daily from Tarnów, making a trip here more practical if you have your own wheels. The Tarnów tourist information centre can help sort out bus timetables and plan a journey.

**Camping Nr 202 Pod Jabłoniami**　　CAMPING GROUND €
(☎14 621 5124; www.camping.tarnow.pl; ul Piłsudskiego 28a; per person/tent/caravan 15/7/17zł, d/tr/q 60/80/100zł; ☺Apr-Nov; 🅿) About 1km due north of the Old Town, this camping ground also has 18 simple bungalows with shared facilities.

## ✕ Eating

**Tatrzańska**　　POLISH €€
(www.kudelski.pl; ul Krakowska 1; mains 15-30zł) This atmospheric restaurant-cafe sports an eclectic menu, with a starters list that includes *żurek* (traditional sour rye soup), carpaccio and spinach pancakes. Mains revert more or less to the mean, with items such as pork tenderloin and fried trout. The traditional 19th-century cafe setting is elegant without being stuffy. It's a good stop for coffees, cakes and ice cream as well.

**Bombay Music**　　INDIAN €€
(www.bombay.pl; ul Krakowska 11a; mains 14-40zł; 🎵) The Bombay serves up somewhat less-than-authentic Indian dishes (plus a few European ones) in elegant surrounds, with the occasional live music set in the evenings. The restaurant is a little hard to find; it's not right on ul Krakowska, but on a small side street just beyond the Hotel Bristol.

**Restauracja Aida**　　ITALIAN €€
(www.restauracja-aida.pl; ul Wałowa 2; mains 15-38zł; ☺11am-11pm Sun-Thu, to midnight Fri & Sat) This small place in a courtyard through an arcade serves excellent Italian dishes as well as more enlightened Polish ones. It's a quiet, almost romantic spot meant for two.

**Bar Łasuch**　　POLISH €
(ul Sowińskiego 4; mains 7-12zł; ☺8am-7pm Mon-Fri, 9am-3pm Sat) Inexpensive milk bar located southwest of the Old Town near the Ethnographic Museum.

## 🍷 Drinking

**Café Piano**　　CAFE
(Rynek 9; ☺10am-midnight; 🛜) Set in beautifully decorated cellars, this studenty place offers plenty of drinks, a few budget dishes and live jazz on some weekends. In summer, they have tables on the Rynek.

**Studio Café**　　CAFE
(ul Żydowska 3; ☺noon-11pm Mon-Sat, 4-11pm Sun) Popular cafe and drinks spot, just off the Rynek.

## ℹ Information

**Bank Pekao** (ul Wałowa 10; ☺8am-6pm Mon-Fri)
**PTTK office** (☎14 622 2200; ul Żydowska 20; ☺9am-1pm & 5-8pm Mon & Thu, 9am-3.30pm Tue, Wed & Fri) Travel agency.
**Tourist office** (☎14 688 9090; www.it.tarnow.pl; Rynek 7; ☺8am-8pm Mon-Fri, 9am-5pm

Sat & Sun May-Oct, 8am-6pm Mon-Fri, 9am-5pm Sat & Sun Nov-Apr) One of the best tourist information offices in the country, offering a wealth of useful brochures, as well as free internet access, bike rental and low-cost accommodation above the office.

### 🛈 Getting There & Away

The train and bus stations are next to each other, just over 1km southwest of the Old Town following ul Krakowska. Bus 9 will take you to the Rynek.

There are frequent buses west to Kraków (15zł, two hours) and regular departures southeast to Krosno (14zł, two hours). For Sandomierz (20zł, three hours), take the bus to Tarnobrzeg (16zł, 2½ hours) and then change.

Trains to Kraków (14zł, 1½ hours) and Rzeszów (15zł to 20zł, 1½ hours) run every hour or so. There are departures every other hour to Nowy Sącz (16zł to 25zł, two hours). Two or three direct trains go to Warsaw (90zł, 4½ hours) daily.

## Rzeszów

POP 157,800

The chief administrative and industrial centre of southeastern Poland, Rzeszów is a surprisingly elegant medium-sized city boasting a handsome square lined with some great clubs, restaurants and hotels, all enlivened by a large student population. It's a highly recommended sojourn if you're looking for some more urbanised fun to balance out your treks in the mountains. It's also a transport hub, meaning you're likely to pass through in any event. As far as stopovers go, this is the most promising around.

Rzeszów started life in the 13th century as a remote Ruthenian settlement. It grew rapidly in the 16th century when Mikołaj Spytek Ligęza, the local ruler, commissioned a church and a fortified castle. It later fell into the hands of the powerful Lubomirski clan, but this couldn't save the town from subsequent decline.

### 🞂 Sights

Rzeszów's main square is a festive spot lined with some lovely Art Nouveau townhouses. In the centre is a **monument to Tadeusz Kościuszko**, honoured by Poles and Americans alike. In the southwest corner, the 16th-century **town hall** was wholly remodelled a century ago in neo-Gothic style.

**Underground Tourist**
**Route**                      UNDERGROUND CELLARS
(Podziemna Trasa Turystyczna; www.mzbm.rzeszow.pl; ul Króla Kazimierza; admission 6zł; ⊘9am-

3.30pm Tue-Fri, noon-6pm Sun Apr-Oct, 9am-3pm Tue-Fri Nov-Mar) Rzeszów's prime attraction took 17 years to link 34 old cellars into a 214m-long route. The cellars date from the 15th to the 20th centuries and are on different levels (the deepest is nearly 10m below the Rynek). Visits are by guided tour and last about 45 minutes. Buy your tickets from the **Rzeszów City Museum** (Muzeum Historii Miasta Rzeszowa; www.muzeum.rzeszow.pl; Rynek 12), around the corner from the entrance.

**Communist Monument**            MONUMENT
(al Cieplińskiego) No visit to Rzeszów would be complete without a photograph of the city's impressively overblown communist monument, erected 'in memory of the heroes of the revolutionary struggles'.

**Rzeszów Regional Museum**            MUSEUM
(Muzeum Okręgowe w Rzeszowie; www.muzeum.rzeszow.pl; ul 3 Maja 19; adult/concession 7/5zł; ⊘9am-3pm Tue-Thu & Sun, 10am-5.30pm Fri) Housed in a one-time Piarist monastery, complete with frescoed vaulting from the 17th century, the Rzeszów Regional Museum contains Polish paintings from the 18th to the 20th centuries and European art from the 16th to the 19th centuries.

**Ethnographic Museum**            MUSEUM
(Muzeum Etnograficzne; www.muzeum.rzeszow.pl; Rynek 6; adult/concession 6/4zł; ⊘9am-3pm Tue-Thu & Sun, to 5.30pm Fri) This museum has traditional folk costumes and old woodcarvings from the region on permanent display.

**Jewish Heritage**            SYNAGOGUES
As a regional hub, Rzeszów was traditionally home to a large number of Jews. The pre-WWII Jewish population numbered around 15,000, or about a third of the city's total. Most of this community perished in 1942 at the German-run extermination camp at Bełżec, near Lublin (p168). Not much trace of this once-vibrant community remains, with the exception of two impressive synagogues, northeast of the Rynek. The 18th-century **New Town Synagogue** (Synagoga Nowomiejska; ul Sobieskiego 18) now houses the **BWA art gallery** (admission free; ⊘10am-5pm Tue-Sun). Note the gate to the cafe on the 1st floor – made of wrought iron and clay, it's the work of the contemporary sculptor Marian Kruczek. The smaller 17th-century **Old Town Synagogue** (Synagoga Staromiejska; ul Bożnicza 4) now houses the city archives and is a centre for Jewish heritage study.

# Rzeszów

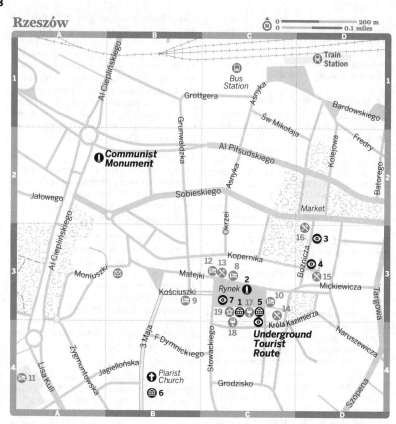

## 🛏 Sleeping

**Grand Hotel** TOP CHOICE  HOTEL €€€

(☑17 250 0000; www.grand-hotel.pl; ul Kościuszki; s/d 400/440zł; P❄@📶) All we can say is 'wow'. This boutique, a block from the Rynek, is one of the swankiest hotels we've seen in Poland outside the traditional tourist hot spots, and an excellent candidate for a splurge. Postmodern touches – such as throw pillows in trendy earth tones scattered around the lobby – adorn this sensitively restored townhouse. The edgy contemporary look of the rooms is straight out of *Wallpaper* magazine. Even if you're not staying here, consider a meal at the 'Patio' restaurant on the ground floor, below a beautiful atrium. Rates drop 10% on weekends.

**Hotel Pod Ratuszem** HOTEL €€

(☑17 852 9770; www.hotelpodratuszem.rzeszow .pl; ul Matejki 8; s/d/apt 125/180/250zł; 📶) This modern, perfectly central hotel is not the fanciest place in town but might just represent the best value, given the excellent location just off the Rynek. One drawback if you're bringing a car is the lack of convenient parking spaces around.

**Hotel Forum** HOTEL €€

(☑17 859 4038; www.hotelforum.pl; ul Lisa Kuli 19; s/d/apt 150/200/320zł; P❄📶) This is another entry in the 'good value for money' category. There's nothing fancy about this cookie-cutter high-rise a few blocks from the Rynek, but the rooms are clean and relatively quiet (ask for a room away from the main road out front), and the bathrooms border on enormous. The breakfast is fresh and the reception friendly.

**Hotel Ambasadorski Rzeszów** HOTEL €€

(☑17 250 2444; www.hotele-rzeszow.com; Rynek 14; s/d 300/380/700zł; P❄📶) This smart

# Rzeszów

four-star hotel occupies a beautifully renovated 17th-century townhouse at the back of the Rynek. The rooms are not quite as eye-catching as those at the Grand, but are plush, comfortable and quiet just the same. The hotel's coffee shop, Cukiernia Wiedeńska, next door at Rynek 14, might very well win the competition for best ice cream and cake concoctions in the city.

**Alko Hostel** HOSTEL **€**
(☏17 853 4430; www.ptsmrzeszow.epodkarpacie .com; Rynek 25; dm 35zł, d/tr from 100/160zł) We're not so sure it's a good idea to call a hostel 'alko', but this is a fairly laid-back affair. There are no amenities to speak of aside from a hard bed, but the Rynek location could hardly be better and the price is definitely right.

## ✗ Eating

**Da Vinci** ITALIAN **€€**
(www.davinci.rzeszow.pl; ul Matejki 4; mains 15-30zł; ⊙1-11pm Mon-Wed, noon-midnight Thu-Sun) Tired of pizza but could do with an infusion of something with lots of tomatoes and garlic? Head for this place, where the walls are covered with the drawings, engravings and writings of the great Renaissance man. We love the cosy room with a fireplace in winter. Excellent choice of wines. The baked cannelloni stuffed with spinach and ricotta is very good.

**Grotesque Restauracja** POLISH **€€**
(http://groteska.eu; Przesmyk 4; mains 20-30zł) Traditional Polish food served in a handsome dining room on a small side street a few steps off the Rynek. The menu features classics such as *wienerschnitzel* (here served Polish-style, with a fried egg on top). *Placki* 'Grotesque' is much better than it sounds, pairing a potato pancake and a ladle of goulash.

**Restauracja Saigon** VIETNAMESE **€**
(http://saigon.rzeszow.pl in Polish; ul Sobieskiego 14; mains 12-20zł; ⬆) Though nominally a Vietnamese restaurant, the food is more reminiscent of old-school Chinese, c 1985. Think sweet-and-sour pork and egg-drop soup. That said, it's still good and a welcome change from pizza and *pierogi*.

**Kryjówka Bar** POLISH **€**
(ul Mickiewicza 19; mains 8-15zł; ⊙9am-10pm Mon-Fri, 10am-10pm Sat) One of the few addresses for a tasty budget meal in the centre, the 'Hideaway Bar' is a pleasant place offering an extensive Polish menu as well as that 21st-century staple, pizza.

## 🍷 Drinking & Entertainment

For pubs and clubs or just hanging out in the sunshine, head for the Rynek.

**TOP CHOICE Graciarnia u Plastików** BAR
(www.graty.itl.pl; Rynek 10; ⊙10am-2am Sun-Thu, to 4am Fri & Sat) Popular student bar beneath and behind the Rynek that defies easy description. Walk down a flight of steep stairs to find thrift-shop furnishings, old lamps, plaster of paris sculptures, caricatures on the wall and a very laid-back vibe.

**Życie jest Pękne** CAFE
(www.zyciejestpiekne.freehost.pl; Rynek 10; ⊙9am-midnight Sun-Thu, to 2am Fri & Sat) Charming

**CARPATHIAN MOUNTAINS RZESZÓW**

**DON'T MISS**

# ŁAŃCUT: HOW THE OTHER HALF LIVED

Just 24km northeast of Rzeszów, Łańcut (*wine*-tsoot) has Poland's largest and richest aristocratic home. The building started life in the 15th century, but it was Stanisław Lubomirski, 100 years later, who turned it into both a mighty fortress and a great residence when he redesigned the building in 1641.

Over the years, the residence has been reshaped and remodelled, gaining Rococo and neoclassical elements. The last important alteration, at the end of the 19th century, gave the building its neo-Baroque facades.

The last private owner, Alfred Potocki, one of the richest men in pre-WWII Poland, accumulated a fabulous collection of art during his tenancy. Shortly before the arrival of the Red Army in July 1944, he loaded 11 railway carriages with the most valuable objects and fled with the collection to Liechtenstein.

Just after WWII, the 300-room castle was taken over by the state and opened as the **Castle Museum** (Muzeum Zamek; ☑17 225 2008; www.zamek-lancut.pl; ul Zamkowa 1; adult/ concession incl entry to castle, stables & coach house 34/26zł, castle only 29/24zł; ⊙11.45am-3pm Mon-Fri, 9.45am-5pm Sat & Sun). Visits are by guided tour only. Among the highlights are the 17th-century **Grand Hall** (Wielka Sień), the Renaissance-style **Eastern Corridor** (Korytarz Wschodni) and the Rococo **Corner Room** (Pokój Narożny). You'll be shown the **Orangery** (Oranżeria), with palms and parrots, and Potocki's collection of 55 carriages and sleighs in the **Coach House** (Wozownia), 300m south of the castle. The **stables** (Stajnie), north of the Coach House, have a fine collection of more than 1000 icons from the 15th century onwards.

Just outside the park is the former **Synagogue** (www.fodz.pl; next to Plac Sobieskiego 15; admission 6zł; ⊙11am-6pm Mon-Wed, Fri & Sat, to 4pm Thu, 2-6pm Sun), built in the 1760s. It has retained much of its original Rococo decoration and some liturgical items are on display.

There are several places to stay. The most atmospheric is the **Hotel Zamkowy** (☑17 225 2671; www.zamkowa-lancut.pl; ul Zamkowa 1; s/d/apt 120/180/260zł; ℗🛜), within the castle complex, though the rooms fall a little short of the overall opulence of the place. There's also a pretty castle **restaurant** (☑17 225 2671; mains 15-25zł), but try to book ahead, especially on weekends when the restaurant tends to close down for wedding parties.

Another sleeping option is the **Pensjonat Pałacyk** (☑17 225 2043; www.palacyk.lancut .pl; ul Paderewskiego 18; r 140zł; ℗🛜). It has seven rooms as well as its own restaurant. To find it from the Rynek, follow Plac Sobieskiego all the way to the end (about 300m). It's on the right side.

The bus station is 500m northeast of the castle along ul Kościuszki; the train station is about 2km to the north. Buses to Rzeszów (7zł, 30 minutes) run every 30 minutes and to Przemyśl (10zł, 1½ hours) every hour or two.

cafe just above and behind Graciarnia u Plastików. It's got the same thrift-shop appeal and the same relaxed, student-friendly atmosphere.

**Tawerna Żeglarska**　　　　BAR
(Rynek 6, enter from ul Króla Kazimierza; ⊙2pm-midnight Mon-Thu, to 1am Fri & Sat, 4pm-midnight Sun)Frequented by students, the 'Sailors' Tavern' is far from the sea but can get pretty stormy when the tide is up on musical evenings.

**Carpe Diem Klub**　　　　CLUB
(www.carpediem.pl; Rynek 4; ⊙10am-2am) Popular dance club in the basement of a Rynek townhouse with a fantastic sound-and-light system.

## ℹ Information

**Bank Pekao** (al Ciepliński 1; ⊙8am-6pm Mon-Fri, 9am-4pm Sat)

**Bank PKO** (ul 3 Maja 23; ⊙8am-6pm Mon-Fri, 9am-1pm Sat) In a lovely neoclassical building.

**City of Rzeszów** (www.rzeszow.pl/en) Municipal website with a small section in English.

**Hard Drive Café** (☑17 852 6141; ul Kościuszki 13; per hr 4zł; ⊙8am-11pm Mon-Sat, 10am-10pm Sun) Internet access.

**Main post office** (ul Moniuszki 1; ⊘7am-8pm Mon-Fri, 8am-2pm Sat)

**Post office** (ul Asnyka 9; ⊘7am-8pm Mon-Fri, 8am-2pm Sat)

## ⓘ Getting There & Around

**AIR Rzeszów International Airport** (⧉17 852 0081; www.rzeszowairport.pl) is at Jasionka, 10km north of the city, and accessible by special airport bus L (8zł), which ferries passengers from the arrivals terminal to the train and bus stations. Taxis from the centre cost about 60zł. There are daily flights to Warsaw as well as regular service to Frankfurt, London, Dublin and a handful of other cities. **LOT** (⧉17 862 0420; Plac Ofiar Getta 6; ⊘8am-6pm Mon-Fri) makes bookings and sells tickets.

**BUS** The bus station is 500m north of the Rynek. Buses depart roughly every hour for Sanok (12zł, 1½ hours), Krosno (10zł, 1½ hours), Przemyśl (14zł, two hours) and Lublin (28zł, 3½ hours). Buses also go to Ustrzyki Dolne (18zł, 2½ hours, five to seven daily) and Ustrzyki Górne (25zł, 3½ hours, three daily), as well as to Zamość (27zł, three hours, two daily). Buses to Łańcut (7zł, 30 minutes) run roughly every half-hour or so and are more convenient than trains, as they stop near the palace.

**TRAIN** The train station is next to the bus station. Trains depart almost hourly for Przemyśl (22zł to 42zł, 1½ hours) and Tarnów (13zł, one hour). A dozen or so daily trains leave for Kraków (21zł, 2½ hours) and several to Warsaw (90zł, five hours).

# Przemyśl

POP 66,600

A sleepy town with an impossible name, Przemyśl (*psheh*-mishl) is close to the Ukrainian border and some way off the usual tourist route. Przemyśl has an attractive main square and some beautiful churches and worthwhile museums to explore.

Founded in the 10th century on terrain long fought over by Poland and Ruthenia (today's Ukraine), Przemyśl changed hands several times before being annexed by the Polish crown in 1340. It experienced its golden period in the 16th century but declined afterwards. During the Partitions (p386) it fell under Austrian administration.

In around 1850 the Austrians began to fortify Przemyśl. This work continued until the outbreak of WWI and resulted in one of the largest fortresses in Europe. It consisted of a double ring of earth ramparts, including a 15km-long inner circle and an outer girdle three times longer, with more than 60 forts placed at strategic points. This formidable system played an important role during the war, but the garrison eventually surrendered to the Russians in 1915 due to a lack of provisions.

Przemyśl was also an important Jewish settlement for centuries leading up to WWII. At the outbreak of the war, the Jewish community numbered around 22,000, a third of the population. The initial situation for Przemyśl's Jews during the war was different to that in other Polish cities owing to Przemyśl's easterly position. For the first two years of the war (when Germany and the Soviet Union carved up Poland between themselves), most of the town found itself in the Soviet occupation zone. The situation deteriorated in 1941 after the Germans invaded the Soviet Union and occupied the entire town. Most of the Jews were eventually sent to their deaths at the German-run Bełżec extermination camp near Lublin in 1942 (p168).

## ◉ Sights & Activities

Perched on a hillside and dominated by four mighty churches, Przemyśl's Old Town is a picturesque place. The sloping **Rynek** has preserved some of its old arcaded houses, mostly on its north and south sides. Many houses bear plaques in English giving the history of the place. Look especially at **Nos 16** and **17**. The former sports a beautifully restored Mannerist facade, while the latter boasts a surviving Renaissance portal from 1560.

**Historic Churches** CHURCHES
The real joy of strolling through Przemyśl is to take in the dramatic sacred architecture, which seems to dwarf the modern-day town with its splendour. Begin with the **Franciscan Church of St Mary Magdalene** (Kościół Franciszkański Św Marii Magdaleny; ul Franciszkańska), a few steps off the Rynek. This church was built between 1754 and 1778 in late-Baroque and classical style, but its monumental facade was remade later. The church has a beautiful Rococo interior with a vaulted and frescoed nave.

Just behind the Franciscan church stands the **former Jesuit church** (Kościół Pojezuicki). Built between 1627 and 1659, it's also a Baroque construction. The church now serves the Uniat congregation as the Greek Catholic Archcathedral and is a popular destination for pilgrims from across the border in Ukraine.

Up the hill behind this church stands the **Carmelite Church of St Teresa** (Kościół Karmelitów Św Teresy). Designed in 1630 by Italian architect Galeazzo Appiani, who also built Krasiczyn castle, the church has preserved some of its original features, including the classical main gate and the white and gold stucco on the vaulting. Note the large wooden pulpit in the shape of a boat, complete with mast, sail, rigging, anchor and two saints bearing oars.

A short walk west along ul Katedralna brings you to the **Cathedral of St John the Baptist** (Katedra Św Jana Chrzciciela; Plac Katedralny), with its 71m-high freestanding bell tower. Just next to the cathedral is the small **Archdiocesan Museum** (Muzeum Archidiecezjalne; Plac Katedralny 2; donation requested; ⊘8am-4pm), which contains the usual range of religious art and vestments.

### Castle
RUIN

A short walk along ul Zamkowa brings you to what is left of the 14th-century castle. Built by King Kazimierz III Wielki (Casimir III the Great) in the 1340s, it mutated into a Renaissance building two centuries later when it acquired its four loopholed towers, two of which have been restored. A local theatre and cultural centre now occupy the restored rooms.

### Przemyśl Regional Museum
MUSEUM

(Muzeum Narodowe Ziemi Przemyskiej; www .muzeum.przemysl.pl; Plac Płk Berka Joselewicza 1; adult/concession 8/5zł; ⊘10.30am-5.30pm Tue & Fri, 10am-3pm Wed, 9am-3pm Thu, 9am-4pm Sat, 11am-3pm Sun) This work in progress is slated to be the most important museum of history and artefacts in this part of Poland when it's eventually finished. There's now a splendid collection of Ruthenian icons and other religious art dating back to the 15th century.

### Jewish Heritage
SYNAGOGUES

The only significant relics of the Jewish legacy left are two synagogues (of four that existed before WWII), both dating from the end of the 19th and beginning of the 20th centuries, renovated after the war and put to other uses. One is in Plac Unii Brzeskiej, off ul 3 Maja on the northern side of the river; the other, now housing the city's public library, is on ul Słowackiego.

### Przemyśl Fortress
FORTRESS

Military buffs will want to see the remnants of Austria–Hungary's Przemyśl Fortress (Twierdza Przemyśl) surrounding the town. As these were mostly earth ramparts, however, they are now overgrown and resemble natural rather than artificial bulwarks. Among the best examples are **Fort I** (Salis Soglio) in Sieliska, **Fort VIII** (Łętownia) in Kuńkowce and **Fort XIII** (San Rideau) in Bolestraszyce. The tourist office can provide information about the sites and transport details. The modest **Przemyśl Fortress Museum** (Muzeum Twierdza Przemyśl; ul Grodzka 8; admission free; ⊘10am-5pm Wed, Sat & Sun) has photographs, postcards, weapons and commemorative mementos connected with the fortress.

Literature fans may be interested in knowing that Czech author Jaroslav Hašek placed part of his classic WWI novel *The Good Soldier Švejk* in Przemyśl, and in fact Hašek's hapless anti-hero, Švejk, even spent some time behind bars here. Town fathers have made a virtue of this dubious connection to world literature and you'll see Czech artist Josef Lada's famous comical illustration of Švejk on signs around town. There's even a little statue of Švejk on the Rynek, where you can pose with him for a photo.

### Museum of Bells & Pipes
MUSEUM

(Muzeum Dzwonów i Fajek; http://muzeum.przemysl .pl in Polish; ul Władycze 3; adult/concession 8/5zł; ⊘10.30am-5.30pm Tue, Thu & Fri, 10am-3pm Wed & Sat, noon-4pm Sun) This curious museum, housed in an 18th-century Baroque clock tower, contains vintage bells as well as elaborately carved wooden and meerschaum pipes and cigar cutters (items that Przemyśl has long been famous for manufacturing). The rooftop affords a panoramic view of the town.

## 🛏 Sleeping

### Hotel Gromada
HOTEL €€

(☎16 676 1111; www.gromada.pl; Wybrzeże Piłsudskiego 4; s/d 160/220zł; P@🌐) Admittedly, the Gromada is one of those souless modern hotels with a whiff of lingering communism about it, but it wins points for effort, good value for money, and an excellent breakfast buffet, with its own little espresso machine. Many of the rooms boast tranquil views out over the river, but they are in varying states of repair, so check out a few before deciding. The hotel is on the southern bank of the San River, about 700m west of the Rynek.

### Hotel Europejski
HOTEL €

(☎16 675 7100; www.hotel-europejski.pl; ul Sowińskiego 4; s/d/tr 120/140/170zł; P🌐) Housed in a renovated old building facing the

DON'T MISS

## FAIRY-TALE CASTLE OF KRASICZYN

The castle (www.krasiczyn.com.pl; adult/concession incl guided tour 10/6zł; ⊙9am-4pm) in the village of Krasiczyn (krah-*shee*-chin), about 11km southwest of Przemyśl, is right out of a fairy tale with its formal rectilinear shape and turreted towers on the corners. The good news is that you can stay the night as well in one of Poland's nicest accommodation options.

The castle was designed in Renaissance style by Italian architect Galeazzo Appiani and built between 1592 and 1618 for the wealthy Krasicki family. The design features a spacious, partly arcaded courtyard.

The cylindrical towers were meant to reflect the social order of the period and were named (clockwise from the southeastern corner) after God, the pope, the king and the nobility. The God Tower (Baszta Boska), topped with a dome, houses a chapel. The King Tower (Baszta Królewska), with its conical roof and little turrets, would make a lovely home for Rapunzel of long-haired fame. On the courtyard side of the castle walls are Renaissance sgraffiti decorations of Biblical scenes and Polish nobility.

Hotel Zamkowy (☑16 671 8321; www.krasiczyn.com.pl; Krasiczyn 179; s/d/tr/ste from 150/240/310/550zł; P🖭) offers several different types of rooms, ranging from suites in the former coach house north of the castle to lovingly restored rooms in the castle itself (doubles/suites 280/550zł). There's even a luxurious five-bed Hunter's Pavilion (1000zł), which has its own kitchen and garden. Within the castle grounds is a restaurant (mains 12-30zł; ⊙2-10pm Mon, 10am-10pm Tue-Sun) that serves mostly Polish dishes in traditional surrounds. The castle is an easy trip from Przemyśl (3zł, 20 minutes) on one of the frequent PKS buses. From Krasiczyn you can also reach Sanok (12zł, one hour, four daily) by bus.

attractive neoclassical train station (1895), this comfortable place has 29 bright rooms with high ceilings and modern bathrooms.

**Dom Wycieczkowy PTTK**
**Podzamcze**                                        HOSTEL €
(☑16 678 5374; http://przemysl.pttk.pl in Polish; ul Waygarta 3; dm 40zł, d/tr 70/90zł; P) The nine rooms (containing 46 beds) at this place have seen some wear but they have had a new lick of paint. It's just a block west of the Rynek.

##  Eating

**ᵀᴼᴾ**
**ᶜᴴᴼᴵᶜᴱ Bar Rubin**                              POLISH €
(ul Kazimierza Wielkiego 19; mains 9-20zł; ⊙9am-8pm) This popular '70s-style diner serves truly delicious traditional Polish food at reasonable prices. With its red laminate walls and chrome chairs, the interior gives the place a milk bar feel. One welcome modern touch, at least on the boiling August day we stopped by for lunch, was air-conditioning.

**Dominikańska**                                     POLISH €€
(Plac Dominikańska 3; mains 14-28zł) You'll find excellent Polish cooking at this upscale restaurant on a small square on the western end of the Rynek. We're a big fan of the home-style *żurek* and the beef roulade stuffed with bacon.

## 🍷 Drinking

For drinking – of the alcoholic or non-alcoholic variety – head to the Rynek. It's lined on all sides with bars and cafes, several of which have outdoor tables in summer.

**Absynt**                                           CAFE
(Plac Dominikańska 4; coffee 6zł; 🖭) You'll find the city's best coffee and espresso-based drinks – but not much absinthe – at this secluded spot on the far western end of the Rynek.

**Kawiarnia Libera**                                 CAFE
(Rynek 26; ⊙10am-midnight; 🖭) This offbeat student cafe is connected to a bookstore of the same name on the Rynek. Walk through a small metal gate to find what feels like a secret student meeting place inside.

**Fiore Cafe**                                       CAFE
(ul Kazimierza Wielkiego 17b; ⊙10am-8pm) If you're looking for ice cream or a slice of something sweet, this modern cafe on a pedestrian street should be your destination.

## ❶ Information

The main commercial artery, ul Jagiellońska, which runs north and east of the Rynek, is a good place to look for ATMs. Internet cafes are few on the ground and several have closed down in recent years.

**Bank Pekao** (ul Jagiellońska 7; ◷9am-5pm Mon-Fri)

**Main post office** (ul Mickiewicza 13; ◷7.30am-8pm Mon-Fri, 8am-2pm Sat)

**PTTK office** (☑16 675 2163; www.przemysl.pl; ul Grodzka 1; ◷10am-6pm Mon-Fri, 9am-5pm Sat & Sun) Travel agency that serves as the tourist information office.

## ❶ Getting There & Away

The train and bus stations are next to each other, on the northeastern edge of the town centre, about 600m from the Rynek.

Up to four buses a day depart for Sanok (12zł, 1½ hours), and there are also departures for Ustrzyki Dolne (14zł, two hours, three to four daily) and Rzeszów (10zł, two hours, 10 daily). Buses to Krasiczyn (3zł, 20 minutes) run as often as twice an hour.

Trains to Rzeszów (24zł, 1½ hours) depart regularly throughout the day. There are half a dozen fast trains and two express trains a day to Kraków (50zł, 4½ hours). One express and several fast trains go daily to Warsaw (120zł, seven hours), and one relatively fast train runs to Lublin (30zł, four hours).

# BIESZCZADY

The region around the Bieszczady (byesh-*chah*-di), in the far southeastern corner of Poland and sandwiched between Ukraine and Slovakia, is one of thick forests and open meadows. Scantily populated and unspoilt, it's one of the most attractive areas of the country. As tourist facilities are modest, roads sparse and public transport limited, the Bieszczady retains its relative isolation and makes for an off-the-beaten-track destination. It's popular with nature-lovers and hikers.

The range's eastern end, the highest and most spectacular part, has been decreed the Bieszczady National Park (Bieszczadzki Park Narodowy), with its headquarters in Ustrzyki Dolne. At 292 sq km, it's Poland's third-largest national park after Biebrza and Kampinos. Its highest peak is Mt Tarnica (1346m).

The region was once much more densely populated than it is today, but Ukrainian nationalists devastated it after the war (see the boxed text, p206). Indeed, many people here say WWII didn't end until 1947.

One of the most exciting developments in recent years is the completion of the 350km bicycle loop known as the **Greenway**

**Bicycle Trail** (Szlak Zielony Rower; www.zielony rower.pl), which links the Bieszczady towns of Sanok, Lesko, Ustrzyki Dolne and Solina before crossing into Ukraine, Slovakia and back into Poland.

The region around Cisna, Wetlina and Ustrzyki Górne forms part of Unesco's tripartite Eastern Carpathian Biosphere Reserve with Slovakia and Ukraine.

## Sanok

POP 39,600

Sanok, nestled in a picturesque valley in the Bieszczady Foothills, is the largest city in the region and a logical base for starting your exploration of the Bieszczady. It has been subjected to Ruthenian, Hungarian, Austrian, Russian, German and Polish rule in its eventful history. Although it contains an important industrial zone (where Autosan, the bus used in intercity and urban transport throughout the land, is produced) it is a picturesque city, with an attractive town square and a few worthy sights of its own. It's also the springboard for the fascinating Icon Trail, a signposted hiking trail that takes in the surrounding countryside's wealth of wooden churches.

## ◎ Sights

**Historical Museum/Icon Museum** MUSEUM (Muzeum Historyczne; www.muzeum.sanok.pl; ul Zamkowa 2; adult/concession 11/7zł; ◷8-noon Mon, 9am-5pm Tue-Sun). Housed in the 16th-century **castle**, this museum is best known for its 700-piece collection of Ruthenian icons. The selection on display consists of about 260 large pieces dating from the 15th to the 18th centuries, most acquired after WWII from abandoned Uniat churches.

The museum's other treasure is the collection of paintings by Zdzisław Beksiński (1929–2005) exhibited on the top floor. Beksiński, who was born and lived in Sanok, was one of Poland's most remarkable contemporary painters, with a fantastical style all his own.

**Museum of Folk Architecture** OPEN-AIR MUSEUM (Muzeum Budownictwa Ludowego; www.mbl.sanok .pl in Polish; ul Rybickiego 3; adult/concession 11/7zł; ◷8am-6pm May-Sep, 9am-4pm Apr & Oct, 8am-4pm Nov-Mar) Sanok's Museum of Folk Architecture is Poland's largest skansen (open-air museum of traditional architecture). You'll find around 120 traditional

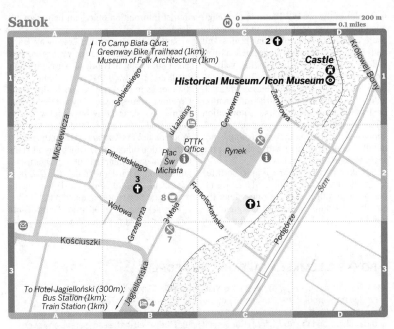

# Sanok

**◎ Top Sights**

| | |
|---|---|
| Castle | D1 |
| Historical Museum/Icon Museum | D1 |

**◎ Sights**

| | |
|---|---|
| **1** Franciscan Church of the Holy Cross | C2 |
| **2** Orthodox Church of the Holy Trinity | C1 |
| **3** Parish Church | B2 |

**🛏 Sleeping**

| | |
|---|---|
| **4** Hotel Pod Trzema Różami | B3 |
| **5** Hotel Sanvit | B1 |

**🍴 Eating**

| | |
|---|---|
| **6** Karczma Jadło Karpackie | C2 |
| **7** Restauracja U Szwejka | B3 |

**🍷 Drinking**

| | |
|---|---|
| **8** Weranda Cafe | B2 |

buildings here and gain insight into the cultures of the Boyks and Lemks (see the boxed text, p206). Among the highlights are four timber churches, an inn, a school and even a fire station. The interiors of many cottages are furnished and decorated as they once were, while some buildings house exhibitions; one of these features a collection of 200 icons. To reach the skansen, walk north from the town centre for around 1km along ul Mickiewicza and ul Białogórska, cross the bridge over the San and turn right.

**Historic Churches**                     CHURCHES

At the southeast corner of the Rynek is the **Franciscan Church of the Holy Cross** (Kościół Franciszkanów Św Krzyża; ul Franciszkańska), the town's oldest, dating to the 1640s. The neo-Romanesque **Parish Church** (Kościół Parafialny; ul Grzegorza), dating from 1886, has Art Nouveau wall paintings and remarkable stained glass behind the main altar. The neoclassical **Orthodox Church of the Holy Trinity** (Cerkiew Św Trójcy; ul Zamkowa) was built in 1784 and initially served the Uniat congregation. The main door behind the grill is left open for you to admire the modern iconostasis.

## 🏃 Activities

Sanok is an excellent base for **hiking**, especially the **Icon Trail** (Szlak Ikon), which takes you past tiny villages and their old Orthodox or Uniat churches. Most of these are traditional wooden ones and a reminder of the pre-WWII ethnic and religious fabric of the region. The most popular route is a 70km-long loop that begins and ends in Sanok and wends along the San River valley north of the city. The net walking time is about 15 hours. The Icon Trial is designated on hiking maps of the Bieszczady available for purchase at the tourist information or PTTK offices. The tourist information office also hands out a free photocopied, simplified version of the trail (though not detailed enough to hike with), showing the main villages and churches.

Sanok is also good for **cycling**, both for mountain biking in the hills and less strenuous, though still rewarding rides along the San River. Hiking maps also designate cycling trails. The helpful staff of the Sanok tourist information office can help plan out a ride.

Sanok lies astride the **Greenway Bicycle Trail** (Szlak Zielony Rower; www.zielonyrower .pl), a sprawling network of bicycle-friendly roads and pathways that covers hundreds of kilometres in all directions (note that some Greenway routes are actually not that 'green', taking you along fairly busy highways). To get started, buy a copy of the *Atlas Szlaków Rowerowych Podkarpackie* from the tourist information office (20zł), which has all of the Greenway paths marked out. Another useful guide, though harder to find, is the *Compass Bieszczady Zielony Rower* (18zł), with all the region's cycling routes mapped out.

Bicycles can be hired from **Camp Biała Góra**, for 7/30zł per hour/day.

## BOYKS & LEMKS: A TALE OF TWO PEOPLES

The Bieszczady, along with the Beskid Niski and Beskid Sądecki further west, were settled from around the 13th century by various nomadic Slavic groups migrating northwards from the south and east. Most notable among them were the Wołosi from the Balkans and the Rusini from Ruthenia. Though they lived in the same areas and even intermarried for centuries, they maintained distinct ethnic identities, which came to be known as Bojkowie and Łemkowie.

The Bojkowie (Boyks) inhabited the eastern part of the Bieszczady, east of Cisna, while the Łemkowie (Lemks) populated the mountainous regions stretching from the western Bieszczady up to the Beskid Sądecki. The two groups had much in common culturally, including a shared Orthodox faith that was similar to that of their Ukrainian neighbours.

After the Union of Brest in 1596, in which some western Orthodox faiths broke with the Patriarch in Constantinople, most Lemks and Boyks turned to the Uniat Church, which accepted the supremacy of Rome but retained the old Eastern liturgy. This lasted until the end of the 19th century, when the Catholic Church began to impose the Latin rite. In response, many Lemks and Boyks chose to revert to the more familiar traditions of the Orthodox Church. By WWII, the total population of Lemks and Boyks was estimated at around 200,000 to 300,000. Ethnic Poles were a minority.

The situation changed dramatically in the aftermath of WWII, when the borders of Poland and the Soviet Union were redrawn. Not everyone was satisfied with the new status quo, particularly a band of Ukrainian nationalists known as the Ukrainian Resistance Army, who were unhappy at finding themselves inside a newly reconstituted Poland. Civil war continued in the region for almost two years after Germany surrendered.

In a bid to rid the region of rebels, the postwar Polish government launched Operation Vistula (Akcja Wisła) in 1947 to expel the inhabitants of the region. Most residents were either deported to the Soviet Union or resettled in the western regions of Poland that had been recently regained from Germany. Ironically, the largest groups to be deported were the Boyks and the Lemks, who had little to do with the conflict. Only 20,000 Lemks, and very few Boyks, were left in the region.

Today, the most visible reminders of their legacy are the wooden Orthodox or Uniat churches dotting the countryside, many dilapidated but others still in decent condition. When hiking on remote trails, especially along the Ukrainian border in the Bieszczady, you'll find traces of destroyed villages, including ruined houses, orchards, churches and cemeteries.

## 🛏 Sleeping

### Hotel Sanvit
HOTEL €€

(📞13 465 5088; www.sanvit.sanok.pl in Polish; ul Łazienna 1; s/d/tr 140/190/240zł; P 🐾 🛜) Clean, reasonably priced and central, just west of the Rynek, the Sanvit is our top choice in Sanok. The 31 rooms are bright and modern, with shiny bathrooms. There's a restaurant and cafe, as well as a wellness centre with sauna, gym and a salt cave.

### Hotel Jagielloński
HOTEL €

(📞13 463 1208; www.hoteljagiellonski.pl; ul Jagiellońska 49; s/d/tr 130/180/215zł; P 🛜) The 19-room Jagielloński, with distinctive wooden furniture, parquetry floors and a very good restaurant, is excellent value. Rooms are spacious and have full facilities.

### Hotel Pod Trzema Różami
HOTEL €

(📞13 464 1243; www.podtrzemarozami.pl in Polish; ul Jagiellońska 13; standard s/d/tr 85/110/130zł, lux r 150zł; P 🛜) About 200m south of the main square, 'Under Three Roses' offers both standard and 'lux' rooms, the latter with full baths and updated decor. Both types of rooms are clean and adequate for a short stay.

### Camp Biała Góra
CAMPING GROUND €

(📞13 463 2818; camp_sanok@poczta.onet.pl; Biała Góra; camping per person/tent 15/15zł, beds in bungalows per person 30-35zł; P) Though not a true camping ground in that there's not much room for caravans and only modest ground to pitch a tent, Biała Góra has plenty of two- and four-person bungalows to rent. There are communal cooking facilities and clean bathrooms, though the property itself is a little run down. You'll find it about 1km north of the Rynek, on the other side of the river from town, just beside the entrance to the skansen.

## 🍴 Eating & Drinking

### Karczma Jadło Karpackie
POLISH €€

(www.karczmasanok.pl; Rynek 12; mains 10-30zł) This amenable, folksy bar and restaurant on the main square serves up unusual Carpathian dishes, including *hreczanyky* (a local dish made with minced pork and buckwheat groats) and *ogórki małosolne* (lightly salted pickles). Enjoy the terrace in nice weather.

### Restauracja U Szwejka
POLISH €€

(www.uszwejka.pl; ul 3 Maja 15; mains 10-30zł) Just down from the bronze statue of the soldier Švejk (from which it takes its name), this place has something for everyone: *pierogi*, pizza and pancakes.

### Weranda Cafe
CAFE

(ul 3 Maja 14) This cosy cafe-bar, with a fire-place glowing in winter and outdoor terrace set up in summer, is a good place to have a drink, alcoholic or otherwise, year-round.

## ℹ Information

**Bank Pekao** (ul Kościuszki 4; ⊘9am-6pm Mon-Fri, to 2pm Sat)

**Main post office** (ul Kościuszki 28; ⊘7am-8pm Mon-Fri, 8am-2pm Sat)

**Prox Internet** (ul Kazimierza Wielkiego 6; per hr 4zł; ⊘9am-6pm Mon-Fri, to 2pm Sat) Internet access.

**PTTK office** (📞13 463 2512; www.pttk.avx.pl in Polish; ul 3 Maja 2; ⊘8am-5pm Mon-Fri) Information about activities; excellent selection of maps.

**Tourist office** (📞13 463 6060; www.sanok.pl; Rynek 14; ⊘9am-5pm Mon-Fri, to 1pm Sat & Sun)

## ℹ Getting There & Away

The train and bus stations are next to each other, connected via a pedestrian overpass, about 1.2km southeast of the Rynek.

There's hourly bus transport to Rzeszów (12zł, 1½ hours). Buses also run to Ustrzyki Dolne (9zł, one hour, 12 daily) and Ustrzyki Górne (15zł, 1½ to 2½ hours, seven daily). Five to six buses run to Cisna (9zł, one hour) and Wetlina (13zł, 1½ to two hours), with additional departures in summer. Several fast buses go directly to Kraków (40zł, three hours), and a smaller number to Warsaw (60zł, four to five hours).

Passenger train service has been scaled back and trains now serve only a handful of destinations, including Rzeszów (22zł, 4 hours) and Krosno (9zł, 1½ hours), but these are better served by bus.

## Lesko

POP 5860

Founded in 1470 on the banks of the San River, Lesko had a mixed Polish-Ruthenian population for centuries, a reflection of the region's history. From the 16th century, many Jews arrived from Spain, fleeing the Inquisition. Their migration continued and by the 18th century Jews made up half of the town's population.

WWII and the years that followed changed the ethnic picture altogether. The Jews were slaughtered by the Nazis, the Ukrainians were defeated by the Polish military and the Lemks were deported. The town was rebuilt and, without having developed any significant industry, is now a small tourist centre. While it may not be the 'Gateway to the Bieszczady' as it likes to call itself – that distinction really goes to Sanok – it is a pleasant stopover on the way south.

## Sights & Activities

Lesko is notable for its Jewish heritage. From the oddly shaped Rynek, with its 19th-century **town hall** in the middle, head 200m north to the town's erstwhile **synagogue** (ul Joselewicza). Built in the Mannerist style in the mid-18th century, the synagogue has an attached tower – a dead giveaway that it was once part of the town's fortifications. Little of the temple's original decoration has survived. The interior houses the **Synagogue Art Gallery** (Galeria Sztuki Synagoga; adult/concession 5/3zł; ⏱10am-5pm May-Oct), which is supposed to showcase artists from the Bieszczady. In the entryway is a list of towns and *shtetls* in the region with Jewish populations of more than 100, a poignant reminder of what the make-up of the region was before the German murderers arrived.

From the synagogue, follow ul Moniuszki north (downhill) about 200m; the stairs on the right lead up to the old **Jewish cemetery**. More than 2000 gravestones, the oldest one dating back to the mid-16th century, are scattered amid trees and ever-consuming ivy, in varying stages of decay. Some of them miraculously retain their rich decoration; others have been defaced.

Just west of the synagogue is the **Parish Church of Our Lady** (Kościół Parafialny Najświętszej Marii Panny; ul Kościuszki). It was built in 1539 and its exterior still retains many Gothic features, including the eastern portal. The freestanding Baroque bell tower was added in the mid-18th century.

## Sleeping & Eating

**Pensjonat Zamek**                    HOTEL €€
(☏13 469 6268; www.zamek.bieszczady.pl; ul Piłsudskiego 7; s/d/tr 110/150/195zł; P🛜) From the exterior, Lesko's aging *zamek* (castle) looks none too inviting. Prospects change, however, once you walk through the door to discover a well-run and atmospheric inn and the best place in town to stay. The public areas have retained a bit of the castle's 16th-century heritage. Alas, the rooms are unadorned, but they are still comfortable. The location is a short walk from the Rynek.

**Hotelik Ratuszowa**                    HOTEL €
(☏13 469 8632; www.lesko.pl; Rynek 12, enter from ul Parkowa; s/d/tr 70/100/130zł; P) The Ratuszowa is the only hotel in Lesko that's right on the Rynek. That said, it's a modest, family-run affair, with eight small and rather plain rooms up under the eaves of its restaurant (mains 10zł to 25zł, open 9am to 9pm), which serves Polish favourites.

**Camping Nad Sanem**           CAMPING GROUND €
(☏13 469 6689; ul Turystyczna 1; beds per person 20-35zł; ⏱May-Sep; P) On the riverside below the castle, the camping ground has 15 bungalows with rooms of different sizes, an area where you can pitch your tent and a restaurant.

## WHEN GOD WAS ON VACATION

Based on the number of day tours to Auschwitz-Birkenau on offer, especially out of Kraków, you would be forgiven for thinking that the nightmare of the Holocaust, the time 'when God was on vacation' as some Jews put it, was played out solely in the German-run extermination camps at Oświęcim in Upper Silesia. But even a cursory trip around Galicia, the Austro-Hungarian province that was heavily Jewish and included many of the towns and cities mentioned in this chapter, will dispel that notion. As dozens of plaques, memorials and crude markers point out, hundreds of thousands of Polish Jews – in fact, a quarter of the three million annihilated – were murdered in their fields and forests at the hands of the Germans. And in some respects it is even more horrible to imagine such crimes committed in the idyllic surrounds of a country town or village.

And the cemeteries… You may have wondered why they are so overgrown, their broken stones pitched this way and that. The answer is simple: there are no relatives left. Brothers, mothers, husbands, lovers, nephews and granddaughters – none survived the Holocaust.

When a Jew dies, a prayer called the Mourner's Kaddish is recited for them. The kaddish is repeated at Yahrzeit, the first anniversary of the death, and annually after that. But virtually no Jews lying in cemeteries such as the one at Lesko have anyone to say this prayer for them.

## ℹ️ Information

**Bank PKO** (ul Przemysłowa 11; ⊘8am-3.30pm Mon-Fri)

**Bieszczady Adventure** (📱13 469 7270; www .krainawilka.pl; Dom Handlowy Bldg, Rynek 2) Specialises in active sport, including rafting, trekking, fly-fishing, off-road and mountain biking.

**Main post office** (ul Parkowa; ⊘7am-8pm Mon-Fri, 8am-2pm Sat)

**Tourist office** (📱013 469 6695; bcit@lesko .pl; ⊘8am-5pm Mon-Sat) Very helpful tourist office in a kiosk in the centre of the Rynek.

## ℹ️ Getting There & Away

The bus station is on ul Piłsudskiego – the road to Sanok – about 1km west of the Rynek. There are plenty of buses to Sanok (5zł, 20 minutes), about 11 of which continue to Krosno (12zł, one hour). A dozen daily buses run to Rzeszów (14zł, two hours) and four express buses go directly to Kraków (45zł, three hours).

For the Bieszczady, three daily buses go to Cisna (8zł, one hour), and some wind up as far as Wetlina (10zł, 1½ hours). As many as 10 buses serve Ustrzyki Górne (12zł, two hours), half of which go via Ustrzyki Dolne.

# Ustrzyki Dolne

POP 9600

An unprepossessing town in the southeastern corner of Poland, Ustrzyki Dolne (oost-*shi*-kee *dol*-neh) is really only an overnight stop for those heading south into the Bieszczady; the headquarters of the Bieszczady National Park is conveniently located here. If you plan on trekking in the mountains independently, Ustrzyki Dolne is the last reliable place to exchange money and stock up on a decent range of provisions.

## ◎ Sights & Activities

There's not much to see in Ustrzyki Dolne except for the **Natural History Museum** (Muzeum Przyrodnicze; www.bdpn.pl in Polish; ul Bełska 7; adult/concession 7/5zł; ⊘9am-5pm Tue-Sat, plus 9am-2pm Sun Jul & Aug) behind the tourist office. It's a good introduction to the geology, flora and fauna of the Bieszczady.

Enquire about horse-riding and riding excursions at the **Galop** (📱13 461 1272; horse@w .polsce.com; ul Chopina 21) shop and travel agency west of the centre.

## 🛏️ Sleeping & Eating

**Hotelik Bieszczadzki**                    HOTEL €
(📱13 461 1071; www.bieszczadzka.com; Rynek 19; d/tr with en suite 100/170zł, s/d/tr with shared

bathroom 50/80/120zł; 🅿️) The most central place in town, the 16-room Bieszczadzki is simple and has a similarly modest pizza **restaurant** (mains 12zł to 22zł; ⊘8am-10pm Mon-Thu, to midnight Fri-Sun).

**Hotel Laworta**                    HOTEL €
(📱13 468 9000; www.laworta.pl in Polish; ul Nadgórna 107; s/d 120/170 zł; 🅿️🛜) This isolated modern high-rise hotel is a good 1.5km walk uphill from the Rynek and the main bus station; nevertheless it offers clean rooms and good facilities, including tennis courts and a sauna. Call or book in advance to make sure someone is at the reception desk on your arrival.

## ℹ️ Information

**Bank Pekao** (Rynek 17; ⊘9am-4.30pm Mon-Fri) Next to the tourist office.

**Bieszczady National Park headquarters** (📱13 461 0650; www.bdpn.pl; ul Bełska 7; ⊘9am-5pm Tue-Sat, plus 9am-2pm Sun Jul & Aug) In the museum.

**Tourist office** (📱13 471 1130; www.cit .ustrzyki-dolne.pl in Polish; Rynek 16; ⊘8.30am-4pm Mon-Fri, 9am-2pm Sat)

## ℹ️ Getting There & Away

The train and bus stations are in one building. You won't get far by train – Zagórz (8zł, 2¾ hours) and Jasło (18zł, 4½ hours) are two of the very few destinations – but bus service is reasonably good. Two dozen daily buses run to Sanok (10zł, one hour), some passing through Lesko (5zł, 30 minutes) on the way. Up to seven buses (several more in summer) go daily to Ustrzyki Górne (9zł, 1½ hours). Destinations further afield include Przemyśl (12zł, two hours, four daily), Rzeszów (18zł, 2½ hours, seven daily) and Kraków (50zł, four hours).

# Ustrzyki Górne

POP 120

Less of a village than a string of houses scattered along the main road, Ustrzyki Górne is the Bieszczady's premier hiking base.

Since the Bieszczady loop road opened in 1962, the mountains have become more accessible. But this is still remote country and Ustrzyki Górne is a good example: it has a few mostly basic places to stay and eat, a little bit of life around the bus station and car park as you enter the village, and not much else. The village springs to life in summer, then sinks into a deep sleep for most of the rest of the year, stirring only a little in winter when the cross-country skiers arrive.

## BEACH BREAK AT SOLINA LAKE

About 30km southwest of Ustrzyki Dolne and accessible by bus is Solina Lake (Jezioro Solińskie), a reservoir 27km long and 60m deep, created in 1968 when the San River was dammed. Today it is the Bieszczady region's most important centre for water sports and recreation.

Polańczyk, the attractive town on the irregularly shaped lake's western shore, offers visitors everything from sailing and windsurfing to fishing and beaches. The **tourist office** (☎13 470 3028; www.esolina.pl; ul Wiejska 2; ⊕8am-6pm Mon-Fri, 10am-6pm Sat), just off Hwy 894 on the way to Lesko, can supply you with all the details.

Ul Zdrojowa, which starts just east of the tourist office, is lined with hotels and sanatoriums offering any number of treatments. Many are huge soulless blocks; instead head for **Pensjonat Korona** (☎013 469 2201; www.pensjonatkorona.pl; ul Zdrojowa 29; s/d 80/140zł), a pleasant guesthouse with 40 beds and its own restaurant just over 1km south down the peninsula.

Though there's no tourist information office here, you can buy hiking maps and some general info from the reception desk at the Hotel Górski. There's a small store at the camping ground and a few small shops around the bus stop to buy provisions.

### 🏃 Activities

The number one activity here, at least in summer, is **hiking**. Ustrzyki Górne is the most popular base for hiking the **Bieszczady National Park** and several great walks start out from here (most from near the camping ground or the bus station and car park). The park is full of fascinating sights and sounds: the remnants of villages abandoned or destroyed during Operation Vistula (see the boxed text, p206), ancient cemeteries, peat reserves (complete with quicksand), and the cry of a lone wolf in the distance.

### 🛏 Sleeping & Eating

Villages such as Ustrzyki Górne usually don't have street names, but general directions should get you there.

**Hotel Górski**　　　　　　HOTEL €€
(☎13 461 0604; www.hotel-pttk.pl; s 95-125zł; d 155-200zł, apt 250-310zł; P@≋) At the northern end of the village on the road to Ustrzyki Dolne and bedecked with flower baskets, this PTTK-run hotel is significantly better than anything else around. With 63 clean, comfortable and modern rooms, all with their own bathrooms, it's also the biggest place in town. The hotel has a gym and sauna, and its own reasonably priced restaurant.

**Schronisko PTTK Kremenaros**　　HOSTEL €
(☎13 461 0605; dm 30zł; ⊕Apr-Oct; P) This hostel is in the last house of the village, on the western side of the road heading towards Wetlina and opposite a huge border station. It's old and basic, but the staff are friendly and the atmosphere good. Rooms have between two and 10 beds. The restaurant has a very short menu but the food is cheap and acceptable.

**Camping Nr 150 PTTK**　　CAMPING GROUND €
(☎13 461 0604; per person/tent 9/11zł, cabins with/without bathroom 40/29zł; ⊕May-Sep; P) The pleasant camping ground next door to the Hotel Górski has some old triple cabins without bathrooms and newer double cabins with en suites.

**Karczma U Eskulapa**　　POLISH €
(mains 10-18zł; ⊕8am-9pm) A convivial spot with an outdoor garden, U Eskulapa is well known for its *pierogi*, trout and *placek po bieszczadzku* (potato pancake filled with goulash). No address, but it's well-signposted, 50m from the car park and bus stop in the direction of the camping ground.

### ℹ Getting There & Away

There are up to seven buses daily to Ustrzyki Dolne (9zł, 1½ hours), two to Krosno (18zł to 19.50zł, three hours), three to Rzeszów (25zł, 3½ hours) and as many as nine a day to Lesko (12zł, two hours) and Sanok (15zł, 2½ hours). A couple more buses run in July and August to the above destinations, while several buses and minibuses go to Wetlina (5zł, 30 minutes) and up to six to Cisna (7zł, 45 minutes).

# Wetlina

POP 300

Wetlina is another popular jumping-off spot for hiking in the Bieszczady. Like Ustrzyki Górne, it stretches along one main road (in this case Hwy 897) and has a limited choice of simple places to sleep and eat.

## 🛏 Sleeping & Eating

**Dom Wycieczkowy PTTK**　　　　HOSTEL €
(☎13 468 4615; www.wetlinapttk.pl; dm 26zł, d 50-70zł; P) This old and very simple hostel offers beds year-round in doubles as well as dorms sleeping five. In summer you can also stay in cabins (30zł per person) or pitch your tent (10zł) on the grounds. The rustic restaurant here has rough pine tables and is decorated with carved wooden figures.

**Camping Górna Wetlinka**　　　HOSTEL €
(☎13 468 4776; per person/tent/car 8/7/10zł, family cabin 200zł; ⊙May-Oct) This excellent and very friendly camping ground also serves as an information point for Bieszczady National Park. Several hiking trails start from here and the staff can organise horse riding (25zł per hour). The home cooking at the on-site restaurant is excellent.

TOP
CHOICE **Stare Sioło**　　　　　POLISH €€
(☎503 124 654; www.staresiolo.com; mains 25-50zł; 🅟) On the Cisna side of Wetlina along the main road, this is easily the best restaurant in this part of Poland and worth a special trip. They pay keen attention to detail, from the custom woodworking in the traditional dining room to the wine list and ultimately to the quality of the cooking. Mains range from fish cooked over a fire to grilled meats, *pierogi* and other relatively simple foods, but done very well. There's a lovely garden and they have live jazz about once a week in summer.

## ❶ Getting There & Away

Up to 10 buses a day go to Sanok (11zł, two hours) via Lesko (9zł, 1½ hours). Count on up to nine buses a day to Ustrzyki Górne (5zł, 30 minutes) to the east and Cisna (5zł, 30 minutes) to the west.

# Cisna

POP 460

Cisna sits on the borderland between the territories once inhabited by the Boyks to the east and the Lemks to the west. The region was densely populated before WWII but today it counts fewer than 500 inhabitants, yet Cisna is still the largest village in the central part of the Bieszczady. Though not attractive in itself, the village has a decent choice of accommodation and is a good base for hiking. It is also the place to board the narrow-gauge tourist train.

---

## HIKING IN THE BIESZCZADY

The Bieszczady is one of the best places in Poland to go hiking. The region is beautiful and easy to walk around, and you don't need a tent or cooking equipment as mountain hostels are a day's walk apart and provide food. The main area for trekking is the national park, with Ustrzyki Górne and Wetlina being the most popular starting points, followed by Cisna.

Bieszczady National Park counts about a dozen well-marked hiking trails, with a total length of 130km. All three jumping-off points have PTTK hostels, with helpful staff who can provide information, and all have boards outlining the trails, complete with walking times, both uphill and downhill. Ascending **Mt Tarnica** (the region's highest peak at 1346m) from Wołosate, southeast of Ustrzyki Górne, will take two to three hours. At least one of the trails reaches (but does not cross) the Ukrainian border at one point. Be sure to carry your passport when hiking in this area.

Mountain hostels will try their best to put you up for the night and feed you regardless of how crowded they get, but bear in mind that in July and August the floor will most likely be your bed, as these places are pretty small. Take a sleeping bag with you.

Get a copy of Galileos' 1:50,000-scale *Bieszczady* map (13zł), which covers the whole region. Agencja Wit's 1:50,000-scale map showing both the Upper and Lower Bieszczady – *Bieszczady Wysokie i Niskie* – costs 18zł. You can buy these maps at the Hotel Górski in Ustrzyki Górne or at the national park offices in Ustrzyki Dolne. The maps are very similar and both are good for hikers.

The **tourist office** (☑13 468 6465; www .cisna.pl; ⊙8am-8pm Mon-Fri, 9am-5pm Sat May-Aug, 8am-4pm Mon-Fri Sep-Apr) is in the county cultural centre in the middle of the village. The staff are extremely helpful; there are also computers on hand to surf the net and even a ping-pong table if you get a rainy day.

## 🏃 Activities

The narrow-gauge train known as the **Bieszczady Forest Railway** (Bieszczadzka Kolejka Leśna; http://kolejka.bieszczady.pl in Polish), based at the station in Majdan, 2km west of Cisna, was built at the end of the 19th century to transport timber between Nowy Łupków and Majdan. The line was extended north to Rzepedź and east to Moczarne, beyond Wetlina. The train on the Majdan–Rzepedź route was in use as recently as 1993, but the line has since been turned into a tourist attraction.

There are two runs on offer. A longer and higher 12km stretch goes from Majdan to Przysłup (adult/child 13/10zł one way, 20/14zł return), midway between Cisna and Wetlina. In July and August it runs once a day during the week at 10am and twice a day on weekends (10am and 1.30pm). The other run – a flatter 9km stretch between Majdan and Balnica (11/9zł one way, 16/12zł return) – follows a similar schedule, running daily during the week at 1.30pm and twice on weekends, at 10.30pm and 1pm. In May, June and September, the trains run once a day on weekends only.

For cycling fans, Ośrodek Wczasowy Perełka rents bikes for 7/25zł per hour/day.

## 🍴 Sleeping & Eating

Cisna has plenty of places of stay, though most of these are in tiny pensions or mountain hostels. The tourist office is happy to help find rooms.

As for eating, at least a half dozen places open in summer near the crossroads (no addresses), though all are more or less Polish-style fast food. Try **Troll** (mains 14-22zł) near the main parking area for pizza. **Grill** (mains 15-22zł), despite the name, is better known for its sweet and savoury pancakes.

**OSW Wołosan**                    GUESTHOUSE €€
(☑13 468 6373; www.wolosan.pl; Cisna 87; s/d 100/160zł; P🛜) By far the classiest place in this part of the Bieszczady, the 27-room Wołosan at the eastern end of Cisna is geared towards hunters (thus the trophies and stuffed animals throughout) but can

organise any number of activities – from quad bikes and snowmobile excursions to off-road jeep safaris.

**Willa Helena**                    PENSION €
(☑502 573 061; http://willa-helena.net.pl; Cisna 107; s/d 35/70zł; P) This pleasant little B&B, opposite the road up to the Wołosan and Pod Honem, has around 10 neat rooms. It's fairly simple, but comfortable and homely.

**Bacówka PTTK Pod Honem**          HOSTEL €
(☑503 137 279; www.podhonem.home.pl in Polish; dm 25zł, d/tr/q 60/80/110zł; P) The 40-bed PTTK mountain hostel is 668m up on a slope at the eastern end of Cisna; it's about 1km up the hill from behind the Wołosan, along a steep dirt track. It's simple and friendly and serves uncomplicated meals.

**Ośrodek Wczasowy Perełka**      BUNGALOWS €
(☑13 468 6325; perelka@naturatour.pl; s/d 40/70zł, cabins per person 30zł; P⛷) The first house on the left as you enter Cisna from the west, this comfortable holiday home has 34 beds in singles and doubles plus another 54 in seasonal A-frame cabins. Also rents bikes.

## ❶ Getting There & Away

Half a dozen buses run daily to Sanok (8zł, one hour) and Wetlina (5zł, 30 minutes). There are more seasonal buses in summer, including up to six to Ustrzyki Górne (8zł, 45 minutes).

# BESKID NISKI

The Beskid Niski (Lower Beskid) is a forest-covered mountain range with gentle slopes that runs for about 85km west to east along the Slovakian frontier. It's bordered on the west by the Beskid Sądecki and on the east by the Bieszczady. As its name suggests, it is not a high outcrop: its tallest peak doesn't exceed 1000m and the range is made for easy walks. Admittedly the Beskid Niski offers less spectacular vistas than the neighbouring Bieszczady. But its dozens of small Orthodox and Uniat churches, especially in the western half of the region, are a strong draw.

## Krosno

POP 47,600
Founded in the 14th century and prosperous during the Renaissance – even nicknamed 'little Kraków' for a time – Krosno slid into

decay from the 18th century onwards. It revived with the trade of linen and Hungarian wine, and, in the mid-19th century, with the development of the oil industry. It is especially known for its ornamental and commercial glassworks.

There's enough here to occupy a half-day of meandering and two very good lodging options, making this a sensible choice for an overnight stay.

## ○ Sights

### TOWN CENTRE

The Old Town's spacious **Rynek** has retained some of its Renaissance appearance, notably in the houses fronted by wide arcaded passageways that line the southern and northeastern parts of the square. The best example is the **Wójtowska Townhouse** (Kamienica Wójtowska; Rynek 7).

### Franciscan Church of the
**Holy Cross** CHURCH
(Kościół Franciszkanów Św Krzyża; ul Franciszkańska) A few steps southeast of the Rynek is the large 15th-century Franciscan church, today filled with neo-Gothic furnishings. The showpiece here is the **Oświęcim Family Chapel** (Kaplica Oświęcimów), just to the left as you enter the church. Built in 1647 by Italian architect Vincenti Petroni, and embellished with magnificent stucco work by another Italian master, Jan Falconi, the chapel is considered one of the best early Baroque chapels in Poland.

### Parish Church of the Holy Trinity CHURCH
(Kościół Parafialny Św Trócy; ul Piłsudskiego) Another huge brick structure, the Parish Church is 50m northwest of the Rynek. Founded in 1402, it was almost completely consumed by fire in the mid-17th century (only the chancel survived) and rebuilt. Note the intricate grape pattern on the wrought-iron main gates. Inside, the renovated gilded high altar is 350 years old, as is the elaborate pulpit. The freestanding onion-domed bell tower (1651) houses three bells called Jan, Marian and Urban. The tower is one of the largest in Poland.

### Subcarpathian Museum MUSEUM
(Muzeum Podkarpackie; www.muzeum.krosno.pl in Polish; ul Piłsudskiego 16; adult/concession 7/4zł; ☺10am-4pm Tue-Sun) One block northwest of the church is the Subcarpathian Museum. Installed in the 15th-century former Bishops' Palace, the museum has interesting historical, archaeological and art sections.

The highlight, however, is its extensive collection of decorative old kerosene lamps, reputedly the largest in Europe.

### Craft Museum MUSEUM
(Muzeum Rzemiosła; www.muzeumrzemiosla.pl in Polish; ul Piłsudskiego 19; adult/concession 5/3zł; ☺9am-5pm Mon-Fri, 10am-2pm Sat & Sun May-Sep, 9am-3pm Mon-Fri, 10am-2pm Sat Oct-Apr) Directly opposite the Subcarpathian Museum is the Craft Museum, featuring displays related to such local crafts and trades as clockmaking, weaving, saddlery and even hairdressing.

### Krosno glassworks GLASS FACTORY
(Krośnieńskie Huty Szkła; www.krosno.com.pl; ul Tysiąclecia 13) About 1km northwest of the Old Town is the famous Krosno glassworks. A **factory shop** (☺9am-5pm Mon-Fri) on site sells a range of its products, including beautiful wine glasses and stemware.

### OUTSIDE THE CENTRE
### Church of the Assumption of
**Mary and Michael the Archangel** CHURCH
(Kościół Wniebowzięcia Matki Boskiej i Św Michała Archanioła) In the village of Haczów (*hah*-choof), about 16km east of Krosno and accessible by PKS bus from Krosno, stands what is considered the largest timber Gothic church in Europe and a Unesco World Heritage site since 2003. The church was built in the mid-15th century on the site of a previous church founded by Władysław Jagiełło in 1388. The walls and coffered ceiling inside are covered in naive paintings dating from the late 15th century and restored in the 1990s.

### Museum of the Oil & Gas Industry MUSEUM
(Muzeum Przemysłu Naftowego i Gazowniczego; www.bobrka.pl; 38-458 Chorkówa; adult/concession 9/5zł; ☺9am-5pm Tue-Sun May-Sep, 7am-3pm Tue-Sun Oct-Apr) The village of Bóbrka, 17km southwest of Krosno, is the cradle of the Polish oil industry. It was here in 1854 that the world's first oil well was sunk by Ignacy Łukasiewicz, inventor of the paraffin lamp. These days, the site where Łukasiewicz first hit pay dirt is a curious open-air museum, and worth the trek out here by bus from Krosno if you have a half day to spend. Among the early wells and derricks on display is the world's oldest surviving hand-dug oil shaft, named Franek and dating back to 1860. From Krosno about 10 buses go daily to Bóbrka village (3zł, 30 minutes), though fewer depart at the weekends. The

skansen is at Chorkówa, about 2km north of where the bus will let you off.

## 🛏 Sleeping

It's a toss-up. Krosno is blessed with two equally good choices to stay depending on what you're looking for: atmosphere and charm or modern convenience.

### Hotel Śnieżka                    HOTEL €€
(☑13 432 3449; www.hotelsniezka.pl; ul Lewakowskiego 22; s/d 110/160zł; P❄@🕾) For atmosphere and charm, this attractive brick-red Victorian townhouse is hard to beat. You'll find 14 cosy rooms, all sparklingly modern, with polished wood floors and big bathrooms. The in-house restaurant is pretty stylish too. The location is within comfortable walking distance of the bus and train stations.

### Hotel Krosno-Nafta               HOTEL €€
(☑13 432 6212; www.hotel.nafta.pl; ul Lwowska 21; s/d/tr 170/240/350zł; P@🕾) In the modern-convenience camp, this is the city's first choice for business clients, but its rates are low enough to appeal to private travellers as well. There are 41 big, comfortable rooms on offer and a decent upmarket restaurant. The hotel is 1km southeast of the centre on the Sanok road. Prices drop 20% at the weekend.

### Pensjonacik Buda                 PENSION €€
(☑13 432 0053; www.buda.krosno.pl; ul Jagiellońska 4; d/tr/ste 150/200/250 zł; P🕾) Despite sitting next to the railway tracks, this B&B is a long 2km walk from the train station and about 1km from the Rynek. Still, it boasts the best restaurant in town and the rooms are clean and comfortable (but not always quiet, owing to the occasional train whistle).

## 🍴 Eating

### TOP CHOICE / Restauracja Buda    POLISH €€
(☑13 432 0053; www.buda.krosno.pl; ul Jagiellońska 4; mains 15-35zł; 🕾) You're not going to believe this as you wend your way out of town, past vacant lots and factory car parks, but this is the best restaurant in Krosno and worth the effort to find it. Excellent traditional Polish cooking with a modern touch – such as roast pork with plum sauce and walnuts – in a refined but not stuffy atmosphere. To get there from the centre, follow ul Czajkowskiego southwest about 1km from Plac Konstytucji 3 Maja and take a left on ul Jagiellońska.

### Royal Hall                       POLISH €€
(Rynek 24; mains 18-24zł) Arguably the best of several similarly nondescript Polish and pizza places that line the Rynek. Offers a good-value daily lunch special, with main, side and dessert, for around 18zł.

### Cukierna Santos                  BAKERY €
(ul Staszica 16; cakes & pastries 2-10zł; ⊘8am-8pm) This very popular little bakery and cafe sells a wide range of fresh-baked pastries, cakes and other sweet and savoury snacks.

## ℹ Information

**Bank PKO** (ul Słowackiego 4; ⊘8.30am-4pm Mon-Fri) Northeast of the Rynek.

**Jack-Pol** (Plac Konstytucji 3 Maja 3; per hr 3zł; ⊘8am-7pm Mon-Fri, 9am-4pm Sat, to 3pm Sun) Internet access south of the Rynek.

**Tourist office** (☑13 432 7707; www.krosno.pl; Rynek 5; ⊘9am-4pm Mon-Fri, 10am-2pm Sat & Sun) At the southeast corner of the main square.

## ℹ Getting There & Away

The train and bus stations sit eyeballing one another 1.5km west of the Rynek.

A dozen or so daily buses head eastwards for Sanok (9zł, 1½ hours), up to four of which continue to Ustrzyki Dolne (18zł, two hours) and two to Ustrzyki Górne (20zł, three hours). Several fast buses depart daily for Kraków (30zł, three hours), and hourly buses go to Rzeszów (12zł, 1½ hours). There are frequent buses south to Dukla (5zł, 45 minutes) and regular buses to Bóbrka (4zł, 30 minutes). For Haczów (3zł, 40 minutes) count on up to 10 buses a day, most of which terminate at Brzozów.

Krosno has lost a lot of its passenger rail service in recent years. Currently, there are three departures daily to Sanok (10zł, 1½ hours) and three to Rzeszów (18zł, 3 hours), but nearly everyone takes the bus to these places too.

## Dukla

POP 2140

Dukla, 19km southwest of Krosno, is close to the Dukla Pass (Przełęcz Dukielska), the lowest and most easily accessible passage over the Western Carpathians. In the 16th century this strategic location brought prosperity to the town, which became a centre of the wine trade on the route from Hungary. Its heyday was in the 18th century, when most of its important monuments were built.

For history buffs, the Dukla Pass is best known as the site of an epic WWII battle in autumn 1944 pitting Nazi Germany on one side and the Soviet Red Army and Slovak partisan units on the other. The battle lasted about a month, with Soviet forces

## HIKING IN THE BESKID NISKI

Two main trails cover the entire length of the Beskid Niski range. The trail marked in blue originates in Grybów, goes southeast to the border and then eastwards all along the frontier to bring you eventually to Nowy Łupków near Komańcza. The red trail begins in Krynica, crosses the blue trail around Hańczowa, continues east along the northern slopes of the Beskid, and arrives at Komańcza. Both these trails head further east into the Bieszczady.

You need four to six days to do the whole of the Beskid Niski on either of these routes, but other trails, as well as a number of rough roads, link the two main trails.

A dozen hostels scattered in small villages throughout the region provide shelter, but most are open only in high summer (July and August). There are also a number of agrotourist farms; these are open for a longer season and sometimes year-round. If you plan on more ambitious trekking, camping gear may be useful. You can buy some elementary supplies in the villages you pass, but you're better off stocking up on essentials before you set out.

The major starting points for the Beskid Niski are Krynica, Grybów and Gorlice from the west; Komańcza and Sanok from the east; and Krosno and Dukla for the central part.

The 1:125,000 *Beskid Niski i Pogórze* map (10zł) from PPWK will give you all the basic information you need for hiking. A more detailed map is Galileos' 1:50,000 *Beskid Niski* (20zł). You can find these maps at tourist offices in Nowy Sącz and Krynica, the PTTK office in Krynica, or at the EMPiK bookshop in Nowy Sącz.

finally breaking through the German lines and crossing into Slovakia in early October. It was one of the fiercest battles of the war, leaving more than 100,000 dead on both sides, and is still commemorated in the Czech Republic and Slovakia. In strategic terms, it was a game-changer, bringing the Red Army south of the Carpathians, from where they eventually met up with other Soviet and Allied units coming up from Hungary for their eventual final push westwards to Prague.

In spite of the area's historic role, these days Dukla is a sleepy place with little in the way of facilities. There's a small **tourist information office** (www.turystyka.karpaty .dukla.pl; ☑13 433 5616; ul Trakt Węgierski 26a; ☉8am-3pm Mon-Sat) at the centre of the town, near the bus stop. You'll find a branch of **Bank PKO** (ul Mickiewicza 1; ☉8am-3.30pm Mon-Fri) south of the parish church.

### ◉ Sights

Dukla's large Rynek boasts a squat **town hall** in the centre. Across the Krosno road to the northwest and next to the tiny Dukielska River is the mighty **Parish Church of St Mary Magdalene** (Kościół Parafialny Św Marii Magdaleny), built in 1765. With its glorious pink and white stuccoed and marbled wood interior, it's a fine example of late Baroque and Rococo architecture.

Diagonally opposite the church is the **Historical Museum** (Muzeum Historyczne; ☑013 433 0085; Trakt Węgierski 5; adult/ concession 6/4zł; ☉10am-6pm Tue-Sun May-Sep, to 3.30pm Tue-Sun Oct-Apr), housed in the decaying 18th-century Mniszech Palace (Pałac Mniszchów). We're huge fans of WWII history and we'd love to give this museum a big thumbs up, but unfortunately it's a disappointment. The static displays of the battle are annotated in Polish only and arranged in a way that makes comprehension nearly impossible. Still, there are some interesting maps and photos, and the park surrounding the palace has a permanent display of 20 heavy weapons, including tanks, big guns, lorries and fighter planes.

### 🛏 Sleeping & Eating

**Dom Wycieczkowy PTTK** HOSTEL €
(☑13 433 0046; Rynek 18; dm 25zł, s/tr 40/80zł; ℗) The local PTTK offers seven stark rooms with bare-bones facilities, but it also has its own pub and cheap restaurant (open 9am to 10pm).

**Dukla Hostel** HOSTEL €
(☑13 433 0886; ptsmdukla@op.pl; Rynek 9; dm 25zł) A basic and very central option on the Rynek, this year-round hostel has 40 beds.

### ⓘ Getting There & Away

About a dozen daily buses head up to Krosno (5zł, 45 minutes) and four south to Barwinek (5zł, 40 minutes), near the Slovak border and the Dukla Pass. Count on four buses to/from Rzeszów (15zł, two hours).

# Biecz

POP 4630

One of the oldest settlements in Poland, Biecz (pronounced bee-ech) was a busy commercial centre from at least the 15th century. It benefited from the wine-trading route heading south over the Carpathians to Hungary, and some 30 crafts developed here. In the 17th century Biecz began to see its prosperity wane when the plague struck and new trade routes bypassed the town. The sleepy atmosphere seems to have remained to this day, though some important historic monuments and a good museum make the town worth a stop.

A small, helpful **tourist information office** (www.biecz.pl; ☑13 447 1114; Rynek 1; ⊘9am-5pm) is at the centre of the Rynek, below the tower. They have a computer terminal on hand in case you need to check your email. **Bank PKO** (Rynek 17; ⊘8.15am-3.30pm Mon-Fri) is also on the main square.

## ⊙ Sights

The location of the town's spacious Rynek is visible for miles around, because of the huge 56m-high octagonal **tower** (adult/concession 3/1.50zł; ⊘8am-3pm Tue-Sat) at its centre. Normally, you can climb the tower, but on our visit it was closed for renovation (though expected to reopen in 2012). The tower, which looks a little like a lighthouse, was built between 1569 and 1581, except for the top, which is a Baroque addition. Its original Renaissance decoration and the unusual 24-hour clock face on its eastern side have been restored in recent years.

**Corpus Christi Parish Church**　CHURCH
(Kościół Parafialny Bożego Ciała) West of the Rynek is the monumental Corpus Christi parish church. This mighty Gothic brick structure, evidence of the town's erstwhile affluence, dates from the 15th century and looks vaguely Flemish. Inside, the chancel holds most of the church's treasures, most notably the late-Renaissance high altar and massive stalls, all from the early 17th century. To the side of the altar is a gilded woodcarving depicting the genealogical tree of the Virgin Mary. Further up is an impressive crucifix from 1639.

Near the church are the remains of the **town walls** and what has become known as **Execution Tower** (Katownia). Biecz was allowed to pass death sentences, and there was even a corporation of executioners who appear to have taken their job pretty seriously. In the year 1614 alone, some 120 brigands were executed here.

**Biecz Regional Museum**　MUSEUM
(Muzeum Ziemi Bieckiej; ⊘8am-3pm Mon-Fri, 10am-6pm Sat & Sun) Most of the collection of the excellent Biecz Regional Museum is housed in two 16th-century buildings, both close to the church. The so-called **House with a Turret** (Dom z Basztą; ul Węgierska; adult/concession 8/4zł) holds the complete contents of an ancient pharmacy, including its laboratory, as well as musical instruments, traditional household utensils, equipment from old craft workshops and a cellar for storing Hungarian wine. The **Kromer Townhouse** (Kamienica Kromerówka; ul Kromera 3; adult/concession 4/2zł) has more historical exhibits on the town's past, plus archaeological and numismatic collections.

## 🛏 Sleeping & Eating

**Hotel Centennial**　HOTEL €€
(☑13 447 1576; www.centennial.com.pl; Rynek 6; s/d/tr 180/190/290zł; 🅿@🛜) The somewhat over-the-top Centennial – all swag drapes, chrome and leatherette settees – offers the best facilities in town, including suites of different size and design in two historic burghers' houses. The hotel's **restaurant** (mains 12zł to 30zł, ⊘10am-10pm) serves excellent and reasonably priced Polish food and pizza.

**Hotel Restauracja Grodzka**　HOTEL €
(☑013 447 1121; grodzka@grodzka.info; ul Kazimierza Wielkiego 35; s 60zł, d 65-70zł, apt 90zł; 🅿) This is a just-acceptable, 16-room, budget option not far from the hostel. It's nothing out of the ordinary, but it does have its own bright and airy **restaurant** (mains 9zł to 17zł, ⊘8am-10pm Mon-Sat, 10am-10pm Sun).

**Biecz Hostel**　HOSTEL €
(☑13 447 1014; ptsmbiecz@o2.pl; ul Parkowa 1; dm 30zł; 🅿) Basic but clean, this hostel with 130 beds is around 1km from the Rynek. It's on the top floor of a large school building and has only doubles and quads, so provides more privacy than most.

## ❶ Getting There & Away

All buses pass through and stop on the northeast and southwest sides of the Rynek. Buses to Jasło (5zł, 35 minutes) run regularly but only a few buses continue to Krosno (10zł, one hour). There are a couple of daily departures to Nowy Sącz (10zł, 1½ hours).

# BESKID SĄDECKI

Fanning out to the south of Nowy Sącz, the Beskid Sądecki (*bes*-keed son-*dets*-kee) is yet another attractive mountain range where you can hike, sightsee or simply have a rest at a mountain spa such as Krynica or Muszyna. The mountains are easily accessible from Nowy Sącz by two roads (Hwy 87 and Hwy 75) that head south along the river valleys, joining up with Hwy 971 to form a convenient loop; public transport is good along this route.

The Beskid Sądecki consists of two ranges, the Pasmo Jaworzyny and the Pasmo Radziejowej, which are separated by the Poprad River valley. There are a number of peaks over 1000m, the highest being Mt Radziejowa (1261m).

The Beskid Sądecki was the westernmost territory populated by the Lemks, and a dozen of their charming rustic churches survive, particularly around Krynica and Muszyna. *Beskid Sądecki* maps (scale 1:50,000; 10zł) published by two different firms (WiT and Demart) are helpful for both hikers and *cerkiew* peepers.

## Nowy Sącz

POP 84,600

Nowy Sącz (*no*-vi sonch), the economic and cultural centre of the Sącz region, is a laid-back town with an attractive main square and a few decent attractions, most notably its large skansen. It can also be a good base for further exploration of the surrounding countryside.

Founded in 1292 and fortified in the middle of the following century by King Kazimierz III Wielki (Casimir III the Great), Nowy Sącz developed rapidly until the 16th century, thanks to its strategic position on trading crossroads. As elsewhere, decline in the 17th century gave way to a partial revival at the close of the 19th century. Nowy Sącz grew considerably after WWII, and its historic district has been largely restored over recent years.

### ◎ Sights

Measuring 160m by 120m, Nowy Sącz's **Rynek** is one of the largest in Poland and is lined on all sides by a harmonious collection of historic houses. The large **town hall**, erected in the middle in 1897, incorporates a number of architectural styles, including Art Nouveau.

**Collegiate Church of St Margaret**      CHURCH
(Kościół Kolegiacki Św Małgorzaty; ul Św Ducha) This church, a block east of the Rynek, dates back to the 14th century but has undergone many changes since then. The small 15th-century image of Christ on the Renaissance main altar suggests a Byzantine influence. Note the remnants of a medieval fresco of the Last Supper on the column to the left as you enter. At the northern end of the same street is the Jesuit **Church of the Holy Spirit** (Kościół Św Ducha) and its massive cloister.

**District Museum**      MUSEUM
(Muzeum Okręgowe; www.muzeum.sacz.pl; ul Lwowska 3; adult/concession 8/5zł, free Sat; ◎10am-3pm Tue-Thu, to 5.30pm Fri, 9am-2.30pm Sat & Sun) The 15th-century Gothic building to the south of St Margaret's houses the district museum. The museum is dedicated to religious art, with naive religious paintings and folk-art woodcarvings collected from rural churches and roadside chapels throughout the region. The collection of Ruthenian Orthodox icons, which includes a splendid iconostasis of the 17th century, is especially fine.

**Jewish Sights**      SYNAGOGUE
(ul Joselewicza 12) For centuries Jews lived in the area just north of the Rynek. This is also the area where the Germans built their wartime Jewish ghetto, before shipping some 25,000 residents to extermination camps in 1942. Not much of the community or the ghetto remains today with the exception of a beautiful 18th-century **synagogue**. Miraculously, it survived the war and now holds a small but interesting **gallery** (admission free; ◎10am-3pm Wed & Thu, to 5.30pm Fri, 9am-2.30pm Sat & Sun) of old black-and-white photos from the community as well as a small display of Judaica. The synagogue was built in the first half of the 18th century in Baroque style but was remodelled in a neo-Moorish style in the 1920s.

Around 500m north of the former ghetto on the other side of the Kamienica River you'll find the **Jewish cemetery** (cmentarz żydowski; ul Rybacka). It contains a couple of hundred derelict headstones amid overgrown grass.

**Royal Castle**      RUIN
(Zamek Królewski; ul Kazimierza Wielkiego) The remains of the royal castle, built by Kazimierz III Wielki in the 1350s, stand along the river about 300m north of the Rynek. The castle

was in use till the early 17th century, when a fire destroyed much of it. You can still see doorways, windows, brick vaults and loopholes.

### OUTSIDE THE CENTRE

**Sącz Ethnographic Park**     OPEN-AIR MUSEUM
(Sądecki Park Etnograficzny; ul Długoszowskiego 83b; adult/concession 14/8zł, free Sat; ⏲10am-5pm Tue-Sun May-Sep, to 2pm Mon-Fri Oct-Apr) About 3.5km southeast of the centre, Sącz Ethnographic Park is one of the largest and best skansens in the country. Houses and other buildings typical of several ethnic cultures from the Carpathian Mountains and foothills are displayed in 10 groups. All in there are almost 70 buildings and other structures, including a farmhouse, forge, windmill, various churches and so on. Visits are in groups guided in Polish; follow along with *The Sącz Ethnographic Park* by Magdalena Kroh, available in English from the skansen shop. Infrequent city buses 14 and 15 go there from the train station, passing the bus station on the way.

## 🛏 Sleeping

**Hotel Panorama**     HOTEL €€
(☎18 443 7110; www.hotelpanoramanowysacz.pl; ul Romanowskiego 4a; s/d/tr/ste 120/180/210/320zł; P@🛜) The recently renovated Panorama, just off the Rynek, is far and away the best place to stay in the Old Town. Its 32 large, clean and comfortable rooms come with updated furniture and modern bathrooms. Ask for a room looking west towards the Dunajec River. Skip breakfast and knock 20zł off the room rate.

**Dom Turysty PTTK**     HOSTEL & CAMPING GROUND €
(☎18 441 5012; ul Nadbrzeżna 40; s/d/tr 85/95/130zł; P🛜) This year-round PTTK hostel has 21 spartan but spick-and-span rooms. It also operates a **camping ground** (per person/tent 13/7zł, open May to September) next door. The hostel is situated outside the centre, about 2km southeast of the Rynek, in the direction of the Sącz Ethnographic Park.

**Hotel Beskid**     HOTEL €€
(☎18 443 5770; www.hotelbeskid.pl; ul Limanowskiego 1; s/d 150/180zł; P@🛜) This austere 81-room hotel offers decent facilities and standards. It's 300m due north of the train station, but a brisk 20-minute hike to the Rynek. Discount rates of 120/140zł for singles/doubles apply at the weekend.

## 🍴 Eating

If none of the following options appeals, consider dinner on the terrace of the Hotel Panorama (mains 15zł to 30zł and the pretty riverside view is free).

---

**WORTH A TRIP**

## COBBLESTONES OF STARY SĄCZ

Stary Sącz (*stah*-ri sonch) is the older and smaller sister of Nowy Sącz, with a pretty, cobblestoned main square and some fetching churches to see. There's also an excellent restaurant in the centre, making it an ideal day trip planned around lunch.

The town owes its existence to 13th-century Duchess Kinga, wife of King Bolesław Wstydliwy (Bolesław the Shy), who in the 1270s founded the convent of the Poor Clares here. After the king's death, Kinga entered the convent, where she lived for the last 13 years of her life, becoming its first abbess.

Though there's a small regional museum here, the main sights are two historic churches. The **Church of the Poor Clares** (Kościół SS Klarysek; Plac Św Kingi) was where the town was born. It was originally Gothic in style and completed in 1332, though it was later given opulent Baroque fittings. The traces of its creator, Kinga, are clearly visible: the Baroque frescoes in the nave depict scenes from her life, and her chapel on the south side boasts a 1470 statue of her on the altar. The pulpit (1671) on the opposite wall is an extraordinary piece of art.

The nearby **Parish Church of St Elizabeth of Hungary** (Kościół Parafialny Św Elżbiety Węgierskiej; ul Kazimierza Wielkiego), two blocks south of the Rynek, dates from the town's 13th-century beginnings but was changed considerably in the 17th and 18th centuries. It's now a textbook example of unbridled Baroque, with five large florid altars.

For lunch or dinner, look no further than **Restauracja Marysieńka** (Rynek 12; mains 12-25zł; ⏲10am-10pm). Nothing fancy – just good Polish food served in a friendly, welcoming atmosphere.

**Restauracja Ratuszowa**　　　POLISH **€€**

(Rynek 1; mains 15-30zł) This restaurant below the Town Hall specialises in *pierogi* and has an impressive range indeed, including some stuffed with nettles, buckwheat groats and black pudding for the especially daring. Eat outdoors behind the Town Hall or downstairs, where you can admire the collection of communist-era propaganda posters on the wall.

**Piwnica Pod Ślepowronem**　　　POLISH **€€**

(ul Lwowska 2; mains 10-20zł; 🍴) This quirky pub-restaurant filled with antiques and curios is housed in a cellar at the southeast corner of the Rynek. On offer is a healthy choice of vegetarian dishes.

**Etc.**　　　CAFE **€**

(ul Romanowskiego 4a; coffee 6zł, cakes 6zł ⊗9.30am-10pm; 🛜) Just next to the Hotel Panorama, this little cafe and pastry shop serves delicious cookies, cakes and coffees. Our fave has to be the cookie made from Nutella: *babeczka z nutellą*. Also sells bottled wines and ice cream.

## ❶ Information

There are plenty of ATMs, banks and *kantors* around the Rynek and along the main pedestrian street that trails south from the Rynek, ul Jagiellońska.

**Bank PKO** (al Wolności 16; ⊗8am-7pm Mon-Fri)

**C@ffe Internet** (ul Kościuszki 22; per hr 3zł; ⊗8am-9pm Mon-Sat, 2-8pm Sun) Internet access.

**EMPiK** (Rynek 17; ⊗9am-6pm Mon-Fri, to 4pm Sat) Maps and English-language books and guides.

**Klub Mega** (1st fl, ul Kościuszki 26; per hr 3zł; ⊗8am-10pm Mon-Fri, 10am-10pm Sat & Sun) Internet access.

**Main post office** (ul Dunajewskiego 10; ⊗9am-5pm Mon-Fri) Located just off the southwest corner of the Rynek.

**PTTK office** (☎18 443 7457; Rynek 9; ⊗7am-3pm Mon, Wed & Thu, 11am-7pm Thu & Fri) Travel agency.

**Tourist office** (☎/fax 18 443 5597; www .nowysacz.pl; ul Piotra Skargi 2; ⊗8am-6pm Mon-Fri, 9am-2pm Sat) Standard tourist office with limited information in English. The office is located just off the northwest corner of the Rynek.

## ❶ Getting There & Away

**BUS** The bus station is midway between the city centre and the train station. Buses to Kraków (16zł, 2½ hours) and Krynica (4zł to 6zł, 1½ hours) depart every half-hour or so and are much faster than the train. There's an hourly service to Szczawnica (8zł, two hours), and up to nine departures to Zakopane (16zł, three hours). Frequent city buses go to Stary Sącz (2.60zł, 20 minutes). There's a handy online timetable at www.pks.pl.

**TRAIN** The main train station is 2km south of the Old Town, but city buses run frequently between the two. A few trains go to Kraków (30zł, four hours), but buses are more useful for this route. Trains run regularly throughout the day to Krynica (11zł, 1½ hours) and pass Stary Sącz (5.50zł, 10 minutes) on their way. There's a reasonable service to Tarnów (20zł, two hours), with trains departing every couple of hours.

# Krynica

POP 12,200

Set in attractive countryside amid the wooded hills of the Beskid Sądecki, Krynica (kri-*nee*-tsah), often known as Krynica-Zdrój (Krynica Spa), is Poland's largest spa and mountain health resort.

Much of the year, patients repair here to drink from around a dozen local mineral springs, each one prescribed for a different ailment, and to relax in the mountain air. In midsummer, though, you can banish any notion about this being a laid-back spa for quiet convalescence amid the pines. It's a full-on summer holiday retreat, chock-a-block with families with prams (strollers), long queues at ice-cream stands, and impromptu rock concerts on the promenade featuring local knock-offs of Axl Rose and Lady Gaga.

It wasn't always this way. In the early decades of the 20th century, Krynica was a fashionable hangout for the artistic and intellectual elite and continued to be so right up until WWII. Splendid villas and pensions were constructed during that period, blending into the wooded landscape. Many of these are still standing (the best are along ul Bulwary Dietla, near the promenade).

Development continued after the war but priorities shifted towards cheap mass tourism, and massive concrete holiday homes and sanatoriums came to occupy the slopes of surrounding hills. Nevertheless, if you're in the mood for it, Krynica can be a lot of fun, and here and there the town has even managed to retain some of that former laid-back, refined atmosphere.

## ◉ Sights & Activities

As with many Polish towns, the main activity in Krynica is drinking, but in this case it's not beer or vodka, rather the bitter water that flows from one of around a dozen medicinal mineral springs.

## Main Pump Room
MINERAL SPRINGS

(Pijalnia Główna; al Nowotarskiego 9; ⏱6.30am-6pm) This hulking communist-era structure on the central pedestrian promenade (al Nowotarskiego) looks more like a retro-futuristic airport terminal (c 1965) than a spa colonnade. Still, it's the main game in town when it comes to taking the cure. Here you can choose to sip from one of eight mineral springs for a mere 1.70zł a glass, including the plastic cup. If you're feeling daring and want to sample the whole bunch, buy a *karnet* of 10 glasses for 13zł.

You can choose from a number of different waters, and displays list the chemical composition of each. By far the heaviest is *Zuber,* which have over 21g of soluble solid components per litre – a record for all liquids of that type in Europe. It's a sulphurous brew that won't be to everyone's taste.

If you'd like to forgo the plastic cup, you can follow local style and buy a kitsch porcelain tankard, complete with a tiny porcelain 'straw', for 10zł. Local practice is to drink the water slowly while walking up and down the promenade.

## Góra Parkowa Funicular
FUNICULAR RAILWAY

(Kolej Linowa na Górę Parkową; www.pkl.pl; al Nowotarskiego 1; adult/concession up & back 12/9zł, up only 8/6zł; ⏱9am-sunset) The Góra Parkowa funicular railway is a fun family outing. The bottom station is near the northern end of the promenade in Park Zdrojowy. Cars depart every 15 minutes; the ascent of 142m takes less than three minutes. At the top, you'll find pretty views in all directions,

as well as a giant slide (3zł) and a tubing run (3zł) for kids. If it's a nice day, buy a one-way ticket and hike back down through the park to town.

## Mt Jaworzyna Cable Car
CABLE CAR

(Kolej Gondolowa na Jaworzynę; www.jaworzyna krynicka.pl; ul Czarny Potok 75; adult/concession up & down 18/15zł, up only 15/12zł; ⏱9am-5pm) A little bit out of the centre but more exciting than the funicular, this cable-car system consists of 55 six-person cars that run from the bottom station in the Czarny Potok Valley, about 6km west of the centre of Krynica, to the top of Mt Jaworzyna (1113m). The route is 2210m long and the cable car climbs 465m in seven minutes.

## 🛏 Sleeping

Krynica has a slew of hotels, pensions and holiday homes – a total of 120 in all. Many places – particularly holiday homes – will offer half or full board, which can be convenient. There are also plenty of private rooms welcoming guests. The tourist office can arrange private accommodation for around 35/40zł per person without/with private bathroom. Remember that in high season (July and August, January and February) few owners will be interested in travellers staying just a night or two.

### Małopolanka
HOTEL €€

(☑18 471 5896; www.malopolanka.eu; ul Bulwary Dietla 13; s/d/apt 140/180/240zł; P@🛜) Małopolanka is an old-fashioned, 20-room pension and spa dating from the 1930s that could almost be the setting for an Agatha Christie mystery. There's a lively bar

## HIKING IN THE BESKID SĄDECKI

Krynica is an excellent springboard for hiking in the Beskid Sądecki. Two marked trails, green and red, head westwards from Krynica up to the top of **Mt Jaworzyna**. It takes three hours to walk there by either trail (or you can get there faster by the Mt Jaworzyna cable car). At the top, you'll get some good views, and may even spot the Tatras on clear days. There's a **PTTK mountain hostel** (☑18 471 2171; dm 30-40zł) just below the summit, where you can eat and stay overnight in doubles or cheap dorms, or you can return to Krynica the same day. You can also continue on the red trail northwest to **Hala Łabowska** (1038m), another three hours' walk from Mt Jaworzyna, where you'll find another **PTTK mountain hostel** (☑18 447 6453; dm/d 20/60zł) providing cheap beds and food. The red trail continues northwest to **Rytro** (four hours' walk). This route, leading mostly through the forest along the ridge of the main chain of the Beskid Sądecki, is spectacular and easy, and because of the accommodation on the way you can travel light. From Rytro, you can go back to Krynica by train or bus. Before setting out, visit the PTTK office in Krynica to pick up maps and ensure there's space in the hostels.

and coffee shop on the ground floor, from where creaky wooden steps lead up to well-appointed, eclectically furnished rooms, many done out in period style and some with hardwood floors. There's a small spa with sauna, massage and various treatments on the premises and the house restaurant is pretty good too.

**Stefania** HOTEL **€€**
(☎18 472 5110; www.hotelstefania.pl; ul Piłsudskiego 13; s/d 135/225zł; P@🛜) The dark green Stefania opened its doors in 2009 and still has the feel of a brand new hotel. The snug rooms have parquet floors and walls painted a creamy yellow – as warm and inviting as a slice of cream cake. The hotel is on the main drag, not far from where the bus drops you from Nowy Sącz.

**Hotel Saol** HOTEL **€€**
(☎18 471 5858; www.hotel.saol.com.pl; ul Zdrojowa 16; s/d/tr 110/200/280zł; P@🛜) This property is one of Krynica's more modern and up-market hotels. Perched above busy ul Zdrojowa not far from the centre, it offers 82 bright, clean rooms, two of which have fireplaces. Facilities include a sauna, solarium, pub and restaurant.

**Pensjonat Witoldówka** PENSION **€€**
(☎18 471 5577; www.witoldowka-krynica.pl; ul Bulwary Dietla 10; per person 90-190zł; P@) Looking like a grand Gothic lodge from the outside, this big wooden hotel is in a great central location, set along the narrow Kryniczanka River and close to the main pump room. The 40 upgraded rooms are comfortable and spacious and there's a bar and restaurant.

## ✖ Eating

Most restaurants offer the standard range of kid-friendly pancakes, *pierogi* and chicken schnitzels. The Małopolanka has an excellent in-house restaurant that takes things up a notch with tablecloth service and well-made local dishes.

**Pod Zieloną Górką** POLISH **€€**
(www.zielonagorka.pl in Polish; Nowotarskiego 5; mains 24-38zł) This atmospheric old-style pub is divided into two sections: an informal family-friendly part with picnic tables on one end and a slightly more upscale dining area with wood-beamed ceilings, lace tablecloths and beautiful porcelain chandeliers on the other. There's also a park-side terrace in fine weather. The menu features Polish favourites, including pork knuckle cooked

in beer, and Czech Pilsner Urquell beer on tap.

**Czekolada i Zdroj** CAFE **€**
(al Nowotarskiego 2; coffee 9zł, cakes 12zł; 🛜) This is a great spot for coffee and cakes, and offers a free and reliable wi-fi connection. It's just opposite the Main Pump Room at the northern end of the Old Spa House (*Stary dom zdrojowy*).

## ℹ Information

**Bank PKO** (ul Zdrojowa 1; ⊗8am-6pm Mon-Fri)
**Post office** (ul Zdrojowa 28; ⊗9am-5pm Mon-Fri)
**PTTK office** (☎18 471 5576; www.krynica.pttk.pl in Polish; ul Zdrojowa 32; ⊗7.30am-5pm Mon-Fri, 9am-11am Sat) More helpful than the tourist office, plus limited Saturday hours. Can advise on mountain walks and arrange coach (bus) tours to neighbouring towns, including across the border in Slovakia.
**Tourist office** (☎18 471 6105; www.krynica.org.pl in Polish; ul Piłsudskiego 8; ⊗9am-4pm Mon-Fri, closed weekends). If you arrive after hours or on the weekend, there's an automated kiosk at the front of the tourist office showing which hotels have vacancies and which are fully booked. Note, as we were researching this book in 2011, there were plans afoot to move the tourist office to a new building at the southern end of the promenade (al Nowotarskiego) by the end of 2012.

## ℹ Getting There & Away

The train and bus stations are next to one another on ul Dr Henryka Ebersa in the southern part of town, about 1.2km from the centre.

Buses to Nowy Sącz (4zł to 6zł, 1½ hours) run every half-hour to one hour. Buses to Grybów (8zł, 50 minutes, six daily) pass through Berest and Polany. There are plenty of buses south to Muszyna (3zł, 25 minutes) via Powroźnik, and a fairly regular service to Mochnaczka and Tylicz (3zł).

There's a regular train service to Nowy Sącz (12zł, 1½ hours) by a roundabout but pleasant route, passing through Muszyna and Stary Sącz. Half a dozen daily trains go to Tarnów (20zł, 3½ hours).

# Around Krynica

The countryside surrounding Krynica, with its beautiful wooded valleys, hills and charming small villages, is worth exploring, particularly for the wealth of old wooden churches still standing. An essential aid for exploring the region is one of the *Beskid Sądecki* maps, readily available in these parts. Most of the churches – all originally

Uniat and Lemk – are accessible by bus, though it's better to be under your own steam in a car or on a bicycle.

To the north of Krynica, 13km and 16km respectively on the road to Grybów, are good *cerkwie* (the plural of *cerkiew*) in **Berest** (1842) and **Polany** (1820). Both retain some of the old interior fittings, including iconostases and wall paintings. Buses ply this route regularly so you shouldn't have problems getting back to Krynica or continuing on to Grybów, from where there's frequent transport west to Nowy Sącz or east to Szymbark and Gorlice.

The 24km loop via Mochnaczka, Tylicz and Powroźnik to the east and south of Krynica is another interesting trip. The 1846 church in **Mochnaczka Niżna** still has its late-17th-century iconostasis. You can also see the small *cerkiew* 600m down the road towards Tylicz on the other side. Built in 1787, it holds a beautiful tiny iconostasis complete with original icons. Several buses run from Krynica to Mochnaczka daily, but take an early one if you want to continue along the route.

The next village, **Tylicz**, boasts two churches, a Catholic one and an Uniat *cerkiew* dating from 1743. The latter is used only for funerals. If you have your own transport, head due east for 3km to **Muszynka**, which is almost at the border with Slovakia. The striking *cerkiew* here dates from 1689.

From Tylicz, a spectacular road skirts the Muszyna River valley for 8km to **Powroźnik**, which features yet another *cerkiew*. This one is the oldest in the region (1606) and the best known. The exterior is beautiful, and inside is an 18th-century iconostasis and several older icons on the side walls.

# Muszyna

POP 5000

Much smaller than Krynica, Muszyna (moo-*shin*-na), 11km to the northeast, is another spa town that exploits its mineral springs for tourism, and there are a number of old-fashioned sanatoriums in the area.

## ◉ Sights & Activities

Worth a look is the tiny **Regional Museum** (Muzeum Regionalne; ul Kity 26; adult/concession 4/2zł; ⊙9am-5pm Tue-Sat, 1-5pm Sun) in an old inn 300m southwest of the V-shaped Rynek. It displays artefacts and old household implements collected from the area.

Two **hiking trails** originate in Muszyna and wend their way northwards up the mountains. The green one will take you to **Mt Jaworzyna** (1113m), while the yellow one goes to the peak of **Mt Pusta Wielka** (1061m). You can get to either in three hours, then continue on to Krynica or Rytro. Any one of the *Beskid Sądecki* maps has all the details.

For a shorter walk, there's also a pretty river promenade along the Poprad River, about 300m beyond the Rynek. To find it, follow ul Kity out of town and cross the rail tracks.

## 🛏 Sleeping

**Sanatorium Uzdrowiskowe Korona**                          HOTEL €€

(☑18 477 7960; www.sanatoriumkorona.pl in Polish; ul Mściwujewskiego 2; s/d/tr 95/170/220zł; 🅿🐾🛜🏊) Perched on a hill above the Poprad River about 1km southwest of the Rynek, this modern hotel-cum-hydrotherapy centre has 120 beds in bright, well-maintained rooms and a good choice of spa treatments. The sanatorium offers a popular weekend package that includes a two-night hotel stay with breakfast, as well as massage, Nordic walking outings, and use of the sauna and jacuzzi, starting at around 550zł per person.

**Hotel Klimek Spa**                          HOTEL €€€

(☑18 477 8222; www.hotel-klimek.com.pl; Złockie 107; s/d/tr/ste 400/500/800/1000zł; 🅿❄🛜🏊) In Złockie, about 3km northwest of the centre of Muszyna, this 53-room spa hotel is one of the best (and most expensive) places around, with a long list of hydrotherapy programmes and treatments on offer, plus a sauna, steam room and small water park. There's also a good restaurant and bar.

## ❶ Information

**Bank PKO** (ul Kity 1; ⊙9am-4pm Mon-Fri) Southwest of the Rynek.

**Post office** (Rynek 24; ⊙7am-7pm Mon-Fri, 8am-2pm Sat)

**Vector travel agency** (☑18 471 8003; www .btvector.com; ul Kity 24; ⊙9am-5pm Mon-Fri, to 1pm Sat) Can provide information, book accommodation and organise tours.

## ❶ Getting There & Away

Buses to Krynica (3zł, 25 minutes) run frequently, and there's also an adequate service to Nowy Sącz (8zł to 9.50zł, 1½ hours). Muszyna is on the rail line linking Krynica (4zł, 20 minutes) and Nowy Sącz (12zł, 1¼ hours), and trains go regularly to both destinations.

# Around Muszyna

Having been in the possession of the bishops of Kraków from 1288 to 1772, Muszyna was traditionally a Polish town; not surprisingly, it has a Catholic church but no *cerkiew*. The surrounding villages, however, were populated for the most part by Lemks, whose wooden Uniat churches still dot the region. There are at least five within 5km of Muszyna.

Three of the churches are north of the town, at **Szczawnik** (built in 1841), **Złockie** (1872) and **Jastrzębik** (1856). Each boasts its original iconostasis. The *cerkiew* at Złockie has a separate bell tower and is somewhat different in style. The belfry of the Jastrzębik *cerkiew* is home to a colony of lesser horseshoe bats and thus off limits. Krynica suburban buses go via Muszyna to these villages sporadically throughout the day.

Two more wooden churches, in **Milik** (1813) and **Andrzejówka** (1864), are west and southwest of Muszyna and have their original iconostases; you can get there by the regular buses or trains heading for Nowy Sącz.

# PIENINY

A startlingly beautiful mountain range between the Beskid Sądecki and the Tatras, the Pieniny is famous for the raft trip down the spectacular Dunajec Gorge, which has become one of Poland's major tourist highlights. Yet there's much more to see and do here. Walkers won't be disappointed with the hiking paths, which offer more dramatic vistas than the Beskid Sądecki or Bieszczady, while lovers of architecture will find some amazing old wooden churches here. There's also a picturesque mountain castle in Niedzica, or you can just take it easy in the pleasant spa resort of Szczawnica.

The Pieniny consists of three separate ranges divided by the Dunajec River, the whole chain stretching east–west for about 35km. The highest and most popular is the central range topped by Mt Trzy Korony (Three Crowns; 981m), overlooking the Dunajec Gorge. Almost all of this area is now the Pieniny National Park (Pieniński Park Narodowy), whose headquarters is at Krościenko. To the east, behind the Dunajec River and south of Szczawnica, lies the Małe Pieniny (Small Pieniny), while to the west extends the Pieniny Spiskie. The latter outcrop, south of Czorsztyn Lake and including

Niedzica, is the lowest and the least spectacular, though the region around it, known as the Spisz, has an interesting blend of Polish and Slovakian cultures.

# Szczawnica

POP 7350

Picturesquely located along the Grajcarek River, Szczawnica (shchahv-*nee*-tsah) has developed into a popular summer resort, while its mineral springs have made it an important spa. It's also the disembarkation point for Dunajec Gorge raft trips.

The town spreads for 4km along the main road, ul Główna, and is divided into two sections, Szczawnica Niżna (Szczawnica Lower) to the west and Szczawnica Wyżna (Szczawnica Upper) to the east, with the bus station more or less in between. Most of the tourist and spa facilities are in the upper section, which also boasts most of the fine old timber houses.

## ◎ Sights & Activities

Szczawnica is a good starting point for **hiking** in both the Pieniny and the Beskid Sądecki ranges. Three trails originate in town and two more begin at Jaworki, 8km to the southeast.

It's also an excellent centre for **biking**, with some demanding mountain bike trails in the hills, and a gentler, more family-friendly run that skirts the Dunajec Gorge for most of its length. The Dunajec Gorge cycling trail starts at the base of the Palenica Chairlift and runs 15km along the Dunajec River to the Slovak town of Červený Kláštor. There are several rental outfits around town, including a couple of big ones at the base of the **chairlift** (4/25zł per hr/day). Most hiking maps also identify cycling trails.

**Szczawnica Spa** MINERAL SPRINGS
(Uzdrowisko Szczawnica; www.uzdrowiskoszczawnica .pl in Polish; ul Zdrojowa 28/Plac Dietla; tastings 1.30zł; ☺7.30am-6pm Mon-Sat, 9am-5pm Sun). Walk uphill from the centre along ul Zdrojowa about 500m to find this handsome spa and mineral springs. On tap are waters from five different springs.

**Palenica Chairlift** CHAIRLIFT
(Kolej Krzesełkowa Palenica; www.pkl.pl; ul Główna 7; up & back 13zł, up only 9zł; ☺9am-8pm) The chairlift near the centre of town makes the ride up to the nearby hill, Palenica (719m), in a few minutes. In winter, this is a popular

snowboard run. In summer, it's a great start to several mountain hikes.

## 🛌 Sleeping

Accommodation in Szczawnica is the same as in many other mountain resorts: plentiful, usually inexpensive and highly varied depending on the season. Plenty of locals also rent out rooms: look for signs along ul Główna and the side streets. Expect to pay from 40zł to 45zł per person for a room with a bathroom (20zł to 30zł without).

**TOP CHOICE ► Hotel Batory**　　　　HOTEL €€
(☑18 262 0207; www.batory-hotel.pl; Park Górny 13; s/d 150/190zł; 🅿🛜) The Batory is a well-run, welcoming hotel with spotlessly clean rooms and a peaceful park location high above Szczawnica. From the outside, it looks like a typically timbered mountain lodge; the rooms are on the plain side but fitted out with quality wooden furnishings. The reception couldn't be friendlier, and downstairs is a charming restaurant with a terrace and a valley view. They light a fire in the fireplace on chilly evenings. The hotel's list of VIP guests includes Nobel laureate Henryk Sienkiewicz, who stayed several times in 1909.

**Solar Spa Centrum**　　　　HOTEL €€
(☑18 262 2411; www.solarspa.pl; ul Zdrojowa 4; s/d 210/400zł high season, incl entry to water park; 🅿@🛜) This huge hotel and spa complex has 103 unadorned though spotless rooms in four separate buildings. The list of spa treatments goes on forever. Best of all is the **water park complex** (Park Wodny; adult/concession from 14/11zł; ⊙10am-9pm), which has pools and slides and is open to non-residents.

## 🍴 Eating

**TOP CHOICE ► Café Helenka**　　　　FRENCH €€
(www.cafe-helenka.pl; Plac Dietla 1; mains 15-25zł; ⊙10am-10pm; ☑) Café Helenka is an unexpected delight: an upmarket cafe and French-inspired restaurant that offers an eclectic menu featuring rarities in these parts such as pumpkin soup, quiches, inventive pasta dishes, and even inspired local dishes such as grilled sheep's cheese served with cranberry jam. The coffee drinks are excellent too. The cafe is right next to the main spa room, about 500m uphill from the centre of town along ul Zdrojowa.

**Eglander Caffe**　　　　CAFE €
(ul Zdrojowa 2; coffee 8zł) Keep this tiny cafe at the bottom of ul Zdrojowa in mind for a late-afternoon refreshment stop. It also does coffee to go.

## ℹ Information

**Bank Spółdzielczy** (ul Główna 1; ⊙8am-6pm Mon-Fri, 7.30am-1pm Sat) Next to the PTTK office; has an ATM.

**PTTK office** (☑18 262 2332; www.pttk .szczawnica.pl in Polish; ul Główna 1; ⊙8am-4pm Mon-Sat) Organises excursions, including Dunajec rafting trips at 10am and 1.30pm, and offers a good selection of hiking maps for sale.

**Szewczyk Travel** (☑18 262 1895; www.szewczyk travel.pl in Polish; ul Zdrojowa 2a; ⊙9am-5pm) *De facto* tourist office in the centre of town; organises excursions, including daily Dunajec rafting trips at 9.30am and 1.45pm for 55zł per person.

## ℹ Getting There & Away

Regular buses run to Nowy Sącz (7zł, two hours) via Stary Sącz (6zł, 1½ hours). Up to eight fast buses go daily to Kraków (18zł, 2½ hours). Buses to Krościenko (2.50zł, 15 minutes) depart frequently.

For the Dunajec Gorge, take a bus (up to four daily in the high season) to Sromowce Wyżne-Kąty (6zł, 30 to 40 minutes) – the driver will set you down at the right place. There are also private minibuses that depart when full.

# Dunajec Gorge

Dunajec Gorge (Przełom Dunajca) is a spectacular stretch of the Dunajec (doo-*nah*-yets) River, which snakes from Czorsztyn Lake (Jezioro Czorsztyńskie) west for about 8km between steep cliffs, some of which are over 300m high. The river is narrow, in one instance funnelling through a 12m-wide bottleneck, and changes incessantly from majestically quiet, deep stretches to shallow mountain rapids. Be advised, however, that this is not a white-water experience but a leisurely pleasure trip.

The gorge has been a tourist attraction since the mid-19th century, when primitive rafts ferried guests of the Szczawnica spa on a day out. Today the raft trip through the gorge attracts hundreds of thousands of people every year, not counting do-it-yourselfers in their own kayaks. The raft itself is a set of five narrow, 6m-long, coffinlike canoes lashed together with rope. Holding 10 to 12 passengers, it is steered by two raftsmen, each decked out in embroidered folk costume and armed with a long navigating pole.

The raft trip begins in the small village of **Sromowce Wyżne-Kąty**, at the **Raft Landing Place** (Przystań Flisacka; ☑18 262 9721; www

## HIKING IN THE PIENINY

Almost all hiking concentrates on the central Pieniny range, a compact area of 40 sq km that now encompasses Pieniny National Park. Trails are well marked and short, and no trekking equipment is necessary. There are three starting points on the outskirts of the park, all providing accommodation and food. The most popular is Krościenko at the northern edge, then Szczawnica on the eastern rim and Sromowce Niżne to the south. Arm yourself with the 1:50,000 *Gorce i Pieniny, Pieniński Park Narodowy* map, which includes a 1:125,000 map of the park showing all hiking routes.

Most walkers start from the Rynek in Krościenko. Follow the yellow trail as far as the **Przełęcz Szopka** pass, then switch to the blue trail branching off to the left and head up to the top of **Mt Trzy Korony** (981m), the highest summit of the central range. If the weather is clear, the reward for this two-hour walk is a breathtaking panorama that includes the Tatras, 35km to the southwest. You are now about 520m above the level of the Dunajec River.

Another excellent view is from **Mt Sokolica** (747m), 2km east as the crow flies from Mt Trzy Korony, or a 1½-hour walk along the blue trail. From Mt Sokolica, you can go back down to Krościenko by the green trail in about 1¼ hours, or to Szczawnica by the blue one in less than an hour.

If you plan on taking the raft trip through the Dunajec Gorge, you can hike all the way to Sromowce Wyżne-Katy, site of the raft landing place. There are several ways to get there and the park map shows them all. The shortest way is to take the blue trail heading west from the Przełęcz Szopka and winding up along the ridge. After 30 to 40 minutes, watch for the red trail branching off to the left (south) and leading downhill. It will take you directly to the wharf in about half an hour.

.flisacy.com.pl; ul Katy 14; ⊙8.30am-5pm May-Aug, 9am-4pm Apr & Sep, to 3pm Oct, closed Nov-Mar). You'll take an 18km-long trip and disembark in Szczawnica. The journey takes about 2¼ hours, depending on the level of the river. Some rafts go further downstream to Krościenko (23km, 2¾ hours), but there's not very much to see on that stretch of the river.

The trip to Szczawnica costs 42/21zł adult/concession, while the one to Krościenko is 51/25zł. Return bus tickets cost an additional 8/6zł.

All of the private travel agencies in Kraków, Zakopane or Nowy Targ offer rafting package tours, including transport, equipment and guides. Prices vary but trips from Zakopane start at around 90zł and from Kraków from around 270zł. The tour sponsored by Szewczyk Travel in Szczawnica is 55zł.

Rafts normally operate from April to October, but trips may be suspended occasionally for a day or two when the river level is high.

Just in front of the ticket office is a branch office of the **Pieniny National Park** (www.pieninpn.pl in Polish; ul Katy 117b), which keeps the same hours as the ticket office.

### ❶ Getting There & Away

Sromowce Wyżne-Katy is serviced by five buses daily from Nowy Targ (10zł, 45 minutes) and, in

season, four from Szczawnica (6zł, 30 minutes). Another way of getting to Sromowce Wyżne-Katy is to hike from Krościenko or Szczawnica (see the boxed text).

If you have private transport, you'll have to either leave your vehicle in Sromowce Wyżne-Katy and come back for it after completing the raft trip in Szczawnica, or drive to Szczawnica and leave your vehicle there, so you'll have it as soon as you complete the trip. There are car parks in both Sromowce Wyżne-Katy and Szczawnica, and the raft operator provides a bus service between the two locations. The cost from Szczawnica back to the raft wharf is 8/6zł adult/concession.

## Niedzica

POP 3000

Five kilometres northwest of Sromowce Wyżne-Katy, Niedzica is known for its castle. Perched on a rocky hill above the south-eastern end of Czorsztyn Lake, the castle was built in the first half of the 14th century as one of the Hungarian border strongholds and was extended in 1601. It remained in private Hungarian hands until the end of WWII. It was partially restored in the 1920s and again 50 years later, but it essentially looks the same as it did in the 17th century, managing to retain its graceful Renaissance shape.

## ⊙ Sights & Activities

The fortress shelters the **Niedzica Castle Museum** (Muzeum Zamkowy w Niedzicy; www .shs.pl in Polish; adult/concession 12/9zł; ☺9am-7pm daily May-Sep, 9am-4pm Tue-Sun Oct-Apr). There's not a tremendous amount to see – some period costumes, furnishings, hunting trophies, a chapel from the late 14th century and collections on the archaeology and history of the Spisz region – but there are fine views over the lake and surrounding area. An ethnographic section of the museum, including Spisz folk art, is presented in season in an old timber **granary** (spichlerz; admission 4zł; ☺May-Sep) 150m from the castle. You can also visit the nearby **Coach House** (Powozownia).

Pleasure boats **Biała Dama I** and **Biała Dama II** (☎18 275 0121; www.turystyka.wolski.pl in Polish) ply the waters of Czorsztyn Lake daily in July and August and at the weekend in May and June. Boats leave the pier at the Harnaś Café beneath the castle to the northwest between 9am and 6pm; the 50-minute trip costs 14/12zł adult/concession. A trip to/from Czorsztyn on the opposite side of the lake costs 6zł.

Czorsztyn Lake is popular as a sailing destination from late May to late August. The **Podhalańskie Towarzystwo Żeglarskie** (Highlanders Sailing Association; ☎609 320 772; www.ptznowytarg.pl in Polish) rents boats and offers sailing lessons from a small office on the northern shore of the lake on the Stylchyn peninsula (below the village of Kluszkowce). Rental rates range, depending on the size of the boat, from 25zł to 45zł per hour.

## 🛏 Sleeping & Eating

**Zespół Zamkowy**      CASTLE €€
(☎18 262 9473; shsniedzica@wp.pl; s/d/tr 200/250/400zł; 🅿🛜) Part of the castle has been turned into a hotel, providing 39 beds in 13 rooms, some of which are in the historic castle chambers and decorated with antique furniture. The castle management also offers cheaper rooms (a couple without private bathroom) in the **Celnica** (d/tw 180/200zł), a fine timber house built in the local style, 200m up the road from the castle.

**Hotel Lokis**      HOTEL €€
(☎18 262 8540; www.lokis.com.pl; Zamek 76; d/tr/apt 260/320/500zł; 🅿🛜) In a wonderful spot overlooking the lake, about 500m from the castle on the road to Nowy Targ, the Lokis is a lovely modern hotel and one of the more attractive places to stay in the Spisz region. It has 23 rooms and a sauna, and there's a big balcony with lake views. Guests can rent bicycles for 25zł a day.

**Hotel Pieniny**      HOTEL €€
(☎18 262 9383; www.niedzica.pl; ul Kanada 38; s/d/tr 100/190/230zł; 🅿@🛜) Halfway between the castle and Niedzica village to the south, this 52-room hotel is a reasonably priced option with plain but comfortable rooms. It also has a tennis court, mini-golf and a sauna, and bikes can be hired for 5/25zł per hour/day.

**Karczma Hajduk**      POLISH €
(Zamek 1; mains 10-22zł; ☺9am-6pm) This little inn, whose name recalls the castle's Hungarian links (the Hajduks were Hungarian mercenaries who fought against the Habsburgs in the 17th and 18th centuries), serves basic Polish dishes right next door to the castle.

## ❶ Getting There & Away

There are about a dozen buses a day from Nowy Targ (6zł, 30 to 40 minutes) to Niedzica village; some but not all of these stop at Niedzica Castle. When buying your ticket, make sure to specify 'Niedzica-Zamek' (castle). Five minibuses a day link the castle to Szczawnica (8zł, 25 minutes).

---

**WORTH A TRIP**

## ABANDONED BEAUTY OF CZORSZTYN

The village of Czorsztyn (*chor*-shtin), across the lake from Niedzica, boasts romantic **castle ruins** (adult/concession 4/2zł; ☺9am-6pm daily May-Sep, 10am-3pm Tue-Sun Oct-Apr) dating from the second half of the 13th century. The fortress was built as the Polish counterpart to the Hungarian stronghold opposite at Niedzica. You get to see a 15th-century gatehouse, courtyards and the remains of an old kitchen. Best of all are the excellent views over the lake, the Dunajec River valley and as far as the Tatras. There's also a small exhibition on the Pieniny region.

The village is just off the Krośnica–Sromowce Wyżne-Kąty road, accessible by the same buses you take for the Dunajec raft trip at Sromowce Wyżne-Kąty (see p224) or you can sail over for an hour or two from the Niedzica side (p225).

# Silesia

POP 9.5 MILLION

## Includes »

## Best Places to Eat

» Bernard (p236)

» Restauracja Zagłoba (p262)

» Ziemiańska (p243)

» Pod Aniołami (p259)

» Złoty Osioł (p266)

## Best Places to Stay

» Hostel Mleczarnia (p235)

» Hotel Patio (p235)

» Villa Navigator (p259)

» Hotel Castle (p257)

» Hotel Śródmiejski (p241)

## Why Go?

Occupying the whole of southwestern Poland, Silesia, or Śląsk (pronounced 'shlonsk') in Polish, is a diverse collection of attractive cities, industrial centres and mountain scenery.

Wrocław is a historical gem and well worth a visit, while attractive smaller centres such as Nysa and Jelenia Góra offer distinctive sights and activities. A natural attraction is presented by the Sudetes Mountains, stretching along the Czech border and home to scenic beauty and idyllic resort towns – popular with hikers, bikers and spa fans alike.

The rich history of the region underpins its charm, with architecture ranging from medieval fortresses to Baroque cathedrals. Silesia also contains the Auschwitz-Birkenau extermination camp complex set up by Nazi Germany, now a grim but moving memorial.

From tumultuous history to modern-day cities and countryside, Silesia affords plenty of opportunities for relaxation, and for immersion in the story of this once-turbulent corner of Europe.

## When to Go

### Wrocław

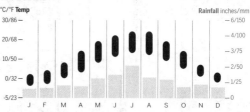

| Mar/Apr | Jun–Aug | Sep |
|---|---|---|
| Spring's vitality is a good match for the Jazz on the Odra festival in Wrocław. | Summer is the season to enjoy hiking in the Sudetes Mountains. | In autumn Polish wine is celebrated at Zielona Góra's Wine Festival. |

# Silesia Highlights

**1** Marvelling at the enormous **Panorama of Racławice** in Wrocław (p231)

**2** Eyeballing bony remains at the macabre **Chapel of Skulls** (p255) near Kudowa-Zdrój

**3** Contemplating the infinite within the tranquil **Church of Peace** (p242) in Świdnica

**4** Hiking between Mt Szrenica and Mt Śnieżka in **Karkonosze National Park** (p249)

**5** Learning the lessons of history at the former Nazi extermination camp at **Auschwitz-Birkenau Memorial & Museum** (p268) in Oświęcim

**6** Visiting the impressive **Książ Castle** (p244) near Świdnica

**7** Exploring the mighty **fortress** at Kłodzko (p252)

**8** Enjoying the peaceful atmosphere of spa town **Cieplice Śląskie-Zdrój** (p248) near Jelenia Góra

**9** Spotting **gnome statues** (p230) in Wrocław Old Town.

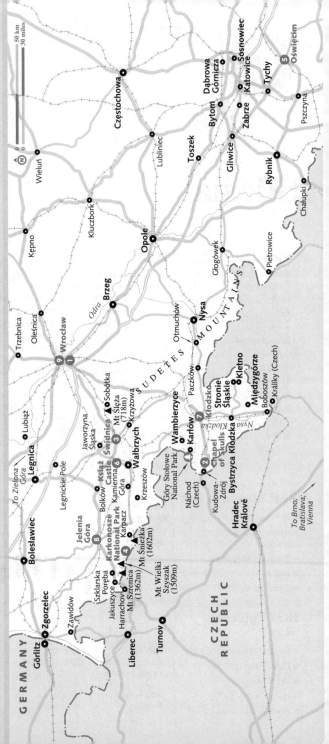

# WROCŁAW

POP 633,000

Everyone loves Wrocław (*vrots*-wahf) and it's easy to see why. Though in some ways it's a more manageable version of Kraków, with all the cultural attributes and entertainment of that popular destination, the capital of Lower Silesia also has an attractive character all its own.

Having absorbed Bohemian, Austrian and Prussian influences, the city has a unique architectural and cultural make-up, symbolised by its magnificent market square. Wrocław's location on the Odra River, with its 12 islands, 130 bridges and riverside parks, is idyllic, and the beautifully preserved ecclesiastical district is a treat for lovers of Gothic architecture.

But Wrocław is not just a pretty face. It is Poland's fourth-largest city and the major industrial, commercial and educational centre for the region; virtually everything in southwestern Poland starts, finishes or is taking place in Wrocław. At the same time it's a lively cultural centre, with several theatres, some major festivals, rampant nightlife and a large student community.

## History

Wrocław was originally founded on Cathedral Island (Ostrów Tumski), and the first recorded Polish ruler, Duke Mieszko I, brought the town, together with most of Silesia, into the Polish state. It must have been a fair-sized settlement by the turn of the first millennium, as it was chosen, along with Kraków and Kołobrzeg, as one of Piast Poland's three bishoprics.

During the period of division in the 12th and 13th centuries, Wrocław was the capital of one of the principalities of the Silesian Piasts. Like most settlements in southern Poland, Wrocław was burned down by the Tatars. The town centre was then moved to the river's left bank.

Wrocław continued to grow under Bohemian administration (1335–1526), reaching the height of its prosperity in the 15th century and maintaining trade and cultural links with the Polish crown. New fortifications were constructed at the beginning of the 16th century, and the remains of the Fosa Miejska (City Moat) show where they were once positioned.

The Habsburgs, who ruled the city for the next two centuries, were less tolerant of the Polish and Czech communities, and things got even worse for the Slavic populations after 1741, when Wrocław fell to Prussia. For the next two centuries the city was increasingly Germanised and became known as Breslau.

As one of the major eastern outposts of the Third Reich, Breslau was given a key defensive role in the last stages of WWII, with the whole city converted into a fortified compound, 'Fortress Breslau'. Besieged by the Red Army in February 1945, the Germans defended their last bastion until May, executing anyone who refused to fight. During the battle, 75% of the city was razed to the ground.

Of the prewar population of more than 600,000, an estimated 30% died, mostly as a result of the fighting and the botched evacuation that preceded it. The handful of Germans who remained were expelled to Germany, and the ruined city was resettled with people from Poland's prewar eastern regions, mostly from Lviv (Lwów in Polish), which had been ceded to the Soviet Union.

The difficult reconstruction of Wrocław continued well into the 1980s, when the city surpassed its prewar population level for the first time.

Since the fall of communism, the city has had some success in attracting new investment, including the presence of LG Electronics in nearby Kobierzyce. Wrocław has also established itself as a centre of finance and tourism. In 2012 the city will host matches in the UEFA Euro football championship, and for 2016 it has been designated a European Capital of Culture by the EU.

## ◉ Sights

### OLD TOWN

Wrocław's extensive Old Town is so full of historic buildings that you could wander round for weeks and still feel like you hadn't seen everything. It's the kind of area that well repays a wander through its backstreets after you've visited the vibrant central square.

**Rynek** SQUARE

Wrocław's market square is Poland's second biggest, after the one in Kraków. The Rynek was laid out in the 1240s and lined with timber houses, which were later replaced with brick structures. The north and south sides were completely destroyed during WWII but have since been rebuilt; they offer an appealing amalgam of architectural styles from Gothic to Art Nouveau. Check out the wave-like glass fountain on the western side of the square, whose curves suggest the mountains of the Sudetes.

### Town Hall
HISTORIC BUILDING

This grand edifice took almost two centuries (1327–1504) to complete, and work on the 66m-high tower and decoration continued for another century.

The eastern facade reflects the stages of the town hall's development, split into three distinct elements. The segment to the right, with its austere early-Gothic features, is the oldest, while the delicate carving in the section to the left shows elements of the early Renaissance style. Prisoners' sentences were once read aloud from the little loggia. The central section dates from the 16th century and is topped by an ornamented triangular roof adorned with pinnacles. The **astronomical clock**, made of larch wood and showing the time and phases of the moon, was built in 1580.

The southern facade, dating from the early 16th century, is the most elaborate, with three projections, a pair of ornate bay windows and carved stone figures.

The western elevation is the most austere, apart from the early-Baroque portal (1615) leading to the **City Museum of Art** (Muzeum Sztuki Mieszczańskiej; www.mmw.pl; Sukiennice 14/15; adult/concession 15/10zł; ☺10am-5pm). The museum's Gothic interiors are every bit as magnificent as the building's exterior, particularly the **Great Hall** (Sala Wielka) on the 1st floor, with carved decorations from the second half of the 15th century. Adjoining it is the **Princes' Room** (Sala Książęca), which was built as a chapel in the mid-14th century. The historic rooms house several exhibitions, including the **Wrocław Treasury** (Wrocławski Skarb) of gold and silverware from the 16th to 19th centuries.

### Hansel & Gretel
HISTORIC BUILDINGS

(Jaś i Małgosia; ul Odrzańska 39/40) Set in the northwestern corner of the Rynek are two charming houses named Jaś i Małgosia, who English and German speakers know better as Hansel and Gretel. They're linked by a Baroque archway from 1728, which once led to the church cemetery (the inscription in Latin reads 'Death is the gateway to life').

### Gnomes of Wrocław
STATUES

(www.krasnale.pl) See if you can spot the diminutive statue of a resting gnome at ground level, just to the west of the Hansel and Gretel houses. A couple of metres away you'll spot some newly installed firemen gnomes, rushing to put out a blaze. These figures are part of a collection of over 150, which are scattered through the city. They're sometimes identified in English as dwarves, as the Polish folkloric character the gnomes are based on (the leprechaun-like *krasnoludek*) resembles a cross between a dwarf and a gnome. Whimsical as they are, they're also a reference to the symbol of the Orange Alternative, a communist-era dissident group that used ridicule as a weapon (see boxed text, p237). You can buy a 'dwarf map' (7zł) from the tourist office and go gnome-spotting.

### Church of St Elizabeth
CHURCH

(Kościół Św Elżbiety; ul Św Elżbiety 1/2) Just north of the Hansel and Gretel houses is this monumental Gothic brick church, with an 83m-high **tower** (admission 5zł; ☺9am-7pm Mon-Fri, 11am-5pm Sat, 1-5pm Sun). You can climb the narrow stairwell with 250-plus steps to the top for a great view of Wrocław.

### University Quarter
HISTORIC SITE

This area occupies the northernmost part of the Old Town, between the riverfront and ul Uniwersytecka. At the quarter's eastern end is the Gothic **Church of SS Vincent and James** (Kościół Św Wincentego i Św Jakuba; Plac Biskupa Nankiera 15a), originally a Romanesque basilica founded in the early 13th century. The largest church in the city, it's now used by the Uniat (Eastern Rite Catholic) faithful.

To the west, the Baroque-Rococo **Church of the Holy Name of Jesus** (Kościół Najświętszego Imienia Jezus; Plac Uniwersytecki), the university church, was built in the 1690s on the site of the former Piast castle. Its spacious interior, crammed with ornate fittings and adorned with fine illusionist frescos of the life of Jesus on its vaulting, is quite spectacular.

The monumental building adjoining the church is the main edifice of the **University of Wrocław** (Uniwersytet Wrocławski; www.uni.wroc.pl; Plac Uniwersytecki 1), built between 1728 and 1742. Enter through the grand blue and gold Rococo gate at the western end and go up to the 1st floor to see the **Aula Leopoldinum** (Plac Uniwersytecki; adult/concession 10/6zł; ☺10am-3.30pm Thu-Tue). Embellished with elaborate stucco work, sculptures, paintings and a trompe l'œil ceiling fresco, it's the city's best Baroque interior. The more modest **Oratorium Marianum**, on the ground floor, is included in the admission fee; as is the **Mathematical Tower**, topped with a sphere and decorated with allegorical figures.

## Church of St Mary Magdalene CHURCH

(Kościół Św Marii Magdaleny; ul Szewska 10) One block east of the Rynek is this mighty Gothic brick building constructed during the city's heyday in the 14th century. Its showpiece is a copy of a Romanesque portal from around 1280 on the south wall, which originally adorned the Benedictine Abbey in Ołbin, but was moved here in 1546 after the abbey was demolished. The original tympanum is on display in Wrocław's National Museum. You can climb the 72m-high **tower** (adult/concession 4/3zł; ⊘10am-6pm Apr-Oct) and cross the so-called **Penance Footbridge**.

### EAST OF THE OLD TOWN

**Panorama of Racławice** MONUMENT
(Panorama Racławicka; www.panoramaraclawicka .pl; ul Purkyniego 11; adult/concession 22/16zł; ⊘9am-5pm) Wrocław's pride and joy is the giant painting housed in this cylindrical building. The canvas measures 15m by 114m, and is wrapped around the internal walls of the rotunda. It's viewed from an elevated central balcony, and three-dimensional items (tree trunks, plants, weapons, roads), special lighting and sound effects bring it to life.

The picture depicts the battle of Racławice (a village 40km northeast of Kraków), fought on 4 April 1794 between the Polish insurrectionist army of regulars and peasants led by Tadeusz Kościuszko, and Russian troops under General Alexander Tormasov. One of the last attempts to defend Poland's independence, the battle was won by the Poles, but it was all for naught: months later the nationwide insurrection was crushed by the tsarist army and the Third Partition put into effect. Poland ceased to exist as a nation until WWI, yet the battle lived on in Polish hearts and minds as the most glorious engagement of the rebellion.

A century after the battle, a group of patriots in Lviv (then the Polish city of Lwów) commissioned the panorama. The two main artists, Jan Styka and Wojciech Kossak, were helped by seven other painters who did the background scenes and details. They completed the monumental canvas in just over nine months, using 750kg of paint. The picture was on display until 1944, when a bomb damaged the canvas.

After the war the painting was sent to Wrocław, but since it depicted a defeat of the Russians (Poland's then official friend and liberator), the communist authorities were reluctant to put it on display. The pavilion built for the panorama in 1967 sat empty until 1985, when the canvas was shown for the first time in more than four decades.

Visits are by 30-minute guided tours, which depart every half-hour. You move around the balcony to inspect each scene in turn while a handheld audioguide provides recorded commentary. The **Small Rotunda** behind the ticket office features a model of the battlefield and the uniforms of forces engaged in the battle. A panorama ticket allows entry to the National Museum on the same day.

## National Museum MUSEUM

(Muzeum Narodowe w Wrocławiu; www.mnwr.art .pl; Plac Powstańców Warszawy 5; adult/concession 15/10zł, free Sat; ⊘10am-5pm Wed-Sun) This treasure trove of fine art is 200m east of the Panorama of Racławice, with extensive permanent collections and a stunning skylit atrium.

The Silesian art collection is a highlight of the museum. Medieval stone sculpture is displayed on the ground floor; exhibits include the Romanesque tympanum from the portal of the Church of St Mary Magdalene, depicting the Assumption of the Virgin Mary, and 14th-century sarcophagi from the Church of SS Vincent and James. The medieval wooden sculpture on the 1st floor features some powerful Gothic triptychs and statues of saints. There are also collections of Silesian paintings, ceramics, silverware and furnishings from the 16th to 19th centuries.

The 2nd floor holds Polish art, mainly paintings, from the 17th century to the present. The collection covers most of Poland's big names, including Jacek Malczewski, Stanisław Wyspiański, Witkacy (Stanisław Ignacy Witkiewicz) and Jan Matejko; be prepared for moody portraits and massive battle scenes. Among the modern painters, Władysław Hasior, Eugeniusz Stankiewicz-Get and Tadeusz Makowski are names to look out for, especially for their humorous takes on war and religion.

## Museum of Architecture MUSEUM

(Muzeum Architektury; ul Bernardyńska 5; adult/concession 10/7zł, free Wed; ⊘11am-5pm) A 16th-century former Bernardine church and monastery contains this collection, which features stone sculptures and stained-glass

# Wrocław

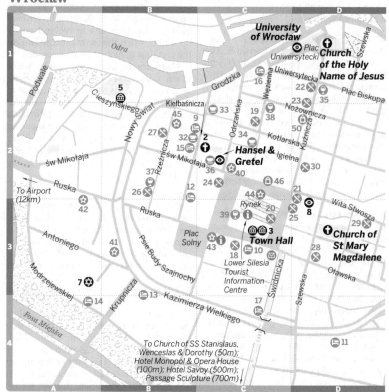

windows from various historic buildings of the region. The oldest exhibit, a Romanesque tympanum on the ground floor, dates from 1165. The museum also has a 12th-century Jewish tombstone, a 1:500 scale model of Wrocław (1740) and a delightful cloister garden.

## ECCLESIASTICAL DISTRICT

The erstwhile Cathedral Island (Ostrów Tumski) – it was connected to the mainland in the 19th century – was the cradle of Wrocław. It was here that the Ślężanie, a tribe of West Slavs who gave their name to the region, constructed their stronghold in the 7th or 8th century. After the town was incorporated into the Polish state and a bishopric established in 1000, Wrocław's first church was built here. Over time a number of churches, monasteries and other religious buildings were constructed, giving a distinctive, markedly ecclesiastical character to the district.

### Cathedral of St John the Baptist  CHURCH

(Katedra Św Jana Chrzciciela; www.katedra.archi diecezja.wroc.pl in Polish; Plac Katedralny 18) The centrepiece of Cathedral Island, this three-aisled Gothic basilica was built between 1244 and 1590. Seriously damaged during WWII, it was reconstructed in its previous Gothic form, complete with dragon guttering. The high altar boasts a gold and silver triptych from 1522 attributed to the school of Veit Stoss, and the western portico is a medieval gem. For once you don't need strong legs to climb the 91m-high **tower** (adult/concession 5/4zł; ⊙10am-6pm Mon-Sat) as there is a lift.

### Church of Our Lady on the Sand  CHURCH

(Kościół Najświętszej Marii Panny na Piasku; ul Św Jadwigi) This lofty 14th-century building dominates the tiny islet known as Sand Island (Wyspa Piasek). Almost all the fittings were destroyed during WWII and the half-dozen old triptychs you see inside have

### Botanical Gardens
GARDENS

(Ogród Botaniczny; www.biol.uni.wroc.pl/obuwr in Polish; ul Sienkiewicza 23; adult/concession 7/5zł; ◷8am-6pm Apr-Oct, 10am-6pm Nov-Mar) If you've had enough of bricks and mortar – sacred or otherwise – Cathedral Island also contains the city's Botanical Gardens, a charming patch of greenery with palm houses.

## WEST & SOUTH OF THE OLD TOWN

### Military Museum
MUSEUM

(Muzeum Militariów; www.mmw.pl; ul Cieszyńskiego 9; adult/concession 7/5zł, free Wed; ◷11am-5pm) Just outside the ring road encircling the Old Town, this collection of militaria is housed within the squat brick **Arsenal** (Arsenał). With two towers and an enormous courtyard, this building is the most significant remnant of the city's 15th-century fortifications. This is also the home of the **Archaeological Museum** (Muzeum Archeologiczne), which opens the same hours and charges the same admission fee.

### Jewish Heritage
RELIGIOUS

Southwest of the Rynek is the restored **White Stork Synagogue** (Synagoga Pod Białym Bocianem; ul Włodkowica 7), built in 1829. Another reminder that this city was once home to more than 20,000 Jews is the **ulica Łąkowa Synagogue Memorial** (ul Łąkowa), 700m further south. Formerly a synagogue built in 1872, it was the country's second largest until it was torched on Kristallnacht (9 November 1938).

The **Old Jewish Cemetery** (Stary Cmentarz Żydowski; www.mmw.pl; ul Ślężna 37/39; adult/concession 7/5zł; ◷10am-6pm), founded in 1856, is about 1.5km south of the train and bus stations. Take tram 9 or 16.

### Church of SS Stanislaus, Wenceslas and Dorothy
CHURCH

(Kościół Franciszkanów Św Stanisława, Wacława i Doroty; Plac Franciszkanski) This massive Gothic affair just south of the Old Town was founded in 1351 to commemorate the meeting between Polish King Kazimierz III Wielki (Casimir III the Great) and his Bohemian counterpart, Charles IV, at which they agreed to leave Silesia in Bohemia's hands. Note the sizeable Rococo tomb at the start of the south aisle.

### Passage
STATUES

(cnr ul Świdnicka & ul Piłsudskiego) This fascinating sculpture depicts a group of seven bronze pedestrians literally being swallowed into the pavement, only to re-emerge on the other side

been collected from other Silesian churches. The wonderful Romanesque tympanum in the south aisle is the only remnant of the original 12th-century church that once stood here. There's a mechanised *szopka* (nativity scene) in the first chapel to the right; make a small donation when one of the assistants turns it on.

### Church of St Giles
CHURCH

(Kościół Św Idziego; Plac Św Idziego) In contrast to the enormous cathedral, the Church of St Giles is barely a cupboard. Built between 1218 and 1230, this is the oldest surviving church in Wrocław, and has an original Romanesque portal.

### Wrocław Archdiocesan Museum
MUSEUM

(Muzeum Archidiecezji Wrocławskiej; Plac Katedralny 16; adult/concession 3/2zł; ◷9am-3pm Tue-Sun) A few steps east of the Church of St Giles is the Wrocław Archdiocesan Museum, with a large collection of sacred art.

# Wrocław

of the street. It was created by Jerzy Kalina and was unveiled in 2005 to mark the 24th anniversary of the declaration of martial law. Look for it 500m west of the train station.

## 👉 Tours

**Wrocław Sightseeing Tours**  GUIDED TOURS
(☑69 890 0123; www.wroclawsightseeingtours.com; ul Wita Stwosza 3) Operates guided walking tours (60zł) and bus tours (100zł) of the city, as well as day trips further afield in Lower Silesia (200zł) and the Sudetes (290zł).

**Gucio** CRUISE
(www.statekpasazerski.pl; Bulwar Piotra Włostowica; ◷11am-7.15pm Mar-Nov) In the warmer months this boat runs 40-minute cruises (13zł) on the Odra departing hourly from the southern end of Sand Island. Hour-long sailings (22zł) depart at 8pm and 9pm on Friday and Saturday.

## ✴ Festivals & Events

**Jazz on the Odra** JAZZ
(www.jnofestival.pl) One of Poland's foremost jazz festivals, in March or April.

**Musica Polonica Nova** MUSIC
(www.musicapolonicanova.pl in Polish) Contemporary music festival held in May.

**Arsenal Nights** MUSIC
(www.wieczorywarsenale.pl) Chamber music festival at the Arsenal in June/July.

**Wratislavia Cantans**      MUSIC
(www.wratislaviacantans.pl) Wrocław's top international music and fine arts festival is held in September.

**Wrocław Marathon**      SPORT
(www.wroclawmaraton.pl) Running event in September.

## 🛏 Sleeping

TOP CHOICE **Hostel Mleczarnia**     HOSTEL €
(🖉71 787 7570; www.mleczarniahostel.pl; ul Włodkowica 5; dm 50zł, d 220zł; 🛜) This hostel on a quiet road not far from the Rynek has bags of charm, having been decorated in a deliberately old-fashioned style within a former residential building. There's a women-only dorm available, along with a kitchen and free laundry facilities. Downstairs is the excellent Mleczarnia cafe-bar.

**Hotel Patio**     HOTEL €€
(🖉71 375 0400; www.hotelpatio.pl; ul Kiełbaśnicza 24; s/d 300/340zł; P🐾@) The Patio offers pleasant lodgings a short hop from the main square, within two buildings linked by a covered, sunlit courtyard. Rooms are clean and light, sometimes small but with reasonably high ceilings, and there's a spectacular breakfast spread.

**Dwór Polski**     HOTEL €€
(🖉71 372 3415; www.dworpolski.wroclaw.pl; ul Kiełbaśnicza 2; s/d 265/325zł; P🛜) You couldn't ask for more character than this: a restored 16th-century house, complete with idiosyncratic rooms, some original dark-wood fittings and fixtures, and a popular restaurant (enter from Rynek 5). The atmospheric internal courtyard is a plus.

**Hotel Monopol**     HOTEL €€€
(🖉71 772 3777; www.monopolwroclaw.hotel.com .pl; ul Modrzejewskiej 2; s/d 600/650zł; 🐾🛜🏊) Wrocław's most elegant hotel, which in its heyday hosted such luminaries as Pablo Picasso and Marlene Dietrich (along with less savoury characters such as Adolf Hitler), has been restored to its former glory. It's opposite the opera house, 350m south of the Rynek off ul Świdnicka. There are two restaurants, three bars, a cafe, a spa and several expensive boutiques within its walls, so you won't be short of pampering options – but might soon be short of cash.

**Art Hotel**     HOTEL €€€
(🖉71 787 7100; www.arthotel.pl; ul Kiełbaśnicza 20; r 380-530zł; P🐾🛜) Elegant but affordable

accommodation in a renovated apartment building, with tastefully restrained decor, quality fittings and gleaming bathrooms. There's a top-notch Polish-French restaurant, and a fitness room for working off any extra weight gained therein. Breakfast is an extortionate additional 50zł per person.

**AS Apartments**     APARTMENTS €€
(🖉71 341 8759; www.asapart.pl; Rynek 18; apt from €50; 🛜) Company offering a choice of villas in the Old Town, many of them with a view of the Rynek itself. The fixtures and fittings can be old-fashioned, but the locations are fabulous for the price. Most apartments come with a kitchen and washing machine, along with free wi-fi access.

**Nathan's Villa Hostel**     HOSTEL €
(🖉71 344 1095; www.nathansvilla.com; ul Świdnicka 13; dm 45zł, r 190zł; 🐾🛜) Sister to the popular Kraków hostel, this place 150m south of the Rynek is a convenient spot to lay your head. Each bunk has its own locker and reading lamp, and there are numerous bathrooms and a laundry service (15zł). Note that it sometimes accepts noisy Polish school groups in addition to backpackers, so check before you check in.

**Hotel Tumski**     HOTEL €€
(🖉71 322 6099; www.hotel-tumski.com.pl; Wyspa Słodowa 10; s/d 280/380zł; P🛜) Located on an islet in the Odra, about 300m north of the river along ul Św Jadwigi, this neat hotel has a riverside setting and is set back from a busy road. There's an attractive rustic-style restaurant serving both Polish and international cuisine.

**Cinnamon Hostel**     HOSTEL €
(🖉71 344 5858; www.cinnamonhostel.com; ul Kazimierza Wielkiego 67; dm 40-60zł, d 135zł; 🛜) Right on the ring road and within spitting distance of pedestrian ul Świdnicka, this charming and upbeat place has rooms (two

to 12 beds) named for spices and herbs, a bright kitchen, a laundry and a comfortable common room.

### Hostel Babel
HOSTEL **€**

(☑71 344 1206; www.babelhostel.pl; ul Kołłątaja 16; dm 45-60zł, d 160zł; ☎) A tatty old staircase leads up to pleasant budget accommodation just 100m from the train station. Dorms are set in renovated apartment rooms with ornate lamps and decorative ceilings. Bathrooms are shiny clean, and guests have access to a kitchen. There's a DVD player for rainy days.

### Hotel Zaułek
HOTEL **€€**

(☑71 341 0046; www.hotel.uni.wroc.pl; ul Garbary 11; s/d 260/350zł; **P**☎) Run by the university, this is a charming guesthouse with friendly staff, accommodating just 18 visitors in a dozen homely rooms. The 1pm checkout is a boon for late sleepers.

### Hotel Europejski
HOTEL **€€**

(☑71 772 1000; www.silfor.pl; ul Piłsudskiego 88; s/d 229/259zł; **@**) Apparently a leopard can change its spots – the formerly drab Europejski is now a smart business hotel just 200m west of the train station. Rooms are clean and bright, and there's a restaurant on the premises.

### Hotel Savoy
HOTEL **€€**

(☑71 344 3071; www.savoy.wroc.pl; Plac Kościuszki 19; s 135zł, d 162-185zł) It may not look like much, but the downbeat Savoy is one of your best shots at a bargain. Pot plants, half-decent furniture and little balconies liven up the best rooms. It's 700m south of the Rynek along ul Świdnicka.

### Hotel Polonia
HOTEL **€€**

(☑71 343 1021; www.odratourist.pl; ul Piłsudskiego 66; s 149-169zł, d 169-229zł; ☎) There's little spectacular about this large hotel 400m west of the train station, but it's close to transport and occasional special promotions make it even better value. Room prices depend on size, and quality of decoration.

### Europeum Hotel
HOTEL **€€**

(☑71 371 4500; www.europeum.pl; ul Kazimierza Wielkiego 27a; s/d 330/380zł; **P**✱☎) Business-oriented hotel with stylish rooms in a great location not far from the Rynek. Rates drop dramatically at weekends, generally by 20%.

### MDK Kopernik Hostel
HOSTEL **€**

(☑71 343 8857; www.mdk.wroclaw.pl; ul Kołłątaja 20; dm/d 40/96zł) A mere 100m from the train station, this is a basic, recently renovated old-style hostel, located in a grand mustard-coloured building. Some dorms are huge and beds are packed close together. Prices are cheaper after the first night.

## ✗ Eating

The market square and its central buildings are jam-packed with eateries, but it's worth checking out the quieter streets for less tourist-happy establishments.

For self-catering supplies, visit **Eko Supermarket** (ul Kuźnicza 48; ☺7am-9pm Mon-Sat, 9am-5pm Sun), **Hala Targowa** (p239) or the supermarket at **Galeria Dominikańska** (p239).

### Bernard
INTERNATIONAL **€€€**

(Rynek 35; mains 25-69zł) Whoever Bernard is, he must be one cool dude – this lively split-level bar-restaurant is a cut above its Rynek rivals. It serves a selection of upmarket comfort food including burgers, steak and fish dishes, along with a Polish choice or two; all washed down with the in-house lager. There's live music most nights, and a breakfast menu from 10am to noon.

### STP
CAFETERIA **€**

(ul Kuźnicza 10; dishes 2.99zł per 100g; ☺10am-9pm; ✗) Short for 'Szybko, Tanio, Pysznie', the name says it all: 'Fast, Cheap, Delicious'. This cafeteria sells food by weight and it's surprisingly good. Just grab a plate, pile it up and it'll be weighed when you reach the cashier.

### Akropolis
GREEK **€€€**

(Rynek 16/17; mains 26-75zł) This restaurant serves excellent Greek food with a view onto the market square, defying the usual rule that restaurants in such a prominent position aren't worth bothering with. The baked lamb in lemon sauce is superb.

### Restauracja JaDka
POLISH **€€€**

(☑71 343 6461; ul Rzeźnicza 24/25; mains 52-87zł) A well-regarded fine-dining option presenting impeccable modern versions of Polish classics and silver-service table settings (candles, crystal, linen) in delightful Gothic surrounds. Bookings are recommended.

### Darea
KOREAN, JAPANESE **€€**

(ul Kuźnicza 43/45; mains 15-150zł) Over time the menu at this place has become steadily more Japanese, but you'll still find authentic Korean dishes like *bibimbab* and *bulgogi* on the list. It's all good Asian food in atmospheric surrounds.

## THE GNOMES ARE REVOLTING

How do unarmed civilians take on a totalitarian regime? For Wrocław University art history graduate Waldemar Fydrych, nicknamed 'Major', the answer was obvious – by ridiculing it.

In the early 1980s, Fydrych set up the **Orange Alternative** (Pomarańczowa Alternatywa), a group that intended to place banana skins beneath the feet of Poland's humourless communist government. It initially painted pictures of gnomes on areas where the authorities had already painted over anti-government graffiti – neatly drawing attention to the negative sentiments that had once been on display there.

In the second half of the decade, the Alternative upped the ante by organising actions intended to both embarrass the regime and encourage independent thought. They handed out items in short supply such as toilet paper and feminine hygiene products; overdressed in red on the anniversary of Russia's communist revolution; and marched to demand the release of Father Christmas. The high point was a demonstration in 1988 in support of gnomes, in which thousands marched while wearing floppy orange hats.

Nowadays the communists are long gone and the gnomes have taken over the streets, in the form of small statues that are said to be a tribute to the icon of the Orange Alternative. 'Major' Fydrych has continued to campaign for change via silliness; in addition to continuing the Alternative's actions, he's twice run for election as Mayor of Warsaw under the slogan 'Merrier and more competent'.

You can read more about the Orange Alternative's history and current activities at its website, www.pomaranczowa-alternatywa.org.

---

**Spice India**  INDIAN €€
(ul Wita Stwosza 15a; mains 7-36zł; 🍴) Tasty, authentic Indian food in a colourful but intimate basement setting. The long menu includes tikka and tandoori variants, along with a generous vegetarian selection.

**Soho**  INTERNATIONAL €€
(ul Szewska 8; mains 20-70zł; ⊘9.30am-10pm; 🍴🛜) Friendly informal eatery with a long and diverse menu including pasta, pizzas, steaks and salads. It has a good vegetarian selection, and also serves breakfast.

**Bar Wegetariański Vega**  VEGETARIAN, VEGAN €
(Sukiennice 1/2; mains 3-7zł; ⊘8am-7pm Mon-Fri, 9am-5pm Sat & Sun; 🍴) This is a cheap, meat-free cafeteria on two floors in the centre of the Rynek, offering vegetarian and vegan dishes in a light green space. There's a good choice of soups and crêpes.

**Amalfi**  ITALIAN €€€
(ul Więzienna 21; mains 29-76zł; ⊘noon-midnight) This pizzeria with a wood-burning stove and a pleasant long terrace is just north of the Rynek. It's the best option for decent Italian cuisine on a street with plenty of Mediterranean offerings.

**Mexico Bar**  MEXICAN €€
(ul Rzeźnicza 34; mains 13-60zł) Compact, warmly lit restaurant featuring sombreros and backlit masks on the walls, serving all the Mexican favourites. There's a small bar to lean on while waiting for a table.

**Karczma Lwowska**  POLISH €€
(Rynek 4; mains 10-45zł; ⊘noon-midnight) Tasty Polish standards in a space with a rustic rural look; try the beer served in big ceramic mugs.

**La Scala**  ITALIAN €€
(Rynek 38; mains 17-70zł; ⊘10am-midnight) Authentic but relatively pricey Italian food; the cheaper trattoria at ground level serves good pizza and pasta.

## 🍷 Drinking

### Cafes

**Mleczarnia**  CAFE-BAR
(ul Włodkowica 5; ⊘8am-4am; 🛜) Hidden away in a backstreet, this atmospheric place is stuffed with chipped old wooden tables bearing lace doilies and candlesticks. It turns out good coffee and light meals, including breakfast. At night the cellar opens, adding another moody dimension.

**Café Artzat**  CAFE-BAR
(ul Malarska 30; ⊘11am-late; 🛜) This low-key cafe just north of the landmark Church of St Elizabeth is one of the best places in town to recharge the batteries over coffee or tea (or a beer) and a good book.

#### Literatka
CAFE-BAR

(Rynek 56/57; ☺10am-late) As the name suggests, this cafe next to a library will suit the literary-minded. The interior is a cosy blend of wood panelling, faded carpet and old books.

#### Afryka
CAFE

(ul Kiełbaśnicza 24; ☺9.30am-10pm) A great place to enjoy a *kawa* (coffee), this cafe blows its chain rivals out of the (hot) water with a superb selection of imported beans and lovely 'front parlour' decor.

#### Czekoladziarnia
CAFE

(ul Więzienna 30; ☺10am-10pm Mon-Fri, noon-10pm Sat & Sun) This little place sells its own shop-made chocolate in both solid and liquid forms.

### Pubs & Bars

#### Abrams' Tower
WINE BAR

(ul Kraińskiego 14; ☺6pm-late) This impressively difficult-to-find bar and wine shop is housed in a 13th-century guard tower and is a superb retreat from the hubbub of the Rynek. It also serves Mexican, Spanish and Thai food. To reach it, step through the pedestrian opening next to the pharmacy at ul Piaskowa 11.

#### Paparazzi
BAR

(ul Rzeźnicza 32/33; ☺noon-late Mon-Fri, 4pm-late Sat & Sun; ☻) This spacious branch of the Polish bar chain is a cut above the rest, with its designer decor, huge rectangular bar and fine cocktails. Try the Wrocław Sling, a mix of vodka and citrus juices.

#### PracOFFnia
PUB

(ul Więzienna 6; ☺noon-late Mon-Fri, 3pm-late Sat & Sun) Housed in what was a prison in the Middle Ages, below a well-concealed courtyard, this eclectic place crammed with old cameras and projectors is Wrocław's most interesting boozer.

#### Spiż
PUB, BREWERY

(Rynek-Ratusz 2; ☺10am-late) Popular microbrewery bar-restaurant buried in a basement under the town hall, with bustling staff scurrying around the copper vats to serve the voracious clientele.

#### Kalogródek
PUB

(ul Kuźnicza 29b; ☺10am-late) Hidden behind some rough-looking wooden hoardings, the big, stepped terrace here is like a playground for students. The open-air vibe and cheap beer make sure it's heaving, even when the weather's uncooperative.

## ☆ Entertainment

Wrocław is an important cultural and nightlife centre, and there's a lot of stuff going on all year round. The monthly freebie *Aktivist* (www.aktivist.pl/wroclaw) has listings in Polish; you can pick up a copy of the bimonthly English-language *The Visitor* (www.thevisitor.pl) from the tourist office.

For a more detailed rundown of clubs, bars and the like, seek out the reliably forthright *Wrocław in Your Pocket* (www.inyourpocket.com/poland/wroclaw) or consult the useful Wrocław Life website (www.wroclaw-life.com).

### Cinema

#### Kino Helios
CINEMA

(www.heliosnet.pl; ul Kazimierza Wielkiego 19a) If you're after a movie, head to this modern multiplex screening English-language films.

### Theatre & Classical Music

#### Wrocławski Teatr Współczesny
THEATRE

(☎71 358 8922; www.wteatrw.pl in Polish; ul Rzeźnicza 12; ☺box office noon-7pm Mon-Fri) Near the centre of town, the Wrocław Contemporary Theatre tends more towards staging productions from modern Polish and international playwrights.

#### Philharmonic Hall
CLASSICAL MUSIC

(Filharmonia; ☎71 342 2459; www.filharmonia.wroclaw.pl; ul Piłsudskiego 19; ☺box office 11am-6pm Mon-Fri) If you're interested in hearing classical sounds, Friday and Saturday evenings are your best bets. It's located 800m southwest of the Rynek.

#### Opera House
OPERA

(Opera Wrocławska; ☎71 370 8880; www.opera.wroclaw.pl; ul Świdnicka 35; ☺box office noon-7pm Mon-Sat, 11am-5pm Sun) This venerable building is the traditional venue for opera and ballet performances.

### Nightclubs

There are two areas to head for if you fancy a big night out: the Rynek, and Pasaż Niepolda off ul Ruska west of the Old Town, which offers a bit more variety.

#### TOP CHOICE PRL
BAR, CLUB

(Rynek-Ratusz 10; ☺24hr) The dictatorship of the proletariat is alive and well in this nonstop tongue-in-cheek venue inspired by communist nostalgia. Disco lights play over a bust of Lenin, propaganda posters line the walls and red-menace memorabilia is scattered through the maze of rooms. Descend to the basement – beneath the portraits of Stalin and Mao – if you'd like to hit the dance floor.

**Novocaina**                                    BAR, CLUB
(Rynek 16; ☺noon-late) Another Rynek cafe-restaurant that dons its party duds late in the evening, this neo-Gothic wet dream with plasma screens and intimate nooks and crannies attracts a fashion-conscious crowd.

**Jazzda**                                        BAR, CLUB
(Rynek 60; ☺9am-late Mon-Sat, 10.30am-late Sun) Looking for a John Travolta kind of evening? This central bar and club with a lit-up, multicoloured dance floor and strobe lights will fit the bill.

**Bezsenność**                                    CLUB
(ul Ruska 51; ☺7pm-late) With its alternative/rock/dance line-up and distressed decor, 'Insomnia' attracts a high-end clientele and is one of the most popular clubs in town.

**Metropolis**                                    CLUB
(ul Ruska 51; ☺9pm-3am) This enormous place has two dance floors, one on the ground floor with dance and techno, and a piano bar in the cellar.

## 🛍 Shopping

### Books

**EMPiK**                                          BOOKS
(Rynek 50; ☺7am-9pm Mon-Sat, noon-9pm Sun) Big range on the Rynek.

**PolAnglo**                                       BOOKS
(ul Kuźnicza 49a) Good selection of books in English.

**Księgarnia Podróżnika**                          BOOKS
(ul Wita Stwosza 19/20) Sells maps and guidebooks.

### Food & Gifts

**Hala Targowa**                               FOOD, GIFTS
(ul Pisarska 17; ☺8am-6.30pm Mon-Fri, 9am-3pm Sat) Lively historic market hall selling food, souvenirs and an endless variety of knick-knacks.

**Galeria Dominikańska**                            MALL
(www.galeria-dominikanska.pl in Polish; Plac Dominikański 3; ☺9.30am-9pm) Big shopping mall with a supermarket and hundreds of shops selling everything under the sun.

## ℹ Information

### Internet Access

**Intermax** (ul Psie Budy 10/11; per hr 4zł; ☺9am-11pm) Enter from ul Kazimierza Wielkiego.

**Internet Netvigator** (ul Igielna 14; per hr 4zł; ☺9am-midnight)

### Websites

**City of Wrocław** (www.wroclaw.pl) Informative official site direct from city hall.

**Wrocław Life** (www.wroclaw-life.com) Interactive information portal on every aspect of life and tourism in Wrocław.

### Post

**Post office** (Rynek 28; ☺24hr)

### Telephone

The best place to pick up a Polish SIM card for your mobile phone is at one of the mobile phone companies' outlets at Galeria Dominikańska.

### Tourist Information

**Lower Silesia Tourist Information Centre** (☎71 342 2291; www.wroclaw-info.pl; Rynek-Ratusz 24; ☺11am-7pm) Covers both Wrocław and the surrounding region.

**Tourist office** (☎71 344 3111; www.wroclaw-info.pl; Rynek 14; ☺9am-9pm)

### Travel Agency

**PTTK** (☎71 343 8331; www.pttk.pl; 1st fl, Rynek-Ratusz 11/12)

## ℹ Getting There & Away

**AIR Wrocław Copernicus Airport** (☎71 358 1381; www.airport.wroclaw.pl) is in Strachowice, 13km west of the city centre. There are direct connections via LOT to Warsaw (six times daily). International links include Dublin via Ryanair (daily), Frankfurt via LOT and Lufthansa (three daily), London via Wizz Air and Ryanair (twice daily), Munich via LOT and Lufthansa (four daily), and Paris aboard Wizz Air (three times weekly).

**LOT** (☎801 703 703; ul Piłsudskiego 36) has an office near the train station.

**BUS** The bus terminal is 1.3km south of the Rynek, behind the train station. Buses run at least hourly to Trzebnica (8zł, 40 minutes), Sobótka (7zł, 55 minutes) and Świdnica (16zł, one hour). They also serve Kudowa-Zdrój (27zł, 2¾ hours, seven daily) and Nysa (15zł, 1½ hours, nine daily). Trains are more convenient for other destinations.

There are also international bus routes to destinations including Prague (from 100zł, 5½ hours, daily). Tickets can be bought at the bus station.

**TRAIN** Trains depart from the impressive mock castle that is Wrocław Główny station, 1.2km south of the Rynek. Trains to Katowice (41zł, three hours, at least hourly) usually pass through Opole (24zł, one hour) on the way. Most continue to Kraków (50zł, five hours). There are 14 daily services to Warsaw, divided between eight TLK trains (57zł, 6½ hours) and six Express InterCity trains (120zł, 5½ hours).

Wrocław also has regular train links with Łódź (45zł, 4¼ hours, three daily), Poznań (38zł, three hours, at least hourly), Gniezno (44zł, 3½ hours, eight daily), Wałbrzych (16zł, 1¾ hours, hourly), Jelenia Góra (22zł, 3¾ hours, seven daily) and Kłodzko (18zł, 1¾ hours, every two hours).

##  Getting Around

**TO/FROM THE AIRPORT** The airport can be reached on bus 406 from the main train station (2.80zł, 30 minutes, every 20 to 40 minutes), or via infrequent night bus 249. A taxi to the airport costs about 50zł.

**CAR & MOTORCYCLE Micar** (☑71 325 1949; www.micar.pl; ul Kamieńskiego 12) has cars with unlimited kilometres starting from 70zł per day.

**PUBLIC TRANSPORT** Wrocław has an efficient network of trams and buses covering the city centre and suburbs. Journeys within the centre cost 2.40zł; longer trips, fast buses and night buses (numbered over 200) are 2.80zł.

**TAXI** These are some of the better-known companies:

**Domino Taxi** (☑71 19625)

**Radio Taxi** (☑71 19622)

**Super Taxi** (☑71 19663)

# AROUND WROCŁAW

## Trzebnica

POP 12,000

A small town 25km north of Wrocław, Trzebnica (tsheb-*nee*-tsah) is noted for its former Cistercian abbey. It's an impressive site and a pleasant half-day trip from Wrocław.

The **abbey church** (ul Jana Pawła II 3) is thought to be one of the first brick buildings erected in Poland. Though it was rebuilt in the 18th century, the structure has preserved much of its original Romanesque shape and, importantly, still boasts two **portals** from that time. The one next to the main entrance, partly hidden behind the Baroque tower added in the 1780s, is particularly fine; on the tympanum, which dates from the 1220s, you can still make out King David on his throne playing the harp to Queen Bathsheba and her lady-in-waiting.

The church's showpiece is **St Hedwig's Chapel** (Kaplica Św Jadwigi), to the right of the chancel. It was built soon after the canonisation of the princess, and the graceful, ribbed Gothic vaulting has been preserved unchanged. Its central feature is

the saint's Gothic sarcophagus, an elaborate work in black marble and alabaster created in stages between 1680 and 1750. To the left of the tomb is the entrance to the three-nave crypt, the oldest part of the church.

The rest of the chapel is full of gilded and marbled altars; in the nave are 18 scenes from the saint's life. The beautiful black organ is striking against the white walls and pastel colours of the ornamentation.

Buses to and from Wrocław (8zł, 40 minutes) run at least hourly.

## Sobótka & Mt Ślęża

POP 6800

Some 34km southwest of Wrocław, the solitary forested cone of **Mt Ślęża** rises to 718m above the surrounding open plain. Mt Ślęża was one of the holy places of an ancient pagan tribe that set up cult sites in the area from at least the 5th century BC till the 11th century AD, when Christianity put a halt to it. The summit was circled by a stone wall marking off the sanctuary where rituals were held, and the remains of these ramparts survive to this day. Mysterious **votive statues** were carved crudely out of granite, and several of them are scattered over the mountain's slopes.

The Ślęża Massif is surrounded by the 15,640-hectare **Ślęża Landscape Park** (Ślężański Park Krajobrazowy). At the northern foot of Mt Ślęża is the small town of Sobótka, the starting point for a hike to the top. The red route will lead you up the mountain, a hike that should take about two hours. You'll find two statues called the Bear (Miś) and the Fish (Ryba) on the way, plus a tall TV mast and a 19th-century church at the top.

Coming down, you can take the steeper but faster (1¼ hours) yellow route directly to the PTTK hostel, about 800m west of your starting point. On the road back into town you'll pass another stone statue, called the Monk (Mnich) but resembling an urn to our untrained eyes.

Sobótka is easily accessible by bus from Wrocław (7zł, 55 minutes, at least hourly) and Świdnica (6zł, 40 minutes, hourly).

# LOWER SILESIA

A fertile lowland extending along the upper and middle course of the Odra River, Lower Silesia (Dolny Śląsk) was settled relatively early on, and is full of interesting old towns and villages. Architecture buffs will have a field day with the wide assortment of castles and churches, and the area's larger towns have more than enough to tempt those with entertainment on their minds.

# Zielona Góra

POP 118,000

The pretty western town Zielona Góra ('Green Mountain') lives up to at least half its name – there's little mountainous about it, but there's much leafy greenness courtesy of the trees shading its pedestrian streets.

The presence of nature is also a reminder that Zielona Góra stands out as Poland's only wine producer. It's a tradition running all the way back to the 14th century, though the climate is less than ideal and viticulture was never a very profitable endeavour here. Though the output today is merely symbolic, the wine association is reflected in the city's attractions.

Like the majority of other towns in the region, Zielona Góra (zhyeh-*lo*-na *goo*-rah) was founded by the Silesian Piasts. It was part of the Głogów Duchy, one of numerous regional principalities, before it passed to the Habsburgs in the 16th century and to Prussia two centuries later. Unlike many other Silesian towns, however, Zielona Góra came through WWII with minimal damage, which is why prewar architecture is well represented here.

## ◉ Sights

**Lubuski Regional Museum** MUSEUM
(Muzeum Ziemi Lubuskiej; www.mzl.zgora.pl; al Niepodległości 15; adult/concession 6/3zł; ⊙11am-4pm) This institution has a large collection of Silesian religious art from the 14th to 18th centuries, a fascinating clock gallery and a permanent exhibition of artwork by Marian Kruczek (1927–83). Kruczek used everyday objects – anything from buttons to spark plugs – to create some striking assemblages, and this is the largest collection of his work in Poland.

In the same building (and included in the ticket price) you'll find the **Wine Museum**, which illustrates the history of winemaking in the region, as well as the **Museum of Torture**. This charming sub-museum holds Poland's largest exhibition on the history of criminal law, the penalty system and torture methods employed from the Middle Ages until the 18th century.

**FREE** **Wine Park** PARK
(Park Winny; ul Wrocławska 12; ⊙10am-10pm Tue-Sun) Located on the site of a historical vineyard, this pleasant park contains a restaurant and cafe, as well as a palm house exhibiting exotic plants. It's a great place to have a meal and unwind.

**Stary Rynek** SQUARE
Lined with brightly painted houses, the renovated old market square is a pleasant and harmonious rectangular space at the end of the long pedestrian stretch along al Niepodległości and ul Żeromskiego. The 18th-century **town hall**, complete with a slim 54m tower, has escaped being over-modernised in spite of changes over the years.

**Ethnographic Museum** MUSEUM
(Muzeum Etnograficzne; www.muzeumochla.pl in Polish; ul Muzealna 5, adult/concession 8/5zł; ⊙10am-5pm Tue-Sun) This outdoor museum is in Ochla, 7km south of the city, and is served by bus 27. Over 60 traditional buildings – many of them residential – have been reassembled over 13 hectares of land.

## ✦ Festivals & Events

**Wine Festival** WINE
Celebration of the grape held in mid-September each year, including concerts, feasts and a parade. The tourist office can inform you about specific events.

## ⌂ Sleeping

**TOP CHOICE** **Hotel Śródmiejski** HOTEL €€
(☎68 415 2415; www.hotel-srodmiejski.pl; ul Żeromskiego 23; s 165-195zł, d 260-350zł; P🌐) A recent modernisation of this accommodation has produced attractive rooms of a contemporary design, and the location is as central as you could want. Weekend discounts are available.

**Hotelik Senator** HOTEL €€
(☎68 324 0436; www.senator.zgora.pl; ul Chopina 23a; s/d 180/210zł; P🌐) Bright hotel with friendly service and simple but comfortable rooms. There's a restaurant on the premises, and it's in a good location for both the train and bus stations and the eating strip along al Niepodległości. Enter from ul Jana Keplera.

**B&B Pokoje Gościnne** HOTEL €
(☎609 058 862; www.zaulekpokoje.pl; Plac Pocztowy 10; s/d from 90/150zł; P🌐) Centrally

located budget lodgings, only a stone's throw from the Stary Rynek. Rooms are modern and comfortable, and a great deal for the price. For longer stays, rates are negotiable.

**Apartamenty Betti**  HOTEL, APARTMENTS **€€**
(☑509 246 205; ul Drzewna 1; s 140-170zł, d 200-220zł, apt 280-350; **P**🛜) Attractive selection of rooms, which are spread through three connected historic buildings near the main square. The three apartments allow self-catering and more elbow room than hotel accommodation.

## ✘ Eating & Drinking

**Essenza**  INTERNATIONAL **€€**
(al Niepodległości 11; mains 22-50zł) Creator of tasty 'fusion cuisine', essentially dishes with a Mediterranean flavour and some Polish influence. The terrace is a pleasant place from which to watch the strolling crowds.

**Ermitaż**  POLISH **€€**
(Plac Pocztowy 16; mains 20-45zł; ⊘8am-late) This cafe-restaurant attracts Zielona Góra's movers and shakers with its stylish decor, good coffee and terrace seating. The menu includes fish dishes and salads, and there's a surprisingly lengthy breakfast selection.

**Pizzeria Gioconda**  PIZZERIA **€**
(ul Mariacka 5; mains 10-20zł) Tuck into the fastest Italian food on the Stary Rynek under the inscrutable gaze of Mona Lisa. It's a simple place in a quiet corner of the square, serving up decent pizzas.

**Haust**  PUB, BREWERY
(Plac Pocztowy; ⊘noon-11pm; 🛜) This lively pub and microbrewery near the Stary Rynek serves five variants of its own beer, from pilsner to porter.

## ❶ Information

**Post office** (ul Bohaterów Westerplatte 21; ⊘7am-8pm Mon-Fri, 9am-3pm Sat, 9am-2pm Sun)

**Tourist office** (☑68 323 2222; www.zielona-gora.pl; Stary Rynek 1; ⊘9am-5pm Mon-Fri, 10am-2pm Sat) In the town hall.

## ❶ Getting There & Away

The bus station is about 1km northeast of the city centre, and the train station's just across ul Dworcowa from the bus station. Major destinations by bus include Poznań (33zł, three hours, five daily), Wrocław (34zł, three hours, six daily) and Jelenia Góra (36zł, 3½ hours, eight daily).

There are eight daily trains to Wrocław (24zł, 3½ hours), six to Poznań (35zł, two hours), four to Szczecin (30zł, four hours), two to Kraków (59zł, 8½ hours) and one to Warsaw (59zł, 5¾ hours).

# Świdnica

POP 59,400

One of the wealthiest towns in Silesia in the Middle Ages, Świdnica (shfeed-*nee*-tsah) escaped major damage in WWII and has retained some important historic buildings, including its disinctive wooden Church of Peace. It's an agreeable place for a stopover and a convenient springboard for the impressive castle at Książ.

Świdnica was founded in the 12th century, and in 1290 became the capital of the Duchy of Świdnica-Jawor. This was one of myriad Silesian Piast principalities but among the most powerful, thanks to its two gifted rulers: Bolko I, who founded it, and his grandson Bolko II, who extended it significantly.

The capital itself was a flourishing commercial centre, well known for its beer, which ended up on the tables of Kraków, Prague and Buda. Until the Thirteen Years' War (1454–66) it was one of the largest Polish towns, with 6000 inhabitants. By 1648, however, the population had dropped to 200, and Świdnica has ever since been dwarfed by its former rival, Wrocław.

## ◎ Sights

TOP CHOICE **Church of Peace**  CHURCH
(Kościół Pokoju; www.kosciolpokoju.pl; Plac Pokoju 6; adult/concession 8/4zł; ⊘9am-1pm & 3-6pm Mon-Sat, 3-6pm Sun Apr-Oct, by reservation Nov-Mar) This magnificent timber church was erected between 1656 and 1657 in just 10 months. The builders were not trying to set any records; the so-called Peace of Westphalia of 1648 allowed the Protestants of Silesia to build a total of three churches as long as they went up in less than a year, had no belfry, and used only clay, sand and wood as building materials. The churches at Świdnica and Jawor still stand, though the one at Głogów burned down in 1758.

The Świdnica church is a shingled structure laid out in the form of a cross and contains not a single nail. The interior is a beautiful, peaceful place to sit in contemplation for a few minutes; the timber structure seems to possess an intimate inclusiveness that big stone churches sometimes lack. The Baroque decoration, with paintings covering the walls and coffered ceiling, has been preserved intact. Along the walls, two storeys of galleries and several small balconies were installed, allowing some 3500 seated worshippers and 4000 standees. The church was added to Unesco's World Heritage List in 2001.

The church is 400m northeast of the Rynek; enter via the arched gateway off ul Kościelna.

### Rynek                                             SQUARE

The Old Town's market square contains a bit of every architectural style from Baroque to postwar concrete structures, the cumulative effect of rebuilding after successive fires and the damage caused by Austrian, Prussian and Napoleonic sieges.

The bright yellow **town hall** dates from the 1710s, and looks a bit squat without its tower, which collapsed in 1967. It contains the **Old Trades Museum** (Muzeum Dawnego Kupiectwa; www.muzeum-kupiectwa.pl in Polish; Rynek 37; adult/concession 5.50/3.50zł, free Fri; ⊙10am-3pm Tue-Fri, 11am-5pm Sat & Sun), with reconstructions of an old tavern, a pharmacy and a shop, and a collection of historic scales and balances.

A **bugle call** sounds from the town-hall tower at 10am, noon, 2pm and 4pm. Alas, however, this is not the live *hejnał* of Kraków, but a recording.

### Church of SS Stanislaus and Wenceslas                           CHURCH

(Kościół Św Stanisława i Wacława; Plac Jana Pawła II 1) The parish Church of SS Stanislaus and Wenceslas, east of the Rynek, is a massive Gothic stone building whose facade is adorned with four elegant 15th-century doorways and an 18m-high window (the stained glass is not original). The **tower**, completed in 1565, is 103m high, making it Poland's tallest historic church tower after that of the basilica in Częstochowa (106m). The spacious interior has a Gothic structure and ornate Baroque decoration and furnishings. The original church was accidentally burned down in 1532 by the town's *burmistrz* (mayor) Franz Glogisch, who fled Świdnica pursued by angry townsfolk who beat him to death in Nysa.

### 🛏 Sleeping

**Hotel Piast-Roman**                         HOTEL €€
(☑74 852 1393; www.hotel-piast-roman.pl; ul Kotlarska 11; s/d 140/180zł; P🐾) The award-winning Piast-Roman, just off the Rynek,

isn't as swish as the ground-floor restaurant might lead you to believe, but it's a good, solid three-star establishment. The rooms are spick and span and you can't top the location.

**Dom Rekolekcyjny**                          HOTEL €
(☑74 853 5260; ul Muzealna 1; s/d 49/79zł; P🐾) Conveniently positioned just one block west of the Rynek (enter from ul Zamkowa), this pleasant accommodation run by the Pentecostal Church is excellent value and nowhere near as monastic as you might expect. Breakfast is not available.

**Park Hotel**                                HOTEL €€
(☑74 853 7098; www.park-hotel.com.pl; ul Pionierów Ziemi Świdnickiej 20; s/d 140/220zł; P🐾🌸) A modern turreted affair on a lovely leafy street within easy walking distance of the Old Town, about 500m south of the train station. It's a smart alternative and offers some big suites with shower or bathtub, and a restaurant.

**Świdnica Hostel**                           HOSTEL €
(☑74 852 2645; www.ssm.swidnica.pl; ul Kanonierska 3; dm 24zł, r 80-110zł; P@) This friendly hostel 700m north of the Rynek offers basic but comfortable accommodation in dorm rooms with three to five beds, as well as private rooms with bathrooms.

### 🍴 Eating & Drinking

**Ziemiańska**                                POLISH €€
(Rynek 43; mains 15-39zł) The interior of this restaurant on the western side of the town hall complex is a little gloomy, but there's no criticising its beautiful courtyard hidden back from the square. The friendly staff serve up a range of tasty Polish dishes.

**Bar Pod Arkadami**                        CAFETERIA €
(ul Trybunalska 2; mains 3-8zł; ⊙9am-6pm Mon-Sat) This tiny snack bar just east of the market square is the place to wrap your mouth around some authentic *barszcz* (beetroot soup) and a *pasztecik* (hot pastry filled with meat, cheese, or cabbage with mushrooms).

**Da Grasso**                                 PIZZERIA €€
(ul Zamkowa 9; mains 15-31zł; 🐾) Just another pizzeria, you might think, but this colourful place 200m west of the Rynek is a slice or two above the usual.

**Baroc**                                        CAFE
(Plac Pokoju 7) This cafe occupying the gatehouse at the entry to the Church of Peace is an attractive place for a quiet drink.

## ⓘ Information

**Library** (ul Franciszkańska 18; per hr 2zł; ☺10am-6pm Mon-Fri, 10am-2pm Sat) Internet access on the ground floor of the public library; turn left through the main door.

**Post office** (Plac Grunwaldzki 1; ☺7am-7pm Mon-Fri, 8am-2pm Sat) Opposite the train station.

**Tourist office** (☎74 852 0290; www.um.swidnica .pl; ul Wewnętrzna 2; ☺10am-6pm Mon-Fri, 10am-3pm Sat, 10am-2pm 1st Sun of month) On the north face of the town hall complex.

## ⓘ Getting There & Away

The train station is a convenient five-minute walk southwest from the Rynek. The PKS bus station is behind it, but you have to go the long way round via the level crossing to reach it.

There are five daily train services to Kłodzko (15zł, 1½ hours).

Hourly buses run to Wrocław (15zł, 1½ hours), while five buses a day depart for Kłodzko (18zł, 1½ hours), including two to Kudowa-Zdrój (21zł, 2½ hours). There are six buses a day to Jelenia Góra (20zł, 1½ hours). Private minibuses to Wrocław depart from a location opposite the bus station. For transport to Książ Castle, see box.

# Książ

With its 415 rooms, the **castle** at Książ (pronounced 'kshonzh') is the largest in Silesia, majestically perched on a steep hill amid lush woods. It was built in the late 13th century by the Silesian Piast Duke Bolko I, acquired by the aristocratic von Hoberg (later Hochberg) family in 1509 and continuously enlarged and remodelled until well into the 20th century. It's thus an amalgam of styles from Romanesque onwards; the central portion, with three massive arcades, is the oldest. The eastern part (to the right) is an 18th-century Baroque addition, while the western segment was built between 1908 and 1923 in a neo-Renaissance style.

During WWII, under Hitler's direct orders, the German authorities confiscated the castle and began construction of a mysterious underground complex beneath the building and surrounding areas (see boxed text, p245). The Soviet military then used it as a barracks until 1946, after which it was pretty much abandoned for a decade and started falling into ruin.

Luckily, restoration work began in 1974. Part of the complex has now been restored and turned into an interesting **museum**

(☎74 664 3850; www.ksiaz.walbrzych.pl; ul Piastów Śląskich 1; adult/concession 15/10zł; ☺10am-5pm).

Approaching the castle from the car park, you pass through a large decorative freestanding **gateway** and get your first view of the castle, standing at end of a beautifully landscaped garden.

Thankfully, this is one stately home in Poland that you can visit without having to accompany a Polish-language tour or wear shower caps over your shoes. As an individual visitor, you follow a prescribed (and rather convoluted) route through the castle, seeing a selection of rooms. The showpiece is **Maximilian Hall**, built in the first half of the 18th century. It's the largest room in the castle and completely restored to its original lavish form, including the ceiling (1733) painted with mythological scenes. The identical fireplaces on either side of the room are sublime. Along with the main rooms, including 'themed' salons (Baroque, Chinese, white etc) on the 1st floor, you'll encounter various temporary exhibits and galleries en route, sometimes with objets d'art for sale. There's also an exhibition of the various dukes up to the castle's last owners, Prince Hans Heinrich XV and his wife Princess Daisy, who was born in Wales.

There are also two tours available, though they're only in Polish unless you apply at least a week ahead for an English-language guide. **Maximilian's Route** (adult/concession 20/15zł, 30min) covers the rooms and their decorative highlights, while **The Mysteries of the Second World War** (adult/concession 22/17zł, 1¼hr) examines the castle's role in the curious wartime Project Riese.

There are several restaurants and cafes dotted about the complex, including a grill and beer garden with leafy views on a terrace within the castle itself.

A five-minute walk east of the castle you can visit the **National Stallion Depot** (Stado Ogierów Skarbu Państwa; ☎74 840 5860; www.stadoksiaz.pl in Polish; ul Jeździecka 3; adult/concession 8/5zł; ☺10am-6pm), once the castle stables. It offers horse-riding sessions (per hour 50zł) on Monday, Wednesday and Thursday evenings, and on weekend afternoons. It's best to book ahead.

## 🛏 Sleeping

**Hotel Przy Oślej Bramie** HOTEL €€ (☎74 664 9270; www.mirjan.pl; ul Piastów Śląskich 1; s/d 165/220zł; 🅿🛜) 'Before the Donkey Gate' has rooms contained in four pretty

## THE ENIGMATIC GIANT

In 1941, the Nazi government of Germany confiscated Schloss Fürstenstein (now Książ Castle) from the aristocratic Hochbergs, its owners for over four centuries. They soon formed their own plan for the property, known as **Project Riese** ('riese' is the German word for 'giant'). As the name suggests, it was of mind-boggling proportions.

From 1943, construction began on a series of sprawling underground complexes beneath the castle and the Eulengebirge (now Góry Sowie) mountain range, part of the Sudetes. It was an enormous undertaking involving the creation of tunnels and chambers using explosives, concrete and steel. In addition to mining specialists, the project used forced labour from both prisoner-of-war and concentration camps.

The sheer scale of the work was a drain on the Nazi regime's resources. As armaments minister Albert Speer later admitted in his memoirs *Inside the Third Reich*, 'The 'Giant' complex alone consumed more concrete than the entire population had at its disposal for air-raid shelters in 1944.'

What's most fascinating about Project Riese is that no one is quite sure what its vast subterranean chambers were for, as they were never completed and key witnesses and documents were lost in the postwar turmoil. Speer referred to a bunker complex, other references were made to bomb-proof underground factories, and many have assumed that Hitler intended to move his headquarters there. The wildest theories suggest that stolen treasures were hidden in the complex, or that the regime was undertaking an atomic bomb programme within its depths.

Whatever the truth, Project 'Giant' retains its giant-sized air of intrigue. For more details on the project and its aftermath, visit www.riese.krzyzowa.org.pl.

little stone buildings to the right before you pass through the gateway to the castle. Just the thing for dyed-in-the-wool romantics.

**Hotel Książ**  HOTEL €€
(☎74 664 3890; www.zamekksiaz.pl; ul Piastów Śląskich 1; s 130-150zł, d 220-240zł; P@) This hotel occupies several outbuildings just past the gateway of the castle complex, with varied standards and facilities. Reception is to the left as you walk up the main path.

### ❶ Getting There & Away

The castle is 7.5km from Wałbrzych; you can reach it from there on city bus 8 (2.40zł, 15 minutes), which runs every 30 to 50 minutes. From Świdnica, 14km to the east, catch minibus 31 to Wałbrzych (5zł, 30 minutes, every 20 minutes) and it will let you off on the main-road turn-off to the castle, reached by an easy 20-minute walk along a paved footpath.

## SUDETES MOUNTAINS

The Sudetes Mountains run for more than 250km along the Czech–Polish border. The highest part of this old and eroded chain of mountains is the Karkonosze, reaching 1602m at Mt Śnieżka. Though the Sudetes don't offer much alpine scenery, they're amazingly varied and heavily covered in forest,

with spectacular geological formations such as those at the Góry Stołowe.

To the north, the Sudetes gradually decline into a belt of gently rolling foothills known as the Sudetes Foothills (Przedgórze Sudeckie). This area is more densely populated, and many of the towns and villages in the region still boast some of their centuries-old timber buildings. Combining visits to these historic settlements with hikes into the mountains and the surrounding countryside is the best way to explore the region.

## Jelenia Góra

POP 84,000

Jelenia Góra (yeh-*lane*-yah *goo*-rah) is set in a beautiful valley surrounded by the Western Sudetes. The city has a relaxed feel and an attractive appearance, and makes a great base for trips into the Karkonosze Mountains.

Jelenia Góra was founded in 1108 by King Bolesław Krzywousty (Bolesław the Wry-Mouthed) – legend has it that the monarch had been following a wounded deer and was so taken by the beauty of the place that he named it 'Deer Mountain'. The border stronghold later came under the rule of the powerful Duchy of Świdnica-Jawor. Gold

# Jelenia Góra

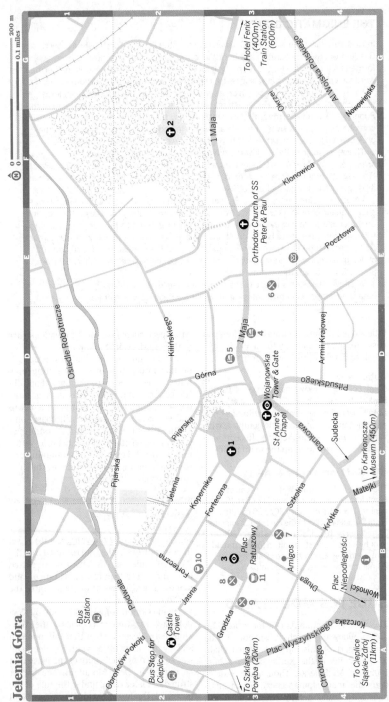

0    200 m
0    0.1 miles

To Hotel Fenix
(400m);
Train Station
(600m)

Al Wojska Polskiego

Nowowiejska

Okrzei

Klonowica

Orthodox Church of SS
Peter & Paul

Pocztowa

1 Maja

6

1 Maja
4

5

Górna

Armii Krajowej

Piłsudskiego

Kilińskiego

Osiedle Robotnicze

Pijarska

Wojanowska
Tower & Gate

St Anne's
Chapel

Bankowa

Sudecka

To Karkonosze
Museum (450m)

1

Pijarska

Jelenia

Kopernika

Forteczna

Szkolna

Matejki

Krótka

Plac
Ratuszowy

7

Amigos

Długa

Plac
Niepodległości

Plac
Wolności

10

3

8
11

9

Forteczna

Jasna

Grodzka

Castle
Tower

Podwale

Bus
Station

Bus Stop for
Cieplice

Obrońców Pokoju

To Szklarska
Poręba (20km)

Plac Wyszyńskiego

Korczaka

Chrobrego

To Cieplice
Śląskie-Zdrój
(11km)

mining in the region gave way to glass production around the 15th century, but weaving gave the town a solid economic base, and its high-quality linen was exported all over Europe.

## ◉ Sights

**Church of the Holy Cross**  CHURCH
(Kościół Św Krzyża; ul 1 Maja 45) Jelenia Góra's main attraction is this massive church; it was built in 1718 for a Lutheran congregation, though it's served a Catholic one since 1947. The three-storey galleries plus the dark, densely packed ground floor can accommodate 4000 people. The ceiling is embellished with illusionist Baroque paintings of scenes from the Old and New Testaments, while the magnificent organ over the high altar dates from 1729.

**Karkonosze Museum**  MUSEUM
(Karkonoskie Muzeum Okręgowe; www.muzeum karkonoskie.pl in Polish; ul Matejki 28; adult/concession 7/3.50zł, free Sun; ⊙9am-4pm) This institution 650m south of the Rynek is renowned for its extensive collection of glass dating from medieval times to the present; the Art Nouveau pieces are wonderful. On the museum grounds is a small skansen (open-air museum of traditional architecture) featuring traditional mountain huts typical of the Karkonosze Mountains.

**Rynek**  SQUARE
The elongated market square, also called Plac Ratuszowy, is lined with a harmonious

group of 17th- and 18th-century houses. Much of their charm is due to their porticos and ground-floor arcades, which provide a covered passageway all around the square. The **town hall** was built in 1749, after its predecessor collapsed.

**Church of SS Erasmus
and Pancras**  CHURCH
(Kościół Św Erazma i Pankracego; Plac Kościelny 1) This place of worship northeast of the Rynek was erected in the 15th century; note the Gothic doorway in the southern entrance portraying Mary and St John at the foot of the cross. The interior, with its theatrical 22m-high Rococo main altar crafted from brick-red marble, boasts mostly Baroque furnishings, including a richly decorated organ.

## ⊨ Sleeping

**Hotel Jelonek**  HOTEL €€
(☑75 764 6541; www.hotel-jelonek.com.pl; ul 1 Maja 5; s 170zł, d 220-350zł; P🕏) Situated in a fine 18th-century burgher's house, this appealing set of lodgings is the nicest in Jelenia Góra. Concentrate on the old prints and antiques in the public areas and turn a blind eye to the Pizza Hut downstairs with its separate entrance. The rooms are stylishly modern, and the more expensive 'lux' rooms are ideal for self-pampering.

**Hotel Fenix**  HOTEL €€
(☑75 641 6600; www.hotelefenix.pl in Polish; ul 1 Maja 88; s/d 169/219zł; P🕏) More convenient for the train station than the centre, the town's flashest hotel offers businesslike modern rooms, and a spa and wellness centre. Even if you're not staying here, it's worth dropping into its excellent restaurant, which serves upmarket Polish dishes.

**Hotel Europa**  HOTEL €€
(☑75 649 5500; www.ptkarkonosze.pl; ul 1 Maja 16/18; s/d 110/168zł; P🕏) This large block east of the Rynek isn't particularly ambient, but the rooms are huge, there's a budget restaurant on site and rates are 20% lower at weekends. Rear rooms look on to the car park.

**Bartek Hostel**  HOSTEL €
(☑75 752 5746; ssm.bartek@wp.pl; ul Bartka Zwycięzcy 10; dm 18-24zł; d 48zł; P) Modest but pleasant and housed in a cabin-like wooden building, this hostel southeast of the Old Town has dorm rooms with between four and 10 beds, as well as a few doubles. From

al Wojska Polskiego, turn onto ul Nowo-wiejska, then left onto ul Bartka Zwycięzcy.

##  Eating

**Metafora** POLISH, ITALIAN €€
(Plac Ratuszowy 49; mains 12-30zł; ☺10am-late Mon-Sat, noon-late Sun; 🛜) It's unclear what the metaphor actually is, but the moody interior of this versatile restaurant-cafe-bar is an attractive place to dine. It serves mostly Polish cuisine, with a dash of Italian in the menu. There's a long drinks list if you just want to sip.

**Restauracja Pokusa** POLISH €€
(Plac Ratuszowy 12; mains 15-22zł) With outdoor tables in the arcaded passageway encircling the Rynek, Pokusa is a very agreeable place, with upbeat decor and a repertoire of mostly Polish food.

**Warka** INTERNATIONAL €
(Plac Ratuszowy 10; mains 9-28zł; ☺10am-late) This lively ground-level eatery has the atmosphere of a cellar premises due to its cosy linked brick-lined rooms, decorated with retro lampshades and photos. Menu items range from Polish standards to pizzas.

**Bar Arnika** CAFETERIA €
(ul Pocztowa 8; mains 7-17zł; ☺10am-5pm Mon-Fri, noon-3pm Sat) One of the cheapest central options, Arnika is a tiny cafeteria serving basic Polish dishes.

##  Drinking

**Pożegnanie z Afryką** CAFE
(Plac Ratuszowy 4; ☺10am-6pm Mon-Fri, 10am-5pm Sat, 11am-5pm Sun) An attractive branch of the cafe chain, 'Out of Africa' peddles any number of imported beans within its dim and character-packed premises and, of course, serves great coffee. Sip and savour.

**Kurna Chata** CAFE-BAR
(Plac Ratuszowy 23/24; ☺10am-late) A small, cosy cafe-bar with a pub feel and folksy decor (think mountain hut and bales of hay), this is a good place on the Rynek for a drink and a snack.

## ℹ️ Information

**Amigos** (📞75 753 2601; ul Długa 4; ☺9am-6pm Mon-Fri, 10am-2pm Sat) Travel agency; enquire here for international bus tickets.
**Main post office** (ul Pocztowa 9/10; ☺7am-9pm Mon-Fri, 9am-3pm Sat)

---

**WORTH A TRIP**

## CIEPLICE ŚLĄSKIE-ZDRÓJ

In the suburbs of Jelenia Góra, Cieplice (cheh-*plee*-tseh) is the oldest spa in the region, and an easy day trip. Its sulphurous **hot springs** have been used for a millennium, and the first spa house was established as early as the late 13th century. The supposedly curative properties of the springs, which come out of the ground at a scalding 90°C, became popular in the late 18th century. This paved the way for the building of the resort and spa town.

The town's core is made up of a large **Spa Park** (Park Zdrojowy), with an embarrassment of lovely *fin-de-siècle* pavilions and buildings, including the domed **Spa Theatre** (Teatr Zdrojowy) and the wooden open-air **Concert Shell** (Muszla Koncertowa). At the western end of pedestrian Plac Piastowski is the 18th-century **Church of St John the Baptist** (Kościół Św Jana Chrzciciela), which contains an altarpiece painted by famed Baroque artist Michael Willmann. Should you wish to sample the local waters, the statue-topped automatic **pump** in a small square near St John's dispenses free water from Cieplice's springs into whatever container you provide.

South of the Spa Park in the timbered **Norwegian Pavilion** (Pawilon Norweski) is the **Natural History Museum** (Muzeum Przyrodnicze; www.muzeum-cieplice.pl; ul Wolności 268; adult/concession 4/3zł, free Sun; ☺9am-5pm Tue-Sun). Its display of birds and butterflies from all over the world stems from the collection of the prominent Schaffgotsch family, local nobles who established the museum in 1876.

Cieplice Śląskie-Zdrój lies 11km south of Jelenia Góra's centre, and can be reached by suburban bus 17 (2.24zł, 20 minutes) from a stop near the bus station on ul Podwale. If you're staying closer to the train station, catch bus 9 or 14 from there instead. Buy your bus ticket from a streetside kiosk, then validate on board.

**Tourist office** (☏75 767 6925; www.jeleniagora .pl; ul Bankowa 27; ⏰9am-6pm Mon-Fri, 10am-2pm Sat) Can arrange free internet access for travellers at the next-door library.

## ❶ Getting There & Away

The train station is about 1.5km east of the Rynek, while the bus station is on the opposite side of town, just northwest of the ring road.

Trains service Szklarska Poręba (9zł, one hour, four daily) and Wrocław (22zł, 3½ hours, eight daily), and there's just one overnight train departing at 7.17pm for Warsaw (61zł, 10½ hours).

Hourly buses run to Karpacz (8zł, 45 minutes), the majority leaving from the train station rather than the bus station. Regular services also head to Szklarska Poręba (8zł, 45 minutes, hourly) and Wrocław (26zł, two hours). There are also useful bus links to Świdnica (20zł, 1½ hours, six daily), Zielona Góra (36zł, 3¼ hours, five daily) and Kłodzko (30zł, 3¼ hours, two daily).

# Karkonosze National Park

**Karkonosze National Park** (Karkonoski Park Narodowy; www.kpnmab.pl; adult/concession 5/ 2.50zł) is a 5575-hectare belt that runs along the Polish–Czech border for some 25km. The two main settlements here are the resort towns of Szklarska Poręba and Karpacz.

The range is divided by the Karkonosze Pass (Przełęcz Karkonoska; 1198m). The highest summit of the eastern section is Mt Śnieżka (1602m), while the western portion is topped by Mt Wielki Szyszak (1509m). The park is predominantly spruce forest up to an altitude of about 1250m.

The characteristic features of the Karkonosze landscape are *kotły* (cirques), huge hollows carved by glaciers during the ice age and bordered with steep cliffs. There are six cirques on the Polish side of the range, the most spectacular being Kocioł Małego Stawu and Kocioł Wielkiego Stawu near Mt Śnieżka, and Śnieżne Kotły at the foot of Mt Wielki Szyszak.

The Karkonosze range is known for its harsh climate, with heavy rainfall (snow in winter) and highly variable weather, including strong winds and mists at any time of year. Statistically, the best chances of good weather are in January, February, May and September.

The national park is the most popular **hiking** territory in the Sudetes and boasts 33 trails covering 100km. The two main gateways are Szklarska Poręba and Karpacz, from where most tourists ascend Mt Szrenica and Mt Śnieżka respectively. For longer walks, the red trail runs right along the ridge between the two peaks, with excellent views on both sides. The trail also passes along the upper edges of the *kotły*. You can walk the whole stretch in six to seven hours. If you start early enough, it's possible to do the Karpacz–Szklarska Poręba (or vice versa) trip within a day, preferably by using the chairlift to Mt Szrenica or Mt Kopa to speed up the initial ascent.

You can break the walk by taking any of the trails that branch off from the main route, or by stopping at one of the half-dozen mountain hostels. The sizeable **Odrodzenie Hostel** (☏75 752 2546; www.schronisko odrodzenie.com in Polish; ul Karkonoska 1, Przesieka; dm 37-47zł, d 134zł) is roughly halfway between Mt Szrenica and Mt Śnieżka, while the **Samotnia Hostel** (☏75 761 9376; www .samotnia.com.pl; ul Na Śnieżkę 16, Karpacz; dm 32-42zł, s/d 47/84) at Kocioł Małego Stawu has the best views in the park. Book in advance.

The national park also has 19 mountain-bike trails totalling some 450km, and the tourist offices in Szklarska Poręba and Karpacz can supply you with an excellent free map of them.

Whatever you're into, take warm, waterproof clothes to deal with the unpredictable weather and get a detailed map of the area. The best one is the 1:25,000 *Karkonosze i Góry Izerskie* (7zł), which also includes the Izera Mountains of the Western Sudetes to the northeast of Szklarska Poręba.

# Szklarska Poręba

POP 6800

At the foot of Mt Szrenica (1362m) at the western end of Karkonosze National Park, Szklarska Poręba (*shklahr*-skah po-*rem*-bah) is usually a lively little place, full of walkers, skiers and souvenir cudgels (mini tomahawks). This major health resort and ski centre, 21km southwest of Jelenia Góra, makes a good base for the region's many outdoor activities. Its main street, ul Jedności Narodowej, skirts the Kamienna River on its way into the hills; the bus station is at the south end and train station at the north end.

## ◉ Sights & Activities

The **Mt Szrenica chairlift** (www.sudetylift.com .pl; ul Turystyczna 25a; one way/return 28/31zł; ⏰9am-4.30pm May-Oct) rises 603m in two stages and deposits you at the top in about 25 minutes; it's used by skiers and snowboarders to reach five trails and two slopes in season, and by hikers the rest of the year. The lower station is 1km south of the centre, uphill along ul Turystyczna. During the ski season there's also a second lift in operation, with greater capacity.

There are some attractions in easy walking distance of town. The road to Jelenia Góra winds east in a beautiful valley along the Kamienna River. Some 3km down the road (or along the green trail on the right bank of the river) is the 13m-high **Szklarka Waterfall** (Wodospad Szklarki). From here the blue trail heads to the mountains and you can follow it to Mt Szrenica in two to three hours.

The road that heads west 4km to the Czech border at Jakuszyce passes rocky cliffs called **Ravens' Rocks** (Krucze Skały). About 500m further on, a red trail branches to the left. It's a 1.5km walk along this trail to **Kamieńczyk Waterfall** (Wodospad Kamieńczyka), the highest (843m) in the Polish part of the Sudetes. Continue for about 1½ hours along the same trail to get to Mt Szrenica. It's possible to hike across the border and join the yellow trail heading south to Vosecká in the Czech Republic.

You can hire bikes from **Wypożyczalnia Rowery & Nosidełka** (ul Turystyczna 19; ☺9am-8pm) for 25zł per day. It also hires out skis and snowboards in winter.

## 🛌 Sleeping

**Fantazja**                              HOTEL €€
(☏75 717 2907; www.fantazja.com.pl; ul Jedności Narodowej 14; s/d 160/260zł; P🛜) This very central accommodation offers comfortable rooms, a solarium, massage services and a popular restaurant serving international dishes. There's also a cafe on the premises.

**Apartamenty Carmen**          APARTMENTS €€
(☏75 717 2558; www.apartamentycarmen.pl; ul Jedności Narodowej 16; apt 160-280zł; P) These apartments provide a spacious modern alternative to hotel rooms, with the bonus of enabling guests to self-cater. They're located in the middle of town, and the largest apartment can house up to four people.

**Hotel Las**                            HOTEL €€€
(☏75 717 5252; www.hotel-las.pl; ul Turystyczna 8, Piechowice; s 200zł; d 260-600zł; P@🐕) Occupying its own forest clearing about 4km

northeast of the centre in Piechowice, the somewhat garish Las offers an astonishing range of sports and fitness facilities, including a **pool** (adult/concession per hr 20/15zł; ☺9am-10pm) that nonresidents can use.

**Mauritius**                            HOTEL €
(☏75 717 2083; www.mauritius.karkonosz.pl in Polish; ul Dworcowa 6; s/d 83/150zł; P🛜) At the northern end of town next to the train station, this exotically named place is a basic holiday home run by the post office. Rooms with balconies, a gym and a cafe-bar add to the attraction.

## 🍴 Eating & Drinking

**Restauracja Młyn Łukasza**          POLISH €€
(ul 1 Maja 16; mains 14-49zł) Its interior has been given the full-on rustic treatment, but this restaurant's outdoor seating alongside a babbling brook is what makes it special. The reasonably priced menu features *pierogi* (dumplings), soups and a range of meat dishes. It's across the river from the bus station.

**Kaprys**                       POLISH, ITALIAN €€
(ul Jedności Narodowej 12; mains 14-49zł) Roomy but mellow restaurant on the main drag, with comfy couch seating and potted plants enlivening the decor. The menu is evenly split between pizzas and pasta, and Polish dishes.

**Metafora**                            POLISH €€
(ul Objazdowa 1; mains 20-45zł) Relaxed venue with a timber interior and a big outdoor area, opposite the bus station across the river. Serves good Polish cuisine and has a breakfast menu. It's also a fine place to have a drink.

## ℹ Information

**Biuro Turystyki WNW** (ul Wzgórze Paderewskiego 4) Travel agency for accommodation, hiking and cycling.

**Post office** (ul Jedności Narodowej 8; ☺8am-6pm Mon-Fri, 9am-3pm Sat)

**Sudety IT** (ul Turystyczna 26) Travel agency specialising in snowsports.

**Tourist office** (☏75 754 7740; www .szklarskaporeba.pl; ul Jedności Narodowej 1a; ☺8am-6pm Mon-Fri, 9am-5pm Sat & Sun)

## ℹ Getting There & Away

Four daily trains go to Jelenia Góra (10zł, one hour), while one heads to Wrocław (37zł, 4¾ hours) and continues to Warsaw (63zł, 12 hours). Also, for the first time in decades, Szklarska

**MOVING ON?**

For tips, recommendations and reviews, head to shop.lonelyplanet.com to purchase a downloadable PDF of the Czech Republic chapter from Lonely Planet's *Eastern Europe* guide.

Poręba now has an international rail connection. At least two trains a day cross the Czech border to Harrachov (4zł, 25 minutes). They then continue to Kořenov, but for this leg you must pay on the train in Czech currency (14Kč, six minutes).

Buses to Jelenia Góra depart at least hourly (8zł, 45 minutes) and there are three daily buses to Wrocław (30zł, 3¼ hours). In July and August there are two daily buses to Karpacz (8zł, 55 minutes). For the Czech Republic, take the bus to Jakuszyce (5zł, 15 minutes) and cross the border to Harrachov, the first Czech village, from where there are onward buses.

# Karpacz

POP 4900

Karpacz (*kar*-pach), 22km south of Jelenia Góra on the slopes of Mt Śnieżka, is one of the most popular mountain resorts in Poland, for skiing in winter and hiking the rest of the year. This small town is a fun place to visit and has some fine wooden buildings.

Karpacz is essentially a village spread over 3km along winding ul Konstytucji 3 Maja, without any obvious centre. The eastern part, known as Karpacz Dolny (Lower Karpacz), has most of the places to stay and eat. The western part, Karpacz Górny (Upper Karpacz), is largely a collection of holiday homes. In the middle of the two districts is the main bus station and the landmark Hotel Biały Jar. About 1km uphill from here is the lower station of the chairlift to Mt Kopa (1377m).

## ⊙ Sights

**Wang Church**                                    CHURCH
(Kościół Wang; www.wang.com.pl; ul Na Śnieżkę 8; adult/concession 7/4zł; ⊗9am-6pm) Karpacz has a curious architectural gem – the Wang Church, the only Nordic Romanesque building in Poland. This remarkable wooden structure in Upper Karpacz was one of about 400 such chapels built at the turn of the 12th century on the bank of Lake Vang in southern Norway; only 28 of these 'stave churches'

survive there today. By the 19th century it became too small for the local congregation, and was put up for sale to make way for a larger church. King Friedrich Wilhelm IV of Prussia bought it in 1841, had it dismantled piece by piece and then had it transported to Karpacz via Berlin. Not only is it the oldest church in the Sudetes, it's also the highest situated (886m).

The church is made of hard Norwegian pine and has been constructed without a single nail. It's surrounded by a cloister that helps to protect it from mountain wind. Part of the woodcarving is original and in excellent shape, particularly the doorways and the capitals of the pillars. The freestanding stone belfry was built when the church was reconstructed here.

## ☆ Activities

Bordered to the south by Karkonosze National Park, Karpacz is an ideal starting point for hiking. Most tourists aim for Mt Śnieżka, and there are half a dozen different trails leading there. The most popular routes originate from the landmark **Hotel Biały Jar** (ul Konstytucji 3 Maja 79) and will take you to the top in three to four hours. When planning a trip to Mt Śnieżka, try to include in your route two picturesque postglacial lakes, Wielki Staw and Mały Staw, both bordered by rocky cliffs. A couple of trails pass near the lakes.

If you prefer not to walk up Mt Kopa, a **chairlift** (ul Turystyczna 4; one way/return 24/29zł; ⊗8.30am-6.30pm), which caters for skiers and snowboarders in winter, will take you up 528m in 17 minutes. From Mt Kopa, you can get to the top of Mt Śnieżka in less than an hour via the black trail.

On Kolorowa Hill in the centre of Karpacz, the **summer sleigh track** (www.kolorowa.pl in Polish; ul Parkowa 10; 1/2/5/10 rides 7/12/25/40zł; ⊗9am-late) is more than 1km long and allows for speeds of up to 30km/h.

## 🛏 Sleeping

The tourist office provides an extensive list of accommodation, including private rooms.

**Hotel Rezydencja**                              HOTEL €€
(✆75 761 8020; www.hotelrezydencja.pl; ul Parkowa 6; s 210-250zł, d 240-280zł; P🖥) The tastefully decorated rooms of this stunner of a hotel, housed in an 18th-century hilltop villa overlooking the centre of Lower Karpacz, are among the most desirable in town. There's

a spa, restaurant and cafe-bar on site, and massage treatments can be arranged.

**Hotel Vivaldi** HOTEL €€€
(☎75 761 9933; www.vivaldi.pl; ul Olimpijska 4; s 250zł, d 330-430zł; P 📶 🏊) A pale-yellow building in the midst of the trees, the Vivaldi is a classy proposition on the winding road up to the chairlift and national park entrance. It contains smart modern rooms and a well-equipped spa with saunas and a whirlpool spa.

**Hotel Kolorowa** HOTEL €€
(☎75 761 9503; www.hotel-kolorowa.pl; ul Konstytucji 3 Maja 58; s/d 90/160zł; P 📶) This hotel opposite the summer sleigh track in Lower Karpacz offers good standards, the all-important sweets on pillows and some rooms with restful hillside views. Restaurant and bar on site.

**Camping Pod Lipami** CAMPGROUND €
(☎504 231 039; www.pod-lipami.pl in Polish; ul Konstytucji 3 Maja 8; per person/tent/caravan 10/9/11zł; P 🏊) This camping ground close to the bus station has its own outdoor pool.

## Eating & Drinking

**Bistro Aurora** POLISH €€
(ul Konstytucji 3 Maja 48; mains 13-32zł) Cosy restaurant and bar that bills itself as a 'mini-museum of Socialist Realism', as the decor features large portraits of communist bigwigs as well as red banners and posters from the era. The slightly mad menu includes such gems as Revolutionary Blintzes and Brezhnev Pork Knuckle.

**Central Bar 49** POLISH €
(ul Konstytucji 3 Maja 49; mains 14-30zł) Atmospheric little cross between a bar and a restaurant, serving up simple but better-than-average Polish dishes such as beetroot soup with croquette and grilled *kiełbasa* (Polish sausage).

**Pizzeria Verde** PIZZERIA €€
(ul Konstytucji 3 Maja 48; mains 17-29zł; ⏰1-9pm Tue-Sun) This eatery in modern premises is an improvement on the average pizzeria, and also offers some decent pasta and meat dishes, along with salads.

## Information

**Biuro Turystyczne Karpacz** (ul Konstytucji 3 Maja 50; ⏰10am-6pm Mon-Sat, noon-4pm Sun) Travel agency.

**Post office** (ul Konstytucji 3 Maja 23; ⏰8am-6pm Mon-Fri, 9.30am-3.30pm Sat)

**Tourist office** (☎75 761 8605; www.karpacz.pl; ul Konstytucji 3 Maja 25a; ⏰9am-5pm Mon-Sat, 10am-2pm Sun) Can advise about bicycle hire.

## Getting There & Away

Buses run regularly to Jelenia Góra (8zł, 45 minutes, hourly), the majority of which terminate at the Jelenia Góra train station rather than the bus station. They go along Karpacz's main road, and you can pick them up at at least half a dozen points, though fewer go all the way to the Upper Karpacz stop. In July and August there are two daily buses to Szklarska Poręba (8zł, 55 minutes).

# Kłodzko

POP 27,700

Kłodzko's strategic position over the centuries is responsible for its big attraction: a monstrously huge brick fortress, begun by the Austrians in 1662 and only completed two centuries later by the Prussians. It's the dominant, somewhat apocalyptic, landmark of the town and the best reason to pay a visit, though the Old Town sits on a hillside and its steep winding streets have a charm of their own.

One of the oldest settlements in Silesia, Kłodzko (*kwots*-koh) started out as a major trade centre thanks to its location on the Nysa Kłodzka River, a tributary of the Odra. Like most settlements in the region, it changed hands every century or so, with Bohemia, Austria and Prussia all having a crack, and only after WWII did the town revert to Poland.

## Sights

TOP CHOICE **Kłodzko Fortress** FORTRESS
(Twierdza Kłodzka; www.twierdza.klodzko.pl in Polish; ul Grodzisko 1; adult/concession 10/8zł, with labyrinth 16/12zł; ⏰9am-6pm mid-Apr–Oct, 9am-3pm Nov–mid-Apr) This mighty fortress, begun under Austrian rule in the mid-17th century, was extended, modernised and modified over the next 200 years. Today it covers 17 hectares, making it the largest and best-preserved fortification of its kind in Poland. The walls in the lower parts measure up to 11m thick, and even at the top they are never narrower than 4m.

The entrance is up the hill north of the town's central Rynek. On entering, you can wander around various pathways and chambers and go to the top of the fortress for a bird's-eye view of town. There are several exhibitions in the grounds, including a lapidarium containing old stone sculptures (mostly tombstones) collected from historic buildings around the region.

However, the real attraction here is the extensive network of defensive tunnels. Guided 40-minute tours of this so-called labyrinth begin on the hour, taking you on a 1km circuit including some passageways that are so low you have to bend over. The average temperature is about 8°C and the humidity is very high.

Altogether 40km of tunnels were drilled around the fortress and served two purposes. Those under the fortifications were principally for communication, shelter and storage, while the others, running up to 500m away from the fortress, were designed to attack and destroy enemy artillery. They were divided into sectors and stuffed with gunpowder; when the enemy happened to move their guns into a particular sector, the relevant chamber was blown up. This bizarre minefield was initiated in 1743 by a Dutch engineer, and by 1807 an immense labyrinth of tunnels had been built. The system was never actually used – at least not here.

### Underground Tourist Route UNDERGROUND
(Podziemna Trasa Turystyczna; ul Zawiszy Czarnego 3) Down the steps from the fortress is one of the entrances to this interesting set of tunnels. The 600m route, scattered with dungeon-type implements, uses some of the medieval storage cellars that were hollowed out under most of the Old Town. You can walk the whole length in 10 minutes, entering from either direction; the other end is in the Old Town. At the time of research the route was closed and undergoing a major renovation, which should be completed by the time you read this – ask at the tourist office for the current entry fee and opening hours.

### Parish Church CHURCH
(Kościół Parafialny; Plac Kościelny; ⊙9.30am-4pm Tue-Thu & Sat & Sun, noon-4pm Mon & Fri) This church, southwest of the Rynek and dedicated to Our Lady of the Assumption, is the most imposing religious building in town. It took almost 150 years before the massive Gothic structure was eventually completed in 1490. Inside, the altars, pulpit, pews,

organ and dozen carved confessionals all blaze with florid Baroque ornamentation, and even the Gothic vaulting, usually left plain, has been sumptuously decorated with plasterwork. Organ recitals are occasionally held in the church – enquire at the tourist office or the Kłodzko Cultural Centre for details.

### Rynek SQUARE
Below the fortress is the town's market square, officially titled Plac Bolesława Chrobrego. Several pastel-coloured houses on its southern side have preserved their original Renaissance and Baroque decor. The town hall was built in 1890 after its predecessor was destroyed by fire; only the 17th-century Renaissance tower survived.

### Kłodzko Regional Museum MUSEUM
(Muzeum Ziemi Kłodzkiej; www.muzeum.klodzko.pl in Polish; ul Łukasiewicza 4; adult/concession 8/6zł; ⊙10am-4pm Tue-Fri, 11am-5pm Sat & Sun) This institution 50m west of the parish church has displays relating to the history of the town and the region, and a collection of contemporary glass by local artists (the region is noted for its glass production).

### Stone Bridge BRIDGE
Southeast of the Rynek is a Gothic stone bridge (1390) spanning the narrow Młynówka River. With half a dozen Baroque statues flanking the sides, it's Kłodko's sized-down answer to the Charles Bridge in Prague.

## 🏃 Activities
The helpful and well-informed tourist office has information on activities as wide-ranging as rock climbing, hiking, cycling, horseback riding, skiing and taking to the waters.

## 🛏 Sleeping

### Casa D'Oro HOTEL €€
(☏74 867 0216; www.casadoro.pl; ul Grottgera 7; s/d 160/180zł; 🛜) Located between the Rynek and the bus and train stations, this attractive small hotel is the handiest accommodation you'll find in Kłodzko. Its pleasantly appointed restaurant is worth dropping into for its light menu of *pierogi* (dumplings) and *naleśniki* (crêpes).

### Hotel Marhaba HOTEL €
(☏74 865 9933; www.marhaba.com.pl; ul Daszyńskiego 16; s 90-100zł, d 100-120zł; 🅿🛜) Basic rooms with shower or full en suite

are the mainstay of this unfussy two-star establishment on the south side of town, backing onto the Młynówka River. Rooms without a bathroom are slightly cheaper, and breakfast is 13zł extra per person.

### Hotel Korona
HOTEL €€

(☑74 867 3737; www.hotel-korona.pl; ul Nowo-rudzka 1; s/d 125/160zł; P 🤶) Located in the far northwestern part of town, this modern establishment is a comfortable option if you're just transiting through Kłodzko for the night. It has a colourful rustic-style restaurant.

### PTSM Hostel
HOSTEL €

(☑74 867 2524; www.ssm-klodzko.pokojegoscinne .eu; ul Nadrzeczna 5; dm 16-22zł; P 🤶) Just 1km north of the Rynek, this simple place has rooms with two to eight beds.

## 🍴 Eating

### Oregano
POLISH, ITALIAN €€

(ul Daszyńskiego 10; mains 10-35zł) This distinctively decorated restaurant opposite the monumental Franciscan church on the south side of the Młynówka River serves a number of Polish dishes, but our money is on the pizza and pasta choices. There's also an inexpensive breakfast menu.

### Restauracja W Ratuszu
POLISH €€

(Plac Bolesława Chrobrego 3; mains 17-60zł; ⊙10am-9pm) Kłodko's most formal restaurant is housed within the town hall. It has

a good range of regional dishes and a tree-shaded terrace open in the warmer months.

### Bar Małgosia
CAFETERIA €

(ul Połabska 2; mains 3-8zł; ⊙7am-7pm Mon-Fri, 8am-6pm Sat, 9am-5pm Sun) This old-fashioned joint is a simple self-service bar that serves hearty Polish dishes at crazily low prices in a soothing green interior, just east of the train and bus stations.

## ℹ Information

**Kłodzko Cultural Centre** (Kłodzko Centrum Kultury; ☑74 867 3364; www.kcksir.pl in Polish; Plac Jagiełły 1) Gives information on cultural events, and screens arthouse films.

**Main post office** (Plac Jagiełły 2; ⊙7.30am-7.30pm Mon-Fri, 8am-3pm Sat)

**PTTK office** (www.klodzko.pttk.pl in Polish; ul Wita Stwosza 1; ⊙8am-3pm Mon-Fri) Travel agency just off the Rynek.

**Tourist office** (☑74 865 4689; www.klodzko .pl; Plac Bolesława Chrobrego 1; ⊙10am-6pm Mon-Fri, 10am-4pm Sat) In the town hall.

## ℹ Getting There & Away

**BUS** The bus station is the transport hub of the region. Buses are frequent to Kudowa-Zdrój (8zł, 50 minutes, hourly). They also run hourly to Bystrzyca Kłodzka (7zł, 30 minutes), and every two hours to Wrocław (16zł, 1¾ hours). There are six daily buses to Nysa (15zł, 1½ hours), most passing through Paczków (12zł, 55 minutes); and two a day to Jelenia Góra (30zł, 3¼ hours).

---

## HEAD CASES

The **Chapel of Skulls** in Czermna, north of Kudowa-Zdrój, was built in 1776 and looks pretty modest from the outside. Inside, however, it's a different story: thousands of neatly arranged skulls and bones decorate the walls, with more suspended from the ceiling. It's the only chapel of its kind in Poland and one of just three in Europe.

The creator of this unusual 'Sanctuary of Silence' was one Václav Tomášek, a Czech parish priest (Czermna belonged to the Prague Archdiocese at that time). He and the local grave-digger spent two decades collecting human skeletons, which they then cleaned and conserved. The 'decoration' of the chapel wasn't completed until 1804. Skulls and bones that didn't fit on the walls and the ceiling were deposited in a 4m-deep crypt.

Since the region was the borderland of the Polish, Czech and German cultures, and Catholic, Hussite and Protestant traditions, many of the bones belonged to victims of nationalist and religious conflicts. The skeletons came mostly from numerous mass graves, the result of two Silesian wars (1740–42 and 1744–45) and the Seven Years' War (1756–63). The cholera epidemic that plagued the region also contributed to such an impressive quantity of raw material.

Several anatomically interesting skulls are displayed on the main altar, including those of a Tatar warrior, a giant and a victim of syphilis. Alongside them are the skulls of the masterminds of the enterprise – the priest and the grave-digger – at one with their work for all eternity.

You can also travel to the Czech Republic from Kłodzko. One daily bus runs across the border from Kłodzko to Náchod (11zł, 1¼ hours), leaving at 8am and travelling via Kudowa-Zdrój. Alternatively, take the daily 6am bus from Kłodzko to Boboszów (11zł, 1½ hours) and walk 2km across the border to Králíky.

**TRAIN** Kłodzko has two useful train stations. The centrally located Kłodzko Miasto station, next to the bus station, has trains to Bystrzyca Kłodzka (6zł, 20 minutes, hourly), Wrocław (18zł, two hours, eight daily) and Świdnica (15zł, 1½ hours, five daily). There are more long-distance trains from the main station, Kłodzko Główne, 2km north.

# Kudowa-Zdrój

POP 10,100

Kudowa-Zdrój (koo-*do*-va zdruy) is an attractive spa town 37km west of Kłodzko, favoured by a mild climate and several mineral springs. Renowned since the 18th century, it's one of the oldest spas in Europe, with well-preserved architecture and a pleasant park off the single main road.

It's the ideal place for recharging before or after enjoying the more strenuous activities the region has to offer, and is the ideal jumping-off point for the marvellous Góry Stołowe National Park.

## ◎ Sights & Activities

**Chapel of Skulls** TOP CHOICE CHURCH
(Kaplica Czaszek; ul Moniuszki 8; adult/concession 4/2zł; ☺9am-5.30pm) You can't miss this macabre chapel in the Church of St Bartholomew's grounds at Czermna, 1km north of Kudowa's town centre. The length of its walls and ceiling are covered with human skulls and bones – about 3000 of them, with another 20,000 to 30,000 filling the crypt below. The overall effect is stunning and will certainly offer you a reality check (see boxed text).

**Spa Park** PARK
Kudowa has an attractive 17-hectare Spa Park (Park Zdrojowy) but most treatments on offer involve room and board at one of the sanatoria. If you want (literally) a taste of what the park has to offer, the **Pump Room** (Pijalnia; adult/concession 1.20/0.60zł; ☺7am-6pm Mon-Sat, 9am-6pm Sun) in the southeastern corner serves up two of the local mineral waters.

The **Galos Salt Caves** (Jaskinie Solno Galos; www.galos.pl; ☺9am-9pm) establishment to the west claims to relieve all your ills via remarkable artificial sea-salt chambers, as do its rival **Solana Salt Grotto** (Grota Solna Solana; www.solana.pl/kudowa.html; ☺9am-9pm), near the tourist office. The prices of their treatments vary with the different packages available, so enquire at each venue.

The **Water World Aqua Park** (Aqua Park Wodny Świat; www.basen.eurograf.pl in Polish; ul Moniuszki 2a; adult/concession 15/13zł; ☺9am-9pm), on the southern edge of the park opposite where the buses stop, offers more active watery fun.

**FREE Frog Museum** MUSEUM
(Muzeum Żaby; ul Słoneczna 31; ☺9am-5pm Mon-Fri) Hop on over to the Góry Stołowe National Park headquarters and check out Poland's only frog museum, which holds thousands of everyday objects with an amphibian theme. The national park was the first in Poland to build tunnels under roads to allow frogs to return to their ponds to spawn without injury. The aim of the museum is to raise awareness of frog conservation issues.

## 🛏 Sleeping

**Pensjonat Akacja** HOTEL €€
(☏74 866 2712; www.akacja.info.pl; ul Kombatantów 5; s/d 120/160zł; P@) This modernised villa is a family-run business providing excellent accommodation in a quiet spot with plenty of space. Some of the rooms on the upper floors have balconies.

**Willa Sanssouci** HOTEL €
(☏74 866 1350; www.sanssouci.info.pl; ul Buczka 3; s/d 120/150zł; P🛜) Located in a lovely villa dating back to 1894, the Sanssouci has comfortable, ample rooms and good service. If you're feeling lucky, give the wishing well in the garden a go.

**Ośrodek Wypoczynkowy Sudety** HOTEL €
(☏74 866 1223; www.kudowa.net.pl in Polish; ul Zdrojowa 32; s 100zł, d 130-150zł; P) This well-placed hotel and recreation centre offers budget accommodation, all with en suites. There's table tennis on the premises, and the management can arrange activities and excursions including hiking and cycling.

**Zespół Uzdrowisk Kłodzkich** SANATORIUM €
(☏74 868 0401; www.zuk-sa.pl; ul Moniuszki 2; dm 39zł; s 75-132zł, d 114-204zł; P@) The Kłodzko Health Resort Company administers five fine old villa sanatoria in the centre of

**WORTH A TRIP**

## GÓRY STOŁOWE

The **Góry Stołowe** (*goo*-ri sto-*wo*-veh), or 'Table Mountains', are among the most spectacular ranges of all the Sudetes, as they're topped by a plateau that is punctuated by fantastic rock formations.

One of the big highlights of the 6300-hectare **Góry Stołowe National Park** is **Szczeliniec Wielki**, the highest outcrop of the range. Both the German poet Goethe and the USA's sixth president John Quincy Adams walked here and admired the dramatic scenery. From a distance, the plateau looks like a high ridge adorned with pinnacles, rising abruptly from the surrounding fields.

From just beyond Karłów, a small village about 1km south of the plateau, you ascend 682 stone steps, which takes about 40 minutes. From there, the one-hour trail around the summit gives excellent views of both the mountain scenery and the rock formations, before arriving back at its starting point.

About 4km to the west, the **Błędne Skały** are another impressive sight, comprising hundreds of gigantic boulders deposited by glaciers in vaguely geometric shapes, forming a vast stone labyrinth. A sometimes very narrow trail runs between the rocks.

The **Góry Stołowe National Park headquarters** (Dyrekcja PNGS; www.pngs.com.pl; ul Słoneczna 31; ⊙7.30am-3.30pm Mon-Fri), 650m southeast of the tourist office in Kudowa-Zdrój, can tell you everything you need to know about the park, and sells maps and English-language guides.

There's only one practical bus to Karłów, which departs Kudowa-Zdrój daily between May and mid-October at 11am (6zł, 20 minutes). It also passes the turn-off to Błędne Skały within the park. The latest return bus from Karłów is at 3.18pm. Private minibuses also run along the same route year-round.

town, providing an unparalleled variety of rooms. The emphasis is on medical treatment but they will accept casual guests. Reception is housed within the elegant Polonia sanatorium.

## 🍴 Eating & Drinking

**Zdrojowa**　　　　　　　　　　CZECH **€€**
(ul Słoneczna 1; mains 9-68zł) This homely but spacious restaurant near the main bus stand serves Czech cuisine, a nod to the neighbours across the mountains. Dishes range from filling soups to tasty schnitzels.

**Café Domek**　　　　　　　　PIZZERIA **€**
(ul Zdrojowa 36; mains 10-32zł; 🛜) This large pizzeria has a huge leafy terrace out front, ideal for relaxing after a day of hiking in the Góry Stołowe National Park.

**Café Pod Palmami**　　　　CAFE-BAR **€**
(ul Łazienki 3; mains 10-36zł; ⊙10am-Thu, 10am-2am Fri & Sat; 🛜) This brick-lined venue in the Spa Park is one of the best places in town to grab a light bite, and stays open till late on weekends for a bit of music-bar action.

## ℹ️ Information

**Arcom** (ul Słoneczna 3; per hr 4zł; ⊙10am-5pm Mon-Fri) Internet access.

**Tourist office** (📞74 866 1387; www.kudowa.pl; ul Zdrojowa 44; ⊙9am-5pm Mon-Fri)

## ℹ️ Getting There & Away

Buses depart from a stand near the corner of ul 1 Maja and ul Poznańska in the town centre – there are hourly departures for Kłodzko (8zł, 50 minutes) and seven a day to Wrocław (27zł, 2¾ hours).

There's one bus a day at 8.55am to Náchod in the Czech Republic. Alternatively, go to the border (3km) and cross it on foot to Náchod, 2km beyond the frontier, from where there are onward buses and trains.

## Bystrzyca Kłodzka

POP 10,500

Bystrzyca Kłodzka (bist-*shi*-tsah *kwots*-kah), perched on a hilltop above the Nysa Kłodzka River, is a sleepy but atmospheric old town that has retained much of its medieval architecture and layout. Though there aren't that many specific attractions, the squares and narrow streets of the Old Town have an appealing character.

Since the 13th century, when it was founded, the town has been destroyed and rebuilt several times, though ironically it survived WWII virtually unmolested.

## ◎ Sights

**Rynek** SQUARE
The houses lining the Rynek, officially known as Plac Wolności, are a blend of architectural styles. The octagonal Renaissance tower (1567) of the Italianate **town hall** in the centre gives the square an almost southern European feel. Next to the town hall is an elaborate Baroque **plague pillar** (1737) dedicated to the Holy Trinity.

**Fortifications** HISTORIC BUILDINGS
In the 14th century the town was granted municipal status and surrounded by fortified **city walls**, some of which are still in place. The most substantial structures include the **Water Gate** (Brama Wodna) just south of the Rynek, and the **Kłodzko Tower** (Baszta Kłodzka; adult/concession 3/2zł; ☺10am-4pm Mon-Sat), which you can climb, on the north side of the Old Town.

**Phillumenistic Museum** MUSEUM
(Muzeum Filumenistyczne; www.muzeum.filumenistyka.pl; Mały Rynek 1; adult/concession 6/4.50zł; ☺8am-4pm Tue-Sat, 10am-3pm Sun) East of the Rynek, the **Knights' Tower** (Baszta Rycerska) was reshaped in the 19th century and turned into the belfry of a Protestant church that had been built alongside. After WWII the church was occupied by the rather esoteric Phillumenistic Museum, which displays lighters, matchbox labels and other paraphernalia related to the match industry. On the square southwest of the museum stands the old **whipping post** from 1566; the Latin inscription on its top reads 'God punishes the impious'.

**Parish Church of St Michael the Archangel** CHURCH
The Gothic Parish Church of St Michael the Archangel (Kościół Parafialny Św Michała Archanioła) sits at the highest point of the Old Town, two blocks northwest of the Rynek. It has a nave and just one aisle with a row of six Gothic columns running right across the middle.

## ⌁ Sleeping & Eating

**TOP CHOICE / Hotel Castle** HOTEL €€
(☎74 812 0560; www.hotelcastle.pl; ul Okrzei 26; s/d 110/190zł; P☎) Housed in an attractive old building fancifully resembling a castle, this hotel offers Bystrzyca Kłodzka's best lodgings. Rooms are tastefully decorated, and there's a good restaurant decked out in baronial splendour. It's 200m north of the tourist office; turn right when leaving the train station.

**Hotel Piast** HOTEL €
(☎74 811 0322; www.hotelpiast.e-wyjazd.pl; ul Okrzei 26; s 35-60zł, d 50-80zł; P☎) About 150m north of the tourist office just outside the Old Town, this hotel offers basic but comfortable rooms.

**Helios** PIZZERIA €
(Plac Wolności 13; mains 7-19zł) Facing the Rynek, this pizzeria also turns out a good range of pasta dishes.

**Secret** CAFE-BAR
(Plac Wolności 4) This poorly named establishment is right on the market square, with a close-up view of the town hall. The outdoor seating is a good place to take in the town's unhurried street life.

## ❶ Information

**Tourist office** (☎74 811 3731; www.bystrzyca klodzka.pl; Mały Rynek 2/1; ☺8am-5pm Mon-Fri, 10am-4pm Sat) On the small square near the Knights' Tower.

## ❶ Getting There & Away

The train station is just east of the tourist office. From here trains connect with Kłodzko Miasto (6zł, 20 minutes, 11 daily) and Wrocław (20zł, two hours, eight daily).

The bus station, on ul Sienkiewicza 200m north of the parish church, has services to Kłodzko (7zł, 30 minutes) at least once every two hours. There are also reasonable bus connections to Boboszów (9zł, one hour) near the Czech border.

# UPPER SILESIA

This part of Silesia presents extreme contrasts. Heavily developed and industrialised, Upper Silesia (Górny Śląsk) occupies just 2% of Poland's territory, yet it's home to a full 9% of the population. Thanks to large deposits of coal, it's traditionally been the nation's centre of heavy industry and the most densely urbanised area in Central Europe. Under socialism this region was the 'reddest' in Poland and relatively well treated as a result.

However, despite the urban sprawl centred on Katowice, the region has its share of attractive cities and towns worth a visit. At the other end of the emotional scale is the Auschwitz-Birkenau extermination camp complex, tragic but unmissable. Upper Silesia is also an easy port of call if you're heading to Kraków or the Czech Republic.

# Nysa

POP 47,300

It has to be admitted that Nysa doesn't boast the harmonious architecture of many other Silesian towns. Around 80% of its buildings were destroyed during fierce battles between German and Soviet forces in 1945, and some of the postwar reconstruction leaves a lot to be desired in aesthetic terms. Still, the mish-mash of old and new is intriguing in its own way, especially the juxtaposition of Nysa's dramatic cathedral to the other historic remnants scattered around its central square.

For centuries Nysa (*ni*-sah) was one of the most important religious centres in Silesia. In the 17th century it became a seat of the Catholic bishops, who were in flight from newly 'Reformed' Wrocław. The bishops soon made Nysa a bastion of the Counter-Reformation; so strong was their hold that the town came to be known as the Silesian Rome.

## ◉ Sights

**Cathedral of SS James and Agnes**    CHURCH
(Katedra Św Jakuba i Agnieszki; www.bazylika-nysa.pl in Polish; Plac Katedralny 7) There's no overlooking Nysa's mighty cathedral on the Rynek, with its imposing blackened bulk and fine stone double portal. Built in 1430, it was remodelled after a fire in 1542, but hasn't changed much since then. The cathedral's 4000-sq-metre roof, supported by 18 brick columns inside, is one of the steepest church roofs in Europe.

The vast interior, much of it dating from the late 19th century, looks distinctly sober and noble, its loftiness being the most arresting feature. On closer inspection, however, you'll see that its side chapels (a total of 18) boast wonderful stained glass and a wealth of tombstones, funeral monuments and epitaphs, making up the largest collection of funerary sculpture in any Silesian church.

The freestanding block next to the cathedral is the **bell tower**, which was begun 50 years after the church was built and was originally intended to be over 100m high. Despite 40 years' work it reached only half that height, and consequently looks truncated and oddly proportioned, especially with the tiny turret tacked onto it.

**Nysa Museum**    MUSEUM
(Muzeum w Nysie; www.muzeum.nysa.pl in Polish; ul Jarosława 11; adult/concession 7/4zł, free Sat; ☺9am-3pm Tue-Fri, 10am-3pm Sat & Sun) To the southeast of the cathedral, this museum is located within the 17th-century **Bishops' Palace**, a spacious double-fronted former Episcopal residence. Exhibits range from archaeological finds to photos documenting war damage, plus a model of the town in its heyday. A more stimulating section deals with witches of the region. The museum also features European paintings from the 15th to the 19th centuries, mostly from the Flemish and Dutch schools.

**Rynek**    SQUARE
The architecture within and along Nysa's vast market square depicts the extent of the damage done in WWII. Only the southern side of the square retains anything like its historic appearance, with its restored houses originally dating from the 16th century. The detached building facing them, the 1604 **Town Weighing House** (Dom Wagi Miejskiej), retains fragments of 19th-century wall painting on a side wall. Just round the corner, on ul Bracka, there are more historic houses and a 1701 copy of the Baroque **Triton Fountain** by Bernini in Rome.

Just past the fountain is the twin-towered **Church of SS Peter and Paul** (Kościół Św Piotra i Pawła), built in 1727 for the Hospitallers of the Holy Sepulchre. It has one of Silesia's best Baroque interiors, complete with an opulent high altar, organ and trompe l'œil wall paintings.

**Fortifications**    HISTORIC BUILDINGS
There are several interesting remains of fortifications around the city. The recently restored 17th-century **St Hedwig's Bastion** (Bastion Św Jadwigi; ul Piastowska 19), two blocks to the northwest of the Rynek, was once home to a Prussian garrison. It's now a cultural centre that houses the tourist office, a restaurant and the **Malachite Museum** (Muzeum Malachit; www.malachit-nysa.pl, in Polish; adult/concession 4/3zł; ☺10am-6pm Tue-Sun),

which has displays devoted to the mineral and its use in jewellery.

The only significant traces of the medieval defences are two 14th-century brick towers: the **Ziębice Tower** (Wieża Ziębicka; ul Krzywoustego), west of the Rynek, with unusual turrets and dragon guttering; and the white-plastered **Wrocław Tower** (Wieża Wrocławska; ul Wrocławska), 200m northeast towards the train station.

## 🛏 Sleeping

TOP CHOICE **Villa Navigator**     HOTEL €€
(📞77 433 4170; www.villanavigator.pl; ul Wyspiańskiego 11; s 90-120zł, d 110-160zł; 🅿🛜) This charming 12-room establishment about 400m west of the Rynek is run by a chatty couple and is exactly what a family-run hotel should be, from the antique furniture, oil paintings and potted plants to the sociable breakfasts in the family parlour. Rooms on the 3rd floor are smaller and simpler but still thoroughly serviceable. For a real visual treat, ask for the Danzig room (number 4) or the Secessionist room (number 3).

**Hotel Piast**     HOTEL €€
(📞77 433 4084; www.hotel-piast.com.pl; ul Krzywoustego 14; s/d 130/180zł; 🅿🛜) Near the Ziębice Tower, this hotel has good if unspectacular standards. Its central location

and small balconies entice guests into what could easily be overlooked as yet another concrete city block.

**Pod Ziębickim Lwem Hostel**     HOSTEL €
(📞77 433 3731; www.schroniskonysa.pl; ul Krakiecka 28; dm 14-27zł; 🅿🛜) About 2km south of the Old Town, this 48-bed hostel has small but smart dorms of two to four beds, providing a little more privacy than many other hostels.

## 🍴 Eating

**Pod Aniołami**     POLISH, ITALIAN €€
(Rynek 24/25; mains 10-38zł; ⏱8am-midnight) Facing the Rynek, this restaurant is furnished with elegant old tables and knick-knacks of bygone eras. It's Nysa's most stylish place, serving inventive Italian and Polish dishes and – wait for it – green beer.

**Pizzeria Piec**     PIZZERIA €
(Rynek 39; mains 9-24zł) Drinkers and diners alike congregate in this den of pasta and pizza attached to the Town Weighing House. The interior is done out in timber and dark green tones, making it a soothing place for a break.

**Bar Popularny**     CAFETERIA €
(Rynek 23/24; mains 3-11zł; ⏱8am-6pm Mon-Fri, 8am-4pm Sat) This unreformed milk bar–cafeteria on the main square looks drab and

---

WORTH A TRIP

## THE WALLS OF PACZKÓW

If you're staying in Nysa or Kłodzko, sleepy Paczków (*patch*-koof) makes a good day trip. It may be small, but the town has one of the most complete sets of medieval fortifications in Poland.

The oval ring of Paczków's **defensive walls** was built around 1350 and was surrounded by a moat. Remarkably, these walls remained in place over the centuries and, as the town escaped major destruction during WWII, they still encircle the historic quarter. They were initially about 9m high for the whole of their 1200m length and had a wooden gallery for sentries below the top.

Four gateways were built, complete with towers (all of which still stand) and drawbridges, and there were two dozen semicircular towers built into the walls themselves (19 have survived, though most are incomplete). The most interesting is the round **Kłodzko Gate Tower** (Wieża Bramy Kłodzkiej), with its irregular loopholes; the oldest is the 14th-century **Wrocław Gate Tower** (Wieża Bramy Wrocławskiej; adult/concession 3/2zł; ⏱6am-6pm Mon-Sat, 9am-4pm Sun), which can be climbed.

There are 10 daily buses to Paczków from Nysa (9zł, 35 minutes) and six from Kłodzko (12zł, 55 minutes).

If there's time to kill before your return service, duck into the surprisingly interesting **Gas Industry Museum** (Muzeum Gazownictwa; www.muzeumgazownictwa.pl, in Polish; ul Pocztowa 6; admission 4/2zł; ⏱8am-2pm Mon-Fri), a short walk north of the Rynek in an old red-brick gasworks that operated from 1902 to 1977. Among its varied gas-related exhibits, it contains an extensive collection of gas meters.

basic, but the food is tasty and there are set meals available which provide an even better bargain.

## Information

**Małpka** (ul Bielawska 7a; per hr 3zł) Internet access 200m southeast of the square.

**Post office** (ul Krzywoustego 21; ⊙8am-7pm Mon-Fri, 8am-2pm Sat)

**PTTK office** (ul Bracka 4; ⊙9am-5pm Mon-Fri) Travel agency.

**Tourist office** (☎77 433 4971; www .informacja-turystyczna.nysa.pl; ul Piastowska 19; ⊙8am-6pm Mon-Fri, 10am-6pm Sat & Sun) Inside St Hedwig's Bastion.

## Getting There & Away

The bus and train stations face one another on ul Racławicka, a 500m walk northeast of the Rynek. By bus, there are services to Paczków (9zł, 35 minutes, 10 daily), Kłodzko (15zł, 1½ hours, six daily), Opole (14zł, 1¼ hours, hourly) and Wrocław (15zł, 1½ hours, nine daily).

Trains are less frequent but may be useful when travelling to Opole (12zł, 1¼ hours, eight daily).

# Opole

POP 126,000

Opole is best known within Poland for the National Festival of Polish Song, which has taken place annually in June since 1963 and is broadcast nationwide on TV. Though it's a fairly large regional industrial centre, it also has an attractive Old Town with pleasant waterside views along the Młynówka Canal, which flows through the historic centre.

Lying on the border of Upper and Lower Silesia, the city is the capital of its own voivodeship (province) called Opolskie. The region is known for an active German minority, one of the few communities of its kind to survive the war. They number about 100,000 and are represented in local government.

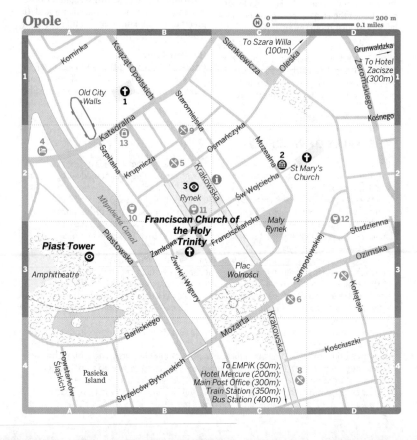

The first Slav stronghold was built here in the 9th century. In the 13th century Opole became the capital of its principality and was ruled by a line of Silesian Piasts until 1532, even though it was part of Bohemia from 1327. Later, Opole fell to Austria, then to Prussia, and after significant destruction in WWII returned to Poland in 1945.

## ◎ Sights

**Rynek**                                                    SQUARE

Though badly damaged during WWII, Opole's central market square was rebuilt after the conflict. It's lined with attractive sand-coloured Baroque and Rococo houses and populated with pubs and bars. The 64m-high tower of the oversized **town hall** in the middle was modelled after the Palazzo Vecchio in Florence and looks a little overly grand here. The original, dating from 1864, collapsed in 1934 but was rebuilt in the same style.

**Franciscan Church of the
Holy Trinity**                                               CHURCH

(Kościół Franciszkanów Św Trójcy; Plac Wolności 2) This church off the southern corner of the Rynek was built of brick around 1330. It boasts an ornate high altar, an 18th-century organ, and a domed Renaissance chapel in the left-hand aisle, separated by a fine, late-16th-century wrought-iron grille. The highlight of the church is the **Chapel of St Anne**, which is accessible from the right-hand aisle through a doorway with a tympanum. The Gothic-vaulted chapel houses a pair of massive double tombs (interring the local dukes) carved in sandstone in the 1380s.

**Opole Silesian Museum**                                    MUSEUM

(Muzeum Śląska Opolskiego; www.muzeum.opole.pl; Mały Rynek 7; adult/concession 5/3zł, free Sat; ☺9am-4pm Tue-Fri, 10am-3pm Sat, noon-5pm Sun) Two blocks east of the market square, this museum is housed in a former Jesuit college (1698). The permanent display features the prehistory and history of the surrounding area and city, and there are always temporary exhibitions. Enter from ul Muzealna.

**Holy Cross Cathedral**                                     CHURCH

(Katedra Św Krzyża; ul Katedralna 2) This Gothic cathedral, a short walk north of the Rynek, features 73m-high towers and mostly Baroque interior furnishing. The lovely bronze gate at the western entrance was erected in 1995 to mark the church's 700th year.

**Piast Tower**                                              TOWER

(Wieża Piastowska; ul Piastowska 14; adult/concession 3/2zł; ☺10am-1pm & 2-6pm Tue-Sun) The only vestige of the dukes' castle is this 33m-tall sturdy watchtower with 3m-thick walls and foundations 6m deep. Built in the 14th century, the castle was pulled down in the 1920s to make room for office buildings. You can climb the 163 steps to the top for a panoramic view over the city.

## 🛏 Sleeping

**Szara Willa**                                          HOTEL €€

(☑77 441 4570; www.szarawilla.pl; ul Oleska 11; s 269-299zł, d 319-329zł; 🅿@) The 'Grey Villa' has a crisp modern feel and design elements with an Asian influence. Its rooms are generously sized, with high ceilings, and four rooms in front look on to a large terrace. A plus is the attached fitness centre

SILESIA OPOLE

with bowling alleys, though the latter can produce some unwelcome noise at night.

### Hotel Piast
HOTEL €€

(☎77 454 9710; www.hotel-piast.com; ul Piastowska 1; s/d 310/369zł; P✳🌐) Commanding the best location of Opole's accommodation, the Piast sits on the northern tip of Pasieka Island, a short trot away from the Old Town. Its rooms are classy and comfortable, and there's a bar on the premises.

### Hotel Zacisze
HOTEL €€

(☎77 453 9553; www.hotel-zacisze.opole.pl; ul Grunwaldzka 28; s 75-140zł, d 150-210zł; P🌐) Located about 700m east of the Rynek, the 18-room Zacisze has a range of small but acceptable single and double rooms in a wonderfully leafy residential area. The cheaper rooms have shared bathrooms.

### Hotel Mercure
HOTEL €€

(☎77 451 8100; www.mercure.com; ul Krakowska 57; s/d 295/315zł; P🌐) A cookie-cutter offering from the international chain, though the quality of its fittings and furnishings aren't quite up to the usual standard. However, there's no denying its handy location near the bus and train stations. It has a bar and restaurant, and you can score a rate up to 50% cheaper by booking online.

## ✕ Eating

The majority of eateries are gathered around the market square. For self-catering supplies, drop into the central **Delikatesy Piast** (Rynek 13; ⊙7am-10pm Mon-Fri, 8am-11pm Sat, 10am-8pm Sun).

### TOP CHOICE / Restauracja Zagłoba
POLISH €€

(ul Krakowska 39; mains 24-35zł; ⊙noon-midnight) One of the best restaurants in provincial Poland, this cellar eatery serves inspired modern Polish food in historic vaults and has won several local awards. Try the excellent Casimir's Delight (pork loin with wild mushroom sauce).

### Kaiseki
JAPANESE €€

(ul Ozimska 4; dishes 9-35zł; ⊙noon-10pm Mon-Sat, noon-9pm Sun) This very stylish and very Japanese eatery, upstairs in a modern shopping mall, serves sushi as well as more substantial mains such as tempura.

### Restauracja U Mnicha
POLISH €

(ul Ozimska 10; mains 10-25zł; ⊙9am-11pm) This modern, monk-themed basement restaurant serves up sandwiches, pizzas and hefty salads

and holds regular summer barbecues in its small garden area. Enter from ul Kołłątaja.

### Smaki Świata
INTERNATIONAL €

(ul Książąt Opolskich 2/6; dishes 2.82zł per 100g; ⊙11am-8pm) 'Tastes of the World' is true to its name, serving Polish, Hungarian, Italian and Chinese cuisine in cheerful cafeteria premises. All food is charged at a flat rate by weight.

## 🍷 Drinking & Entertainment

### John Bull Pub
PUB

(Rynek-Ratusz; ⊙noon-late; 🌐) This facsimile of a pub from provincial Britain boasts a huge terrace section on the market square that stays open late in the warmer months. Look for the red telephone box.

### Kawiarnia Artystyczna Dworek
CAFE-BAR

(ul Studzienna 1; ⊙noon-late) A leafy terrace tucked out the back of the Old Town, the 'Artistic Cafe Manor' shelters a laid-back pub, cafe and music club.

### Highlander Klub
PUB, CLUB

(ul Szpitalna 3; ⊙11am-late) A good place for a beer and dance, this friendly (but not very Scottish) venue hosts DJs playing anything from house to Latin.

## 🛍 Shopping

### Cepelia
ARTS & CRAFTS

(ul Koraszewskiego 25) Opole is famed for its porcelain hand-painted with fine floral motifs, and this is where you'll find the widest selection.

### EMPiK
BOOKS

(ul Krakowska 45/47; ⊙9am-10pm Mon-Sat, noon-9pm Sun) Books, newspapers and magazines.

## ❶ Information

**HMS Computers** (ul Krakowska 26; per hr 4zł; ⊙9am-5pm Mon-Fri, 9am-2pm Sat) Internet access.

**Main post office** (ul Krakowska 46; ⊙24hr)

**PTTK office** (☎77 454 5113; www.opole.pttk.pl; ul Krakowska 15; ⊙9am-5pm Mon-Fri, 9am-1pm Sat) Travel agency.

**Tourist office** (☎77 451 1987; www.opole.pl; Rynek 23; ⊙9am-6pm Mon-Fri, 10am-5pm Sat)

## ❶ Getting There & Away

The train station and bus station face each other at the end of ul Krakowska, south of the Old Town.

Opole is on the main line between Katowice (32zł, two hours, at least hourly) and Wrocław

## WORTH A TRIP

## PASS THE CROWBAR, JEEVES

The small town of Toszek is worth a side trip simply to look around its impressive Gothic **castle** (ul Zamkowa), but there's a literary footnote awaiting book lovers on the other side of town.

In May 1940 popular British novelist **PG Wodehouse**, creator of the masterful valet Jeeves and his hapless employer Bertie Wooster, was captured by the German army at his home in France. In September he was moved to a civilian internment camp in German Tost, now Toszek.

The prison was set up within the grounds of the **psychiatric hospital** (ul Gliwicka 5a), and its sinister story didn't end with the Germans – after the war it operated as a political prison of the Soviet Union's feared NKVD secret police. Though you can't enter, you can get a good view of its grim red-brick exterior from the dishevelled park across the road. Within the complex are grounds that were used as an exercise yard for the prisoners, beyond which was their dining hall and hospital.

Wodehouse, then 58, coped well with the privations of camp life, but was unimpressed with what he could see of Toszek through the barred windows, writing: 'If this is Upper Silesia, what must Lower Silesia be like?'

The internationally famous author was treated well by his captors, being allowed to work on a rented typewriter. Then, in 1941, he was invited by the German authorities to make a series of radio broadcasts to reassure his readers in still-neutral America of his good health. Naively, Wodehouse agreed, unaware of the defiant mood in the UK after the Blitz and the Battle of Britain. The broadcasts caused an outpouring of indignation and accusations of collaboration.

Although British intelligence secretly cleared Wodehouse of any wrongdoing after the war, the incident left its mark. The author never returned to Britain, living out his days on Long Island, New York.

Sir Pelham Grenville Wodehouse died in 1975, aged 93, just six weeks after receiving a belated knighthood from his homeland. He is survived by almost 100 books, including the one he completed while a prisoner in Toszek – *Money in the Bank*.

If you're interested in visiting Toszek, there are 10 trains a day from Opole (12zł, 50 minutes). From the station, turn left and take a 20-minute walk along ul Dworcowa to the town centre.

(24zł, one hour, at least hourly). Most Katowice trains continue to Kraków (41zł, four hours), and there are seven trains daily to Częstochowa (24zł, two hours). To Warsaw there are four TLK trains (56zł, 5½ hours) and four Express InterCity trains (122zł, 4¾ hours).

Useful buses head to Nysa (10zł, one hour, hourly) and Kłodzko (19zł, 2½ hours, seven daily).

# Katowice

POP 307,000

Katowice (kah-to-*vee*-tseh) is at the centre of the so-called Upper Silesian Industrial District (Górnośląski Okręg Przemysłowy, or GOP). The GOP contains 14 cities and a number of neighbouring towns, forming one vast conurbation with a population of well over three million.

Historically, Katowice is a product of the 19th-century industrial boom, but it only became a city in the interwar period. After WWII, at the height of the Stalinist cult craze, the city was renamed Stalinogród, but reverted to its old name soon after Comrade Joe died in 1953. Katowice has few significant historical monuments, but it's a major commercial and cultural centre and holds sufficient attractions to make it worth a stopover.

## Sights

Rynek       SQUARE

The city's central market square is not lined with historic burghers' houses as you'd find elsewhere in Silesia, but instead is encircled by drab postwar blocks. It's a showpiece of the 'early Gierek style' – the term Poles sarcastically give to architecture spawned during the fleeting period of apparent prosperity in the early 1970s, when Edward Gierek's communist government took out hefty loans from the West to fancifully make Poland a 'second Japan'.

# Katowice

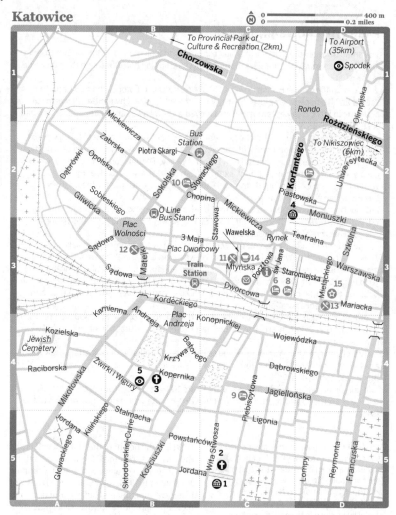

## Silesian Museum
MUSEUM

(Muzeum Śląskie; www.muzeumslaskie.pl; al Korfantego 3; adult/concession 12/7zł, free Sat; ⊙noon-5pm) North of the Rynek, the Silesian Museum features Polish paintings from 1800 to 1939, as well as various temporary displays from its vast collections (fine art, archaeology, ethnography and local history and culture).

## Upper Silesian Ethnographic Park
MUSEUM

(Górnośląski Park Etnograficzny; www.skansen chorzow.pl; ul Parkowa 25; adult/concession 6/4zł; ⊙8am-4pm Mon, 9am-5pm Tue-Fri, 11am-7pm Sat & Sun May-Sep) This sprawling open-air museum contains scores of traditional wooden buildings spread over 20 hectares. It's situated within the even bigger **Provincial Park of Culture and Recreation**, which also houses a stadium, zoo, amusement grounds and a planetarium. The park is about 3km northwest of the centre; reach it from the centre on tram 6, 11, 19 or 23.

## Cathedral of Christ the King
CHURCH

(Katedra Chrystusa Króla; www.katedra.katowice .opoka.org.pl in Polish; ul Plebiscytowa 49a) Some 800m south of the Rynek is Poland's largest

# Katowice

cathedral, its base measuring 89m by 53m. The massive sandstone structure was erected between 1927 and 1955. The spacious interior is topped with a large dome that rises 59m from the floor, but apart from colourful stained-glass windows and an unusual 'wheel' crucifix, it's fairly plain. Behind it, the **Archdiocesan Museum** (ul Jordana 39; admission free; ⊙2-6pm Tue & Thu, 2-5pm Sun) has a collection of sacred art from the late 14th century, including some beautiful Gothic altarpieces. Enter it from ul Wita Stwosza.

**Museum of Katowice History at Nikiszowiec**     MUSEUM
(ul Rymarska 4; adult/concession 12/7zł; ⊙10am-4pm Tue-Fri, 11am-3pm Sat & Sun) This branch of the historical museum is based in the distinctive suburb of **Nikiszowiec**, about 5km southeast of the city centre. The district is a unique housing estate created for miners (and their families) who worked at a nearby shaft between 1908 and 1924. Built of attractive red brick, with a network of streets between them, the nine blocks are interconnected by gateways. The complex was designed to be self-sufficient, with shops, restaurants, a swimming pool, a hospital, a school and a detention centre. The museum adds context to this interesting architectural gem. Bus 30 (2.60zł) goes here from the centre.

**Skyscraper**     HISTORIC BUILDING
(Drapacz Chmur; ul Żwirki i Wigury 15) This blocky, 14-storey, 60m-tall structure was Poland's tallest building from 1934 until 1955. It's considered the best example of Functionalism in Poland. Nearby is the lofty **Garrison Church of St Casimir** (Parafia Wojskowa Św Kazimierza; ul Skłodowskiej-Curie 20), which opened just a year before Skyscraper, with lovely Art Deco interiors.

## 🛏 Sleeping

**Jopi Hostel**     HOSTEL €
(☎32 204 3432; www.jopihostel.pl; ul Plebiscytowa 23; dm 41-51zł, s/d 82/108zł; 🛜) Modern hostel south of the train station, with a well-equipped kitchen and comfortable lounge/dining area. Rooms are painted a cheery orange-yellow shade, lending a touch of brightness to the interior.

**Hotel Diament**     HOTEL €€
(☎32 253 9041; www.hoteldiament.pl; ul Dworcowa 9; s/d 279/369zł; 🅿🛜) This business-friendly member of a Silesian hotel chain is comfortable, convenient and reliably friendly, with a good restaurant downstairs. Booking online usually secures a much lower rate.

**Hotel Monopol**     HOTEL €€€
(☎32 782 8282; www.hotel.com.pl; ul Dworcowa 5; s/d 490/580zł; 🅿❄🛜⛲) A tasteful reincarnation of Katowice's most celebrated prewar hotel, with friendly, helpful staff. Rooms are full of stylish walnut and chrome surfaces, with huge shower heads. There are also two restaurants, a fitness centre with two saunas, and a swimming pool. Check out the fabulous 19th-century floor mosaic under glass in the foyer.

**Pokoje Gościnne Zacisze**     HOTEL €€
(☎515 272 124; www.noclegizacisze.pl in Polish; ul Słowackiego 15; s/d 120/240zł; 🛜) Don't let the creaky old staircase put you off – this accommodation offers pleasantly appointed rooms in an old building near the bus station. Not much English is spoken, however, and there's no breakfast available.

**Hotel Katowice**     HOTEL €€
(☎32 258 8281; www.hotel-katowice.com.pl; al Korfantego 9; s/d 192/270zł; 🅿🛜) Only a Soviet central planner could admire the exterior of this communist-era relic, but the rooms have been renovated and the city centre's a light stroll away. Amenities include a bar, restaurant and cake shop.

## ✗ Eating

Several pedestrian strips hold Katowice's highest concentrations of eateries: ul Stawowa, just north of the train station, has plenty of snack bars and unfussy restaurants; the areas around ul Staromiejska and ul Wawelska, northeast of the station, are a bit more cosmopolitan and upmarket.

**Złoty Osioł** VEGETARIAN €
(ul Mariacka 1; mains all 11zł; ✐) A cheerful, popular vegetarian cafe, the 'Golden Donkey' has cool hippy decor (think psychedelic walls and distressed furniture) and a tasty range of meat-free dishes, including some vegan options.

**La Grotta** ITALIAN €€
(ul Wawelska 3; mains 13-47zł; ✐9am-10pm Mon-Sat, 11am-10pm Sun) On a short but bustling pedestrian street by the train station, this charming two-floor trattoria is Katowice's best Italian eatery and reaches far beyond the usual pizza and pasta offerings.

**Restauracja A Dong** ASIAN €€€
(ul Matejki 3; mains 30-85zł) This is the place to find authentic Asian food in Katowice. Dishes include Sichuan squid, Malaysian shrimps, Vietnamese octopus and lobster Saigon-style.

## 🍷 Drinking & Entertainment

**Gaudi Café** CAFE
(ul Wawelska 2; ✐9am-10pm Mon-Sat, 10am-10pm Sun) In tribute to the acclaimed Spanish architect, this is the coolest cafe on the centre's coolest pedestrian street. The coffee and cakes are good, but it's the out-there interior that'll leave you in awe.

**Lemoniada** CLUB
(ul Mariacka 4; ✐9pm-late Wed-Sat) Arguably the best nightclub on this nightlife strip. A glamorous interior awaits, along with Katowice's beautiful people.

## ℹ Information

**Copy Self Xero** (ul 3 Maja 19; per hr 5zł; ✐7.30am-7pm Mon-Fri, 9am-1pm Sat) Internet access.

**Post office** (ul Pocztowa 9; ✐24hr)

**Tourist office** (☎32 259 3808; www.katowice .eu; Rynek 13; ✐9am-6pm Mon-Fri, 9am-4pm Sat) If you're interested in finding out more about Katowice's distinctive interwar architecture, ask here for the architectural walking trail brochure.

## ℹ Getting There & Away

**AIR Katowice Airport** (☎32 392 7385; www .katowice-airport.com) is in Pyrzowice, 35km north of the city. There are domestic flights to Warsaw (three daily), with international services to numerous European cities, including Frankfurt (up to four daily) aboard Lufthansa and Wizz Air, London (three daily) via Ryanair and Wizz Air, Dublin (three weekly) on Ryanair, Munich (twice daily) aboard LOT, and Paris (three weekly) via Wizz Air. **LOT** (☎32 203 6900; www.lot.com; ul Piastowska 1; ✐9am-5pm Mon-Fri) has an office near Hotel Katowice.

You can transfer between the airport and Katowice train station via seven daily shuttle services offered by **Matuszek** (☎32 236 1111; www.matuszek.com.pl; one way/return 20/40zł). Buying on the bus rather than booking online incurs an extra 5zł fee each way. The company also runs services from Katowice Airport to Kraków; see p145 for details.

**BUS** The bus station, on ul Piotra Skargi some 500m north of the train station, handles buses to most destinations around the region, with plenty of long-distance and international services as well. For most journeys the train will be a better option, though the five daily buses to Oświęcim (8zł, 1½ hours) may be useful.

However, the best bus option to Oświęcim is the 'O Line' bus (7zł, 55 minutes), which departs for the Auschwitz-Birkenau Museum seven times a day from Monday to Saturday between 6am and 4.30pm from a stop at ul Sokolska 3, next to the concert hall. The last return is at 6.25pm.

**TRAIN** Trains are the main means of transport in the region and beyond. The train station is in the city centre and trains depart for Oświęcim (9zł, one hour, three daily), Pszczyna (9zł, 50 minutes, at least hourly), Kraków (19zł, two hours, at least hourly), Opole (32zł, two hours, at least hourly), Wrocław (41zł, three hours, at least hourly), Poznań (56zł, 5¾ hours, 11 daily), Częstochowa (17zł, 1¾ hours, at least hourly) and Warsaw (116zł, 2¾ hours, hourly). International destinations include Berlin, Bratislava, Budapest, Prague and Vienna.

## Pszczyna

POP 25,000

One of the oldest towns in Silesia (its origins go back to the 11th century), Pszczyna (*psh-chi*-nah), the 'pearl of Silesia', is an attractive burg with an impressively palatial castle.

The town was home for centuries to the Piast dynasty. In 1847, after centuries of changing ownership, it became the property of the powerful Hochberg family of Prussia.

In the last months of WWI, Pszczyna was the flashpoint of the first of three consecutive Silesian uprisings in which Polish peasants took up arms and demanded that the region be incorporated into Poland. Their wishes were granted in 1921, following a plebiscite held by the League of Nations.

## ◎ Sights

### Castle
CASTLE

This grandiose former residence (which looks more like a palace) dates back to the 12th century, when the Opole dukes built a hunting lodge here. It has been enlarged and redesigned several times, most recently in 1870.

The Hochbergs, who owned the castle until 1945, furnished their home according to their status – they were among the richest families in Europe, ruling vast swathes of land from their Silesian family seat, the castle at Książ. Priceless works of art completed the scene, but most were lost during WWII.

Today the palace houses the **Castle Museum** (Muzeum Zamkowe; www.zamek-pszczyna .pl; ul Brama Wybrańców 1; adult/concession 14.50/8.50zł; ☺10am-3pm Mon & Tue, 10am-4pm Wed-Sun), with about a dozen rooms open over three floors. Those wanting more detailed information should pick up a copy of the English-language guidebook *The Castle Museum in Pszczyna* (17zł) from the ticket office or tourist office.

The castle's interiors feature bedchambers, drawing rooms and salons filled with tapestries, ceramics, paintings and hunting trophies. Unforgettable are the **library** (adult/concession 5/3zł), panelled entirely in walnut, and the stunning **Mirror Chamber**, which hosts occasional chamber music concerts. Some of the palace's rooms also contain themed exhibitions, including a **collection of armour** in the basement and one of miniscule portraits in the **Cabinet of Miniatures** (adult/concession 3/2zł) on the 3rd floor. Behind the castle is the extensive English-style **Castle Park** along the Pszczynka River.

### Rynek
SQUARE

The castle looks on to this elongated and leafy market square, lined with old burghers' houses dating mostly from the 18th and 19th centuries. On its northern side is the **Protestant church** and, next to it at number 2, the **town hall**, both remodelled last century. Behind the town hall is the 14th-century **parish church**, extensively rebuilt over the years, with a typically lavish interior featuring a ceiling painting of the Ascension.

### Pszczyna Farm Village
MUSEUM

(Zagroda Wsi Pszczyńskiej; www.skansen.pszczyna.pl; ul Parkowa; adult/concession 6/4zł; ☺10am-3pm Tue-Fri, 10am-6pm Sat & Sun Apr-Oct) A five-minute walk east of the Rynek is this small but interesting open-air museum with half a dozen 200-year-old timber houses – including a mill, smithy and barn – collected from the region.

## 🛏 Sleeping

### Pensonjat Piano Nobile
HOTEL €€

(☎32 447 7881; www.pianonobile.com.pl; Rynek 16; s 170zł, d 220-280zł; @) Small hotel within an impressively renovated 200-year-old residence in a convenient location right on the market square. Provides comfortably appointed rooms and an atmospheric restaurant.

### Hotel Zamkowy
HOTEL €€

(☎32 449 1720; www.hotelzamkowy.eu; Rynek 20; s/d 220/260zł; @) Attractive small hotel housed in a renovated 18th-century burgher's house. If the marble floors in the public areas and the guestrooms' enormous bathrooms don't impress, the views of the square and the castle will.

### Villa Retro
HOTEL €

(☎32 210 2245; www.retro.pl; ul Warowna 31; s 80-100zł, d 120-140zł; P @) Named (and decorated) long before retro became a byword for cool, this guesthouse with rooms in two buildings is a friendly and central choice. The more expensive rooms are bigger, but otherwise the same standard.

### Hotel U Michalika
HOTEL €

(☎32 210 1355; www.umichalika.com.pl; ul Dworcowa 11; s/d 110/150zł; P 🛜) This hotel is owned and operated by local chef-turned-entrepreneur Stefan Michalika and offers 16 modern and upbeat rooms. The in-house restaurant is very good. Enter from behind the building.

## 🍴 Eating & Drinking

### Restauracja Kmieć
POLISH €€

(ul Piekarska 10; mains 13-55zł; ☺noon-9pm) Set in a historic townhouse dating from 1756, this long-established family restaurant serves a solid range of old-fashioned Polish food and is hugely popular for it.

### Café U Telemanna
CAFE €

(ul Brama Wybrańców 1; dishes 6-14zł; ☺9am-9pm Mon-Thu, 9am-11pm Fri & Sat, 10am-9pm Sun) Located in the courtyard of the castle, this is a good pit stop for a drink or a snack after viewing the building. The cafe is named after composer Georg Philip Telemann (1681–1767), who lived here for four years in the early 18th century.

**Barocco** PUB
(ul Bednarska 3; ⊘11am-late) This pub is a bit more relaxed than the places on the square and makes a good spot for a leisurely beer.

## ❶ Information

**Post office** (ul Batorego 1; ⊘7am-7.30pm Mon-Fri, 7am-1pm Sat)

**Tourist office** (☑32 212 9999; ul Brama Wybrańców 1; ⊘8am-4pm Mon-Fri, 10am-4pm Sat & Sun) Just inside the castle gate.

## ❶ Getting There & Away

The bus and train stations are to the east of the centre, about 200m apart. Trains to Katowice (9zł, 50 minutes) run at least hourly, and there are two buses daily to Kraków (18zł, two hours).

# Oświęcim

POP 39,900

Oświęcim (osh-*fyen*-cheem) is a quiet, medium-sized industrial city on the border between Silesia and Małopolska, about 30km southeast of Katowice and about 40km west of Kraków. The Polish place name may be unfamiliar to most foreigners, but the German version, Auschwitz, is not. This was the scene of the largest attempt at genocide in human history. Though visiting it is a grim experience, it's an essential element in understanding the full evil of the Holocaust.

## ◉ Sights

**Auschwitz-Birkenau Memorial & Museum** MUSEUM
(Miejsce Pamięci i Muzeum Auschwitz-Birkenau; www.auschwitz.org.pl; ul Więźniów Oświęcimia 20; ⊘8am-7pm Jun-Aug, 8am-6pm May & Sep, 8am-5pm Apr & Oct, 8am-4pm Mar & Nov, 8am-3pm Dec-Feb) The Auschwitz extermination camp was established in April 1940 by the German occupiers in prewar Polish army barracks on the outskirts of Oświęcim. Auschwitz was originally intended for Polish political prisoners, but the camp was then adapted for the wholesale extermination of the Jews of Europe in fulfilment of Nazi ideology. For this purpose, the much larger camp at Birkenau (Brzezinka), also referred to as Auschwitz II, was built 2km west of the original site in 1941 and 1942, followed by another one in Monowitz (Monowice), several kilometres to the west.

It is now estimated that in total this German-run death factory eliminated well over a million people of 27 nationalities, including around a million Jews, 150,000 Poles and 23,000 Roma.

The name Auschwitz often describes the whole Auschwitz-Birkenau complex. In 2007, its Unesco World Heritage listing was changed from 'Auschwitz Concentration Camp' to 'Auschwitz-Birkenau: German Nazi Concentration & Extermination Camp (1940–45)'.

Both Auschwitz and Birkenau are open to the public, and the museum's visitor centre is at the entrance to the Auschwitz site. Photography and filming are permitted throughout the camp without the use of a flash or stands. There's a self-service snack bar by the entrance as well as a *kantor* (private currency-exchange office), free left-luggage room and bookshops with publications about the place.

If not on a tour, get a copy of the museum-produced *Auschwitz Birkenau Guidebook* (5zł). It has plans of both camps and gets you round the grounds.

*Auschwitz*

Auschwitz was only partially destroyed by the fleeing Nazis, and many of the original brick buildings stand to this day as a bleak testament to the camp's history. Some 13 of the 30 surviving prison blocks now house museum exhibitions – either general, or dedicated to victims from particular countries or ethnic groups that lost people at Auschwitz.

Between April and October it's compulsory to join a tour if you arrive between 10am and 3pm. The four-hour English-language **tours** (adult/concession 25/20zł) of Auschwitz and Birkenau leave every half-hour between 9.30am and 3.30pm between May and September, and hourly from 10pm to 3.30pm in April and October. From November to March the English-language tour price jumps to adult/concession 39/28zł and they're only available at 10.30am, 11.30am and 1.20pm. All tours include entry to view the 17-minute **documentary film** (adult/concession 3.50/2.50zł; ⊘hourly on the hr) about the liberation of the camp by Soviet troops on 27 January 1945, which is screened in the visitor centre. The film is not recommended for children under 14 years old.

From the visitor centre in the entrance building, you enter the barbed-wire encampment through the infamous gate, displaying the grimly cynical message in German: *'Arbeit Macht Frei'* (Work Brings Freedom).

The sign is in fact a replica, which replaced the original when it was stolen in late 2009. Though it was recovered within a few days, it had been cut into pieces by the thieves and took 17 months to restore. At the time of research, it was envisaged that the replica would remain in place while the original sign would eventually be put on exhibition within the museum.

*Birkenau*

It was actually at Birkenau, not Auschwitz, that most of the killing took place. Massive (175 hectares) and purpose-built to be efficient, the camp had more than 300 prison barracks (they were actually stables built for horses, but housed 300 people each). Birkenau had four huge gas chambers complete with crematoria. Each could asphyxiate 2000 people at one time, and there were electric lifts to raise the bodies to the ovens.

Though much of Birkenau was destroyed by the retreating Nazis, the size of the place, fenced off with long lines of barbed wire and watchtowers stretching almost as far as your eye can see, will give you some idea of the scale of the crime; climb the tower at the entrance gate to get the full effect. Some of the surviving barracks are open to visitors for viewing, silent contemplation and prayer. If you're not part of a tour, make sure to leave enough time (at least an hour) to walk around the camp.

FREE Auschwitz Jewish Centre MUSEUM
(www.ajcf.org; Plac Skarbka 5; ☺8.30am-8pm Sun-Fri Mar-Oct, 8.30am-6pm Sun-Fri Nov-Feb) In the centre of the town of Oświęcim, this institution approaches the Holocaust from another angle, with permanent exhibitions about Oświęcim's thriving Jewish community in the years before WWII. Within the restored synagogue (1913) are photos and Judaica found beneath the town's Great Synagogue in 2004. It's hard to forget you're looking at the last remnants of Polish Jewry, an all but exterminated culture.

## 🛏 Sleeping & Eating

**Hotel Olecki** HOTEL €€
(☎33 847 5000; www.hotelolecki.pl; ul Leszczyńskiej 12; s/d/ste 180/210/350zł; P@) This hotel near the entrance to Auschwitz is the most comfortable and conveniently located accommodation in Oświęcim. Its restaurant serves both Polish and international cuisine, and has a beer garden.

**Centre for Dialogue and Prayer** HOTEL, CAMPGROUND €€
(☎33 843 1000; www.centrum-dialogu.oswiecim.pl; ul Kolbego 1; camping per person 30zł; s/d 110/220zł; P@) This Catholic facility is 500m southwest of the tourist office, providing comfortable and quiet accommodation in rooms of two to 10 beds (most with en suite) and a restaurant. Full board is available.

**International Youth Meeting Centre** HOTEL €€
(☎33 843 2107; www.mdsm.pl; ul Legionów 11; s/d 120/170zł; P@) This German-built centre, 1km east of the train station, is essentially for long-staying groups, but they'll take anyone if there are vacancies. Meals are available.

## ℹ️ Information

**Tourist office** (☎33 843 0091; www.mpit-oswiecim.neostrada.pl; ul Leszczyńskiej 12; ☺8am-6pm Mon-Fri, 8am-3pm Sat & Sun) Near the Auschwitz site.

## ℹ️ Getting There & Around

For most tourists, the jump-off point for Oświęcim is Kraków. Buses (12zł, 1½ hours, 11 daily) can be a more convenient option than trains, as they generally drop you off in the parking lot opposite the entrance to Auschwitz. There are also numerous minibuses to Oświęcim from the minibus stands off ul Pawia, next to Galeria Krakowska.

The alternative is catching a train from Kraków (14zł, 1½ hours, hourly), then walking 1.5km to the museum entrance. If you don't fancy walking from the Oświęcim train station to the museum, take any southbound city bus (2.40zł).

If Katowice is your starting point, there are three daily trains (9zł, one hour) and five buses (8zł, 1½ hours) to Oświęcim. The best option, however, is the dedicated 'O Line' bus (7zł, 55 minutes), which heads directly to the museum seven times a day from Monday to Saturday. It operates between 6am and 4.30pm from a stop at ul Sokolska 3, next to Katowice's concert hall. The last return from Oświęcim is at 6.25pm.

From mid-April to late October, there's a free bus linking Auschwitz with Birkenau. It departs hourly, from 11.30am to 4.30pm from outside the entrance to the visitor centre (buses run to 5.30pm in May and September, and until 6.30pm from June to August). Alternatively, it's any easy 2km walk between the two sites.

Most travel agencies in Kraków offer organised tours of Auschwitz (including Birkenau), from 90zł to 120zł per person. Check with the operator for exactly how much time the tour allows you at Auschwitz, as some run to a very tight schedule.

# Wielkopolska

POP 3.4 MILLION

## Includes »

## Best Places to Eat

- » Warung Bali (p281)
- » Tapas Bar (p281)
- » Cymes (p281)
- » Restauracja Ratuszowa (p290)
- » Antonio (p293)

## Best Places to Stay

- » Brovaria (p280)
- » Hotel Stare Miasto (p280)
- » Frolic Goats Hostel (p280)
- » Hotel Europa (p292)
- » Hotel Atelier (p289)

## Why Go?

If you want to distil the essence of Poland's eventful history, head for Wielkopolska. The region's name means Greater Poland, and this is where the Polish state was founded in the Middle Ages. Centuries later, the local population has an understandable pride in its long history.

Though Poznań is a city focused on commerce, it has a lively character and plenty of sights; and beyond, the Wielkopolska countryside offers a selection of charming towns and rural scenery. Among the region's attractions are castles, steam trains, palaces, churches, nature reserves and a memorable Iron Age settlement. And at the heart of it all is the great cathedral of Gniezno, the birthplace of Catholic Poland.

It's an impressive menu, but Wielkopolska is also a great place to strike out on your own. Wherever you end up, you'll be sure to find something of historic interest...it's that kind of place.

## When to Go

### Poznań

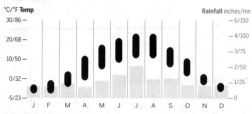

| Mar–May | Jul | Sep |
|---|---|---|
| Welcome spring by hiking through Wielkopolska National Park near Poznań. | Summer is the time for alternative theatre and other arts at Poznań's Malta Festival. | Iron Age culture is commemorated in autumn at the archaeological festival in Biskupin. |

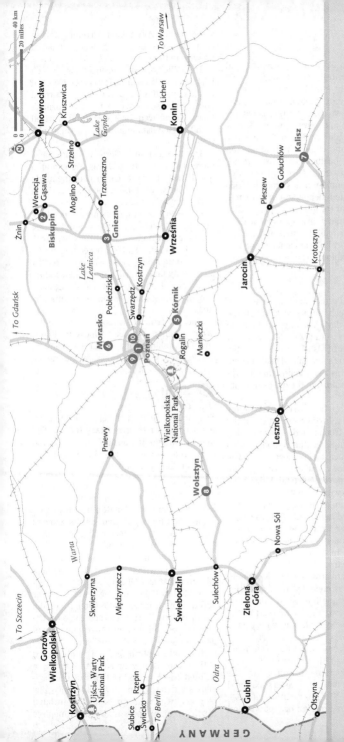

## Wielkopolska Highlights

**1** Sampling the lively **entertainment** (p283) within Poznań's Old Town

**2** Travelling back to the Iron Age at the fortified village of **Biskupin** (p290)

**3** Exploring Gniezno's monumental historic **cathedral** (p287)

**4** **Cycling** (p277) through the Wielkopolska countryside

**5** Visiting the small, distinctive castle at **Kórnik** (p285)

**6** Encountering meteorite craters at **Morasko** (p286)

**7** Viewing the intriguing 1920s architecture of central **Kalisz** (p292)

**8** Catching a steam train to **Wolsztyn** (p287)

**9** Watching mechanised goats butting horns on the **Town Hall** in Poznań (p272)

**10** Walking through Poland's earliest history on the island of **Ostrów Tumski** (p276)

# POZNAŃ

POP 552,000

If you arrive in Poznań any evening and stroll into its central market square, you'll receive an instant introduction to the characteristic energy of Wielkopolska's capital. The city's Old Town district is buzzing at any time of the day, and positively jumping by night, full of people heading to its many restaurants, pubs and clubs. The combination of international business travellers attending its numerous trade fairs and the city's huge student population has created a distinctive vibe quite independent of tourism.

In addition to its energetic personality, Poznań offers many historical attractions in its centre, particularly museums, and its plentiful transport links make it a great base from which to explore the quieter surrounding countryside.

## History

The history of Poznań and the history of Poland were much the same thing in the nation's earliest days. The city was founded as a 9th-century settlement on the easily defensible island of Ostrów Tumski, during the reign of Poland's first ruler, Duke Mieszko I. Some historians even claim that it was here, not in Gniezno, that the duke's baptism took place in 966.

Mieszko's son, the first Polish king, Bolesław Chrobry, further strengthened the island, and the troops of the Holy Roman Empire that conquered the region in 1005 didn't even bother to lay siege to it. The Bohemian Prince Bratislav (Brzetysław), however, liked a challenge and damaged the town considerably in 1038. This marked the end for Poznań as the royal seat (though kings were buried here until 1296), as subsequent rulers chose Kraków as their capital.

Poznań continued to develop as a commercial centre – in 1253 a new town centre was laid out on the left bank of the Warta River. Soon afterwards a castle was built and the town was encircled with defensive walls. Poznań's trade flourished during the Renaissance period, and by the end of the 16th century the population had passed the 20,000 mark.

But into every city's life a little rain must fall. From the mid-17th century on, Swedish, Prussian and Russian invasions, together with a series of natural disasters, battered the city. In the Second Partition of 1793, Poznań fell under Prussian occupation and was renamed Posen, later becoming part of Germany and experiencing steady industrial growth up to the outbreak of WWI.

The Wielkopolska insurrection, which broke out in Poznań in December 1918, led to the city's addition to the newly reformed Polish state (see boxed text, p275). Poznań's long trading traditions were then revived with the establishment of regular trade fairs in 1921.

The city fell into German hands once more during WWII, and was incorporated into Hitler's Third Reich. In 1945 the battle for its liberation took a month and did a huge amount of damage.

In the postwar era, Poznań was one of the first cities to feel the forceful hand of the communist regime, during a massive workers' strike in June 1956 (see boxed text, p276). The spontaneous demonstration, cruelly crushed by tanks, turned out to be the first of a wave of popular protests on the long and painful road to overcoming communist rule.

Since the return of democracy, Poznań has taken advantage of its business traditions and favourable location near Germany to develop its role as an important educational and industrial centre.

## ◉ Sights

### OLD TOWN

The historic heart of the city is centred on the lively and attractive **Stary Rynek** (Old Market Square). It was laid out in 1253 and contains a vibrant mix of sights, restaurants and entertainment outlets.

**Town Hall**                    HISTORIC BUILDING
(Ratusz; Stary Rynek 1) Poznań's Renaissance town hall, topped with a 61m-high tower, instantly captures your attention. Its graceful form replaced the 13th-century Gothic town hall, which was consumed by fire in the early 16th century, along with much of the town. It was designed by Italian architect Giovanni Battista Quadro and constructed from 1550 to 1560; only the tower is a later addition, built in the 1780s after its predecessor collapsed. The crowned eagle on top of the spire, with an impressive wingspan of 2m, adds some Polish symbolism.

The main eastern facade is embellished with a three-storey arcade. Above it is a painted frieze depicting kings of the Jagiellonian dynasty, and a clock. Every day at noon two metal goats appear through a pair of small doors above the timepiece and butt their horns together 12 times, in deference to an old legend. Apparently two goats intended for a celebratory banquet escaped and ended up clashing horns above the about-to-be-unveiled clock, much to the amusement of the assembled dignitaries. The clockmaker was duly ordered to add the errant animals' images to his piece.

**Historical Museum of Poznań**     MUSEUM
(Muzeum Historii Miasta Poznania; www.mnp.art
.pl; Stary Rynek 1; adult/concession 7/5zł, Sat free;
⊙9am-3pm Tue-Thu, noon-9pm Fri, 11am-6pm Sat
& Sun) This museum inside the town hall displays an interesting and well-presented exhibition on the town's history, and the building's original interiors are worth the entry price on their own.

The Gothic vaulted **cellars** are the only remains of the first town hall. They were initially used for trade but later became a jail.

The 1st floor is home to three splendid rooms. The largest, the richly ornamented **Renaissance Hall**, is a real gem, with its original stuccowork and paintings from 1555. The 2nd floor contains artefacts from the Prussian/German period, documents illustrating city life in the 1920s and '30s, and a collection of interesting memorabilia from the past two centuries.

In front of the building, near the main entrance, is the **whipping post** (*pręgierz*), once the site of public floggings – and of more serious penalties. The original miniature model executioner which accompanied the post, dating from 1535, is on display in the museum.

**Museum of Applied Arts**     MUSEUM
(Muzeum Sztuk Użytkowych; www.mnp.art.pl; Góra
Przemysława 1) Housed within Poznań's **castle** (which looks more like a palace), this museum's collection includes furniture, gold and silverware, glass, ceramics, weapons, clocks, watches and sundials from Europe and the Far East. At the time of research it was undergoing a major renovation as part of a restoration of the castle's original structure, but should have reopened by the time you read this – check with the tourist office for opening hours and entry fees.

**Parish Church**     CHURCH
(Kościół Farny; ul Gołębia) A few steps south of the museum, this church was originally built for the Jesuits by architects from Italy after more than 80 years of work (1651–1732). The impressive baroque structure has an ornamented facade, and a lofty interior supported on massive columns which is crammed with monumental altars.

**Museum of the Wielkopolska Uprising**     MUSEUM
(Muzeum Powstania Wielkopolskiego; Stary Rynek
3; adult/concession 4/2zł, Sat free; ⊙9am-5pm
Tue-Fri, 10am-4pm Sat & Sun) In the old guardhouse on the western side of the buildings in the centre of the Rynek, this museum details the battles waged by Polish fighters seeking independence from Germany after the end of WWI (see boxed text, p275). It's an interesting if compact institution with displays of military uniforms, weaponry, photographs, and documents created for the newborn Polish state that the Uprising hoped to help create.

**Museum of Musical Instruments**     MUSEUM
(Muzeum Instrumentów Muzycznych; www.mnp.art
.pl; Stary Rynek 45; adult/concession 5.50/3.50zł,
Sat free; ⊙9am-3pm Tue-Thu, noon-9pm Fri, 11am-
6pm Sat & Sun) Institution housing hundreds of instruments, from whistles to concert pianos; including intriguing musical devices such as a typewriter for musician notation and a polyphon, the precursor of the record player.

**Fish Sellers' Houses**     HISTORIC BUILDINGS
(Domki Budnicze) South of the town hall is an endearing row of small arcaded buildings, known as the Fish Sellers' Houses. They were built in the 16th century on the site of fish stalls and later reconstructed after major WWII damage.

**Weigh House**     HISTORIC BUILDING
(Waga Miejska) Behind the town hall is the Weigh House, a postwar replica of the 16th-century building designed by Giovanni Battista Quadro that was dismantled in the 19th century.

**Wielkopolska Military Museum**     MUSEUM
(Wielkopolskie Muzeum Wojskowe; www.mnp.art.pl;
Stary Rynek 9; adult/concession 7/5zł, Sat free;
⊙9am-3pm Tue-Thu, noon-9pm Fri, 11am-6pm Sat
& Sun) Holds exhibits of arms from Poland's many conflicts over the centuries, dating from the 11th century to the present.

**Arsenal City Art Gallery**     GALLERY
(Galeria Miejska Arsenał; www.arsenal.art.pl; Stary
Rynek 3; adult/concession 5/3zł; ⊙11am-6pm Tue-
Sat, to 3pm Sun) The site of a former arsenal now houses this art gallery, which partly atones for its ugly architecture by hosting interesting temporary exhibitions of modern art.

# Greater Poznań

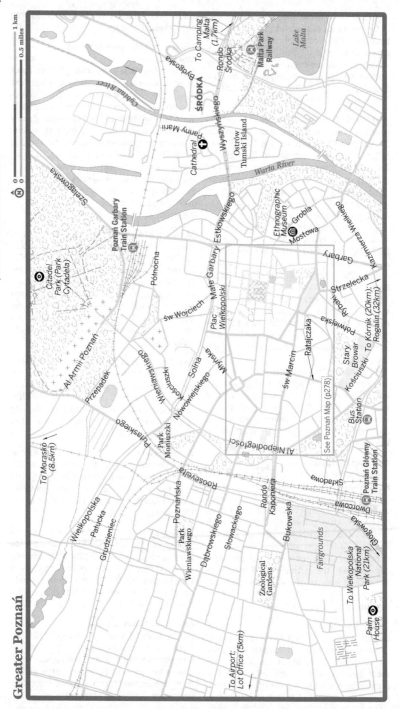

N

0                1 km
0          0.5 miles

To Morasko
(8.5km)

To Airport;
Lot Office (5km)

Wielkopolska

Pałucka

Grudzieniec

Park
Wieniawskiego

Poznańska

Dąbrowskiego

Słowackiego

Zoological
Gardens

Palm
House

To Wielkopolska
National
Park (21km)

Fairgrounds

Bukowska

Rondo
Kaponiera

Roosevelta

Park
Moniuszki

Pułaskiego

Wieniawskiego

Kościuszki

Nowowiejskiego

Solna

Młyńska

Przepadek

Al Armii Poznań

Citadel
Park (Park
Cytadela)

Szelągowska

Poznań Garbary
Train Station

Północna

św Wojciech

Plac
Wielkopolski

Małe Garbary

Estkowskiego

Ethnographic
Museum

Grobla

Mostowa

Garbary

Warta River

Cathedral

Ostrów
Tumski Island

Panny Marii

Wyszyńskiego

Cybina River

Bydgoska

To Camping
Malta (1.7km)

Rondo
Śródka

ŚRÓDKA

Malta Park
Railway

Lake
Malta

św Marcin

Ratajczaka

Al Niepodległości

See Poznań Map (p278)

Stary
Browar

Bus
Station

Kościuszki

św Marcin

Strzelecka

Półwiejska

Rybaki

Kazimierza Wielkiego

To Kórnik (20km);
Rogalin (32km)

Poznań Główny
Train Station

Składowa

Dworcowa

Głogowska

Skłodowska

## LINE IN THE SAND

Europe breathed a deep sigh of relief on 11 November 1918, the day the guns fell silent in WWI. But for Poles living in Wielkopolska, the fight was just beginning.

Germany had sued for peace in the west, but in the east it had been militarily successful against newly communist Russia, and still held firm authority in the ethnically Polish portions of its empire. However, change was in the wind – US President Woodrow Wilson had foreshadowed the creation of an independent Poland as a buffer state between Germany and Russia.

But where would the border of a new Poland fall? The Polish-majority inhabitants of Wielkopolska were unwilling to risk Poland's oldest province staying within Germany, and on 27 December 1918 a full-scale rebellion, the Wielkopolska Uprising, broke out in Poznań. Sparked by a stirring speech by acclaimed pianist Ignacy Paderewski (who later became prime minister of the new nation), the Uprising was led by Polish soldiers who had been drafted into the German army in the war, and was endorsed by underground citizens' committees.

The insurrection quickly escalated into a full-blown civil war that raged across Wielkopolska through the winter, as Polish forces liberated town after town. Their successful capture of Poznań's airport in early January 1919 even enabled them to launch airborne bombing raids on German targets in Frankfurt an der Oder a few days later.

Though a ceasefire was signed in February, skirmishes continued over the following months. But the Uprising had achieved its aim: on 28 June 1919, just over six months after hostilities had broken out, the Treaty of Versailles awarded Wielkopolska to the newly formed Poland.

### Archaeological Museum    MUSEUM

(Muzeum Archeologiczne; www.muzarp.poznan.pl; ul Wodna 27; adult/concession 6/3zł, Sat free; ☺10am-4pm Tue-Fri, to 6pm Sat, to 3pm Sun) Located off the southeastern corner of the Rynek, inside the 16th-century **Górka Palace**. Before going in, stop and have a look at the fine Renaissance doorway on the building's eastern facade. The museum presents the prehistory of the region, from the Stone Age to the early medieval period, as well as housing an extensive Egyptian collection.

### Franciscan Church    CHURCH

(Kościół Franciszkanów; ul Franciszkańska 2) Just west of the Rynek is the richly decorated baroque Franciscan Church. Its **Chapel of the Virgin Mary** in the left transept has a carved oak altar and a tiny, reputedly miraculous image of St Mary.

### Ethnographic Museum    MUSEUM

(Muzeum Etnograficzne; www.mnp.art.pl; ul Grobla 25; adult/concession 7/5zł, Sat free; ☺9am-3pm Tue-Thu, noon-9pm Fri, 11am-6pm Sat & Sun) Southeast of the Rynek is this good collection of folk woodcarving and traditional costumes of the region. Of particular note are the large roadside posts and crosses on display.

### WEST OF THE OLD TOWN

Stretching west from Plac Wolności to the trade-fair buildings and the train station is this area of broad thoroughfares and grand buildings from the 19th and 20th centuries.

### Monument to the Victims of June 1956    MONUMENT

(Pomnik Poznańskiego Czerwca 1956) On **Plac Mickiewicza** you'll find one of Poznań's most significant memorials, which commemorates the ill-fated workers' protest of 1956 (see boxed text, p276). The monument, consisting of two 20m-tall crosses bound together, was unveiled on 28 June 1981, the 25th anniversary of the strike, at a ceremony attended by more than 100,000 people. It's a huge, evocative landmark, similar to the Monument to the Fallen Shipyard Workers in Gdańsk.

### Museum of Poznań June 1956    MUSEUM

(Muzeum Poznańskiego Czerwca 1956; ul Św Marcin 80/82) Within the grand neo-Romanesque **Kaiserhaus**, built from 1904 to 1910 for German Emperor Wilhelm II, this museum offers details of the massive 1956 strike.

### National Museum    MUSEUM

(Muzeum Narodowe; www.mnp.art.pl; al Marcinkowskiego 9; adult/concession 12/8zł, Sat free; ☺9am-3pm Tue-Thu, noon-9pm Fri, 11am-6pm

## STRIKING OUT

The June 1956 industrial strike in Poznań was the first mass protest in the Soviet bloc, breaking out just three years after Stalin's death.

It originated in the city's largest industrial plant, the Cegielski metalworks (then named after Stalin), which produced railway stock. When the workers demanded the refund of an unfairly charged tax, the factory management refused and simply threw the workers' delegates out of the meeting room. This sparked a spontaneous strike the next day, in which the metalworkers, joined by workers from other local industrial plants, headed for Plac Mickiewicza (then named Plac Stalina).

The 100,000-strong crowd that gathered (a quarter of the city's total population) demanded 'bread and freedom', insisting that changes had to be introduced to improve working conditions, and requested that authorities come and discuss the issue. The demonstration was disregarded by city officials.

Matters soon got out of hand. The angry crowd stormed police headquarters and the Communist Party building, and released 257 prisoners from jail after disarming the guards. Shortly afterwards, a battle for the secret-police headquarters broke out, and it was there that the bloodshed began when police started firing at people surrounding the building. Tanks were introduced into the action, and troops were hastily brought from Wrocław and told they were there to pacify a German riot.

Fierce street battles continued for the whole night and part of the next day, resulting in a total of at least 76 dead and 900 wounded. More than 300 people were arrested, 58 of whom were indicted.

These figures make the protest the most tragic in communist Poland, yet it was underreported and for a long time underestimated. The historic importance of the revolt has only recently been appreciated and given the status it deserves, as an event on a par with the internationally famous shipyard strikes in Gdańsk.

Sat & Sun) Extensive collection of Polish and European art displayed in numerous rooms. Polish painting of the last two centuries is represented by almost all the big names, including Jan Matejko, Stanisław Wyspiański and Jacek Malczewski. Look out for the distinctive work of Tadeusz Makowski, a 20th-century artist who created curious human figures from basic geometric shapes. An older noteworthy curiosity is the museum's collection of coffin portraits.

**Palm House**　　　　　　　　　　GARDENS
(Palmiarnia; www.palmiarnia.poznan.pl in Polish; ul Matejki 18; adult/concession 7/5zł; ⏰9am-5pm Tue-Sun) A short walk from the main train station along ul Głogowska, Park Wilsona contains one of the biggest greenhouses in Europe. Constructed in 1910, it houses many thousands of species of tropical and subtropical plants, including the continent's largest cactus collection and its tallest bamboo trees.

### NORTH OF THE OLD TOWN
**Monument to the Poznań Army**　　MONUMENT
(Pomnik Armii Poznań; Plac Niepodległości) This stark modern monument 500m north of the Old Town is dedicated to the local armed force that resisted the German invasion of 1939 for almost two weeks. It's just opposite the sloping **Cemetery of the Meritorious**, the oldest existing graveyard in the city (1810).

**Citadel Park**　　　　　　　　　　PARK
(Wzgórze Cytadela) A large park laid out on what was once a massive Prussian fortress. It was involved in one major battle, when the Germans defended themselves for four weeks in 1945; as a result it was destroyed apart from a few fragments.

Today Citadel Park incorporates two museums: the **Poznań Citadel Museum** (Muzeum Cytadeli Poznańskiej; adult/concession 4/2zł, Fri free; ⏰9am-4pm Tue-Sat, 10am-4pm Sun) and the **Poznań Army Museum** (Muzeum Armii Poznań; adult/concession 4/2zł, Fri free; ⏰9am-4pm Tue-Sat, 10am-4pm Sun). There are also cemeteries for Polish, Soviet, British and Commonwealth soldiers, all on the southern slopes of the hill.

### OSTRÓW TUMSKI
To the east, over the Warta River, is the island of Ostrów Tumski. You're walking

through deep history here, the place where Poznań was founded, and with it the Polish state. The original 9th-century settlement was gradually transformed into an oval stronghold surrounded by wood-and-earth ramparts, with an early stone palace. Mieszko I added a cathedral and further fortifications, and by the end of the 10th century Poznań was the most powerful stronghold in the country.

In the 13th century, when Poznań had spread beyond the island and the newly designed town was laid out, Ostrów Tumski lost its trade and administrative importance, but remained the residence of the Church authorities.

### Cathedral                            CHURCH
(www.katedra.archpoznan.org.pl in Polish; ul Ostrów Tumski 17; admission free) Ostrów Tumski's quiet ecclesiastical quarter is dominated by Poznań's monumental, double-towered cathedral. Basically Gothic with additions from later periods, most notably the Baroque tops of the towers, the cathedral was badly damaged in 1945 and took 11 years to rebuild.

The aisles and the ambulatory are ringed by a dozen chapels containing numerous tombstones. The most famous of these is the **Golden Chapel** behind the high altar, its golden ceiling decorated with various saints. Dating from the 15th century, the chapel was completely rebuilt in the 1830s as the mausoleum of the first two Polish rulers, Mieszko I and Bolesław Chrobry. Enveloped in Byzantine-style decoration are the double tomb of the two monarchs on one side and their bronze statues on the other.

The rulers' original burial site was the **crypt** (adult/concession 3/1.50zł), accessible from the back of the left-hand aisle. Apart from the fragments of what are thought to have been their tombs, you can see the relics of the first pre-Romanesque cathedral dating from 968 and of the subsequent Romanesque building from the second half of the 11th century, along with dozens of coins tossed in by more recent Polish visitors. A diorama explains the development of the cathedral over the centuries.

### Archdiocesan Museum              MUSEUM
(Muzeum Archidiecezjalne; www.muzeum.poznan.pl in Polish; ul Lubrańskiego 1; adult/concession 6/4zł; ◷10am-5pm Tue-Fri, 9am-3pm Sat) This museum north of the cathedral is located within the former Lubrański Academy, the first high school in Poznań (1518). Within its walls you'll find a collection of sacred art from the 12th century onwards.

### Cathedral Island Heritage Centre   MUSEUM
(Interaktywne Centrum Historii Ostrowa Tumskiego; www.trakt.poznan.pl; ul Gdańska) At time of research, planning was underway for this cutting-edge multimedia museum which will tell the tale of the island's eventful history via holograms and other technological trickery. It'll be located opposite the island's eastern shore and will be linked by a footbridge. It should be open in 2013; check with the tourist offices for construction updates, and details of entry fees and opening hours.

### LAKE MALTA
### Malta Park Railway                  RAILWAY
(Kolejka Parkowa Maltanka; www.mpk.poznan.pl /turystyka/maltanka; ul Jana Pawła II 1; adult/concession 5/3.50zł; ◷10am-6.30pm May-Sep) East of Ostrów Tumski on the far bank of the river, beyond the Rondo Śródka, you'll find the terminus of this tourist railway. It runs miniature trains along the shoreline of the 70-hectare artificial **Lake Malta** (Jezioro Maltańskie), a favourite summer spot for families, picnickers and boating enthusiasts.

The railway terminates at the **New Zoo** (Nowe Zoo; www.zoo.poznan.pl in Polish; ul Krańcowa 81; adult/concession 20/10zł; ◷9am-7pm). This sprawling institution covers 116 hectares at the eastern end of the lake, and houses diverse species including Baltic grey seals in a leafy pine-forest environment.

## 🏃 Activities

If you're challenged for time in Poznań, a good way to get a quick feel for the city's history is to follow one or more of the six self-guided walking routes, outlined in free brochures available from the tourist office. A more ambitious stroll is the **Royal-Imperial Route**, mapped out in another free brochure, which takes you from the shores of Lake Malta to the city's west, passing dozens of sights along the way.

Poznań's flat terrain is also good for cycling, with plenty of bike trails through the city and beyond. To get started, ask the tourist office for both the Poznań cycling map (9zł) and the free brochure *Cycle Trails in Wielkopolska*. Bicycles can be hired from **Malta Bike** (www.maltabike.pl in Polish; ul Jana Pawła II; ◷10am-9pm Apr-Oct) at the western end of Lake Malta, for 7zł per hour or 30zł per day.

WIELKOPOLSKA POZNAŃ

# Poznań

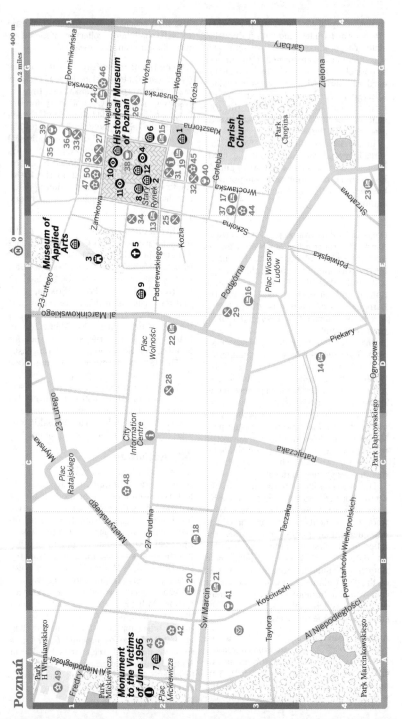

**Monument to the Victims of June 1956**

**Museum of Applied Arts**

**Historical Museum of Poznań**

**Parish Church**

Park H Wieniawskiego

Park Mickiewicza

Plac Mickiewicza

Al Niepodległości

Fredry

23 Lutego

Mlyńska

Plac Ratajskiego

Mielżyńskiego

27 Grudnia

Św Marcin

Kościuszki

Taczaka

Taylora

Powstańców Wielkopolskich

Ratajczaka

Al Niepodległości

Park Marcinkowskiego

Park Dąbrowskiego

Ogrodowa

Plac Wolności

City Information Centre

23 Lutego

al Marcinkowskiego

Paderewskiego

Kozia

Zamkowa

Szkolna

Wrocławska

Gołębia

Podgórna

Plac Wiosny Ludów

Piekary

Półwiejska

Strzałowa

Zielona

Park Chopina

Klasztorna

Stary Rynek

Wielka

Szewska

Dominikańska

Woźna

Ślusarska

Kozia

Wodna

Garbary

0            400 m
0            0.2 miles

N

# Poznań

##  Festivals & Events

Poznań's trade fairs are its pride and joy, though few are of interest to casual visitors. The main ones take place in January, June, September and October, with dozens of other trade shows of varying size throughout the year. July, August and December are almost free of fairs.

**Poznań Jazz Festival**       JAZZ

A range of local and international jazz performers strut their stuff at various venues. Held in March.

**St John's Fair**       CRAFT, ANTIQUES

Held on the Stary Rynek in June. Buy craft items and local foods from the stalls, and take in street-artist performances.

**Malta Festival**       THEATRE

(www.malta-festival.pl) Fringe and alternative theatre, in July. This unconventional celebration of the arts takes place across the city, often in squares and streets, as well as on the shores of Lake Malta.

**Tzadik Poznań Festival**       JEWISH

(www.tzadikpoznanfestival.pl) Annual celebration of Jewish culture, with an emphasis on modern interpretations of music, film, design and poetry. Held in July.

**Wieniawski International
Violin Competition**       CLASSICAL MUSIC

(www.wieniawski.pl) Named after ace violinist Henryk Wieniawski (1835–80) and held every five years in October (next due in 2016).

**St Martin's Day** PARADE

Parades and festivities descend on the town on 11 November, but the highlight is the baking and eating of special St Martin's sweet croissants.

## 🛏 Sleeping

Try not to arrive in Poznań during one of the city's numerous trade fairs – they wreak havoc on the city's accommodation range, doubling prices and reducing available beds. You can check the dates of the fairs online at www.mtp.pl.

Outside trade fair periods, room prices drop significantly on weekends. Prices given here are standard weekday rates for 'off-fair' periods. The tourist offices are knowledgeable about lodging options and can help you find a bed. In addition, the private agency **Biuro Zakwaterowania Przemysław** (☑61 866 3560; www.przemyslaw.com.pl; ul Głogowska 16; ☉10am-6pm Mon-Fri, to 2pm Sat), located opposite the train station, can organise accommodation in private rooms.

**Brovaria** HOTEL €€

(☑61 858 6868; www.brovaria.pl; Stary Rynek 73/74; s 250-290zł, d 290-330zł; ✳🛜) This multitalented hotel also operates as a restaurant and bar, but most impressive is its in-house boutique brewery, whose operations you can view within the building. The elegant rooms have tasteful dark timber tones, and some have views onto the Rynek.

**Hotel Stare Miasto** HOTEL €€

(☑61 663 6242; www.hotelstaremiasto.pl; ul Rybaki 36; s/d 215/340zł; P✳🛜) Stylish value-for-money hotel with a tasteful chandeliered foyer and spacious breakfast room. Rooms can be small but are clean and bright with lovely starched white sheets. Some upper rooms have skylights in place of windows.

**Frolic Goats Hostel** HOSTEL €

(☑61 852 4411; www.frolicgoatshostel.com; ul Wrocławska 16/6; dm 39-60zł, r 190zł; 🛜) Named after the feisty goats who fight above the town hall clock, this popular hostel is aimed squarely at the international backpacker. The pleasant green lounge complements tidy, reasonably uncrowded dorms, and bike hire is available for 30zł per day. Enter from ul Jaskółcza.

**Rezydencja Solei** HOTEL €€

(☑61 855 7351; www.hotel-solei.pl; ul Szewska 2; s/d/ste 199/299/389zł; 🛜) Temptingly close to the Rynek, this tiny hotel offers small but cosy rooms in an old-fashioned residential style, with wallpaper and timber furniture striking a homely note. The attic suite is amazingly large and can accommodate up to four people.

**Blow Up Hall 50 50** HOTEL €€€

(☑61 657 9980; www.blowuphall5050.com; ul Kościuszki 42; r 880-1400zł; P✳🛜) Wild art hotel housed within the solid ex-brewery walls of the Stary Browar shopping mall, 750m south of the Rynek. Each room has an individual hyper-modern design whose colour scheme can range from dazzling white to gleaming black, with shiny angular furniture and fittings. The restaurant and bar are equally impressive.

**Capital Apartments** APARTMENTS €€

(☑61 852 5300; www.toppoznanhotels.com; ul Piekary 16; apt €50-80; 🛜) This company maintains a number of modern apartments dotted around the city centre, all within walking distance of the Stary Rynek. They're a good-value option if you're tired of hotel breakfasts and want to prepare your own food, or if the lack of laundrettes in Poland is making you desperate for a washing machine.

**Hotel Royal** HOTEL €€

(☑61 858 2300; www.hotel-royal.com.pl; ul Św Marcin 71; s/d/ste 272/336/400zł; ✳🛜) Tasteful terracotta tones predominate in this smart, refined hotel, situated on the main road leading into the centre. Opt for the spacious suite for extra elbow room, or just hang around the lobby perusing the photos of famous Polish TV stars who've laid their heads here.

**Hostel Cameleon** HOSTEL €

(☑61 639 3041; ul Świętosławska 12; dm 55zł, s 120-175zł, d 165-200zł; 🛜) Centrally located hostel offering budget accommodation within an interior of a contemporary design, featuring earthy tones. There's a spacious kitchen and lounge, and all beds have reading lamps and lockers. The cheaper private rooms have shared bathrooms, and there's also a washing machine available.

**Fusion Hostel** HOSTEL €

(☑61 852 1230; www.fusionhostel.pl; ul Św Marcin 66/72; dm 55-69zł, s 119-180zł, d 199zł; 🛜) Hostel with a view, perched on the 7th floor of a scuffed commercial building. The decor is modern and bright, and guests have access to a lounge, a kitchen and bicycle hire

(20zł per day). The lift is hidden behind the security booth in the foyer.

### Don Prestige Residence
APARTMENTS €€

(☑61 859 0590; www.donprestige.com; ul Św Marcin 2; apt from 380zł; 🅿✳🛜) Some hotels try to make you feel like you're at home – the Don Prestige makes you wish your home was a bit more like this. Its luxury serviced apartments come with stylish interiors, kitchens and more mod cons than a New York penthouse.

### Hotel Rzymski
HOTEL €€

(☑61 852 8121; www.hotelrzymski.pl; al Marcinkowskiego 22; s/d 260/325zł; @) If walls could talk, this hotel would have a story worth listening to. It began life as the German-owned Hotel de Rome, changed to Polish ownership, was used in WWII as a hotel for the German military, then became Polish-owned once more, still with the same name (Rzym is Rome in Polish). The rooms are comfortable and the multilingual staff helpful.

### Dom Polonii
ROOMS €€

(☑61 852 7121; poznan@swp.org.pl; Stary Rynek 51; s/d 140/230zł) Dating from 1488, the Dom Polonii is tucked into a corner of Poznań's market square, offering just two double rooms to anyone who's organised enough to book sufficiently in advance. The only way you could get more central would be by tunnelling under the town hall.

### Hotel Lech
HOTEL €€

(☑61 853 0151; www.hotel-lech.poznan.pl; ul Św Marcin 74; s/d 200/295zł; 🛜) A comfortable choice, with basic fittings but high ceilings. It's located midway between the train station and the Old Town, and the accommodating staff are used to dealing with tourists. Flash your ISIC card for a substantial discount.

### Hotel Mercure Poznań
HOTEL €€€

(☑61 855 8000; www.mercure.com; ul Roosevelta 20; s/d from 400/500zł; 🅿✳🛜) In a gigantic modern building off a busy main road 500m west of the Kaiserhaus, this hotel offers all the expected facilities for business travellers, including a gym, a restaurant and a bar. The 'big box' look is softened by musical designs on bedspreads and curtains, a reference to the nearby Philharmonic Hall. Breakfast is a breathtaking additional 70zł.

### Hotel Ibis
HOTEL €€

(☑61 858 4400; www.ibishotel.com; ul Kazimierza Wielkiego 23; r 245zł; 🅿✳🛜) A typical hotel in this reliable business chain, Poznań's Ibis offers a multitude of predictably well maintained rooms, an easy 700m walk southeast of the Rynek. If you don't like surprises, this is a good place to hang your hat.

### Camping Malta
CAMPGROUND €

(☑61 876 6203; www.campingmalta.poznan.pl; ul Krańcowa 98; camping per person 15zł, per tent 12zł, s/d 150/230zł; 🅿) Malta is the best of Poznań's camping grounds and the closest to the centre – it's on the northeastern shore of Lake Malta, 3km east of the Old Town. Heated bungalows provide good all-year shelter.

## 🍴 Eating

Poznań's sophisticated dining scene centres on the Old Town, whose narrow streets contain eateries offering every cuisine imaginable.

### 🔺 TOP CHOICE Warung Bali
INDONESIAN €€

(ul Żydowska 1; mains 20-49zł; 🥢) Excellent Indonesian restaurant not far from the main square, with a tastefully decorated interior full of blonde wood furniture, hanging gold cloth and shadow puppets. Indonesian music plays softly while you order *gado gado*, satays, *nasi goreng* and other delicious classics from the former East Indies.

### Tapas Bar
TAPAS €€

(Stary Rynek 60; mains 31-54zł; ⊙9am-late) This atmospheric place dishes up authentic tapas and Spanish wine in a room lined with intriguing bric-a-brac, including jars of stuffed olives, Mediterranean-themed artwork and bright red candles. Most tapas dishes are 21zł to 25zł, so forget the mains and share with friends. There's a breakfast menu too.

### Cymes
JEWISH €€

(☑61 851 6638; ul Woźna 2/3; mains 26-38zł; ⊙4pm-late) If you're tired of pork for dinner, this ambient Jewish restaurant is the logical place to go. The interior is warm and cosy, done out like a residential dining room with ceramic plates on the walls. On the menu are various poultry and fish dishes, including a whole goose for eight people, to be ordered 24 hours beforehand.

### Wiejskie Jadło
POLISH €€

(Stary Rynek 77; mains 15-49zł) Compact Polish restaurant hidden a short distance back from the Rynek along ul Franciszkańska. It offers a range of filling dishes including *pierogi* (dumplings), soups, and pork in all its varied possibilities, served in a homely rustic space with flowers on the table.

### Shivaz
INDIAN €€

(ul Podgórna 6; mains 16-38zł; ) Forget the usual flocked wallpaper – this modern Indian restaurant is done out in an east-meets-nightclub style, with dark purple decor, black timber furniture and couch seating. The set menu for two is good value at 80zł. And here's a historical curiosity – interwar German president Paul von Hindenburg was born in this building in 1847.

### Gospoda Pod Koziołkami
POLISH €€

(Stary Rynek 95; mains 12-27zł) Homely bistro within Gothic arches on the ground floor, and a grill in the cellar. The menu is crammed with tasty Polish standards, including some distinctive Wielkopolska specialities.

### Trattoria Valpolicella
ITALIAN €€

(ul Wrocławska 7; mains 26-69zł; ⊙1-11pm; 𝄫) This stayer in the turbulent Poznań dining scene serves a wide variety of pasta and other Italian specialities, well suited to a glass of vino, in convincingly rustic Mediterranean surroundings. Look for the faded Italian flag which makes you think of Ireland.

### Restauracja Delicja
FRENCH, ITALIAN €€€

(Plac Wolności 5; mains 50-85zł; ⊙1-10pm) One of Poznań's top restaurants, tucked away off Plac Wolności, with its own miniature courtyard and an illustrious reputation for top-notch international cuisine along French-Italian lines. Refinement and elegance are *de rigueur*.

### Bar Wegetariański
VEGETARIAN €

(ul Rybaki 10; mains 11-17zł; ⊙11am-6pm Mon-Fri, to 3pm Sat; 𝄫) This cheap eatery 500m south of the Rynek offers tasty meat-free dishes, including its signature wholemeal crêpes stuffed with mushrooms and cabbage. It's in a homely little space, with dishes prepared in a domestic-style open kitchen behind the counter.

### Sioux
AMERICAN €€

(Stary Rynek 93; mains 21-50zł) As you'd expect, this is a 'Western'-themed place, complete with waiters dressed as cowboys. Oddly named dishes such as 'Apache Trout' are on the menu, along with lots of steaks, ribs, grills and enchiladas.

### Stary Browar Food Court
INTERNATIONAL €

(ul Półwiejska 42; ⊙9am-9pm) The dining section of this gigantic shopping mall 750m south of the Rynek offers decent food in chic surrounds, including Chinese, Italian and seafood dishes. There are also cafes scattered through the complex, and the building's spectacular old-meets-new architecture is worth a visit in its own right.

### Bar Mleczny Apetyt
CAFETERIA €

(ul Szkolna 4; mains 4-11zł; ⊙9am-10pm Mon-Sat, 10am-10pm Sun; 𝄫) The latest-closing *bar mleczny* (milk bar) in town enjoys a good, central location. The food is exactly what you'd expect, and none the worse for that, with *naleśniki* (crêpes) choices galore.

## 🍷 Drinking

Once you've done the rounds of the beer gardens on the Rynek, there are plenty of places elsewhere in town worth seeking out for a drink. Ul Woźna and ul Nowowiejskiego have plenty of student-oriented bars, while ul Żydowska caters for a more mature audience and the southern Old Town has a bit of everything.

### TOP CHOICE Ptasie Radio
CAFE, BAR

(ul Kościuszki 74; ⊙8am-midnight Mon-Fri, 10am-midnight Sat & Sun) This funky drinking hole, 'Bird Radio', is a retro riot of chipped wooden tables, pot plants and bird images everywhere along its shelves and walls (the name comes from a famous Polish poem). It's a mellow place for a coffee or something stronger.

### Proletaryat
BAR

(ul Wrocławska 9; ⊙1pm-late Mon-Sat, 3pm-late Sun) Bright red communist-nostalgia bar with an array of socialist-era gear on the walls, including military insignia, portraits of Brezhnev and Marx, and the obligatory bust of Lenin in the window. Play 'spot the communist leader' while sipping a boutique beer from the Czarnków Brewery.

### Post Office Café
CAFE

(Stary Rynek 25/29; ⊙10am-11pm) Housed in one of the colourful Fish Sellers' Houses, this compact cafe has an interesting gimmick – it sells stamps and postcards, so you can write to loved ones while sipping coffee. There's even a posting box on the premises.

### PRL
BAR

(ul Żydowska 11; ⊙6pm-late) Not easy to find even with a map and compass, this tiny subterranean bar is decorated with communist-era memorabilia, from uniforms to chunky appliances. It's grungy but fun. Enter through the narrow door on ul Mokra.

**Atmosfera** CAFE, BAR
(ul Mokra 2; ☺noon-11pm; 🛜) If you're on the run from the Foreign Legion, or just trying to escape the hordes in the Stary Rynek, you could do worse than head for this hidden-away cafe in tiny ul Mokra. The decor is a faded blue showcase of floral wreaths and abstract art, just worn enough to give it character. To become even more unfindable, head to the upstairs room.

**Bodega** CAFE, BAR
(ul Żydowska 4; ☺11am-11pm Sun-Thu, to midnight Fri & Sat) On a street populated with cafes, Bodega's sleek modern lines stand out. The geometrically sharp interior is composed of mellow chocolate and gold tones, with candles on the tables, and chatting locals enjoying the relaxed vibe. Good coffee is accompanied by snacks and sweet temptations.

**Czarna Owca** BAR, CLUB
(ul Jaskółcza 13; ☺noon-late Mon-Fri, 5pm-late Sat) Calling your bar the 'Black Sheep' hardly encourages good behaviour, so sipping a quiet pint is seldom on the agenda here. When you've finished boozing in the dark, intimate bar, join the herd on the downstairs dance floor for DJs playing house, pop, rock, Latin or retro sounds, depending on the night.

## ☆ Entertainment

Poznań's comprehensive monthly *iks* (4.10zł) contains listings on everything from museums to outdoor activities, with a short summary of the most important events in English. It's available from the tourist offices. The free monthly *Aktivist* can also be helpful, especially for nightlife, and the free *In Your Pocket* pulls no punches with its colourful descriptions of local clubs.

### Live Music & Clubs
**Johnny Rocker** LIVE MUSIC
(ul Wielka 9; ☺5pm-late) This super-smooth basement venue with a curvy bar is crammed with happy drinkers sitting cabaret-style in front of a stage that features live blues, jazz or rock acts every weekend. If the sounds are overwhelming, you can always retreat to the stylish 'red room'.

**Lizard King** LIVE MUSIC
(Stary Rynek 86; ☺noon-late) Simultaneously happening and laid-back, this venue is in prime position on the Rynek. Friendly crowds sit drinking and eating in the split-level space, casting the occasional glance at the lizard over the bar. There's often live music at night, including rock, jazz and blues.

**Van Diesel Music Club** CLUB
(Stary Rynek 88; ☺9pm-late) Happening venue on the main square, with DJs varying their offerings between pop, house, R&B, soul and dance. Given the variety, you're sure to find a night that suits you here.

**Club FBI** CLUB
(ul Jaskółcza 15a; ☺9pm-late) Though it looks seriously official from the outside, you don't have to be Mulder or Scully to gain access to this lively club's below-ground dance floor. Drinks are served by bar staff in law-enforcement get-up.

**Deep** CLUB
(ul Wrocławska 5; ☺8pm-late Tue-Sat) This underground den is a hotbed of sportswear, short skirts and bumpin' black music. It's the kind of place that's good for rowdy nights out with your mates.

**Blue Note Jazz Club** JAZZ
(ul Kościuszki 76/78) Major live jazz spot and occasional dance club within the Kaiserhaus. It hosts regular concerts and jam sessions by local groups, with occasional big-name gigs.

### Classical Music, Opera & Theatre
**Philharmonic Hall** CLASSICAL MUSIC
(Filharmonia; ☏61 853 6935; www.filharmonia.poznan.pl; ul Św Marcin 81) Just west of the Kaiserhaus, this musical institution holds concerts at least weekly by the house symphony orchestra. Poznań also has Poland's best boys' choir, the Poznańskie Słowiki (Poznań Nightingales), who can be heard here.

**Teatr Wielki** OPERA, BALLET
(☏61 659 0280; www.opera.poznan.pl; ul Fredry 9) The usual stage for opera, ballet and various visiting performances.

**Teatr Polski** THEATRE
(☏61 852 5628; www.teatr-polski.pl; ul 27 Grudnia 8/10) The Polish Theatre is Poznań's main repertory stage.

**Centrum Kultury Zamek** CONCERT VENUE
(Castle Cultural Centre; www.zamek.poznan.pl; ul
Św Marcin 80/82) Active cultural hub located
in the Kaiserhaus, hosting cinema, art and
music events.

## ℹ Information

### Internet Access

In addition to the following providers, there's
free wireless access available in the Stary
Rynek, though it can be a little flaky.

**Adax** (ul Półwiejska 28; per hr 4zł; ⊙8am-9pm
Mon-Fri, 10am-9pm Sat, noon-9pm Sun) Near
the Stary Browar shopping mall.

**Salon Gier** (ul Dworcowa 1; per hr 4.50zł; ⊙24hr)
Beneath the main train station concourse.

### Post

**Main post office** (ul Kościuszki 75; ⊙7am-8pm
Mon-Fri, 8am-3pm Sat)

### Tourist Information

**City Information Centre** (☏61 851 9645;
www.cim.poznan.pl; ul Ratajczaka 44; ⊙10am-
7pm Mon-Fri, 10am-5pm Sat)

**Glob-Tour** (☏61 866 0667; www.globtourfb
.poznan.pl; Poznań Główny, ul Dworcowa 1;
⊙24hr) In the main train station.

**Tourist office** (☏61 852 6156; www.poznan.pl;
Stary Rynek 59/60; ⊙9am-8pm Mon-Fri,
10am-8pm Sat & Sun)

### Travel Agencies

**Almatur** (☏61 855 7633; ul Ogrodowa 9/43)

**LOT** (☏801 703 703; www.lot.com) At the
airport.

## ℹ Getting There & Away

**AIR** Poznań's **airport** (www.airport-poznan.com
.pl; ul Bukowksa 285) is in the western suburb of
Ławica, 7km from the centre. There are flights
from Poznań to Warsaw (four to five daily) via
LOT; Barcelona (five weekly) on Ryanair and
Wizz Air; Bristol (twice weekly) via Ryanair;
Copenhagen (daily) via SAS; Dublin (four weekly)
via Ryanair; Edinburgh (twice weekly) on
Ryanair; Frankfurt (twice daily) on LOT or
Lufthansa; Liverpool (twice weekly) via Ryanair;
London (twice daily) on Ryanair or Wizz Air;
Munich (four daily) via LOT or Lufthansa; Prague
(daily) via Czech Airlines; and Stockholm (three
weekly) on Wizz Air. For other destinations,
check the airport's website.

**BUS** The bus terminal is about 750m east of
the train station. Buses run regularly to Kórnik
(10zł, 40 minutes). On longer routes, you could
also use buses to get to Kalisz (26zł, 2½ hours,
10 daily) and Zielona Góra (33zł, three hours,
five daily).

**TRAIN** Poznań is a busy railway hub. From
Poznań Główny train station there are 15 daily
trains to Warsaw, including four TLK trains (54zł,
3½ hours) and four Express InterCity trains
(119zł, 3¼ hours). Equally frequent services run
to Wrocław (38zł, three hours), Szczecin (44zł,
2¾ hours) and Kraków (59zł, 7¾ hours).

Trains to Gdańsk (54zł, 5½ hours, six daily)
and Toruń (37zł, 2½ hours, 10 daily) all pass

---

## HAVE BIKE, WILL TRAVEL

Since communism fell and took its travel restrictions with it, Poles have been making
up for lost time, journeying to more far-flung locales each year. But they'd have to put in
some serious trekking to catch up with their compatriot Kazimierz Nowak.

In 1931, this Poznań resident fetched up in Tripoli, Libya, as a press correspondent,
covering the Italian military campaign there. When his colleagues returned to Europe,
however, Nowak stayed behind. He had a dream: to travel the entire length of Africa by
bicycle.

On 4 November 1931 he set off, passing through Egypt before heading south. On his
journey, he often shared stories with locals around their campfires, and cast a critical eye
on colonial settlers from Europe. He also took photographs, which he sold to Polish and
German newspapers to supplement his funds.

Nowak reached Cape Town in May 1934. Then, amazingly, he turned his bike around
and rode the entire length of the continent again, on a western route this time. In
November 1936, five years after his odyssey had begun, he reached the Mediterranean
at Algiers. He had covered 40,000km on bicycle and foot.

Returning to Poznań, Nowak wrote a book about his exploits and gave ethnographic
lectures at the Apollo Cinema, while planning a new expedition in Asia. It was not to be:
on 13 October 1937 Kazimierz Nowak died of malaria, no doubt contracted on his epic
trek. The great traveller was gone, but not forgotten – nowadays you can see a plaque
commemorating his journey, with a map of the route, on the far wall of the concourse at
Poznań Główny train station.

through Gniezno (16zł, 40 minutes, hourly). Six trains depart for Zielona Góra daily (35zł, two hours). There are also five daily trains to Wolsztyn (16zł, 1¾ hours), including steam trains (see boxed text, p287).

Five international trains run to Berlin daily, including three EuroCity services taking just 2½ hours. There's also one direct train to Cologne each day (nine hours).

## ❶ Getting Around

**TO/FROM THE AIRPORT** Poznań's airport is accessible by express bus L from the main train station (4.40zł, 20 minutes), which travels via the 'Bałtyk' stop near Rondo Kaponiera. Buses 48, 59 and night bus 242 also head to the airport from the 'Bałtyk' stop (3zł, 25 minutes). A taxi should cost around 20zł to 30zł (20 minutes).

**PUBLIC TRANSPORT** Tickets for the city's trams and buses cost 2zł for a 15-minute ride, 3zł for half an hour and 4zł for up to one hour. Approximate journey times are posted at stops. A day ticket costs 12zł.

# AROUND POZNAŃ

## Kórnik

POP 6800

The town of Kórnik, 20km southeast of Poznań, is proof that mad German kings didn't have a monopoly on eccentric castle design. Its unconventional castle was built by the powerful Górka family in the 15th century. Nowadays it's more like a mansion than a castle; anyone who's visited a stately home in the English countryside will experience déjà vu (it even has tasteful tea rooms outside the main gate).

Its present-day appearance dates from the mid-19th century, when its owner, Tytus Działyński, gave the castle a somewhat outlandish mock-Gothic character, partly based on a design by German architect Karl Friedrich Schinkel. The building now looks as though two halves of completely different castles were spliced together, perhaps by force, and provides some interesting photos from varying angles.

The interior, too, was extensively (though more consistently) remodelled to provide a plush family home and accommodate the owner's vast art collection. On the 1st floor a spectacular Moorish hall was created (clearly influenced by the Alhambra in Granada) as a memorable setting for the display of armour and military accessories. The collection

was expanded by Działyński's son Jan and his nephew Władysław Zamoyski; the latter donated the castle and its contents to the state in 1924.

The castle luckily survived the war and, miraculously, so did its contents. Part of it is now open as a **museum** (www.bkpan.poznan .pl; ul Zamkowa 5; adult/concession 12/7zł; ◷10am-4pm Tue-Sun Feb-Nov). You can wander through its fully furnished and decorated 19th-century interiors, dotted with items collected by the family. The collection is well presented in a surprisingly light-filled space, and includes some intriguing pieces like elaborately designed furniture, medieval weaponry and centuries-old books, including a copy of Copernicus' masterwork, *De Revolutionibus Orbium Coelestium*.

Behind the castle is a large, English-style park known as the **Arboretum** (www.idpan .poznan.pl; adult/concession 6/4zł; ◷10am-6pm), which was laid out during the castle's reconstruction, and stocked with exotic species of trees and shrubs from Europe's leading nurseries. Today the Arboretum is run by a scientific research institute and has some 2500 plant species and varieties; the best times to visit are May to June and September to October, when the greatest number of specimens come into flower.

Some of the castle's outbuildings are also used for exhibitions. **Galeria Klaudynówka**, a servants' house from 1791, displays contemporary paintings, while the **coach house** on the opposite side of the road holds three London coaches, brought from Paris by Jan Działyński in 1856.

## ❶ Getting There & Away

There's frequent bus transport from Poznań to Kórnik (10zł, 40 minutes), which deposits you at the Rynek in Kórnik, a three-minute walk from the castle. Follow the road as it veers to the right past the town hall and becomes ul Zamkowa.

## Rogalin

POP 700

The tiny village of Rogalin, 12km west of Kórnik, was the seat of yet another Polish aristocratic clan, the Raczyński family, who built a palace here in the closing decades of the 18th century, and lived in it until WWII. Plundered but not damaged during the war, the palace was taken over by the state. In 1991, Count Edward Raczyński, who had been Polish ambassador to Britain at the outbreak of WWII and a leading figure in the Polish government in exile, confirmed the use of the palace as a **National Museum branch** (☑61 813 8030; www.mnp.art.pl; adult/ concession 10/7zł, Wed free; ☺9.30am-4pm Tue-Sat & 10am-6pm Sun).

Less visited than Kórnik's castle and much more Germanic in its appearance, the Rogalin palace consists of a massive, two-storey, Baroque central structure and two modest symmetrical wings linked to the main body by curving galleries, forming a giant horseshoe around a vast forecourt. Within the main house you can peruse an exhibition on the history of the palace and the Raczyński family, and see an exact replica of the London study of Count Raczyński. Entry to the main building involves a compulsory tour; English-language tour guides can be organised in advance for 85zł.

Just beyond the left wing is the **Gallery of Painting** (Galeria Obrazów), an adapted greenhouse displaying Polish and European canvases from the 19th and early 20th centuries. The Polish collection includes some first-class work, with Jacek Malczewski best represented. The dominant work, though, is Jan Matejko's *Joan of Arc*.

In the **coach house**, near the front courtyard, are a dozen old coaches, including Poznań's last horse-drawn cab, and a restaurant.

Opposite the main house is a small French garden, which leads into the larger **English landscaped park**, originally laid out in primeval oak forest. Not much of the park's design can be deciphered today, but the ancient oak trees are still here, some of them centuries old. The three most imposing specimens have been fenced off and baptised with the names Lech, Czech and Rus, after the legendary founders of the Polish, Czech and Russian nations.

One more place to see is the **chapel**, on the eastern outskirts of the village, built in the 1820s to serve as a mausoleum for the Raczyński family. It's a replica of the Roman temple known as the Maison Carrée in Nîmes, southern France.

### ⓘ Getting There & Away

There are several buses each day from Poznań to Rogalin (9zł, 45 minutes). Buses back to Poznań pass through every couple of hours until late afternoon.

# Wielkopolska National Park

Just a few kilometres southwest of Poznań's administrative boundaries is the 76-sq-km **Wielkopolska National Park** (Wielkopolski Park Narodowy; www.wielkopolskipn.pl). About 80% of the park is forest – pine and oak being the dominant species – and its postglacial lakes give it a certain charm.

**Hiking** is the main attraction here, and a good point to start your stroll is the town of Mosina (21km from Poznań), which is served regularly by both train and bus from Poznań. From Mosina, follow the blue-marked trail heading northwest to Osowa Góra (3km). Once you reach small Lake Kociołek, switch to the red trail, which winds southwestwards. After passing another miniature lake, the trail reaches Lake Góreckie, the most beautiful body of water in the park. The trail then skirts the eastern part of the lake and turns northeast to bring you to the town of Puszczykowo, from where trains and buses can take you back to Poznań. It's about a 17km walk altogether, through the most attractive area of the park.

If you want to do more walking, there are four more trails to choose from. Get a copy of the TopMapa *Wielkopolski Park Narodowy* map (scale 1:35,000), which has all the details.

The two towns sit conveniently on the eastern edge of the park, just 4km apart on the Poznań–Wrocław railway line. There are regular slow trains from Poznań Główny to Puszczykowo (5zł, 17 minutes, hourly) and Mosina (6zł, 25 minutes, hourly).

# Morasko

Great balls of fire! Just 10km from the centre of Poznań is the **Morasko Meteorite Reserve** (Reserwat Meteoryt Morasko), one of just two registered impact sites in Europe. The idea of flaming space rock crash-landing in the peaceful forest here may seem bizarre, but that's exactly what happened roughly 10,000 years ago, and eight craters are still clearly visible, some filled with water. The largest is over 100m across and 13m in depth, and while it's overgrown enough not to look like the surface of the moon, the extent of the dent is still pretty impressive.

To get to the reserve you can catch tram 12 or 14 from the train station to the Osiedle

## ALL STEAMED UP

Almost everywhere in Europe, the grand age of steam is over. The steam trains that still operate are confined to picturesque tourist railways, functioning as museum pieces on wheels. But not in the town of Wolsztyn, 65km southwest of Poznań.

Thanks partly to the enthusiasm of British trainspotters, PKP still runs regular steam-train services between Poznań Główny and Wolsztyn. Each day at least one steam train hauls passengers along the route – check at the station for the current timetable (*pociąg parowy* means 'steam train').

In addition to the Poznań services, there's a steam train a day in each direction between Wolsztyn and Leszno, which is also linked directly by rail to Poznań. PKP also operates special one-off steam services throughout the warmer months, including an annual Wolsztyn–Wrocław train.

So where do those train enthusiasts come in? They're the eager customers of the **Wolsztyn Experience** (☏+44 1628 524876; www.wolsztyn.co.uk), a steam-train course which instructs would-be drivers and gives them a chance to actually drive a train on its regular run.

Also, in May each year Wolsztyn is home to the Steam Parade, a festival featuring steam locomotives from across Europe. And if too much steam is never enough, the town also offers a steam-train museum, within its working engine depot south of the train station at ul Fabryczna 1.

Sobieskiego tram terminus and follow the 4km walking trail, or change to bus 88 to Morasko village and pick up the trail from there, about 1km from the reserve.

# EASTERN WIELKOPOLSKA

## Gniezno

POP 69,500

Appearances can be deceptive – on first glance at the relaxed centre of Gniezno (*gnyez*-no), you'd never guess the huge part it played in the founding of Poland. Its Old Town, attractively renovated on the 1000th anniversary (in 2000) of the establishment of the city's historic bishopric, is a charming collection of winding streets and colourful, slope-roofed buildings centred on a pleasant cobblestone square and the city's famous cathedral. Its historic cathedral is well worth a visit, and it is also a great place to catch your breath after the hustle of Poznań.

It may be slow-paced now, but in its day Gniezno has been both a royal and a religious seat. It is also considered to be the cradle of the Polish state, as it was here that the various tribes of the region were first united as Poles in the 10th century. In a key development, Duke Mieszko I is thought to have been baptised here in 966, thus raising the autonomous region of Wielkopolska from obscurity to the rank of Christianised nations. Later, in 1025, Bolesław Chrobry was crowned in the local cathedral as the first Polish king.

The town has retained its status as the seat of the Church of Poland and is still the formal ecclesiastical capital, despite the fact that the archbishops are only occasional guests these days.

## ◉ Sights

**Cathedral** CHURCH

(ul Łaskiego 9; admission free; ⊘9am-5pm Mon-Sat, 1-6pm Sun) Gniezno's history and character are inextricably intertwined with its cathedral, an imposing, double-towered, brick Gothic structure. The present church was constructed after the 1331 destruction of the previous Romanesque cathedral by the Teutonic Knights (see boxed text, p331). It changed a lot in later periods: chapels sprouted all around it, and the interior was redecorated in successive styles. After considerable damage in WWII, it was rebuilt according to the original Gothic structure.

Its focal point is the elaborate silver **sarcophagus of St Adalbert**, which is in the chancel. The Baroque coffin was the work of Peter van der Rennen and was made in 1662 in Gdańsk. It's topped with the semi-reclining figure of the saint, who looks remarkably lively considering his unfortunate demise.

# Gniezno

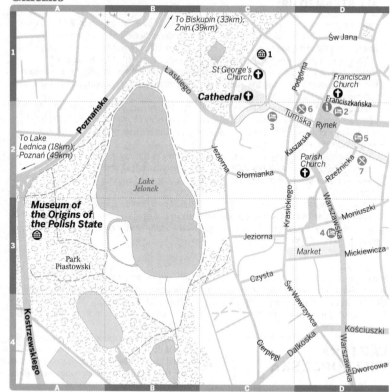

Adalbert was a Bohemian bishop who passed through Gniezno in 997, on a missionary trip to convert the Prussians, a heathen Baltic tribe inhabiting what is now Masuria in northeastern Poland. The pagans were less than enthusiastic about accepting the new faith and terminated the bishop's efforts by cutting off his head. Bolesław Chrobry recovered the bishop's body, paying its weight in gold, then buried it in Gniezno's cathedral in 999. In the same year, Pope Sylvester canonised the martyr. This contributed to Gniezno's elevation to an archbishopric a year later, and also led to the placing of several important memorials to the saint in the church.

One example is the pair of Romanesque **bronze doors** from about 1175, in the back of the right-hand (southern) aisle, at the entrance from the porch. Undeniably one of the best examples of Romanesque art in Europe, the doors depict, in bas-relief, 18 scenes from the life of St Adalbert.

Framing the doors is the exquisite 15th-century **Gothic portal** with the scene of the Last Judgement in its tympanum. In the opposite porch, right across the nave, is another elaborate **Gothic portal**, dating from the same period, this one with the scene of the Crucifixion in its tympanum.

The nearby entrance in the back wall of the church leads downstairs to the **basement**, where the relics of the previous Romanesque cathedral can be seen, along with the Gothic tombstones of the bishops.

Also on this back wall are two carved tombstones. To the left is the red-marble **tomb of Primate Zbigniew Oleśnicki**, attributed to Veit Stoss, and to the right is the late-15th-century bronze **tomb of Archbishop Jakub** from Sienna. Also note an expressive wooden crucifix from around 1440, placed high on the rood beam at the entrance to the chancel.

## Gniezno

**◎ Top Sights**

**◎ Sights**

**⊜ Sleeping**

**⊗ Eating**

**Museum of the Origins of the Polish State** MUSEUM

(Muzeum Początków Państwa Polskiego; www.mppp.pl in Polish; ul Kostrzewskiego 1; adult/concession 5.50/3.50zł; ⊙10am-5pm Tue-Sun) This museum on the far side of Lake Jelonek illustrates Gniezno's pivotal role in Polish history. The permanent collection contains archaeological finds and works of art related to the development of the Polish nation from pre-Slavic times to the end of the Piast dynasty. The museum also runs an audiovisual presentation about Poland under the Piasts.

**Archdiocesan Museum** MUSEUM

(Muzeum Archidiecezji Gnieźnieńskiej; www.muzeumag.pl in Polish; ul Kolegiaty 2; adult/concession 6/4zł; ⊙9am-5.30pm Mon-Sat, to 4pm Sun) North of the cathedral behind St George's Church, this museum holds a collection of sacred sculptures and paintings, liturgical fabrics, coffin portraits and votive offerings.

## ⊨ Sleeping

**Hotel Atelier** HOTEL €€

(✆61 424 8550; www.hotelatelier.pl; ul Tumska 5; s 210zł, d 240-280zł; P❋⊛⧖) This classy four-star hotel is set within a residential building that once housed a photographer's studio, or *atelier*. The tastefully appointed green-hued rooms contain elegant timber furniture, and there's a restaurant and cafe-bar to take advantage of.

**Hotel Pietrak** HOTEL €€

(✆61 426 1497; www.pietrak.pl; ul Bolesława Chrobrego 3; s/d 180/210zł; ⧖) Located in

All along the aisles and the ambulatory are **chapels**, built from the 15th to 18th centuries, and separated from the aisles by decorative wrought-iron screens. There are 17 screens in all, ranging in style from Gothic and Renaissance to Baroque, and constituting one of the most beautiful collections of its kind to be gathered in a single church in Poland. Inside the chapels are some fine tombstones, altarpieces, paintings and wall decorations – well worth a closer look.

One interesting modern artwork sits in the body of the church: a **statue of Cardinal Stefan Wyszyński**, the Polish primate credited with persuading the Soviets to relax their antireligious stance during the communist era. The panelled piece shows various scenes from the cardinal's eventful life and career.

For city views, you can climb the **tower** (adult/concession 3/2zł; ⊙9.30am-5.15pm Mon-Sat, 1-5.45pm Sun).

**WORTH A TRIP**

## THE PIAST TRAIL

The Piast Trail (Szlak Piastowski) is a tourist trail weaving together a selection of sites related to Poland's early history. Dozens of attractions are strung out in a giant figure eight stretching from Poznań in the west to Inowrocław in the east, with Gniezno at the centre. The trail provides good inspiration for a driving holiday through Wielkopolska. If pressed for time, you could do a simple loop from Poznań through Gniezno and back, or use Gniezno as a base for day trips along the trail in all directions. For more details, drop into the Gniezno tourist office and ask for the free Szlak Piastowski brochure.

Highlights along the trail include the following:

» **Lake Lednica** – a postglacial lake containing the island of Ostrów Lednicki, a 10th-century stronghold. Museums here exhibit archaeological remains and 19th-century rural architecture.

» **Gniezno** – where Poland's connection with the Catholic faith began.

» **Biskupin** – much older than the Piasts with its reconstructed Iron-Age town site.

» **Strzelno** – boasts two of the best Romanesque churches in the region.

» **Kruszwica** – with its Mouse Tower, the only remainder of a 14th-century castle built by King Kazimierz III Wielki.

two 18th-century burghers' houses just shy of the Rynek, the Pietrak provides good facilities, including a fitness centre with a spa. The restaurant serves up quality food, and operates a colourful beer garden in the street during summer.

**Hotel Awo**　　　　　　　　　　　HOTEL €€
(☑61 426 1197; www.hotel-awo.pl; ul Warszawska 32; s/d 160/210zł; P🛜) A midrange place with neat, clean rooms, a pleasant courtyard with a beer garden, and a restaurant on the premises. Note that it's right by the city market, making it potentially noisy for south-facing rooms.

**City Hotel**　　　　　　　　　　　HOTEL €
(☑61 425 3535; www.hotelgniezno.com; Rynek 15; s/d from 80/100zł; 🛜) This hotel doesn't make much effort to live up to its prestigious position on the Rynek – inside its rooms, you'll find fairly basic furnishings. But the price is right, and the rooms and the cafe look out onto the square. Enter via the kebab shop downstairs.

### ✗ Eating

**Restauracja Ratuszowa**　　　　POLISH €€
(ul Bolesława Chrobrego 41; mains 15-48zł) A restaurant with an elegantly old-fashioned interior within the town hall building, and a spacious deck on the street in the warmer months. There are plenty of meaty options on the menu, along with fish and pasta dishes.

**Kredens Cechowy**　　　　　　POLISH €€
(ul Tumska 15; mains 12-45zł) Attractive eatery with a touch of green, both in the decor and the pot plants scattered through its dining space. The menu covers all the bases from crêpes to steaks.

### ℹ Information

**Post office** (ul Bolesława Chrobrego 36)
**Tourist office** (☑61 428 4100; www.szlak piastowski.com.pl in Polish; Rynek 14; ⏰8am-6pm) Also provides free internet access.

### ℹ Getting There & Away

There are eight daily buses running to Żnin (9zł, one hour), where you can change for the narrow-gauge train to Biskupin.

Trains run regularly throughout the day to Poznań (16zł, 40 minutes, hourly). There are also departures to Toruń (18zł, 1¾ hours, 10 daily), Gdańsk (50zł, five hours, six daily) and Wrocław (44zł, 3½ hours, eight daily).

## Biskupin

Forget static museum displays in dimly lit rooms – Biskupin's re-created Iron Age town site, with its wooden palisades, thatched roofs and costumed historical re-enactors, is a stimulating way to learn about the distant pre-Polish past.

The fortified lake town was built about 2700 years ago by a tribe of the Lusatian culture, then accidentally rediscovered in 1933 by a school teacher who noticed some wooden stakes poking out of the lake. The town's remnants were then unearthed from beneath a thick layer of turf. It is the only known surviving Iron Age town in Poland, and proves that the region was already inhabited by well-organised social groups more than 1600 years before the Polish state was born.

## Sights & Activities

The Iron Age town is situated within the **Archaeological Reserve** (Rezerwat Archeologiczny; 52 302 5055; www.biskupin.pl; adult/concession 8/6zł; 8am-6pm) You can just wander through the grounds, or organise an English-speaking guide in advance for 110zł. The ticket office also sells some publications about the site in English.

Once past the gate, follow the path to the **museum**, which presents finds excavated on and around the island, together with background information about the place and the people. There's also a model of the town as it once looked.

The **Iron Age town** lies further along, on the peninsula in the northern end of the park. The gateway, a fragment of the defensive wall and two rows of houses have been reconstructed to give some idea of what the town once looked like. The interiors of a few houses have been fitted out as they may have been 2700 years ago. Within the thatched structures you'll find various stalls selling handcrafted arrows, jewellery and replica coins, and a man in period garb giving hatchet-throwing demonstrations out front. From the wharf near the gateway, a **pleasure boat** (trips 6zł) departs several times a day for a short trip around the lake.

In September each year, an **archaeological festival** is held at the reserve. In addition to demonstrations of ancient cultures including dance, handcrafts and food, it's an annual excuse to stage rousing re-enactments of battles between Germanic and Slavic tribes, providing a colourful (and photogenic) spectacle.

## Getting There & Away

**BUS** From the bus stop at the entrance to the Archaeological Reserve, buses run every hour or two north to Żnin (4zł, 15 minutes, Monday to Friday) and south to Gąsawa (3zł, five minutes, Monday to Friday). From either of these places, regular buses go to Gniezno (9zł, one hour). If you miss your bus, Gąsawa is an easy 2km walk away.

---

**WORTH A TRIP**

### ŻNIN DISTRICT RAILWAY

For an entertaining day trip on narrow rails, step aboard a train running along the **Żnin District Railway** (Żnińska Kolej Powiatowa; www.ciuchciaznin.pl; ul Potockiego 4, Żnin; one way/return 11/19zł). This narrow-gauge line was opened in 1894 to carry sugar beets to the local sugar factory, and also functioned as public transport. The passenger service was cancelled in 1962, but the line lives on as a tourist attraction.

Once the train leaves the dinky narrow-gauge station at Żnin (east of the town's bus station), it trundles very slowly through a succession of low green hills covered with crops, pausing briefly at a stop serving the village of Wenecja before reaching the **Wenecja Narrow Gauge Railway Museum** (Muzeum Kolei Wąskotorowej w Wenecji; adult/concession 8/6zł; 9am-6pm), a showcase of narrow little engines, carriages and their associated memorabilia. Across the rails from the museum are the **ruins** of a 14th-century castle.

The next stop on the line is the Archaeological Reserve at Biskupin, a major attraction; then the train finally reaches the village of Gąsawa. The main sight of interest here is **St Nicholas' Church** (Kościół Św Mikołaja; ul Żnińska 1), a 17th-century wooden structure with an unusual mix of architectural styles: Gothic, Baroque, neoclassical and more modern additions all jostling together. When the church was renovated in 1999, the workers discovered original frescoes that had been covered up by a mixture of reeds and plaster. The paintings depict saints and other Biblical figures, and have been revealed by careful 'excavation'.

If you take an early train from Żnin, it's possible to stop off at the railway museum, Biskupin and Gąsawa, then return to Żnin by the last train of the day. Five trains depart from Żnin daily from May to September between 9am and 2.40pm (in July and August there's an extra departure at 4pm), then make the return journey from Gąsawa.

**TRAIN** A narrow-gauge tourist train (see boxed text, p291) operates from May to September, from Żnin to Gąsawa (one way/return 11zł/19zł, one hour), passing Biskupin on the way (40 minutes). The Biskupin station is right by the entrance to the reserve. In Żnin, the station is 150m east of the bus station; in Gąsawa it's 700m southwest of the Rynek on the Gniezno road.

# SOUTHEASTERN WIELKOPOLSKA

## Kalisz

POP 107,000

Given how little the average traveller knows about Kalisz (*kah*-leesh), its centre comes as a pleasant surprise, revealing a charming collection of city parks, gently curving streets and simple but harmonious architecture.

Kalisz has the longest documented history of any town in Poland: it was mentioned by Claudius Ptolemy in his renowned *Geography* of the 2nd century AD as Calisia, a trading settlement on the Amber Route between the Roman Empire and the Baltic Sea.

In more modern times, Kalisz was razed to the ground by the invading Germans in the first days of WWI. Within a month, the population dropped from 70,000 to 5000 and most buildings were reduced to ruins. The town was rebuilt on the old street plan, but in a new architectural style. Luckily, given the circumstances, most of the new buildings survived WWII without much damage.

### ⦿ Sights

The Old Town sits in the angle between the Prosna and Bernardynka Rivers, with a dozen small bridges and the **City Park** (Park Miejski) stretching to the southeast.

#### Główny Rynek                    SQUARE

Start your sightseeing in the low-key but attractive Main Market Square by heading for the **Town Hall tower** (admission 3zł; ⊙10am-2pm Mon-Fri, to 1pm Sat & Sun). There are fine views from the top, and an exhibition relating the history of Kalisz.

#### Kalisz Regional Museum          MUSEUM

(Muzeum Okręgowe Ziemi Kaliskiej; www.muzeum .kalisz.pl; ul Kościuszki 12; adult/concession 4/2zł, Sun free; ⊙10am-3pm Tue, Thu, Sat & Sun, noon-5.30pm Wed & Fri) Presenting an in-depth examination of the city's story, this museum features archaeological and historical exhibits from Kalisz and surrounding areas. It's 500m southwest of the Rynek, across the Prosna River.

#### Centre of Figurative & Graphic Arts          GALLERY

(Centrum Figuracje i Grafiki; ☑62 757 2999; ul Kolegialna 4; adult/concession 4/2zł, Sun free; ⊙10am-3pm Tue, Thu & Fri, to 5.30pm Wed, to 2.30pm Sat & Sun) Displays temporary exhibits of drawings and graphic arts, including works by Tadeusz Kulisiewicz (1899–1988), a Kalisz-born artist known mainly for his drawings. Enter from ul Łazienna.

#### Zawodzie Archaeological Reserve          MUSEUM

(Rezerwat Archeologiczny Zawodzie; ul Pobożnego 87; adult/concession 5/3zł; ⊙10am-3pm Tue-Fri, to 6pm Sat & Sun) Located upon the site of an ancient village from 10,000 years ago, this recently opened attraction includes full-sized facsimiles of timber structures of the era, along with authentic archaeological remains. A pleasant way to get there from the vicinity of the Hotel Europa is to walk east along al Wolności, following it to the right past the theatre as it becomes ul Częstochowska. Once across the Prosna River, turn left and follow the riverbank as far as ul Zawodzie. This street will take you to the reserve (it's about a one-hour walk in total).

#### Historic Churches          CHURCHES

In the northern part of the Old Town are a brace of interesting churches. The oldest, **St Nicholas' Church** (Kościół Św Mikołaja; ul Kanonicka 5), is one block northwest of the Rynek and dates from the 13th century. It was originally Gothic, but has been modernised several times.

About 250m north of Plac Jana Pawła II is the 1607 **Bernardine Church** (Kościół Pobernardyński; ul Stawiszyńska 2), with a spectacular interior featuring sumptuous Baroque decoration.

Just off Plac Jana Pawła II, the **Collegiate Church** (Sanctuary of St Joseph; Plac Jana Pawła II 3) is a lavish place of worship, built in 1353 and rebuilt in the 18th century. It boasts a Baroque interior flooded with gilt and glitter.

### ⌷ Sleeping

##### TOP CHOICE ⁄ Hotel Europa          HOTEL €€

(☑62 767 2032; www.hotel-europa.pl; al Wolności 5; s 170zł, d 210-395zł, ste 590zł; ⓟ❀ ) If you've schlepped through numerous three-star hotels in a hot Polish summer, you'll weep with joy on encountering this excellent central hotel's deluxe doubles with air-conditioning, kettles and gleaming bathrooms. Go crazy and shell out for the Egyptian-themed suite. You'll find it just south of the Old Town across the Prosna River.

**Hotel Roma** HOTEL €€
(☑62 501 7555; www.restauracje-kalisz-turek.pl; ul Chopina 9; s/d 180/240zł; P❄🖭) A nice surprise in a shabbier part of town, this white villa-style accommodation 500m northwest of the Rynek offers just seven spacious rooms with skylights, above the in-house Italian restaurant with a garden courtyard.

**Hotel Calisia** HOTEL €€
(☑62 767 9100; www.hotel-calisia.pl; ul Nowy Świat 1-3; s/d 170/220zł; P🖭) The corridors are boxy and the rooms are a touch faded, but the service is good. There's a restaurant and bar on the premises, which are located 750m south of the main square.

**PTSM Hostel** HOSTEL €
(☑62 757 2404; sosw@ecentrum.kalisz.pl; ul Handlowa 30; dm 25zł) This youth hostel is halfway between the train station and the Old Town, in a pleasant location near the trees and ponds of Park Przyjaźni. Check in before 9pm.

## 🍴 Eating & Drinking

As usual, there are plenty of eating options on the Rynek and the streets around it. In summer a gaggle of beer gardens and snack stalls springs up around the top end of al Wolności, near the Hotel Europa.

**Antonio** ITALIAN €€
(ul Śródmiejska 21; mains 30-50zł) If you're not hungry after smelling the garlic aroma drifting up to the street from this cellar restaurant just southwest of the Rynek, we'll be amazed. The dining area features red-checked tablecloths, candlelight, roses, Renaissance-inspired artwork and quality Italian food.

**Baja Mexico** MEXICAN €€
(Główny Rynek 3; mains 7-37zł) All the well-known Tex-Mex dishes are on offer at this central theme bar just off the Rynek, and fajitas and enchiladas do make a nice change from the usual rounds of cutlets and dumplings. Enter off ul Piskorzewska.

**Bar Maleński** CAFETERIA €
(ul Parczewskiego 2-3; mains 6-15zł; ⊙8am-6pm Mon-Fri, 9am-3pm Sat) *Maleński* means tiny, a

fitting title for this diminutive cafeteria not far west of Plac Jana Pawła II. It's the best place in town for an ultrabudget meal, from roast chicken to more adventurous choices like beans Breton-style.

**Złoty Róg** PUB BREWERY
(al Wolności 3; ⊙10am-11pm Mon-Fri, 1-11pm Sat & Sun) A good place for a drink, right next to the Hotel Europa. Sample one of the four boutique beers brewed out the back, and recuperate from sightseeing within the cool timber interior.

## ☆ Entertainment

**Centre of Culture & Arts** CINEMA
(Centrum Kultury i Sztuki; www.ckis.kalisz.pl in Polish; ul Łazienna 6) This institution a block southeast of the Rynek hosts a variety of events, including screenings of art-house movies.

## ℹ Information

**Cafe Alisia** (al Wolności 6; per hr 5zł; ⊙10am-9pm) Internet access east of the Hotel Europa.

**Post office** (ul Zamkowa 18/20; ⊙8am-8pm Mon-Sat)

**Tourist office** (☑62 598 2731; www.cit.kalisz.pl; ul Chodyńskiego 3; ⊙10am-5pm Mon-Fri, to 2pm Sat) Enter from ul Zamkowa.

## ℹ Getting There & Around

The bus and train stations are close to each other, about 2km southwest of the Old Town. To get to the centre, take bus 5 from the train station, or bus 2 or 4 from the main road next to the bus station (2.40zł).

**BUS** There are 10 buses to Poznań daily (26zł, 2½ hours) via Gołuchów (8zł, 25 minutes). There are also eight buses to Wrocław (26zł, three hours) and two to Toruń (34zł, four hours). The hourly suburban bus 12A to Pleszew Szpital also passes through Gołuchów (4.80zł, 40 minutes); it picks up from Plac Jana Pawła II in central Kalisz.

**TRAIN** Trains to Łódź (20zł, two hours) run about every two hours throughout the day. There are also trains to Warsaw (48zł, 4½ hours, three daily), Wrocław (35zł, 2¼ hours, five daily) and Poznań (22zł, 2½ hours, three daily).

## Gołuchów

POP 1200

This small village near Kalisz is unremarkable save for its attractive castle, which provides sufficient reason for a day trip.

## ⊙ Sights

### Castle                                    MUSEUM

(www.mnp.art.pl; ul Działyńskich 2; adult/concession 8/5.50zł, Sat free; ⊙10am-4pm Tue-Sun) Gołuchów's castle began life around 1560 as a small fortified mansion with four octagonal towers at the corners, built by the Leszczyński family. Some 50 years later it was enlarged and reshaped into a palatial residence in late-Renaissance style. Abandoned at the end of the 17th century, it gradually fell into ruins until the Działyński family, the owners of Kórnik castle, bought it in 1856. It was completely rebuilt between 1872 and 1885, and it was then that it acquired its French appearance.

The castle's stylistic mutation was essentially the brainchild of Izabela Czartoryska, daughter of Prince Adam Czartoryski and wife of Jan Działyński. She commissioned the French architect Viollet le Duc to reinvent the residence; under his supervision many architectural bits and pieces were brought from abroad, mainly from France and Italy, and incorporated into the building.

Having acquired large numbers of works of art, Izabela crammed them into her new palace, which became one of the largest private museums in Europe. During WWII the Nazis stole the works of art but the building itself survived relatively undamaged. Part of the collection was recovered and is now once more on display in its rightful home.

On exhibition inside the building is a wealth of furniture, paintings, sculptures, weapons, tapestries, rugs and the like. One of the highlights is a collection of Greek vases from the 5th century BC. You enter the castle through a decorative 17th-century doorway, which leads into a graceful arcaded courtyard; admission is strictly limited, with tours running for a set number of visitors every half-hour.

### Museum of Forestry                       MUSEUM

(Muzeum Leśnictwa; ul Działyńskich 2; adult/concession 5/3zł; ⊙10am-3pm Tue-Fri, to 4pm Sat & Sun) To the south of the castle is this museum, housed in a former distillery which was considerably extended in 1874 and adapted as a residence. It contains displays on the history of Polish forestry and the timber industry, along with a collection of contemporary art on the subject.

Entry includes the museum's **annexe**, east of the castle, displaying ecological exhibits in an old coach house. The collection includes a number of curious *księgi drzewne* (wooden books), boxes shaped like books, which were used to collect seeds and other plant matter.

Another outpost you can visit as part of the same entry fee is the **Museum of Forest Techniques**, 750m beyond the castle in the far north of the park. It contains tools and machinery used in forestry.

Several bison live relatively freely in a large, fenced-off **bison enclosure** (⊙7am-sunset), west of the park, 500m beyond the forestry techniques museum (follow the Żubry signs).

## ⓘ Getting There & Away

Suburban bus 12A goes roughly hourly to/from Kalisz (4.80zł, 40 minutes). Get off at the bus stand next to the cemetery, cross the main road, and walk around the church to find the park entrance. About 10 PKS buses each day run both to Poznań (23zł, 2¼ hours) and Kalisz (8zł, 25 minutes).

# Gdańsk & Pomerania

POP 6.5 MILLION

## Why Go?

Cream-hued beaches shelving smoothly into the nippy Baltic Sea, wind-crafted dunes vivid against leaden skies, stern red-brick churches and castles erected by a medieval order of pious knights, and silenced shipyards that once seethed with anti-communist tumult – this is Pomerania, Poland's north, a place with many faces.

The epicentre of Pomerania is Gdańsk, northern Poland's metropolis, a forward-looking city with a fascinatingly photogenic historical centre. Like most of the region, Gdańsk has changed hands many times over the centuries, each invader and overseer bequeathing a layer of architecture and culture for today's tourists to ogle.

Away from the beaches and Gdańsk's miracles in red brick you'll discover Kashubia, a region that keeps the traditional fires burning, including its own language – the perfect place to slow down and escape Poland's beaten tracks.

## Best Places to Eat

» Velevetka (p313)
» Błękitny Pudel (p320)
» Restauracja Pod Łososiem (p313)
» Restauracja Gdańska (p313)

## Best Places to Stay

» Hotel Apollo (p348)
» Kamienica Gotyk (p311)
» Hotel Podewils (p311)
» Hotel Karczma Spichrz (p327)

## When to Go
### Gdańsk

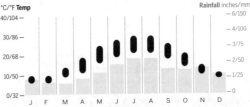

**Apr**
Go amber hunting after spring's high tides along Pomerania's white-sand beaches.

**Aug**
Enjoy a spot of bric-a-brac hunting and local culture during Gdańsk's Dominican Fair.

**Dec**
Explore the deserted dunes and lakes of the Słowiński National Park.

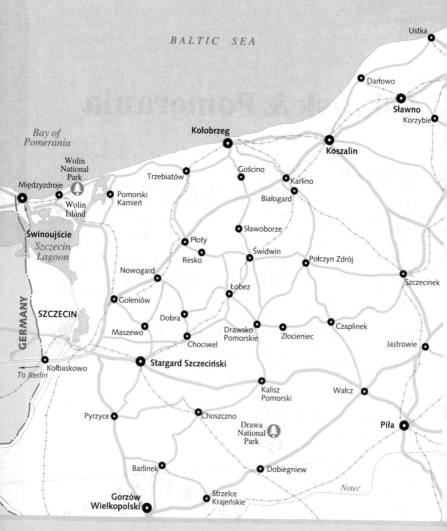

## Gdańsk & Pomerania Highlights

① Exploring the recent past at the **Roads to Freedom Exhibition** (p309), tracing Gdańsk's part in the fall of communism

② Boogying on the beach at one of **Sopot's** (p317) many nightclubs

③ Admiring the architecture of **Gdańsk's Długi Targ** (p301),

one of Poland's grandest thoroughfares

④ Wandering the halls, corridors and chapels of **Malbork Castle** (p335)

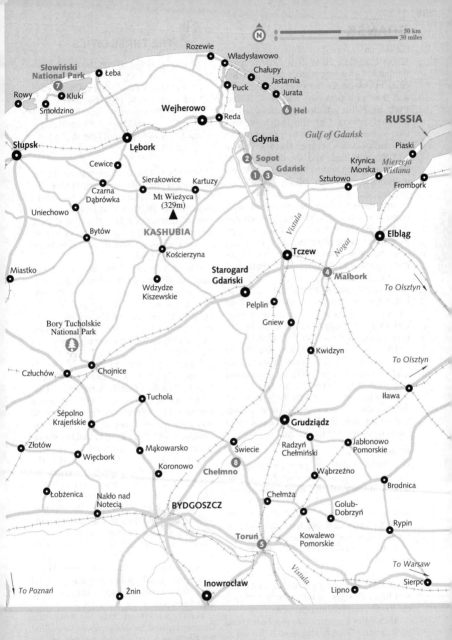

Europe's biggest medieval
fortress

**5** Marvelling at the Gothic
masterpieces that make **Toruń**
(p324) one of Poland's most
intriguing destinations

**6** Going to **Hel** (p321) and
back to see the seals

**7** Doing a spot of dune
surfing in the intriguing
**Słowiński National Park**
(p343)

**8** Revelling in the off-beat
ambience of **Chełmno's
walled town** (p332), a real
blast from the Polish past

# GDAŃSK

POP 456,000

Like a mini-state all to itself, Gdańsk has a unique feel that sets it aside from all other cities in Poland. Centuries of maritime ebb and flow as a port city; streets of distinctively un-Polish architecture influenced by a united nations of wealthy merchants who shaped the city's past; the to-ing and fro-ing of Danzig/Gdańsk between Teutonic Prussia and Slavic Poland; and the destruction of WWII have bequeathed this grand old dame a special atmosphere millions now come to enjoy.

And those visitors are coming in ever greater numbers to wander the narrow cobbled streets of the Main Town, to gaze in wonder at monster red-brick churches, to scatter along its historical thoroughfares lined with grand, elegantly slender buildings, and to duck and dive in and out of characterful cafes, amber shops and intriguing museums. Tourism hasn't turned its back on the water, with pleasure-boat cruises upriver and a wealth of maritime history to view in between brews at dockside beer gardens.

Though an old city with a tumultuous past, and the historic scars to prove it, 21st-century Gdańsk is an energetic destination crammed with diverse sights and many ways to have fun. With the best transport links in the north it's also an ideal launch pad for much of the Polish Baltic coast and many other inland attractions.

## History

Describing Gdańsk's past as 'eventful' would be a major understatement. The official history of the much fought-over city is counted from the year 997, when the Bohemian Bishop Adalbert arrived here from Gniezno and baptised the inhabitants. The settlement developed as a port over the following centuries, expanding northwards into what is today the Old Town. The German community then arrived from Lübeck in the early 13th century, the first in a succession of migrants that crafted the town's cosmopolitan character.

In 1308 the Teutonic order (see boxed text, p331) seized Gdańsk and quickly turned it into a major trade centre, joining the Hanseatic League (see boxed text, p308) in 1361. In 1454 the locals decided on a spot of regime change, razing the Teutonic Knights' castle, and pledging allegiance to the Polish monarch instead.

### THE THREE CITIES

When in and around Gdańsk, you're sure to come across the term Tri-City (Trójmiasto in Polish) on everything from tourist brochures to bus timetables. The three cities in question are tourist magnets Gdańsk, Sopot and the much less visited port of Gdynia.

From here, the only way was up: by the mid-16th century, the successful trading city of 40,000 was Poland's largest city, and the most important trading centre in Central Europe. Legions of international merchants joined the local German-Polish population, adding their own cultural influences to the city's unique blend.

Gdańsk was one of the very few Polish cities to withstand the Swedish Deluge of the 1650s, but the devastation of the surrounding area weakened its position, and in 1793 Prussia annexed the shrinking city. Just 14 years later, however, the Prussians were ousted by the Napoleonic army and its Polish allies.

It turned out to be a brief interlude – in 1815 the Congress of Vienna gave Gdańsk back to Prussia, which became part of Germany later in the century. In the years that followed, the Polish minority was systematically Germanised, the city's defences were reinforced and there was gradual but steady economic and industrial growth.

After Germany's defeat in WWI, the Treaty of Versailles granted the newly re-formed Polish nation the so-called Polish Corridor, a strip of land stretching from Toruń to Gdańsk, providing the country with an outlet to the sea. Gdańsk itself was excluded and designated the Free City of Danzig, under the protection of the League of Nations. With the city having a German majority, however, the Polish population never had much political influence, and once Hitler came to power it was effectively a German port.

WWII started in Gdańsk when the German battleship *Schleswig-Holstein* fired the first shots on the Polish military post at Westerplatte. During the occupation of the city, Nazi Germany continued to use the local shipyards for building warships, with Poles as forced labour. The Red Army arrived in March 1945; during the fierce battle that ensued the city centre virtually ceased to exist. The German residents fled, or died in the conflict. Their place was eventually taken by Polish newcomers, mainly from the territories lost to the Soviet Union in the east.

The complex reconstruction of the Main Town took over 20 years from 1949, though work on some interiors continued well into the 1990s. Nowhere else in Europe was such a large area of a historic city reconstructed from the ground up.

In December 1970 a huge workers' strike broke out in the shipyard and was 'pacified' by authorities as soon as the workers left the gates, leaving 44 dead. This was the second important challenge to the communist regime after that in Poznań in 1956. Gdańsk came to the fore again in 1980, when another popular protest paralysed the shipyard. This time it culminated in negotiations with the government and the foundation of Solidarity. Lech Wałęsa, the electrician who led the strike and subsequent talks, later became the first freely elected president in postwar Poland.

Postcommunist Gdańsk has consolidated its role as the region's leading administrative and industrial city, with some diversification into high-tech; tourism has been another huge and rather unexpected success story. In 2012 Gdańsk will be one of four Polish host cities for the UEFA European Football Championships and has recently decided to throw its hat into the ring to become a European city of culture in 2016, all evidence of the city's optimistic, vibrant approach.

## ◉ Sights

### MAIN TOWN

Gdańsk's jewel in the crown is its Main Town (Główne Miasto; Map p304), which looks much as it did some 300 to 400 years ago, during the height of its prosperity. As the largest of the city's historic quarters, and the richest architecturally, it was the most carefully restored after WWII. Prussian additions from the Partition period were airbrushed out of this remarkably impressive re-creation, so the result is a snapshot of Gdańsk up to the end of the 18th century.

The town was originally laid out in the mid-14th century along a central axis consisting of ul Długa (Long Street) and Długi Targ (Long Market). The latter was designed for trading, which would have taken place in the Rynek (Main Market Square). This axis is also known as the Royal Way.

**Royal Way**  HISTORIC THOROUGHFARE

Lined by the city's grandest facades, the Royal Way was the route along which the Polish kings traditionally paraded during their periodic visits. Of the three Royal Ways in Poland (Warsaw, Kraków and Gdańsk), the Gdańsk one is the shortest – only 500m long, but it's architecturally perhaps the most refined.

The traditional entry point for kings was the **Upland Gate** (Brama Wyżynna; Map p304), at the western end of Royal Way. The gate was built in 1574 as part of the city's new fortifications, which were constructed outside the medieval walls to strengthen the system. The authorities weren't happy with the original structure, so in 1586 they commissioned a Flemish artist, Willem van den Block, to embellish it. It was covered with sandstone slabs and ornamented with three coats of arms: Prussia (with unicorns), Poland (with angels) and Gdańsk (with lions).

Just behind the Upland Gate is a large 15th-century construction known as the **Foregate** (Przedbramie; Map p304). It consists of the **Torture House** (Katownia) to the west and a high **Prison Tower** (Wieża Więzienna) to the east, linked to one another by two walls.

When the Upland Gate was built, the Foregate lost its defensive function and was turned into a jail. The Torture House then had an extra storey added as a courtroom and was topped with decorative Renaissance parapets. A gallows was built on the square to the north, where public executions of condemned foreigners were held (locals had the 'privilege' of being hanged on Długi Targ). The Foregate was used as a jail till the mid-19th century. It was damaged during WWII and the restoration that began in 1951 is still ongoing. Nowadays it's the home of the **Amber Museum** (Muzeum Bursztynu; Map p304; www.mhmg.pl; adult/concession 10/5zł, free Mon; ◎11am-3pm Mon, 10am-6pm Tue-Sat, 11am-6pm Sun), where kilograms of 'Baltic gold' radiate a prehistoric glow.

Further to the east is the **Golden Gate** (Złota Brama; Map p304). Designed by Abraham van den Block, son of the decorator of the Upland Gate, and built in 1612, it's a sort of triumphal arch ornamented with a double-storey colonnade and topped with eight allegorical statues. The four figures on the side of the Prison Tower represent Peace, Liberty, Wealth and Fame, which Gdańsk was always struggling to achieve against foreign powers (sometimes including the Polish

GDAŃSK & POMERANIA GDAŃSK

# Tri-City Area

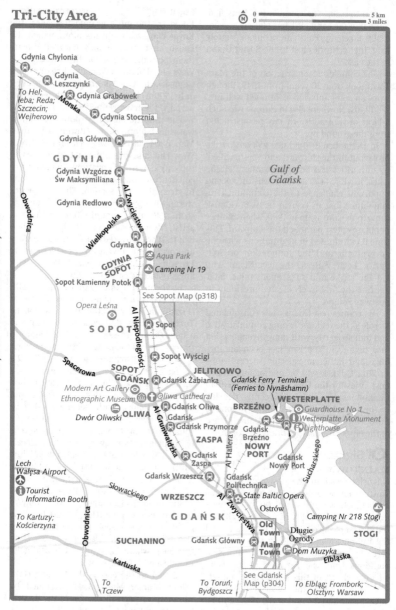

kings). The sculptures on the opposite side symbolise the burghers' virtues: Wisdom, Piety, Justice and Concord. Today's figures are postwar copies of the 1648 originals.

Once you pass the Golden Gate, you are on the gently curving **ulica Długa,** one of the loveliest streets in Poland, which, despite its name (meaning 'Long Street'), is only 300m in length. In 1945 it was just a heap of smoking rubble. Stop at the **Uphagens' House** (Dom Uphagena; Map p304; www .mhmg.pl; ul Długa 12; adult/concession 10/5zł, free

Mon; ☺11am-3pm Mon, 10am-6pm Tue-Sat, 11am-6pm Sun) to see the restored historic interior, a collection of sumptuously decorated rooms with period furniture from the 18th century. As you pass beyond the kitchen, take a minute to browse the family tree and history of the Uphagen family, outlined in English.

**Historical Museum of Gdańsk**    MUSEUM
(Muzeum Historii Miasta Gdańska; Map p304; www .mhmg.pl; ul Długa 47; adult/concession 10/5zł, free Mon; ☺11am-3pm Mon, 10am-6pm Tue-Sat, 11am-6pm Sun) Reaching the eastern end of ul Długa, take a moment to gaze up at the pinnacle of the **Town Hall**. This tall, slim tower, Gdańsk's highest at 81.5m, has a life-sized gilded figure of King Zygmunt II August on top – a reward for his generosity in granting the city certain privileges.

The Town Hall has both Gothic and Renaissance elements. The first building is said to have appeared here in the 1330s, but it grew and changed until the end of the 16th century. In 1945 it was almost completely burnt out and the authorities were on the point of demolishing the shell, before vehement local protests made them change their mind.

After half a millennium of municipal administration, the city bureaucrats didn't return after WWII and today this grand building houses the main branch of Gdańsk's museum. Enter the building by twin flights of balustraded stairs and go through an ornate Baroque doorway (1766), which is topped by the city's coat of arms guarded by two lions that, unusually, are both looking towards the Golden Gate, supposedly awaiting the arrival of the king. The doorway was the final addition to the external decoration of the building.

Inside are several rooms embellished in period style, either original or re-created by postwar restorers from old photographs, drawings and engravings. The showpiece is the **Red Room** (Sala Czerwona), done up in Dutch Mannerist style from the end of the 16th century and once the venue for the town council's musings. The large, richly carved fireplace (1593) and the marvellous portal (1596) all attract the eye but the real centre of attention is the ornamented ceiling – 25 paintings dominated by an oval centrepiece entitled *The Glorification of the Unity of Gdańsk with Poland*. The painter, Isaac van den Block, yet another member of the Flemish family of artists, incorporated various themes into the painting, from everyday scenes to the panorama of Gdańsk on the top of the triumphal arch. All this room's decoration is the real original deal; it was dismantled in 1942 and hidden outside the city until the bombing was done with.

The 2nd floor houses exhibitions related to Gdańsk's history, including photos of the destruction of 1945. From here you can enter the **tower** for great views across the city.

**Długi Targ**    HISTORIC THOROUGHFARE
Długi Targ (Long Market) was once the main city market and is now the major focus for visitors. Sadly it's all got a bit tacky in recent years and is now hemmed with tourist-class eateries, dubious amber stalls, quick-tongued touts and sun-shades keeping overpriced beer and their drinkers out of the sun.

According to local legend, the **Neptune Fountain** (Fontana Neptuna; Map p304), next to the Town Hall, once gushed forth with the trademark Gdańsk liqueur, Goldwasser. As the story goes, it spurted out of the trident one merry night and Neptune found himself endangered by crowds of drunken locals who couldn't believe their luck. Perhaps that's why, in 1634, the fountain was fenced off with a wrought-iron barrier. The bronze statue itself was the work of another Flemish artist, Peter Husen; made between 1606 and 1613, it is the oldest secular monument in Poland. A menagerie of stone sea creatures was added in the 1750s during the restoration of the fountain.

The nearby 1618 **Golden House** (Złota Kamienica; Map p304), designed by Johan Voigt, has the richest facade in the city. In the friezes between storeys are 12 elaborately carved scenes interspersed with busts of famous historical figures, including two Polish kings.

The Long Market is flanked from the east by the **Green Gate** (Zielona Brama; Map p304), marking the river end of the Royal Way. It was built in the 1560s on the site of a medieval defensive gate and was supposed to be the residence of the kings. However, the damp and chilly lodge never hosted a Polish monarch (they preferred the houses nearby, particularly those opposite the Artus Court) but one Polish leader, former President Lech Wałęsa, did like the building – he had his offices here for many years.

**Artus Court**    HISTORIC BUILDING
(Dwór Artusa; Map p304; www.mhmg.pl; Długi Targ 43/44; adult/concession 10/5zł, free Mon; ☺11am-

## SONS OF DANZIG

As a lively cultural and intellectual centre, Gdańsk has spawned some famous personalities over the years. Here are the biggest names:

» **Johannes Hevelius** (1611–87) – Astronomer who produced one of the first detailed maps of the moon's surface.

» **Gabriel Daniel Fahrenheit** (1686–1736) – Inventor of the mercury thermometer.

» **Arthur Schopenhauer** (1788–1860) – Philosopher who felt that irrational human behaviour was driven by a force he called the 'will to live'.

» **Günter Grass** (b 1927) German author, Nobel laureate and perhaps Gdańsk's most famous living son. Best known for his first novel *The Tin Drum*.

» **Lech Wałęsa** (b 1943) – Former Gdańsk dockyard electrician, Solidarity leader and Polish president.

» **Jacek Kaczmarski** (1957–2004) – Poet and singer-songwriter whose fierce opposition to the communist regime led to his exile in the 1980s.

» **Donald Tusk** (b 1957) – Current prime minister, criticised in 2011 for spending millions of złoty flying home to Gdańsk from Warsaw every weekend!

3pm Mon, 10am-6pm Tue-Sat, 11am-6pm Sun) Rising in all its embellished grandeur behind the Neptune Fountain, the Artus Court is perhaps the single best-known house in Gdańsk. The court has been an essential stop for passing luminaries ever since its earliest days, and a photo display in the entrance shows an enviable selection of famous visitors, from King Henry IV of England to a host of contemporary presidents.

Built in the middle of the 14th century, the court was given its monumental facade by Abraham van den Block in the 1610s. Inside there's a huge hall, topped by a Gothic vault supported on four slim granite columns, decorated with hunting murals and dominated by a vast painting depicting the Battle of Grunwald. There are also large models of masted sailing ships suspended from its ceiling! Wealthy local merchants used the building as a communal guildhall, holding meetings, banquets and general revelries in the lavishly decorated interior.

Like most of the centre, the court was comprehensively destroyed in WWII, but has been painstakingly restored from old photographs and historical records, recapturing at least a glimpse of its remarkable past. The hall is still the undisputed centrepiece, but the adjoining chambers hold historical artefacts and some exquisite pieces of classic Danzig furniture in the darkwood style synonymous with the city's golden age.

The plainly renovated upper floors hold a selection of historical exhibits, including a photographic 'simulacrum' of how the great hall would have looked at its peak – even in two dimensions it's a breathtaking space, filled from top to bottom with paintings, models and stuffed animals.

One unique feature of the interior is its giant Renaissance **tiled stove**, standing in the corner of the hall and almost touching the ceiling. It's reputedly the highest stove of its kind in Europe. Looking like a five-tier tower, 10.65m high, the stove is also lavishly ornamented, with a wealth of decoration portraying, among other things, rulers, allegorical figures and coats of arms. Built in 1546 by George Stelzener, the stove survived virtually unchanged until 1943, when local conservators dismantled the upper part and hid it outside the city. The fragments were collected after the war, and after a long and complex restoration, the whole thing was eventually put together and revealed to the public in 1995. It contains 520 tiles, 437 of which are originals.

### Waterfront

Beyond the Green Gate is the Motława River. It was once a busy quay, crowded with hundreds of sailing ships loading and unloading their cargo, which was stored either in the cellars of the burghers' houses in town or in the granaries on the other side of the river, on Spichlerze Island. Today it's a well-liked promenade lined with cafes, small art galleries and souvenir emporia.

In medieval times, the parallel east–west streets of the Main Town all had defensive gates at their riverfront ends. Some of them still exist, though most were altered in later periods. Walking north along Długie Pobrzeże (literally, Long Waterfront), you first reach the **Bread Gate** (Brama Chlebnicka; Map p304), at the end of ul Chlebnicka. It was built around 1450, still under the Teutonic order, as shown by the original city coat of arms consisting of two crosses. The crown was added by King Kazimierz Jagiellończyk in 1457, when Gdańsk was incorporated into the kingdom.

Enter the gate and walk a few steps to see the palatial **House Under the Angels** (Dom Pod Aniołami; Map p304), which is also known as the English House (Dom Angielski) after the nationality of the merchants who owned it in the 17th century when it was the largest burgher's house in Gdańsk.

### ulica Mariacka                                    STREET

The most atmospheric of all the streets in Gdańsk and one of Poland's most characterfully photogenic lanes is this length of cobbles between the waterfront **St Mary's Gate** (Brama Mariacka; Map p304) and the red-brick hulk of St Mary's Church. Almost completely re-created after WWII, mostly on the basis of old documents, photographs and illustrations, every ornamental detail unearthed from the debris, including countless scary gargoyles, was incorporated. It's the only street with a complete row of terraces, which lends the scene enormous charm. Despite its quaint attractiveness it's still a pretty quiet, residential lane with just a few artisan amber jewellery shops, a couple of cafes and one of northern Poland's best hotels (Kamienica Gotyk) showing any life. Some of the best stalls are set up here during the Dominican Fair (p311).

### Gdańsk Crane                     HISTORIC BUILDING

(Żuraw Gdański; Map p304; ul Szeroka 67/68; adult/concession 8/5zł; ☉10am-6.30pm daily Jul & Aug, shorter hours rest of yr) Just beyond the modest **Gate of the Holy Spirit** (Brama Św Ducha; Map p304) on the waterfront rises the oh-so conspicuous Gdańsk Crane. Built in the mid-15th century as the biggest double-towered gate on the waterfront, it also served to shift heavy cargoes directly onto or off vessels docked at the quay. For this purpose two giant wheels – 5m in diameter – were installed as a hoist with a rope wound around the axle; the whole contraption was set in motion by people 'walking' along the inner circumference like mice in a wheel.

Incredibly, this people-power could hoist loads of up to 2000kg, making it the largest crane in medieval Europe. Early-17th-century wheels were added higher up for installing masts.

Blasted to pieces in 1945, everything was carefully pieced back together in the postwar decades, making it the only fully restored relic of its kind in the world. Inside you'll find exhibits relating to the history of shipping, plus a collection of shells, corals and other marine life; English notes are available on laminated sheets. You can also climb up into the section overlooking the water and have a closer look at the hoisting gear (but sadly not a go on the wheel).

### Central Maritime Museum           MUSEUM

(Centralne Muzeum Morskie; Map p304; www.cmm.pl; Ołowianka 9/13; adult/concession 18/10zł, ticket valid for the museum, Gdańsk Crane & ferry) At the time of research the main annexe of the museum, right next door to the Gdańsk Crane, was undergoing an extensive, €8.6 million expansion to create a brand new **Maritime Cultural Centre**. Work on the incongruously modern-looking structure was supposed to be wrapped up in summer 2011 but looked far from completion when we visited.

The museum is housed in three reconstructed granaries on Ołowianka Island in the Motława River. The museum's own **ferry service** (one way/return 1/2zł, free with museum ticket) shuttles between the crane and the island. Exhibits illustrate the history of Polish seafaring from the earliest times to the present and include models of old sailing warships and ports, a 9th-century dugout, navigation instruments, ships' artillery, flags and the like. An interesting exhibit is a collection of salvaged items from the *General Carleton*, a British ship that disappeared mysteriously in the Baltic in 1785. In 1995 Polish scuba divers happened upon the wreck, and the museum's later excavation turned up the ship's bell with its name engraved clearly in the metal.

Moored next to the island, the **MS Sołdek** (Map p304) was the first vessel to be built at the Gdańsk Shipyard in the postwar years. Retired in 1981, this old seadog is now part of the museum and can be scrambled around almost at will.

### St Mary's Church                     CHURCH

(Bazylika Mariacka; Map p304) Dominating the heart of the Main Town, St Mary's Church is

# Gdańsk

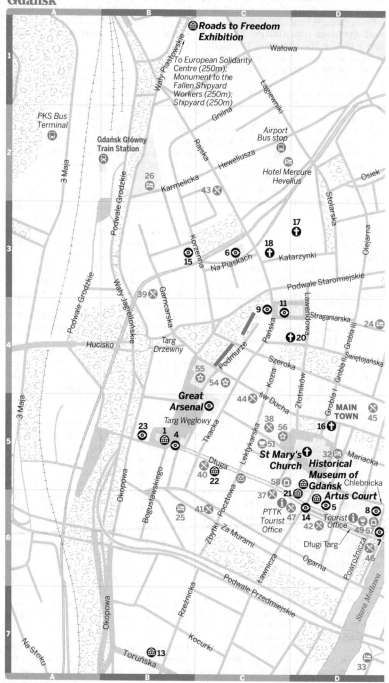

Roads to Freedom Exhibition

To European Solidarity Centre (250m); Monument to the Fallen Shipyard Workers (250m); Shipyard (250m)

Wałowa

Łagiewniki

Gnilna

PKS Bus Terminal

Gdańsk Główny Train Station

Airport Bus stop

Hotel Mercure Hevelius

Osiek

Karmelicka

Rajska

Heweliusza

Stolarska

Olejarna

26

43

17

Korzenna

18

Na Piaskach

Katarzynki

15

6

Podwale Staromiejskie

39

Garncarska

Podwale Grodzkie

Wały Jagiellońskie

Hucisko

Targ Drzewny

Podmurze

9

11

Ławendowa

Straganiarska

24

20

Pańska

Szeroka

Kozia

Złotników

Grobla II · Grobla II · Grobla III

Świętojańska

55

54

Great Arsenal

Targ Węglowy

św Ducha

44

MAIN TOWN

45

23

1

4

Tkacka

Lektykarska

38

56

16

Grobla I · Grobla II

Okopowa

Bogusławskiego

Długa

40

22

Pocztowa

St Mary's Church

Historical Museum of Gdańsk

51

32

Mariacka

Chlebnicka

Artus Court

58

37

21

5

8

25

41

PTTK Tourist Office

47

14

Tourist Office

42

Tourist Office

49 57

Zbytki

Za Murami

Ławnicza

Długi Targ

Ogarna

Powroźnicza

7

46

Podwale Przedmiejskie

Stara Motława

Rzeźnicka

Kocurki

Toruńska

13

Na Stoku

Okopowa

3 Maja

3 Maja

Wały Piastowskie

33

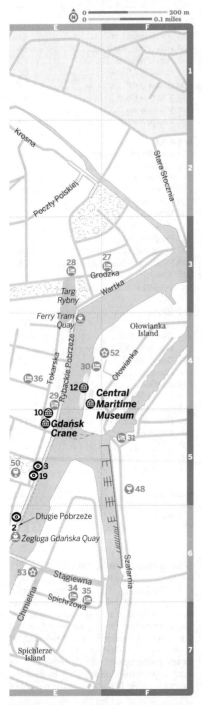

often cited as the largest old brick church in the world. Some 105m long and 66m wide at the transept, its massive squat tower climbs 78m high into the Gdańsk cityscape. Around 25,000 people can fit easily into its 5000-sq-metre (0.5-hectare) interior, and – this being Poland – that stat might have been tested for real a couple of times. Even from streets away, this awe-inspiring colossus looms sin-isterly in a million red bricks, dwarfing the houses at its oversize Gothic feet.

Begun in 1343, St Mary's didn't reach its present gigantic proportions until 1502. It served as the parish church for the Catholic congregation until the Reformation blew into town. It passed to the Protestants in 1572, to be used by them until WWII.

The church was a sitting duck for the Red Army shells in 1945, when half of the vault collapsed and the interior was largely burnt out. Fortunately, locals were wise enough to hide the most valuable works of art before the carnage commenced. Long and complex reconstruction was completed when these were returned.

The church's elephantine size is arresting and you feel even more antlike when you enter the building. Illuminated with natural light passing through 37 large windows (the biggest is 127 sq metres, the same area as a very large apartment), the three-naved, whitewashed interior, topped by an intricate Gothic vault, is astonishingly bright and spacious. It was originally covered with frescos, the sparse remains of which are visible in the far right corner.

On first sight, the church looks almost empty, but walk around its 30-odd chapels to discover how many outstanding works of art have been accumulated. In the floor alone, there are about 300 tombstones. In the chapel at the back of the left (northern) aisle is a replica of Memling's *The Last Judgment* – the original is in the National Museum's Department of Early Art. The extraordinary Baroque organ manages enough puff to fill the space with its tones.

The high altar boasts a Gothic polyptych from the 1510s, with the Coronation of the Virgin depicted in its central panel. Large as it is, it's a miniature in this vast space. The same applies to the 4m crucifix high up on the rood beam. Directly below it is a lofty wooden sacrarium from 1482, elaborately carved in the shape of a tower.

One object that does stand out, in terms of both its size and rarity, is the 15th-century

# Gdańsk

**astronomical clock**, placed in the northern transept. Another attraction of the church is its **tower** (adult/concession 4/2zł; ☉9am-5.30pm Mon-Sat, 1-5.30pm Sun), offering unrivalled vistas from its tiny viewing platform, 405 steps above the city.

**Great Arsenal**          HISTORIC BUILDING
(Wielka Zbrojownia; Map p304) To the west of St Mary's Church, ul Piwna (Beer St) ends at the Great Arsenal. This being Gdańsk, even such an apparently mundane building

as an armoury is an architectural gem. It's the work of Antonius van Opbergen, built at the beginning of the 17th century and, like most of Gdańsk's architecture, clearly shows the influence of the Low Countries. The main eastern facade, framed within two side towers, is floridly decorated and guarded by figures of soldiers on the top. Military motifs predominate, and the city's coat of arms guards the doorways. A small stone structure rather like a well, in the middle of the facade, is the lift that was used for hoisting heavy ammunition from the basement. At the time of research the building stood eerily empty.

### Royal Chapel
CHURCH

(Kaplica Królewska; Map p304) Squeezed between two houses just to the north of St Mary's Church, and completely overshadowed by its bulky neighbour, the small Royal Chapel is the only Baroque church in old Gdańsk. It was built between 1678 and 1681 to fulfil the last will of the primate of Poland at the time, Andrzej Olszowski. The chapel was designed by famous royal architect Tylman van Gameren, with the facade its most attractive feature.

### St Nicholas' Church
CHURCH

(Bazylika Św Mikołaja; Map p304; ul Świętojańska) Erected by the Dominican order on its arrival from Kraków in 1227, this is one of Gdańsk's oldest places of Christian worship and it certainly feels that way inside. Amazingly, it was the only central church to escape damage in WWII – according to one story, the attacking Soviet troops deliberately avoided shelling it, due to Orthodox believers' high regard for St Nicholas. Unlike most of the other Gothic churches in the city, the interior of St Nick's is very richly decorated with black-and-gold Baroque altars and ornately carved pews lining the nave. The magnificent late-Renaissance high altar of 1647 first catches the eye, followed by the imposing Baroque organ made a century later.

### National Museum's Department of Early Art
MUSEUM

(Muzeum Narodowe Oddział Sztuki Dawnej; Map p304; ul Toruńska 1; adult/concession 10/6zł; ⊙10am-5pm May-Sep, 9am-4pm Oct-Apr) Located just outside the Main Town, in an otherwise fairly uninteresting quarter called the Old Suburb, the National Museum's Department of Early Art is housed in the vaulted interiors of a former Franciscan monastery. Among the best art museums in the country, it covers the broad spectrum of Polish and international art and crafts, boasting extensive collections of paintings, woodcarvings, gold and silverware, embroidery, fabrics, porcelain, faience, wrought iron and furniture. It has the original figure of St George from the spire of the defunct Court of the Fraternity of St George; an assortment of huge, elaborately carved Danzig-style wardrobes (typical of the city, from where they

were sent all over the country); and several beautiful ceramic tiled stoves.

The 1st floor is given over to paintings, with a section devoted to Dutch and Flemish work. The jewel of the collection is Hans Memling's (1435–94) triptych of *The Last Judgment,* one of the earlier works of the artist, dating from 1472 to 1473. You'll also find works by the younger Brueghel and Van Dyck, and the beautifully macabre *Hell* by Jacob Swanenburgh, who was the master of the young Rembrandt.

### Market Hall
MARKET

(Hala Targowa; Map p304; Plac Dominikański; ⊙9am-6pm Mon-Fri, 9am-5pm Sat) Built on the site of a Dominican monastery, the 19th-century Market Hall is more interesting for its wrought-iron 19th-century railway-station architecture than for the procession of butchers, bakers and wedding-dress makers inside.

### Hyacinthus' Tower
HISTORIC BUILDING

(Baszta Jacek; Map p304; Plac Dominikański) The tall octagonal tower rising in front of the market hall is a remnant of the medieval fortifications and dates from around 1400. Today it houses a photo shop.

## OLD TOWN

Despite its name, Gdańsk's Old Town (Stare Miasto; Map p304) was not the cradle of the city. The earliest inhabited site, according to archaeologists, was in what is now the Main Town area. Nonetheless, a settlement existed in the Old Town from the late 10th century and developed parallel to the Main Town.

Under the Teutonic order, the two parts merged into a single urban entity, but the Old Town was always poorer and had no defensive system of its own. One other difference was that the Main Town was more 'German' while the Old Town had a larger Polish population. During WWII it suffered as much as its wealthier cousin but, apart from a handful of buildings (mainly churches), it was not rebuilt in its previous shape. The most interesting area today is along the Radunia Canal, between ul Garncarska and ul Stolarska.

### St Bridget's Church
CHURCH

(Kościół Św Brygidy; Map p304; ul Profesorska 17) Founded 700 years ago, St Bridget's was reduced to medieval brick dust in 1945, and until 1970 only the outer walls were left standing. Very little of the prewar furnishings survived, but if you've taken a fancy to

## IN A LEAGUE OF ITS OWN

It wasn't easy being a merchant in the Middle Ages, without the benefit of chambers of commerce or Rotary Clubs, and very little respect from the ruling classes. Travelling salesmen were seen as easy pickings by local lords, paying heavy tolls as they moved from province to province in Central Europe. Taking to the sea wasn't much better, as merchants' slow-moving boats were subject to attack by pirates.

The answer to their problems was to band together in the Hanseatic League, a group of trading ports that formed in the late 13th century and wielded unprecedented economic power. The Hansa (from a German word for 'association') was centred on Germany, making good use of its central location, with members also scattered throughout Scandinavia, across the Baltic to Russia, and west to the Netherlands. The League also had trading posts in cities like London and Venice. As a result, it could trade wax from Russia with items from English or Dutch manufacturers, or Swedish minerals with fruit from the Mediterranean.

The League took a far more muscular approach than that of today's business councils. It bribed rulers, built lighthouses and led expeditions against pirates, and on one memorable occasion raised an armed force that defeated the Danish military in 1368.

At its height the League had over a hundred members, including major cities now within Poland such as Danzig (Gdańsk), Stettin (Szczecin), Thorn (Toruń) and Elbing (Elbląg).

But it was all downhill from there. With no standing army and no government beyond irregular assemblies of city representatives, the League was unable to withstand the rise of the new nation-states of the 15th century and the shift of trade to Atlantic ports after the discovery of the New World. The assembly met for the last time in 1669, and its membership had been reduced to the core cities of Hamburg, Bremen and Lübeck by the time of its eventual disintegration in 1863.

The memory of the League lives on, however, in the **New Hanse** (www.hanse.org), founded in 1980 and bringing together the former Hansa member cities in a body promoting cultural cooperation and tourism.

amber you're sure to appreciate the spectacular 174cm-high amber monstrance depicting the tree of life and the monumental high altar, the highlight of the interior and a recent construction containing a record-breaking 6500kg of polished prehistoric tree resin.

Lech Wałęsa attended Mass here when he was an unknown electrician in the nearby shipyard. With the wave of strikes in 1980 the church became a strong supporter of the dockyard workers, and its priest, Henryk Jankowski, took every opportunity to express their views in his sermons. The church remains a record of the Solidarity period, with several contemporary craftworks related to the trade union and to modern Polish history in general. You'll find the tombstone of murdered priest Jerzy Popiełuszko, the Katyń epitaph, a collection of crosses from the 1980 and '88 strikes, and a door covered with bas-reliefs of scenes from Solidarity's history – all in the right-hand (northern) aisle.

**St Catherine's Church** CHURCH
(Kościół Św Katarzyny; Map p304; ul Profesorska 3) The largest monument of the Old Town is St Catherine's Church, which is the oldest in Gdańsk, begun in the 1220s. It was the parish church for the whole town until St Mary's was completed. As is common, the church evolved over centuries and only reached its final shape in the mid-15th century (save for the Baroque top to the tower, added in 1634).

Unfortunately, a major fire in May 2006 collapsed the church roof and caused damage to its interiors. Restoration work was in progress at the time of research, with some areas inaccessible to visitors, including the museum and tower, which were expected to be closed for some time. Although open to visitors, the interior was looking a bit ragged and it will be a long time before this wonderful church returns to its former glory.

**Great Mill** HISTORIC BUILDING
(Wielki Młyn; Map p304; ul Na Piaskach) Standing conspicuously opposite St Catherine's

Church, the Great Mill certainly lives up to its name. Created by the Teutonic Knights in northern Poland's typical red brick around 1350, it was medieval Europe's largest mill at over 40m long and 26m high. With a set of 18 monster millstones, each 5m in diameter, the mill produced 200 tonnes of flour per day right up until 1945. No longer serving the purpose for which it was built, the mill is now a mall.

**Old Town Hall**                    HISTORIC BUILDING
(Ratusz Staromiejski; Map p304; ul Korzenna 33) Behind the Great Mill, across a small park, the Old Town Hall was once the seat of the Old Town council. A well-proportioned Renaissance building crowned with a high central tower typical of its Flemish provenance, it was designed at the end of the 16th century by Antonius van Opbergen, the architect later responsible for the Great Arsenal. The brick structure is delicately ornamented in stone, including the central doorway and a frieze with the shields of Poland, Prussia and Gdańsk.

The Old Town Hall now houses the Baltic Sea Culture Centre and an exhibition hall. Go upstairs to see the foyer, notable for its rich decoration, which was partly assembled from old burghers' houses. Note the arcaded stone wall (1560) with three Roman gods in bas-relief. This composition, older than the town hall itself, was moved here from one of the houses in the Main Town. One of the doors leads to the Great Hall, which can also be visited. Concerts are held here – check the program for details.

### SHIPYARD AREA

TOP
CHOICE **Roads to Freedom**
**Exhibition**                              MUSEUM
(Drogi do Wolności; Map p304; www.fcs.org.pl; ul Wały Piastowskie 24; adult/concession 6/4zł; ☺10am-6pm Tue-Sun) Housed in a bunker deep beneath thundering ul Wały Piastowskie, this exhibition tracing the Polish struggle against communist rule is essential viewing for every visitor to the Tri-City. The story, all related with English captioning, begins with the uprisings in European capitals (Berlin, Budapest) against postwar communism, before moving on to the events around the Lenin Shipyard in the 1970s and '80s. Listen to Wałęsa's rabble-rousing speeches with subtitles, see the rather odd Pope-themed clown pen he used to sign the August Agreements, try to decipher the Unesco-

protected plywood board on which the handwritten, occasionally fantastical, demands of the dockers were displayed (Three-year maternity leave! Retirement at 50!) and watch the harrowing film showing the imposition of martial law in July 1983. All in all, an outstanding exhibition and a superbly interactive way of learning about the events in Gdańsk that still echo around Eastern Europe to this day.

**Shipyard**                                SHIPYARD
(Stocznia Gdańska; off Map p304) Gdańsk's former Lenin Shipyard to the north of the city centre is a key fragment of 20th-century European history. It was here that the first major cracks in Eastern Europe's communist wall appeared when discontent with the communist regime boiled over into strikes and dissent, brutally stamped out by armed force in 1970. A decade later an electrician named Lech Wałęsa emerged to rouse crowds of strikers here, leading to the formation of the Solidarity movement and ultimately to democracy for Poland and most of the Eastern Bloc.

However, since the giddy years of the Wałęsa presidency, the yard has largely lost its haloed status and for some time the vast area has been slated for redevelopment and general gentrification, though structures with historic significance will probably remain in place.

Near the entrance, the huge structure being thrown up at the time of research will become the **European Solidarity Centre** (off Map p304; www.ecs.gda.pl; Plac Solidarności), an exhibition hall, information centre and archive, plus the headquarters of an organisation observing human rights around the globe.

**Monument to the Fallen**
**Shipyard Workers**                       MONUMENT
(Pomnik Poległych Stoczniowców; off Map p304; Plac Solidarnści) Just in front of the shipyard gates, the Monument to the Fallen Shipyard Workers commemorates the workers killed in the riots of 1970. Unveiled on 16 December 1980, 10 years after the massacre, the monument is a set of three 42m-tall steel crosses, with a series of bronze bas-reliefs in their bases. One of the plates contains a fragment of the poem "You Who Wronged", by late Nobel laureate Czesław Miłosz: 'You who wronged a simple man/Do not feel safe. A poet remembers./You can kill one, but another is born.'

The first monument in a communist regime to commemorate the regime's victims, it became an instant symbol and landmark.

## WESTERPLATTE & NOWY PORT

Westerplatte (Map p300) is a long peninsula at the entrance to the harbour, 7km north of the historical centre. When Gdańsk became a free city after WWI, Poland was permitted to maintain a post at this location, at the tip of the port zone. It served both trading and military purposes and had a garrison to protect it.

The area is famous for one thing – it was here, at 4.45am on 1 September 1939 that the first shots of WWII were fired during the German invasion of Poland. The German battleship *Schleswig-Holstein* began shelling the Polish guard post and the first bullets fired back at them came from the windows of the Nowy Port **Lighthouse** (Latarnia Morska; Map p300; www.latarnia.gda.pl; ul Przemyslowa 6a; adult/concession 7/5zł; ☺10am-6pm Sat & Sun May–mid-Jun, daily mid-Jun–August, 10am-5pm Sat & Sun Sep). There are incredible views across the Bay of Gdańsk, including the Hel Peninsula, from the top.

On the other side of the harbour, the Westerplatte garrison, which numbered just 182 men, held out for seven days before surrendering. The site is now a memorial, with some of the ruins left as they were after the bombardment, plus a massive **monument** (Map p300) put up in memory of the defenders. The surviving **Guardhouse No 1** (Wartownia Nr 1; Map p300; ul Sucharskiego; adult/concession 3/2zł, free Mon; ☺9am-6pm mid-May–mid-Sep) houses a small exhibition describing the events of early September 1939.

Bus 106 goes to Westerplatte from the main train station, but a more attractive way to get here is by boat. Ferries, paddle steamers and a replica galleon depart several times daily for Westerplatte from the wharf next to the Green Gate (Map p304). The lighthouse in Nowy Port can be reached by tram 95 from outside Gdańsk Główny train station.

## OLIWA

A desirably gentrified suburb about 9km from the historic centre, Oliwa (Map p300) boasts a fine cathedral set in a quiet park, and provides an enjoyable half-day break from the dense attractions of the Main Town. To get here, take the commuter train from central Gdańsk and get off at Gdańsk Oliwa station, from where it's a 10-minute walk.

**Oliwa Cathedral**  CHURCH
(Map p300; ul Cystersów 10) The beginnings of Oliwa go back over 800 years, when the Pomeranian dukes who then ruled Gdańsk invited the Cistercians to settle here in 1186 and granted them land together with privileges, including the revenues from the port of Gdańsk.

The abbey didn't have an easy life. The original church from around 1200 was torched first by the pagan Baltic Prussians, then by the Teutonic Knights. A new Gothic church, built in the mid-14th century, was ringed with defensive walls, but that didn't save it from further misfortunes. When in 1577 the abbots supported King Stefan Batory in his attempts to reduce the city's independence, the citizens of Gdańsk burned the church down in revenge. The monks rebuilt their holy home once more, but during the Swedish wars the church fell prey to repeated looting, losing its organ and pulpit in the process. The monks' woes came to an end in 1831, but only when the Prussian government decided to expel them from the city altogether. The church was handed to the local parish and, in 1925, raised to the rank of cathedral. A safe distance from the city centre, it came through the war almost unscathed, and is a significant, and somewhat unusual, example of ecclesiastical architecture.

The first surprise is the facade, a striking composition of two slim octagonal Gothic towers with a central Baroque portion wedged between them. You enter the church by going downstairs as the floor is more than a metre below ground level. The interior looks extraordinarily long, mainly because of the unusual proportions of the building – the nave and chancel together are 90m long but only 8.3m wide. At the far end of this 'tunnel' is a Baroque high altar (1688), while the previous oak-carved Renaissance altar (from 1606) is now in the left-hand transept. Opposite, in the right transept, is the marble tombstone of the Pomeranian dukes (1613).

The showpiece of the church is the **organ** (www.gdanskie-organy.com). This glorious instrument, begun in 1763 and completed 30 years later, is renowned for its fine tone and the mechanised angels that blow trumpets and ring bells when the organ is in action. In July and August, recitals take place on Tuesday and Friday evenings, but 20-minute performances are held daily every hour or two between 10am and 3pm or 4pm (in the afternoon only on Sunday). Check the schedule with the tourist offices before setting off.

**Modern Art Gallery** GALLERY
(Oddział Sztuki Nowoczesnej; Map p300; ul Cystersów 18; adult/concession 10/6zł; ⊙10am-5pm Tue, Wed & Fri-Sun, noon-7pm Thu) Behind the cathedral is the 18th-century abbots' palace, now home to the Polish modern art branch of the National Museum of Gdańsk.

**Ethnographic Museum** MUSEUM
(Oddział Etnografii; Map p300; ul Cystersów 19; adult/concession 8/4zł; ⊙10am-5pm Tue, Wed & Fri-Sun, noon-7pm Thu) This interesting collection of rural household implements and crafts from the region is installed in an unusual granary.

## ✨ Festivals & Events

Aside from the Dominican Fair held annually in August, other major events in Gdańsk include the following:

**International Festival of Open-Air & Street Theatre** THEATRE
(FETA; www.feta.pl) Held in July.

**International Organ, Choir & Chamber Music Festival** MUSIC
(www.gdanskie-organy.com) Concerts every Friday in July and August in St Mary's Church.

**International Organ Music Festival** MUSIC
(www.filharmonia.gda.pl) Held in the Oliwa Cathedral with twice-weekly organ recitals from mid-June till the end of August.

**International Shakespeare Festival** THEATRE
(www.shakespearefestival.pl) Every August; performances mostly take place at the Teatr Wybrzeże but the festival is likely to move to the new Shakespeare Theatre, due for completion sometime in 2012.

**Sounds of the North Festival** MUSIC
(www.ars-baltica.net) Held every two years in August (next in 2012 and 2014), featuring traditional folk music from the Baltic region.

## 🛏 Sleeping

At the bottom end of the market, the city has some long-established hostels; at the top end look out for discounted rates at weekends and off season (October to April).

**DON'T MISS**

## DOMINICAN FAIR

Gdańsk's biggest bash of the year is the August **Dominican Fair** (Jarmark Dominikański; www.mtgsa.pl), held in the city since 1260. Launched by Dominican monks on Plac Dominikański as a feast day, the fun has spread to many streets in the Main Town and lasts for three weeks from the last Saturday of July. Amid the stalls selling cheap Chinese charms, dubious antiques, general bric-a-brac and craft items, interesting events take place on four stages and various other venues around the city centre. It's a great time to be in Gdańsk, but accommodation can be madly expensive and unfilled beds rare during the festivities.

On the rare occasion when Gdańsk is fully booked, consider staying in Sopot and use the cheap SKM train commute into the city centre.

**TOP CHOICE** **Kamienica Gotyk** GUESTHOUSE €€
(Map p304; ☑58 301 8567; www.gotykhouse.eu; ul Mariacka 1; s/d 280/310zł) Wonderfully located at the St Mary's Church end of ul Mariacka, Gdańsk's oldest house is filled by this neat, clean, Gothic-themed guesthouse. The seven rooms have Gothic touches such as broken-arched doorways and hefty drapery, though most are thoroughly modern creations and bathrooms are definitely of the third millennium. There's a small Copernicus museum in the cellar and a gingerbread shop on the ground floor.

**TOP CHOICE** **Hotel Podewils** HOTEL €€€
(Map p304; ☑58 300 9560; www.podewils.pl; ul Szafarnia 2; s/d 480/570zł; ☏☎) The view from the Podewils across the river to the Main Town can't be beaten, though the owners probably wish they could lift its cheery Baroque facade and move it away from the incongruously soulless riverside development that's sprouted next door. Guestrooms are a confection of elegantly curved timber furniture, classic prints and distinctive wallpaper; a restaurant, bar and two saunas keep guests occupied when not out sightseeing.

## APARTMENTS

As across Poland's north, a good way to save a bagful of złoty is to rent a room or a flat. The following agencies have ample digs if this is the way you decide to go:

**Grand-Tourist** (Map p304; ☑58 301 2634; www.gt.com.pl; ul Podwale Grodzkie 8) Located within the City Forum shopping centre opposite the train station, this efficient agency handles private rooms and apartments for up to six people. The basic rooms in ul Złotników couldn't be more central, but if you're banished to the suburbs, find out how close the place is to the SKM commuter train. Prices start at 60zł for a single room.

**Apartments Apart** (☑22 351 2250; www.apartmentsapart.com) Warsaw-based company offering a selection of apartments scattered around the Main Town, suitable for up to four people. Prices start at around 160zł per night for a studio apartment.

**Zappio Hostel**  HOSTEL €
(Map p304; ☑784 398 957; www.zappio.pl; ul Świętojańska 49; dm/s/d from 49/99/178zł; @⊛); Occupying a labyrinthine, chunky-beamed former merchant's house, the Zappio is so big that families with kiddies and party animals won't get in each other's way. In addition to high-ceilinged dorms sleeping up to 14, and 13 rooms of various medieval shapes and sizes, this remarkable hostel also has its own pub, bike rental, guest kitchen and 24-hour reception.

**Dom Muzyka**  HOTEL €€
(Map p300; ☑58 326 0600; www.dommuzyka.pl; ul Łąkowa 1/2; s 250zł; d 340-360zł; P@⊛) During the day, this understated hotel within a music college has a background soundtrack of random sounds and tuneful melodies. Its light-filled rooms hoist elegantly high ceilings and are discreetly decorated with old prints. Sparkling bathrooms complete the graceful look, and there's a classy restaurant and bar off the foyer. It's located about ten minutes' walk from the waterfront, across the river.

**Happy Seven Hostel**  HOSTEL €
(Map p304; ☑58 320 8601; www.happyseven.com; ul Grodzka 16; dm 45-70zł; @⊛) Hostels are at their most memorable and fun when the owners apply a touch of imagination to the dorms, and that's exactly what you'll experience here. The 'Library' has walls jam-packed with old volumes, the 'Warehouse' sports hefty metal shelving, while old suitcases hang from the ceiling in the 'Travel' dorm. Facilities include a guest kitchen and a small retro-styled common room equipped with Playstation 3. The hostel has another more upmarket annex nearby.

**Willa Litarion**  HOTEL €€
(Map p304; ☑58 320 2553; www.litarion.pl; ul Spichrzowa 18; s/d 255/330zł; ⊛) Another new kid on the block...well, island to be exact, Spichlerze Island. The 13 stylishly furnished, light-flooded rooms are bedecked in well-tuned browns, creams and golds with the odd splash of other hues, and bathrooms are crisp. More often than not this place is booked up to the back teeth, always a good sign.

**Hotel Królewski**  HOTEL €€€
(Map p304; ☑58 326 1111; www.hotelkrolewski.pl; ul Ołowianka 1; s 380zł, d 470-520zł; P⊛) This stylish hotel manages to marry its historical old granary-building exterior with an interior of 21st-century rooms and top-notch service. The waterside location, just a hop across the Motława to the Main Town, makes this an outstanding base if you've got the cash to splash.

**Dwór Oliwski**  HOTEL €€€
(Map p300; ☑58 554 7007; www.dwor-oliwski .com.pl; ul Bytowska 4; s 350-620zł, d 420-680zł; P⊛⊠) Retreat to the country (almost) at this luxuriously magnificent 17th-century manor house, a compelling reason to head out to Oliwa. The sophisticated five-star accommodation is housed in traditional buildings set amid extensive gardens and there's a spa and excellent French restaurant.

**Villa Pica Paca**  HOTEL €€€
(Map p304; ☑58 320 2070; www.picapaca.com; ul Spichrzowa 20; s/d 340/440zł; ⊛) One of a cluster of small boutique and design hotels to have sprung up on Spichlerze Island's ul Spichrzowa, the Pica Paca won't quite do it for seasoned boutique hotel dwellers, but it's an attention-grabbing place to tarry nonetheless. The eight cosily funky rooms and seven suites are all named after famous personalities, though some are better known than others (Nina Soentgerath room anyone?). The celebrity-obsessed theme

continues in the Germanically minimalist breakfast room.

### Qubus Hotel HOTEL €€€
(Map p304; 🖉58 752 2100; www.qubushotel.com; ul Chmielna 47/52; r from 450zł; P❄@🗫) The only hotel in Pomerania owned by the Polish Qubus chain, this 110-room mammoth in the city centre's southern reaches caters for both business clients and tourists. Inoffensively decorated rooms are generously cut and bathrooms pristine, but breakfast is 70zł extra. The hotel's own dinky little boat takes guests to the city centre (from 10am to 4pm), meaning you don't have to negotiate the grotty underpass beneath Podwale Przedmiejskie to reach it.

### Dom Aktora HOTEL €€
(Map p304; 🖉58 301 5901; www.domaktora.pl; ul Straganiarska 55/56; s/d 250/330zł, apt 380-560zł; P🗫) The no-nonsense apartments at this former thespians' dorm are affordable and have simply equipped kitchens, making this a prime target for self-caterers. Bathrooms throughout are 21st-century conceptions but otherwise not much has changed here decor-wise since the mid-1990s.

### Dom Harcerza HOTEL €€
(Map p304; 🖉58 301 3621; ul Za Murami 2/10; s 51zł, d 122-223zł, tr 152-263zł) Though occupying a former cinema, the 'Scouts' House' has a decidedly un-Hollywood feel. The simple, snug rooms are nothing fancy, but they're clean and tidy. Downstairs there's an old-fashioned restaurant serving standard Polish dishes. As the name suggests, this place deals with overexcited scout groups so things can get high-spirited, but the location near ul Długa is a winner.

### Hostel Targ Rybny HOSTEL €
(Map p304; 🖉58 301 5627; www.gdanskhostel .com.pl; ul Grodzka 21; dm/s/d from 45/100/200zł; @🗫) Once top hostel dog in Gdańsk, this long-established waterfront hostel sits within a picturesque old building with a sloping roof. Both the dorm area and rooms are a bit too snug, but that's made up for by their cleanliness. The free breakfast only makes sporadic appearances and some guests have complained about rude staff.

### Hotel Hanza HOTEL €€€
(Map p304; 🖉58 305 3427; www.hotelhanza.pl; ul Tokarska 6; s/d 440/500zł; P❄@🗫) A late-20th-century structure plonked right on the waterfront, with better views from it than

of it, this popular choice has just acceptable rooms for this price range, oversize bathrooms and pleasant staff, but could do with an update in parts. There's a well-populated riverside cafe-bar terrace with attractive views of old granaries across the water.

### Camping Nr 218 Stogi CAMPGROUND €
(Map p300; 🖉58 307 3915; www.kemping-gdansk .pl; ul Wydmy 9; site per adult/child 13/9zł, cabins 100zł; ☺May-Sep) Located in a pine forest in the suburb of Stogi, about 5.5km northeast of the centre, this is the most convenient of Gdańsk's three camping grounds. Just 200m away is one of the city's best beaches, with the cleanest water you'll find for miles. Tram 8 from the main train station passes here (25 minutes).

## 🍴 Eating

Plenty of eateries throughout the centre cater to every budget. Variety is also on the increase with everything from milk-bar basics to molecular fusion on the menu in the city centre.

### TOP CHOICE Velevetka KASHUBIAN €€€
(Map p304; ul Długa 45; mains 30-60zł) Go Kashubian at this delightful new eatery opposite the Town Hall, which manages to evoke a rural theme without a single ancient agricultural knick-knack or trussed waitress in sight. Admire the crisp interior of heavy wooden furniture, lightened with big-print traditional motifs and soothing scenes of the Kashubian countryside, while munching through finely crafted regional dishes.

### Restauracja Gdańska POLISH €€€
(Map p304; www.gdansk.pl; ul Św Ducha 16; mains 50-80zł; ☺noon-midnight) Dining in any of the five banqueting rooms and salons here is a bit like eating out in a well-stocked regional museum, surrounded as you are by massed antique furniture, oil paintings, model ships and random objets d'art. The upper-end traditional menu of herring, white Gdańsk-style *żurek* (traditional sour rye soup), duck with apple and cranberry, and slabs of cheesecake is as heavy as the sumptuous drapery.

### Restauracja Pod Łososiem POLISH €€€
(Map p304; ul Szeroka 52/54; mains 50-80zł; ☺noon-last customer) Founded in 1598 and particularly famous for its salmon dishes, this is one of Gdańsk's oldest and most highly regarded restaurants. Red leather seats, brass chandeliers and a gathering of

gas lamps fill out the rather sombre interior, illuminated slightly by the speciality drink here – Goldwasser. This gooey, sweet liqueur with flakes of gold suspended in it was invented and produced in its cellars from the late 16th century until WWII.

### Kresowa
EASTERN EUROPEAN €€

(Map p304; ul Ogarna 12; mains 20-40zł; ⊙noon-10pm) Take your tastebuds to Poland's long-lost east and beyond at this two-level, 19th-century period restaurant with the mood of an Imperial-era Chekhovian parlour. Start with Ukrainian borscht, order a main of Georgian lamb and finish off with a piece of Polish cheesecake while sipping Russian *kvas* (partially fermented bread and water) or vodka.

### Filharmonia
FUSION €€€

(Map p304; ul Ołwianka 1; mains 30-50zł; ⊙noon-midnight) Occupying a red-brick corner of the Philharmonia building facing the Targ Rybny across the river, the cooks here dabble in Heston Blumenthal–style molecular cuisine to admirable effect. If you came to Pomerania to glut out on braised flesh and ale, then the fernickety creations here will disappoint with their finesse, attention to detail and obsessive focus on taste.

### Bar Mleczny Neptun
POLISH €

(Map p304; ul Długa 33/34; mains 5-14zł; ⊙7.30am-8pm Mon-Fri, 10am-5pm Sat & Sun; 🕾) It's surprising just where some of Poland's communist-era milk bars have survived and this one, right on the tourist drag, is no exception. However, the Neptun is a cut above your run-of-the-mill *bar mleczny,* with

---

### TRI-CITY TOURIST CARD

The **'Gdańsk–Sopot–Gdynia Plus' tourist card** (adult/concession 15/11zł for 24hr, 34/22zł for 72hr) provides discounts or free admission at 200 museums, galleries, cultural institutions, hotels, restaurants and clubs, as well as serving as a pass for the entire Tri-City public transport system. With so many service providers taking part, the ticket comes with a usefully thick booklet giving details on every location you can unsheathe it and what discounts to expect. It's available from any tourist office in the Tri-City area.

---

potted plants, decorative tiling and free wi-fi – whatever next?!

### Green Way
VEGETARIAN €

(Map p304; ul Garncarska 4/6; mains 8-17zł; ⊙10am-8pm Mon-Fri, noon-7pm Sat & Sun; 🖋) A kind of 21st-century *bar mleczny* only serving generous portions of vegetarian and organic fare. This being Eastern European, don't expect much spice. There's another, more central, branch at ul Długa 11.

### Czerwone Drzwi
POLISH €€

(Map p304; ul Piwna 52/53; mains 20-70zł; ⊙10am-10pm) Step through the Red Door into a relaxed, refined cafe atmosphere, which helps you digest the small but interestingly seasonal menu of Polish and international meals.

### Pellowski Bakery
CAFE €

(Map p304; ul Rajska 5; cakes & snacks from 2zł; ⊙7am-8pm Mon-Fri, 7am-3pm Sat, 9am-4pm Sun) The bakeries belonging to this chain are located throughout the city centre and are great for a coffee-and-pastry breakfast.

### Tawerna
POLISH €€€

(Map p304; ul Powroźnicza 19/20; mains 29-119zł; ⊙11am-late) A historic eatery within a dark, restfully gloomy interior. It's nautically themed, hence the fish-o-centric menu.

### Kuchnia Rosyjska
RUSSIAN €€

(Map p304; Długi Targ 11; mains 9-42zł) Russian restaurant on the main tourist route decorated with the inevitable *matryoshka* dolls, samovars and folksy utensils.

##  Drinking

Getting a dose of Arabica, a jug of ale or something a lot, lot stronger is pretty easy in central Gdańsk, with cafes and bars assembling anywhere tourists do. More characterful nooks can be found in ul Mariacka and ul Piwna, and even the new development across the Motława has a few worthwhile places.

### Brovarnia
MICROBREWERY

(Map p304; ul Szafarnia 9; ⊙1-11pm) Northern Poland's best microbrewery cooks up award-winning dark, wheat and lager beers in polished copper vats amid sepia photos of old Gdańsk. Tables are tightly packed but this place lacks a beer-hall feel, possibly as it's squeezed into vacant granary space in the posh Hotel Gdańsk.

# AMBER GAMBLER

For some visitors, one of the main reasons to come to Gdańsk is to source jewellery made of Baltic gold – fossilised tree resin found on the Baltic shores of Poland and Russia, commonly known as amber.

But beware: at some smaller, less-reputable stalls, you may not be getting the real deal, with some pieces containing well-crafted chunks of Russian or Chinese plastic.

Here are three ways locals recommend you can tell if the amber you are being offered is bona fide prehistoric sap. Not all shopkeepers will be happy to see you testing their wares in these ways, for a variety of obvious reasons.

» Take a lighter and put amber into the heat – it should give off a characteristic smell, like incense.

» Amber floats in 20% salt water, while plastic or synthetic amber won't.

» Rub amber against cloth and the static electricity produced attracts tiny pieces of paper.

**Degustatornia Dom Piwa** PUB
(Map p304; ul Grodzka 16; ☺3pm-midnight Mon-Thu, until 1am Fri & Sat, & 10pm Sun) If beer brings you cheer, then the 180 types of ale, lager, porter and myriad other hop-based concoctions at this pub will have you ecstatic. Some 80 Polish bottled beers are poured alongside such gems as Czech Radegast, Kentish Spitfire, dark Erdinger wheat beer, Belgian strawberry ale and cloudy Ukrainian Chernihivske.

**Goldwasser** CAFE
(Map p304; Długie Pobrzeże 22; ☺10am-8pm) Experience the spirit of the interwar Free City of Danzig in both atmosphere and in your glass at the home of three tasty local tipples – Goldwasser, Kurfüsten and locally produced Machandel vodka. Enter from Długi Targ.

**Cafe Absinthe** CAFE
(Map p304; ul Świętego Ducha 2; ☺10am-4am Mon-Fri, until 6am Sat) By day this unassuming bar occupying an inconspicuous corner of the Teatr Wybrzeże building is the haunt of a few coffee-cradling newspaper readers. But when darkness falls, the inebriated debauchery starts – when there's no dance floor, use the tables.

**Pi Kawa** CAFE
(Map p304; ul Piwna 5/6; ☺10am-10pm) This cafe on Beer Street has a relaxed interior with a country kitchen feel, sporting timber tables, original artwork for sale, and a fish tank. It's a good hide-out from the tourist crowds on ul Długa.

**Kamienica** CAFE
(Map p304; ul Mariacka 37/39; ☺10am-11pm) The pick of the bunch on ul Mariacka is this excellent two-level cafe with a calm, sophisticated atmosphere and the best patio on the block. As popular for a daytime caffeine-and-cake halt as it is for a sociable evening bevvy.

##  Entertainment

Check the local press for up-to-date cultural and entertainment listings. As anyone in town will tell you, Sopot is the place to go for a serious night out.

### Clubs & Live Music

**Miasto Aniołów** CLUB
(Map p304; www.miastoaniolow.com.pl; ul Chmielna 26; ☺9pm-late) The City of Angels covers all the bases – late-night revellers can hit the spacious dance floor, crash in the chill-out area, or hang around the atmospheric deck overlooking the Motława River. Nightly DJs play disco and other dance-oriented sounds.

**Parlament** CLUB
(Map p304; www.parlament.com.pl; ul Św Ducha 2; ☺8pm-late) Popular though pretty mainstream club with strutting nights devoted to hits of yesteryear, pop, dance, R'n'B and the inevitable Polish hip-hop phenomenon.

**Yesterday** CLUB
(Map p304; www.yesterday-klub.pl; ul Piwna 50/51; ☺8pm-late) Groovy cellar venue decked out in 1960s flower-power decor, including a large Yellow Submarine and a fluorescent portrait of Chairman Mao. DJs play a variety of sounds from 9pm every night, and there's the occasional live gig.

## Opera, Classical Music & Theatre

**Baltic Philharmonic Hall**　CLASSICAL MUSIC
(Map p304; ☑58 320 6262; www.filharmonia.gda
.pl; ul Ołowianka 1) The usual home of chamber music concerts also organises many
of the major music festivals throughout
the year.

**State Baltic Opera**　OPERA
(Map p300; ☑58 763 4906; www.operabaltycka.pl;
Al Zwycięstwa 15) Founded in 1950, Gdańsk's
premier opera company resides in this opera
house in the Wrzeszcz district, next to the
Gdańsk Politechnika train station. Alongside the usual operatic repertoire, it stages
regular ballets. Symphonic concerts are also
held here.

**Teatr Wybrzeże**　THEATRE
(Map p304; ☑58 301 1328; www.teatrwybrzeze.pl;
Targ Węglowy 1) Top productions of Polish and
foreign classics next to the Great Arsenal in
the Main Town.

## 🔒 Shopping

Gdańsk shopping isn't all about amber –
Goldwasser makes an unusual take-home
item and pretty Kashubian handicrafts are
also worth considering.

**Burztynowa Komnata**　JEWELLERY
(Map p304; Długie Pobrzeże 1; ☻10am-6pm)
Attractive creations in local amber as well as
polishing demonstrations.

**Millennium Gallery**　JEWELLERY
(Map p304; Długi Targ 25/27; ☻10am-6pm) Certi-
fied pieces of exquisite amber jewellery.
Second branch at Długie Pobrzeże 2.

**Cepelia**　ARTS & CRAFTS
(Map p304; ul Długa 47; ☻10am-6pm Mon-Fri, to
2pm Sat) The most obvious place to head for
Kashubian trinkets.

## ℹ️ Information

### Internet Access
**Jazz'n'Java** (Tkacka 17/18; per hr 6zł; ☻10am-
10pm)
**PTTK Tourist Office** (ul Długa 45; per 15 min
3zł; ☻8am-8pm daily Jun-Aug, 9am-4pm
Mon-Fri, 9am-5pm Sat & Sun Sep-May)

### Internet Resources
**http://guide.trojmiasto.pl** Detailed Tri-City
tourist guide.
**www.gdansk4u.pl** Gdańsk's official tourist
website.
**www.gdansk.pl** Excellent city information site.

**www.lonelyplanet.com/poland/pomerania
/gdansk** For planning advice, author
recommendations, traveller reviews and insider
tips.

### Money
**Bank Millennium** Eastern Main Town (Długi
Targ 17/18); Western Main Town (ul Wały
Jagiellońskie 14/16)
**Bank Pekao** (ul Garncarska 23)
**PBK Bank** (ul Ogarna 116)

### Post
**Post office** (Map p304; ul Długa 23/28)

### Tourist Information
**PTTK Tourist Office** (Map p304; ☑58 301
9151; www.pttk-gdansk.pl; ul Długa 45; ☻8am-
8pm daily Jun-Aug, 9am-4pm Mon-Fri, 9am-
5pm Sat & Sun Sep-May)
**Tourist office** Train station (ul Podwale
Grodzkie 1; ☻9am-5pm Mon-Sat, to 4pm Sun
high season); Main Town (Map p304; ☑58 301
4355; Długi Targ 28/29; ☻10am-5pm Mon-Sat,
to 4pm Sun high season); Airport (Map p300;
ul Słowackiego 200; ☻9am-5pm Mon-Sat, to
2pm Sun high season) Efficient but occasionally
visitor-weary info points. The train station
branch is hidden in the underpass leading to
the city centre.

### Travel Agencies
**JoyTrip** (☑58 320 6169; www.pl.joytrip.eu;
ul Fieldorfa 11/13) Whatever you need to do in
the Tri-City, these guys can help you do it.
**Travel Plus** (☑58 346 3118; www.travel-plus.eu;
ul Szeroka 50/51) Gdańsk and Pomerania-wide
tours.
**PTTK** (☑58 301 9151; www.pttk-gdansk.pl;
ul Długa 45, PTTK Tourist Office) Arranges
foreign-language tours and other excursions.

## ℹ️ Getting There & Away

### Air
**Lech Wałęsa airport** (Map p300; ☑58 348
1163; www.airport.gdansk.pl) is in Rębiechowo,
14km west of Gdańsk. The **LOT office** (☑58
301 2822; Wały Jagiellońskie 2/4) is next to the
Upland Gate.

There are domestic flights with LOT to Warsaw (at
least four times daily) and Eurolot to Kraków (up to
nine weekly) and Wrocław (at least four weekly).

International flights to many European capitals
and regional destinations in the UK and across
Europe are operated by budget airlines **Ryanair**
(www.ryanair.com) and Hungarian low-cost
carrier **Wizz Air** (www.wizzair.com).

### Boat
**Polferries** (www.polferries.pl) operates car
ferries from Gdańsk Nowy Port (Map p300)

to Nynäshamn in Sweden (adult/concession Skr750/640, 19 hours, daily departures in high season).

### Bus

Gdańsk's bus terminal is right behind the central train station, linked to it by an underground passageway. Buses are handy for regional destinations, which have rare or no trains.

Gdańsk has the following bus connections:

**Elbląg** 14zł, 1½ hours, nine daily

**Frombork** 18zł, three hours, daily (alternatively change in Elbląg)

**Kartuzy** 7zł, one hour, half-hourly (bus 801 from the road outside the bus station)

**Kościerzyna** 16zł, 1½ hours, hourly

**Lidzbark Warmiński** 30zł, three to 3½ hours, daily

**Olsztyn** 33zł, four hours, six daily

**Warsaw** 56zł, six hours, eight daily

There are plenty of connections from Gdańsk to Western European cities plus daily services east to Kaliningrad (50zł, five hours), and Vilnius (150zł, 16 hours) via Olsztyn.

### Train

The grand main train station, **Gdańsk Główny**, on the western outskirts of the Old Town, handles all services.

Almost all long-distance trains to/from the south originate and terminate in Gdynia, while trains running along the coast to western destinations start in Gdańsk and stop at Gdynia (and Sopot) en route.

Gdańsk has the following rail connections:

**Lębork** (for Łeba) 11zł, 1¾ hours, hourly (SKM)

**Malbork** 12zł, 50 minutes, many

**Olsztyn** 39zł, three hours, six daily

**Poznań** 54zł, five hours, six daily

**Szczecin** 56zł, five hours, three daily (or change in Słupsk)

**Toruń** 44zł, four hours, nine daily

**Warsaw** 56zł to 119zł, 5¾ to 7¼ hours, 11 daily (two overnight services)

**Wrocław** 61zł, eight hours, three daily (or change in Poznan)

### 🛈 Getting Around

#### To/From the Airport

The **Airport Bus** (www.airportbus.com.pl) goes to the airport seven times a day from outside the Hotel Mercure Hevelius (9.90zł, 35 minutes), or you can take cheaper bus 110 to/from Gdańsk Wrzeszcz (2.50zł, 35 minutes).

#### Boat

From May until September, **Żegluga Gdańska** (Map p304; www.zegluga.pl) runs pleasure boats and hydrofoils from Gdańsk's wharf, near the Green Gate, to Sopot (adult/concession 30/15zł) and Westerplatte (30/20zł).

To Hel (adult/concession 20/10zł, four daily) take the **Ferry Tram** (Tramwaj Wodny; Map p304; www.ztm.gda.pl), which departs from a point further up the wharf near Targ Rybny. Bicycles cost an extra 3zł to transport.

**Ustka-Tour** (www.rejsyturystyczne.pl) operates cruises to Westerplatte (adult/concession return 40/22zł, hourly) aboard the *Galeon Lew* and the *Perła*, replica 17th-century galleons.

#### Train

A commuter train, known as the SKM (Szybka Kolej Miejska; Fast City Train), runs constantly between Gdańsk Główny and Gdynia Główna (35 minutes), stopping at a dozen intermediate stations, including Sopot (3.40zł). The trains run every five to 10 minutes at peak times and every hour or so late at night. You buy tickets at the stations and validate them in the big yellow boxes at the platform entrance (not in the train itself), or purchase them prevalidated from vending machines on the platform.

#### Tram & Bus

These are a slower means of transport than the SKM but cover more ground, running from 5am until around 11pm, when a handful of night lines take over. Tickets cost 2.80zł for any one way journey and 3.80zł for one hour's travel. A day ticket valid for a 24-hour period from the first time it is franked costs 11zł. Remember to validate your ticket in the vehicle, so it's stamped with the date and time.

# AROUND GDAŃSK

## Sopot

POP 38,800

The junior partner in the Tri-City set-up (along with Gdańsk and Gdynia), Sopot is a kind of Schizophrenia-on-Sea, a mix of elegant villas and marauding clubbers, an overdeveloped 21st-century seafront just streets away from typically Polish soot-cracked facades. Like the British seaside towns of Brighton and Eastbourne rolled into one, Sopot is about moneyed Poles flashing their cash in ritzy eateries standing alongside old Polish literary-themed cafes, a strutting club scene illuminating pensioners taking the waters while kids on the beach build sandcastles. Whatever Sopot has become, it certainly remains popular, with international visitors mingling with the Slavic waffle-and-ice-cream crowds on hot

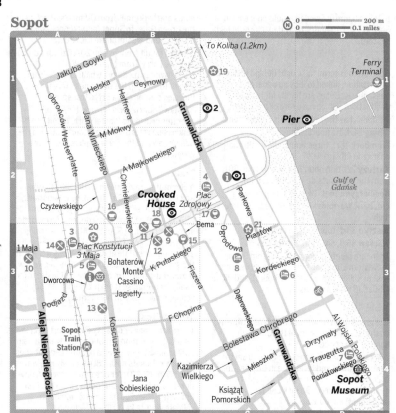

Sopot

GDAŃSK & POMERANIA SOPOT

summer days then getting down at the beachside clubs of a balmy Baltic eve.

Sopot's incarnation as a fashionable resort arose in 1823 when Jean Georges Haffner, a former doctor in Napoleon's army, popularised sea-bathing here. The settlement, originally established in the 13th century as a fishing village, rapidly became the beach destination of the rich and famous, particularly after WWI when it was included in the territory of the Free City of Danzig. Since 1990 it's once again become the playground of wealthy entrepreneurs and A-Z-list celebrities, and remains unrivalled among the Baltic's resorts for glitz and pretentiousness.

## ☉ Sights & Activities

**ulica Bohaterów Monte Cassino** STREET
Sopot's unavoidable spine is Heroes of Monte Cassino Street, an attractive and invariably crowded mall stretching from the railway line to the pier. Many of Sopot's

eateries and places of entertainment line its pedestrianised length, some of which can be found in the unmissable **Crooked House** (Krzywy Domek; Map p318; ul Bohaterów Monte Cassino 53), a warped structure and a typical piece of post-communist-era architectural experimentation. Concealed within its twin-level innards are a dozen bars and restaurants, and several shops. Love it or hate it, most wander in to investigate at some point.

**Sopot Museum** MUSEUM
(Muzeum Sopotu; Map p318; www.muzeumsopotu .pl; ul Poniatowskiego 8; adult/concession 5/3zł, free Thu; ☉10am-4pm Tue, Wed & Fri, noon-6pm Thu, 11am-6pm Sat & Sun) At the southern end of the beachfront, the Sopot Museum showcases 19th-century furniture and fittings within a grand villa of that era, including some enormous, ornately carved wardrobes. Other displays include old sepia photos and maps of German Zoppot and other Baltic

# Sopot

resorts. The building, an early-20th-century holiday home of a wealthy merchant, is worth a look in itself.

**Pier**      WATERFRONT
(Map p318; www.molo.sopot.pl) At the end of Monte Cassino, beyond Plac Zdrojowy, is the famous Molo, Europe's longest wooden pier, built in 1928 and jutting 515m out into the Bay of Gdańsk. Various attractions along its length come and go with the seasons.

**Opera Leśna**      AMPHITHEATRE
(Forest Opera; Map p300; www.bart.sopot.pl; ul Moniuszki 12) In a wooded hilly area of the town stands the Opera Leśna, an amphitheatre that seats 5000 people and is host to the prestigious **International Sopot Festival** (www.sopotfestival.onet.pl; ⊙Aug), a Eurovision-style song contest and festival famous across Central and Eastern Europe. The arena has been closed in recent years for renovation, but was set to reopen for the summer of 2012.

**Aqua Park**      AMUSEMENT PARK
(Map p300; www.aquaparksopot.pl; ul Zamkowa Góra 3/5; per hr 24zł; ⊙8am-10pm) This large Aqua Park has tubes, slides, spas and a wild river ride, plus something called 'The World of Saunas'.

**Art Gallery**      GALLERY
(Państwowa Galeria Sztuki; Map p318; www.pgs.pl; Plac Zdrojowy 2; adult/concession 10/7zł; ⊙11am-7pm Tue-Sun) Funded by the town of Sopot, this glitzy new art gallery within the reconstructed

Dom Zdrojowy (Spa House) has changing exhibitions of mostly Polish art.

FREE **Dom Zdrojowy**      BATHHOUSE
(Spa House; Map p318; Plac Zdrojowy 2; ⊙10am-6pm) Take the space-age glazed lift to the 3rd floor of the new Spa House to enjoy a free sip of Sopot's natural, mineral-rich spring water.

**Grand Hotel**      LANDMARK
North of the pier is the landmark 1927 Grand Hotel, adjoining the long waterfront spa park that first popularised the town.

## 🛏 Sleeping

TOP CHOICE **Hotel Bayjonn**      HOTEL €€€
(Map p318; ☎58 732 7563; www.bayjonnhotel.pl; ul Powstańców Warszawy 7; s 475-599zł, d 550-699zł; P🐾) Occupying an architecturally striking corner of the newly erected Haffner Centre, this recently-minted design hotel is all retro stripes and faux '70s browns, but with stunningly contemporary bathrooms and little nods to the past in the shape of old German-era maps of Zoppot. Facilities are kept shiny, staff are friendly enough and the location is superb. When you've finished admiring the interior, head to the ground-floor Thai restaurant then work it off in the small gym.

**Central Hostel Sopot**      HOSTEL €
(Map p318; ☎58 719 2473; www.hostelcentral.pl; ul Bohaterów Monte Cassino 15; dm 55-80zł, d 230zł) Hurray, Sopot has a hostel, and it's a good

one, too. Spacious both horizontally and vertically, this three-storey former workers' hostel has dorms containing four to 10 beds, space-saving under-bunk lockers and the occasional renovated bathroom. Breakfast is included in the price, there's cycle hire and tours are planned.

**Pensjonat Eden** GUESTHOUSE €€
(Map p318; ☎58 551 1503; www.hotel-eden.pl; ul Kordeckiego 4/6; s 110-200zł, d 190-300zł; P) The crumbly facade of this early-20th-century villa doesn't promise much; but once inside this family-run guesthouse you'll receive a friendly welcome before being shown up to one of the 26 well-kept rooms, flaunting stylishly high ceilings and lots of fun-and-fusty furniture straight from granny's parlour.

**Hotel Rezydent** HOTEL €€€
(Map p318; ☎58 555 5800; www.hotelrezydent.pl; Plac Konstytucji 3 Maja 3; s from 420zł, tw from 450zł; P❄@🛜) The Rezydent is the most elegant hotel in town, though you'll need an inelegantly fat wallet to stay here. Its rooms' tasteful tones are set off by stylish carpets, timber furniture and lustrous bathrooms. When you're done luxuriating, there's a classy restaurant and pub downstairs, along with an art gallery, a sauna and massage services.

**Camping Nr 19** CAMPGROUND €
(Map p300; ☎58 550 0445; www.kemping19.cba.pl; ul Zamkowa Góra 25; site 14zł) A large but often chock-full camping ground located at the northern end of town near the beach (a five-minute walk from the Sopot Kamienny Potok train station).

**Pensjonat Wanda** GUESTHOUSE €€
(Map p318; ☎58 550 3037; www.bws-hotele.pl; ul Poniatowskiego 7; s 280-320zł, d 300-360zł; P🛜) A traditional, 25-room guesthouse with en-suite rooms, some with balconies overlooking the sea and sand. There's a reasonably priced restaurant on the premises.

**Willa Zacisze** APARTMENTS €€
(Map p318; ☎58 551 7868; ul Grunwaldzka 22a; apt 260zł; P) These apartments with modern furniture and fittings allow some savings on meals, as they're fitted out with kitchens. Great location close to the beach.

## Eating

Much of Sopot's cuisine scene is seasonal, particularly in the beach area, but there's no shortage of good year-round options.

TOP CHOICE **Błękitny Pudel** CAFE €€
(Map p318; ul Bohaterów Monte Cassino 44; mains 19-37zł; ⏲9am-11pm) This top pub-cafe is a real knick-knack fest with the cobbled interior bedecked in wooden tennis rackets, balalaikas, richly upholstered divans and seemingly everything in between. A cafe by day and beer/cocktail spot after dark; choose between the cosy interior and an outdoor pew for a bit of people watching on ul BMC.

**Kebabistan** KEBAB €
(Map p318; ul Bohaterów Monte Cassino 36; kebabs 10-20zł; ⏲11am-late) Not hard to guess what this places serves up – *döner,* in a box, in bread, plus *baklava* and drinks. Great name and popular stop-off for those stumbling/crawling their way to the SKM at 3am.

**Pub Kinski** PUB €€
(Map p318; ul Kościuszki 10; mains 25-35zł; ⏲1pm-3am) The house and birthplace of legendary German actor and psychopath Klaus Kinski has been converted into an offbeat bar-restaurant, with film posters and decadent crimson tablecloths within a cosy, candlelit setting. The man himself probably would have trashed the place, but in a loving way.

**Green Way** VEGETARIAN €
(Map p318; Al Niepodległości 786; mains 8-18zł; ⏲10am-7pm Mon-Sat, from 11am Sun; ✎) Generous portions of budget veggie nosh in no-frills surroundings. There's another branch at ul Bohaterów Monte Cassino 47.

**Tesoro Express** PIZZERIA €€
(Map p318; ul Bohaterów Monte Cassino 11; mains 10-30zł; ⏲noon-8pm Mon-Thu, to 10pm Fri & Sat, from 1pm Sun) Real Italian pizzas made by real Italians plus real cheap beer.

## Drinking

**Spatif** BAR
(Map p318; ul Bohaterów Monte Cassino 54; ⏲4pm-1am) Head up the steps off ul BMC to find this unmissable, avant-garde place packed with charity-shop leftovers and backstage kitsch. The crowd ranges from wannabe novelists to Warsaw boob-job gals, the atmosphere more vodka-inspired the later things get.

**Młody Byron** CAFE
(Map p318; ul Czyżewskiego 12; ⏲3-11pm Mon-Fri, noon-midnight Sat & Sun) This newly renovated mini-palace houses a quaint little cafe (the former U Hrabiego), far from the lubricated

wannabes on ul BMC, where more bookish types take the cake and engage in highbrow banter.

### Mandarynka
BAR
(Map p318; www.mandarynka.pl; ul Bema 6) This very cool confection of timber tables, scarlet lampshades and huge orange cushions is about as loungey as it gets. There's a food menu, and a DJ in action upstairs most nights.

### Zaścianek
CAFE
(Map p318; ul Haffnera 3; ⊙11am-10pm) Delightful olde-worlde cafe full of antique bric-a-brac, potted plants, oil paintings and intimate tables for two.

## ☆ Entertainment

Sopot has a vibrant club and live-music culture that's always changing; ask the locals about the current hot favourites. The scene here is also notably gay-friendly.

### Papryka
CLUB
(Map p318; www.klubpapryka.pl; ul Grunwaldzka 11; ⊙3pm-late) This appealing timbered villa near the beach buzzes on all levels – the two floors, balcony and beer garden are set in an attractive park surrounding the club. Music includes house, dub and alternative sounds.

### Organica
CLUB
(Map p318; www.organicaclub.pl; ul Bohaterów Monte Cassino 17; ⊙9pm-5am Thu-Sat) This completely third-millennium dance nook in black and neon, punctuated with red lightning strikes creeping across the walls, has silken sipping booths and local DJs pumping out chilled tunes for well-tailored revellers.

### Cream
CLUB
(Map p318; www.creamsopot.pl; Al Mamuszki 2; ⊙9pm-late Thu-Sat) The biggest, brashest and busiest of the beachfront clubs, where northern Poland's rich, young and beautiful can be found gyrating to DJs from across the *rzeczpospolita* (republic) and beyond.

### Koliba
CLUB
(off Map p318; www.koliba.pl; beach entrance 5, ul Powstanców Warszawy 90; ⊙24hr) A beach hike or bike ride north along the Baltic, this traditional timber mountain chalet is a restaurant by day but at night the tables and chairs are pushed back to create the Tri-City's most unlikely and unpretentious nightclub. Great beach access and Baltic-side terrace.

## ❶ Information

**Post office** (Map p318; ul Kościuszki 2)

**Tourist office** Dom Zdrojowy (Map p318; ☑58 550 3783; www.sts.sopot.pl; Plac Zdrojowy 2; ⊙9am-6pm high season); Dworcowa (Map p318; ☑58 341 4073; ul Dworcowa 4; ⊙9am-6pm high season)

## ❶ Getting There & Away

All trains between Gdańsk and Gdynia stop in Sopot – see p317. SKM commuter trains to Gdańsk (3.40zł) run every five to 10 minutes at peak times.

A ferry service dubbed the **Ferry Tram** (Tramwaj Wodny; www.ztm.gda.pl) heads from Sopot to Hel or Gdańsk three times a day in summer. The landing site is at the pier.

# Hel Peninsula

Located north of the Tri-City, the Hel Peninsula (Półwysep Helski) is a 34km-long, crescent-shaped sandbank arcing out into the Baltic Sea. A mere 300m wide at the base, it's no wider than 500m for most of its length though does expand out to around 3km at the end to accommodate the 'capital', Hel. Reaching just 23m above sea level, much of the landscape is covered with trees – picturesque, wind-deformed pines predominate – and there's also a number of typical coastal plant varieties including sand sedge and dune thistle.

The peninsula was formed over the course of about 8000 years by sea currents and winds, which gradually formed an uninterrupted belt of sand. At the end of the 17th century, as old maps show, the sandbar was still cut by six inlets, making it a chain of islands. In the 19th century the peninsula was cut into separate pieces several times by storms. The edges have been strengthened and the movement of the sand has been reduced by vegetation, but the sandbar continues to grow.

The peninsula is bookended by two fishing ports: the aforementioned Hel at its tip and Władysławowo at its base. Between them is a third port, Jastarnia, and three villages: Chałupy, Kuźnica and Jurata. All are tourist resorts during the short summer season (July and August) and are linked by a railway line and a surprisingly good road running the peninsula's entire sandy length.

The northern shore is one long stretch of beautifully sandy beach and, except for small areas around the resorts (which are

GDAŃSK & POMERANIA HEL PENINSULA

usually packed with holidaymakers), they're clean and deserted.

The Hel Peninsula is easily accessible from the Tri-City by train, bus and boat. The bus and train can take you anywhere you want, while boats and hydrofoils link Hel with Gdańsk and Sopot.

## HEL
POP 3900

Most English-speakers can't help cracking a smirk as they ask for their ticket to Hel. But this relaxed holiday town at the end of its long slender sandbar is far from purgatory. In fact it's quite a pleasant getaway, and feels a long way from Poland's post-communist cares. The beach is the obvious main draw when it's hot; the rest of the year the town shows few vital signs.

Throughout history, Hel benefited from its strategic location at the maritime gateway to Gdańsk. By the 14th century Hel was a prosperous fishing port and trading centre. However, it was constantly threatened by storms and the shifting coastline, and declined in importance in the 18th century before reinventing itself as a popular seaside resort.

### ◉ Sights

**Fokarium**                                    AQUARIUM
(www.fokarium.com; ul Morska 2; admission 2zł; ☺9.30am-7pm) Just off the beach in the centre of town is the Fokarium, where Baltic grey seals can be seen in captivity. The three large pools are home to half a dozen of the creatures, and feeding takes place at 11am and 3pm (and other times when large school groups turn up) when keepers put these incredibly obedient animals through their paces for fishy rewards. You'll need a 2zł piece to unlock the main turnstile and another if you want to visit the small museum once inside.

**Museum of Fishery**                           MUSEUM
(Muzeum Rybołówstwa; Bulwar Nadmorski 2; adult/concession 6/4zł; ☺10am-6pm daily Jul & Aug, shorter hours rest of yr). Hel's Gothic church dates from the 1420s, making it the oldest building in town. Pews and monstrances have given way to exhibits on fishing and boat-building, a display of stuffed sea birds and a collection of old fishing boats. The tower provides views of the peninsula and Gulf of Gdańsk.

**Memorial**                                    MEMORIAL
As you walk from the train station to the town centre, you'll notice a park containing a memorial to the 1939 defence of the town during the German invasion. Hel was the last place in Poland to surrender; a garrison of some 3000 Polish soldiers defended the town until 2 October. The peninsula became a battlefield once more on 5 April 1945, when about 60,000 Germans were caught in a bottleneck by the Red Army and didn't lay down their arms until 9 May, making it the last piece of Polish territory to be liberated.

**Lighthouse**                                  LIGHTHOUSE
(ul Bałtycka 3; adult/concession 6/4zł; ☺10am-2pm & 3-7pm Jul & Aug, shorter hours May, Jun & Sep) Around 1km north of town, the 42m-high brick lighthouse looks like a rocket about to take off.

### 🛏 Sleeping

There are beds in ample numbers during the summer months though few classic hotels or guesthouses. The best place to start if you're looking to stay over is the official **Hel website** (www.gohel.pl) which has lots of listings and an interactive map. Many locals rent out rooms in their homes for around 65zł a night – just ask around. Unfortunately you'd be lucky to find anyone willing to let you bed down for just one night.

**Duna Guesthouse**                    GUESTHOUSE €
(☑58 351 2063; www.duna.org.pl; ul Morska; d/tr 140/180zł) This beachside place has fresh, well-tended rooms and apartments with flat-pack furniture and modern bathrooms. Outside of the high season you can pay as little as 55zł per person.

### ❶ Getting There & Away

To reach Hel by train, you'll first have to make your way to Gdynia (from Gdańsk on the SKM, 5zł, 30 minutes) and change there (15.60zł, two hours, hourly); even in low season there are fairly regular services. When you arrive, follow the brick footpath 500m to the town centre.

You can also get to Hel via the **Ferry Tram** (Tramwaj Wodny; www.ztm.gda.pl) from Gdańsk or Sopot (see p317).

Another waterborne option is the Żegluga Gdańska pleasure boat/hydrofoil from May to September from Gdańsk (p317).

## Kashubia

If you believe the legend, the region of Kashubia (Kaszuby) was created by giants, whose footprints account for the many hills and lakes that characterise the landscape. Stretching for 100km southwest of Gdańsk, it's a picturesque area noted for its small, traditional villages, and a lack of cities and industry.

In contrast to most of the other groups who gradually merged to form one big family of Poles, the Kashubians have managed to retain some of their early ethnic identity, expressed in their distinctive culture, dress, crafts, architecture and language.

The Kashubian language, still spoken in the home by some 50,000, mostly elderly locals, is the most distinct Polish dialect. It's thought to derive from the old Slavic Pomeranian language; other Poles have a hard time deciphering it.

The area between Kartuzy and Kościerzyna is the most topographically diverse part of the region, including the highest point of Kashubia, Mt Wieżyca (329m). This is also the most touristy area of Kashubia, with the most facilities. Public transport between Kartuzy and Kościerzyna is fairly regular, with buses running every hour or two.

Unless you have your own transport, you miss out on some of the region by being limited to the major routes. Public transport becomes less frequent the further off the track you go. Visiting the two regional destinations Kartuzy and Wdzydze Kiszewskie will give a taste of the culture of Kashubia, though less of its natural beauty.

### KARTUZY
POP 15,000

The town of Kartuzy, 30km west of Gdańsk, owes its birth and its name to the Carthusians, a religious order that was brought here from Bohemia in 1380. Originally founded in 1084 near Grenoble in France, the order was known for its austere monastic rules – its monks passing their days in the contemplation of death, following the motto 'Memento Mori' (Remember You Must Die).

When they arrived in Kartuzy the monks built a church and, beside it, 18 hermitages laid out in the shape of a horseshoe. The church (ul Klasztorna 5) seems to be a declaration of the monks' philosophy; the original Gothic brick structure was topped in the 1730s with a Baroque roof that looks like a huge coffin. On the outer wall of the chancel there's a sundial and, just beneath it, a skull with the 'Memento Mori' inscription. The adjacent cemetery continues the morbid theme.

The maxim is also tangibly manifested inside, on the clock on the balustrade of the organ loft. Its pendulum is in the form of the angel of death armed with a scythe that swings unnervingly above your head as you enter.

The interior is a Baroque riot beneath Gothic vaulting; the intricately carved stalls catch the eye while the church's oldest artefact, an extraordinary panel from a 15th-century Gothic triptych, is in the right-hand chapel.

Slavophiles will love Kartuzy's other attraction, the surprisingly good and delightfully old-school **Kashubian Museum** (Muzeum Kaszubskie; www.muzeum-kaszubskie.gda.pl; ul Kościerska 1; adult/concession 10/6zł; ⊘8am-4pm Tue-Sat year-round, 10am-2pm Sun May-Sep), south of the train station near the tracks. Amid the inevitable wooden farm implements and kitchen utensils there are some beautiful toffee-brown and metallic-black pottery so typical of the region, wonderfully simple textiles and hefty rural furniture. One room is given over to the Carthusians.

Whether you're looking to stay on or move on, the brand-new **tourist office** (⊘58 684 0201; ul Klasztorna 1; ⊘9am-6pm Mon-Fri, to 3pm Sat & Sun) can help out. The office is also a superb source of information on Kashubian culture throughout the region.

Gryf buses (not PKS) shuttle between Gdańsk (7zł, one hour) and Kartuzy every half an hour.

### WDZYDZE KISZEWSKIE
POP 200

Some 16km south of Kościerzyna, Wdzydze Kiszewskie is a tiny village with a big attraction, namely the **Kashubian Ethnographic Park** (Kaszubski Park Etnograficzny; www.muzeum-wdzydze.gda.pl; adult/concession 12/9zł; ⊘10am-6pm Tue-Sun Jul & Aug, shorter hours rest of yr), an open-air museum displaying the typical rural architecture of Kashubia. Established in 1906 by the local schoolmaster, this was Poland's first open-air museum of traditional architecture. Many have followed in its wake. Pleasantly positioned on the lakeside, it now contains a score of buildings rescued from central and southern Kashubia, including cottages, barns, a school, a windmill and an 18th-century church used for Sunday Mass. Some of the interiors boast authentic furnishings, implements and decorations, showing how the Kashubians lived a century or two ago.

Eight buses daily link Wdzydze with Kościerzyna (7zł, 40 minutes), which has very frequent services to/from Gdańsk (16.50zł, 1½ hours, half-hourly).

# LOWER VISTULA

The fertile land within the valley of the Lower Vistula, bisected by the wide, slowly flowing river, was prized by invaders for centuries. Flat, open and dotted with green farms, this region developed during the 13th and 14th centuries into a thriving trade centre, via the many ports established along the Vistula's banks from Toruń to Gdańsk. The history of these towns is intertwined with that of the Teutonic order, the powerful league of Germanic knights who by then occupied much of the valley. Remnants from the order's heyday now comprise some of the most prominent sights in the region.

Though the Lower Vistula suffered much destruction in the closing months of WWII, what survived is a rich cultural inheritance of great depth and interest.

## Toruń

POP 193,100

If you've spent your time so far in Poland jostling with the stag and hen crowds in Kraków and wandering Warsaw's concrete, wondering why you came, then Toruń will come as a mini-revelation. This magnificently walled Gothic town on the Vistula should be high on every traveller's list, possibly as its delights seem low on everyone else's, leaving visitors who make it here to revel unrestricted in its wealth of red-brick buildings, Unesco-listed sites and medieval city defences, all of which WWII mercifully decided to ignore.

Beyond architecture, Toruń is also well known as the birthplace of Nicolaus Copernicus (1473–1543). His name (Mikołaj Kopernik in Polish) is all over town, and you can even buy gingerbread shaped in his image. This other Toruń icon – its *pierniki* (gingerbread) – is famous across Poland.

### History

Toruń was kickstarted into prominence in 1233, when the Teutonic Knights transformed the existing 11th-century Slav settlement into one of their early outposts. The knights surrounded the town, then known as Thorn, with walls and a castle. Rapid expansion as a port meant that newly arriving merchants and craftspeople had to settle outside the city walls and soon built what became known as the New Town. In the 1280s Toruń joined the Hanseatic League, giving further impetus to its development.

Toruń later became a focal point of the conflict between Poland and the Teutonic order, and when the Thirteen Years' War finally ended in 1466, the Treaty of Toruń returned a large area of land to Poland, stretching from Toruń to Gdańsk.

The following period of prosperity ended with the Swedish wars, and the city fell under Prussian domination in 1793, later becoming part of Germany. Toruń didn't return to Poland until the nation was recreated after WWI.

After WWII, Toruń expanded significantly, with vast new suburbs and industries. Luckily, the medieval quarter was unaffected and largely retains its old appearance.

## ◎ Sights

**Regional Museum**       MUSEUM
(Muzeum Okręgowe; www.muzeum.torun.pl; Rynek Staromiejski 1; adult/concession 10/6zł; ⊙10am-6pm Tue-Sun May-Sep, 10am-4pm Tue-Sun Oct-Apr) The **Old Town Hall** (Ratusz Staromiejski) was built at the end of the 14th century and hasn't changed much since, though some Renaissance additions lent an ornamental touch to the sober Gothic structure. It was once used as the municipal seat and a market, but today the building is home to the main branch of the Regional Museum. Displays within its original interiors include a collection of Gothic art (painting, woodcarving and stained glass), a display of local 17th- and 18th-century crafts, and a gallery of Polish paintings from around 1800 to the present. You can also ascend the **tower** (adult/concession 10/6zł; ⊙10am-8pm May-Sep, 10am-5pm Oct-Apr) for a fine panoramic view of Toruń's Gothic townscape.

**Cathedral of SS John the Baptist & John the Evangelist**     CHURCH
(Katedra Św Janów; ul Św Jana & ul Kopernika) Under heavy and seriously needed renovation at the time of research, Toruń's mammoth Gothic Cathedral of SS John the Baptist & John the Evangelist was begun around 1260 but was only completed at the end of the 15th century. Its massive tower houses Poland's second-largest historic bell (after the one in the Wawel Royal Cathedral of Kraków), the **Tuba Dei** (God's Trumpet). Cast in 1530, it weighs 7238kg and is rung for significant religious and national events. On the southern side of the tower, facing the Vistula, is a large 15th-century clock; its original face and

single hand are still in working order. Check out the dent above the VIII – it's from a cannonball that struck the clock during the Swedish siege of 1703.

The interior is a light-filled environment with elaborate altars resting beneath the whitewashed vaulting. Its most striking murals are the monochrome paintings set high at the back of each aisle, which depict a monk and a devil or plague figure; created by an unknown artist, the black-and-white style is highly unusual for this kind of church art.

The high altar, adorned with a Gothic triptych and topped with a crucifix, has as a background a superb stained-glass window in the best medieval style. The last chapel in the right-hand aisle holds the oldest object in the church, the font where Copernicus was baptised. To one side is his epitaph.

### House of Nicolaus Copernicus    MUSEUM
(Dom Mikołaja Kopernika; ul Kopernika 15/17; adult/concession 10/7zł; ⊘10am-6pm Tue-Sun May-Sep, 10am-4pm Tue-Sun Oct-Apr) As is often the case with 'birthplaces' in Central and Eastern Europe, local Toruń historians often lock horns over the issue of whether Copernicus was actually born in this red-brick mansion. This, and a lack of English captioning, rather takes the oomph out of the Regional Museum's second-biggest attraction, which is torn between displays of old furniture, astronomy and Copernicus' life story. More engaging, if ridiculously overpriced, is its short **audiovisual presentation** (adult/concession 12/7zł) regarding Copernicus' times in Toruń, with a **model** of the town during that period. There are soundtracks in several languages, English included.

The third element of the museum is the extravagantly titled **World of Toruń's Gingerbread** (Świat Toruńskiego Piernika; adult/concession 10/6zł), which offers insights into the arcane art of *pierniki* creation. Visitors are guided by a costumed medieval townsperson and given the chance to bake their own.

### House Under the Star    MUSEUM
(Kamienica Pod Gwiazdą; Rynek Staromiejski 35; adult/concession 7/4zł; ⊘10am-6pm Tue-Sun May-Sep, 10am-4pm Tue-Sun Oct-Apr) The House Under the Star is a chunk of madly stuccoed architectural confectionery embellishing the Main Square. Inside you'll discover another outpost of the Regional Museum, this time a small but elegant collection of Asian art, including Japanese swords, Indian statues and Chinese pottery from the Tang dynasty. The building's ornate Baroque fittings include striking polychrome ceilings and a statue of Minerva.

### City Defences    HISTORIC BUILDINGS
Lost count of the museum's myriad branches? Teeth aching from too much gingerbread? Could be time to take a break and stroll the remnants of the town's original medieval fortifications, a popular activity with no admission to pay. Take a picnic if the weather's good.

To the east, in a triangle squeezed between the Old and New Towns, are the **ruins of the castle**, built by the Teutonic Knights. It was destroyed by the town's inhabitants in 1454 as a protest against the order's economic restrictions (they must have been really miffed – those Teutonic castles were sturdily built).

Following the old city walls west around from the castle, you'll come to the first of three surviving city gates, the **Bridge Gate** (Brama Mostowa). A 700m-long bridge was built here between 1497 and 1500 and survived for over three centuries. Continue along the walls to find the other two gates, the **Sailors' Gate** (Brama Żeglarska) and the **Monastery Gate** (Brama Klasztorna). At the far western end are a few medieval granaries and the **Leaning Tower** (Krzywa Wieża).

### Explorers' Museum    MUSEUM
(Muzeum Podróżników; ul Franciszkańska 11; adult/concession 8/5zł; ⊘10am-6pm Tue-Sun May-Sep, 10am-4pm Tue-Sun Oct-Apr) Usually the last subdivision of the Regional Museum on visitors' mental itineraries, the Explorers' Museum is commendably interesting in an eccentric sort of way. It contains artefacts from the amassed collection of seasoned nomad Antonio Halik, including his hats, travel documents, souvenirs of his many

## JUST THE TICKET

If you're planning to visit all six attractions affiliated with the Regional Museum in Toruń, why not buy a single pass costing 40zł (concessions 25zł) valid for two days. Otherwise visit on a Wednesday when the whole caboodle (except the Town Hall tower) is free.

GDAŃSK & POMERANIA TORUŃ

# Toruń

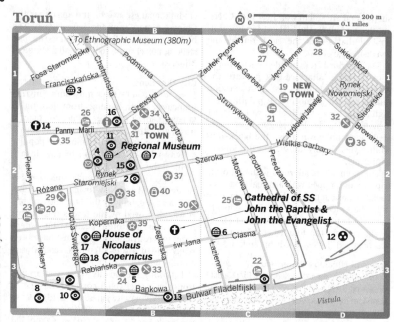

journeys and a criminal number of pilfered hotel keys!

## St Mary's Church
CHURCH

(Kościół NMP; ul Panny Marii) Toruń's third great Gothic structure in the Old Town (after the Town Hall and Cathedral) is St Mary's Church, erected by the Franciscans at the end of the 13th century. Austere and plain from the outside, the highly strung interior has tall, intricate stained-glass windows and a prominent golden altarpiece.

## House of the Esken Family
MUSEUM

(Dom Eskenów; ul Łazienna 16) The Gothic House of the Esken Family, set behind the cathedral, was converted into a granary in the 19th century. It normally contains city history displays on the 1st floor, and on the 2nd floor a collection of medieval weaponry and archaeological exhibits from the Iron and Bronze Ages, but was under comprehensive renovation at the time of research.

## Ethnographic Museum
MUSEUM

(Muzeum Etnograficzne; www.etnomuzeum.pl; Wały Sikorskiego 19; adult/concession 9/6zł; ⏰9am-4pm Wed & Fri, 9am-5pm Tue & Thu, 10am-6pm Sat & Sun) The thatched cottages in

parkland to the north of the city centre aren't relics from some former age but belong to this undervisited museum of rural life.

## Gingerbread Museum
MUSEUM

(Muzeum Piernika; www.muzeumpiernika.pl; ul Rabiańska 9; adult/concession 9.50/8zł; ⏰9am-6pm) Learn about gingerbread's history and create a spicy toothrotter under the enlightened instruction of a mock-medieval gingerbread master.

## Wozownia Art Gallery
GALLERY

(ul Rabiańska 20; admission varies, free Tue; ⏰11am-6pm Tue-Fri, from noon Sat & Sun) This small art gallery has changing displays of contemporary art, providing some contrast to the Gothic frenzy outside.

## ⚡ Festivals & Events

### Jazz Odnowa
(www.jazz.umk.pl) One of Poland's top jazz festivals, held in February.

### Polish Speedway Grand Prix
(www.speedway.torun.pl) Held in late April at Europe's largest speedway stadium.

### Probaltica Music & Art Festival of Baltic States
(www.probaltica.art.pl) Held in May.

# Toruń

**Kontakt International Theatre Festival**
(www.teatr.torun.pl) Held every other year in
May (next in 2012 and 2014).

**Toruń Days**
City festival held on 24 June.

# 🛏 Sleeping

Toruń has plenty of central places to stay,
but as hotels tend to be small, finding a
room can be tricky at peak times; weekdays
are busiest, and many owners offer reasonable weekend discounts. Toruń has a vast
number of three-star hotels housed within
historic buildings in the centre of town, and
competition keeps standards high.

### Hotel Karczma Spichrz

TOP CHOICE | HOTEL €€
(☑56 657 1140; www.spichrz.pl; ul Mostowa 1; s/d
from 230/290zł; P❋🌐) Wonderfully situated within a historic waterfront granary,
this hotel's 19 rooms are well supplied with
personality, featuring massive exposed
beams above characterful timber furniture

and contemporary bathrooms. There's a
restaurant and bar, a billiards room, and
the location by the river is within walking distance of the sights but away from
the crowds.

### B&B

HOTEL €€
(☑56 621 8100; www.hotelbb.pl; ul Szumana 8;
r 140-199zł; ❋🌐P) Had enough of smoke-
tainted mattresses, Solidarity-era TVs and
dust-layered frilliness? Then take one of
the 93 rooms in this purpose-built cube
near the bus station north of town, the
first B&B to open in Poland. Despite its
location just metres from the busy ring
road, absolutely no traffic din will disturb
your sleep in the rooms that provide the
basics every 21st-century traveller needs:
bed, breakfast, shower and wi-fi in a basic,
easily maintainable but by no means
spartan environment. If you want local
character, go elsewhere. Breakfast is an
extra 22zł.

### Hotel Kopernik    HOTEL €€

(✆56 652 25 73; www.kopernik.torun.pl; ul Wola Zamkowa 16; s 170-260zł; d 200-350zł; ⓟ🛜) This former army hostel has long been a favourite among travellers to Toruń and continues to offer a great deal on the eastern edge of the Old Town. Rooms are basic with pine furniture and cheap carpets, and bathrooms are standard-issue, but staff are superb and the no-frills breakfast taken in the basement provides a filling set-up for the day.

### Green Hostel    HOSTEL €

(✆52 561 4000; www.greenhostel.eu; ul Małe Garbary 10; d/tr 100/150zł; 🛜) Located up a 14th-century set of steeply spiralling stairs behind an inconspicuous entrance opposite Hotel Heban, this dorm-less hostel offers 34 beds over four floors, bathrooms on each floor and 24-hour reception. Rates are per person – you pay for the whole room and there are no singles, so this is definitely a better deal if you're travelling in a two- or moresome. Rooms are a trifle cramped. Commendably hushed digs for people who prefer to do their partying outside the hostel.

### Hotel Petite Fleur    HOTEL €€

(✆56 621 5100; www.petitefleur.pl; ul Piekary 25; s/d from 168/216zł) One of the best midrange options in Toruń has understated rooms containing slickly polished timber furnishings and elegant prints, though the singles can be a touch space-poor. The French brick cellar restaurant is one of Toruń's better hotel eateries.

### Hotel Heban    HOTEL €€

(✆56 652 1555; www.hotel-heban.com.pl; ul Małe Garbary 7; s/d 190/290zł; ⓟ🛜)Atmospherically billeted in a prettily gabled townhouse in quiet ul Małe Garbary, the Heban has a floral-themed restaurant, a relaxingly stylish lounge in olive green and 22 light and airy, if not over-stylishly fitted-out, rooms.

### Hotel Pod Orłem    HOTEL €€

(✆56 622 5025; www.hotel.torun.pl; ul Mostowa 17; s 132-223zł, d 167-223zł; ⓟ) The Pod Orłem is one of Toruń's oldest hotels, with a history going back more than a century. Leather-padded doors open onto some pretty spacious rooms; the cheaper ones are strangely like staying in your grandma's spare room. Buffet breakfast is an extra 16zł.

### Hotel Pod Czarną Różą    HOTEL €€

(✆56 621 9637; www.hotelczarnaroza.pl; ul Rabiańska 11; s/d 170/210zł) 'Under the Black Rose' fills out both a historic inn and a newer wing facing the river, though its interiors present a uniformly clean, up-to-date look with the odd antique reproduction. Buffet breakfast included.

### Hotel Trzy Korony    HOTEL €€

(✆56 622 6031; www.hotel3korony.pl; Rynek Staromiejski 21; s 125-195zł, d 140-190zł) Amazingly, this budget hotel's glorious history includes sleepovers by three illustrious monarchs (hence the name, meaning 'three crowns'). Today the only crowned head you'd encounter would be hiding from a Facebook-inspired revolution in one of its 30 bog-standard rooms, neatly furnished with wholly un-royal flat-pack pine furniture. The cheaper quarters have shared bathrooms.

### Dom Turysty PTTK    HOSTEL €

(✆56 622 3855; www.pttk.torun.pl; ul Legionów 24; s/d/tr/q 70/85/120/140zł) The 65-bed PTTK hostel is in a residential house, a 10-minute walk north of the Old Town (five minutes from the bus terminal), with 24-hour reception and a snack bar. Rooms are simple but clean and functional.

### Hotel Gotyk    HOTEL €€

(✆56 658 4000; www.hotel-gotyk.com.pl; ul Piekary 20; s/d 190/270zł) Yet another beautifully restored townhouse hotel. Pass the suit of armour in the foyer and up green carpeted stairs you'll find individually decorated rooms and classic furniture.

### Orange Hostel    HOSTEL €

(✆56 652 0033; www.hostelorange.pl; ul Prosta 19; dm/s/d 30/50/90zł; @🛜) Modern, friendly base with a range of cheap, private rooms, a guest kitchen and clean washing facilities. There's a second branch at ul Jęczmienna.

### Fort IV    HOSTEL €

(✆56 655 8236; www.fort.torun.pl; ul Chrobrego 86; dm 23-25zł, s/d 31/62zł) Toruń is encircled by the ruins of 19th-century forts but this is the only one to put up guests for the night in basic, iron-bedded dorms. Take bus 14 to the end of the line.

## ✖ Eating

### Oberża    POLISH €

(ul Rabiańska 9; mains 6-15zł; ⊙11am-11pm Mon-Thu, to 1am Fri & Sat, to 9.30pm Sun; 🛜) This large self-service canteen stacks 'em high and sells 'em cheap for a hungry crowd of locals and tourists. Find your very own thatched mini-cottage or intimate

## STRANGE STATUARY

Toruń's main square is furnished with a number of interesting pieces of statuary, but relatively few locals know the stories behind them.

Starting a few steps from the Old Town Hall entrance, the **statue Copernicus** is one of the oldest monuments dedicated to the stargazer and a regular feature in holiday snaps.

West of the Town Hall, opposite the post office, is an intriguing small **fountain** dating from 1914. Bronze-cast frogs sit on its rim, admiring a statue of a violin-playing boy known as Janko Muzykant, Toruń's very own answer to the Pied Piper. Legend has it that a witch once came to the town, but wasn't welcomed by the locals. In revenge, she invoked a curse, and the town was invaded by frogs. The mayor offered a sackful of gold and his daughter to anyone who would rescue the town. A humble peasant boy then appeared and began to play his rustic fiddle and the frogs, enchanted by the melodies, followed him to the woods and the town was saved.

On the opposite side of the Rynek, at the corner of ul Chełmińska, you'll find another curious critter-related statue at knee-level, depicting a **dog** and an **umbrella**. The pooch's name is Filus, and he starred in a famous long-running Polish comic strip as the pet of brolly-wielding Professor Filutek.

The **bronze donkey** in the southeast corner (dubbed the 'brass ass' by some Americans) has a much more sinister story attached. Few tourists straddling its back are aware that this is actually a copy of a wooden donkey that stood here in medieval times, to which criminals were strapped and flogged.

hideout lost amid stained-glass windows, cartwheels, bridles and other rural knick-knackery of yesteryear to enjoy 11 types of *pierogi* (dumplings), soups, salads and other Polish mains from a menu tuned to low-cost belly-packing. And don't forget your wireless-enabled device.

**Bar Mleczny**　　　　　　　POLISH €
(ul Różana 1; mains 3-9zł; ⊙9am-7pm Mon-Fri, 9am-4pm Sat & Sun) The city centre's last remaining *bar mleczny* offers substantial Polish stodge for a fistful of złoty. The outdoor window serves up waffles, ice cream and perhaps northern Poland's best *zapiekanki* (Polish pizza).

**Prowansja**　　　　　　　FRENCH €€
(ul Szewska 19; mains 15-26zł; ⊙noon-10pm Sun-Thu, noon-11pm Fri & Sat) This charming little place does a reasonable impression of a French restaurant. In fact the quiche, crêpes and salads could make you think you were in Provence, but only if you've never been there. Pretty good wine list and some Polish fare on the menu.

**Kuranty**　　　　　　　BISTRO €€
(Rynek Staromiejski 29; mains 15-50zł; ⊙11am-2am) With leathery seating and lots of exposed wood, this place resembles a Victorian British boozer but with flat-screen TVs hanging from the bar. A list of *pierogi* filled with

almost any other foodstuff, Italian pastas, soups and meat dishes populate the menu.

**Masala (Gospoda Pod Modrym Fartuchem)**　　　　　INDIAN €€
(Rynek Nowomiejski 8; mains 10-35zł; ⊙10am-10pm) Though still retaining its medieval character, this 15th-century building now hosts an Indian bar-restaurant, but one with a muddled menu of borscht, tortillas and biryani dishes to satisfy any (or no) palate. The outdoor seating on the New Town Square is still a great place for a post-dusk brew.

**Green Way**　　　　　　VEGETARIAN €
(ul Łazienna 13; mains 8-19zł; ⊙11am-7pm Mon-Sat, noon-6pm Sun; ✍) This being Toruń, even this vegetarian canteen, part of a national chain, resides in high-ceilinged, attractively wood-panelled premises.

## 🍷 Drinking

**Tantra**　　　　　　　BAR
(ul Ślusarska 5) Forget those Gothic bricks – this bar takes the colour red to new heights in its astonishingly decorated interior. It's done out in an Indian and Tibetan theme and layered with cloth and other artefacts from the subcontinent, including some tastefully rendered images of erotic temple statuary. Relax on the cushion-strewn

divans, order a drink from the long list and meditate on the infinite.

### Cafe Molus
CAFE

(www.cafemolus.pl; Rynek Staromiejski 19) This stylish cafe fulfils the desires of the sweet-toothed and caffeine-cravers under broken Gothic arches, painted ceilings and some of the chunkiest beamery you're ever likely to see. But the highlight here must be the secluded little Renaissance-style courtyard out back where you can leave the city distantly frenzying as you take cake. Rooms available.

### Atmosphera
CAFE

(ul Panny Marii 3) Try a gingerbread-flavoured coffee (*kawa po Toruńsku*) and a hefty wedge of cheesecake at this unassuming caffeine stop littered with odd tables and a jumble of chairs. Over 100 different kinds of tea, plus a globalised wine list.

## ☆ Entertainment

### Dwór Artusa
PERFORMING ARTS

(☎56 655 4939; www.artus.torun.pl; Rynek Staromiejski 6) The Artus Court, one of the most impressive mansions on the main square, is now a major cultural centre and has an auditorium hosting musical events, including concerts and recitals.

### Art Cafe
CLUB

(ul Szeroka 35; ☺8pm-late) The insider's address for everything new and cool in electronic music, from house to hardcore, with occasional hip-hop nights thrown in. Posters outside the door outline upcoming acts.

### Lizard King
LIVE MUSIC

(www.lizardking.pl; ul Kopernika 3) Live-music venue with gigs ranging from local tribute bands to quite big rock acts from around Eastern and Central Europe.

## 🛍 Shopping

Gingerbread is Toruń's signature souvenir but it's so scrumptious we doubt much of it actually makes it out of the country. The following two stores are traditional gingerbread emporia, but this sweetmeat can be found in many other gift shops and even the local supermarkets.

### Pierniczek
FOOD

(ul Żeglarska 25; ☺9am-8pm) *The* place to buy gingerbread, though don't expect low prices just because it's a factory shop.

### Sklep Kopernik
FOOD

(Rynek Staromiejski 6) Another place to purchase Toruń's favourite nibble, housed in the Artus Court on the southern side of the main square.

## ❶ Information

**Bank Pekao** (ul Wielkie Garbary 11)

**Emporium** (☎56 657 6108; www.emporium .torun.com.pl; ul Piekary 28; ☺10am-6pm Mon-Fri, to 4pm Sat year-round, plus 10am-4pm Sun Jul & Aug) Great little souvenir shop offering cycle hire (per hour/day 5/25zł), handy luggage store (per hour 1zł) and city maps.

**Ksero Uniwerek** (ul Franciszkańska 5; per hr 6zł; ☺8am-7pm Mon-Fri, 9am-4pm Sat) Internet access.

**Post office** (Rynek Staromiejski 15)

**Tourist office** (☎56 621 0931; www.it.torun.pl; Rynek Staromiejski 25; ☺9am-4pm Mon & Sat, 9am-6pm Tue-Fri year-round, 11am-3pm Sun May-Sep) Free internet access, heaps of info and very professional staff who know their city.

## ❶ Getting There & Away

**BUS** The PKS terminal, close to the northern edge of the Old Town, handles services to:

**Chełmno** 9zł, 1½ hours, many

**Golub-Dobrzyń** 8zł, one hour, many

**Szczecin** 50zł to 60zł, six hours, five daily (one overnight service)

**Warsaw** 37zł to 53zł, three hours, hourly

**TRAIN** Toruń has two stations – Toruń Główny is about 2km south of the Old Town, on the opposite side of the Vistula, while the more convenient Toruń Miasto is located on the Old Town's eastern edge. Not all services stop at both stations.

Trains head to:

**Gdańsk** 44zł, 3¼ to five hours, nine daily

**Grudziądz** 13zł, 1½ hours, seven daily

**Kraków** 61zł, 7¾ to 9¼ hours, four daily

**Malbork** 21zł to 31zł, 2½ hours, six daily

**Olsztyn** 26zł, 2½ hours, eight daily

**Warsaw** 37zł to 46zł, three hours, 11 daily

# Golub-Dobrzyń
POP 13,000

Golub-Dobrzyń may sound like a minor character in *The Lord of the Rings*, but it is in fact a town about 40km east of Toruń. Dobrzyń, on the southern bank of the Drwęca River, is a boxy, uninteresting place, but Golub was founded in the 13th century as a border outpost of the Teutonic Knights, who left behind one of their

## A THOUSAND AND ONE KNIGHTS

It's impossible to travel anywhere in Pomerania without encountering the ghosts of the Teutonic Knights, the military monks who ended up ruling great swathes of modern-day Germany and Poland.

Their rise is a spectacular tale worthy of a mega-budget Hollywood treatment, involving foreign origins, holy war, conquest, defeat and an unexpected sideline in charitable works.

The Order of the Hospitallers of Saint Mary of the Teutons in Jerusalem, as it was formally known, was founded in Palestine in 1190, as a medical body to treat Germanic knights fighting in the Crusades.

In this religion-infused landscape, the order attracted many fighters wanting to take holy orders. From this potent military and spiritual mix emerged the Teutonic Knights, warrior monks who wore a distinctive white habit with a black cross.

Back in Europe, their big break came when the Polish Duke Konrad I of Mazovia needed help subduing the pagan Prussians of the Lower Vistula. By the end of the 13th century, the Teutonic Knights had conquered all of Prussia. They then set about consolidating their rule by building castles, importing German peasants to build up the population, and developing trade. Towns such as Thorn (Toruń) and Elbing (Elbląg) became important Teutonic centres, and the castle at Marienburg (Malbork) was a potent symbol of the order's might.

Inevitably, territorial tensions arose with the neighbouring and newly resurgent Kingdom of Poland. After a century of friction, the Knights fell to combined Polish and Lithuanian forces at the Battle of Grunwald (1410). But their greatest defeat at Polish hands was yet to come – the Thirteen Years' War saw the order's own subjects turn against it, and the Treaty of Toruń in 1466 forced it to give up much of Pomerania, Warmia and the banks of the Vistula.

The Teutonic Knights were on the way out. In 1525 the order's Grand Master Albert transformed Prussia into a secular state, ending the knights' rule and naming himself duke. Then, after centuries of decline, Napoleon declared the Teutonic order dissolved in 1809.

Curiously though, the order refused to die. In 1834 the Austrian Emperor Franz I re-established the Teutonic order as a religious body, restricted to charitable and nursing activities – neatly returning the body to its medieval roots. Nowadays the Grand Master holds office at Singerstrasse 7 in Vienna, where the Teutonic order operates a museum and archive. It even has a website: www.deutscher-orden.at (in German).

typically impressive castles. If Toruń hasn't quite satisfied your appetite for Gothic-era red-brick structures, then an easy half-day excursion to G-D may do the trick.

### Sights

**Golub Castle** CASTLE
(Zamek Golubski; www.zamekgolub.pl; adult/concession 10/8zł; ⊘9am-7pm May-Sep, 9am-3pm Oct-Apr) Golub's brawny, square-set castle overlooks the town from a hill, the prominent structure consisting of a massive Gothic brick base topped with a slightly more refined Renaissance cornice. The original 14th-century castle was converted into a Renaissance palace in the early 17th century during the tenureship of its most famous resident, Princess Anna Waza, sister of Polish King Zygmunt III Waza. In fact, it's believed she still occasionally floats around her former pile in the form of a benevolent white lady, granting the wishes of locals and visitors.

Somewhat bizarrely, the only way to see the castle's rather bare interiors is on an hour-long guided tour. Tagging along with a Polish group, the visit starts with an excruciatingly dull film then progresses into the various austere rooms housing modest ethnographical and archaeological exhibits. However, the Gothic architecture is pretty impressive, as are the views out across the town and the forests beyond.

### Festivals & Events

Every July the castle hosts the **International Knights' Tournament**, a huge mock-medieval jamboree including jousting, music and lots of costumes.

## 🛏 Sleeping & Eating

**Dom Wycieczkowy PTTK**  HOSTEL, HOTEL €€
(☑56 683 2455; hostel dm/d 30/80zł; hotel s/d 160/230zł; P) The castle's upper floor houses some of the cheapest fortification accommodation in Poland. There are two standards on offer: one a basic PTTK hostel with dorm beds and simple doubles, the other consisting of hotel-type rooms. There's a restaurant and cafe downstairs.

## ❶ Getting There & Away

Buses run regularly to/from Toruń (8zł, one hour) and many other towns and cities in the region. When coming from Toruń alight at the bus stop at the foot of the castle. On your way back, wait at the stop on the other side of the road as it's a long hike to Dobrzyń bus station.

# Chełmno

POP 20,500

The most worthwhile day trip from Toruń 40km to the south, Chełmno (*heum*-no) is one of those enjoyably forgotten places that seems to lead a provincial life all of its own, with only occasional intrusions from the outside world. Its chipped and faded facades, sooty air and old red-brick institutions belong to the Poland of two decades ago, its churches and impressively beefy ring of defensive walls to a medieval golden era that's unlikely to return anytime soon.

Like Toruń, Chełmno was once an important settlement in the swathe of northern Poland controlled by the Teutonic Knights. Though it had been Polish since the late 10th century, the Teutonic Knights bookmarked it as a potential capital when they arrived in the late 1220s. Their castle was completed by 1265, bolstering Chełmno's profitable position on the Vistula trade route, and its lucrative affiliation to the Hanseatic League.

After the Treaty of Toruń, Chełmno was returned to Poland, but a devastating plague and a series of wars rendered the town a forgotten backwater by the time it was annexed by Prussia in 1772. It was returned to Poland in 1920 and survived WWII without major damage.

## ◉ Sights & Activities

**Regional Museum**  MUSEUM
(Muzeum Ziemi Chełmińskiej; Rynek 28; adult/concession 4/2zł; ◐10am-4pm Tue-Fri, 10am-3pm Sat, 11am-3pm Sun) The epicentre of Chełmno's chessboard of streets is the **Rynek**, in the middle of which stands the compact little Renaissance **Town Hall**, built around 1570 on the site of the previous Gothic structure. It now houses the Regional Museum, whose collection traces the town's history, though the building's interiors, including a spectacular courtroom, are equally distracting.

Outside, affixed on the rear wall of the Town Hall is the old Chełmno measure, the 4.35m-long *pręt chełmiński*. The entire town was laid out according to this measure, setting all the streets exactly the same width apart. It is divided into 'feet' a little smaller than an English foot. This unique system was used until the 19th century, and the town also had its own weights.

**City Walls**  HISTORIC BUILDINGS
Chełmno is encircled by 2.2km of defensive walls, which have survived almost in their entirety. There once were 23 towers along their length and some still exist, though they're not all in good shape. Alas, it's not possible to walk around the entire circumference as various gardens and buildings block the way.

Walking along ul Dworcowa from the bus terminal, you'll enter the Old Town through the **Grudziądz Gate** (Brama Grudziądzka), the only surviving medieval gateway. It was remodelled in the 17th century to incorporate a chapel. Note an expressive pietà in the niche in the gate's eastern facade.

**Parish Church**  CHURCH
(ul Szkolna) Just off the Rynek, this massive, Gothic church was commissioned by the Teutonic Knights in the late 13th century. The magnificent interior is crammed with ornate Baroque and Rococo furnishings, and also holds some supposed relics of St Valentine, patron saint of lovers, locked within the right-hand pillar as you face the altar (hence the marketing campaign by the local authorities entitled 'Chełmno, the Town of Lovers').

**Church of SS John the Baptist & John the Evangelist**  CHURCH
(Kościół Św Jana Chrzciciela i Jana Ewangelisty; ul Dominikańska) At the far western tip of the Old Town, this church was built between 1266 and 1325 and has a richly gilded high altar with an ornate organ to the side. Underneath the organ is a black-marble tombstone from 1275, one of the oldest in the region.

**Church of SS Peter & Paul**  CHURCH
(ul Wodna) Occupying the town's northern corner, the impressive red-brick stepped

gable of this 14th-century church fronts an interior containing doored Rococo stalls, a huge Baroque altar straddled by a star-studded globe, and the tomb of the first bishop of Chełmno, Heidenreich. At the time of research the whole architectural caboodle was just about to be restored to its former glory.

## 🛏 Sleeping & Eating

Sleepy Chełmno has just a handful of places to stay and very few restaurants. From around Easter to September a few beer gardens sprout on the Rynek, which also has a couple of bakery cafes.

**Restauracja Spichlerz**  POLISH €€
(ul Biskupia 3; mains 7-35zł; ☺10am-midnight Mon-Thu, 10am-2am Fri & Sat, 11am-midnight Sun) Ask anyone in Chełmno where to head when it's feeding time and they'll point you in the direction of this pub-restaurant just off the Rynek. The fare is mostly Polish and hearty, the crowd a mix of vodka-swigging old-timers and beer-caressing youths.

**Karczma Chełmińska**  HOTEL €€
(☑56 679 0605; www.karczmachelminska.pl; ul 22 Stycznia 1b; s/d 190/240zł; 🅿🛜) This tourist-friendly courtyard hotel, in the southwestern corner of the Old Town, offers neat rooms with great stone-effect bathrooms. The courtyard restaurant, with waiters in traditional garb, serves up tasty grub including interesting seasonal specials.

**Hotelik**  HOTEL €
(☑56 676 2030; www.hotelik.info; ul Podmurna 3; s/d 100/140zł;🛜) Located 60m to the right of the Grudziądz Gate as you enter the Old Town, this very well-maintained half-timbered mini-hotel offers a jumble of good-value en-suite rooms, some small and cosy, others more spacious with antique elements.

**Europejskie Centrum Wymiany Młodzieży**  HOSTEL, CAMPGROUND €
(☑56 686 3067; www.ecwm-chelmno.pl; ul Jastrzębskiego 5; s/d 100/150zł; ☺May-Sep) On Lake Starogrodzkie, 2km west of the walled town, the European Centre of Youth Exchange offers basic rooms, a camping ground and heaps of sporting and recreation facilities.

## ℹ Information

**Tourist office** (☑56 686 2104; www.chelmno.pl; Ratusz, Rynek; ☺8am-3pm Mon, 8am-4pm Tue-Fri, 10am-3pm Sat, 11am-2pm Sun) In the museum entrance within the Town Hall.

## ℹ Getting There & Away

Buses depart roughly hourly to/from Toruń (8zł, 1½ hours) and Grudziądz (8zł, one hour).

# Grudziądz

POP 96,000

Grudziądz (*groo*-jonts), located some 30km down the Vistula River from Chełmno, probably doesn't have enough to warrant a special trip but could be a minor diversion on the way between Toruń and Malbork. Post-WWII renovation of the Old Town has finally gathered pace in recent years and trams still trundle through the cosy main square lending it atmosphere. Unfortunately the remainder of Grudziądz is made up of thundering motorways and blocky communist-era tenements of little interest to anyone.

Grudziądz may not be too focused on appearances, but its history is certainly colourful. It started life as an early Piast settlement, came under the rule of the Teutonic Knights as Graudenz in the 1230s, then returned to the Polish crown in 1466. The city was caught up in the 17th-century wars with Sweden – it was burnt down while being liberated by Polish troops in 1659. In the First Partition of 1772, Grudziądz was swallowed by Prussia, developing as an industrial centre before returning to Poland in the aftermath of WWI.

Grudziądz was severely damaged in 1945 but was rebuilt and developed into a bustling, if fairly unremarkable, urban centre.

## ◎ Sights

**Regional Museum**  MUSEUM
(www.muzeum.grudziadz.pl; ul Wodna 3/5; adult/concession 7/3.50zł, free Tue; ☺10am-4pm Tue-Thu, 10am-6pm Fri, 10am-3pm Sat & Sun) Based in a former Benedictine convent at the southern end of the old quarter, the Regional Museum is worth an hour or so's perusal. The main building houses contemporary paintings from the region and temporary exhibitions, with further sections on local archaeology and history in two old granaries just to the west. The ticket is valid for all five sites.

**Granaries**  HISTORIC BUILDINGS
(Spichrze) The extraordinary row of crumbling granaries was built along the whole length of the town's waterfront to provide storage and protect the town from invaders. Begun in the 14th century, they were

gradually rebuilt and extended until the 18th century, and some were later turned into housing blocks by knocking through windows in the walls. These massive buttressed brick buildings – most of them six storeys high – are an impressive sight rising high above the Vistula, which has swollen to quite a width by the time it reaches Grudziądz.

### Church of St Francis Xavier            CHURCH
(Kościół Św Franciszka Ksawerego; ul Kościelna) A few buildings in the centre retain their historical significance, the most impressive of which is this early 18th-century church. Most of the narrow interior is taken up by a beautiful Baroque high altar, and the surrounding ornamentation includes some unusual chinoiserie, a decorative style drawing on Chinese art.

## Sleeping & Eating

### Hotel RAD            HOTEL €€
(☑56 465 5506; www.hotelrad.pl; ul Chełmińska 144; s/d 150/190zł; ℗) Located on the Toruń road 2.5km south of the centre, this is Grudziądz's best option with neatly appointed rooms and a decent restaurant. Take tram 2 to the Wiejska stop.

### Baza Noclegowa – Centrum Kultury            GUESTHOUSE €
(☑56 462 0900; www.teatr.grudziadz.pl; ul Focha 19; s/d 49/98zł; ℗) Decent digs hidden inside a cultural complex, cheek-to-cheek with a theatre. Just a short walk from the Old Town. Phone ahead if possible so they know you're coming.

### Camping 134            CAMPGROUND €
(☑56 462 2581; www.moriw.pl; ul Zaleśna 1; bungalows 60-175zł; ℗ 🗐) Two-star camping ground on a lake 5km south of town boasting a long list of facilities.

### Da Grasso            PIZZERIA €€
(Rynek 13; pizzas from 14zł, other mains 10-20zł; ☺11am-10pm Mon-Thu, 11am-1am Fri & Sat, noon-10pm Sun; ☑) Facing the market square and its dramatic military statue, this retro-styled eatery in slabs of green and red serves up monster wheels of pizza and lots of vegetarian dishes.

## Information

**Tourist office** (☑56 461 2318; www.it.gdz.pl; Rynek 3/5; ☺8am-5pm Mon-Fri, 8am-2pm Sat May-Sep, 10am-2pm Sun Jul-Aug, shorter hr Oct-Apr)

## Getting There & Away

**BUS** The bus station is a short walk north of the train station. Buses leave for the following:

**Chełmno** 8zł, one hour, hourly

**Gdańsk** 22zł, 2½ hours, seven daily

**Toruń** 10zł to 20zł, 2½ hours, hourly

**TRAIN** The post-apocalyptic train station is about 1km southeast of the Old Town, a 15-minute walk or a quick trip on tram 1. Grudziądz has the following rail connections:

**Kwidzyn** 10zł, 40 minutes, six daily

**Malbork** 16zł, 1½ hours, six daily

**Toruń** 14zł, 1½ hours, six daily (or change in Jabłonowo Pomorskie)

# Kwidzyn

POP 38,000

Kwidzyn is a sleepy town that would be wholly unremarkable were it not for the presence of a mammoth Gothic castle and cathedral. Located 40km downriver from Grudziądz, it's yet another medieval stronghold of the Teutonic order and was formerly known as Marienwerder. Under the rule of German authorities for most of its history, the town became part of Poland after 1945.

## Sights

The square **castle**, with its central courtyard, was built in the first half of the 14th century. It experienced many ups and downs in subsequent periods and suffered a serious loss in 1798 when the Prussians pulled down two sides (eastern and southern) and the main tower. Unlike many of its red-brick peers, it survived WWII unscathed.

Most of the building now houses the **Kwidzyn Museum** (www.zamek.kwidzyn.pl; ul Katedralna 1; adult/concession 10/5zł; ☺9am-5pm Tue-Sun May-Aug, 9am-4pm Tue-Fri, 9am-3pm Sat & Sun Sep-Apr), which has several sections, including displays on medieval sacred art, regional folk crafts and plenty of farming implements, as well as a display in the cellar detailing the German-funded archaeological excavations around the site. There are some grim sets of manacles hanging off the dungeon walls for effect, and some inexplicably placed cannons beside them. You won't find any English labelling, but the fine original interiors justify a visit, and there are some good views over the countryside from some of the windows.

The most curious feature of the castle is the two unusual towers standing some distance away from the western and southern

## GNIEW

Not to be outdone by its neighbours, the small town of Gniew (pronounced 'gnyef') has an equally prominent and remarkably well-maintained castle on the other side of the Vistula. The town has also retained its original medieval layout in its tiny old centre. With few interruptions from modern life, it's a charming place to visit for a couple of hours.

The first stronghold of the Teutonic order on the left bank of the Vistula, the **castle** was built in the late 13th century and is a massive, multistorey brick structure with a deep courtyard. In 1464 it came under Polish rule and remained so until the First Partition of 1772. The Prussians remodelled it to accommodate barracks, a jail and an ammunition depot. It was seriously burnt out in 1921, but the 2m-thick walls survived and it was later restored.

The castle now houses the **Archaeological Museum** (www.zamek-gniew.pl; ul Zamkowa 3; adult/concession 10/8zł; ⊗9.30am-4.30pm Tue-Sun May-Sep, by appointment Oct-Apr). The archaeological exhibition is in two rooms, but you will also get to see the chapel and temporary exhibitions in other rooms, and wander through most of the castle. All visits are guided and the tour takes up to 1½ hours. At weekends historical performances are held twice a day.

Gniew's bus terminal is about 200m northwest of the Rynek. There are seven mostly morning services to Tczew (9zł, 40 minutes), morning and afternoon buses to Gdańsk (14.50zł, 1½ hours) and three services to Toruń (30zł, two hours).

sides, linked to the main building by arcaded bridges. One (the smaller tower) held a well, while the other served as the *gdaniska* (knights' toilet), a long drop if ever there was one. They once stood above the river, which later changed course leaving them (and the knights) high and dry. You can visit both while wandering the interior, but it's also worth seeing them from the outside.

The **cathedral** attached to the castle is the familiar Gothic brick blockbuster, which has a suitably defensive appearance, thanks to its 19th-century tower. Look for the interesting ceramic mosaic (from around 1380) in the external wall above the southern porch.

### 🛏 Sleeping & Eating

**Hotel Centrum**      HOTEL €€
(📞55 613 1366; www.centrumhotel.pl; ul Kopernika 32; s 260-320zł; d 310-370zł; 🅿🛜) Shockingly clean-cut and trendily designed for rural Poland, these new digs boast 32 en-suite rooms, and some of the best facilities you're likely to find outside the big tourist centres, including a swanky restaurant.

**Hotel Kaskada**      HOTEL €
(📞703 400 440; www.hotelkaskada.emeteor .pl; ul Chopina 42; s 110-140zł; d 140-160zł; 🅿🛜) Cheap and opposite the train station, this is a handy option if you decide to stay over. The restaurant is a simple affair, as are the rooms; rates include breakfast.

### ❶ Getting There & Away

The bus and train stations are set 200m apart, both around a 10-minute walk from the castle.

**BUS** Kwidzyn has the following bus services:
**Grudziądz** 13zł, 45 minutes, two daily
**Malbork** 17zł, 45 minutes, two daily
**TRAIN** Trains head to the following:
**Grudziądz** 10zł, 40 minutes, six daily
**Malbork** 10zł, 40 minutes, nine daily
**Toruń** 18zł, 2½ hours, five daily

## Malbork

POP 36,500

Around 30km southeast of Gdańsk, the quiet, rural town of Malbork would be bypassed by 99% of foreigners were it not for its astounding castle, one of the unmissables of any trip to Poland and a stunning spectacle both inside and out. Top dog among Polish fortifications, the magnificent Unesco-listed structure is a classic example of the medieval fortress, and Europe's largest Gothic castle to boot. The fortress is an easy day trip from Gdańsk by train, but it's probably not worth overnighting here as there's precious little to Malbork other than its Gothic pile.

### ◉ Sights

**Castle**      CASTLE
(Muzeum Zamkowe; www.zamek.malbork.pl; ul Starościńska 1; adult/concession incl audio tour

39/29zł; ◎9am-7pm Tue-Sun mid-Apr–mid-Sep, 10am-3pm Tue-Sun mid-Sep–mid-Apr) Malbork's blockbuster attraction is its show-stoppingly massive castle that sits on the banks of the sluggish Nogat River, an eastern arm of the Vistula. The **Marienburg** (Fortress of Mary) was built by the Teutonic Knights and was the headquarters of the order for almost 150 years. Its vast bulk is an apt embodiment of its weighty history.

The immense castle took shape in stages. First was the so-called High Castle, the formidable central bastion that was begun around 1276 and finished within three decades. When Malbork became the capital of the order in 1309, the fortress was expanded considerably. The Middle Castle was built to the side of the high one, followed by the Lower Castle still further along. The whole complex was encircled by three rings of defensive walls and strengthened with dungeons and towers. The castle eventually spread over 21 hectares, making it the largest fortress built anywhere in the Middle Ages.

The castle was only seized by the Polish army in 1457, during the Thirteen Years' War, when the military power of the knights had started to erode. Malbork then became the residence of Polish kings visiting Pomerania, but from the Swedish invasions onwards it gradually went into decline. After the First Partition in 1772, the Prussians turned it into barracks, destroying much of the decoration and dismantling sections of no military use.

In the 19th century the Marienburg was one of the first historic buildings taken under government protection, becoming a symbol of medieval German glory. Despite sustaining damage during WWII, almost the entire complex has been preserved, and the castle today looks much as it did six centuries ago, dominating the town and the surrounding countryside. The best view is from the opposite side of the river (you can get there via the footbridge), especially in the late afternoon when the brick turns an intense red-brown in the setting sun.

The fortress now operates as a **museum** with an ever-greater number of the rooms and chambers open to visitors, and housing dozens of exhibitions on various historical and archaeological topics.

The first thing to do when you arrive at the castle is buy your ticket from the office around 100m east of the main entrance. Mercifully, the castle management no longer insists you tag along with a tour and entry is now with an iPod audio tour – a vast improvement on the guides of yore with their jaded quips and dodgy English. The audio tours are picked up just by the main gate and come with a numbered map showing the rather complicated route you should take. Of course, without the human guide you are now free to wander at will and due to the vastness of the castle you're more than likely to get lost at some point anyway. Allow at least two hours to do the place justice.

The entrance to the complex is from the northern side, through what used to be the only way in. From the main gate, you walk over the drawbridge, then go through five iron-barred doors to the vast courtyard of the **Middle Castle** (Zamek Średni). On the western side (to your right) is the **Grand Masters' Palace** (Pałac Wielkich Mistrzów), which has some splendid interiors. Alongside is the **Knights' Hall** (Sala Rycerska), which is the largest chamber in the castle at 450 sq metres. The remarkable ceiling has its original palm vaulting preserved. The building on the opposite side of the courtyard houses a collection of armour and an excellent display of amber, both of which come towards the end of the prescribed audio tour.

The tour proceeds to the **High Castle** (Zamek Wysoki), over another drawbridge and through a gate (note the ornamented 1280 doorway) to a spectacular arcaded courtyard that has a reconstructed well in the middle.

One of the most striking interiors is **St Mary's Church**, accessed through a beautiful Gothic doorway, known as the Golden Gate. This is where the brothers would have met to pray every three hours, 24/7, but was the part most damaged during the bombardment of 1945. Renovation work has been slow and hasn't really progressed much since 2006. In fact a decision may be taken to leave the church in its ruinous state as a memorial. Underneath the church's presbytery is St Anne's Chapel, with the grand masters' crypt below its floor.

Other highlights of the tour include the **Gdaniska**, the knights' loo perched high atop its own special tower and connected to the castle by a walkway. Perhaps it was one of the order who coined the phrase 'long drop' as he reached for the cabbage leaves they used for toilet paper. The knights' **kitchen** also sticks in the memory, fragrant with its calendar of fast days (the knights seemed to have liked two things – fasting and drinking beer). Also look out for the interesting underfloor heating system in many of the rooms and the little Gothic stucco figures pointing the way to the nearest WC.

The view from the castle's main square tower is also pretty impressive and gives a sense of the building's scale and how it fits into the surrounding landscape.

**Skwer Esperanto**                    PARK
(Plac Zamenhofa) If you've seen the castle and have more time to kill in Malbork, walk south along the line of the river, past impressive remnants of the old city walls, to this square behind Hotel Stary Malbork. This scrappy park isn't much to look at, but around its edge are commemorative stones placed by keen international speakers of Esperanto from as far away as Korea and Congo, in honour of the world language invented by Ludwig Zamenhof. There's a monument to the great man in the middle of the park. The explanatory signage is in Polish... and Esperanto, naturally.

## Sleeping

**Hotel Grot**                    HOTEL €€
([phone]55 646 9660; www.grothotel.pl; ul Kościuszki 22d; s/d 199/289zł; [P][wifi]) British and Australian travellers may crack a smirk as they check into the Grot, but there's nothing unhygienic about this place. In fact it's pretty classy for its price range, with contemporary furniture and spotless bathrooms. On the ground floor you'll find an impressive restaurant and a small travel agency selling international bus and plane tickets.

**Hotel Stary Malbork**                    HOTEL €€
([phone]55 647 2400; www.hotelstarymalbork.com.pl; ul 17 Marca 26/27; s 210-250zł, d 340-360zł; [P][wifi]) This graceful hotel is the best value in town, with airy, relaxing rooms raising high ceilings and adorned with period touches. The singles have double beds and the very spacious deluxe doubles, costing just a fraction more than an ordinary room for two, are a quantum leap up the guestroom food chain. There's a sauna, cafe and restaurant on the premises.

**Hotel Zamek**                    HOTEL €€
([phone]55 272 8400; www.hotelprodus.pl; ul Starościńska 14; s/d 210/310zł; [P]) Nestled in a restored medieval building in the Lower Castle (a former hospital), Hotel Zamek far

from lives up to its name. The interiors are dim and drab and the rooms a throwback to the Wałęsa era, but it's the location that makes this place worth considering. The in-house restaurant is a sound option, though often heaving with shouty German tour groups.

**Pokoje Gościnne Szarotka**                    HOTEL €
([phone]55 612 1444; ul Dworcowa 1a; s/d 45/70zł; [wifi]) Occupying a high-ceilinged building on the way from the train and bus stations to the town centre, this cheap and fairly well-maintained crash pad has basic shared bathrooms, a guest kitchen and garishly no-frills rooms of mismatched decor and haphazard furniture. You may want to have a sleeping bag handy as the lumpy bedding is decidedly grotty.

## Eating

**Polska Kuźnica Smaku**                    POLISH €
(ul Grunwaldzka 9; mains 8-15zł; ⊘8am-6pm Mon-Sat, 11am-5pm Sun) Occupying an old red-brick building surrounded by market stalls, this unassuming eatery puts the emphasis firmly on wholesome Polish fare prepared fresh to order: *pierogi*, *żurek* (sour rye soup), *gołąbki* (cabbage rolls). The Croatian owner worked in the UK for five years, hence the 'Croatian cuisine days' and a menu containing three magic little words – Full English Breakfast.

**Restauracja Piwniczka**                    POLISH €€
(ul Starościńska 1; mains 25-50zł; ⊘10am-7pm) Situated in an atmospheric cellar beneath the west wall of the castle, facing the river, this restaurant dishes up excellent, flavoursome Polish standards along with specials like Castle's Pot Soup (pork and mushroom) and The Knight's Plate (two kinds of pork and a chicken shashlik).

**Pizzeria Patrzałkowie**                    INTERNATIONAL €
(ul Kościuszki 25; pizzas 7-20zł, other mains 10-16.50zł; ⊘10am-9pm Sun-Thu, 10am-10pm Fri & Sat; [wifi]) At the station end of town, this pizzeria-cafe serves up helpings of pizza, pasta, *pierogi*, salads and soups, including some decent vegetarian options, to a mixed crowd of locals and tourists.

## Information

**Post office** (ul 17 Marca 38) Has a currency exchange office.
**Tourist office** ([phone]55 647 4747; www.visitmalbork.pl; ul Kościuszki 54; ⊘8am-7pm Mon-Fri,

10am-3pm Sat & Sun Jul & Aug, 8am-4pm Mon-Fri Sep-Jun) Large welcome centre with free internet access (plus wi-fi hotspot), free left-luggage service and a library.

### ⓘ Getting There & Away

The train station and bus terminal are at the eastern end of the town centre, 1km from the castle. Coming from Gdańsk by train, you'll catch a splendid view of the castle; watch out to your right when crossing the river. Malbork sits on the busy Gdańsk–Warsaw railway route, and has services to the following destinations:

**Elbląg** 7zł, 30 minutes, 18 daily
**Gdańsk** 12zł to 16zł, 50 minutes, two hourly
**Grudziądz** 16zł, 1½ hours, six daily
**Kwidzyn** 10zł, 40 minutes, nine daily
**Olsztyn** 20zł to 35zł, two hours, six daily
**Warsaw** 50zł to 110zł, five hours, nine daily

## Elbląg

POP 127,500

Few used to linger longer than a night in Elbląg (*el*-blonk), at one end of the Elbląg–Ostróda Canal (see p367), as boats moor up long after it's possible to get anywhere else. However, in the 1990s the authorities decided to give canal navigators a reason to stay on by rebuilding the Old Town, levelled by the Red Army in 1945. But instead of a painstakingly precise, budget-bustingly expensive rebuild, the new structures are computer-generated versions of what stood here before the shells began to fall. While full marks should be awarded for effort, the old-new streets are a touch sterile and lifeless, leaving visitors with the impression that Elbląg is happening elsewhere (don't worry, it isn't). It's all still a work in progress and might come good yet, and amid the stylised medieval gables in metal tubing and period-faithful plastic windows a few reminders of a more glorious red-brick past do survive.

Centuries before WWII turned its historical centre into landfill, Elbląg became a stronghold and port of the Teutonic Knights. In the 13th century, the Vistula Lagoon (Zalew Wiślany) extended further south than it does today, allowing the town to develop as a maritime centre and a member of the Hanseatic League. When Elbląg came under Polish rule after the Treaty of Toruń, it was a major gateway to the sea. Later, Swedish invasions and the gradual silting up of the waterway capsized the town's prosperity, though a partial revival came with industrial development in the late 19th century.

### ◉ Sights & Activities

**St Nicholas' Church**                                    CHURCH
(Kościół Św Mikołaja; Stary Rynek) One blast from the past amid the evolving rebuild of the Old Town is this sturdy, red-brick island of true oldness, noted for its 95m-high, carefully reconstructed tower. Within, you'll find some of the original wood-carving, including several triptychs, which escaped war damage. On summer mornings the beautiful stained-glass windows speckle the marble floors with ecclesiastical disco light.

**Elbląg Museum**                                          MUSEUM
(www.muzeum.elblag.pl; Bulwar Zygmunta Augusta 11; adult/concession 10/5zł, free Sun; ⊙9am-5pm Tue-Sun) A five-minute walk south along the riverbank is the Elbląg Museum. Occupying two large buildings, the museum has sections on archaeology and the town's history, plus a photographic record of Elbląg from the 19th century to WWII.

**Market Gate**                                  HISTORIC BUILDING
(Brama Targowa; Stary Rynek) The northern entrance to the Old Town was once through the Market Gate, the only surviving gate from the medieval fortifications. In front of it is a **statue** of a baker who legendarily saved the town in the 16th century when he spotted the approaching Teutonic Knights, bent on invasion, and cut the ropes that held the gates open. At the time of research the tourist office was just about to leave the building and it wasn't yet clear if it would remain open for visitors. If it does, climb to the top for views across the town.

**Galeria El**                                             GALLERY
(ul Kuśnierska 6; admission varies with exhibition; ⊙10am-6pm Mon-Sat, 10am-5pm Sun) Some 200m to the north of the Market Gate is the Galeria El, formerly St Mary's Church. Another massive Gothic brick structure, the original church was gutted and now houses a gallery of contemporary art, with occasional concerts and events. It's worth a visit just to see the imposing interior, and the large modern-art objects dotted through the grounds. It was all under heavy, EU-funded renovation at the time of research, but should have reopened by the time you get there.

## 🛏 Sleeping

**TOP CHOICE** **Hotel Pod Lwem** HOTEL €€
(📞55 641 3100; www.hotelpodlwem.pl; ul Kowalska 10; s/d 250/330zł; P❄🖭) Occupying one of Elbląg's old-new reconstructions, the town's only design hotel is a stylish place to spend a night prior to, or following, a trip on the canal. Room decor unites cream leather, dark wood and flurries of white punctuated with exclamations of colour, and the dominance of light tones makes some rooms feel bigger than they are. Buffet breakfast is taken in the smart cellar restaurant.

**Pensjonat Boss** GUESTHOUSE €€
(📞55 239 3729; www.pensjonatboss.pl; ul Św Ducha 30; s/d 160/230zł) This Old Town guesthouse offers 13 clean but ordinary rooms above its own bar. The building is a more attractive example of the new-look architecture, especially when the colourful window boxes are in bloom.

**Hotel Sowa** HOTEL €€
(📞55 233 7422; www.sowa.elblag.biz.pl; ul Grunwaldzka 49; s/d 155/190zł) A handy, cheap but unexciting option opposite the train station.

**Camping Nr 61** CAMPGROUND €
(📞55 641 8666; www.camping61.com.pl; ul Panieńska 14; site per adult/child 12/6zł; ⏰May-Sep) Elbląg's pleasantly shaded camping ground occupies an unusually convenient spot on the Elbląg River, close to the Old Town.

## 🍴 Eating

**Wędrowiec** INTERNATIONAL €€
(ul Wigilijna 12; mains 9-33zł; ⏰11.30am-11.30pm) Characterfully stuccoed three-level eatery with an exotic mixed-bag menu, an antiques roadshow of furniture, period wallpaper and stylish light fittings.

**Cafe Carillon** CAFE €€
(ul Mostowa 22; mains 8-18zł; ⏰10am-10pm) Elbląg's best cafe with Art Deco–style stained glass and a view of St Nicholas' Church.

**Cztery Pory Roku** ITALIAN €€
(ul Wieżowa 15; mains 9-25zł; ⏰noon-10pm) Attractive pizzeria and cafe also serving, pasta, soups and fish dishes within its brown-and-white pseudo-Mediterranean interior.

**Restauracja Pod Aniołami** LATIN AMERICAN €€
(ul Rybacka 23/24B; mains 17-30zł; ⏰noon-midnight) Tempting tourists and hip locals alike, the Latin American menu here adds a welcome dash of chilli.

## ℹ Information

**Bank Pekao** (Stary Rynek 18a)
**Post office** (Plac Słowiański 1)
**Tourist office** (📞55 239 3377; www.ielblag.pl; Stary Rynek 25; ⏰10am-6pm Apr-Sep, 9am-5pm Mon-Fri Oct-Mar)

## ℹ Getting There & Away

**BOAT** Boats heading for the Elbląg–Ostróda Canal depart from the quay next to the Old Town. Information and tickets are available from **Żegluga Ostródzko-Elbląska** (📞55 232 4307; www.zegluga.com.pl; ul Wodna 1b) just back from the quay.

**BUS** The bus terminal is next to the train station 1km southeast of the centre. Buses run to the following:
**Gdańsk** 16zł, 1½ hours, many
**Frombork** 6.80zł, 40 minutes, at least twice hourly
**Warsaw** 50zł, 4½ to 5½ hours, hourly (two overnight services)

**TRAIN** From the newly renovated train station there are services to the following:
**Gdańsk** 15.60zł to 20.50zł, 1½ hours, 10 daily
**Malbork** 10zł, 30 minutes, 17 daily
**Olsztyn** 24zł, 1½ hours, 10 daily

# Frombork

POP 2500

Tucked away on the northeast edge of coastal Poland, just a few kilometres shy of Russia's Kaliningrad enclave, Frombork is actually in Warmia (we won't tell if you don't) but is included here due to transport links with Pomerania. Its impressive walled complex overlooking the tranquil town and the water beyond is what people come here to see, and the town makes for an enjoyable day trip from Elbląg or even Gdańsk if you plan things right.

Alighting from the bus on the main road, what looks like a castle above you is, in fact, a cathedral, established by the Warmian bishops (see p361) in the 13th century after a forced departure from nearby Braniewo, following an uprising of pagan Prussians. Later, from 1466 to 1772, Frombork was part of Poland, before it shifted to Prussian control as Frauenburg.

The town took a serious pummelling in WWII, but the cathedral miraculously survived. Frombork was repopulated by Poles exiled from territories annexed by the Soviet Union and many locals speak passable Russian to this day.

The complex is the main draw in Frombork, but the icing on the cake is its association with Nicolaus Copernicus. It was here that he spent the latter half of his life and conducted most of the observations and research for his heliocentric theory. Copernicus was buried in the cathedral, having survived just long enough to have the first printed copy of his great work placed in his hands – or so the legend goes.

## ◉ Sights

The Cathedral Hill complex (Wzgórze Katedralne) is today the **Nicolaus Copernicus Museum** (Muzeum Mikołaja Kopernika; www.frombork.art.pl). It covers several sights within the fortified complex, each visited on a separate ticket; the cathedral and the Old Bishop's Palace are the main two sights. The entrance is from the southern side through the massive **Main Gate** (Brama Główna), where you'll find the museum ticket office.

**Old Bishops' Palace**                          MUSEUM
(Stary Pałac Biskupi; adult/concession 6/3zł; ⊘9am-4.30pm Tue-Sun) The museum's main exhibition space can be found in the southeastern corner of the complex, though the entrance can take a bit of finding. The ground floor is taken up with objects discovered during postwar archaeological excavations, while the other levels are largely devoted to the life and work of Copernicus, along with temporary displays and a collection of old navigational aids.

The most interesting section is on the 1st floor, where modern artists' interpretations of the great man, in sculpture and oils, are presented, before you pass into the room containing books and other artefacts from his time.

Though Copernicus is essentially remembered for his astronomical achievements (supplanting the old geocentric Ptolemaic system with his revelation that the earth revolves around the sun), his interests extended across many other fields, including medicine, economics and cartography. Apart from an early edition of his famous *De Revolutionibus Orbium Coelestium* (On the Revolutions of the Celestial Spheres), there are copies displayed of his treatises and manuscripts on a range of subjects, together with astronomical instruments and other scientific bric-a-brac. The exhibits are well lit and creatively placed, but English captioning is sadly lacking.

If you've little'uns in tow then the top-level hall packed with hands-on scientific experiments is a sure-fire winner.

**Cathedral**                                    CHURCH
(adult/concession 6/3zł; ⊘9am-4.30pm Mon-Sat) Tickets for the cathedral must be bought from a separate office at ul Katedralna 11, 50m to the left of the Main Gate as you exit the complex.

Filling the middle of the courtyard with its huge Gothic-brick facade and with a slim octagonal tower at each corner, this impressive building was erected between 1329 and 1388, and was the largest church ever built by the Warmian bishops. So chuffed were they with the result that it became a blueprint for most of the subsequent churches they founded across the region.

Frombork's cathedral certainly doesn't save the best till last: there it is, right in front of you as you enter the main door – the highlight of a visit for most – the tomb of Nicolaus Copernicus himself. Buried under the floor, his casket is visible through an illuminated glass panel.

The rest of the chilly, elongated main nave is cluttered with a riot of Baroque altars and other 18th-century embellishment. Magnificent in powder blue, gold and silver, the Baroque organ, dating from 1683, is a replacement for the one nicked by the Swedes in 1626. The instrument is noted for its rich tone, best appreciated during the Sunday recitals held annually from late June to late August, as part of Frombork's **International Festival of Organ Music** (www.frombork-festiwal.pl in Polish).

**Copernicus Tower**                              TOWER
At the northwestern corner of the complex is this 14th-century tower (Wieża Kopernika), believed to be the place from which the astronomer took some of his observations. The top floor is set up to recreate his study but at the time of research the tower was indefinitely closed to visitors.

**Belfry**                             HISTORIC BUILDING
(Dzwonnica; adult/concession 6/3zł; ⊘9.30am-5pm) The high tower at the southwestern corner of the defensive walls is the former cathedral belfry, which can be ascended for cracking views of the Cathedral Hill, the town and the Vistula Lagoon and Vistula Spit.

**Water Tower**                                   TOWER
(Wieża Wodna; ul Elbląska 2; adult/concession 5/3zł; ⊘10am-7pm Apr-Aug) Across the main

road from the cathedral, down in the town, this tower was built in 1571 as part of one of the first water-supply systems in Europe and was used for two centuries to provide Cathedral Hill with water through oak pipes. The admission fee gets you to the top and there's a cafe on the ground and 1st floors.

### Planetarium                    PLANETARIUM
(adult/concessions 8/5zł) Located at the base of the belfry, the planetarium presents half-hour shows in Polish six times daily. Get there 10 minutes before the shows start.

### Hospital of the Holy Ghost           MUSEUM
(Szpital Św. Ducha; ul Stara; adult/concession 6/3zł; ⊗9.30am-5pm Tue-Sun) The 15th-century Hospital of the Holy Ghost, formerly St Anne's Chapel, contains exhibitions of religious art and medical history. It's a short and well-signposted walk east of the cathedral.

## 🛏 Sleeping & Eating

Several private homes around town rent rooms to visitors for around 50zł per night. Look out for the *kwatery prywatne* signs or head to ul Kaplańska 5 or ul Ogrodowa 24. There's a cheap Biedronka supermarket on the Rynek for snackers, picnickers and self-caterers.

### Hotelik Dom Familijny Rheticus      HOTEL €
(☑55 243 7800; www.domfamilijny.pl; ul Kopernika 10; s/d 110/130zł, apt 120-270zł; P🐾) This fine, family-run establishment offers nine very spacious apartments with full-blown kitchens, and each sleeping up to five people, in the main building; plus a new annex with standard hotel doubles and singles. The internationally flavoured Don Roberto restaurant attached to the new building is Frombork's finest. Breakfast is an extra 15zł.

### Hotel Kopernik                HOTEL €€
(☑55 243 7285; www.hotelkopernik.com.pl; ul Kościelna 2; s/d 130/190zł; P🐾) The incongruously recent-looking Hotel Kopernik has 37 neat but small rooms, its own budget restaurant and the only *kantor* (currency exchange office) in town. The motel look doesn't sit well with Frombork's more traditional buildings, but some south-facing rooms have attractive cathedral views.

### Camping Frombork            CAMPGROUND €
(☑506 803 151; www.campingfrombork.pl; ul Braniewska 14; site 5zł, plus per person 10zł, dm 25zł, d/tr 50/75zł; ⊗May-Sep) Privately owned camping ground at the eastern end of town, on the Braniewo road.

### Restauracja Akcent            RESTAURANT €€
(ul Rybacka 4; mains 7-29zł; ⊗10am-11pm) An alternative to the hotel eateries listed above,

GDAŃSK & POMERANIA FROMBORK

---

## MIERZEJA WIŚLANA

If you long to escape the tourist hordes of Gdańsk, head east to the Mierzeja Wiślana (Vistula Spit). This long, narrow sandbar is flanked by the Gulf of Gdańsk to the north and the Zalew Wiślany (Vistula Lagoon) to the south, a vast estuary that stretches all the way to Kaliningrad in Russia. The peninsula is also part Russian, being neatly bisected by the international border.

On the route from Gdańsk to the spit is **Sztutowo**, some 30km from the city. Here you'll find **Stutthof**, the former extermination camp in which the Nazis disposed of Polish resisters from the beginning of WWII, and which later became part of their Final Solution against Jews. Nowadays it's a sombre museum presenting exhibitions and documentaries about the German occupation of the region.

Continuing on to the Mierzeja Wiślana, there's a wealth of natural attractions, including pine forests, giant sand dunes, a cormorant reserve at Kąty Rybackie, and places to hire sailboats, yachts and catamarans. **Krynica Morska** is the major town on the peninsula, with a popular swimming beach, accommodation in old-fashioned villas and a lighthouse open to visitors. You can reach Krynica Morska by bus or car from Gdańsk, or by ferry from Elbląg.

For that all-over Baltic tan, there's even a nude beach near Piaski, 12km east of Krynica Morska on the far Polish end of the spit. And while you're enjoying the Mierzeja Wiślana beaches, don't forget to have a look for fragments of amber on the shore, washed up by storms in spring.

this is a decent place with a sightline to the castle and a menu that goes beyond the basics.

## ❶ Information

**Tourist office** (☑55 243 7500; ul Elbląska 2; ◷10am-7pm Apr-Aug) Privately run, seasonal information point within a gift shop at the base of the Water Tower. Rents out a very well appointed apartment around 2km from Frombork.

## ❶ Getting There & Away

PKS buses and private minibuses running between Elbląg (7zł, 40 minutes, hourly) and Braniewo stop on the main drag through town, just below the Cathedral Hill.

Just north of the station is the marina; from here pleasure boats go to Krynica Morska (return adult/concession 42/30zł, 1½ hours) and on to Elbląg (86/60zł, four hours).

# NORTHERN & WESTERN POMERANIA

Stretching northwest from Gdańsk, the Baltic coast is Poland's key summer-holiday strip. It may not be as well known as Spain's Costa del Sol, but it's an attractive coastline of dunes, woods and coastal lakes, fronted by pristine white sandy beaches.

The numerous resort towns stretching all the way from Hel to Świnoujście are engaging places to spend some time. Often blessed with historic architecture, they also contain pleasant, green parks and a good mix of restaurants, bars and other diversions. Outside the urban centres, there are also two interesting national parks on the Pomeranian coast.

As you move around, you'll notice that northern and western Pomerania is basically a rural, sparsely populated region, with compact towns and little industry. This blend of natural beauty with the delights of low-key resort towns makes it a pleasing region to explore, whatever the season.

---

# Łeba

POP 3800

Summertime in Łeba (*weh*-bah) brings Polish and German holidaymakers by the bus-load, who create a relaxed, good-humoured buzz as they stroll the streets, eat out and enjoy the amusements that spring up to keep them diverted. Outside the high season this small fishing port slams the shutters and hunkers down to survive another long Baltic winter.

Most come here for the generous expanse of wide sandy beach and clean water for swimming. The town is also within day-trip distance from Gdańsk, and the attractive Słowiński National Park is within walking distance.

The sea and sand that put Łeba on the tourist map were almost its undoing in the past. In the 16th century the town moved from the western to the eastern bank of the Łeba River after a huge storm flattened the settlement, but even then, Łeba was prey to the peril of shifting sand dunes, which threatened to cover its buildings and disrupt shipping. However, at the end of the 19th century a new port was constructed and forests were planted to impede the sands.

The train and bus stations are next to each other in the southwestern part of Łeba, two blocks west of ul Kościuszki, the main drag. This shopping street crosses the Chełst canal then runs north to the port, on a brief stretch of the Łeba River that joins Lake Łebsko to the sea. The river divides Łeba's beachfront into two sections – the east and the quieter west.

## 🛏 Sleeping

Accommodation options vary according to the season, with July and August by far the busiest months. Low-season room rates drop like a pebble in the Baltic.

**Na Rogu**                              GUESTHOUSE €
(☑59 866 1225; www.narogu.maxmedia.pl; ul Sosnowa 2; per person 60-80zł) Countless locals proffer rooms in their houses during the season, but the difference at Na Rogu is the owner, Maciej. Fluent in English, this former Gdańsk shipyard worker can arrange any activity in Łeba you care to think up, and he's many a tale to tell from Solidarity days. His seven rooms are huge, bright and colourful – some of the bathrooms are as big as hotel singles. Breakfast is an extra 20zł.

**Hotel Neptun**                              HOTEL €€€
(☑59 866 1432; www.neptunhotel.pl; ul Sosnowa 1; s 500-620zł, d 745-850zł; P🛉🛱⛱) One of the finest places to lay your head by the Baltic. The 32 rooms at this early-20th-century beachside villa are studies in understated elegance, all antique-style furniture, regency wall coverings and multi-pillowed beds. The cherry on the cake is the terrace pool area

overlooking the beach, and a bar where sunsets and sundowners can be enjoyed simultaneously. Rates nose-dive when temperatures outside do likewise.

**Hotel Gołąbek** HOTEL €€
(📷59 866 2945; www.hotel-golabek.leb.pl; ul Wybrzeże 10; s/d 240/350zł; P🖥) It may be named after a cabbage roll (actually the owner's surname), but the Gołąbek exudes style on the edge of the wharf, with charming old fishing boats and port views. Bright, cheerful rooms, a sauna, solarium and waterfront restaurant all add up to make this a great deal, but booking ahead is essential.

**Dom Turysty PTTK** HOSTEL €
(📷59 866 1324; ul Kościuszki 66; dm 40-50zł; ☺May-Sep) Occupying a high-ceilinged building, home to a hotel of some kind since before WWI, this large PTTK hostel has 100 beds spread between cosy, no-frills dorms, some with en-suite facilities, others sharing tired shower rooms and toilets. Breakfast is an extra 20zł, full board 40zł.

**Camping Nr 41 Ambré** CAMPGROUND €
(📷59 866 2472; www.ambre.leba.pl; ul Nadmorska 9a; site per adult 15zł, bungalows 240-400zł) This camping ground has a handy range of rooms, a restaurant and delicatessen, and neat, cared-for grounds and facilities.

## ℹ Information

**Post office** (ul Kościuszki 23)
**Tourist office** (📷59 866 2565; www.lotleba.pl; ul 11 Listopada 5a; ☺8am-8pm Mon-Fri, 8am-6pm Sat, 10am-4pm Sun Jun-Aug, 8am-4pm Mon-Fri Sep-May)
**Town library** (ul 11 Listopada 5a; per hr 4zł; ☺noon-8pm Mon-Fri, 10am-2pm Sat) Internet access, next to the tourist office.

## ℹ Getting There & Away

The usual transit point to/from Łeba is Lębork, 29km to the south, which is well connected to the Tri-City area by SKM services. Trains to/from Lębork (10zł, 40 to 50 minutes) depart eight times daily in summer. Buses (5zł, 35 minutes) do the run at least every hour, supplemented by regular minibuses (6zł, 25 minutes).

# Słowiński National Park

The 186-sq-km **Słowiński National Park** (Słowiński Park Narodowy; www.slowinskipn.pl; adult/concession 6/3zł; ☺7am-9pm May-Sep,

8am-4pm Oct-Apr) takes up the 33km stretch of coast between Łeba and the tourist fishing village of **Rowy**, complete with two large lakes, the Łebsko and the Gardno, and their surrounding belts of peat bog, meadows and woods. It's named after the Slav tribe of the Slovincians (Słowińcy), a western branch of the Kashubians whose descendants inhabited this part of the coast right up until the 19th century. In 1977 the park was placed on Unesco's list of World Biosphere Reserves.

## ◎ Sights

**Shifting Dunes** LANDSCAPE
The most unusual feature of the national park is the **shifting dunes** (wydmy ruchome), which create a genuine desert landscape (see boxed text, p344). They're on the sandbar separating the sea from Lake Łebsko, about 8km west of Łeba. Rommel's Afrika Korps trained in this desert during WWII, and the site was also a secret missile testing ground from 1940 to 1945.

The dunes are easily reached from Łeba: take the road west to the hamlet of **Rąbka** (2.5km), where there's a car park and the gate to the national park. Private minibuses, open-sided electric cars and motorised trains (15zł) ply this road in summer, from a stop on Al Wojska Polskiego, north of the canal. It's also an easy walk.

The sealed road continues into the park for another 3.5km to the site of the rocket launcher, now an outdoor **museum**. From here a wide path goes on through the forest for another 2km to the southern foot of the dunes, where half-buried trees jut out of the sand. As you walk round the bend from the woods, it's quite a sight – the pale, immense dunes open up in front of you like a desert dropped into the middle of a forest, with a striking contrast at the line where the trees meet the sand. Continue up the vast dunes for a sweeping view of desert, lake, beach, sea and forest.

No cars or buses are allowed beyond the car park. You can walk to the dunes (45 minutes), buy a ticket on one of the small electric cars, or rent a bicycle (per hour/day 10/40zł). Coming back, you can either retrace your steps or walk to Łeba along the beach (8km), perhaps stopping for a swim – something you certainly can't do in the Sahara.

**Lakes** LAKES
There are four lakes in the park, two large and two small. They are shallow lagoons that started life as bays and were gradually

## SHIFTING SANDS

The 'walking' dunes in the Słowiński National Park are composed of sand thrown up on the beach by waves. Dried by wind and sun, the grains of sand are then blown away to form dunes that are steadily moving inland. The 'white mountain' progresses at a speed of 2m to 10m a year, burying everything it meets on its way. The main victim is the forest, which is gradually disappearing under the sand, to reappear several decades later as a field of skeletal trees.

The process started at least 5000 years ago, and so far the dunes have covered an area of about 6 sq km and reached a height of 30m to 40m, with the highest peak at 42m. They continue to spread inland over new areas, creating a kind of miniature Sahara-by-the-Sea.

cut off from the sea by the sandbar. With densely overgrown, almost inaccessible marshy shores, they provide a habitat for about 250 species of birds, which live here either permanently or seasonally. Large parts of the lake shores have been made into strict no-access reserves, safe from human interference.

About 16km long and 71 sq km in area, **Lake Łebsko** is the biggest in Pomerania and the third-largest in Poland, after Śniardwy and Mamry in Masuria. It's steadily shrinking as a result of the movement of the dunes, the growth of weeds, and silting.

### Kluki                                    VILLAGE

Set on the southwestern shore of Lake Łebsko, the tiny isolated hamlet of Kluki was the last holdout of Slovincian culture, now showcased in the centrally located **skansen** (Muzeum Wsi Słowińskiej; www.muzeumkluki.pl; adult/concession 10/8zł; ⊗9am-4pm Mon, 9am-6pm Tue-Sun Jun-Aug, 9am-4pm Tue-Sun Sep-May). It's modest but authentic, comprising original *in situ* buildings. The long, two-family, white-washed houses are fitted with traditional furniture and decorations.

Buses run to Kluki from Słupsk (10.10zł, one hour, five daily).

### Smołdzino                                VILLAGE

West of Kluki, outside the park's boundaries, Smołdzino boasts a fine **Natural History Museum** (Muzeum Przyrodnicze; adult/concession 4/2zł; ⊗9am-5pm May-Sep, 7.30am-3.30pm Mon-Fri Oct-Apr), which features collections of flora and fauna from the park's various habitats.

Just 1km southwest of the village is **Mt Rowokół**, the highest hill in the area at 115m above sea level. On its top is a 20m **observation tower**, providing sweeping views over the forest, the lakes and the sea. The path up the hill begins next to the petrol station and you can get to the top in 15 minutes.

Buses to/from Słupsk (8zł, 45 minutes) go at least hourly throughout the day.

## Słupsk

POP 98,700

Sometimes it's the anonymous, unpromising names on the map that turn out to be the most charming halts, and that certainly could be said of Słupsk (pronounced 'swoopsk'). A regional service centre with a country town pace, Słupsk has everything that makes a small Polish town just that, with its milk bar, PKP, PKS, PTTK and even a branch of Cepelia all in place. Wide 19th-century avenues lined with mature trees and park benches create an easy-going feel; throw in a touch of architectural interest and you have yourself a pleasant alternative to the busier centres on the coast, as well as a handy base between Gdańsk and Szczecin for flits to the seaside resorts of Darłowo and Ustka.

Like all Pomeranian cities, Słupsk's history involves a complex list of owners: it began life in the 11th century as a Slav stronghold on the Gdańsk–Szczecin trading route, then was ruled by Gdańsk dukes from 1236, passed to the Brandenburg margraves in 1307 and later became part of the West Pomeranian Duchy. In 1648 it reverted to the Brandenburgs, and became part of Prussia, then Germany, until returning to Polish rule after WWII.

### ⊙ Sights

**Museum of Central Pomerania**          MUSEUM
(Muzeum Pomorza Środkowego; www.muzeum .slupsk.pl; ul Dominikańska 5-9; admission 10zł, valid for Museum & Mill; ⊗10am-4pm Wed-Sun) The Museum of Central Pomerania is

housed within Słupsk's main attraction, its commanding 16th-century castle. Beyond its impressive blocky tower are sacral woodcarvings, historic furniture and other exhibits illustrating the town's history. The highlight is a 200-piece collection of portraits by Stanisław Ignacy Witkiewicz (1885–1939), the controversial writer, photographer and painter popularly known as Witkacy.

### Mill
MUSEUM
(ul Dominikańska; ☉10am-4pm Wed-Sun) The building opposite the castle gate is the 14th-century mill, an annex to the museum. Its three floors focus on two themes: the first examines old ethnic groups that once inhabited Pomerania; the second is an exhibition looking at Poles who arrived in the area from the Polish-speaking territories of the east during the 20th century.

### St Hyacinthus' Church
CHURCH
(Kościół Św Jacka) Next to the mill is the 15th-century St Hyacinthus' Church, aka St Jack's as the tourist signposting would have it. The main body of the church is often closed outside service times, but its fine organ can be heard at regular summer concerts, held midweek in July and August.

### Witches' Tower
HISTORIC BUILDING
(Baszta Czarownic; Al F Nullo 8; adult/concession 6/4zł; ☉10am-6pm Tue-Sun) Only two remnants of the 15th-century fortified walls that once encircled the town survive: the **Mill Gate** (Brama Młyńska), beside the mill, and the Witches' Tower a bit further north. The latter has had a sensational career, having been a 17th-century jail for women suspected of witchcraft; in total, 18 women were executed here up to 1714. Nowadays the tower houses temporary exhibitions for the Baltic Gallery of Contemporary Art.

### St Mary's Church
CHURCH
(ul Nowobramska) Fans of red brick and stained glass should check out this chunky Gothic church with its vibrantly coloured, postwar windows.

### Town Hall
HISTORIC BUILDING
(Plac Zwycięstwa) The elaborate Renaissance-Gothic Town Hall has an impressive main tower, which can be ascended for a full Słupsk panorama.

### Baltic Gallery of Contemporary Art
GALLERY
(www.baltic-gallery.art.pl; ul Partyzantów 31a; adult/concession 6/4zł; ☉10am-6pm Mon-Fri) The main building of Słupsk's gallery specialises in short-term instalments of Polish and international artists.

## 🛏 Sleeping

Most of Słupsk's accommodation options hide behind striking 19th-century facades.

### Hotel Staromiejski
HOTEL €€
(☏59 842 8464; www.przymorze.com.pl; ul Jedności Narodowej 4; s 172-222zł, d 274-304zł; P🖥🛜) Right next door to Hotel Piasta, a couple of blocks west of the Stary Rynek, the Staromiejski is top dog in Słupsk with renovated rooms featuring vibrant carpets and timber furniture. The fancy in-house restaurant plates up quality Polish fare for democratic prices.

### Hotel Atena
HOTEL €€
(☏59 842 8814; www.hotelatena.ta.pl; ul Kilińskiego 7; s/d 160/210 zł; 🛜) You'll be disappointed/relieved to hear that the Hellenic theme doesn't go far beyond the name at this smart hotel just across the river from the Old Town. The rooms are a bit of a mishmash but everything's kept spick and span and the restaurant is a godsend in eatery-starved Słupsk.

### Hotel Piast
HOTEL €€
(☏59 842 5286; www.hotelpiast.slupsk.pl; ul Jedności Narodowej 3; s 139-206zł, d 173-246zł; P🖥@) Affordable accommodation in a grand 1897 structure, with options ranging from basic guesthouse-style rooms to proper luxury suites. The corridors are a bit grim, but the staff are friendly and the rooms are pleasantly light and airy.

### Hotel Mikołajek
HOTEL €
(☏59 842 2902; ul Szarych Szeregów 1; s 90zł, d 140zł) Don't be fooled here by the reception's elegant darkwood panelling and curvaceously grand staircase – this is an old

---

### WISH YOU WERE HERE

Słupsk is the birthplace of Heinrich von Stephan (1831–97), the reputed inventor of the postcard. He was born at former Holstentorstrasse 31, approximately where today's ul Piekiełko meets ul Grodzka. Pause for a moment and pay homage to the creator of the indispensable part of travel culture at the information board that marks the spot.

ratbag of a PTTK hotel, sorely in need of an update. The survivable, tobacco-smoke-infused rooms have rickety fittings and time-thinned duvets, but high ceilings lift the mood a tad and showers gush scalding hot. It's just across the river from the Old Town.

## ✕ Eating & Drinking

For a town the size of Słupsk, eating options are thin on the ground. Bakery-cafes gather around the town-centre end of Al Wojska Polskiego.

### Pizza Jadło w Piwnicy                    INTERNATIONAL €
(ul Bema 9; mains 8-17zł; ☺noon-10pm Sun & Mon, 11am-10pm Tue-Thu, 11am-11pm Fri & Sat) Tuck into decent pizzas and various grilled-meat dishes at northern Poland's strangest tables, each one made from a cross-section of tree trunk. Medieval weaponry and stuffed animals threaten from the walls.

### Bar Mleczny Poranek                              POLISH €
(Al Wojska Polskiego 46; mains 3-8zł; ☺7.30am-6pm Mon-Fri, 9am-5pm Sat & Sun) Polish food at its socialist-era zenith in an unashamedly unrenovated *bar mleczny* setting. This place heaves at mealtimes – hopefully you won't be afterwards. The number of dishes on offer dwindles towards the end of the day.

### Caffeteria Retro                                   CAFE €
(Al Sienkiewicza 3; ☺9am-midnight Mon-Fri, 11am-midnight Sat, 11am-11pm Sun) Down a set of steps off busy Al Sienkiewicza, Caffeteria Retro is one of the town's more characterful spots to grab a cuppa joe.

## ⓘ Information

**Post office** (ul Łukasiewicza 3)
**Tourist office** (☎59 842 4326; www.slupsk.pl; ul Starzyńskiego 8; ☺8am-6pm Mon-Fri, 9am-3pm Sat, 10am-2pm Sun Jun–mid-Sep, 8am-4pm Mon-Fri mid-Sep–May) Cycle hire and free internet access. Can arrange tours into the Słowiński National Park.

## ⓘ Getting There & Away

**BUS** Myriad companies run buses to Ustka (5zł, 15 to 20 minutes, several hourly) from the first bus stop on the right when heading along al Wojska Polskiego from the train station. Tickets are bought from the conductor.

Other destinations include the following:
**Darłowo** 10.60zł, 1½ hours, 11 daily
**Łeba** 12zł, 1½ hours, two daily
**Kluki** 10zł, one hour, six daily
**Smołdzino** 8zł, 45 minutes, five daily

**TRAIN** Słupsk has the following train connections:
**Gdańsk** 16.60zł, 2½hours, 13 daily (some SKM)
**Szczecin** 46zł, 2¾ to four hours, eight daily
**Warsaw** 61zł to 123zł, 8½ to 10 hours, three daily (one overnight)

## Ustka
POP 16,200

With a leafy, primly maintained centre and streets of graceful architecture, this fishing port is one of the Baltic's more refined resort towns. German sun-seekers certainly seem to think so; they've been flocking to Ustka's white-sand beach ever since the 19th-century when 'Iron Chancellor' Otto von Bismarck built an elaborate beach shack here. To cater for this ongoing Teutonic invasion, the town has ample, good-quality digs and an animated seaside promenade, at least in the summer season.

## 🛏 Sleeping & Eating

If you've not booked ahead in July and August, the best place to start looking for sheet space is the helpful tourist office. At quieter times you could try your luck in ul Żeromskiego, which is lined with grand old villas offering cheap rooms.

### Hotel Rejs                                        HOTEL €€
(☎59 814 7850; www.hotelrejs.com; ul Marynarki Polskiej 51; s/d 240/360zł; ℗@☎) Studies in understated luxury, the rooms at Ustka's top hotel effortlessly marry all mod cons with polished-wood antique finery. The award-winning restaurant is also arguably the best in town. Booking ahead essential.

### Villa Red                                   GUESTHOUSE €€
(☎59 814 8000; www.villa-red.pl; ul Żeromskiego 1; s/d 290/380zł; ℗☎) A grand old red-brick pile built in 1886 for Otto von Bismarck, this is one of the most characterful places to slumber on the Baltic coast. Rooms resemble well-stocked antique emporia and the theme continues in the restaurant.

### V Starym Kinie                             GUESTHOUSE €€
(☎602 772 575; www.kino.ustka.pl; ul Marynarki Polskiej 82; r 120-160zł) They pack 'em in so tightly in Ustka that even the old cinema has been commandeered to put up guests. Each of the smartly done up, comfortable rooms is named after a Hollywood star, and there's a small kitchen.

## Camping Słoneczny  CAMPGROUND €

(☑59 814 5586; ul Grunwaldzka 35; dm 35zł, cabins 100zł) The most convenient of the two seasonal camping grounds, about 1.2km away from the beach.

## Pensjonat Oleńka  GUESTHOUSE €€

(☑59 814 8522; ul Zaruskiego 1; d 250zł, ste 400-550zł) In the middle of the granary row, the Oleńka has three elegantly stylish rooms and four suites.

## ℹ Information

**Doma Ustka** (☑59 814 5623; www.doma.ustka .pl; ul Wilcza 22) Accommodation-finding service.

**Post office** (ul Marynarki Polskiej 47)

**Tourist office** (☑59 814 7170; www.ustka.pl; ul Marynarki Polskiej 87; ⊙8am-6pm Mon-Sat, 10am-3pm Sun mid-Jun–Aug, 9am-5pm Mon, 8am-4pm Tue-Fri Sep–mid-Jun) Can provide information on fishing tours, horse riding, canoeing and hiking in the area.

## ℹ Getting There & Away

The train station is diagonally opposite the tourist office. The bus station is a five-minute walk further north along al Marynarki Polskiej. Trains to Słupsk depart approximately every other hour (5.30zł, 20 minutes) in summer, and there are several buses per hour (5zł, 15 to 20 minutes). Regular buses also go to Rowy (one hour), on the edge of Słowiński National Park. In July and August, at least three bus services a day run direct to Warsaw (65zł to 84zł, nine hours).

# Darłowo

POP 14,400

Inland Darłowo and little seaside sister Darłówko on the Wieprza River form an interesting pair of siblings. The former Hanseatic trading port of Darłowo still retains traces of its wealthy medieval past, contrasting starkly with hedonistic Darłówko and its seasonal fish friers, creamy beach and as-tacky-as-they-come promenade of Chinese-made souvenirs. Inevitably it's Darłówko that forms the main draw for visitors and the town has the lion's share of accommodation and places to eat. The only 'sight' there is the pedestrian drawbridge uniting the western and eastern sides of the river, which opens when boats go into or out of the bay. The two communities are linked by a river taxi and local buses that run along both sides of the river. Otherwise it's around 30 minutes on foot.

## ⊙ Sights

### Museum of Pomeranian Dukes  MUSEUM

Muzeum Zamku Książąt Pomorskich; www.muzeum darlowo.pl; ul Zamkowa 4; adult/concession 11/7zł; ⊙10am-6pm May-Sep) South of Darłowo's central Rynek is its well-preserved 14th-century **castle**, erected in 1352 and renovated in 1988. It was the residence of the Pomeranian dukes until the Swedes devastated it during the Thirty Years' War, and the Brandenburgs took it following the Treaty of Westphalia. The dethroned King Erik, who ruled Denmark, Norway and Sweden between 1396 and 1438 and became known as the 'last Viking of the Baltic', lived in the castle for the last 10 years of his life. He is believed to have hidden his enormous ill-gotten treasure here; so far it remains undiscovered, so keep your eyes peeled as you wander!

The castle's grand halls and noble quarters are now a museum but your self-guided tour begins in the claustrophobic brick basement where beer and prisoners were once kept. Amid the impressive interiors, old farming implements, art from the Far East and old postcards from Rügenwalde (the German name for Darłowo), what sticks in the memory is the impressive collection of antique furniture, which includes a late-Renaissance Italian four-poster and some Danzig wardrobes of truly preposterous proportions.

Vista junkies should ascend the castle's main **tower** (admission 3.50zł).

### St Mary's Church  CHURCH

(ul Kościelna) Behind the attractively renovated Baroque **Town Hall** on Darłowo's large Rynek rises this massive brick church. Begun in the 1320s and enlarged later, it has preserved its Gothic shape pretty well. Worth special attention are the three **tombs** placed in the chapel under the tower. The one made of sandstone holds the ashes of King Erik, who died in Darłowo in 1459. His tombstone, commissioned in 1882 by the Prussian Emperor Wilhelm II, isn't as impressive as the two mid-17th-century, richly decorated tin tombs standing on either side of it, which contain the remains of the last West Pomeranian duke, Jadwig, and his wife Elizabeth. The grounds contain some interesting old German gravestones rescued from the surrounding villages.

### St Gertrude's Chapel  CHURCH

(Kaplica Św Gertrudy; ul Św Gertrudy; ⊙8am-8pm) A few hundred metres north of the Rynek stands a truly quirky piece of medieval architecture. This 12-sided chapel topped with a high, shingled central spire was once the cemetery chapel but became a church in 1997. The outside is reminiscent of a Carpathian timber church but inside the ceiling is a huge piece of Gothic star vaulting supported by six hefty octagonal columns.

## 🛏 Sleeping

Most places to stay are in Darłówko. Many locals rent out rooms in their homes, from 40zł per person.

**TOP CHOICE Hotel Apollo**  HOTEL €€€
(☑94 314 2453; www.hotelapollo.pl; ul Kąpielowa, Darłówko; s 220-320zł, d 380-500zł, apt 750zł; P❄@❒) Surely one of northern Poland's best places to linger, this tasteful hotel, crafted from a palatial spa house just steps from the Baltic briny, is welcoming, spacious and crisply luxurious. The 16 contemporary rooms are all the same, just the colour schemes differ, but stumping up a bit more cash gets you one with a knock-dead sea view. The circular beach cafe is good for a coffee in style even if you aren't a guest.

**Hotel Irena**  GUESTHOUSE €€
(☑94 314 3692; www.irena.darlowo.info.pl; Al Wojska Polskiego 64, Darłowo; s/d 110/170zł; P❒) The best deal in either settlement is this neat little guesthouse (it's not a hotel) in central Darłowo, with easy access to the castle and the bus station. The owner speaks no English but can usually communicate that smokers should go elsewhere without the use of words.

**Róża Wiatrów**  CAMPGROUND €
(☑94 314 2127; www.rozawiatrow.pl; ul Muchy 2, Darłówko; site per adult/child 12/8zł) This multifaceted holiday complex near the sea has camping space for 100 bodies and offers plenty of other accommodation, from plain to glam.

## ⓘ Information

**Post office** (ul Pocztowa 2)
**Tourist office** (☑504 992 452; Plac Kociuszki; ⊙10am-5pm Jul & Aug only)

## ⓘ Getting There & Away

The bus terminal is at the southwestern end of Darłowo, a 10-minute walk from the Rynek. A bus runs at 9.15am to Ustka (12.50zł, one hour) and there are seven services to/from Słupsk (10.60zł, one to 1½ hours).

## ⓘ Getting Around

Minibuses shuttle between Darłowo and Darłówko but a more interesting way to make the short trip is by **water tram** (one way 9zł; ⊙10am-6.30pm May-Sep), basically a boat that leaves on the hour from Darłowo and on the half-hour from Darłówko.

# Kołobrzeg

POP 45,000

The biggest resort on the Polish Baltic coast, Kołobrzeg (ko-*wob*-zhek) has much more than just its share of the north's pristine white sand. This atmospheric town of seafront attractions, spa traditions, beer gardens and summer crowds of strolling Germans is big enough to offer urban distractions on top of the delights of swimming and sunbathing.

It's actually one of Poland's oldest settlements, having been founded in the 7th century when salt springs were discovered here. In 1000 it became a seat of the Polish bishopric, putting it on a par with Kraków and Wrocław.

However, the good times couldn't last and the town became a popular destination for military invaders, including Swedes, Brandenburgs, Russians and the French forces under Napoleon. Once this phase was over, Kołobrzeg reinvented itself as a sunny spa resort, only to be demolished by the two-week battle for the city in the closing months of WWII.

Almost seven decades since the destruction of 1945, Kołobrzeg still bears the scars. The town was never rebuilt and the modern 'medieval-style' architecture that now packs the old centre (in the same ilk as Elbląg) is pretty unconvincing. However the bombs also created a lot of parkland, and along with the beach and seafront these combine to make this Baltic base a relaxing, if not particularly aesthetically pleasing, place for a couple of days' exploration.

## ⊙ Sights & Activities

Not much remains of Kołobrzeg's old quarter, but the odd survivor of WWII can be found among the old-new imitations.

**Cathedral**  CHURCH
(ul Katedralna) The 14th-century cathedral is the most important historic sight in town. Though badly damaged in 1945, it has been rebuilt close to its original form. For such a massive building, it has a surpris-

ingly light-filled interior, illuminated by its extremely tall and narrow windows of beautifully patterned stained glass. Its colossal two conjoined towers occupy the whole width of the building, and the facade is a striking composition of windows placed haphazardly.

No, you haven't had too much vodka, those columns on the right side of the nave really are leaning. But don't worry, you don't have to rush out to avoid being crushed – they've been that way since the 16th century. Still, the impression they create is slightly unnerving.

Old fittings include three 16th-century triptychs and a unique Gothic wooden chandelier (1523) in the central nave. There are some even older objects, such as the bronze baptismal font (1355) featuring scenes of Christ's life; a 4m-high, seven-armed candelabrum (1327); and the stalls in the chancel (1340). Outside is a striking modern monument celebrating 1000 years of Polish Catholicism; the design, a symbolic split cross joined by a peace dove, depicts influential rulers Bolesław Chrobrego and Otto III.

**Polish Arms Museum**                    MUSEUM
(Muzeum Oręża Polskiego; ul Gierczak 5; adult/ concession 10/7zł; ☺10am-6pm May-Aug, shorter hrs Sep-Apr) This large museum isn't as dull as you might expect and is well worth a look if you've time on your hands. The displays cover the history of weaponry across the ages, with examples of swords, armour, halberds and more modern military technology, including an outdoor display (extra 4zł) of suitably daunting weapons and vehicles. The huge display of cannonballs are calling cards left by Kołobrzeg's many invaders, and the 1945 destruction is impressively brought to life using war debris arranged against a panorama of the city ablaze.

**History Museum**                         MUSEUM
(ul Armii Krajowej 13; adult/concession 10/7zł, with Polish Arms Museum 15/10zł; ☺10am-6pm Tue-Sun May-Aug, shorter hrs Sep-Apr) Housed in an Empire-style merchant's house called the **Braunschweig Palace**, the sister institution to the Polish Arms Museum has a neatly presented collection, with an emphasis on weights and scales. Head downstairs for an interesting audiovisual presentation (in English on request) about the city's history, using images of old postcards.

**Beach**                                   BEACH
In the seaside sector, the white-sand beach itself is the top attraction, supplemented by the usual seasonal stalls, waffle kiosks, amusement arcades, novelty boat trips, buskers and other street life. At intervals along the sands you can hire a double-seater beach chair, popular among those who've enjoyed too many waffles. Walk out 200m over the sea on the **pier**, an obligatory activity for holidaymakers. Oddly enough, an eyrar of swans gathers on the sand beneath the structure, kept well fed by holidaying passers-by. To the west, by the harbour and its newly constructed cluster of waterside apartments, stands the red-brick **lighthouse** (Latarnia Morska; adult/child 4/3zł; ☺10am-5pm, until sunset Jul & Aug), which you can climb for panoramic views.

**Town Hall**                    HISTORIC BUILDING
(main entrance on ul Armii Krajowej) The Town Hall, just east of the cathedral, is a neo-Gothic structure designed by Karl Friedrich Schinkel and erected by Ernst Friedrich Zwirner (who also built Cologne Cathedral) in the early 1830s after the previous 14th-century building was helpfully razed to the ground by Napoleon's troops in 1807. The area in the front of the main entrance is populated by beer gardens in summer, providing pleasant places to sit and admire the architecture. One of its wings houses a **modern art gallery** (adult/concession 5/3zł; ☺10am-5pm Tue-Sun).

**Powder Tower**                 HISTORIC BUILDING
(Baszta Prochowa; ul Dubois 20) The Powder Tower is a 15th-century survivor from the original city walls and was given its current name in 1945, in honour of an earlier tower that exploded into oblivion in 1657 when its gunpowder store caught fire. It now houses the Kołobrzeg branch of the PTTK, meaning you can get a look inside for free.

**Viking Ship**                            CRUISE
(cnr ul Towarowa & ul Cicha; adult/child 25/20zł; ☺10am-5pm) A replica Viking ship and 18th-century galleon both head out into the Baltic for regular 45-minute mini-cruises.

## 🛏 Sleeping

The summer hordes make a real dent in Kołobrzeg's substantial accommodation range, though private rooms are on offer from locals loitering around the train station brandishing *wolne pokoje* (rooms free) signs, even in low season. As a foreigner you can expect to pay about 50zł per person for these rooms – Poles bargain the price down to around 40zł. Owners are very reluctant to rent for just one night.

### Maxymilian Hotel HOTEL €€
(☑94 354 0012; www.maxymilian-hotel.pl; ul Borzymowskiego 3; s/d 170/300zł; P 🛜 ✉) Popular with German tour groups, the splendidly classy Maxymilian offers a quiet location and stylishly furnished rooms. The elegant building it occupies stands in stark contrast to the Sand Hotel opposite, which casts a long shadow. A spa, restaurant, sauna and very accommodating staff make this a great deal, but book ahead as this place gets chockers before anywhere else. Room rates include breakfast.

### Sand Hotel HOTEL €€€
(☑94 353 4111; www.sandhotel.pl; ul Zdrojowa 3; s 259-279zł; d 379-509zł; ❄ 🛜 ✉) Even the economy rooms at this newly minted glass-and-steel colossus are lessons in elegantly clean-cut retro styling, and more than get you in the mood for all the pampering and pummelling available at the hotel's spa. Rooms are pretty spacious, the modern gym is awash with technology and there's not a waffle in sight at the much-lauded restaurant.

### Hotel Centrum HOTEL €€
(☑94 354 5560; www.ckp.info.pl; ul Katedralna 12; s/d 110/180zł; P @) Generously cut rooms behind an unpromisingly sooty facade often have park or garden views, but it's a bit of a hike to the beach. The hotel and associated eateries are staffed by students training to work in the hospitality industry, often a guarantee of old-world courtesy, little textbook touches not found in other places and the occasional spillage. Probably the best value for money in town for what you get.

### Etna HOTEL €€
(☑94 355 0000; www.hoteletna.pl; ul Portowa 18; s/d 180/240zł; P ❄) This massive beach-area building looks unpromising from the outside, but the rooms are spacious and bright, and you can indulge in a full range of spa treatments and physio here.

## ✕ Eating & Drinking

Half- and full board is the way to go at most hotels and guesthouses, and homestay owners normally allow guests to use their kitchens. Seasonal fast-food outlets and cafes abound, but there are also several worthwhile year-round options.

### Pergola INTERNATIONAL €€€
(bul Jana Szymańskiego 14; mains 30-60zł; ⊙10am-11pm) Elevated above the snaffling promenaders and serving a Mediterranean and Polish menu, this the best of the countless eateries that gather around the lighthouse. Recommended for its fish dishes and grandstand views of the Baltic.

### Restauracja Pod Winogronami INTERNATIONAL €€€
(ul Towarowa 16; mains 28-79zł; ⊙11am-midnight) Extremely popular among the ambling crowds, 'Under the Grapes' has a slightly French air, but the meat-heavy menu draws mainly on Polish and German cookbooks. The 'grilled boar in juniper sauce' sounds delicious, the puzzling 'elephant's ear' less so.

### Gospoda Pod Dwoma Łabędziami POLISH €€
(ul Armii Krajowej 30b; mains 17-40zł; ⊙10am-10pm) Cosy and low-lit, this subterranean eatery has a stone floor, faux rustic decor and English-speaking staff. Good for a hearty lunch or dinner of Polish standards, or a few frothy Lech ales after dark.

### Bar Syrena POLISH €
(ul Zwycięzców 11; mains 10-17zł; ⊙noon-6pm Mon-Sat, until 5pm Sun) The *bar mleczny* brought almost into the 21st century, serving Polish standards in a spick-and-span tiled dining room with abstract prints on the walls. You'll forgive the plastic trees when you fork the filling fare shoved through the serving hatch behind the bar – just the ticket after a wind-blasted day by the Baltic.

### Kalla Pizza PIZZERIA €€
(ul Armii Krajowej 32; mains 10-31zł; ⊙10.30am-11pm) Pizza place with a popular warm-weather beer garden outside the main entrance to the Town Hall.

## ℹ Information

**Albatros** (☑94 354 2800; www.albatros.turystyka.pl; ul Morska 7a; ⊙9am-4pm Mon-Fri, 9am-1pm Sat) Accommodation service.

**Post office** (ul Armii Krajowej 1)

**PTTK** (☑94 352 2311; www.pttk.kolobrzeg.pl; Baszta Prochowa, ul Dubois 20; ⊙9am-5pm Mon-Fri) Can help find accommodation and has a wealth of information on Kołobrzeg and activities in the surrounding area.

**Tourist office** (www.kolobrzeg.pl) train station (☎94 352 7939; ul Dworcowa 1; ⏰8am-5pm Jul & Aug, 8am-4pm Mon-Fri Sep-Jun) city centre (☎94 354 7220; Plac Ratuszowy 2/1; ⏰8am-5pm); harbour (☎94 352 0855; Morska 2; ⏰8am-4pm Mon-Fri) The train station tourist office is in an unmarked building opposite the station.

**Vobis** (1st fl,ul Armii Krajowej 20c; per hr 6zł; ⏰10am-6pm Mon-Fri, 10am-3pm Sat) Internet access.

## 🛈 Getting There & Away

**BOAT Kołobrzeska Żegluga Pasażerska**
(☎94 352 8920; www.kzp.man.pl; ul Morska 2) operates regular catamaran cruises to Nexø on Bornholm Island, Denmark (one way/return 130/180zł, 4½ hours). The service sails daily in July, August and September, and three times a week in June.

**BUS** Buses head to the following:
**Świnoujście** 25zł, 2½ hours, four daily
**Szczecin** 19zł to 25zł, 2½ to three hours, seven daily
**Warsaw** 74zł to 90zł, 10 hours, up to nine in summer

**TRAIN** Kołbrzeg has the following rail connections:
**Gdańsk** 36zł to 101zł, 4¼ hours, four daily (or change in Koszalin)
**Szczecin** 22zł, two hours, eight daily
**Warsaw** 63zł to 125zł, 10 hours, three daily (one overnight)

# Świnoujście

POP 41,000

As far northwest as you can get in Poland without leaving the country, Świnoujście (shvee-no-*ooysh*-cheh) is an attractive seaside town occupying the eastern end of Uznam Island with a touch of faded grandeur along its waterfront promenade, and a relaxed atmosphere despite its role as a major port and naval base. There are plenty of green parks and a choice of water views over sea or river, something that may have inspired its famous literary residents from its 19th-century German past (when it was known as Swinemünde), including novelist and travel writer Theodor Fontane and poet Ernst Schrerenberg. Other notable visitors included Kaiser Wilhelm II and Tsar Nicholas II, who met here in 1907, sparking fruitless hopes that their friendship would avert a European war.

The town remains popular with Germans, mostly elderly day-trippers from the former GDR. Of all the Baltic's resorts, Świnoujście attracts the most sedate crowd and those looking to rave by the sea should move on quickly.

Świnoujście's location makes the city a handy entry point for travellers across the Baltic, via ferry services from Sweden and Denmark; it also has a border crossing with Germany.

## ◉ Sights & Activities

Świnoujście isn't big on sights, with most visitors coming to laze on the **beach**, one of the widest and longest in Poland. Back from the sands, the resort district still retains a certain *fin-de-siècle* air in places, with some elegant villas. This runs down to the seafront where the (at)tack begins in the shape of waffle stands and fluffy toy seals.

**Museum of Sea Fishery** MUSEUM
(Muzeum Rybołówstwa Morskiego; Plac Rybaka 1; adult/concession 6/4zł; ⏰9am-5pm Tue-Sun) If you're keen on stuffed sea life, you'll be delighted by the static displays of albatrosses, sharks and seals, along with fishing paraphernalia and model boats. The museum's saving grace is its three tanks of exotic fish, including a real live piranha. There are also displays on the town's history, including historic official seals of a nonaquatic nature, but no captions in English.

**Air Raid Shelter** HISTORIC BUILDING
(ul Wyspiańskiego 51) One of many to be built before WWII, this last remaining shelter was once used by residents seeking protection from heavy Allied bombing. The exterior is inexplicably decorated with nautical memorabilia including anchors and ropes. It's not open for viewing, but there's an explanatory plaque in English.

## 🛏 Sleeping

Świnoujście has plenty of places to get some shut-eye but you may have to approach the tourist office or accommodation agency if you decide to turn up unannounced during the short July-August season.

**Biuro Zakwaterowań Barton** ACCOMMODATION SERVICES
(☎91 321 1155; www.barton.com.pl; Wybrzeże Władysława IV) For private rooms, head to this small office by the ferry landing. Rates average around 50zł to 60zł per person; note that most are in the southwestern suburbs, with almost none in the beach area.

**WORTH A TRIP**

## WOLIN NATIONAL PARK

Best accessed from the resort of Międzyzdroje, **Wolin National Park** (Woliński Park Narodowy; www.wolinpn.pl) occupies the central section of Wolin Island. With a total area of about 50 sq km, it's one of the smaller Polish parks, yet it's picturesque enough to warrant a day or two's walking.

The park's northern edge drops sharply into the sea, forming an 11km-long sandy cliff nearly 100m high in places.

Back from the coast are a number of lakes, mostly on the remote eastern edge of the park. The most beautiful is the horseshoe-shaped **Lake Czajcze**. Away from the lakeland, there's **Lake Turkusowe** (Turquoise), named after the colour of its water, at the southern end of the park, and the lovely **Lake Gardno** close to the seashore, next to the Międzyzdroje–Dziwnów road. The lakes are surrounded by mixed forest, with beech, oak and pine predominating. The flora and fauna is relatively diverse, with a rich bird life. The last wild bison in Pomerania were wiped out in the 14th century, but there's a small **bison reserve** inside the park, 2km east of Międzyzdroje.

### Activities

The best way to explore the park is by **hiking**, and the small area means a good walk needn't be too taxing. Three marked trails wind into the park from Międzyzdroje. The red trail leads northeast along the shore, then turns inland to **Wisełka** and continues through wooded hills to the small village of **Kołczewo**. The green trail runs east across the middle of the park, skirts the lakeland and also ends in Kołczewo. The blue trail goes to the southern end of the park, passing Lake Turquoise on the way. It then continues east to the town of **Wolin**.

All the trails are well marked and easy. Get a copy of the detailed *Woliński Park Narodowy* map (scale 1:30,000), and consult the park headquarters in Międzyzdroje for further information.

**Willa Paw** GUESTHOUSE €€
(☏91 321 4325; ul Żeromskiego 25; s/d 150/180zł; P🖧) The seven rooms here above a relaxing cafe are big enough to swing a four-pawed animal (actually the name means peacock in Polish) and are a cut above your average bog-standard guesthouse with darkwood furniture and monster bathrooms. Slightly nonplussed staff.

**Hotelik Belweder** HOTEL €€
(☏91 327 1677; www.hotel-belweder.pl; ul Wyspiań-skiego 1; s/d 180/240zł; P🖧) Quite different to the town's villa-based guesthouses, this purpose-built hotel in its own compound around 600m back from the beach has bright, well-tended rooms, friendly staff and cycle hire.

**Hotel Ottaviano** HOTEL €€
(☏91 321 4403; www.ottaviano.pl; ul Monte Cassino 3; s/d 200/300zł; P🖧) Located in the very centre of town, and handy for the ferry crossing, the Ottaviano is a pretty good deal. Rooms are colourful, furnished with imagination and have warm, uncarpeted wood-effect floors. The in-house restaurant has views across the attractive paved street.

**Camping Nr 44 Relax** CAMPGROUND €
(☏91 321 3912; www.camping-relax.com.pl; ul Słowackiego 1; site 11zł, plus per person 16zł) A large, popular camping ground superbly located between the beach and the spa park.

**Willa Merry** APARTMENTS €
(☏91 321 2619; www.villa-merry.com; ul Żerom-skiego 16; d 90-120zł, apt 330-460zł; P) One of the top self-catering options in town, Merry's two swish Art Nouveau buildings contain several kitchen-equipped apartments with lots of space but cheapo furniture.

## ✖ Eating

**Restauracja Gryfia** POLISH €€
(ul Piłsudskiego 10; mains 10-30zł; ◷11am-late) This town-centre eatery gives off a semi-fancy air but still serves no-nonsense Polish fare and a cheap lunch menu (16zł). Tightly packed tables mean you might get to know your fellow diners sooner rather than later.

### Restauracja Centrala  POLISH €€

(ul Armii Krajowej 3; mains 10-45zł; ⊘10am-midnight) Chilled-out space with a burnt-orange interior and striking frescos featuring primitive figures; grab a seat for marina views. The apple strudel with vanilla cream is particularly good, and there's live jazz here at regular intervals.

## ⊕ Information

**Bank Pekao** ul Monte Cassino (ul Monte Cassino 7) ul Piłsudskiego (ul Piłsudskiego 4)
**Biuro Podróży Partner** (☏91 322 4397; ul Bohaterów Września 83/14) Information and ferry tickets; enter via Pasaż Żeglarski.
**Post office** (ul Piłsudskiego 1)
**Tourist office** (☏91 322 4999; www.swinoujscie .pl; Plac Słowiański 6; ⊘9am-5pm Mon-Fri, 10am-2pm Sat & Sun high season)

## ⊕ Getting There & Away

The most convenient overland crossing to/from Germany is 2km west of town. The first town on the German side, Ahlbeck, handles transport further into the country.

**BOAT** Tickets for all boat services are available at the terminals and from most travel agencies around town.

The German company **Adler-Schiffe** (www .adler-schiffe.de) runs cruises from Świnoujście to Zinnowitz via Ahlbeck, Heringsdorf and Bansin in Germany, up to four times daily. The tourist office has information on times and prices.

Major carrier **Polferries** (www.polferries.pl) operates ferries to Ystad, Sweden (adult/concession Skr590/490, seven hours, daily) and Copenhagen (520/460kr, nine hours, daily). **Unity Line** (www.unityline.pl) also runs daily ferries to Ystad (Skr600/500, seven hours).

All ferries depart from the ferry terminal on Wolin Island, on the right bank of the Świna River (across the river from the main town).

**BUS** Ostseebus 290 (one way/return 7/13zł) links the Polish and German sides of Uznam Island every 30 minutes between 9am and 6pm. A day pass costs 24zł, or €6 in Germany. Otherwise Świnoujście has the following domestic bus and minibus connections:
**Kołobrzeg** 25zł to 35zł, three hours, four daily
**Międzyzdroje** 4.50zł, 15 minutes, 17 daily
**Szczecin** 15zł, 1½ hours, many daily

**CAR & MOTORCYCLE** Cars not belonging to local residents can only use the shuttle ferry between Uznam and Wolin Islands (between the railway station on one side and the town centre on the other) at weekends and between 10pm and 5am on weekdays; otherwise you'll have to head for the crossing serving Karsibór Island,

7km south of Świnoujście. Expect to wait during the peak season (usually no longer than a couple of hours). Passage for both vehicles and passengers is free.

**TRAIN** The bus terminal and train station are next to each other on the right bank of the Świna River. Passenger ferries shuttle constantly between the town centre and the stations (free, 10 minutes).

Świnoujście has the following rail connections:
**Kraków** 71zł, 11 to 13½ hours, five daily
**Międzyzdroje** 4.20zł, 15 minutes, hourly
**Poznań** 54zł, four to five hours, eight daily
**Szczecin** 18zł, 1½ hours, hourly
**Warsaw** 64zł, eight to 9½ hours, three daily
**Wrocław** 59zł, seven to eight hours, eight daily

## Szczecin

POP 406,000

Well off any track (non-German) tourists beat, the western port city of Szczecin (*shcheh*-cheen) is a lively city awash with students and a muddle of architecture inherited from wildly different ages. Crumbly German-era tenements and mansions, some now undergoing renovation, echo a past splendour but historical style is patchy. The authorities seem to have given up on the idea of rebuilding, choosing instead to fill the gaps in the city centre with glass-and-steel malls, sacrificing entire streets in the name of retail.

A busy working port, though you'd never know it wandering the city centre, Szczecin has just enough to warrant a stopover.

### History

Szczecin's beginnings go back to the 8th century, when a Slav stronghold was built here. In 967 Duke Mieszko I annexed the town for the newborn Polish state, but was unable to hold or Christianise it. It was Bolesław Krzywousty who recaptured the town in 1121 and brought the Catholic faith to the locals.

Krzywousty died in 1138 and the Polish Crown crumbled; Pomerania formally became an independent principality. Periods of allegiance to Germanic and Danish rulers followed, before Western Pomerania was unified by Duke Bogusław X in 1478, with Szczecin being chosen as the capital.

The next major shift in power came in 1630, when the Swedes conquered the city. Sweden then ceded Szczecin to Prussia in 1720, which as part of Germany held the region until WWII. Under Prussian

# Szczecin

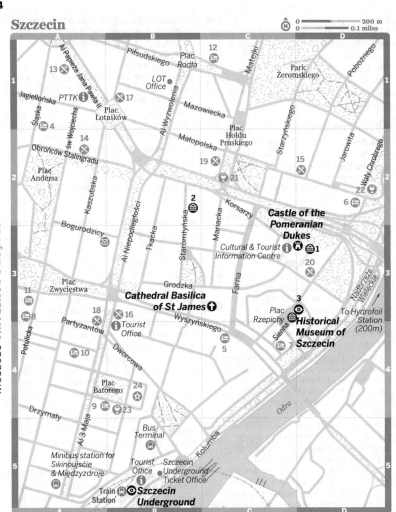

rule, Szczecin (Stettin in German) grew considerably, becoming the main port for landlocked Berlin. By the outbreak of WWII the city had about 300,000 inhabitants.

In April 1945 the Red Army passed through on its way to Berlin, leaving 60% of the urban area in ruins. Only 6000 souls remained of the former population, most of the others having fled.

With new inhabitants, mostly drawn from territories lost by Poland to the Soviet Union, the battered city started a new life, developing into an important port and industrial centre for the postwar nation.

## Sights & Activities

**Castle of the Pomeranian Dukes** CASTLE
(Zamek Książąt Pomorskich; www.zamek.szczecin
.pl; ul Korsarzy 34; admission 8zł; 10am-6pm
Tue-Sun) The mother of all Szczecin monuments is the Castle of the Pomeranian Dukes. This vast, blocky building looms over the Old Town, but the square central courtyard and simple Renaissance-style decoration atop the walls have a certain understated grace (spot the repeated circular pattern that resembles the Yin and Yang symbol). The castle was originally built in the mid-14th century and

# Szczecin

grew into its current form by 1577, but was destroyed by Allied carpet-bombing in 1944 before being extensively restored. Admire the colourful historic clockface from the courtyard, with its jester figure chiming in each new hour, then climb to the top of the 58.6m **bell tower** (adult/concession 4/3zł) for a view of the city.

The castle also accommodates the **Castle Museum**. Its star exhibits are six spectacular sarcophagi of the Pomeranian dukes. These large tin boxes are decorated with a fine engraved ornamentation and were made between 1606 and 1637 by artists from Königsberg. Following the death of the last Pomeranian duke, Bogusław XIV, the crypt was walled up until the sarcophagi were discovered during restoration work in 1946, after the castle's wartime destruction. The remains of the dukes were deposited in the cathedral, while the least-damaged sarcophagi were restored for display.

Various temporary exhibitions and displays of art take place in other rooms of the castle. In summer, concerts are held on Sunday in the courtyard or the former chapel, which occupies nearly half the northern side.

**Historical Museum of Szczecin**   MUSEUM
(Muzeum Historii Miasta Szczecina; www.muzeum
.szczecin.pl; ul Ks. Mściwoja II 8; adult/concession 10/5zł; ☉10am-6pm Tue-Fri, to 4pm Sat &

Sun) A short walk south will bring you to the 15th-century Gothic **Town Hall**, one of the most architecturally fascinating buildings in the city with its monster red-brick gable. This is the only relic of the Old Town, having miraculously survived the near-total destruction of the surrounding streets in WWII. Szczecin never enjoyed the meticulous postwar reconstruction of other Polish cities, but the Old Town has been partially recreated with an attractive line of stylised burghers' houses right behind the Town Hall (in striking contrast to the unbecoming communist-era blocks opposite). The area is populated with a few fashionable cafes and upmarket bars, but remains quiet most of the time.

The Town Hall is home to the Historical Museum, a well-curated exhibition filling the light-filled interior. The most fascinating exhibit is a medieval treasure trove unearthed in 2001 during building works elsewhere in the city, a multimillion-dollar collection of silver coins, buttons, rings and other jewellery – and the small iron pot the loot was stashed in.

**Szczecin Underground**   UNDERGROUND
(www.schron.szczecin.pl; ul Kolumba 1; adult/concession single tour 15/14zł, both tours 25/23zł; ☉tours noon & 1pm Mon-Sat) This award-winning attraction near the train station is

made up of a sprawling set of concrete tunnels beneath the city streets, designated as a bomb shelter in the 1940s and as a fallout shelter thereafter. Tours alternate between a WWII or Cold War theme. Buy tickets from the office at ul Kolumba 1 at least 15 minutes before the tour begins then make your way to the entrance on Platform 3 of the train station.

**Cathedral Basilica of St James**　CHURCH
(Bazylika Katedralna pw Św Jakuba Apostoła; ul Wyszyńskiego; admission 4zł) Head downhill from the city centre to explore Szczecin's 12th-century cathedral, partially destroyed by Red Army shells in 1945 and reconstructed in 1972. It's this early 70s renovation you'll notice first, the incongruously modern facade more reminiscent of a derelict factory than a place of worship. As a foreigner you'll be cherry-picked to shell out the 4zł admission, then proceed to the nave where a forest of red-brick columns provides perspective to an interior lacking atmosphere. On the right, almost at the end of the nave, a plaque remembering those who perished in the Smolensk air disaster sits below another to the Katyń victims they were on their way to honour. Otherwise possibly the world's tiniest crypt and some impressive stained glass are the only other distractions, except for the **tower** (admission 8zł; ⊗11am-6pm Tue-Sat, from noon Sun) where a lift winches you up to striking views of the river.

**National Museum's Department of Early Art**　MUSEUM
(Galeria Sztuki Dawnej; www.muzeum.szczecin.pl; ul Staromłyńska 27; adult/concession 10/5zł; ⊗10am-6pm Tue-Fri, to 4pm Sat & Sun) The National Museum's Department of Early Art resides in an 18th-century palace that formerly served as the Pomeranian parliament. It displays a collection of religious art, particularly woodcarving from the 14th to 16th centuries, and you can also take a peek at the Pomeranian crown jewels.

**Maritime Museum**　MUSEUM
(Muzeum Morskie; www.muzeum.szczecin.pl) Closed at the time of research, the National Museum's Maritime Museum is set to move into a purpose-built complex which will also house a library and culture centre. The project is still at the planning stage and it's not clear when the new centre will open.

## 🛏 Sleeping

**Hotel Focus**　HOTEL €€
(☏91 433 0500; www.hotelfocus.com.pl; ul Małopolska 23; s/d from 229/269zł; P🛜) If all you are looking for is a place to snooze, breakfast and surf the web, this big, new, shiny business hotel overlooking the river is the base for you. High standards throughout, cheery staff, a filling breakfast and an absence of tobacco odour earn this laudable newcomer glowing reviews from all who overnight here. Rooms are standard throughout but tick all 21st-century boxes.

**Youth Hostel**　HOSTEL €
(☏91 422 4761; www.ptsm.home.pl; ul Monte Cassino 19a; dm 22-24zł, s/d 50/56zł; P@) Everything is pleasant about this place, with its simple but bright rooms, located in a leafy neighbourhood. There's a laundry for guest use, and out in the well-kept garden there are concrete table-tennis tables. It's 2km northwest of the centre; take tram 3 from the station to Plac Rodła and change for the westbound tram 1 to the 'Piotra Skargi' stop.

**Hotel Rycerski**　HOTEL €€
(☏91 814 6601; www.hotelewam.pl; ul Potulicka 1a; s 150-230zł, d 270-290zł; P🛜) Serving a mainly weekday business clientele, this red-brick pile hides in its own walled grounds off a quiet city-centre street. Receptionists speak no English and communal spaces are a touch too utilitarian, but rooms are well sustained, very comfortable and a nifty deal at the lower end of the price scale. Rates can go up as well as down at weekends.

**Hotel Victoria**　HOTEL €€
(☏91 434 3855; www.hotelvictoria.com.pl; Plac Batorego 2; s/d 150/205zł) Just uphill from the bus terminal and train station, this well-mannered option, popular with German groups, has cheaply furnished but neatly kept rooms, a quiet-ish location, but an unexpected facility in the shape of the Tango Nightclub, mercifully fired up weekends only. May win the prize for Poland's grandest restaurant/breakfast room.

**Dom Pracy Twórczej Sztukateria**　HOTEL €€
(☏91 851 1911; ul Śląska 4; s 100-120zł, d 140-160zł) Don't be fooled by the rather austere, chlorine-scented corridors at this place – turn the key in your door to reveal very well appointed, spacious rooms with new furniture and spotless bathrooms. A real bargain at these prices, despite the views of

Szczecin's soot-streaked backyards from the windows. Breakfast is an extra 15zł.

### Hotel Campanile
HOTEL €€
(☎91 481 7700; www.campanile.com.pl; ul Wyszyńskiego 30; r 209zł; P❄️🛜) Part of a French chain, this modern hotel is in pole position for sightseeing, as it's an easy walk from the castle, the Old Town, the train and bus stations, and the city's main drag. Rooms are compact but pristine and comfortable, with tea- and coffee-making facilities. There's a bar and restaurant off the foyer.

### Hotel Podzamcze
GUESTHOUSE €€
(☎91 812 1404; www.podzamcze.szczecin.pl; ul Sienna 1; s/d 209/264zł) Nestling in the partially renovated Old Town, this cosy, 32-bed guesthouse sits above a pub-restaurant. Rooms are clean and looked after, if not particularly classy, and you can knock off almost 60zł at weekends by forgoing breakfast.

### Hotelik Elka-Sen
HOTEL €
(☎91 433 5604; www.elkasen.szczecin.pl; al 3 Maja 1a; s/d 120/140zł) Sounding like the name of an indigestion cure, these lodgings have a location almost as strange as their title: a lift acts as the front door and rooms occupy a basement space in the incredibly ugly School of Economics, itself next door to the local prison. The foyer's a little gloomy but the pine-furnished rooms receive natural light from half-moon windows, and bathrooms twinkle.

### Hotelik Słowiański
HOTEL €
(☎91 812 5461; ul Potulicka 1; s 80-125zł, d 98-135zł) Formerly a police dorm, this is Szczecin's hotel of last resort offering unadorned rooms scented with that oh-so Polish aroma – second-hand, low-grade tobacco smoke. However it's clean, receptionists speak some German and the high ceilings add perspective to the smallish rooms. There's a choice of en-suite or shared bathrooms.

### Radisson SAS Hotel
HOTEL €€€
(☎91 359 5595; www.radissonsas.com; Plac Rodła 10; s from 400zł, d from 460zł; P❄️@🛜🏊) Szczecin's swankiest option, if not its prettiest, features smart rooms within a supercentral salmon-pink complex.

### Camping Marina
CAMPGROUND €
(☎91 460 1165; www.camping marina.pl; ul Przestrzenna 23; site per adult/child 15/7zł, cabins 60-100zł; ☺May-Sep) Good camping ground with cabins on the shore of Lake Dąbie in

Szczecin Dąbie, about 7km southeast of the city centre.

##  Eating

*The* place to head in summer for a light pasta lunch, full-blown steak dinner or a coffee and ice-cream halt (or a few beers) is the new strip of al fresco eateries, interspersed with splashing fountains, which extends the entire length of al Papieża Jana Pawła II. If you prefer a roof over your food, try the following options.

### Karczma Polska Pod Kogutem
POLISH €€
(Plac Lotników 3; mains 24-67zł; ☺11am-midnight Sun-Thu, to 1am Fri & Sat) The rustic barn look is enduringly popular with restaurants serving traditional Polish food, and Karczma Polska doesn't disappoint – there's even a mock pigsty on the way downstairs to the toilets. Its external wooden deck is a great vantage point over the picturesque square opposite, and the menu is a veritable zoo of defunct grunters, squawkers and even rutters.

### Restauracja Chata
POLISH €€
(Plac Hołdu Pruskiego 8; mains 20-70zł; ☺11am-11pm Mon-Thu, to 2am Fri, noon-2am Sat, noon-11pm Sun) Charmingly muralled place dishing up hearty Polish fare in faux-rustic timber surroundings, decked out with the odd folksy-looking item. Variously-stuffed *pierogi* and a comprehensive range of Polish soups make tasty starters to main courses of wild boar, beef steak and mixed grill.

### Avanti
ITALIAN €€
(al Papieża Jana Pawła II 43; mains 13-65zł; ☺noon-11pm Mon-Sat, noon-10pm Sun) The best Italian job in town serves meticulously crafted Apennine fare in a refined ambience to a foodie crowd that definitely prefers their pizza without pineapple chunks. The menu is reassuringly short and changes daily.

**Restauracja Bombay** INDIAN €€
(www.india.pl; ul Partyzantów 1; mains 25-45zł; ☺1-11pm) Possibly the last thing you might expect amid Szczecin's chipped facades and wonky tramlines: quality Indian food, including items such as thali meals, served in tastefully exotic surrounds by waiters with impeccable English. It's owned by a former Miss India (1973 vintage), and boasts an appropriately international wine list.

**Bar Mleczny Turysta** POLISH €
(ul Obrońców Stalingradu 6; mains 3-8.50zł; ☺7.30am-6.30pm Mon-Fri) With its chequered tile floor, tiny stools bolted to the floor, time-warped menu boards in 1970s plastic lettering and brusque, ladle-wielding dinner ladies, this is the belly-filling *bar mleczny* experience Szczecin-style. There's a milkshake bar next door (4zł per glass).

**Ukraineczka** UKRAINIAN €€
(ul Panieńska 19; mains 12-42zł; ☺11am-10pm Mon-Thu, to 11pm Fri-Sun) Simple, small, neat place in a new building offering authentically traditional Ukrainian and Lithuanian dishes, Obolon and Lvivske beers and Georgian wines.

**Bar Rybarex** POLISH €
(ul Małopolska 45; mains 7-13.50zł; ☺8am-7pm Mon-Fri, 10am-6pm Sat & Sun) This recently relocated budget fish cafeteria has a wide range of piscine dishes to choose from. Funkily designed interior.

**Dom Chleba** CAFE €
(al Niepodległości 2; ☺6am-7pm Mon-Fri, 7am-5pm Sat, 8am-3pm Sun) If your digs don't do breakfast, this place will in the form of brain-rousing coffees and monster pastries for a couple of złoty.

## 🍷 Drinking

**Stara Komenda** MICROBREWERY
(Plac Batorego 3) Still a building site at the time of research, this long-awaited microbrewery-pub had plans to concoct its own wheat beer and lagers and was expected by most to become Szczecin's premier elbow-bending venue for orthodox fans of the hop. Go and see if they were right.

**Christopher Columbus** BAR
(ul Wały Chrobrego 1; ☺10am-1am Sun-Thu, 10am-2am Fri & Sat) Pass the huge plastic shark strung up outside to discover Szczecin's best beer garden offering widescreen, if not particularly exciting, views of the river.

Occasional live music in the shade of mature trees.

**Brama Jazz Cafe** CAFE
(Plac Hołdu Pruskiego 1; ☺10am-midnight) Housed in the Baroque Royal Gate, another fragment of lost history, the Brama has a DJ playing different styles of jazz on Tuesday nights. Have a drink in the relaxed outdoor area beneath a stern circle of carved Prussian eagles.

## ☆ Entertainment

Szczecin has a sizeable student population that keeps things lively on the nightlife scene, at least in term time. For the latest club and event info pick up a copy of *Echo* or *hot* – they're both in Polish only but listings usually need little translation. The website www.clubbing.szn.pl (Polish only) is also a good place to start.

**Alter Ego Club** LIVE MUSIC
(www.alterego.art.pl; Czerwony Ratusz; Plac Batorego 4) Low-lit, red-brick live-music venue featuring local rock bands and occasional indie, jazz and reggae acts.

**Kafe Jerzy** CLUB
(www.kafejerzy.pl; ul Jagiellońska 67; from 7pm Thu-Sat) Difficult to find, but worth it for the packed-out nights, guest DJs and easy-going crowd. Head west from al Jana Pawła II along ul Jagiellonska for seven blocks until you reach the traffic lights on al Bohaterów Warszawy. The club is across the street along an alleyway of garages on the left. Taking a taxi will save a lot of searching around.

**City Hall** CLUB
(www.cityhall.pl; Czerwony Ratusz, ul 3 Maja 18; ☺6pm-late) The basement of the massive Red Town Hall just off ul Maja packs in up to 400 mad-for-it clubbers for some of the biggest nights in town.

## ℹ Information

**Bondi** (al Wyzwolenia 1; per hr 5zł; ☺8am-11pm) Internet access within a 24-hour currency exchange office.

**Deutsche Bank** (al Wyzwolenia 12)

**Post office** main post office (al Niepodłegości 41/42); station branch (ul Dworcowa 20b)

**Cultural & Tourist Information Centre** (☎91 489 1630; Entrance I, ul Korsarzy 34; ☺10am-6pm) In the castle.

**Tourist office** main branch (☎91 434 0440; al Niepodległości 1a; ☺9am-5pm Mon-Fri, 10am-4pm Sat high season); train station (☺8am-8pm high season)

## MOVING ON?

For tips, recommendations and reviews, head to shop.lonelyplanet.com to purchase a downloadable PDF of the Germany chapter from Lonely Planet's *Western Europe* guide.

## ℹ Getting There & Away

AIR The **airport** (☎91 484 7400; www.airport .com.pl) is in Goleniów, about 45km northeast of the city. A shuttle bus (14.50zł) operated by **Interglobus** (www.interglobus.pl; ul Kolumba 1; ⊙8.30am-6.30pm Mon-Fri, to 2.30pm Sun) picks up from stops outside the LOT office and the train station before every flight, and meets all arrivals. **LOT** (☎801 703 703; al Wyzwolenia 17) runs a similar service (25zł); enquire about tickets at its office. Alternatively, a taxi should cost around 140zł.

There are services to Warsaw (up to three daily) with LOT. London (four weekly), Dublin (two weekly) and Liverpool (two weekly) are all served by Ryanair.

BOAT A new **hydrofoil** (www.wodolot.info.pl; one way/return 55/110zł) now buzzes up to Świnoujście at least five times a week from April to October. Departures from the Dworzec Morski (River Station) on riverfront ul Jana z Kolna are at 9am and either 3pm or 4pm, returning 90 minutes later.

BUS The bus terminal is uphill from the train station and handles regular summer buses to nearby beach resorts, but limited services to Świnoujście and Międzyzdroje (for Wolin National Park) – go by train instead or take one of the regular minibuses operated by **Emilbus** (www.emilbus.com.pl) that depart from a special stand at the southern end of al 3 Maja.

**Berlineks** (☎0668 223 667) runs comfortable minibuses to Berlin (52zł, 2½ hours; seven daily) from outside the train station. **Interglobus** (www.interglobus.pl) operates similar services starting from 45zł one way, as well as other trips and transfers.

TRAIN The main train station, Szczecin Główny, is on the bank of the Odra River, 1km south of the centre. As well as domestic connections there are also cross-border trains to Berlin (two hours, three daily) and long-distance services to Prague (6¾ hours, daily). The city has the following domestic rail connections:

**Gdańsk** 47zł, five hours, three daily (or change in Słupsk)

**Kołobrzeg** 22zł, 2½ hours, eight daily

**Kraków** 66zł, 11 hours, seven daily

**Poznań** 30zł to 38zł, 2¾ hours, 15 daily

**Słupsk** 30zł, three to four hours, eight daily

**Warsaw** 61zł to 127zł, 6½ hours, seven daily

# Warmia & Masuria

POP 4.1 MILLION

## Includes »

## Best Places to Stay

» Hotel Zamek Ryn (p372)

» Hotel Willa Port (p366)

» Hotel Wileński (p363)

» Zajazd Pod Zamkiem (p371)

## Best Lakes

» Lake Śniardwy (p369)

» Lake Niegocin (p373)

» Lake Łuknajno (p377)

» Lake Mamry (p369)

## Why Go?

There's something in the water in these two northeast regions bordering the Russian enclave of Kaliningrad – mostly hundreds of sailors, windsurfers and kayakers who come to make a splash in the Great Masurian Lakes, which dominate the landscape. There's more aqua fun to be had here than in the rest of the country put together, and if water sports are your thing, this is your place.

Away from the lakes, one of the world's most intriguing canal trips – the Elbląg-Ostróda experience – and countless rivers, wetlands and swamps mean you're never far from a soaking in these parts. The Łyna and Krutynia Rivers are kayaking bliss, and Warmia even boasts a small stretch of Baltic coastline.

When you've had your fill of water fun, the region has bags of red-brick architecture left by the Warmian Bishops and is home to Hitler's wartime hideout, the Wolf's Lair – one of Europe's most significant WWII sites.

## When to Go

### Olsztyn

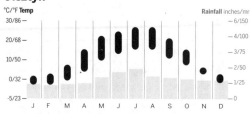

**Jan**
Cross lakes in Masuria on a pair of skis, when the whole region turns to ice.

**Aug**
Join the pilgrimage to Święta Lipka during the Feast of the Assumption.

**Oct**
See the lakes reflect the fiery autumnal shades of the region's many forests.

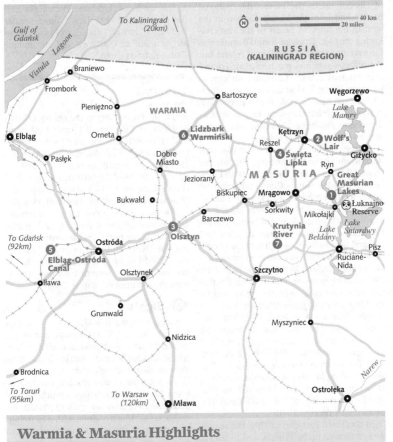

## Warmia & Masuria Highlights

**1** Joining the yachting set for a tour of the **Great Masurian Lakes** (p369)

**2** Scrambling around the **Wolf's Lair** (p375), Hitler's secret wartime bunker

**3** Doing a spot of cobblestone-surfing in **Olsztyn's Old Town** (p362)

**4** Joining the faithful throngs at **Święta Lipka** (p368), a major place of Polish Catholic pilgrimage

**5** Wondering at the spectacle of boats travelling over dry land on the **Elbląg-Ostróda Canal** (p367)

**6** Exploring the halls of Lidzbark Warmiński's mammoth Gothic **Castle** (p368), the architectural highlight of the region

**7** Paddling along the **Krutynia River** (p364) in a kayak

## History

Despite being lumped together administratively today, Warmia and Masuria have always been separate entities with separate populations, and their histories, though broadly similar, are largely independent.

Warmia is imaginatively named after its original inhabitants, the Warmians, who were wiped out by the Teutonic Knights in the 13th century, after which the Knights

set up a Teutonic province. For more than five centuries this was largely an autonomous ecclesiastical state run by all-powerful Catholic bishops.

The Warmian diocese was the largest of four that were created by the papal bulls of 1243. Though administratively within the Teutonic state, the bishops used papal protection to achieve a far-reaching autonomy. Their bishopric extended from the north of Olsztyn up to the present-day national border, and from the Vistula Lagoon in the west to the town of Reszel in the east. Following the 1466 Treaty of Toruń, Warmia was incorporated into the kingdom of Poland, but the bishops retained much of their control over internal affairs, answering directly to the pope. When the last grand master adopted Protestantism in 1525, Warmia became a bastion of the Counter-Reformation. In 1773 the region fell under Prussian rule, along with swathes of western Poland.

In the medieval period, Masuria was dealing with its own upheavals. The Jatzvingians (Jaćwingowie), the first inhabitants, belonged to the same ethnic and linguistic family as the Prussians, Latvians and Lithuanians. For farmers they were unusually warlike, and caused plenty of headaches for the Mazovian dukes, as they invaded and ravaged the northern outskirts of the principality on a regular basis and even pressed as far south as Kraków. In the second half of the 13th century, however, the Teutonic Knights expanded eastwards over the region, and by the 1280s they had wiped them out too.

Both Warmia and Masuria quickly became a bone of contention between the Teutonic order and Lithuania, and remained in dispute until the 16th century. At that time the territory formally became a Polish dominion, but its colonisation was slow. Development was also hindered by the Swedish invasions of the 1650s and the catastrophic plague of 1710.

In the Third Partition of 1795, the region was swallowed up by Prussia, and in 1815 it became a part of the Congress Kingdom of Poland, only to be grabbed by Russia after the failure of the November Insurrection of 1830. After WWI Poland took over the territory, though not without resistance from Lithuania, but the region remained remote and economically unimportant. Warmia was finally restored to Poland after WWII, and the two halves became a single administrative zone.

# THE OLSZTYN REGION

The Olsztyn region is principally Warmia and the land to the south of the region's capital, Olsztyn. Like Masuria, its landscape is dotted with lakes and sporadically cloaked in forest. There are several important architectural monuments here and relics of the bishops that once ruled the area. Of particular note

is the castle of Lidzbark Warmiński and the church in Święta Lipka; more secular highlights include the impressive open-air museum at Olsztynek and the unique Elbląg-Ostróda Canal.

## Olsztyn

POP 176,000

By far the biggest city in the region, Olsztyn (*ol*-shtin) is the natural jumping off point and transport hub for many other towns and attractions in Warmia and Masuria. However, it's worth spending a couple of days in this bustling settlement to explore the cobblestoned Old Town and enjoy the laid-back, slightly off-the-beaten-track feel.

The town was founded in the 14th century as the southernmost outpost of Warmia, and only came under Polish control following the Treaty of Toruń in 1466. With the First Partition of Poland in 1772, Olsztyn became Prussian (renamed Allenstein) and remained so until the end of WWII.

### ◉ Sights

**Museum of Warmia & Masuria** MUSEUM
(Muzeum Warmii i Mazur; www.muzeum.olsztyn.pl; ul Zamkowa 2; adult/concession 9/7zł; ⊙9am-5pm Tue-Sun Jun-Sep, 10am-4pm Tue-Sun Oct-May) This massive redbrick 14th-century **castle** is the most important historic building in town. It's in excellent shape despite its age, and now houses an art gallery, restaurant and open-air theatre, along with a museum. Two rooms on the 1st floor are dedicated to astronomer Nicolaus Copernicus, who was the administrator of Warmia and lived in the castle from 1516 to 1520. He made some of his astronomical observations here, and you can still see the diagram he drew on the cloister wall to record the equinox and thereby calculate the exact length of the year. Models of the instruments he used are on display in his former living quarters, and a set of narrow steps lead up to his toilet – a dark, uninviting place, but at least private. A third room was used as a chapel by the great astronomer, and traces of the original 14th-century ceiling pattern can still be seen above the alcoves. The rest of the 1st floor has displays of silverware and religious icons, and the 2nd floor houses temporary exhibitions, normally of a contemporary nature. The castle tower affords views of the town through narrow gaps in the brickwork.

# Olsztyn

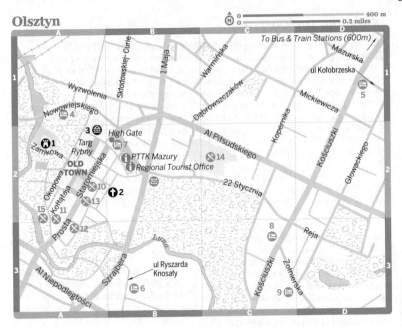

To Bus & Train Stations (600m)

High Gate

PTTK Mazury
Regional Tourist Office

OLD TOWN
Targ Rybny
Zamkowa

ul Ryszarda Knosały

---

## Olsztyn

### ◉ Sights

### 🛏 Sleeping

### ✕ Eating

---

**House of the Olsztyn Gazette**  MUSEUM
(Dom 'Gazety Olsztyńskiej'; Targ Rybny 1; adult/
concession 6/4zł; ⊙9am-5pm Tue-Sun Jul & Aug,
slightly shorter hrs rest of yr) Just to the west, on
the quiet old fish-market square, is the Museum of Warmia & Masuria's main annexe,
housed in the former *Gazeta Olsztyńska*
newspaper building. The paper was famed
for its outspoken politics under Nazi occupation, which swiftly led to the arrest and
execution of its publisher in 1940 and the
destruction of the offices. Reconstructed,
the building now has exhibitions about the
city's and region's past, and the political role
of journalism.

**Cathedral**  CHURCH
(ul Jana Długosza) The Gothic cathedral on the
eastern side of the Old Town dates from the
same period as the castle, though its huge
60m tower was only added in 1596. As in
the castle, the most impressive architectural
feature is the webbed vaulting in the aisles,
reminiscent of Gaudí's Sagrada Família in
Barcelona. The nave, however, has netlike
arches dating from the 17th century. Among
the remarkable works of art are the 16th-
century triptych at the head of the left aisle,
and a shimmering gold and silver altarpiece
of the Virgin Mary.

## 🛏 Sleeping

**TOP CHOICE Hotel Wileński**  HOTEL €€
(☎89 535 0122; www.hotelwilenski.pl; ul Ryszarda
Knosały 5; s 243-290zł, d 288-340zł; ❀⒜) Opened
in 2009, the elegant Wileński is proof that

## KAYAKING THE KRUTYNIA

The travel agency **PTTK Mazury** (☑89 527 4059; www.mazurypttk.pl in Polish; ul Staromiejska 1) runs 10-day kayaking tours along the **Krutynia River route** (known as Szlak Kajakowy Krutyni). The 103km trip begins at **Stanica Wodna PTTK** in Sorkwity, 50km east of Olsztyn, and goes down the Krutynia River and Lake Bełdany to Ruciane-Nida. It's regarded as Poland's top kayak trip and few come away disappointed. Tours depart daily from May to October, and the price (around 1150zł) includes a kayak, food, insurance, lodging in cabins and a Polish-, English- or German-speaking guide.

You can also do the trip on your own, hiring a kayak (20zł to 35zł per day) from the Stanica Wodna PTTK in Sorkwity, but check availability in advance. You can use the same overnight bases as the tours but you can't always count on cabins, so be prepared to camp.

Brochures in English and German, with a detailed description and maps of the Krutynia route, are available at the PTTK Mazury office. Information in German is also available online (www.masuren-online.de).

a new boy can go straight to the top of the class. Installed in a row of knocked-through 19th-century townhouses, elegant corridors lead to formally furnished quarters with big-print wall coverings and imaginative bathrooms. The downside – some rooms have a view of McDonald's across the road, but bulky curtains black out the golden 'M'.

**Villa Pallas**  GUESTHOUSE €€
(☑89 535 0115; www.villapallas.pl; ul Żołnierska 4; s 170-220zł, d 200-250zł; P@) This sophisticated villa is named after the Greek goddess Athena, whose statue makes up part of the mix 'n' match decor. Negotiate the maze of stairways to find relatively well-furnished, spotless rooms and some decent suites. A smart restaurant and small spa centre complete the picture. Rooms are cheaper at weekends.

**Hotel Wysoka Brama**  HOSTEL €
(☑89 527 3675; www.hotelwysokabrama.olsztyn.pl; ul Staromiejska 1; s 55-100zł, d 70-120zł) Superbly located on the edge of the Old Town, actually occupying a section of the High Gate – the last remaining entrance in the medieval town walls – this PTTK hotel has somewhat scuffed private rooms and a handful of much nicer en suites. Predictably, it's crammed with travellers in summer.

**Hotel Pod Zamkiem**  GUESTHOUSE €€
(☑89 535 1287; www.hotel-olsztyn.com.pl; ul Nowowiejskiego 10; s/d 170/220zł; P☏) Occupying a large early 20th-century villa, once the home of the influential Sperl family, this stylish guesthouse has character in spades. Wooden beams, murals and lots of pine provide atmosphere, and the park setting puts you right by the castle and the Old

Town. It's on a busy road so request a room at the back.

**PTSM Youth Hostel**  HOSTEL €
(☑89 527 6650; www.ssmolsztyn.pl; ul Kościuszki 72/74; dm 25-33zł, s/d 50/80zł) This sometimes gloomy hostel has a large kitchen, bike hire and generously cut rooms that sleep up to six. In winter you can often have the place to yourself.

**Camping 173 Dywity**  CAMPGROUND €
(☑89 512 0646; www.dywity.com.pl; ul Barczewskiego 47; camp sites per person/car/tent 14/10/12zł; ☺May-Sep) Perfectly situated campground on an isolated bend of the Łyna River, 10km north of Olsztyn.

**Hotel Warmiński**  HOTEL €€
(☑89 522 1400; www.hotel-warminski.com.pl; ul Kołobrzeska 1; s 269-340zł, d 289-370zł; ☏) This very well appointed hotel knows what business travellers need and provides it with a smile. Rooms are top-notch and rates fall a bit at weekends.

## 🍴 Eating

In the summer months beer gardens serving food sprout around the edges of the Rynek (Old Town Sq). Snackers and self-caterers should head for the better-than-average **Supermarket Spożywczy** within the Alfa Centrum shopping mall on al Piłsudskiego.

**Weranda Grill**  INTERNATIONAL €€
(ul Kołłątaja 15; mains 16-28zł) Meat lovers will flock to this large restaurant for a menu packed with loin chops, grilled ribs and sausages; vegetarians will be disappointed with a small selection of salads. A compromise

is easy to find though; grab a beer and kick back on the enormous summer terrace along the banks of the Łyna River.

### Feniks Cafe
CAFE €

(ul Prosta 7/9; ⊙7am-8pm Mon-Sat, from 9am Sun) A great little caffeine and cake stop on the main thoroughfare through the Old Town with better-than-average coffees and calorie-packed treats for the sweet-toothed such as *szarlotka* (apple cake), sticky filled buns, *sernik* (cheesecake) and that Polish favourite, wafer tubes filled with whipped cream (*rurki z bitą Śmietaną*).

### Chilli
INTERNATIONAL €€

(ul Kołłątaja 1; mains 18-49zł; ⊙9am-last customer) By day, this imperial-purple lounge serves an international menu amid B&W images of 20th-century USA and to cucumber-cool tunes on the CD deck. When the streetlamps flick on it gradually morphs into a smooth club with a lengthy cocktail menu.

### Greenway
VEGETARIAN €

(ul Prosta 10/11; mains 7.50-17zł; ⊙10am-8pm Mon-Sat, noon-8pm Sun; ♪) A branch of the popular Polish chain. Monster portions of the usual offerings, such as Mexican goulash, enchiladas and spinach quiche, are great belly fillers but this branch is too small for a city of this size, and the queues can be long.

### Bar Dziupla
POLISH €

(ul Staromiejska; mains 4-19zł; ⊙8am-10pm Mon-Sat, 9am-10pm Sun) Dziupla puts a stylish spin on the milk-bar 'franchise' to provide the best budget fare in the Old Town, including nine delicious takes on *pierogi* (Polish dumplings).

### ⓘ Information

**Biblioteka** (Library; ul Stare Miasto 33; ⊙9am-7pm Mon-Fri, 9am-2pm Sat) Free internet access on 2nd floor.

**Main post office** (ul Pieniężnego 21)

**Regional tourist office** (☏89 535 3565; www .mazury.travel; ul Staromiejska 1; ⊙8am-6pm Mon-Fri, 10am-3pm Sat & Sun Jul & Aug, shorter hrs rest of yr) Helpful office with heaps of information on cycling paths, walking trails and waterways in the region.

### ⓘ Getting There & Away

The queue-plagued bus and train stations are both in a big, semi-derelict L-shaped building on Plac Konstytucji 3 Maja. Walk to the Old Town (15 minutes) or take one of the frequent city buses that drop off in front of the High Gate.

**BUS** Buses run from Olsztyn to numerous towns:

**Elbląg** 18zł, 1½ to 2½ hours, nine daily

**Gdańsk** 28zł, 3½ hours, seven daily

**Giżycko** 20zł, 2¾ hours, 11 daily

**Kaliningrad** 29zł, four hours, four weekly (with Ecolines, from a stop on ul Partyzantów)

**Kętrzyn** 17zł, 1½ to 2¼ hours, half-hourly

**Lidzbark Warmiński** 8zł, one hour, ten daily

**Olsztynek** 5zł, 50 minutes, many

**Ostróda** 5zł, 1¼ hours, many

**Warsaw** 27-41zł, three to 4½ hours, hourly

**TRAIN** Olsztyn has rail connections to a number of towns:

**Elbląg** 24zł, 1¾ hours, ten daily

**Gdańsk** 39zł, three hours, six daily

**Toruń** 32zł, 2½ hours, eight daily

**Warsaw** 46zł, four hours, four daily (or change in Iława)

## Olsztynek
POP 7600

Around 25km southwest of Olsztyn, Olsztynek is a small town with one big attraction: the **Museum of Folk Architecture** (Muzeum Budownictwa Ludowego; www.muzeum olsztynek.com.pl; ul Leśna 23; adult/concession 10/6zł; ⊙9am-6pm high season). Tucked away on the northeastern outskirts of town, this skansen (open-air ethnographic museum) features about 40 examples of regional timber architecture from Warmia and Masuria, and also has a cluster of Lithuanian houses. There's a variety of peasant cottages complete with outbuildings, various windmills and a thatched-roof church. A number of buildings have been furnished and decorated inside in traditional period manner and the effect is impressive.

Above the skansen's rustic restaurant is a small museum that is split in two; one half is filled with the usual collection of folk art and farming tools, while the other contains a detailed account (in Polish) of Stalag 1B Hohenstein, a POW camp located on the outskirts of the village during WWII. Some 650,000 captured soldiers passed through the camp, consisting mostly of French, Belgian, Italian and Russian nationals.

The area to the south and east of the town is popular with Poles for its lakes and horse riding. Agritourism accommodation is common here, and information on this, and local activities, can be picked up at the **tourist office** (☏89 519 5477; it@olsztynek.com .pl; Ratusz, Rynek 1; ⊙8am-5pm Mon-Fri).

## ❶ Getting There & Away

The train station is 1km northeast of the centre, close to the skansen. At least six trains run to Olsztyn (9.60zł, 30 minutes) daily.

The bus terminal is 250m south of the Rynek, but many regional buses call in at the train station. Buses and minivans run to Olsztyn (5zł, 50 minutes, two or three hourly), Grunwald (4-10zł, 30 minutes, five daily) and Ostróda (8.50zł, 30 minutes to one hour, 11 daily).

## Grunwald

Grunwald is hard to find, even on detailed maps, yet the name is known to every Pole. Here, on 15 July 1410, the combined Polish and Lithuanian forces (supported by contingents of Ruthenians and Tatars) under King Władysław II Jagiełło defeated the army of the Teutonic Knights (see p331). A crucial moment in Polish history, the 10 hours of carnage left the grand master of the Teutonic order, Ulrich von Jungingen, dead and his forces decimated. This was reputedly the largest medieval battle in Europe, with an estimated 70,000 troops aiming to hack each other to bits.

The battlefield is an open, gently rolling meadow adorned with three monuments. Built on the central hill is the **Museum of the Grunwald Battlefield** (Muzeum Bitwy Grunwaldzkiej; adult/concession 7/4zł; ⊙9am-5pm 1 May-Sep), which has a minuscule display of period armour, maps and battle banners. Its redeeming feature is a small cinema that plays scenes from *Bitwa pod Grunwaldem* (1931), a classic Polish flick about the battle. Five hundred metres from the museum are the ruins of a **chapel**, erected by the order a year after the battle, on the spot where the grand master is supposed to have died. All signs are in Polish, but the shop by the entrance to the battlefield sells brochures in English and German.

The best time to visit the place is in July during the **Days of Grunwald festival** (www.republika.pl/grunwald), a medieval extravaganza with heaps of stalls, tournaments, concerts and costumed characters, culminating in an epic re-enactment of the battle itself.

Only three buses a day run to the battlefield from Olsztyn (14.50zł, 1½ hours). Other buses and minivans operate to/from Olsztynek (4-10zł, 30 minutes, five daily) and Ostróda (8.50zł, 50 minutes, 10 daily).

## Ostróda

POP 33,500

Drowsy Ostróda is the southern terminus of the Elbląg-Ostróda Canal, and if you take a boat in either direction you'll probably end up spending a night here. Apparently Napoleon once ruled Europe from this quiet corner; he wouldn't look twice at it now, but Polish holidaymakers love the leisurely pace of life here, attracted by its location on placid, swan-infested Lake Drwęke.

## 🛏 Sleeping & Eating

The tourist office has lists of private rooms in and around the town; they're pasted on the door when the office is closed. There's a 3zł fee if the staff book for you.

**TOP CHOICE** **Hotel Willa Port** HOTEL €€€
(☑89 642 4610; www.willaport.pl; ul Mickiewicza 17; d from 340zł; P✳︎❄︎☎︎❄︎) Perched on the lake edge, this bold new hotel is a real treat if you decide to linger longer in Ostróda. Liberally tailored rooms are a delight of funky retro veneer; spots of audacious colour contrasting with beiges and greys, sinks like halved boiled eggs with the yokes removed and all-glass showers. Competition is high for lakeside rooms and the knock-'em-dead views from the balconies are worth the extra. Staff fluent in English, innovative design throughout and a trendy restaurant make this one of northeast Poland's finest sleeps.

**Tawerna** POLISH €€
(Gen Roji 1; mains 15-30zł) Tawerna occupies a lovely spot on a small lake inlet at the northern end of town. Its large wooden deck is the perfect place for an aperitif or a hearty Polish meal. With the lake just metres away, burn it all off by hiring a kayak for 5/30zł per hour/day.

## ❶ Information

**Tourist office** (☑89 642 3000; www.mazury-zachodnie.pl, www.it.ostroda.pl; Plac 1000-lecia Państwa Polskiego 1a; ⊙9am-6pm Mon-Fri, 10am-4pm Sat, 10am-2pm Sun Jun-Aug, shorter hrs rest of yr) Located on the main square.

## ❶ Getting There & Away

The train and bus stations are next to each other, 500m west of the wharf. Ostróda has connections to the following towns:

**BOAT** In July and August a boat to Elbląg leaves every other day at 8am (p367).

## BARGING IN

The rich forests of the Ostróda region have attracted merchants from Gdańsk and Elbląg since medieval times, yet until the 19th century the only way of getting timber down to the Baltic was a long water route along the Drwęca and Vistula Rivers via Toruń. Engineers considered building a canal as a short cut but quickly found that the terrain was rugged and too steep for conventional locks.

In 1836 Prussian engineer Georg Jakob Steenke (1801–82), from Königsberg, produced a sophisticated design for an Elbląg-Ostróda Canal incorporating slipways, but Prussian authorities rejected the project as unrealistic and too costly. Steenke didn't give up, however, and eventually succeeded in getting an audience with the king of Prussia. With typical kingly shrewdness, the monarch approved the plan, not because of its technical or economic aspects but because nobody had ever constructed such a system before.

The part of the canal between Elbląg and Miłomłyn, which included all the slipways, was built between 1848 and 1860, and the remaining leg to Ostróda was completed by 1872. The canal proved to be reliable and profitable, and it cut the distance of the original route along the Drwęca and Vistula almost fivefold. Various extensions were planned, including one linking the canal with the Great Masurian Lakes, 120km to the east, but none were ever built.

The canal was damaged during the 1945 Red Army offensive but was repaired soon after liberation and opened for timber transport in 1946. A year later, the first tourist boat sailed the route. It remains the only canal of its kind in Europe and continues to operate, though the timber boats are a distant memory.

BUS **Olsztyn** 5zł, one hour, hourly
**Olsztynek** 8.50-15zł, 30 minutes to one hour, 11 daily
**Grunwald** 8.50zł, 50 minutes, 10 daily
**Elbląg** 12.50-19zł, 1¼ hours, 12 daily
TRAIN **Olsztyn** 9.50zł, 40 minutes, hourly
**Toruń** 26-33zł, two hours, seven daily
**Warsaw** 70zł, 4½ hours, 10 daily (change in Iława)

## Elbląg-Ostróda Canal

The 82km Elbląg-Ostróda Canal is the longest navigable canal still in use in Poland. It's also the most unusual. The canal deals with the 99.5m difference in water levels by means of a unique system of **slipways**, where boats are physically dragged across dry land on rail-mounted trolleys (see the boxed text).

The canal follows the course of a chain of six lakes, most of which are now protected conservation areas. The largest is **Lake Drużno** near Elbląg. It was left behind by the Vistula Lagoon, which once extended deep into this region.

The five slipways are on a 10km stretch of the northern part of the canal. Each slipway consists of two trolleys tied to a single looped rope, operating on the same principle as a funicular. They are powered by water.

## 🏃 Activities

### Boat Excursions

From May to September, pleasure boats operated bycy **Żegluga Ostródzko-Elbląska** (📞in Ostróda 89 646 3871; www.zegluga.com.pl) sail the main part of the canal between Ostróda and Elbląg. They depart Ostróda at 8am and Elbląg an hour later every other day, arriving at the opposite end at about 8pm (adult/concession 144/119zł). Luggage and bicycles are transported free of charge.

If you don't feel like committing to the full 11-hour stretch, take the boat from Elbląg as far as Buczyniec (95/73zł, 4½ hours), which covers the most interesting part of the canal, including all five slipways. This is a good solution for motorists leaving their vehicles in Elbląg as the company puts on buses to transport passengers back to Elbląg.

The boats, which have a capacity of 65, only run when at least 20 passengers turn up. You can expect regular services in July and August (sometimes two boats are required to meet the demand) and on hot summer days it may be an idea to book ahead. Outside this period there are fewer services. It's worth ringing Żegluga Ostródzko-Elbląska a couple of days in advance to find out about the availability of tickets and the current timetable status. Boats have snack bars on board, which serve some basic snacks and drinks.

# Lidzbark Warmiński

POP 16.400

Lidzbark Warmiński, 46km north of Olsztyn, is a rough and ready town with a massive Gothic castle. Its past is certainly more glorious than its present; it was the capital of the Warmian bishopric for over four centuries. In 1350 the bishops chose it as their main residence; a castle and a church were built and the town swiftly became an important religious and cultural centre. The astronomer Copernicus lived here between 1503 and 1510, serving as doctor and adviser to his uncle, Bishop Łukasz Watzenrode.

When the Reformation arrived in the 16th century, Lidzbark, along with most of the province, became a citadel of Catholicism, and it remained so until the First Partition of 1772. Deprived of his office, the last bishop, Ignacy Krasicki, turned to literature, becoming an outstanding satirist and all-round man of letters.

Today there's little trace of the town that was reputedly the richest and most cultured in Warmia, but the castle alone is enough to justify a day trip.

## ◉ Sights

**Castle**                                    CASTLE

This stocky, square-set redbrick fortress, adorned with corner turrets, is probably Warmia's most significant cultural gem. Enter from the south through the palatial, horseshoe-shaped building surrounding Plac Zamkowy, which was extensively rebuilt in the 18th century. A wide brick bridge runs up to the main castle gate.

The castle was commissioned in the late 14th century on a square plan with a central courtyard, the whole surrounded by a moat and fortified walls. When the bishops' era ended with the 18th-century Partitions, the castle fell into decline and served a variety of purposes, including use as barracks, a warehouse, a hospital and an orphanage. In the 1920s, restoration was undertaken and within 10 years the castle had been more or less returned to its original form. Miraculously, it came through the war unharmed, and today it is easily one of Poland's best-preserved medieval castles.

Most of the interior, from the cellars up to the 2nd floor, now houses a branch of the **Museum of Warmia & Masuria** (Muzeum Warmii i Mazur; www.muzeum.olsztyn.pl; Plac Zamkowy 1; adult/concession 8/6zł; ⊘9am-5pm Tue-Sun Jun-Aug, 10am-4pm Tue-Sun Sep-May). The first thing you'll notice is a beautiful courtyard with two-storey arcaded galleries all round it. It was constructed in the 1380s and has hardly been altered since then.

The castle's two-storey vaulted cellar, cool on even the hottest of days, is largely empty aside from a few marble fireplaces and cannon barrels. The cannons once belonged to the bishops, who maintained their own small army.

Most of the attractions are housed on the 1st floor, which holds the main chambers; the vaulted **Grand Refectory** (Wielki Refektarz) is quite remarkable. The chessboard-style wall paintings, dating from the end of the 14th century, feature the names and coats of arms of bishops who once resided here. In stark contrast is an adjoining tiny room centred on a dank, dark pit, which was once used as a prison cell. Exhibitions on this floor include medieval art from the region, such as some charming Madonnas and fine silverware. The adjoining chapel was redecorated in Rococo style in the mid-18th century and is quite overbearing compared to the rest of the castle.

The top floor contains several exhibitions, including cubist and surrealist 20th-century Polish painting, a collection of icons dating from the 17th century onwards, and spiffy army uniforms and evening gowns from the early 1800s.

## ❶ Getting There & Away

The bus terminal occupies the defunct train station, about 500m northwest of the castle. There are 10 buses a day to Olsztyn (8zł, one hour), supplemented by private minibuses.

# Święta Lipka

Polish Catholics flock to this tiny hamlet for one reason only – to visit its celebrated church. The origins of Święta Lipka (*shfyen*-tah *leep*-kah), which means 'Holy Lime Tree', are linked to one of Poland's most famous miracle stories. As the tale goes, a prisoner in Kętrzyn castle was visited the night before his execution by the Virgin Mary, who presented him with a tree trunk so he could carve an effigy of her. The resulting figure was so beautiful that the judges took it to be a sign from heaven and gave the condemned man his freedom. On his way home he placed the statue on the first lime tree he encountered, which happened to be in

Święta Lipka (though it obviously wasn't called that at the time).

Miracles immediately began to occur, and even sheep knelt down when passing the shrine. Pilgrims arrived in increasing numbers, including the last grand master of the Teutonic order, Albrecht von Hohenzollern, who walked here barefoot (ironically, he converted to Lutherism six years later). A timber chapel was built to protect the miraculous figure, and was later replaced with the present building. It's perhaps the most magnificent baroque church in northern Poland, a huge attraction and still a major pilgrimage site.

## ◎ Sights

### Church of Our Lady CHURCH
(www.swlipka.org.pl; admission free; ⊗8am-6pm except during Mass) Built between 1687 and 1693, and later surrounded by an ample rectangular cloister, the hugely popular church was built around four identical corner towers, all housing chapels. The best artists from Warmia, Königsberg (Kaliningrad) and Vilnius were commissioned for the furnishings and decoration, which were completed by about 1740. Since then the church has hardly changed, neither inside nor out, and is regarded as one of the purest examples of a late-Baroque church in the country.

The entrance to the complex is an elaborate wrought-iron gateway. Just behind it, the two-towered cream facade holds a stone sculpture of the holy lime tree in its central niche, with a statue of the Virgin Mary on top.

Once inside (appropriate clothing is required to enter), the visitor is enveloped in colourful and florid, but not overwhelming, Baroque ornamentation. All the frescoes are the work of Maciej Mayer of Lidzbark, and display trompe l'œil images, which were fashionable at the time. These are clearly visible both on the vault and the columns; the latter look as if they were carved. Of course Mayer also left behind his own image – you can see him in a blue waistcoat with brushes in his hand, in the corner of the vault painting over the organ.

The three-storey, 19m-high altar, covering the whole back of the chancel, is carved of walnut and painted to look like marble. Of the three paintings in the altar, the lowest one depicts the Virgin Mary of Święta Lipka with the Christ child, complete with subtle lighting for effect.

The pulpit is ornamented with paintings and sculptures. Directly opposite, across the nave, is a holy lime tree topped with the figure of the Virgin Mary, supposedly placed on the spot where the legendary tree itself once stood.

The pride of the church is its breathtaking organ, a sumptuously decorated instrument of about 5000 pipes. The work of Johann Jozue Mosengel of Königsberg, it is decorated with mechanical figures of saints and angels that dance around when the organ is played. Short demonstrations are held every hour on the half-hour from 9.30am to 5.30pm, May to September, and at 10am, noon and 2pm in October.

The cloister surrounding the church is ornamented with frescoes, also masterminded by Mayer. The artist painted the corner chapels and parts of the northern and western cloister, but died before the work was complete. It was continued in the same vein by other artists, but without the same success.

## ❶ Getting There & Away
Buses from Święta Lipka:
**Kętrzyn** 5.50zł, 20 minutes, half-hourly
**Olsztyn** 15.50zł, 1¾ hours, hourly
**Lidzbark Warmiński** 15zł, one hour, daily (early morning)

# THE GREAT MASURIAN LAKES

The Great Masurian Lake district (Kraina Wielkich Jezior Mazurskich), east of Olsztyn, is a verdant land of rolling hills dotted with countless lakes, healthy little farms, scattered tracts of forest and small towns. The district is centred on **Lake Śniardwy** (114 sq km), Poland's largest lake, and **Lake Mamry** and its adjacent waters (an additional 104 sq km). Over 15% of the area is covered by water and another 30% by forest.

The lakes are well connected by rivers and canals to form an extensive system of waterways. The whole area has become a prime destination for yachtspeople and canoeists, and is also popular among anglers, hikers, bikers and nature-lovers. Any boating enthusiast worth their (freshwater) salt should make Masuria their first port of call.

The main lakeside centres are Giżycko and Mikołajki and Węgorzewo. All the lake

# The Great Masurian Lakes

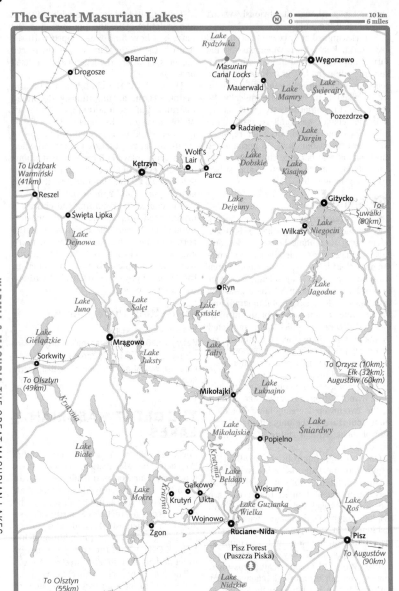

towns lead a frenetic life in July and August, take it easy in June and September, and retire for a long snooze the rest of the year.

## ⓘ Getting Around

Yachties can sail most of the larger lakes, all the way from Węgorzewo to Ruciane-Nida. These larger lakes are interconnected and form the district's main waterway system. Kayakers will perhaps prefer more intimate surroundings alongside rivers and smaller lakes. The best established and most popular kayak route in the area originates at Sorkwity and follows the Krutynia River and Lake Bełdany to Ruciane-Nida (see p364). If you're not up for doing everything yourself, you can enjoy the lakes in comfort from the deck of one of the pleasure boats operated by the **Żegluga Mazurska** (www.zeglugamazurska .com.pl). These large boats have an open deck above and a coffee shop below, and can carry backpacks and bicycles.

Theoretically, boats run between Giżycko, Mikołajki and Ruciane-Nida daily from May to September, and to Węgorzewo from June to August. In practice, trips can be cancelled if fewer than 10 passengers turn up, so the service is most reliable from late June to late August. Schedules are clearly posted at the lake ports.

The detailed *Wielkie Jeziora Mazurskie* map (scale 1:100,000; 8zł), produced by Copernicus, is a great help for anyone exploring the region by boat, kayak, bike, car or on foot. The map shows walking trails, canoeing routes, accommodation options, petrol stations and much more.

## Kętrzyn

POP 28,000

Busy Kętrzyn (*kent*-shin) is the best base for daytrips to both the Wolf's Lair and Święta Lipka, though the town itself has little to offer visitors. It was founded in the 14th century by the Teutonic Knights and for most of its history was known as Rastenburg. Though partly colonised by Poles, it remained Prussian until WWII, after which it became Polish. The name derives from Wojciech Kętrzyński (1838–1919), a historian who documented the history of the Polish presence in the region.

### ◎ Sights

**Castle**                                                CASTLE
Plac Zamkowy 1; adult/concession 6/3zł; ⊘10am-5pm mid-Jun–mid-Sep, shorter hours mid-Sep–mid-Jun) Kętrzyn's Teutonic past lives on in the form of its mid-14th-century brick castle on the southern edge of the town centre. Today the building is home to the disappointingly scrappy Regional Museum, which displays exhibits tracing the town's history in very un-castle-like interiors. Highlights include a Prussian standing stone reminiscent of Central Asia's Scythian figures, old photos of Rastenburg and some beautiful old trunks. On the day we visited we were watched throughout and the place reeked of cigarettes.

**St George's Church**                                    CHURCH
(Kościół Św Jerzego; ul Zamkowa; tower adult/concession 4/2zł; ⊘9am-5pm) With its squat, square tower, the Gothic church looks like

the town's second fortress from a distance. Its interior has furnishings and decoration dating from various periods, indicating a number of alterations over time. It's a bit further up the street from the castle.

### ⊨ Sleeping & Eating

**TOP CHOICE** **Zajazd Pod Zamkiem**          GUESTHOUSE €
(⊘89 752 3117; www.zajazd.ketrzyn.pl; ul Struga 3; s/d 100/140zł; P📶) Sitting pretty above a superb Polish restaurant and the town's best beer garden, the four generously cut rooms (sleeping up to four) all have identical layouts but different decor and colour schemes, with antiques thrown into the mix here and there. The 19th-century villa setting, proximity to the castle and filling breakfasts make this Kętrzyn's top choice. However, with so few rooms booking ahead is absolutely essential come summer.

**Hotel Koch**                                            HOTEL €€
(⊘89 752 2058; www.masuren2.de; ul Traugutta 3; s/d 150/200zł; P📶) Bog-standard rooms with large bathrooms are a bit overpriced at this central option, but there's a decent restaurant (a rarity in these parts) and a competent tour company on the premises that can get you on the water at the drop of several hundred złoty.

### ❶ Information

**Tourist office** (⊘89 751 4765; it@ketrzyn.com .pl; Piłsudskiego 1; ⊘8am-6pm Mon, 7.30am-3.30pm Tue-Fri) Brand new office with heaps of information on the lakes, the Wolf's Lair and other attractions.

### ❶ Getting There & Away

The train and bus stations are next to each other, 600m southeast of the town centre.

**BUS** For the Wolf's Lair take a service heading for Węgorzewo via Radzieje and alight at Gierłoż. At weekends it's advisable to take a taxi (30zł) from the large ul Szkolna rank in the town centre, as buses operate a why-bother-at-all kind of service. Otherwise buses run to the following towns:

**Giżycko** 11zł, 50 minutes, eight daily
**Węgorzewo** 11zł, one hour, hourly
**Olsztyn** 17zł, 1½ to 2¼ hours, half-hourly
**Święta Lipka** 5zł, 20 minutes, half-hourly

**TRAIN** Kętrzyn has the following train services:
**Gdańsk** 50zł, 4½ hours, two daily
**Elbląg** 41zł, three hours, two daily
**Giżycko** 7.30zł, 30 minutes, seven daily
**Olsztyn** 23.50zł, 1½, two daily

# Węgorzewo

POP 11,600

The small but busy town of Węgorzewo (ven-go-*zheh*-vo) on Lake Mamry is the north-ernmost lakeside centre for both excursion boats and independent sailors. The main town itself isn't quite on the lake shore but is linked to it by a 2km river canal.

It's less overrun by tourists than its southern cousins, except on the first week-end of August, when the town hosts a large craft fair, attracting plenty of artisans from around the region and beyond.

## 🛏 Sleeping & Eating

As the focus of activity is on the lake area, you won't find too many places to stay around the centre. There are dozens of pensions and larger leisure facilities spread out in the surrounding area, par-ticularly in the lakeside suburb of Kal, but they can be tricky to reach and usually only open in summer.

**Pensjonat Nautic** GUESTHOUSE €€
(☑87 427 2080; www.nautic.pl; ul Słowackiego 14; s 120zł, d 220zł; 🅿) An excellent and versa-tile family guesthouse near the canal and the boat wharf. Rooms range from com-fortable standard en suites with blue wood fittings to a pair of amazing apart-ments with their own kitchenettes and terraces. The restaurant here also comes recommended.

**Camping Rusałka** CAMPGROUND €
(☑87 427 2191; www.cmazur.pl; ul Leśna 2; site per adult/child 13/8zł; ⊙May-Sep) With its pleasant wooded grounds, a restaurant, and boats and kayaks for hire, Rusałka is a good base and well run, though most cabins are pretty basic. It's on Lake Święcajty, 4km from Węgorzewo off the Giżycko road. Infrequent PKS buses go there in season; if you don't want to wait, take any bus to Giżycko, get out at the Lake Święcajty turn-off and walk the last 1km.

## ℹ Information

**Tourist office** (☑87 427 4009; www.wegorzewo .pl; Plac Wolności 11; ⊙9am-5pm mid-Jun–mid-Sep, 8am-4pm Mon-Fri mid-Sep–mid-Jun)

## ℹ Getting There & Away

**BOAT** From July to August, a single **Żegluga Mazurska** (www.zeglugamazurska.pl) boat sails from the wharf at Lake Mamry for Giżycko at 3pm.

**BUS** There are no trains so head for the bus terminal 1km northwest of the centre, from where there are services to the following towns:

**Giżycko** 9zł, 45 minutes, half-hourly
**Kętrzyn** 11zł, one hour, half-hourly
**Warsaw** 44zł, 5¼ hours, four daily

---

**DON'T MISS**

## LUSCIOUS LAKESIDE LODGINGS

There are lots of characterful places to stay around the Great Masurian Lakes, besides those listed in the towns we include in this chapter. Here are four of the best:

**Hotel Zamek Ryn** (☑87 429 7000; www.zamekryn.pl; plac Wolności 2, Ryn; s/d from 175/295zł; 🅿🎿📶⛱) Without doubt top digs in the region, and one of Poland's top hotels. The 161 deluxe rooms here fill a red-brick and stone castle in the town of Ryn, around halfway between Mrągowo and Giżycko.

**Bałdygówka** (☑89 741 0438; Hacerska 6, Mrągowo; s/d 40/80zł; 🅿) Located right on the shore of Lake Juno in the northern suburbs of quietly historical Mrągowo. The three comfortable rooms at this superb guesthouse sleep up to 10 and give onto a large communal hall absolutely crammed with old communist-era knick-knacks. There's a grill, a kitchen and a billiards and table tennis room, and the water is a two-minute walk away.

**Klasztor Wojnowo** (Wojnowo 76; s/d 40/80zł) A former Old Believers cloister overlooking a small lake in the village of Wojnowo, 6km west of Ruciane-Nida. Travellers are put up in tranquilly meditative surroundings.

**Potocki** (☑87 425 7073; www.galkowo.pl; Gałkowo 46; s 60-110zł, d 80-145zł) A rural tourism complex 10km west of Ruciane-Nida. It has farm cottages with stylishly simple rooms and camp-fire sites. It's a great base for horse riding and hiking trips around the southern end of the lakes.

# Giżycko

POP 29,800

Positioned on the northern shore of **Lake Niegocin**, Giżycko (ghee-*zhits*-ko) is the largest sailing centre in the lakes, and the focal point of the seasonal tourist trade. It's not an aesthetically pleasing town, with a lake frontage more tacky than tasteful, but it's one of the few Masurian towns with a buzz and its huge fortress is worth at least an hour of your time.

The town started life under the Teutonic Knights but was destroyed on numerous occasions by Lithuanians, Poles, Swedes, Tatars, Russians and Germans in turn. Today it's essentially a transport hub and provisions base for the holiday homes and watersports centres that have grown up outside the town, and for the hordes of lake-bound holidaymakers who arrive en masse in the short summer season.

## ◎ Sights

**Boyen Fortress**                    HISTORIC SITE

(Twierdza Boyen; www.boyengizycko.pl; adult/concession fortress & museum 7/4zł; ⊙9am-8pm mid-Apr–mid-Nov) The Boyen Fortress was built between 1844 and 1856 to protect the kingdom's border with Russia, and was named after the then Prussian minister of war, General Hermann von Boyen. Since the frontier ran north–south along the 90km string of lakes, the stronghold was strategically placed in the middle, on the isthmus near Giżycko.

The fortress, situated by the lake to the west of the town centre, which consists of several bastions and defensive towers surrounded by a moat, was continually modified and strengthened, and successfully withstood Russian attacks during WWI. In WWII it was a defensive outpost of the Wolf's Lair, given up to the Red Army without a fight during the 1945 offensive. The fortifications have survived in surprisingly good shape, and some of the walls, bastions and barracks can safely be explored. Inside the museum you'll find a scale model of the fortress and a few odd items, such as a section of wall with a Russian soldier painted on it, used as target practice by the Prussians.

**Water Tower**                 HISTORIC BUILDING

(Wieża Ćiśień; cnr ul Warszawska & Wodociągowa; adult/concession 10/5zł; ⊙9am-10pm) Built in 1900 in neo-Gothic style, Giżycko's seven-storey Water Tower supplied the city with running water until 1997. Today the tall redbrick structure houses a cafe and memorabilia exhibition, but the main attraction is of course the views from the top, accessed by lift. The tower is located a short walk along ul Warszawska from the main Plac Grunwaldzki.

**Rotary Bridge**                      LANDMARK

(ul Moniuszki) Giżycko's working rotary bridge was built in 1889 and is the only one of its kind in the country. Despite weighing more than 100 tonnes, it can be turned by one person, and is opened six times daily to allow boats through, closing to traffic for between 20 minutes and 1½ hours each time. If you're travelling by car, circumvent the wait and take the long way round via ul Obwodowa. Pedestrians can take the footbridge a little further up the canal.

## ✦ Activities

**Yacht Charters**

Giżycko has the largest number of yacht-charter agencies in the area, and accordingly offers the widest choice of boats. The town is also a recognised centre for disabled sailors, with regular national regattas, and many companies provide specialist equipment, advice and training.

With yachting such a huge business here, the boat-charter market is highly volatile and operators often change. The tourist office is likely to have the current list of agents (sometimes up to 40) and can provide advice.

Finding anything in July and August without advance booking can be difficult. Securing a boat in early June or late September is much easier, but shop around, as prices and conditions vary substantially and bargaining may be possible with some agents.

In July and August, expect to pay somewhere between 200zł and 500zł per day for a sailing boat large enough to sleep around four to five people. Prices depend on the size of cabins, toilet and kitchen facilities and so on, and are significantly lower in June and September – often half of the high-season prices. You pay for your own petrol. A boat with skipper included costs on average 300zł per day.

Check the state of the boat and its equipment carefully, and report every deficiency and bit of damage in advance to avoid hassles on return. Come prepared with your own equipment, such as a sleeping bag, sturdy rain gear and torch.

Local charter operators:

**Bełbot** (☏87 428 0385; www.marina.com.pl)

**Grzymała** (☏87 428 6276; http://czarter.mazury .info.pl)

**Interjacht** (☏660 222 880; www.interjacht.pl)

**Osmolik Romuald** (☏87 428 1011; www .osmolik.trinet.pl)

**PUH Żeglarz** (☏602 580 593; www.zeglarz -czartery.pl)

### Ice Sailing

The Masurian Lake district is one of Poland's coldest regions in winter; lake surfaces often freeze over from December to April. During this time the lakes support ice sailing and ice windsurfing, mostly on crisp, clear days. The tourist office has a list of operators renting boats and giving lessons if you're interested.

### Diving

**CK Diver**                                     DIVING
(☏87 428 4362; www.ckdiver.suw.pl; ul Mickiewicza 9; ◷9am-5pm Mon-Fri) Offers scuba-diving courses for all levels throughout the year, in groups or on an individual basis. Prices start at 100zł for a taster session, going up to 1600zł for advanced tuition. To find the office, walk north from Plac Grunwaldzki along al 1 Maja for around 150m, then take a left into ul Mickiewicza.

### Cross-Country Skiing

Skiing on and around the frozen lake is a popular cold-weather activity. Ask the tourist office about where to hire the necessary gear.

## 🛏 Sleeping

The tourist office has a long list of accommodation options available in town, most of which consists of holiday cottages, pensions and private rooms. The majority only open in July and August – outside these months few places are open. Much of Giżycko's accommodation displays the pressures of mass occupation.

**Hotel Cesarski**                          HOTEL €€
(☏87 732 7670; www.cesarski.eu; Plac Grunwaldzki 8; s/d 160/230zł; P🞸) This very comfy hotel couldn't be more central, located as it is on the main town square near the tourist office. Rooms are all creamy and cosy, but best of all is the large roof terrace where breakfast can be taken.

**Centralny Ośrodek Sportu**        CAMPGROUND €
(COS; ☏87 428 2335; www.gizycko.cos.pl; ul Moniuszki 22; sites/s/d/cabins 15/115/165/96zł; P) The COS is a large activity centre on Lake Kisajno. Accommodation is in a variety of cabins and hotel rooms, plus a handful of camping sites. It's crowded with eating and sports facilities, including boat and bicycle hire and yacht charters.

**Gościniec Jantar**                  GUESTHOUSE €€
(☏87 428 5415; www.jantar-gizicko.pl; ul Warszawska 10; s/d 120/160zł; P🞸) Stacked above its own traditional restaurant in the centre of town, this is a decent little guesthouse with 12 pine-filled rooms, thick rugs and personable staff. It's let down slightly by a faint tobacco odour in some of the rooms.

**Hotel Wodnik**                            HOTEL €€
(☏87 428 3871; www.cmazur.pl; ul 3 Maja 2; s/d 190/265zł; P🞸) From the outside this looks like the worst kind of Socialist-era slab but the renovated rooms inside have only occasional reminders of Poland's yesteryear hospitality industry. Chunky radios and an overdose of woodchip wallpaper aside, the small rooms are well maintained. Book ahead as this place fills up even in midwinter. It's located just off the main Plac Grunwaldzki.

## ✗ Eating

In the high season you only have to wander down to the waterfront to find dozens of temporary cafes, kiosks and snack bars catering for the holiday crowds. Outside these times you'll have to choose from the hotel restaurants and a handful of other eateries in the centre.

**Kuchnia Świata**                   INTERNATIONAL €€
(Plac Grunwaldzki 1; mains 9-39zł; ◷10am-11pm Mon-Thu, 10am-1am Fri & Sat, noon-11pm Sun) The best year-round place to eat in town, the 'Cuisines of the World' certainly lives up to its name, with countless reminders of the culinary world you've left behind, such as king prawns, Greek salads and Chinese dim sum, populating the huge menu.

**Bar Hornet**                              POLISH €€
(Plac Grunwaldzki 12; mains 8-30zł) The suitably yellow Hornet splits itself into two sections, a self-service cafeteria and a smarter sit-down restaurant. The only difference between them is the waiters, but it's nice to have a choice! The food's decent value anyway, with a fine selection of quick eats and a salad bar, and the wooden deck is good for warm evenings.

## WOLF'S LAIR

Hidden in thick forest near the hamlet of Gierłoż, 8km east of Kętrzyn, is one of Poland's eeriest historical relics – 18 overgrown hectares of huge, partly destroyed concrete bunkers. This was Hitler's main headquarters during WWII, baptised with the German name of Wolfsschanze, or **Wolf's Lair** (Wilczy Szaniec; www.wolfsschanze.pl; adult/concession 12/8zł; ☉8am-sunset).

The location was carefully chosen in this remote part of East Prussia, far away from important towns and transport routes, to be a convenient command centre for the planned German advance eastwards. The work, carried out by some 3000 German labourers, began in autumn 1940; about 80 structures were finally built, including seven heavy bunkers for the top leaders. Martin Bormann (Hitler's adviser and private secretary), Hermann Göring (Prussian prime minister and German commissioner for aviation) and Hitler himself were among the residents. Their bunkers had walls and ceilings up to 8m thick.

The whole complex was surrounded by multiple barriers of barbed wire and artillery emplacements, and a sophisticated minefield. An airfield was built 5km away and there was an emergency airstrip within the camp. Apart from the natural camouflage of trees and plants, the bunker site was further disguised with artificial vegetation-like screens suspended on wires and changed according to the season of the year. The Allies did not discover the site until 1945.

Hitler arrived at the Wolf's Lair on 26 June 1941 (four days after the invasion of the Soviet Union) and stayed there until 20 November 1944, with only short trips to the outside world. His longest journey outside the bunker was a four-month stint at the Ukraine headquarters of the Wehrmacht (the armed services of the German Reich) in 1942, overseeing the advancing German front.

Having survived an assassination attempt within the bunker in July 1944, Hitler left the Wolf's Lair as the Red Army approached a few months later. The Nazi-German army prepared the bunkers to be destroyed, should the enemy have attempted to seize them. The complex was eventually blown up on 24 January 1945 and the Germans retreated. Three days later the Soviets arrived, but the extensive minefield was still efficiently defending the empty ruins. It took 10 years to clear the 55,000 mines within the complex.

Today, the site has succumbed to Mother Nature; bunkers are slowly disappearing behind a thick wall of natural camouflage. It's best to pick up a site map or booklet sold from stands in the parking area. If you're in a group, organise a guide to show you around; English-, German- and Russian-speaking guides charge 60zł per 1½-hour tour. All structures are identified with numbers and marked with big signs telling you not to enter the ruins, advice that many people ignore, including some guides (bunker 6 appears to be the most popular one to enter). Of Hitler's bunker (13) only one wall survived, but Göring's 'home' (16) is in relatively good shape. A memorial plate (placed in 1992) marks the location of Colonel Claus von Stauffenberg's 1944 assassination attempt on Hitler and a small exhibition room houses a scale model of the original camp layout.

You can also continue 200m past the entrance towards Węgorzewo, and take a small road to the right signposted 'Kwiedzina (5km)'. On either side of this narrow path is a handful of crumbling bunkers that can be explored free of charge.

See (p371) for details on how to reach the Wolf's Lair.

WARMIA & MASURIA GIŻYCKO

**Grota** INTERNATIONAL €€
(ul Nadbrzeżna 3a; mains 15-30zł; ☉11am-midnight summer only) Restaurants on the marina may draw the crowds with their lake-front views, but Grota gets the locals' vote for its food. Wood-oven-baked pizzas and a mix of Polish and German cuisine fill the menu, and there's seating along the canal in summer. To find Grota, head to the Rotary Bridge from Plac Grunwaldzki, but take a left before you cross the river; it's on the left-hand side about 150m along.

## ❶ Information

**Centrum Podróży** (☎87 428 3112; ul Dąbrowskiego 3; ☉9am-5pm Mon-Fri) Travel agency.

**Main post office** (ul Pocztowa 2) Three hundred metres north of Plac Grunwaldzki.

**Romix Internet** (ul Olsztyńska 11b; per hr 5zł; ☺9am-5pm Mon-Fri) Located 150m west of Plac Grunwaldzki.

**Tourist office** (☑87 428 5265; www.gizycko .turystyka.pl; ul Wyzwolenia 2; ☺9am-6pm Mon-Fri, 10am-4pm Sat & Sun May-Sep, slightly shorter hrs rest of yr) Friendly, award-winning office with loads of info on the region and free internet access. Enter from Plac Grunwaldzki.

## ⓘ Getting There & Away

**BOAT** **Żegluga Mazurska** (www.zegluga mazurska.com) boats operate from May to September, with extra services in July and August. Check the website or the timetable at the wharf (near the train station) for sailing times and prices.

**BUS** Next to the train station, the bus terminal handles services to the following towns:

**Kętrzyn** 11zł, 50 minutes, eight daily

**Mikołajki** 12zł, one hour, nine daily

**Olsztyn** 20zł, 2¾ hours, 11 daily

**Suwałki** 18zł, two hours, six daily

**Warsaw** 36zł to 65zł, 4¾-6 hours, eight daily (most services summer only)

**Węgorzewo** 9zł, 50 minutes, at least hourly

**TRAIN** The train station is on the southern edge of town near the lake. Trains run to the following towns:

**Białystok** 36.50zł, 2½ hours, two daily

**Ełk** 11.50zł, 50 minutes, seven daily

**Gdańsk** 54zł, five hours, two daily

**Kętrzyn** 7.30zł, 30 minutes, seven daily

**Olsztyn** 19.70zł, two hours, six daily

**Warsaw** 56zł, five hours, daily

# Mikołajki

POP 3800

More intimate and scenically pleasing than Giżycko, lively lakeside Mikołajki (mee-ko-*wahy*-kee) perches on picturesque narrows crossed by three bridges. Tourism has all but taken over here, and its recently spruced up waterfront is filled to overflowing with promenading families and pleasure boats in summer. Like most of its neighbours, Mikołajki is a big hit with German tourists, especially those from the former GDR.

## 🏃 Activities

As in Giżycko, yacht hire is big business here in summer, and around 10 companies vie for the seasonal trade.

**Wioska Żeglarska** BOATING
(☑87 421 6040; www.wioskazeglarskamikolajki.pl; ul Kowalska 3) The Wioska Żeglarska, on the waterfront, has sailing boats for hire, or staff may be able to advise you on other companies if it's booked out. See p373 for more information on yacht charters.

**Port Rybitwa** BOATING
(☑87 421 6163; www.portrybitwa.pl; ul Okrężna 5) For shorter-term excursions, Port Rybitwa hires out low-powered motorboats (from 95zł per hour, 475zł per day) from near the town's swimming beach. The owner can suggest plenty of DIY excursions on the connecting lakes.

## 🛏 Sleeping & Eating

Surprisingly there aren't too many hotels in Mikołajki, but the tourist office can supply a bewilderingly long list of rooms for rent (40zł to 60zł per person). However, few owners will consider single-night stays, especially during July and August; in fact most will expect you to linger at least five nights in the high season. If you're here just for a night or two, try to book ahead with one of the following.

**TOP**
**CHOICE** **Pensjonat Mikołajki** GUESTHOUSE €€
(☑87 421 6437; www.pensjonatmikolajki.pl; ul Kajki 18; s/d from 120/180zł; ⓟ⌖) In this part of Poland accommodation is all about lake views, and if you book early here that's exactly what you'll get. But the other surprisingly contemporary rooms aren't bad either – all are fragrant with pine and boast well-maintained fittings and lemon-fresh bathrooms. There's handy cycle hire for 8zł per hour (30zł per day).

**Hotel Mazur** HOTEL €€
(☑87 421 6941; www.hotelmazur.pl; Plac Wolności 6; s/d 230/315zł; ⓟ⌖) Occupying Mikołajki's grandest edifice, the former town hall on the main square, the Mazur is the town's finest digs, with liberally cut rooms and pristine bathrooms, though for these prices the pine furniture feels cheap. The wood-panelled salon and brick cellar restaurant are Mikołajki's swankiest dining nooks.

**Król Sielaw** GUESTHOUSE €€
(☑87 421 6323; ul Kajki 5; s/d 100/160zł) Rustic beams and twee crafts provide the usual touch of colour in these very reasonable rooms. The country theme continues in the unpretentious fish restaurant downstairs.

The lake is only a block away and there are discounts for staying more than three nights.

### Camping Wagabunda
CAMPGROUND **€**

(☏87 421 6018; www.wagabunda-mikolajki.pl; ul Leśna 2; camp sites per person/tent 14/14zł; ☺May-Sep) The Wagabunda is the town's main camping ground. It's across the bridge from the centre and a 600m walk southwest. In addition to the camping area it has plenty of small cabins that vary in standard and price, and bicycles, boats and canoes are available for hire.

### Restauracja Prohibicja
POLISH **€€**

(Plac Handlowy 13; mains 8-46zł) Possibly Mikołajki's best eating option has a stylishly done gangster-jazz theme. The walls are covered in pictures of famous silver-screen mobsters and celebrated jazz musicians doing their thing, as well as photos of Polish celebs who have parked buttocks here. There's a vine-shaded terrace outside and cheap rooms upstairs.

## ℹ Information

**Library** (Biblioteka; ul Kolejowa 6, ground fl; ☺8am-3pm Mon, 10am-5pm Tue, Thu & Fri, 10am-6pm Wed, 9am-1pm Sat) Free internet access on flashy Apple Macs at the library. Enter from ul Papieża Jana Pawła II.

**Tourist office** (☏87 421 6850; www.mikolajki .pl; ul Żeglarska; ☺10am-8pm Jul & Aug, 10am-6pm May, Jun, Sep & Oct)

## ℹ Getting There & Away

**BOAT** From May to September, **Żegluga Mazurska** (www.zeglugamazurska.com) boats leave Mikołajki for Giżycko at 10.30am and 3pm. Round trips on Lake Śniardwy sail regularly.

**BUS** There are no trains to or from Mikołajki so that just leaves the tiny bus station on small plac Kościelny near the church at the top of the main street (ul 3-go Maja), which handles services to the following towns:

**Giżycko** 12zł, one hour, nine daily

**Mrągowo** 6zł, 40 minutes, 17 daily

**Olsztyn** 19zł, 2¼ hours, five daily (or change in Mrągowo)

**Warsaw** 36-46zł, 4½-5½ hours, nine daily (most summer only)

# Łuknajno Reserve

The shallow 700-hectare **Lake Łuknajno**, 4km east of Mikołajki, shelters Europe's largest surviving community of wild swans *(Cygnus olor)* and is home to many other birds – 128 species have been recorded here. The 1200- to 2000-strong swan population nests in April and May but stays at the lake all summer. A few observation towers beside the lake make swan viewing possible.

A rough road from Mikołajki goes to the lake, but there's no public transport. Walk 3.5km until you get to a sign that reads '*do wieży widokowej*' (to the viewing tower), then continue for 10 minutes along the path to the lake shore. The track can be muddy in spring and after rain, so choose your shoes wisely. Depending on the wind, the swans may be close to the tower or far away on the opposite side of the lake. Accommodation is available near the lake at **Folwark Łuknajno** (☏87 421 6862; www.luknajno.pl; s/d 120/180zł, camp sites per person/tent 10/15zł; P), a lovely country house with its own restaurant and pier on Lake Śniardwy. Bicycles and canoes are available for rent.

# Understand
# Poland

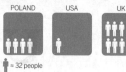

**population per sq km**

POLAND  USA  UK

≈ 32 people

# Poland Today

## Recession? What Recession?

While much of the rest of the world struggles along through a lacklustre economic recovery following a whopper of a global recession in 2009 and 2010, Poland's economy continues to defy gravity.

Poland was one of the fastest-growing economies in the European Union in 2011, clipping along at around 4% growth, and was expected to slow only modestly in 2012 to around 3.6%, according to the International Monetary Fund. Indeed, the Polish central bank likes to boast Poland was the only country in the European Union whose economy didn't shrink during the recession. In fact, there was no recession.

It's a remarkable feat, especially to anyone who remembers the Polish economy under the bad old days of communism. Back then it was one of Europe's chronic basket cases, deeply in debt, racked by high inflation and with no prospects for improvement.

So what's underpinning the growth? At least part of it is good old-fashioned government stimulus, particularly the massive public investments the country is making to co-host the UEFA Euro 2012 football championship. It's not just new stadiums, but billions of euros of new roads, bridges, train lines and other infrastructure.

## President of Europe

While Poland's politicians have had their ups and downs leading their country since the fall of communism, they seem to have had better luck in guiding the entire European Union. Poland assumed the EU's rotating six-month presidency on 1 July 2011, putting it in charge – temporarily at least – of the bloc's 27 member states.

The Polish presidency came at a time of unparalleled economic challenges facing the bloc, with the euro crisis, lingering economic

---

» GDP
(per head):
US$19,700

» Inflation:
2.6% (2010)

» Unemployment: 9.4%
(2011)

» Number of
lakes: 9000

» Number of
bison in the
wild: 700

» Proportion of
population who
died in WWII:
20% (UK 0.9%;
USA 0.2%)

---

## Top Films

**Katyń** (Andrzej Wajda) Moving depiction of the WWII massacre.
**Amator** (Krzysztof Kieślowski) Early Kieślowski effort on self-censorship under communism.
**The Pianist** (Roman Polański) Oscar-winning film about life in Warsaw's WWII Jewish ghetto.

## Do and Don'ts

» Do flavour your beer with raspberry soda and drink it through a straw. OK don't.

» Don't wave your arms in a crowded restaurant to attract attention, but it's perfectly OK to fetch the menu yourself.

» Don't forget to say hello – *dzień dobry* – even to strangers.

» Do take flowers – or better, a bottle of vodka – when invited to someone's home.

## belief systems
(% of population)

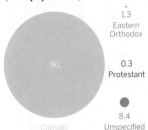

1.3
Eastern
Orthodox

0.3
Protestant

90

8.4
Unspecified

Catholic

## if Poland were 100 people

97 would be Polish
3 would be other ethnic backgrounds

problems in the United States, and a host of big political changes in the Middle East, and elsewhere. That said, at least as this book goes to press, things seem to have gone as well as could be expected.

On the domestic front, the country's politics seem as muddled as ever. Polish parliamentary elections in October 2011 reaffirmed the dominance of the centre-right Civic Platform party, but set off the usual scramble to form a coalition that was capable of getting something accomplished.

## Euro Fever!

And we're not talking about the woes of the European Union's common currency. Poland has gone football (soccer) mad and it's all tied to the country's role as co-host, with Ukraine, of the UEFA Euro 2012 football championship.

The tournament kicks off on 8 June 2012 with the Polish team taking the pitch at the new national stadium in Warsaw's Praga district (which was still hastily under construction as this book was being researched). The final is set for 1 July in the Ukrainian capital, Kiev. Other Polish cities chosen to host games include Gdańsk, Poznań and Wrocław.

In many ways UEFA was taking a risk by selecting Poland and Ukraine as co-hosts. Forget about the countries' less-than-stellar performances in past UEFA Cup games. The massive amounts of money needed to build new stadiums, roads and everything else to host an event of this size would stretch any country's budget, let alone the budgets of two countries still working off a 40-year communist hangover.

In the beginning there were some concerns that neither Poland nor Ukraine would meet their deadlines. But as we peeked in at construction sites during 2011, all was proceeding apace. Indeed, the whole of Poland seemed to be one big construction site.

Poland is ranked 21st among the most-polluting countries of the world. Much of this pollution is concentrated in the industrial area of Upper Silesia. The country is a signatory to the Kyoto Protocol and has pledged to reduce emissions by 30% to 40% by 2020.

## Myths

» Vodka is the number one drink among Poles. Not true. The day-to-day drink is beer.

» Poles eat nothing but *pierogi* and *kiełbasa*. Not true...well not entirely. There's much more on the menu.

## Top Books

**The Polish Officer** (Alan Furst) Gripping spy novel set in Poland on the eve of WWII.

**God's Playground: A History of Poland** (Norman Davies) Highly readable two-volume set on 1000 years of Polish history.

**The Painted Bird** (Jerzy Kosiński) Page-turner on the travails of an orphan boy on the run during WWII.

**Survival in Auschwitz** (Primo Levi) Classic of Holocaust literature that hasn't lost a drop of impact.

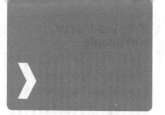

# History

It would be no overstatement to say that Polish history has been characterised by a series of epic climbs, cataclysmic falls and back-from-the-brink recoveries.

The Poland that we would recognise today got its start around the first millennium, with the conversion to Christianity of Duke Mieszko I in 966. The early years, like the surrounding kingdoms at that time, were filled with wars, conquests and Mongol invasions, but the kingdom thrived. The rule of Kazimierz III Wielki in the 14th century was particularly benign and brought the royal capital, Kraków, one of Central Europe's first centres of higher learning, today's Jagiellonian University, in 1364.

A major triumph came in 1410 with the defeat of the Teutonic Knights by a combined force of Poles and Lithuanians. A little over a century later, in 1569, the Poles and Lithuanians formalised their union, creating for a time Europe's largest country.

The people of Warsaw had special reason to celebrate the union, as it meant shifting the capital there from Kraków around 1600. The rest of the 17th century, though, can be written off as a wash. Poland got sucked into a series of tragic wars, including a melee with Sweden that cost the country a quarter of its territory and a third of its people.

A vastly weakened Poland in the 18th century proved too tempting for neighbours Prussia, Russia and Austria, who agreed to carve up the country among themselves, leaving Poland off world atlases until the end of WWI.

The newly independent Poland got off to a decent start, but the country's position between Germany and the Soviet Union was precarious. Both Hitler and Stalin coveted Polish territory and eventually went to war over it. Poland lost around a fifth of its population during WWII, including nearly all of the country's three million Jews.

The war ended up shifting Poland's border around 200km westward, while at the same time putting it firmly in the Soviet-controlled

Norman Davies' two-volume *God's Playground: A History of Poland* is beautifully written, easy to read and a perfect key to understanding 1000 years of the Polish nation. *Heart of Europe: A Short History of Poland* is a condensed version, with a greater emphasis on the 20th century.

| TIMELINE | 700 BC | Before AD 500 | Before AD 500 |
|---|---|---|---|
| | During the Iron Age, the Lusatian tribe, present on the territory of modern-day Poland, builds a remarkable fortified settlement in the town of Biskupin. | Slavs begin settling the area of present-day Poland, though the exact date of arrival of the first Slavic tribes is unknown. | Establishment of the first Polish town, Gniezno, by Lech, one of three mythical brothers who in legend founded the three Slavic nations (Poland, Ruthenia and Bohemia). |

Eastern bloc. Communism was a period of hardship and stagnation that was eventually overcome as Soviet-backed regimes collapsed in Eastern Europe in 1989.

The early years of the newly democratic Poland were rocky, but accession to the European Union leaves reason to hope for a brighter future.

## Before the Poles

The lands of modern-day Poland have been inhabited since the Stone Age, with numerous tribes from the east and west calling its fertile plains home. Archaeological finds from both the Stone and Bronze Ages can be seen in many Polish museums, but the greatest example of pre-Slavic peoples resides in Biskupin: its fortified town from the Iron Age was built by the Lusatian tribe around 2700 years ago. The Celts, followed by the Germanic tribes and then the Baltic folk, all established themselves on Polish soil, but it wasn't until the coming of the Slavs that Poland began to shape itself into a nation.

## Slavic Origins & the Piast Dynasty

Although the exact date of the arrival of the first Slavic tribes is unknown, historians agree Slavs began settling the area between the 5th and 8th centuries. From the 8th century onwards, smaller tribes banded together to form greater conglomerations, thus establishing themselves more fully on the lands of the future Polish state.

The country's name derives from one of these tribes, the Polanie (literally, 'the people of the fields'), who settled on the banks of the Warta River near present-day Poznań. Their tribal chief, the legendary Piast, managed to unite the scattered groups of the surrounding areas into a single political unit in the 10th century, and gave it the name Polska (later Wielkopolska, meaning Great Poland). It wasn't until the coming of Piast's great-great grandson, Duke Mieszko I, that much of Poland was united under one dynasty, the Piast.

## Christianity & Conquering

After Duke Mieszko I converted to Christianity, he did what most early Christian rulers did and began conquering the neighbours. Soon the entire coastal region of Pomerania (Pomorze) fell under his sovereignty, along with Śląsk (Silesia) to the south and Małopolska (Little Poland) to the southeast. By the time of his death in 992, the Polish state was established within boundaries similar to those of Poland today, and the first capital and archbishopric were established in Gniezno.

By that time, towns such as Gdańsk, Szczecin, Poznań, Wrocław and Kraków already existed. Mieszko's son, Bolesław the Brave, continued

**National Heroes**

» Marshal Józef Piłsudski

» Tadeusz Kościuszko

» Nicolaus Copernicus

» Frédéric Chopin

» Marie Curie

» Lech Wałęsa

**HISTORY BEFORE THE POLES**

| 966 | 970s | 1038 | 1226 |
|---|---|---|---|
| Polska's first recorded ruler, Duke Mieszko I, converts to Christianity, possibly as a political move against Otto the Great. It marks the formal birth of the Polish state. | Duke Mieszko I builds Poland's first cathedral at Gniezno, and a second at Poznań. The Catholic religion begins its long hold on the Polish people. | Under the rule of Piast Kazimierz I, the Polish capital is moved from Gniezno to Kraków. The city would remain the seat of royal Poland for the next 550 years. | Duke Konrad of Mazovia calls in the Teutonic Knights to help him subdue a band of pagan Prussians, allowing the Knights to gain a firm foothold on Polish soil. |

his father's work, even pushing the Polish border as far east as Kyiv. The administrative centre of the country was moved from Wielkopolska to the less vulnerable Małopolska, and by the middle of the 11th century Kraków was established as the royal seat.

When pagan Prussians, from the region that is now the north-eastern tip of Poland, attacked the central province of Mazovia in 1226, Duke Konrad of Mazovia called for help from the Teutonic Knights, a Germanic military and religious order that had made its historic mark during the Crusades. The knights soon subjugated the pagan tribes but then bit the hand that fed them, building massive castles in Polish territory, conquering the port city of Gdańsk (and renaming it Danzig), and effectively claiming all of northern Poland as their own.

They ruled from their greatest castle of all, at Malbork, and within a matter of decades became a major European military power.

## The Reign of Casimir III the Great

Under the rule of Kazimierz III Wielki (Casimir III the Great; 1333–70), Poland gradually became a prosperous and powerful state. Kazimierz Wielki regained suzerainty over Mazovia, then captured vast areas of Ruthenia (today's Ukraine) and Podolia, thus greatly expanding his monarchy in the southeast.

Kazimierz Wielki was also an enlightened and energetic ruler on the domestic front. Promoting and instituting reforms, he laid down solid legal, economic, commercial and educational foundations. He also passed a law providing privileges for Jews, thus establishing Poland as a safe house for the Jewish community for centuries to come. Over 70 new towns were founded, and the royal capital of Kraków flourished.

In 1364 one of Europe's first universities was established at Kraków, and an extensive network of castles and fortifications was constructed to improve the nation's defences. There is a saying that Kazimierz Wielki 'found Poland built of wood and left it built of stone'.

## The Defeat of the Knights

The close of the 14th century saw Poland forge a dynastic alliance with Lithuania, a political marriage that increased Poland's territory five-fold overnight and that would last for the next four centuries. The union benefited both parties – Poland gained a partner in skirmishes against the Tatars and Mongols, and Lithuania received help in the fight against the Teutonic Knights.

Under Władysław II Jagiełło (1386–1434), the alliance finally defeated the Knights in 1410 at the epic battle of Grunwald and recovered eastern Pomerania, part of Prussia and the port of Gdańsk.

**1241–42**
Mongol invasions leave Poland and much of Europe in ruin. This allows room for German settlers to move east into Poland, but also Poland to expand eastwards into Ukraine.

**1333**
Kazimierz III Wielki (Casimir the Great) assumes the throne and under his near-40-year rule, Poland gradually becomes a prosperous and powerful state, extending into areas of today's Ukraine.

**1493**
Poland's lower house of parliament, or Sejm, is established. The first Sejm consists of bishops and noblemen, and is largely present to keep an eye on the monarchy.

STU/WIDMANDORF/ALAMY ©

» Kazimierz III Wielki

For 30 years the Polish empire was Europe's largest state, extending from the Baltic to the Black Sea.

But it was not to last. Threat of invasion became apparent towards the end of the 15th century – this time the main instigators were the Ottomans from the south, the Tatars of Crimea from the east, and the tsars of Moscow from the north and east. Independently or together, they repeatedly invaded and raided the eastern and southern Polish territories, and on one occasion managed to penetrate as far as Kraków.

## Poland's Golden Age

The early 16th century brought the Renaissance to Poland and during the reigns of Zygmunt I Stary (Sigismund I the Old; 1506-48) and his son Zygmunt II August (Sigismund II Augustus; 1548-72), the arts and sciences flourished. This is traditionally viewed as the kingdom's 'golden age'.

The bulk of Poland's population at this time was made up of Poles and Lithuanians but included significant minorities from neighbouring countries. Jews constituted an important and steadily growing part of the community.

On the political front, Poland evolved during the 16th century into a parliamentary monarchy, with most of the privileges going to the *szlachta* (the feudal nobility), who comprised roughly 10% of the population. In contrast, the status of the peasants declined, and they gradually found themselves falling into a state of virtual slavery.

Hoping to strengthen the monarchy, the Sejm (an early form of parliament reserved for the nobility) convened in Lublin in 1569, unified Poland and Lithuania into a single state, and made Warsaw the seat of future debates. Since there was no heir apparent to the throne, it also established a system of royal succession based on direct voting in popular elections by the nobility, who would all come to Warsaw to vote.

## Royal Republic

The 'Royal Republic' refers to the practice of 'electing' the kings by the nobility, a dubious idea that got its start when Zygmunt II August died without an heir. The decision to consider foreign candidates almost led to the unravelling of the 'republic'. For each royal election, foreign powers promoted their candidates by bargaining and bribing voters. During this period, no fewer than 11 kings ruled Poland; only four were native Poles.

The first elected king, Henri de Valois, retreated to his homeland to take up the French crown after only a year on the Polish throne. His successor, Stefan Batory (Stephen Bathory; 1576-86), prince of

**Who Poland Fought in the 17th Century**

» Russia
» Sweden
» Turkey
» Prussia
» Ukraine
» Transylvania

HISTORY POLAND'S GOLDEN AGE

| Early 16th Century | 1541 | 1569 | 1570s |
|---|---|---|---|
| Arts and sciences flourish under the reigns of Zygmunt I Stary and his son Zygmunt II August. This is often viewed as the kingdom's 'golden age'. | Nicolaus Copernicus proposes that the earth orbits the sun and changes the course of science forever. Poles say that Copernicus 'stopped the sun and moved the earth'. | The Kingdom of Poland and the Grand Duchy of Lithuania unite as a single state to counteract the rising threat of the Moscow tsars. The union lasts until 1791. | Poland uniquely establishes a parliamentary monarchy, with most of the privileges going to the feudal nobility. This eventually proves a disaster when the nobles cannot agree on many key issues. |

Transylvania, was a much wiser choice. Batory, together with his gifted commander and chancellor Jan Zamoyski, conducted a series of successful battles against Tsar Ivan the Terrible and came close to forming an alliance with Russia against the Ottoman threat.

After Batory's premature death, the crown was offered to the Swede Zygmunt III Waza (Sigismund III Vasa; 1587–1632), and during his reign Poland achieved its greatest extent ever, more than three times the size of present-day Poland. Despite this, Zygmunt is best remembered for moving the Polish capital from Kraków to Warsaw between 1596 and 1609.

## Eastern Interlopers & the Deluge

The beginning of the 17th century marked a turning point in Poland's fortunes. The increasing political power of the Polish nobility undermined the authority of the Sejm; the country was split up into several huge private estates, and nobles, frustrated by ineffective government, resorted to armed rebellion.

Meanwhile, foreign invaders were systematically carving up the land. Jan II Kazimierz Waza (John II Casimir Vasa; 1648–68), the last of the Vasa dynasty on the Polish throne, was unable to resist the aggressors – Russians, Tatars, Ukrainians, Cossacks, Ottomans and Swedes – who were moving in on all fronts. The Swedish invasion of 1655–60, known as the Deluge, was particularly disastrous.

The last bright moment in the long decline of the Royal Republic was the reign of Jan III Sobieski (John III Sobieski; 1674–96), a brilliant commander who led several victorious battles against the Ottomans. The most famous of these was the Battle of Vienna in 1683, in which he defeated the Turks and checked their advancement into Western Europe.

## The Rise of Russia

By the start of the 18th century, Poland was in decline and Russia had evolved into a mighty expansive empire. The tsars systematically strengthened their grip over the flailing country, and Poland's rulers effectively became puppets of the Russian regime. This became crystal clear during the reign of Stanisław August Poniatowski (1764–95), when Catherine the Great, empress of Russia, exercised direct intervention in Poland's affairs. The collapse of the Polish empire was just around the corner.

The Ottoman Empire, though an ancient enemy of the Poles, was the only European power that never recognised the Partition of Poland.

## Poland Under Partition

During your travels in Poland, you're likely to hear reference to the 'partition', the period at the end of the 18th century when Poland was carved up between its more-powerful neighbours, Prussia, Russia and Austria. The partition period lasted all the way to the end of WWI. For 123 years Poland disappeared from world maps.

| 1596–1609 | Early 17th Century | 1655–60 | 1683 |
| --- | --- | --- | --- |
| After 550 years, Kraków loses the capital crown to Warsaw. The city is chosen as the seat of Polish power because of its central location, and closer proximity to Vilnius. | Under King Zygmunt III Waza (Sigismund III Vasa), Poland achieves its greatest territorial extent ever, more than three times the size of present-day Poland. | During the Deluge, Poland loses a quarter of its territory, cities are plundered and the economy is destroyed. From a population of 10 million, four million succumb to war, famine and plague. | Jan III Sobieski leads a Polish force in a battle against the Ottoman Turks at the gates of Vienna. His victory saves the city, but weakens Poland's own military defences. |

The partition initially led to immediate reforms and a new, liberal constitution, and Poland remained relatively stable. Catherine the Great could tolerate no more of this dangerous democracy, though, and sent Russian troops into Poland. Despite fierce resistance, the reforms were abolished by force.

Enter Tadeusz Kościuszko, a hero of the American War of Independence. With the help of patriotic forces, he launched an armed rebellion in 1794. The campaign soon gained popular support and the rebels won some early victories, but Russian troops, stronger and better armed, defeated the Polish forces within a year.

Despite the partition, Poland continued to exist as a spiritual and cultural community, and a number of secret nationalist societies were created. Since revolutionary France was seen as their major ally in the struggle, some leaders fled to Paris and established their headquarters there.

In 1815 the Congress of Vienna established the Congress Kingdom of Poland, but Russian oppression continued. In response, armed uprisings broke out, the most significant of which occurred in 1830 and 1863. An attempted insurrection against the Austrians also occurred in 1846.

In the 1870s Russia dramatically stepped up its efforts to eradicate Polish culture, suppressing the Polish language in education, administration and commerce, and replacing it with Russian. However, it was also a time of great industrialisation, with cities like Łódź experiencing a booming economy. With the outbreak of WWI in August 1914, the fortunes of Poland changed once again.

## WWI & the 'Second Republic'

Though most of the fighting in WWI, at least on the eastern front, was staged on Polish land and caused staggering loss of life and livelihood, paradoxically, the war led to the country's independence by pitting Poland's occupiers against each other.

On the one side were the Central Powers, Austria-Hungary and Germany (including Prussia); on the other, Russia and its Western allies. Since no formal Polish state existed, there was no Polish army to fight for the national cause. Even worse, some two million Poles were conscripted into the Russian, German or Austrian armies, and were obliged to fight one another.

After the October Revolution in 1917, Russia plunged into civil war and no longer had the power to oversee Polish affairs. The final collapse of the Austrian empire in October 1918 and the withdrawal of the German army from Warsaw in November brought the opportune moment. Marshal Józef Piłsudski took command of Warsaw on 11 November 1918, declared Polish sovereignty, and usurped power as the head of state.

The French general Napoleon Bonaparte spent a great deal of time in Poland, and was revered by the Poles as a potential national saviour. Speaking in Italy in 1797, he personally vowed to reverse the Polish partition that had been imposed on the country by Russia.

| 1764 | 1772 | 3 May 1791 | 1793 |
|---|---|---|---|
| King Stanisław August Poniatowski assumes the throne. He is a popular but weak ruler who allows Russia's Catherine the Great to exercise direct intervention in Poland's affairs. | First Partition of Poland at the instigation of Catherine the Great. Russia, Prussia and Austria annex substantial chunks of the country, amounting to roughly 30% of Polish territory. | The world's second written constitution (the first was in the USA) is signed in Warsaw. It places peasants under direct protection of the government, and attempts to wipe out serfdom. | Second Partition of Poland, with Russia and Prussia grabbing over half the remaining Polish territory. Poland shrinks to around 200,000 sq km and a population of four million. |

## Rise & Fall of the Second Republic

The Treaty of Versailles in 1919 that formally ended WWI called directly for the creation of a newly independent Poland, and thus the 'Second Republic' was born.

Poland began its new incarnation in a desperate position – the country and its economy lay in ruins, and an estimated one million Poles had lost their lives in WWI. All state institutions – including the army, which hadn't existed for over a century – had to be built up from scratch.

The treaty awarded Poland the western part of Prussia, providing access to the Baltic Sea. The city of Gdańsk, however, was omitted and became the Free City of Danzig. The rest of Poland's western border was drawn up in a series of plebiscites, which resulted in

### PIŁSUDSKI: PATRIOT, SOLDIER, STATESMAN

All around Poland, you'll see statues bearing the stern, moustached visage of Marshal Józef Piłsudski, a controversial political figure in the 1920s and '30s who is nevertheless revered as a Polish patriot and superb military commander.

Piłsudski was born in 1867 in the Russian-occupied Vilnius region and joined the anti-tsarist movement while a teenager. He spent many of his early years in prison: five years in Siberia, a brief stint in Warsaw's Citadel, and more jail time in St Petersburg, before returning to Poland to lead the Polish Legions in WWI.

At the end of the war, Piłsudski returned to Warsaw to declare the birth of a new Polish state on 11 November 1918. Arguably, though, his greatest moment came immediately after the war when he launched a massive offensive to the east, capturing vast territories that had been Polish before the 18th-century partitions. A Soviet counteroffensive reached as far as Warsaw, but in the Battle of Warsaw in August 1920, the Polish army, under Piłsudski's command, outmanoeuvred and defeated the Red Army.

Once independent Poland was safely back on the map and a modern democratic constitution had been adopted in 1921, Piłsudski stepped down in 1922.

He reappeared on the scene four years later, however, to declare an effective coup d'état in order to rescue the country from what he saw as a political stalemate and economic stagnation. Piłsudski's sudden return spurred three days of street fighting that left 400 dead and over 1000 wounded.

After the government resigned, the National Assembly elected Piłsudski as president. He refused to take that post and opted instead for the office of defence minister, which he maintained until his death. There are few doubts, though, that it was Piłsudski who ran the country behind the scenes until he died in 1935.

Despite his dictatorial style, he was buried with ceremony among Polish kings in the crypt of Kraków's Wawel Cathedral.

| 1795 | 1807 | 1810 |
|---|---|---|
| The Third Partition of Poland. The country ceases to exist completely, and will only again become a republic after the end of WWI in 1918. | Napoleon Bonaparte establishes the Duchy of Warsaw after crushing the Prussians on Polish soil. After Napoleon's defeat at the hands of the Russians, the duchy returns to Russia and Prussia. | The birth year of Frédéric Chopin, Poland's most beloved musician and a perennial favourite around the world. He's honoured by Poles but spent much of his life in France. |

TOMASZ BIDERMANN/DREAMSTIME.COM ©

» Chopin monument (p59)

Poland acquiring some significant industrial regions of Upper Silesia. The eastern boundaries were established when Polish forces defeated the Red Army during the Polish–Soviet war of 1919–20.

When Poland's territorial struggle ended, the Second Republic covered nearly 400,000 sq km and had a population of 26 million. One-third was of non-Polish ethnic background, mainly Jews, Ukrainians, Belarusians and Germans.

After Piłsudski retired from political life in 1922, the country experienced four years of unstable governments until the great military commander seized power once again in a military coup in May 1926. Parliament was gradually phased out but, despite the dictatorial regime, political repression had little effect on ordinary people. The economic situation was relatively stable, and cultural and intellectual life prospered.

On the international front, Poland's situation in the 1930s was unenviable. In an attempt to regulate relations with its two hostile neighbours, Poland signed nonaggression pacts with both the Soviet Union and Germany. Nevertheless, it soon became clear that the pacts didn't offer any real guarantee of safety.

On 23 August 1939 a pact of nonaggression between Germany and the Soviet Union was signed in Moscow by their respective foreign ministers, Ribbentrop and Molotov. This pact contained a secret protocol in which Stalin and Hitler planned to carve up the Polish state.

## WWII

If Poles had been asked in the 1930s to sketch out a nightmare scenario for the future, many would likely have said 'Germany fighting the Soviet Union over Poland', and that's more or less exactly what happened.

The war that would vastly reshape the country started at dawn on 1 September 1939 with a massive German invasion. Fighting began in Gdańsk (at that time the Free City of Danzig) when German forces encountered a stubborn handful of Polish resisters at Westerplatte. The battle lasted a week.

Simultaneously, another German line stormed Warsaw, which finally surrendered on 28 September. Despite valiant resistance, there was simply no hope of withstanding the numerically overwhelming and well-armed German forces; the last resistance groups were quelled by early October.

Hitler's policy was to eradicate the Polish nation and Germanise the territory. Hundreds of thousands of Poles were deported en masse to forced-labour camps in Germany, while others, primarily the intelligentsia, were executed in an attempt to exterminate the spiritual and intellectual leadership.

HISTORY WWII

Marshal Józef Piłsudski's most famous quotation was: 'To be defeated and not to submit, that is victory; to be victorious and rest on one's laurels, that is defeat.'

When God Looked the Other Way, by Wesley Adamczyk, is a gripping and terrible tale of a Polish family deported to southern Siberia in WWII.

| 1815 | 1830 | 1863 | Late 19th Century |
| --- | --- | --- | --- |
| Congress Kingdom of Poland is established at the Congress of Vienna. The Duchy of Warsaw is swept away and Poland once again falls under the control of the Russian tsar. | First of a number of insurrections against the ruling Russians, known as the November Insurrection. Within a year the rebellion is defeated, and deportations of Poles to Siberia begin. | January Insurrection against Russian rule. The insurgency is crushed, and Russia abolishes Congress Poland. Polish lands and its citizens are incorporated directly into the Russian Empire. | Despite Poland's political problems, the industrialisation of the 19th century proves an economic boom, particularly for working-class cities like Łódź. |

## THE WARSAW RISING

In early 1944, with German forces retreating across Poland in the face of an advancing Soviet army, the Polish resistance (Armia Krajowa; AK) in Warsaw was preparing for the liberation of its city. On 1 August 1944, orders were given for a general anti-German uprising, with the intention of establishing a Polish command in the city before the Red Army swept through.

The initial 'rising' was remarkably successful and the AK, creating barricades from ripped-up paving slabs and using the Warsaw sewers as underground communication lines, took over large parts of the city. It hoped to control the city until support came from both the Allies and the Soviets. But none arrived. The Allies were preoccupied with breaking out of their beachhead in Normandy after the D-Day landings, and the Red Army, which was camped just across the Vistula River in Praga, didn't lift a finger. On learning of the rising, Stalin halted the offensive and ordered his generals not to intervene or provide any assistance in the fighting, instead allowing the Germans to break the back of any potential Polish resistance to a communist takeover of the country.

The Warsaw Rising raged for 63 days before the insurgents were forced to surrender; around 200,000 Poles were killed. The German revenge was brutal – Warsaw was literally razed to the ground, and, on Hitler's orders, every inhabitant was to be killed. It wasn't until 17 January 1945 that the Soviet army finally marched in to 'liberate' Warsaw, which by that time was little more than a heap of empty ruins.

For the Poles, the Warsaw Rising was one of the most heroic – and most tragic – engagements of the war. The events of the rising are commemorated in the Warsaw Rising Museum and the Monument to the Warsaw Uprising.

---

The Jews were to be eliminated completely. At first they were segregated and confined in ghettos, then shipped off to extermination camps scattered around the country. Almost the whole of Poland's Jewish population (three million) and roughly one million other Poles died in the camps. Resistance erupted in numerous ghettos and camps, most famously in Warsaw (see the boxed text, p58).

*A Surplus of Memory: Chronicle of the Warsaw Ghetto Uprising,* by Yitzhak Zuckerman, is a detailed narrative of this heroic act of Jewish resistance.

## Soviet Invasion

Within a matter of weeks of the German invasion, the Soviet Union moved into Poland and claimed the country's eastern half. Thus, Poland was yet again partitioned. Mass arrests, exile and executions followed, and it's estimated that between one and two million Poles were sent to Siberia, the Soviet Arctic and Kazakhstan in 1939–40. Like the Germans, the Soviets set in motion a process of intellectual genocide.

| Late 19th Century | 1903 | 1914 | 11 November 1918 |
| --- | --- | --- | --- |
| At the end of the century around four million Poles, from a total population of 20 to 25 million, emigrate to avoid harsh Russian rule. Most go to the USA. | Warsaw-born Marie Curie wins the Nobel Prize for physics. The first woman to win, she becomes the first person to win two when she gets a second in 1911, for chemistry. | Start of WWI. The occupying powers – Germany and Austria to the west and south, Russia to the east – force Poles to fight each other on Polish soil. | The date of the founding of the Second Republic, so named to create a symbolic bridge between itself and the Royal Republic that existed before the partitions. |

## Government-in-Exile & Homegrown Resistance

Soon after the outbreak of war, a Polish government-in-exile was formed in France under General Władysław Sikorski, followed by Stanisław Mikołajczyk. It was shifted to London in June 1940 as the front line moved west.

The course of the war changed dramatically when Hitler unexpectedly attacked the Soviet Union on 22 June 1941. The Soviets were pushed out of eastern Poland by the onslaught and all of Poland lay under Nazi German control. The Führer set up camp deep in Polish territory (see the boxed text, p375), and remained there for over three years.

A nationwide resistance movement, concentrated in the cities, had been put in place soon after war broke out to operate the Polish educational, judicial and communications systems. Armed squads were set up by the government-in-exile in 1940, and these evolved into the Armia Krajowa (AK; Home Army), which figured prominently in the Warsaw Rising.

Amazingly, considering the Soviet treatment of Poles, Stalin turned to Poland for help in the war effort against the German forces advancing eastwards towards Moscow. The official Polish army was re-formed late in 1941, but was largely under Soviet control.

You can find a library of wartime photographs chronicling the horror and destruction of the Warsaw Rising at www.warsawuprising.com.

## The Tide Turns

Hitler's defeat at Stalingrad in 1943 marked the turning point of the war on the eastern front, and from then on the Red Army successfully pushed westwards. After the Soviets liberated the Polish city of Lublin, the pro-communist Polish Committee of National Liberation (PKWN) was installed on 22 July 1944 and assumed the functions of a provisional government. A week later the Red Army reached the outskirts of Warsaw.

Warsaw at that time remained under Nazi German occupation. In a last-ditch attempt to establish an independent Polish administration, the AK attempted to gain control of the city before the arrival of the Soviet troops, with disastrous results. The Red Army continued its westward advance across Poland, and after a few months reached Berlin. The Nazi Reich capitulated on 8 May 1945.

At the end of WWII, Poland lay in ruins. Over six million people, about 20% of the prewar population, lost their lives, and out of three million Polish Jews in 1939, only 80,000 to 90,000 survived the war. Its cities were no more than rubble; only 15% of Warsaw's buildings survived. Many Poles who had seen out the war in foreign countries opted not to return to the new political order.

Winston Churchill observed that 'Poland was the only country which never collaborated with the Nazis in any form and no Polish units fought alongside the German army'.

| 28 June 1919 | August 1920 | 12–14 May 1926 | 1 September 1939 |
| --- | --- | --- | --- |
| The Treaty of Versailles that formally ends WWI awards Poland the western part of Prussia and access to the Baltic Sea, but leaves Gdańsk a 'free city'. | Poland defeats the Red Army in the Battle of Warsaw. The battle helps to secure large portions of land in what is now Belarus and Ukraine. | Poland's postwar experiment with democracy ends when Marshal Józef Piłsudski seizes power in a military coup, phases out parliament and imposes an authoritarian regime. | The Nazis use a staged attack on a German radio station by Germans dressed as Poles as a pretext to invade Poland. WWII starts. |

## MASSACRE AT KATYŃ

In April 1943, German troops fighting Soviet forces on the eastern front came across extensive mass graves in the forest of Katyń, near Smolensk, in present-day Russia. Exploratory excavations revealed the remains of several thousand Polish soldiers and civilians who had been executed. The Soviet government denied all responsibility and accused the Germans of the crime. After the communists took power in Poland the subject remained taboo, even though Katyń was known to most Poles.

It wasn't until 1990 that the Soviets admitted their 'mistake', and two years later finally made public secret documents showing that Stalin's Politburo was responsible for the massacre. Meanwhile, in the summer of 1991, further mass graves of Polish soldiers were discovered in Myednoye and Kharkov, both in central Russia.

The full horror of Katyń was finally revealed during exhumations of the mass graves by Polish archaeologists in 1995–96. Here's what happened: soon after their invasion of Poland in September 1939, the Soviets took an estimated 180,000 prisoners, comprising Polish soldiers, police officers, judges, politicians, intellectuals, scientists, teachers, professors, writers and priests, and crammed them into various camps throughout the Soviet Union and the invaded territories.

On Stalin's order, signed in March 1940, about 21,800 of these prisoners, including many high-ranking officers, judges, teachers, physicians and lawyers, were transported from the camps to the forests of Katyń, Myednoye and Kharkov, shot dead and buried in mass graves. The Soviet intention was to exterminate the intellectual elite of Polish society.

No one has been brought to trial for the atrocity, as Russia states that Katyń was a military crime rather than a genocide, war crime, or crime against humanity.

## Communist Poland

Though Poland emerged from WWII among the victorious powers, it had the misfortune of falling within the Soviet-dominated Eastern bloc.

The problems started at the Yalta Conference in February 1945, when the three Allied leaders, Roosevelt, Churchill and Stalin, agreed to leave Poland under Soviet control. They agreed that Poland's eastern frontier would roughly follow the Nazi Germany–Soviet demarcation line of 1939. Six months later Allied leaders set Poland's western boundary along the Odra (Oder) and the Nysa (Neisse) Rivers; in effect, the country returned to its medieval borders.

The radical boundary changes were followed by population transfers of some 10 million people: Poles were moved into the newly defined Poland, while Germans, Ukrainians and Belarusians were resettled outside its boundaries. In the end, 98% of Poland's population was ethnically Polish.

| 17 September 1939 | 22 June 1941 | 1942 | 19 April 1943 |
|---|---|---|---|
| The Soviet Union fulfils its side of the Molotov-Ribbentrop Pact, a blueprint for the division of Eastern Europe between it and Nazi Germany, and invades eastern Poland. | Nazi Germany abrogates the Molotov-Ribbentrop Pact and declares war on the Soviet Union. This creates an uneasy alliance between Poland and the Soviet Union against their common foe. | Nazi Germany establishes 'Operation Reinhard', the name given to its plan to murder the Jews in occupied Poland, and builds secret extermination camps in Poland's far eastern regions. | The date of the start of the Ghetto Uprising in Warsaw. The Jewish resistance fighters hold out against overwhelming German forces for almost a month. |

As soon as Poland formally fell under Soviet control, Stalin launched an intensive Sovietisation campaign. Wartime resistance leaders were charged with Nazi collaboration, tried in Moscow and summarily shot or sentenced to arbitrary prison terms. A provisional Polish government was set up in Moscow in June 1945 and then transferred to Warsaw. General elections were postponed until 1947 to allow time for the arrest of prominent Polish political figures by the secret police. After rigged elections, the new Sejm elected Bolesław Bierut president.

In 1948 the Polish United Workers' Party (PZPR), henceforth referred to as 'the Party', was formed to monopolise power, and in 1952 a Soviet-style constitution was adopted. The office of president was abolished and effective power passed to the first secretary of the Party Central Committee. Poland became an affiliate of the Warsaw Pact.

In 1944 Stalin was quoted as saying 'fitting communism onto Poland was like putting a saddle on a cow'.

## Bread & Freedom

Stalinist fanaticism never gained as much influence in Poland as in neighbouring countries, and soon after Stalin's death in 1953 it all but disappeared. The powers of the secret police declined and some concessions were made to popular demands. The press was liberalised and Polish cultural values were resuscitated.

In June 1956 a massive industrial strike demanding 'bread and freedom' broke out in Poznań. The action was put down by force and soon afterwards Władysław Gomułka, a former political prisoner of the Stalin era, was appointed first secretary of the Party. At first he commanded popular support, but later in his term he displayed an increasingly rigid and authoritarian attitude, putting pressure on the Church and intensifying persecution of the intelligentsia.

It was ultimately an economic crisis, however, that brought about Gomułka's downfall; when he announced official price increases in 1970, a wave of mass strikes erupted in Gdańsk, Gdynia and Szczecin. Again, the protests were crushed by force, resulting in 44 deaths. The Party, to save face, ejected Gomułka from office and replaced him with Edward Gierek.

Another attempt to raise prices in 1976 incited labour protests, and again workers walked off the job, this time in Radom and Warsaw. Caught in a downward spiral, Gierek took out more foreign loans, but, to earn hard currency with which to pay the interest, he was forced to divert consumer goods away from the domestic market and sell them abroad. By 1980 the external debt stood at US$21 billion and the economy had slumped disastrously.

By then, the opposition had grown into a significant force, backed by numerous advisers from the intellectual circles. When, in July 1980, the government again announced food-price increases, the outcome was

WAJDA

Acclaimed Polish director Andrzej Wajda's 2007 film *Katyń* is a powerful and moving piece of work about the massacre of Polish officers in the Soviet Union on Stalin's orders during WWII. It's given added emotional impact by the fact that Wajda's own father was one of those officers.

### 1 August 1944

Start of the Warsaw Rising. The entire city becomes a battleground, and after the uprising is quelled, the Germans decide to raze Warsaw to the ground.

### 27 January 1945

The Soviet Red Army liberates Germany's Auschwitz-Birkenau extermination camp. Some of the first photos and film footage of the Holocaust are seen around the world.

### February–August 1945

Poland's borders are redrawn. The Soviet Union annexes 180,000 sq km to the east, while the Allies return 100,000 sq km of Poland's western provinces after centuries of German rule.

» Auschwitz-Birkenau (p268)

predictable: fervent and well-organised strikes and riots spread like wildfire throughout the country. In August, they paralysed major ports, the Silesian coal mines and the Lenin Shipyard in Gdańsk.

Unlike most previous popular protests, the 1980 strikes were non-violent; the strikers did not take to the streets, but stayed in their factories.

Learn more about the communist years at www .ipn.gov.pl, the website of the Institute of National Remembrance.

## Solidarity & the Collapse of Communism

The end of communism in Poland was a long and drawn-out affair that can be traced back to 1980 and the birth of the Solidarity trade union.

On 31 August of that year, after protracted and rancorous negotiations in the Lenin Shipyard, the government signed the Gdańsk Agreement. It forced the ruling party to accept most of the strikers' demands, including the workers' right to organise independent trade unions, and to strike. In return, workers agreed to adhere to the constitution and to accept the Party's power as supreme.

Workers' delegations from around the country convened and founded Solidarity (Solidarność), a nationwide independent and self-governing trade union. Lech Wałęsa, who led the Gdańsk strike, was elected chair.

It wasn't long before Solidarity's rippling effect caused waves within the government. Gierek was replaced by Stanisław Kania, who in turn lost out to General Wojciech Jaruzelski in October 1981.

The trade union's greatest influence was on Polish society. After 35 years of restraint, the Poles launched themselves into a spontaneous and chaotic sort of democracy. Wide-ranging debates over the process of reform were led by Solidarity, and the independent press flourished. Such taboo historical subjects as the Stalin-Hitler pact and the Katyń massacre could, for the first time, be openly discussed.

Not surprisingly, the 10 million Solidarity members represented a wide range of attitudes, from confrontational to conciliatory. By and large, it was Wałęsa's charismatic authority that kept the union on a moderate and balanced course.

*Mad Dreams, Saving Graces: Poland, a Nation in Conspiracy,* by Michael T Kaufman, is a trip through the dark times of martial law and the gloomy period up until 1988 – as readable as it is informative.

## Martial Law & Its Aftermath

In spite of its agreement to recognise the Solidarity trade union, the Polish government remained under pressure from both the Soviets and local hardliners not to introduce any significant reforms.

This only led to further discontent and, in the absence of other legal options, more strikes. Amid fruitless wrangling, the economic crisis grew more severe. After the unsuccessful talks of November 1981 between the government, Solidarity and the Church, social tensions increased and led to a political stalemate.

| 8 May 1945 | 1947 | June 1956 | 1970 |
|---|---|---|---|
| WWII officially ends with the surrender of Nazi Germany. There's great joy throughout Poland, but also apprehension as the war's end finds the country occupied by the Soviet Red Army. | Despite Stanisław Mikołajczyk – the government-in-exile's only representative to return to Poland – receiving over 80% of the vote in elections, 'officials' hand power to the communist government. | Poland's first industrial strike, in Poznań. Around 100,000 people take to the streets; the Soviet Union crushes the revolt with tanks, leaving 76 dead and over 900 wounded. | West German chancellor Willy Brandt signs the Warsaw Treaty that formally recognises the country's borders. Brandt famously kneels at a monument to the victims of the Warsaw Ghetto Uprising. |

When General Jaruzelski unexpectedly appeared on TV in the early hours of the morning of 13 December 1981 to declare martial law, tanks were already on the streets, army checkpoints had been set up on every corner, and paramilitary squads had been posted to possible trouble spots. Power was placed in the hands of the Military Council of National Salvation (WRON), a group of military officers under the command of Jaruzelski himself.

Solidarity was suspended and all public gatherings, demonstrations and strikes were banned. Several thousand people, including most Solidarity leaders and Wałęsa himself, were interned. The spontaneous demonstrations and strikes that followed were crushed, military rule was effectively imposed all over Poland within two weeks of its declaration, and life returned to the pre-Solidarity norm.

In October 1982 the government formally dissolved Solidarity and released Wałęsa from detention, but the trade union continued underground on a much smaller scale, enjoying widespread sympathy and support. In July 1984 a limited amnesty was announced and some members of the political opposition were released from prison. But further arrests continued, following every public protest, and it was not until 1986 that all political prisoners were freed.

## The Gorbachov Impact

The election of Mikhail Gorbachov as leader in the Soviet Union in 1985, and his *glasnost* and *perestroika* programmes, gave an important stimulus to democratic reforms throughout Central and Eastern Europe.

By early 1989, Jaruzelski had softened his position and allowed the opposition to challenge for parliamentary seats.

These 'semifree' elections – semifree in the sense that regardless of the outcome, the communists were guaranteed a number of seats – were held in June 1989, and Solidarity succeeded in getting an overwhelming majority of its candidates elected to the Senate, the upper house of parliament. The communists, however, reserved for themselves 65% of seats in the Sejm.

Jaruzelski was placed in the presidency as a stabilising guarantor of political changes for both Moscow and the local communists, but a non-communist prime minister, Tadeusz Mazowiecki, was installed as a result of personal pressure from Wałęsa.

This power-sharing deal, with the first non-communist prime minister in Eastern Europe since WWII, paved the way for the domino-like collapse of communism throughout the Soviet bloc. The Communist Party, haemorrhaging members and confidence, historically dissolved itself in 1990.

**Good Reads on the '89 Revolution**

» *The Magic Lantern: The Revolution of '89*, by Timothy Garton Ash

» *1989: The Struggle to Create Post–Cold War Europe*, by Mary Elise Sarotte

» *The Year that Changed the World*, by Michael Meyer

HISTORY SOLIDARITY & THE COLLAPSE OF COMMUNISM

» Pope John Paul II (p193)

### 1978

Karol Wojtyła, archbishop of Kraków, becomes Pope John Paul II. His election and triumphal visit to his homeland a year later dramatically increase political ferment.

### November 1980

Solidarity, the first non-communist trade union in a communist country, is formally recognised by the government. A million of the 10 million members come from Communist Party ranks.

### 13 December 1981

Martial law is declared in Poland. It is debatable whether the move is Soviet driven or an attempt by the Polish communists to prevent Soviet military intervention. It lasts until 1983.

# The Rise & Fall of Lech Wałęsa

In November 1990, Solidarity leader Lech Wałęsa won the first fully free presidential elections and the Third Republic of Poland was born. For Wałęsa it marked the high point of his career and for Poland the start of a very rocky rebirth.

In the first few months of the new republic, the government's finance minister, Leszek Balcerowicz, introduced a package of reforms that would change the centrally planned communist system into a free-market economy almost overnight. His economic plan, dubbed 'shock therapy' for the rapid way that it would be implemented, allowed prices to move freely, abolished subsidies, tightened the money supply, and sharply devalued the currency, making it fully convertible with Western currencies.

The effect was almost instant. Within a few months the economy appeared to have stabilised, food shortages became glaringly absent and shops filled up with goods. On the downside, prices skyrocketed and unemployment exploded. The initial wave of optimism and forbearance turned into uncertainty and discontent, and the tough austerity measures caused the popularity of the government to decline.

As for Wałęsa, while he was a highly capable union leader and charismatic man, as president he proved markedly less successful. During his statutory five-year term in office, Poland witnessed no fewer than five governments and five prime ministers, each struggling to put the newborn democracy back on track. His presidential style and accomplishments were repeatedly questioned by practically all of the political parties and the majority of the electorate.

Over time, his quirky behaviour and capricious use of power prompted a slide from the favour he had enjoyed in 1990 to his lowest-ever level of popular support in early 1995, when polls indicated that only 8% of the country preferred him as president for the next term.

## The Country Turns to the Left

Wałęsa was defeated in the 1995 presidential election by Aleksander Kwaśniewski – a former communist. Though the election was close, it marked quite a comedown for Solidarity and for Wałęsa, its anti-communist folk hero.

With the post of prime minister in the hands of another former communist, Włodzimierz Cimoszewicz, and parliament moving to the left as well, the country that had spearheaded the anti-communist movement in Central and Eastern Europe oddly found itself with a firmly left-wing government – a 'red triangle' as Wałęsa himself had warned.

The Catholic Church, much favoured by Wałęsa during his term in the saddle, also lost out and didn't fail to caution the faithful against the danger of 'neopaganism' under the new regime.

**More Reading on Poland in WWII**

» *No Simple Victory: World War II in Europe*, by Norman Davies

» *Rising '44: The Battle for Warsaw*, by Norman Davies

» *Bloodlands: Europe between Hitler and Stalin*, by Timothy Snyder

» *Between Two Evils*, by Lucyna B Radło

| April 1989 | 1990 | 1995 | 1999 |
| --- | --- | --- | --- |
| Poland becomes the first Eastern European state to break free of communism. In so-called round-table negotiations, Poland's opposition is allowed to stand for parliament and Solidarity is re-established. | Not a great year for Polish communists. The Party dissolves, the first democratic presidential election takes place and the country becomes a free-market economy. | Former communist Aleksander Kwaśniewski defeats Lech Wałęsa for the presidency in what ends up being a humiliating climb-down for the former leader of the Solidarity trade union. | Poland becomes a member of NATO. The country has come full circle, moving from the Warsaw Pact with the former Soviet Union to an alliance with the West. |

President Kwaśniewski's political style proved to be much more successful than Wałęsa's. He brought much-needed political calm to his term in office, and was able to cooperate successfully with both the left and right wings of the political establishment. This gained him a degree of popular support, and paved the way for another five-year term in office in the presidential election in October 2000. Wałęsa, trying his luck for yet another time, suffered a disastrous defeat, collecting just 1% of the vote this time around.

On 1 May 2004, under Kwaśniewski's presidency, Poland fulfilled its biggest post-communist foreign-policy objective, joining the European Union along with seven other countries from Central and Eastern Europe.

The website www .polishroots .org shows how Poland's borders have shifted over the past 200 years since Partition.

## The Disaster at Smolensk

Outside of the traditional ups and downs of Poland's electoral politics, the year 2010 brought epic tragedy to the leadership that affected both the right and left of the political establishment and threw the entire country into prolonged sorrow.

On 10 April that year a Polish air-force jet carrying 96 people, including president Lech Kaczyński, his wife and a high-level Polish delegation of 15 members of parliament, crashed near the Russian city of Smolensk. There were no survivors. The plane had been flying in from Warsaw for a memorial service to mark the 70th anniversary of the WWII-era massacre of Polish officers at Katyń Forest.

The pilot attempted to land the plane in heavy fog at a military airport, struck a tree on the descent and missed the runway. An initial high-level Russian commission placed the blame on pilot error, though an official Polish government report, released in 2011, assigned blame to both the Polish side and to air-traffic controllers on the Russian side.

The crash brought overwhelming grief to the country and a procession of high-level funerals. However, it also served to unite the country's fractured politics – albeit briefly – and ultimately proved the strength of the country's democracy. While many leading officials were killed, there was no ensuing succession crisis.

Following the disaster, the presidency fell to parliamentary speaker Bronisław Komorowski, who promptly called for early elections. Komorowski, of the right-leaning Civic Platform party, won in a run-off against the late president's twin brother, Jarosław Kaczyński.

| 1 May 2004 | July 2006 | April 2010 | 9 October 2011 |
|---|---|---|---|
| Poland joins the EU. Despite massive support, there is fear that the country is swapping one foreign governing power for another, and EU membership will spark a wave of emigration. | Twin brothers Lech and Jarosław Kaczyński occupy the presidential and prime minister seats respectively. Their nationalistic and conservative policies alienate many people. | President Lech Kaczyński, his wife and more than 90 others die in a tragic plane crash near the Russian city of Smolensk. The country unites in grief. | Parliamentary elections confirm the leadership of the right-leaning Civic Platform party, but the socially liberal Palikot Movement polls a historic 10% of the vote. |

# Jewish Heritage

For centuries up until WWII, Poland was home to Europe's biggest population of Jews. Warsaw was the second-biggest Jewish city in the world, after New York. It goes without saying that in many, many ways the saddest result of WWII was the near total destruction of this community and culture at the hands of Nazi Germany. Poland, and the world, is all the poorer for it.

While interest in Jewish history and the Holocaust in Poland languished during the communist period, the good news is that the country is rediscovering its Jewish heritage. Many cities have established Jewish heritage trails, the number of Jewish cultural festivals and events is increasing, and interest in Jewish music is on the rise.

**Cities with Important Jewish Heritage**

» Warsaw – the former Jewish ghetto

» Kraków – Kazimierz and Podgórze

» Lublin – the Jewish heritage trail

» Łódź – the Litzmannstadt ghetto

## Early Days

Jews began arriving in what is now Poland around the turn of the first millennium, just as the Polish kingdom was being formed. Many of these early arrivals were traders, coming from the south and east along established trading routes.

From the period of the early Crusades (around 1100), Poland began to develop a name for itself as a haven for Jews, a reputation it would maintain for centuries. At least some of the early Jewish inhabitants were coin-makers, as many Polish coins from the period bear Hebrew inscriptions.

## The Enlightened Kazimierz

The Polish ruler most often associated with the growth of Poland's Jewish population is Kazimierz III Wielki (Casimir III the Great; 1333–70), an enlightened monarch who passed a series of groundbreaking statutes that expanded privileges for Jews. It's no coincidence that the Kazimierz district near Kraków and Kazimierz Dolny, both important Jewish centres, bear his name.

'If a Christian desecrates or defiles a Jewish cemetery in any way, he should be punished severely as demanded by law' – written in 1264 by Bolesław the Pious, inviting Jewish settlement.

All was not a bed of roses and the good times were punctuated by occasional deadly pogroms, often as not whipped up by the clergy. The Catholic Church, at the time, was not as fond of Jews as were the king and nobility, who relied on Jewish traders as middlemen.

The 16th century is considered the golden age of Poland's Jews; the century saw a dramatic leap in the kingdom's Jewish population, driven in part by immigration. Much of Europe at this time was an intolerant place, and Jews were being forced out of neighbouring countries. Many new arrivals were Sephardim, descendants of Spanish Jews who'd been tossed out of Spain by King Ferdinand and Queen Isabella in 1492. By the end of the 16th century, Poland had a larger Jewish population than the rest of Europe combined.

## Pogroms & Partition

If the 16th century was good, the 17th century was an unprecedented disaster, both for the country and its Jewish population.

The Cossack insurrection of the 1650s in neighbouring Ukraine, led by Bohdan Chmielnicki, resulted in massive pogroms and the slaughter of tens of thousands of Jews in the southeastern parts of the Polish kingdom.

The war with Sweden, the 'Deluge', laid waste to much of the kingdom. Jews found themselves caught in the middle, ruthlessly hunted by Swedes on one side and Poles on the other.

After the partitions of the 18th and early 19th centuries, conditions for Jews differed greatly depending on what area they found themselves in. In the southern and eastern parts of the country that went to Austria, Jews enjoyed a gradual move towards religious tolerance. This was expanded slowly, in fits and starts, to other areas of the former kingdom over the 19th century.

Industrialisation in the 19th century led to higher living standards for Jews and non-Jews alike. Many Jews chose to leave the *shtetl* (small Jewish villages in the countryside) for greater opportunities in rapidly growing cities like Łódź. Urbanisation accelerated the process of assimilation, and by the 20th century, urban Jews and Poles had much more in common than they had apart.

Any existing legal distinctions between Jews and Poles vanished after WWI with the establishment of independent Poland, which declared everyone equal under the law regardless of religion or nationality.

A 1931 census showed Poland's Jews numbered just under three million people, or around 10% of the population.

## WWII & the Holocaust

It goes beyond the scope of this section to describe in any detail the near-total slaughter of Poland's Jewish population by Nazi Germany starting in 1939. The numbers speak for themselves: of around three million Jews living in Poland in 1939, fewer than 100,000 survived the war. Whole communities, large and small, were wiped out.

In the early stages of the war, in 1940 and '41, the German occupiers forced Jews to live in restricted ghettos, such as in Warsaw, Łódź, Kraków

---

The book *Jews in Poland: A Documentary History*, by Iwo Cyprian Pogonowski, provides a comprehensive record of half a millennium of Polish-Jewish relations in Poland.

---

**Most Important Holocaust Memorial Sites & Camps**

» Auschwitz-Birkenau
» Majdanek
» Bełżec
» Treblinka
» Sobibór

---

### READING UP ON THE HOLOCAUST

The genre of Holocaust literature is immense and it's not possible to mention all of the excellent titles, many written by Holocaust survivors and rich with detail.

As far as historic works go, we like Laurence Rees' *Auschwitz: A New History*, which combines excellent scholarship with personal anecdote to explain how the changes in official Nazi policy during the war were felt at camps like Auschwitz-Birkenau. It sounds dry, however it's anything but.

An occasionally overlooked masterpiece is *Fatelessness*, by Hungarian Nobel Prize–winner Imre Kertész. The novel tells the Auschwitz story through the eyes of a 15-year-old boy separated from his family in Budapest.

In many ways, the gold standard of Holocaust literature remains Primo Levi's *Survival in Auschwitz*. Levi, an Italian Jew, survived the war as a prisoner in the Monowitz camp at Auschwitz. It's a brilliant read, filled with honest sentiment of a young man simply trying to comprehend the insanity around him and stay alive.

To see the camps from a Polish author's perspective, pick up a copy of Tadeusz Borowski's *This Way for the Gas, Ladies and Gentlemen*, in English translation. Borowski was not a Jew, but a political prisoner. His Auschwitz is a madhouse of boxing matches and brothels and filled with unlucky souls willing to risk everything simply to steal a potato.

and scores of smaller cities around the country. In some cases, these were de facto internment camps; in others, like at Łódź, they were labour camps, harnessed directly to Germany's war effort.

Living conditions were appalling and thousands died of disease, exhaustion and malnutrition. To this day, Polish cities like Lublin, Częstochowa and Radom still bear the scars of their former ghettos; parts of these cities remain bleak and depressed.

After Germany declared war on the Soviet Union in the summer of 1941, Nazi policy towards the Jews shifted from one of internment to full-scale extermination. For many, death would come quickly. By the end of 1942 and early 1943, the majority of Poland's Jewry was gone. Most of the victims were shot in the fields and forests around their villages, or deported to hastily erected extermination camps at Treblinka, Sobibór and Bełżec (see p168 for more).

The extermination camps at Auschwitz-Birkenau and other places would grind on through 1944, but by then most of the victims were European Jews from outside Poland.

*Auschwitz: The Nazis and the Final Solution* is a BBC documentary that attempts to deal with the horrific events at Auschwitz-Birkenau.

## Disillusionment & Emigration

In the aftermath of WWII, many surviving Jews opted to emigrate to Israel or the USA. A small percentage decided to try to rebuild their lives in Poland – to decidedly mixed results.

It seems hard to believe now, but in the months and years after the war, there was not much sympathy in Poland for Holocaust survivors. Poland was a ravaged country, and every person to some extent had been made a victim by the war.

The low point came in Kielce in July 1946, when around 40 Jews were attacked and killed by an angry mob of Poles. The origins of the pogrom are unclear – some believe the attack was instigated by communist authorities – but it marked a watershed in Jewish attitudes. Emigration rates rose and few Jews chose to stay.

Additionally, Poland's position within the Soviet-controlled Eastern bloc greatly complicated the way the Holocaust was taught and commemorated. The Soviet Union had waged a mighty struggle to defeat Nazi Germany and the official line was to milk that effort for all it was worth. To that end, the suffering of the Jews was politicised, viewed as

---

### JEWISH TOURS

Several tour companies and organisations offer guided tours to Poland's most significant Jewish heritage sights, as well as to important Holocaust destinations. Outside of the companies listed below, local tourist offices can provide information on a particular area's Jewish sights and history.

**Our Roots** (☎22 620 0556; http://our-roots.jewish.org.pl) This Warsaw-based tour group specialises in tours of Jewish sites around the city and region. It offers a standard five-hour 'Jewish Warsaw' tour for around 500zł. Other tours, including to Auschwitz-Birkenau and Treblinka, can be organised on request.

**Jarden Tourist Agency** (☎12 421 7166; www.jarden.pl; ul Szeroka 2) Based in Kraków, this tour operator specialises in Jewish heritage tours around town. The most popular one, 'Retracing Schindler's List' (two hours by car), costs 60zł per person for groups of four or more.

**Momentum Tours & Travel** (☎in the USA 305 466 0652; www.momentumtours.com) One of the best of many international tourist agencies that offer specialised tours of Jewish heritage sites in Poland. The company's eight-day Poland tour includes off-the-beaten-track destinations like Tykocin, Kazimierz Dolny and Tarnów, among others.

part of a greater struggle of the working class over fascism. Even today, many Holocaust memorial sites – such as Majdanek near Lublin – are marred by wildly overblown communist-era statuary that appear to cast the Holocaust as part of an epic battle, instead of more appropriately being memorials to honour the lives lost.

## Jewish Revival

The years since the collapse of the communist regime have seen a marked improvement in local attitudes towards Jewish culture and history, and what might even be termed a modest Jewish revival.

Kraków, especially the former Jewish quarter of Kazimierz, has led the way. The city's annual Jewish Culture Festival (p21) is filled with theatre, film and, most of all, boisterous klezmer music. The festival has emerged as one of the city's – and the country's – cultural highlights. In 2010, Kraków opened the doors to an impressive new museum covering the Nazi-German occupation of the city during WWII – housed in the former enamel factory of Oskar Schindler, of *Schindler's List* fame (p127).

Kazimierz itself is a mixed bag of serious Jewish remnants and cheesy-but-fun Jewish restaurants, where the *Fiddler on the Roof* theme is laid on so thick that even Zero Mostel would probably blush. Still, the energy is infectious and has exerted a positive influence on other cities, including Warsaw, Lublin and Łódź to embrace their own Jewish heritage.

In the past few years, the tourist office in Łódź has marked out an important Jewish landmarks trail (p85) that you can follow through that city's former Jewish area and learn the tragic but fascinating story of what was the country's longest-surviving ghetto during the war. Lublin, too, now has a self-guided tour that highlights that city's rich Jewish heritage (p165).

Warsaw, which was home to the biggest Jewish population and wartime ghetto, had long been a laggard in the effort to embrace the country's Jewish past, but the new Museum of the History of Polish Jews (p56), set to open in 2012, looks ready to put that legacy to rest once and for all.

**JEWISH HERITAGE**

### Cities with Beautiful Synagogues

» Kraków
(Kazimierz district)

» Zamość

» Oświęcim

» Nowy Sącz

### Best Jewish Festivals

» Jewish Culture Festival, Kraków

» Festival of Klezmer Music and Tradition, Kazimierz Dolny

» Four Cultures, Łódź

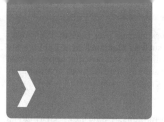

# The Arts

Poles punch well above their weight when it comes to contributing to the arts. Literature and cinema are where the country excels. Poland has produced no fewer than four Nobel Prize winners in literature and several household names when it comes to film, including Andrzej Wajda, Roman Polański and Krzysztof Kieślowski.

Judging from the number of concerts and festivals around the country, the performing arts, including classical music, theatre and dance, are alive and kicking. Despite modern trends, folk arts and music remain popular, particularly at summer folk fests.

**Must-Reads by Polish Writers**

» *The Painted Bird*, Jerzy Kosiński

» *The Street of Crocodiles*, Bruno Schulz

» *The Polish Complex*, Tadeusz Konwicki

» *The Captive Mind*, Czesław Miłosz

» *Solaris*, Stanisław Lem

## Literature

In Poland, as in many Central European countries, literature holds a special place in the hearts of citizens. It has served as the only outlet for resentment against foreign rule during occupation, and has often captured the spirit of a struggling country.

### Novelists

The Nobel Prize for literature was first awarded in 1901, and it was only four years later that Henryk Sienkiewicz (1846–1916) became the first of four Polish writers to be so honoured. Sienkiewicz took the prize for *Quo*

---

### POLISH PROSE IN EXILE

A number of Polish émigrés have made a name for themselves outside the country. Józef Teodor Konrad Nałęcz Korzeniowski (1857–1924) was born into a family of impoverished but patriotic gentry in Berdichev, now in western Ukraine. He left the country in 1874 and, after 20 years travelling the world as a sailor, settled in England. Though fluent in Polish, he dedicated himself to writing in English. He is known throughout the world by his adopted name of Joseph Conrad, and his novels (*Heart of Darkness* and *Lord Jim*, to name but two) are considered classics of English literature.

American Nobel Prize–winner Isaac Bashevis Singer (1902–91) spent his formative years in Poland before moving to the USA in 1935 in the face of rising fascism. Singer originally wrote in his native tongue of Yiddish, before translating his work into English for an American audience. Two of his most memorable stories are *Enemies, a Love Story* and *Yentl;* the latter was made into a film starring Barbra Streisand.

During the late '60s and early '70s, Ryszard Kapuściński (1932–2007) was one of Poland's only foreign correspondents, mostly covering wars and revolutions in Africa, Asia and the Americas. He went on to pen literary works of some standing, including *Imperium,* dealing with the Soviet Union, and *The Emperor,* covering the demise of Haile Selassie's Ethiopian regime.

Despite controversy surrounding the authenticity of some of Jerzy Kosiński's (1933–91) works, the author is known for two highly regarded novels, *The Painted Bird* and *Being There*. Kosiński was born Josek Lewinkopf in Łódź and emigrated to the USA in 1957.

*Vadis?*, an epic novel chronicling the love affair between a pagan Roman and a young Christian girl in ancient Rome.

Novelist and short-story writer Władysław Reymont (1867–1925) became another Nobel Prize winner in 1924 for *The Peasants* (Chłopi), a four-volume epic about Polish village life.

Between the wars, several brilliant avant-garde writers emerged who were only fully appreciated after WWII. They included Bruno Schulz (1892–1942), Witold Gombrowicz (1904–69) and Stanisław Ignacy Witkiewicz (also known as Witkacy; 1885–1939).

Despite penning only a handful of books, Schulz is regarded as one of Poland's leading literary lights; his *The Street of Crocodiles* is a good introduction to his ingenious, imaginative prose. As a Jew caught in the maelstrom of WWII, he stood little chance of surviving the German occupation.

The Polish Way: A Thousand-Year History of the Poles and their Culture (1988) by Adam Zamoyski is one of the best accounts of Polish culture from its birth to the recent past. It is fully illustrated and exquisitely written.

## The Post-WWII Generation

The postwar period presented Polish writers with a conundrum: adopt communism and effectively sell out, or take a more independent path and risk persecution.

Czesław Miłosz (1911–2004), who broke with the communist regime, offered an analysis of this problem in *The Captive Mind* (Zniewolony Umysł). Miłosz, a long-time émigré who spent the last 40 years of his life in the USA, occupies the prime position in Polish postwar literature, and the Nobel Prize awarded to him in 1980 was recognition of his achievements.

Novelist, screenwriter and film director Tadeusz Konwicki (b 1926) is another remarkable figure of the postwar literary scene. A teenage resistance fighter during WWII, Konwicki's pre-1989 works had communist censors tearing their hair out. He has written more than 20 novels, among which the best known are the brilliant *A Minor Apocalypse* (Mała Apokalipsa) and *The Polish Complex* (Kompleks Polski).

Stanisław Lem (1921–2006) is without doubt Poland's premier writer of science fiction. Around 27 million of his books, translated into 41 languages, have been sold around the world. Of the 30 or so novels he wrote, the most famous is *Solaris*.

## Poetry

The 19th century produced three exceptional poets: Adam Mickiewicz (1798–1855), Juliusz Słowacki (1809–49) and Zygmunt Krasiński (1812–59). Known as the Three Bards, they captured a nation deprived of its independence in their romantic work.

The website www.polishwriting.net is a guide to around 20 contemporary Polish novelists whose works are available in English, and includes short biographies, interviews, articles and extracts from their works.

The greatest of the three, Mickiewicz, is to the Poles what Shakespeare is to the British, and is as much a cultural icon as a historical and creative figure. Born in Navahrudak, in what is now Belarus, he was a political activist in his youth and was deported to central Russia for five years. He left Poland in the 1830s, never to return, and served as a professor of literature in Lausanne and Paris.

Mickiewicz' most famous poem, known to all Polish schoolchildren, is the epic, book-length *Pan Tadeusz* (1834). It is a romantic evocation of a lost world of 18th-century Polish-Lithuanian gentry, torn apart by the Partition of 1795.

Interestingly, Poland's last Nobel Prize (in 1996) went to a poet, Wisława Szymborska (b 1923). The Swedish academy described her as 'the Mozart of poetry' with 'something of the fury of Beethoven'. For those wanting to sample her work in English, a good introduction is the volume entitled *View with a Grain of Sand*, published in 1995.

# Cinema

Though the invention of the cinema is attributed to the Lumière brothers, some sources claim that a Pole, Piotr Lebiedziński, should take some of the credit; he built a film camera in 1893, two years before the movie craze took off.

The first Polish film was shot in 1908, but large-scale film production only took off after WWI. Little work produced between the wars reached international audiences; the country's greatest contribution to world cinema at the time was actress Pola Negri (1897–1987), a star of Hollywood's silent flicks of the 1920s.

## The Polish School

Polish cinema came to the fore from 1955 to 1963, the period known as the Polish School. The school drew heavily on literature and dealt with moral evaluations of the war – its three greatest prodigies, Andrzej Wajda (b 1926), Roman Polański (b 1933) and Jerzy Skolimowski (b 1938), all attended the Łódź Film School and went on to international acclaim.

Wajda produced arguably his best work during this time, the famous trilogy A Generation (Pokolenie), Canal (Kanał) and Ashes and Diamonds (Popiół i Diament). Since then, the tireless Wajda has produced a film every couple of years, the best of which include Man of Marble (Człowiek z Marmuru), its sequel Man of Iron (Człowiek z Żelaza), and The Promised Land (Ziemia Obiecana), which was nominated for an Oscar. In 2007, Wajda shot to the top of Polish cinema once again with his controversial and deeply moving film, Katyń, about the massacre of Polish officers by the Soviet Union in the Katyń Forest during WWII.

Polański and Skolimowski began their careers in the early '60s; the former made only one feature film in Poland, Nóż w Wodzie (Knife in the Water), before continuing his career in the West. The latter shot four films, of which the last, Ręce do Góry (Hands Up), made in 1967, was kept on the shelf until 1985. He also left Poland for more receptive pastures, and while he gained an international following, it was nothing compared to the recognition Polański received. Polański's body of work includes such remarkable films as Cul-de-Sac, Revulsion, Rosemary's Baby, Chinatown, Bitter Moon and The Pianist.

## After the Polish School

Poland's film-makers never reached the heights of the Polish School after 1963, yet they continued to make exemplary works. The communist era produced a string of important directors, including Krzysztof Zanussi, Andrzej Żuławski and Agnieszka Holland, and in 1970 Marek Piwowski shot The Cruise (Rejs), Poland's first cult film.

One name that regularly tops the list of art-house favourites is Krzysztof Kieślowski (1941–96), the director of the extraordinary trilogy Three Colours: Blue/White/Red. He started in 1977 with Blizna (Scar), but his first widely acclaimed feature was Amator (Amateur). After several mature films, he undertook the challenge of making Dekalog (Decalogue), a 10-part TV series that was broadcast all over the world.

More recently, Poland has produced a number of world-class cinematographers, including Janusz Kamiński, who was awarded two Oscars for his work on Steven Spielberg's Schindler's List and Saving Private Ryan. Allan Starski is another Pole to win an Oscar for Schindler's List, this time for art and set direction.

---

**Don't-Miss Films by Polish Directors**

» The Pianist, Roman Polański

» The Three Colours Trilogy, Krzysztof Kieślowski

» Ashes and Diamonds, Andrzej Wajda

» Katyń, Andrzej Wajda

» The Double Life of Veronique, Krzysztof Kieślowski

---

Check out the Polish Film Institute's website at www.pisf.pl for up-to-date information on the Polish film industry.

# Music

## Classical

The foremost figure in the history of Polish music is Frédéric Chopin (1810–49), who crystallised the national style in classical music, taking inspiration from folk or court dances and tunes such as *polonez* (polonaise), *mazurek* (mazurka), *oberek* and *kujawiak*. No one else in the history of Polish music has so creatively used folk rhythms for concert pieces, nor achieved such international recognition.

Chopin was not the only composer inspired by folk dances at the time. Stanisław Moniuszko (1819–72) used his inspiration to create Polish national opera; two of his best-known pieces, *Halka* and *Straszny Dwór,* are staples of the national opera-house repertoire. Henryk Wieniawski (1835–80), another remarkable 19th-century composer, also achieved great heights in the world of Polish music.

By the start of the 20th century, Polish artists were beginning to grace the world stage. The first to do so were the piano virtuosos Ignacy Paderewski (1860–1941) and Artur Rubinstein (1886–1982), the latter performing right up until his death. Karol Szymanowski (1882–1937) was another musical personality of the first half of the 20th century; his best-known composition, the ballet *Harnasie,* was influenced by folk music from the Tatra Mountains, which he transformed into the contemporary musical idiom.

In the 1950s and 1960s a wealth of talent began to emerge once more, including Witold Lutosławski, with his *Musique Funèbre* and *Jeux Vénitiens,* and Krzysztof Penderecki, with his monumental dramatic forms such as *Dies Irae, Ubu Rex, Devils of Loudun, Seven Gates of Jerusalem* and *Credo.*

## Rock & Pop

Unlike most countries, pop plays third fiddle to rock and hip-hop in Poland. The country's first rock pioneer was Tadeusz Nalepa (1943–2007), who began his career in the late 1960s and went on to nationwide success. Other veterans of the rock-pop scene include Lady Pank, Republika, Budka Suflera, Maanam, Bajm, T.Love and Hey. Recent years have seen a rash of productions covering just about every musical genre and style from salsa to rap. Brathanki and Golec uOrkiestra are both popular

**Where to Find Frédéric Chopin**

» Chopin Museum, Warsaw

» Holy Cross Church, Warsaw

» Warsaw University (Chopin studied here)

» Żelazowa Wola, Warsaw

THE ARTS MUSIC

### ALL THAT JAZZ

Jazz clubs come and go, but jazz as a music form retains a passionate following in Poland. This possibly owes something to the fact that jazz was officially frowned upon by the former communist government for nearly 40 years.

Krzysztof Komeda (1931–69), a legendary pianist, became Poland's first jazz star in the postwar decades and an inspiration to many who followed, including Michał Urbaniak (violin, saxophone), Zbigniew Namysłowski (saxophone) and Tomasz Stańko (trumpet), all of whom became pillars of the scene in the 1960s. Urbaniak opted to pursue his career in the USA, and is perhaps the best-known Polish jazz musician on the international scene.

Of the younger generation, Leszek Możdżer (piano) is possibly the biggest revelation thus far, followed by several other exceptionally skilled pianists such as Andrzej Jagodziński and Włodzimierz Pawlik. Other jazz talents to watch out for include Piotr Wojtasik (trumpet), Maciej Sikała (saxophone), Adam Pierończyk (saxophone), Piotr Baron (saxophone) and Cezary Konrad (drums).

Several Polish cities hold annual jazz festivals. One of the best is Kraków's All Souls' festival (p22), held in November.

groups that creatively mix folk and pop rhythms, and the likes of Wilki, Dżem and Myslovitz are keeping the country's rock traditions alive.

## Painting

For a comprehensive look at the last 100 years of Poland's poster art, log on to www.theartof poster.com.

The country's first major painter was no Pole at all. Bernardo Bellotto (c 1720–80) was born in Venice, the nephew (and pupil) of that quintessential Venetian artist, Canaletto. He specialised in *vedute* (town views) and explored Europe thoroughly, landing the job of court painter in Warsaw during the reign of King Stanisław August Poniatowski (1764–95). An entire room in Warsaw's Royal Castle (p49) is devoted to his detailed views of the city, which proved invaluable as references during the reconstruction of the Old Town after WWII. Bellotto often signed his canvases *'de Canaletto',* and as a result is commonly known in Poland simply as Canaletto.

## Development of Polish Artists

By the middle of the 19th century, Poland was ready for its own painters. Born in Kraków, Jan Matejko (1838–93) created stirring canvases that glorified Poland's past achievements. He aimed to keep alive in the minds of his viewers the notion of a proud and independent Polish nation, during a time when Poland had ceased to exist as a political entity. His best-known work is *The Battle of Grunwald* (1878), an enormous painting that took three years to complete. It depicts the famous victory of the united Polish, Lithuanian and Ruthenian forces over the Teutonic Knights in 1410 and is displayed in Warsaw's National Museum (p59).

Poles who became household names include Antoni Patek (cofounder of watchmakers Patek Philippe & Co), Max Factor (the father of modern cosmetics) and the four Warner brothers (founders of Warner Bros).

The likes of Józef Brandt (1841–1915) and Wojciech Kossak (1857–1942) also contributed to the documentation of Polish history at this time; Kossak is best remembered as co-creator of the colossal *Panorama of Racławice,* which is on display in Wrocław (p231).

## Theatre

Although theatrical traditions in Poland date back to the Middle Ages, theatre in the proper sense of the word didn't develop until the Renaissance period and initially followed the styles of major centres in France and Italy. By the 17th century the first original Polish plays were being performed on stage. In 1765 the first permanent theatre company was founded in Warsaw, and its later director, Wojciech Bogusławski, came to be known as the father of the national theatre.

Theatre development was hindered during Partition. Only the Kraków and Lviv theatres enjoyed relative freedom, but even they were unable to stage the great Romantic dramas, which were not performed until the

### POST-WWII PAINTING

From the end of WWII until 1955, the visual arts were dominated by Socialist Realism, canvases of tractors, landscapes, peasants and factories that became, officially at least, all the rage in those days.

On a more positive note, at least from an artistic standpoint, this was also a time when poster art came to the fore, building on a tradition dating back to the turn of the century. One of the most influential artists was Tadeusz Trepkowski (1914–54), who produced his best posters after WWII. His works, and those by other poster artists, can be seen at Warsaw's Poster Museum (p61).

From 1955 onwards, Poland's painters began to experiment with a variety of forms, trends and techniques. Zdzisław Beksiński (1929–2005) is considered one of the country's best contemporary painters; he created a mysterious and striking world of dreams in his art.

## POLAND'S SKANSENS

Skansen is a Scandinavian word referring to an open-air ethnographic museum. Aimed at preserving traditional folk culture and architecture, a skansen gathers together a selection of typical, mostly wooden, rural buildings (dwellings, barns, churches, mills) collected from the region, and often reassembles them to look like a natural village. The buildings are furnished and decorated in their original style, incorporating a range of traditional household equipment, tools, crafts and artefacts, and offer an insight into the life, work and customs of the period.

There are about 35 skansens in Poland focusing on distinctive regional traits. They are sometimes called *muzeum budownictwa ludowego* (museum of folk architecture), *muzeum wsi* (museum of the village) or *park etnograficzny* (ethnographic park), but the term skansen is universally applied.

It's difficult to form a hard-and-fast 'Skansen Top 10' list, but you shouldn't miss the ones in Sanok (p204) and Nowy Sącz (p218).

THE ARTS FOLK ARTS

beginning of the 20th century. By the outbreak of WWI, 10 permanent Polish theatres were operating. The interwar period witnessed a lively theatrical scene with the main centres situated in Warsaw and Kraków.

After WWII, Polish theatre acquired an international reputation. Some of the highest international recognition was gained by the Teatr Laboratorium (Laboratory Theatre), which was created in 1965 and led by Jerzy Grotowski in Wrocław. This unique experimental theatre, remembered particularly for *Apocalypsis cum Figuris,* was dissolved in 1984, and Grotowski concentrated on conducting theatrical classes abroad until his death in early 1999.

Another remarkable international success was Tadeusz Kantor's Cricot 2 Theatre of Kraków, formed in 1956. Unfortunately, his best creations, *The Dead Class* (Umarła Klasa) and *Wielopole, Wielopole,* will never be seen again; Kantor died in 1990 and the theatre was dissolved a few years later.

**Theatre Directors to Look Out For**

» Jerzy Jarocki
» Jerzy Grzegorzewski
» Krystian Lupa
» Maciej Prus

## Folk Arts

Poland has long and rich traditions in folk arts and crafts, but there are significant regional distinctions. Folk culture is strongest in the mountains, especially in the Podhale at the foot of the Tatras, but other relatively small enclaves, such as Kurpie and Łowicz (both in Mazovia), help to keep traditions alive.

Industrialisation and urbanisation have increasingly encroached on traditional customs. People no longer wear folk dress except for special occasions, and the artefacts they make are mostly for sale as either tourist souvenirs or museum pieces; in any case, they are not used for their original purposes. The country's many open-air folk museums, called skansens, are the best places to see what is left.

# Landscape & Wildlife

## A Varied Landscape

With primeval forest, wind-raked sand dunes, coastal lakes, endless beaches, reedy islands, caves, craters, a desert and even a peninsula called 'Hel', it's fair to say that the Polish landscape is one of Europe's most varied.

Poland's bumps and flat bits were largely forged during the last ice age, when the Scandinavian ice sheet crept south across the plains and receded some 10,000 years later. This left five discernable landscape zones: the Sudetes and Carpathian Mountains in the south; the vast central lowlands; the lake belt; the Baltic Sea in the north; and the north-flowing rivers.

## Southern Mountains

The southern mountains stretch from the Sudetes range in the southwest, via the Tatras to the Beskids in the southeast. The Sudetes are geologically ancient hills, their millennia-rounded peaks reaching their highest point at the summit of Śnieżka (1602m) in the Karkonosze range. Poland's highest point is Mt Rysy (2499m) in the Tatras, a jagged, alpine range shared with Slovakia.

To the north of the Tatra lies the lower (but much larger) densely forested range of the Beskids, with its highest peak at Babia Góra (1725m). The southeastern extremity of Poland is occupied by the Bieszczady, part of the Carpathian arc and arguably the most picturesque and lonely procession of peaks in the country.

## Central Lowlands

The central lowlands stretch from the far northeast all the way south to around 200km shy of the southern border. The undulating landscape of this, the largest of Poland's regions, comprises the historic areas of Lower Silesia, Wielkopolska, Mazovia and Podlasie. Once upon a time, streams flowing south from melting glaciers deposited layers of sand and mud that helped produce some of the country's most fertile soils. As a result, the central lowlands are largely farmland and Poland's main grain-producing region. In places, notably in Kampinos National Park to the west of Warsaw, fluvioglacial sand deposits have been blown by wind into sand dunes up to 30m high, creating some of the largest inland natural sand structures in Europe.

Fuel for the 19th-century industrial revolution was extracted from the vast coal deposits of Upper Silesia in the western part of the lowlands.

---

**Vital Stats**

Area – 312,685 sq km

Countries bordered – seven

Total length of border – 3582km

Number of lakes – 9300

Highest mountain – Mt Rysy (2499m)

Longest river – Vistula (1090km)

---

Some 52% of Polish territory is agricultural; almost 30% is forested.

# Water, Water, Everywhere

Not only does Poland enjoy a long stretch of the Baltic coast, it also has countless lakes and rivers, popular with yachtsmen, anglers, swimmers and divers, as well as thousands of species of flora and fauna.

## Poland's Lakes

The lake zone includes the regions of Pomerania, Warmia and Masuria. The latter contains most of Poland's 9300 lakes – more than any other European country except Finland. The gently undulating plains and strings of post-glacial lakes were formed by sticky clay deposited by the retreating ice sheet. The lake region boasts the only remaining *puszcza* (primeval forest) in Europe, making Białowieża National Park and the wildlife inhabiting it one of the highlights of the country.

## Baltic Coast

The sand-fringed Baltic coast stretches across northern Poland from Germany to Russia's Kaliningrad enclave. The coastal plain that fringes the Baltic Sea was shaped by the rising water levels after the retreat of the Scandinavian ice sheet and is now characterised by swamps and sand dunes. These sand and gravel deposits form not only the beaches of Poland's seaside resorts but also the shifting dunes of Słowiński National Park, the sand bars and gravel spits of Hel, and the Vistula Lagoon.

## Poland's Rivers

Polish rivers drain northwards into the Baltic Sea. The biggest is the mighty 1090km-long Vistula (Wisła), originating in the Tatra mountains. Along with its right-bank tributaries – the Bug and the Narew – the Vistula is responsible for draining almost half of the country and is known as the 'mother river' of Poland, given its passage through both Kraków and Warsaw. The second-largest river, the Odra, and its major tributary, the Warta, drains the western third of Poland and forms part of the country's western border. Rivers are highest when the snow and ice dams melt in spring and are prone to flooding during the heavy rains of July.

# Wildlife

Wildlife-spotters certainly have a lot to look forward to in Poland. Grazing bison in the Białowieża National Park and storks nesting atop telegraph poles are easy to find; brown bears and lynx may be harder to track down. Poland's varied landscapes also provide habitats for a vast array of plants.

## Animals

There is a rich bounty of zoological and ornithological treasure in Poland. Its diverse landscapes provide habitats for mammal species such as wild boar, red deer, elk and lynx in the far northeast, and brown bears and wildcats in the mountain forests of the south. Rare bird species found in Poland include thrush nightingales, golden eagles, white-backed and three-toed woodpeckers, and hazel grouses, among 200 other species of nesting bird.

### Wolves

Grey wolves, the largest members of the canine family, are individually distinct animals who travel and hunt in hierarchical units. In the days of old, wolf hunting was a favourite pastime of Russian tsars. This, and diminishing habitats, drove their numbers into the red until wolves had all but disappeared in the 1990s. After specialised legislation to protect

LANDSCAPE & WILDLIFE WATER, WATER, EVERYWHERE

## THE BISON: BACK FROM THE BRINK

The European bison (*Bison bonasus*, *żubr* in Polish) is the largest European mammal, its weight occasionally exceeding 1000kg. These large cattle, which can live for as long as 25 years, look pretty clumsy but can move at 50km/h when they need to.

Bison were once found all over the continent, but the increasing exploitation of forests in Western Europe pushed them eastwards. In the 19th century the last few hundred bison lived in freedom in the Białowieża Forest. In 1916 there were still 150 animals but three years later they were gone, hunted to extinction. At that time only about 50 bison survived in zoos across the world.

It was in Białowieża that an attempt to prevent the extinction of the bison began in 1929, by bringing several animals from zoos and breeding them in their natural habitat. The result is that today there are more than 300 bison living in freedom in the Białowieża Forest alone and about 350 more have been sent to a dozen other places in Poland. Many bison from Białowieża have been distributed among European zoos and forests, and their total current population is estimated at about 2500.

them was passed in 1998, the wolf census conducted in 2001 revealed that the numbers had already begun to climb.

### Horses

Prize-winning children's book *Bocheck in Poland* by Josepha Contoski is a beautifully rendered story of the relationship between white storks and Polish people.

Poles and horses go way back. Poland has a long tradition of breeding Arabian horses and the Polish plains were once home to wild horses. Several species of wild horse have been preserved in zoos, including the tarpan, which is extinct out of captivity. Luckily, Polish farmers used to crossbreed tarpans with their domestic horses and the small Polish konik horse is a result of this mix, keeping the tarpan genes alive. Konik horses are now being used to breed the tarpan back. The hucul pony is a direct descendant of the tarpan living in the Carpathians.

### Bird Life

The diverse topography of Poland is like flypaper for a range of bird species and orni-tourists. The vast areas of lake, marsh and reed bed along the Baltic coast, and the swampy basins of the Narew and Biebrza Rivers, are home to many species of waterfowl, and are visited by huge flocks of migrating geese, ducks and waders in spring and autumn. A small community of cormorants lives in the Masurian lakes.

In addition to their baby-delivery service, *bociany* (storks) are also known in Poland to bring good luck. Poles will often place wagon wheels and other potential nesting foundations on their roofs to attract the white stork. Telecommunications companies even go to lengths to ensure that their structures are stork-friendly.

Storks, which arrive from Africa in spring to build their nests on the roofs and chimneys of houses in the countryside, are a much-loved part of the rural scene. The expression 'every fourth stork is Polish' is based on the fact that Poland welcomes around one quarter of Europe's 325,000 white storks each year, most of which make their summer homes in Masuria and Podlasie in the northeast.

The *orzeł* (eagle) is the national symbol of Poland and was adopted as a royal emblem in the 12th century. Several species can be seen, mostly in the southern mountains, including the golden eagle and short-toed eagle, as well as the rare booted eagle, greater spotted eagle and lesser spotted eagle. The white-tailed eagle, supposedly the inspiration for the national emblem, lives in national parks along the Baltic coast.

### Plant Life

Poland contains the only surviving fragment of the forest that covered much of Europe in prehistoric times. This original forest of Białowieża National Park is still home to majestic five-centuries-old oak trees and a range of flora that is, quite literally, ancient.

The most common plant species in Poland is the pine, which covers 70% of the total forested area, but the biological diversity and ecological resilience of forests are increasing thanks to the proliferation of deciduous species such as oak, beech, birch, rowan and linden. The forest undergrowth hosts countless moss and fungus species, many of the latter suitable for rich sauces or to be fried in breadcrumbs.

In the highest mountain regions, coniferous forests of dwarf mountain pines are capable of resisting harsher climates, while the lowlands and highlands are hospitable for dry-ground forests and marsh forests. Distinctly Polish plants include the Polish larch *(Larix polonica)* and the birch *(Betula oycoviensis)* in the Ojców region.

## Conservation Areas in Poland

Currently 30% of Poland is forested and the majority of forests are administered by the state. Around 23% of the country is under some sort of protection as a national park, landscape park or other type of conservation area.

### National Parks

There are 23 *parki narodowe* (national parks) in Poland, covering about 3200 sq km – around 1% of the country's surface area. Other than a concentration of six in the Carpathian Mountains, they are distributed fairly evenly and therefore exhibit the full range of landscapes, flora and fauna the country possesses (see p31). The oldest national park in Poland, Białowieża, was established in 1932.

### Landscape Parks

In addition to Poland's national parks, the *parki krajobrazowe* (landscape parks) also play a key role in conservation efforts. As well as their aesthetic contribution, landscape parks are often of key historic and cultural value.

### Reserves

Poland has a number of *rezerwaty* (reserves) – usually small areas containing a particular natural feature such as a cluster of old trees, a lake with valuable flora or an interesting rock formation. Nine biosphere reserves have been recognised by Unesco for their innovative approach to sustaining various ecological elements.

Check out the English-language website www.wildpoland.com for heaps of information on wildlife spotting in Poland's national parks

LANDSCAPE & WILDLIFE CONSERVATION AREAS IN POLAND

Of the 110 species of mammal and 424 species of bird known to inhabit Poland, 12 of each are considered threatened.

# Survival Guide

# Directory A–Z

## Accommodation

Poland has a wide choice of accommodation options to suit most budgets, including hotels, pensions and guesthouses, hostels, apartment rentals and camping grounds. Prices across all of these categories have increased in recent years, but are still generally lower than comparable facilities in Western Europe.

This book divides accommodation options into three categories based on price: budget, midrange and top end. Budget properties normally include hostels, camping grounds and some cheaper guesthouses. Midrange accommodation includes hotels, pensions and better guesthouses. Top end means corporate chains, luxury hotels and high-end boutiques.

### PRICE CATEGORIES

| Budget ($) | < 150zł |
| --- | --- |
| Midrange ($$) | 150-400zł |
| Top End ($$$) | > 400zł |

» Warsaw is the most expensive place to stay, followed by Kraków, Wrocław, Poznań and other major cities. The further away from the big cities you go, the cheaper accommodation gets.

» Watch for seasonal fluctuations on rates. Summer resorts, particularly on the Baltic coast, in the mountains or near the Great Masurian Lakes, have higher prices in July and August. Ski centres increase prices in winter, particularly over the Christmas and New Year holidays.

» Hotels in large cities often offer discounts on the weekend. Similarly, resort properties may offer lower room rates during the week.

» Prices normally include breakfast but not parking, which can range from 10zł a night in smaller properties up to 100zł a night for garaged parking in Warsaw and Kraków.

» Room rates include VAT and should be the final price you pay. A small number of municipalities levy a 'tourist tax' on lodging, but this seldom amounts to more than 1zł or 2zł a night per room.

» Prices are quoted in złoty, though some larger hotels geared to foreign clients may also quote rates in euros for guests' convenience. All hotels accept złoty as payment.

## Types of Rooms

Polish hotels offer a standard mix of rooms, including singles, doubles, and apartments or suites. Often hotels will also have rooms for three or four people. Hotels normally display a sign at the reception desk, listing the types of rooms and prices. Look for the following:

| Single room | *pokój 1-osobowy* |
| --- | --- |
| Double room | *pokój 2-osobowy* |
| With bathroom | *z łazienką* |
| Without bathroom | *bez łazienki* |
| Basin in room only | *z umywalką* |

» Prices for double rooms may vary depending on whether the room offers twin beds or one full-sized bed, with the latter generally more expensive.

» Some properties do not have dedicated single rooms, but may offer a double at a reduced rate. It never hurts to ask.

## Hotels

Hotels account for the majority of accommodation options in Poland, encompassing a variety of old and new places, ranging from basic to ultra-plush.

At the top end are the various international and Polish hotel chains that offer high-standard accommodation to a mostly business-oriented clientele, usually at prices aimed at corporate expense accounts.

Going down the chain, there are plenty of smaller, privately owned hotels that cater to the midrange market. Many of these can be very nice and represent excellent value, but it always pays to check the room before accepting an offer. Don't be fooled by the hotel reception areas, which may look great in contrast to the

## PRACTICALITIES

» **Radio** The state-run Polskie Radio is the main radio broadcaster, operating on AM and FM in every corner of the country; all programs are in Polish.

» **Television** Poland has two state-owned, countrywide TV channels: TVP1 and the more educational and culture-focused TVP2. There are also several private channels, including the countrywide PolSat.

» **Newspapers & Magazines** Catch up on Polish current affairs in the *Warsaw Voice* (www.warsawvoice.pl), a weekly available from major newsagencies. Foreign newspapers can be found at EMPiK stores, bookshops and newsstands in the lobbies of upmarket hotels.

» **Weights & Measures** Poland uses the metric system.

» **Smoking** As of 2010, Poland has banned smoking in all public indoor spaces, including bars and restaurants. While some establishments defy the ban, most have complied. Most hotels are also entirely smoke-free.

rest of the establishment. If you ask to see a room, you can be pretty sure they won't give you the worst one, which may happen otherwise. While rates at these places vary, expect to pay around 150zł for a single and from 180zł for a double room.

Close to the bottom rung are sport hotels. In many aspects they are similar to municipal hostels: they seldom have singles, offer mostly shared facilities, and you can usually pay just for your bed, not the whole room.

### Pensions

*Pensjonaty* (pensions) are small, privately run guest-houses that provide breakfast and occasionally half or full board. By and large, these are clean, comfortable, friendly and good value.

While prices vary depending on the location and comfort level, they are usually a bit cheaper than comparable hotels. Singles/doubles typically run around 120/160zł. We're big fans of Polish pensions. Our only gripe is that the breakfast buffets can sometimes lack imagination (mostly simple ham and cheese plates) and they often serve only instant coffee.

### Hostels

This heading is a catch-all that includes both the new breed of privately owned hostels and the older, publicly run or municipal hostels. There are big differences. We also include here the simple, rustic mountain lodges operated by PTTK (Polish Tourist & Countryside Association).

### PRIVATE HOSTELS

These can usually only be found in big cities like Kraków, Warsaw, Zakopane, Wrocław, Poznań and Łódź. Standards are often higher than for basic youth hostels at prices that are roughly the same. They typically offer shared dorm-room accommodation, with prices dropping depending on how many beds the room has. They usually also offer a smaller number of private doubles and singles at prices that are normally well below hotels.

» Private hostels usually provide group kitchens, laundry facilities and sometimes a lounge and bar.

» Beds normally come with sheets included, and rooms should have lockers to guard your things when you're not around.

» They often have free wi-fi and computers on hand to surf the net, as well as friendly multilingual staff to answer questions.

» While they normally market themselves to backpackers, there are no age restrictions or curfews.

### PUBLIC HOSTELS

Poland has around 600 *schroniska młodzieżowe* (youth hostels), which are operated by the **Polskie Towarzystwo Schronisk Młodzieżowych** (PTSM; Polish Youth Hostel Association; www.ptsm.org.pl), a member of Hostelling International (HI).

Of these, around 20% are open year-round and the rest in July and August only.

» Hostels are normally marked with a sign featuring a green triangle with the PTSM logo inside, placed over the entrance.

» Curfew is normally 10pm, and almost all hostels are closed between 10am and 5pm.

» Facilities and conditions of public hostels differ markedly. Some hostels are in poor shape, while others are good and modern.

» All-year hostels have more facilities, including showers, a place to cook and a dining room.

» Seasonal hostels are normally located in schools while pupils are on holidays, and conditions are much more basic, with some lacking showers, kitchens and hot water. Bed sheets may not be available, so bring your own.

» Youth hostels are open to all, members and non-members alike, and there is no age limit.

## PTTK & MOUNTAIN HOSTELS

The **Polskie Towarzystwo Turystyczno-Krajoznawcze** (PTTK; Polish Tourist & Countryside Association; www .pttk.pl) has built up a network of its own hostels, called *dom turysty* or *dom wycieczkowy*.

They are aimed at budget travellers, providing basic accommodation for hikers and backpackers. Single rooms are a rarity, but you'll always have a choice of three- and four-bed rooms, usually with shared facilities, where you can often rent just one bed (not the whole room) for around 35zł to 45zł.

PTTK also runs a network of *schroniska górskie* (mountain hostels). Conditions are usually simple but prices are low and hot meals are usually available. The more isolated mountain hostels will usually try to take in all-comers, regardless of how crowded they get, which means that in the high season (summer and/or winter) it can sometimes be hard to even find a space on the floor. These hostels are open all year, though it's always best to check at the nearest regional PTTK office before setting off.

### Private Rooms

As you're travelling around Poland, you'll see many private homes offering rooms to let for the night. These are particularly prevalent in mountain areas or places that draw large amounts of visitors. Look for signs reading '*pokoje*', '*noclegi*' or '*zimmer frei*' in the window.

Private rooms are often a lottery: you don't know what sort of room you'll get or who your hosts will be. It's therefore a good idea to take the room for a night or two and

then extend if you decide to stay longer.

» Private rooms may or may not offer their own bathrooms.

» Breakfast and other meals may be available but not included in the basic room rate. It's best to sort this all out at the beginning before taking the room.

» Expect to pay 40zł for singles and from 60zł to 100zł for doubles, depending on the standard.

## Agrotourist Accommodation

Known as *kwatery agroturystyczne*, agrotourist accommodation refers to rooms on farms and in country houses and cottages. Meals can normally be provided on request, and sometimes there are opportunities for horse riding, fishing, canoeing, cycling and such. They're a great way to meet locals on their own turf, sample home-cooked regional food and enjoy a bit of country lifestyle.

In most cases, rooms are simple and rarely have private bathrooms, but prices are reasonable, usually between 40zł and 60zł per bed.

The owners of these places are affiliated with *stowarzyszenia agro-turystyczne* (agrotourist associations), which have 30-plus regional offices around the country; contact local tourist information centres for more details.

While this accommodation type is generally not included in this book (as most require your own transport to get to), information is easy to track down – most local tourist offices have a list of places in their region.

## Short-Term Apartment Rental

In recent years, fully equipped apartments available for short-term rental have become handy accommodation options in larger cities such as Warsaw and Kraków. They range from simple studios to two-bedroom luxury establishments, and are often centrally located. Apartments normally only make sense for stays of three days or longer because of the coordination hassles involved with picking up keys and making payment.

» Expect apartments to be fully equipped with towels and bed sheets. Better places may have a washing machine as well as small kitchen appliances (toasters, coffee-makers), allowing you to self-cater and cook meals.

» Note that payment is usually made in cash upfront or by credit card transfer over the internet. If you have the option, it's always a good idea to try to take a look at the property first before surrendering any money.

### Camping

Poland has over 500 camping and bivouac sites registered at the **Polish Federation of Camping & Caravanning** (www.pfcc .eu). The sites are distributed throughout the country and can be found in all the major cities (usually on the outskirts), in many towns and in the countryside.

Private camping grounds also exist in Poland. They range from small back gardens with a bathroom in the owner's house to large grounds with bungalows, cafes, shops, bike and boat hire, and so on.

About 40% of registered sites are camping grounds with full facilities, including lighting, electricity, running water, showers, kitchen and caravan pitches. The remaining 60% are bivouac sites, the equivalent of very basic camp sites, usually

---

### BOOK YOUR STAY ONLINE

For more accommodation reviews by Lonely Planet authors, check out hotels.lonelyplanet.com/Poland. You'll find independent reviews, as well as recommendations on the best places to stay. Best of all, you can book online.

equipped with toilets and not much else.

» Many places also have wooden cabins for rent, which are similar to very basic hotel rooms.

» Most camping grounds are open from May to September, but some run only from June to August.

» Fees are usually charged per tent site, plus an extra fee per person and per car. Some camping grounds levy an additional fee for electricity use.

## Business Hours

Most places adhere roughly to the hours following. Shopping centres and malls generally have longer hours and are open from 9am to 8pm on Saturday and Sunday. Museums are almost invariably closed on Mondays, and have shorter hours outside of the high season. In this guide, we've removed opening hours for restaurants that adhere to standard business hours.

**OPENING HOURS**

| | |
|---|---|
| Banks | 8am-5pm Mon-Fri, 9am-1pm Sat (varies) |
| Offices | 8am-5pm Mon-Fri, 9am-1pm Sat (varies) |
| Shops | 8am-6pm Mon-Fri, 8am-2pm Sat |
| Post Offices | 8am-8pm Mon-Fri, 8am-1pm Sat (cities) |
| Restaurants | 11am-11pm daily |

## Children

Travelling with children in Poland doesn't create any specific problems. Children enjoy privileges on local transport, and with accommodation and entertainment; age limits for particular freebies or discounts vary from place to place, but are not often rigidly enforced; and basic supplies for children are easily available in cities. There are quite a few shops devoted to kids' clothes, shoes and toys, and you can buy disposable nappies (diapers) and baby food in supermarkets and pharmacies. For general suggestions on how to make a trip with kids easier, pick up a copy of Lonely Planet's *Travel with Children*.

## Customs Regulations

» Travellers arriving from non-EU countries can bring in up to 200 cigarettes, 50 cigars or 250g of pipe tobacco, up to 2L of non-sparkling wine, and up to 1L of spirits.

» Travellers arriving from an EU member state can import up to 800 cigarettes, 200 cigars or 1kg of pipe tobacco, and up to 110L of beer, 90L of wine and 10L of spirits. This is seldom checked.

» The export of items manufactured before 9 May 1945 is prohibited without an export permit (*pozwolenie eksportowe*). Official antique dealers may offer to help you out with the paperwork, but the procedure is bureaucratic and time-consuming.

## Discount Cards

Several cities and regions offer special short-term 'tourist' cards. These usually provide discounted or free admission to museums, galleries and cultural institutions. Some also provide free public transport. Check online for details. Cards are normally available at tourist information offices and other sales points.

Popular tourist discount cards include the **Warsaw Tourist Card** (www.warsaw card.com; 1-day card 20zł), the **Kraków Card** (www .krakowcard.com; 2-day card 50zł) and the **Tri-City Tourist Card** (www.gdansk4u .pl; 1-/3-day card 15/34zł), for use in Gdańsk and Sopot.

## Hostel Cards

A HI membership card can gain you 10% to 25% discount on youth-hostel prices, though some hostels don't give discounts to foreigners. Bring the card with you, or get one issued in Poland at the provincial branch offices of the PTSM in the main cities. Go to www.ptsm.org.pl to find an office.

## Student Cards

Students receive great discounts in Poland, including discounts on most museum entries, as well as on some public transport. To qualify you need to be under the age of 26 and have a valid International Student Identity Card (ISIC). ISIC cards are available in Poland at the **Almatur Student Bureau** (www.almatur.pl), which has offices in most major cities.

## Electricity

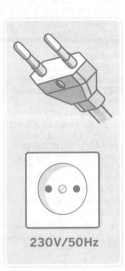

230V/50Hz

## Embassies & Consulates

The website http://embassy -finder.com maintains an up-to-date list of consulates and embassies around the world. Embassies are located in Warsaw, while several countries maintain consulates in other cities around the country.

**Australia** (☎22 521 3444; 3rd fl, ul Nowogrodzka 11, Warsaw)

**Belarus** Białystok (☎85 664 9940; ul Elektryczna 9); Warsaw (☎22 742 0990; ul Wiertnicza 58)

**Canada** (☎22 584 3100; ul Matejki 1/5, Warsaw)

**France** (☎22 529 3000; ul Piękna 1, Warsaw)

**Germany** Gdańsk (☎58 340 6540; Al Zwycięstwa 23); Kraków (☎12 424 3000; ul Stolarska 7); Warsaw (☎22 584 1700; ul Jazdow 12); Wrocław (☎71 377 2700; ul Podwale 76)

**Ireland** (☎22 849 6633; ul Mysia 5, Warsaw)

**Japan** (☎22 696 5000; ul Szwoleżerów 8, Warsaw)

**Lithuania** Sejny (☎87 517 3790; ul 22 Lipca 9); Warsaw (☎22 625 3368; Al Ujazdowskie 14)

**New Zealand** (☎22 521 0500; Al Ujazdowskie 51, Warsaw)

**Slovakia** (☎22 525 8110; ul Litewska 6, Warsaw)

**South Africa** (☎22 625 6228; 6th fl, ul Koszykowa 54, Warsaw)

**UK** Katowice (☎32 206 9801; ul PCK 10); Kraków (☎12 421 7030; ul Św Anny 9); Szczecin (☎91 487 0302; ul Starego Wiarusa 32); Warsaw (☎22 311 0000; ul Kawalerii 12); Wrocław (☎71 344 8961; ul Oławska 2)

**Ukraine** (☎22 622 4797; Al Szucha 7, Warsaw)

**USA** Kraków (☎12 424 5100; ul Stolarska 9); Warsaw (☎22 504 2000; Al Ujazdowskie 29/31)

## Food

We've included an in-depth discussion of Polish food and eating habits on p36. In this guide we've broken down eating listings into three price categories: budget, midrange and top end, depending on the price of an average main-course item.

### RESTAURANT PRICES

| Budget ($) | < 20zł |
|---|---|
| Midrange ($$) | 20-40zł |
| Top End ($$$) | > 40zł |

## Gay & Lesbian Travellers

Homosexuality is legal in Poland but not openly tolerated. Polish society is overwhelmingly conservative and for the most part remains hostile towards homosexuality.

The Polish gay and lesbian scene is fairly discreet; Warsaw and Kraków are the best places to find bars, clubs and gay-friendly accommodation, and Sopot is noted as gay-friendly compared to the rest of Poland. The best sources of information for Poland's scene are http://warsaw.gayguide .net and www.innastrona.pl.

## Insurance

Insurance can cover you for medical expenses, theft or loss, and also for cancellation of, or delays in, any of your travel arrangements. There are a variety of policies and your travel agent can provide recommendations.

Worldwide travel insurance is available at www.lonely planet.com/travel_services. You can buy, extend and claim online anytime – even if you're already on the road.

Always read the small print of a policy carefully and make sure the policy includes health care and medication in Poland. Some policies specifically exclude 'dangerous activities' such as scuba diving, motorcycling, skiing, mountaineering and even trekking.

## Internet Access

### Wi-Fi

Poland is well wired, and the majority of hotels, above a basic pension, offer some form of internet access (normally wi-fi) for you to log on with your own laptop, smartphone or tablet device. Additionally, many bars, cafes and restaurants, including McDonald's and Costa Coffee outlets nationwide, offer free wi-fi for customers, though the strength and reliability of the signal can vary considerably. In this guide, we've used the ⊚ icon to identify hotels, restaurants, cafes and bars that have wi-fi access.

### Finding a Computer

Locating a computer to use for a few minutes of surfing has become more problematic. Many hotels seem to be dropping the practice of making a computer terminal available for guests, though some still do, including many private hostels. Larger hotels will sometimes have a business centre for guests to use. In this guide, we've used the @ icon to indicate hotels that have computers available for guests.

The situation with internet cafes is much the same. As more and more Poles purchase their own computers the number of internet cafes has dropped. Still, there are some internet cafes around (and we've done our best to find them and identify them in the destination chapters). Other alternatives for finding a computer include tourist information offices, which may have a terminal on hand for a few minutes of gratis surfing, or local libraries.

## Legal Matters

Foreigners in Poland, as elsewhere, are subject to the laws of the host country. While your embassy or consulate is the best stop in any emergency, bear in mind that there are some things it can't do for you, like getting local laws or regulations waived because you're a foreigner, investigating a crime, providing legal advice or representation in civil or criminal cases, getting you out of jail and lending you money.

A consul can, however, issue emergency passports, contact relatives and friends, advise on how to transfer funds, provide lists of reliable local doctors, lawyers and interpreters, and visit you if you've been arrested or jailed.

## Maps

Poland produces good quality, inexpensive maps that can be purchased at tourist information offices, bookstores and many large petrol stations.

You probably won't need to buy special maps for large cities and major tourist hot spots, since many of these are provided in this book and the local tourist information office will have good free maps to hand out.

Where you will need maps, though, is in smaller cities and on hiking and biking trips. Stock up on maps for these in big cities as you go along, since they may not be available locally.

**Demart** (www.demart.com .pl) is one of the best map makers; its city plans, with orange covers, are excellent. Maps, usually costing anywhere between 10zł and 20zł, include tram and bus routes, alphabetical lists of streets, post offices, hotels, hospitals, pharmacies and the like.

Decent maps are also essential if you plan on driving. The book format *Atlas Samochodowy* (Road Atlas) includes sketch maps of major cities, Polish road signs and a full index. Find it at bookshops and large petrol stations.

Don't forget to bring along your satellite-navigation system if driving or you plan on renting a car. Polish navigation maps are usually included in most companies' European maps packages.

## Money

The official Polish currency is the *złoty* (literally, 'golden'), abbreviated to zł and pronounced *zwo*-ti. It is divided into 100 *groszy,* which are abbreviated to gr. Banknotes come in denominations of 10zł, 20zł, 50zł, 100zł and 200zł, and coins in 1gr, 2gr, 5gr, 10gr, 20gr and 50gr, and 1zł, 2zł and 5zł. It's a stable currency that has held its own with respect to the euro and US dollar in recent years.

Try to keep some small-denomination notes for shops, cafes and restaurants – getting change for the 100zł notes that ATMs often spit out can be a problem.

### ATMs

ATMs are ubiquitous in cities and towns, and even the smallest hamlet is likely to have at least one. The majority accept Visa and MasterCard.

The easiest way to carry money is in the form of a debit card, withdrawing cash as needed from an ATM. Charges are usually minimal, but check with your home bank about transaction fees and withdrawal limits.

### Cash

Change money at banks or, more commonly, *kantors* (private currency-exchange offices). You can find these in town centres as well as at travel agencies, train stations, post offices and department stores. Rates vary, so it's best to shop around.

» *Kantors* are usually open between 9am and 6pm on weekdays and to 2pm on Saturday, but some open longer and a few stay open 24 hours.

» *Kantors* usually exchange cash only and normally only accept major world currencies and some neighbouring countries' currencies. The most common and most easily changed are US dollars, euros and UK pounds.

» There's no commission on transactions – the rate you get is what is written on the board (every *kantor* has a board displaying its exchange rates).

### Credit Cards

Visa and MasterCard are widely accepted for goods and services. The only time you may experience a problem is at very small establishments or for a very small transaction. American Express cards are typically accepted at larger hotels and restaurants, though they are not as widely recognised as other cards.

Credit cards can also be used to get cash advances, and most banks will advance cash on a valid major credit card.

### International Transfers

Have money sent to you through the **Western Union** (www.westernunion.com) money-transfer service. Money is usually received within 15 minutes of the sender transferring it (along with the transaction fee) at any of the 30,000 Western Union agents scattered worldwide. Western Union outlets can be found in all Polish cities and most large towns, including at many branches of Bank Pekao.

### Taxes

Poland's VAT is calculated at various rates depending on the product. The top rate is 23%. The tax is normally included in the prices of goods and services as marked.

## Tipping

» In restaurants, tip 10% of the bill to reward good service. Leave the tip in the pouch that the bill is delivered in or hand the money directly to the waiter.

» Tip hairdressers and other personal services around 10% of the total.

» Taxis drivers won't expect a tip, but it's fine to round the fare up to the nearest 5zł or 10zł increment to reward special service.

» Tipping in hotels is essentially restricted to the top-end establishments, which usually have decent room service staff and porters, who all expect to be tipped.

## Post

Postal services are provided by **Poczta Polska** (www.poczta -polska.pl). In large cities there will be a dozen or more post offices, of which the *poczta główna* (main post office) will have the widest range of facilities, including (sometimes) poste restante and fax.

» Postal service is generally reliable. Letters and postcards sent by air from Poland take less than a week to reach a European destination and two weeks if sent anywhere else.

» A standard letter up to 50g costs 2.40zł to mail within Europe and 2.50zł to the rest of the world. It's always best to have letters and packages weighed at the post office to ensure proper postage.

## Telephone

### Domestic & International Calls

All Polish telephone numbers, landline and mobile, have nine digits. Poland recently dropped its former system of city codes and it's no longer necessary to dial a '0' before calling between cities within Poland. Simply dial the unique nine-digit number.

In keeping with local practice, this book lists landlines as ☏12 345 6789, with the first two numbers corresponding to the former city code. Mobile phone numbers are listed as ☏123 456 789.

To call abroad from Poland, dial the international access code (☏00), then the country code, then the area code (minus any initial zero) and the number. To dial Poland from abroad, dial your country's international access code, then 48 (Poland's country code) and then the nine-digit local number.

### Mobile/Cell Phones

Poland uses the GSM 900/1800 network, which covers the rest of Europe, Australia and New Zealand, but isn't compatible with most mobile phones in North America or Japan, though some North American cell phones have GSM 1900/900 phones that will work in Poland.

If you have a GSM phone, check with your service provider about using it in Poland, and beware of calls being routed internationally (very expensive for a 'local' call).

A cheaper – and often better – option is to buy a Polish prepaid SIM card. They sell for as little as 10zł and can be organised relatively quickly and painlessly at any provider shop (GSM, Orange etc). No ID is required, and top-ups can be bought at phone shops, news-paper kiosks and even some ATMs. Before purchasing a SIM card, be sure your phone is unlocked (able to accept foreign SIM cards).

The situation is more complicated if you plan on using a 'smartphone' like an iPhone, Android or Blackberry that may not be easily unlocked to accommodate a local SIM card. With these phones, it's best to contact your home telephone provider to consider short-term international calling and data plans appropriate to what you might need.

Smartphones can still be used as wi-fi devices, but switch your phone to 'airplane' mode on arrival, which blocks out calls and text messages but still allows wi-fi. Also turn off your phone's 'data roaming' setting on arrival to avoid unwanted roaming fees.

### Phonecards

Public phones usually require a phonecard, which you can buy from post offices, newspaper kiosks, and some tourist offices and hotel reception desks. TP cards cost 9/15/24zł for a 15-/30-/60-*impuls* (unit) card. A 60-*impuls* card is enough for a 10-minute call to the UK, or an eight-minute call to the USA.

Alternatively, you can buy a calling card from a private telephone service provider, such as **Telegrosik** (www.tele grosik.pl), whose international rates are even cheaper.

## Time

All of Poland lies within the same time zone, GMT/UTC+1, which is the same as most of continental Europe. Polish local time is one hour ahead of London and six hours ahead of New York.

Poland observes Daylight Saving Time (DST), and puts the clock forward one hour at 2am on the last Sunday in March, and back again at 3am on the last Sunday in October.

The 24-hour clock is used for official purposes, including all transport schedules. In everyday conversation, however, people commonly use the 12-hour clock.

## Toilets

» Toilets are labelled '*toaleta*' or simply 'WC'.

» Men should look for '*dla panów*' or '*męski*', or a door marked by an upside-down triangle.

» Women should head for '*dla pań*' or '*damski*', or a door marked with a circle.

## SHIFTING BORDERS

Poland is a member of the EU's common border area, the Schengen zone, and travel to neighbouring EU countries, including Germany, the Czech Republic, Slovakia and Lithuania, no longer requires passports or visas.

The same situation does not apply for visiting Belarus or Ukraine. For Belarus, most travellers will need to secure a visa in advance from a Belarusian consulate (see p418). You'll need a valid passport, photo and application. Fees vary but can be expensive. See the Belarusian foreign ministry website for details: www.mfa.gov.by.

The situation for Ukraine is mixed: EU, US and Canadian citizens do not need a visa for stays up to 90 days, but citizens of Australia and New Zealand (as of this writing) still need to get a visa in advance. Check the Ukrainian foreign ministry website (www.mfa .gov.ua) for details.

» Some small establishments, like bars, will often have shared facilities.

» Public toilets in Poland are few and far between and often not very clean.

» The fee for a public toilet is usually 1zł or 2zł, collected by a toilet attendant sitting at the door. Have small change ready.

## Tourist Information

Poland's official tourist information portal is www .poland.travel. It's a treasure trove of useful information, with a large English-language section on festivals and events, accommodation and tips on what to see and do.

On the ground in Poland, many towns have set up local tourist information offices that vary greatly in terms of helpful information and language ability, though at the very least they should be able to provide a free walking map of the city and practical advice on places to stay and eat.

In places where there are no general tourist offices, look for a PTTK office. PTTK was once a helpful organisation, focusing on outdoor activities such as hiking, sailing, cycling and camping. Today it's just another travel agency, but many of its offices are well-stocked with maps and trekking brochures, can arrange guides and accommodation, and provide tourist information.

## Travellers with Disabilities

Poland is not well equipped for people with disabilities, even though there has been a significant improvement over recent years. Wheelchair ramps are available only at some upmarket hotels and restaurants, and public transport will be a challenge for anyone with mobility problems. Few offices, museums or banks provide special facilities for travellers with disabilities, and wheelchair-accessible toilets are few and far between.

There are several useful websites for travellers with disabilities. If your Polish language is up to snuff, try www. niepelnosprawni.pl for up-to-date information on the current situation for people with disabilities in Poland.

In the USA, travellers with disabilities may like to contact the **Society for Accessible Travel & Hospitality** (www .sath.org). In the UK a useful contact is the **Royal Association for Disability & Rehabilitation** (www.radar .org.uk).

## Visas

Citizens of EU countries do not need visas to visit Poland and can stay indefinitely. Citizens of the USA, Canada, Australia, New Zealand, Israel, Japan and many other countries can stay in Poland for up to 90 days without a visa.

Other nationalities should check current visa requirements with the Polish embassy or consulate in their home country.

Note that Poland is a member of the EU's common border and customs area, the Schengen Zone, which imposes its own 90-day visa-free travel limit on visitors from many countries outside the European Union. In practice, this means your time in Poland would count against your stay within the entire Schengen Zone – so plan your travel accordingly. There's more information on the Polish **Ministry of Foreign Affairs** (www.mfa.gov.pl) website.

## Work

Without a high standard of Polish, most people will need to arrange a job in Poland through an international company or be prepared to teach English. English teachers remain in high demand, with schools popping up in cities and towns across the country. Teacher standards are generally high, however, and you'll probably need a TEFL (Teaching English as a Foreign Language) certificate to secure a job. The website **Teaching English in Poland** (www.teachingenglishinpoland .com) offers some handy tips for getting started.

# Transport

## GETTING THERE & AWAY

### Entering the Country

#### Passport

See p421 to find out which countries require a visa to travel to Poland. Theoretically, the expiry date of your passport should not be less than three months after the date of your departure from Poland. Additionally, some airlines may deny travel to passengers whose passports are within six months of expiration.

### Air

#### Airports & Airlines

The majority of international flights to Poland arrive at **Warsaw-Frédéric Chopin Airport** (WAW; ☎22 650 4220; www.lotnisko-chopina.pl). Other international air gateways include:

**Gdańsk – Lech Wałęsa** (GDN; ☎58 348 1163; www.airport.gdansk.pl)

**Katowice** (KTW; ☎32 392 7385; www.katowice-airport.com)

**Kraków-Balice** (KRK; ☎12 639 3000; www.lotnisko-balice.pl)

**Łódź** (LCJ; ☎42 688 8414; www.airport.lodz.pl)

**Rzeszów** (RZE; ☎17 852 0081; www.rzeszowairport.pl)

**Wrocław** (WRO; ☎71 358 1381; www.airport.wroclaw.pl)

Poland's national carrier is **LOT** (www.lot.com). It's one of the world's oldest national carriers, with a generally good safety record in the post-communist era.

LOT offers regular service to Poland from throughout Europe, including from most capital cities. Outside Europe it has direct flights to/from Chicago, New York, Tel Aviv and Toronto, and other destinations.

Many other national and major world carriers operate regular flights to Poland, normally between their national capital and/or major city and Warsaw.

Additionally, many budget carriers service the Polish market. These include EasyJet, Jet2, GermanWings, Ryanair, Wizz Air and some others. These usually service smaller airports such as Łódź, Katowice and Rzeszów, though several fly to Kraków as well.

The following airlines fly to and from Poland:

**Aeroflot** (www.aeroflot.ru)
**Air France** (www.airfrance.com)
**Alitalia** (www.alitalia.com)
**Austrian** (www.aua.com)
**British Airways** (www.british-airways.com)
**Czech Airlines** (www.czechairlines.com)
**Delta Airlines** (www.delta.com)
**EasyJet** (www.easyjet.com)
**GermanWings** (www.germanwings.com)
**KLM** (www.klm.com)
**Lufthansa** (www.lufthansa.com)
**Malev** (www.malev.hu)
**Norwegian** (www.norwegian.com)
**Ryanair** (www.ryanair.com)
**SAS** (www.flysas.com)
**WizzAir** (www.wizzair.com)

#### Tickets

Fares vary greatly depending on the route, the time of year, and the day of the week. Poland's high season is summer (June to August) and a short period around Christmas. The rest of the year is quieter and cheaper. Weekday flights tend to be more expensive than weekends, or trips that include a weekend stay.

For flights within Europe, travellers have the choice of dozens of major, full-fare carriers and budget carriers. Budget options from Britain are particularly good, as several low-cost carriers operate regular services from airports around the UK to airports throughout Poland.

The best advice is simply to shop around for the best deal, keeping in mind that you're likely to pay less the further in advance you can plan your travel. If you're booking on short notice (that is, less than around three or four weeks before departure), national carriers sometimes offer better prices than budget airlines.

On transatlantic and long-haul flights your travel agent is probably still the best source of cheap tickets, although there is an increasing number of online booking agencies. One feasible option is to find the best deal to a European hub, like London, and then try to find a budget flight from there. That might land you the cheapest deal, but bear in mind that budget airlines rarely use main airports, and you're likely to have to change not just planes en route but airports too.

# Land
## Border Crossings

Sitting in the middle of Europe and sharing its borders with seven countries, Poland has plenty of rail and road crossings. Border crossings are more numerous with Germany to the west and the Czech and Slovak republics to the south than they are with Ukraine, Belarus, Lithuania and Russia to the east and northeast.

Remember that part of Poland's eastern border is now one of the external borders of the EU. If you're travelling overland to Russia, be aware that you may need a Belarusian transit visa, which must be obtained in advance.

Following is a list of 24-hour border crossings for heading east out of Poland by road:

**Belarusian border** (south to north): Terespol, Kuźnica Białostocka

**Lithuanian border** (east to west): Ogrodniki, Budzisko

**Russian border** (east to west): Bezledy, Gronowo

**Ukrainian border** (south to north): Medyka, Hrebenne, Dorohusk

# Belarus, Lithuania, Ukraine & Russia
## BUS

**Eurolines Polska** (www.euro linespolska.pl) has daily buses to Warsaw from Minsk (from 97zł, 12 hours) in Belarus and Vilnius (from 80zł, 12 hours) in Lithuania. It's also possible to cross the border into Belarus by bus from Białystok, though service is erratic. As we were researching this guide, there were two daily buses to Grodno (35zł, two hours), departing at 2.20pm and 3.30pm.

## TRAIN

Warsaw has direct trains to Kyiv (from €60, 15 hours) in Ukraine that bypass Belarus and do not require a Belarusian visa. There is also a regular train service to Minsk (from €40, 10 hours). These trains are sleeper only, and you'll be automatically sold a sleeping berth when buying your ticket.

The fastest option from Warsaw to Vilnius (€24, 9½ hours) in Lithuania travels through Suwałki and requires a change in Šeštokai across the border. It's a good option as there is no need to arrange a transit visa for Belarus.

It's possible to travel to St Petersburg (from €90, 24 hours) in Russia from

Warsaw, but unless you've got a Belarus transit visa, you'll have to choose your train carefully. Make sure to select the route that passes through Vilnius (via Suwałki with a change in Šeštokai). You can also get to Moscow (from €80, 20 hours) from Warsaw, but the train passes through Minsk and requires a Belarus transit visa.

# Czech Republic
## BUS

**Eurolines CZ** (www.eurolines .cz) runs regular buses from Prague to Warsaw (125zł, 14 hours) via Wrocław (115zł, five hours).

## TRAIN

There are daily express trains from Prague to Warsaw (€60, 9½ hours) via Katowice, and to Kraków (€46, 8½ hours).

# UK
## BUS

**Eurolines** (☎8717 818177; www.eurolines.co.uk) runs buses from London to Warsaw (one way about UK£65, 26½ hours) via Poznań and Łódź, and to Kraków (UK£65, 26¾ hours) via Wrocław and Katowice. The frequency of the service varies depending on the season: it's as often as daily in summer and slows down to twice weekly the rest of the year. Tickets can be bought from any National Express office and a number of travel agencies.

## TRAIN

You can travel from London to Warsaw via the Channel Tunnel, with a single change of train at Brussels (20 hours). The normal 2nd-class, one-way fare is around €170.

# Western Europe
## BUS

**Eurolines** (www.eurolines .com) operates an extensive network of bus routes all over Western Europe. Standards, reliability and comfort vary from bus to

## THINGS CHANGE

The information in this chapter is particularly vulnerable to change. Check directly with the airline or a travel agent to make sure you understand how a fare (and ticket you may buy) works and be aware of the security requirements for international travel. Shop carefully. The details given in this chapter should be regarded as pointers and are not a substitute for your own careful, up-to-date research.

bus, but on the whole are not bad. Most buses are from the modern generation, and come equipped with air-conditioning, toilet facilities and a DVD player.

As a rough guide only, average one-way fares and journey times between some Western European cities and Warsaw are as follows:

| TO | FARE | TIME |
| --- | --- | --- |
| Amsterdam | €76 | 21hr |
| Brussels | €75 | 21hr |
| Cologne | €62 | 20hr |
| Frankfurt | €70 | 19hr |
| Hamburg | €49 | 17hr |
| Munich | €72 | 20hr |
| Paris | €77 | 27hr |
| Rome | €108 | 27hr |

### TRAIN

A number of German cities are linked by train (direct or indirect) with major Polish cities. Direct connections with Warsaw include Berlin, Cologne, Dresden and Leipzig. There are also direct trains between Berlin and Kraków (via Wrocław; around €50, 9½ hours).

The Warsaw–Berlin route (via Frankfurt/Oder and Poznań; €40, six to 8½ hours) is serviced by five trains a day.

There are no direct trains from Brussels (Bruxelles-Nord) to Warsaw (from €91, 14½ hours); if making this trip the quickest route is via Cologne. From Paris to Warsaw (€160, 16½ hours), a change is often required in Cologne.

## Sea

Poland has regular car-ferry services plying the routes from Denmark and Sweden to Gdańsk and Świnoujście on the coast of Poland. The fares quoted here are for a foot passenger throughout the year.

### Denmark

**Polferries** (www.polferries.pl) Operates regular ferry service between Copenhagen and Świnoujście (adult/concession 520/460kr, nine hours, daily).

### Sweden

**Polferries** (www.polferries.pl) Operates car ferries from Nynäshamn to Gdańsk's Nowy Port (adult/concession Skr750/640, 19 hours, daily departures in high season) and from Ystad to Świnoujście (adult/concession Skr590/490, seven hours, daily).

**Stena Line** (www.stenaline.com) From Karlskrona to Gdynia (from Skr400, 11 hours, daily).

**Unity Line** (www.unityline.pl) From Ystad to Świnoujście (adult/concession Skr600/500, seven hours, daily).

# GETTING AROUND

## Air

**LOT** (www.lot.com) operates a domestic network of domestic routes. There are regular flights between Warsaw and Bydgoszcz, Gdańsk, Katowice, Kraków, Poznań, Rzeszów, Szczecin and Wrocław. All flights between regional cities travel via Warsaw and connections aren't always convenient.

The regular one-way fare on any of the direct flights to/from Warsaw starts at around 200zł and can reach up to 600zł and higher. Tickets can be booked and bought at any LOT office, and from some other travel agencies.

There's no departure tax on domestic flights.

## Bicycle

Poland has great potential as a place to tour by bicycle – most of the country is flat and you can throw your bike on a train to cover long distances quickly. Camping equipment isn't essential, as hotels and hostels are usually no more than a day's ride apart, although carrying your own camping gear will give you more flexibility.

Cycling shops and repair centres are popping up in large cities, and in some of the major tourist resorts.

Likewise, the number of shops offering bike rentals is on the increase; you'll be able to hire a bike in most major cities.

### Road Conditions

Major roads carry heavy traffic and are best avoided. Instead, plan your route along minor roads, which are usually much less crowded and in reasonable shape.

Stock up on detailed hiking maps, which normally show bike trails as well as walking trails.

Some drivers hug the side of the road to give cars and trucks more room to overtake, passing perilously close to cyclists. Note that in Poland cyclists are not allowed to ride two abreast.

Cities are often not the most pleasant places to cycle either, though many cities now have dedicated cycle paths and more are planned for the future. The main problem is drivers who often don't give a damn about two-wheeled travellers.

### Taking Your Bike on the Train

Many – but not all – trains allow you to transport bikes. When buying your ticket at the station, inform the ticket seller you have a bike and they will let you know whether it's allowed onboard. Bikes usually require a separate ticket, ranging in price from 5zł to 10zł. Online timetables usually note whether bikes are permitted.

Some trains have special carriages equipped to carry

## CLIMATE CHANGE & TRAVEL

Every form of transport that relies on carbon-based fuel generates $CO_2$, the main cause of human-induced climate change. Modern travel is dependent on aeroplanes, which might use less fuel per kilometre per person than most cars but travel much greater distances. The altitude at which aircraft emit gases (including $CO_2$) and particles also contributes to their climate change impact. Many websites offer 'carbon calculators' that allow people to estimate the carbon emissions generated by their journey and, for those who wish to do so, to offset the impact of the greenhouse gases emitted with contributions to portfolios of climate-friendly initiatives throughout the world. Lonely Planet offsets the carbon footprint of all staff and author travel.

bicycles and these will be marked. Other times you'll have to stow the bike in a baggage car. If the train has no baggage car, bikes are only permitted in the first and last carriages of the train. If you have to stow your bike there, try to sit near it and keep it out of the way of other passengers. Bikes cannot be taken on sleeping cars.

### Security

Poland is famous for bike theft. Don't trust your bike for even a couple of minutes unattended, regardless of how strong the lock is.

Many hotels have secured luggage rooms, which are normally fine for overnight, though if in doubt take your bike with you into your room. If your hotel can't store your bike, then the in-room option is the only one you have.

Trains pose particular risks of theft. If you have to leave your bike in a baggage car, try to sit near the car and check on it periodically. Lock your bike to a fixed part of the railcar if possible.

### Boat

Poland has a long coastline and lots of rivers and canals, but passenger-boat services are limited and operate only in summer. There are no regular boats running along the main rivers or along the coast.

Several cities, including Szczecin, Gdańsk, Toruń, Poznań, Wrocław and

Kraków, have local river cruises during the summer, and a few coastal ports (Kołobrzeg and Gdańsk) offer sea excursions. There are also trips out of Elbląg to Frombork and Krynica Morska.

Tourist boats are available in the Augustów area where they ply part of the Augustów Canal (p107). Arguably the most unusual canal trip is the cruise along the Elbląg-Ostróda Canal (p367).

### Bus

Poland has a comprehensive bus network (far greater than the rail network) covering most villages accessible by road. Buses are often more convenient than trains over a short distance and occasionally longer ones when, for instance, the train route involves a long detour.

The frequency of service varies greatly: on the main routes there may be a bus leaving every quarter of an hour or so, whereas some small remote villages may get only one bus a day. Ticket prices also vary greatly due to fierce competition between bus companies, so shop around.

### Bus Companies

Most of Poland's bus transport is operated by the former state bus company, PKS (Państwowa Komunikacja Samochodowa), although deregulation of the country's bus system has

made room for a plethora of private operators. What this means for travellers is a broader range of options and frequent promotions; don't automatically assume PKS offers the lowest prices and best service.

PKS can be a good code word when seeking directions to bus stations – it's now a term for buses in general.

You can find details of its services online at its various websites, which mostly take the form www.pks.warszawa .pl, www.pks.krakow.pl etc. Just insert the city or town you will depart from before '.pl' in the web address. Very few sites have English versions, but with a little time and effort it's easy enough to find timetables.

Normally the *dworzec autobusowy PKS* (local PKS bus station) is found alongside the train station, but in some towns it's centrally located. Bus stations normally have pitiful facilities (no left-luggage service or even a place for coffee), but most do have some sort of information counter.

PKS has many private competitors, both locally and on the national scene. The main competitor nationwide is **Polski Bus** (www.polskibus .com), which runs handy long-haul services between many major cities on buses that are modern and comfortable. It has a very easy to use English-language timetable.

Minibuses are an additional option to the bigger buses of PKS and Polski Bus. They are generally more frequent and much faster than their bigger brothers, and service more routes. There is rarely any sort of information counter at minibus stands, but schedules are clearly displayed. Minibus stations are usually in the vicinity of the PKS station.

## Costs

The approximate fares for intercity bus journeys are as follows:

| DISTANCE | FARE |
| --- | --- |
| 20km | 6-8zł |
| 40km | 10-12zł |
| 60km | 12-14zł |
| 80km | 15-18zł |
| 100km | 18-20zł |
| 150km | 22-25zł |
| 200km | 27-30zł |
| 250km | 32-38zł |
| 300km | 40-45zł |

Note that while prices listed were accurate at the time of research, don't be surprised to find them a few złoty different when you hit the road. The entire bus system is still in a state of flux.

## Station Timetables

Timetables are posted on boards either inside or outside PKS bus terminal buildings. There are also notice boards at all bus stops along the route. The timetable of *odjazdy* (departures) lists *kierunek* (destinations), *przez* (the places passed en route) and departure times.

Also check any additional symbols that accompany the departure time. These symbols can mean that the bus runs only on certain days or in certain seasons. They're explained in the key at the end of the timetable, but can be very difficult to decipher.

## Tickets

The only place to buy PKS tickets is at the bus station itself, either from the information/ticket counter or the bus driver. If you get on the bus somewhere along the route, you buy the ticket directly from the driver.

Tickets for Polski Bus can be bought online at www.polskibus.com.

# Car & Motorcycle

## Automobile Associations

The **Polski Związek Motorowy** (PZM, Polish Automobile & Motorcycle Federation; www.pzm.pl, in Polish) is Poland's national motoring organisation. It provides a 24-hour national **roadside assistance** (☑9637) service and if you are a member of an affiliated automobile association, it will help you on roughly the same terms as your own organisation would. If not, you must pay for all services.

## Bringing Your Own Car

Many Western tourists bring their own vehicles into Poland. There are no special formalities: all you need at the border is your passport (with a valid visa if necessary), your driving licence, vehicle registration document and third-party insurance (called a Green Card). Fines are severe if you're caught without insurance. A nationality plate or sticker must be displayed on the back of the car.

## Driving Licences

Foreign driving licences are valid in Poland for up to 90 days. Strictly speaking, licences that do not include a photo ID need an international driving permit as well, although this rule is rarely enforced.

## Fuel

*Benzyna* (petrol) is readily available at petrol stations throughout the country. There are several different kinds and grades of petrol available, including 95- and 98-octane unleaded and diesel. The price of fuel can differ from petrol station to petrol station by up to 10%. Nearly all petrol stations accept credit cards.

Virtually all petrol stations have adopted a self-service system and offer services commonplace in the West.

## Car Hire

Car-hire agencies will require you to produce your passport, a driving licence held for at least one year, and a credit card. You need to be at least 21 or 23 years of age (depending on the company) to hire a car, although hiring some cars, particularly luxury models and 4WDs, may require a higher age.

One-way hire within Poland is possible with most companies (usually for an additional fee), but most will insist on keeping the car within Poland. No company is likely to allow you to take its car beyond the eastern border.

High insurance premiums mean that car hire in Poland is not cheap, and there are seldom any promotional discounts. As a rough guide only, economy models offered by reputable local companies cost about 160/800zł per day/week (including insurance and unlimited mileage). Rates at the big international agencies start at around 225/1000zł per day/week. It's usually cheaper to book your car from abroad or over the internet.

Major car-rental firms in Warsaw include the following:

**Avis** (☑22 572 6500; www.avis.pl)

**Budget** (☑22 868 3336; www.budget.pl)

## ROAD DISTANCES (KM)

| | Białystok | Bydgoszcz | Częstochowa | Gdańsk | Katowice | Kielce | Kraków | Łódź | Lublin | Olsztyn | Opole | Poznań | Rzeszów | Szczecin | Toruń | Warsaw | Wrocław |
|---|---|---|---|---|---|---|---|---|---|---|---|---|---|---|---|---|---|
| Bydgoszcz | 389 | | | | | | | | | | | | | | | | |
| Częstochowa | 410 | 316 | | | | | | | | | | | | | | | |
| Gdańsk | 379 | 167 | 470 | | | | | | | | | | | | | | |
| Katowice | 485 | 391 | 75 | 545 | | | | | | | | | | | | | |
| Kielce | 363 | 348 | 124 | 483 | 156 | | | | | | | | | | | | |
| Kraków | 477 | 430 | 114 | 565 | 75 | 114 | | | | | | | | | | | |
| Łódź | 322 | 205 | 121 | 340 | 196 | 143 | 220 | | | | | | | | | | |
| Lublin | 260 | 421 | 288 | 500 | 323 | 167 | 269 | 242 | | | | | | | | | |
| Olsztyn | 223 | 217 | 404 | 156 | 479 | 394 | 500 | 281 | 370 | | | | | | | | |
| Opole | 507 | 318 | 98 | 485 | 113 | 220 | 182 | 244 | 382 | 452 | | | | | | | |
| Poznań | 491 | 129 | 289 | 296 | 335 | 354 | 403 | 212 | 465 | 323 | 261 | | | | | | |
| Rzeszów | 430 | 516 | 272 | 642 | 244 | 163 | 165 | 306 | 170 | 516 | 347 | 517 | | | | | |
| Szczecin | 656 | 267 | 520 | 348 | 561 | 585 | 634 | 446 | 683 | 484 | 459 | 234 | 751 | | | | |
| Toruń | 347 | 46 | 289 | 181 | 364 | 307 | 384 | 159 | 375 | 172 | 312 | 151 | 470 | 313 | | | |
| Warsaw | 188 | 255 | 222 | 339 | 297 | 181 | 295 | 134 | 161 | 213 | 319 | 310 | 303 | 524 | 209 | | |
| Wrocław | 532 | 265 | 176 | 432 | 199 | 221 | 268 | 204 | 428 | 442 | 86 | 178 | 433 | 371 | 279 | 344 | |
| Zielona Góra | 601 | 259 | 328 | 411 | 356 | 422 | 427 | 303 | 542 | 453 | 245 | 130 | 585 | 214 | 281 | 413 | 157 |

Europcar (☎22 650 2564; www.europcar.com.pl)
Hertz (☎22 500 1620; www.hertz.com)
Local Rent-a-Car (☎22 826 7100; www.lrc.com.pl)

## Road Conditions

Driving in Poland for long distances is no fun. Roads are crowded and a massive explosion in road building and road repair, some of it spurred by Poland's preparations to co-host the UEFA 2012 football championship, has led to many detours and delays.

Poland currently has only a few motorways in the proper sense of the word, but an array of two- and four-lane highways criss-cross the country. Secondary roads are narrower but they usually carry less traffic and are OK for leisurely travel. The paved minor roads, which are even narrower, are also often in acceptable condition, though driving is harder work as they tend to twist and turn, are not so well signposted and pass through every single village along the way.

## Road Hazards

Drive carefully on country roads, particularly at night. There are still horse-drawn carts on Polish roads, and the further off the main routes you wander, the more carts, elderly cyclists, tractors and other agricultural machinery you'll encounter. These vehicles are often lit poorly or not at all.

## Road Rules

Road rules are the same as in the rest of Europe. A vehicle must be equipped with a first-aid kit, a red-and-white warning triangle and a nationality sticker on the rear; the use of seat belts is compulsory. Drinking and driving is strictly forbidden – the legal blood alcohol level is 0.02%. Police can hit you with on-the-spot fines for speeding and other traffic offences (be sure to insist on a receipt).

Polish speed limits are 20km/h to 50km/h in built-up areas (to 60km/h from 11pm to 5am), 90km/h on open roads, 110km/h on dual carriageways and 130km/h on motorways.

Car headlights must be on at all times, even during a sunny day. Motorcyclists should remember that both rider and passenger must wear helmets.

Some potentially unfamiliar traffic signs include the following:

**Blue disc with red border and red slash** No parking on the road.

**Yellow diamond with white border** You have right of way; a black slash through it means you no longer have right of way.

**Yellow triangle (point down) with red border** Give way (yield).

## Hitching

*Autostop* (hitching) is never entirely safe anywhere in the world. Travellers who decide to hitch should understand that they are taking a small but potentially serious risk. Those who choose to hitch will be safer travelling in pairs, and letting someone know where they are planning to go.

That said, hitching does take place in Poland; locals can often be seen thumbing a ride from one small village to the next. Car drivers rarely stop though, and large commercial vehicles (which are easier to wave down) expect to be paid the equivalent of a bus fare.

## Local Transport

### Bus, Tram & Trolleybus

Polish cities offer excellent public transport. Every large and medium-sized city will have a comprehensive *autobus* (bus) network, while some cities will also have *tramwaj* (tram) and *trolejbus* (trolleybus) systems. Warsaw is the only city with a metro.

» Public transport normally operates daily from around 5am to 11pm. Service is less frequent on weekends.

» Trams and buses are likely to be crowded during rush hour (7am to 9am and 4.30pm to 6.30pm Monday to Friday).

» Timetables are usually posted at stops, but don't rely too much on their accuracy.

#### TICKETS AND FARES

Each city has a slightly different system of ticketing and fares, so be prepared to watch what the locals do and do likewise.

Most cities have a fare system based on the duration of the ride, with a standard 60-minute ticket costing around 2.50zł. There may be slightly cheaper tickets available for shorter rides (20 or 30 minutes) and more expensive tickets for longer ones (90 minutes).

While it is becoming increasingly rare, some smaller cities may still have the older equipment and charge a flat fare per ride, with the duration and the distance making no difference. If you change vehicles, you need to validate another ticket. In these cases, too, a standard ticket costs in the vicinity of 2.50zł.

There are many common features across Polish buses and trams:

» There are no conductors on board buses and trams. Buy tickets beforehand and punch or stamp them in one of the little machines installed near the doors once you enter the bus or tram.

» Buy tickets from newspaper kiosks like Ruch or Relay or from street stalls around the central stops, recognisable by the *bilety* (tickets) boards they display.

» Buy several tickets at once since you may find yourself at a far-flung stop with no chance to buy tickets locally. Note that ticket kiosks may be closed on Sunday.

» Plain-clothed ticket inspectors are always on the prowl and foreigners are not exempt. These inspectors tend to be officious, dogged and singularly unpleasant to deal with.

### Taxi

Taxis are easily available and not too expensive. As a rough guide, a 5km taxi trip will cost around 20zł, and a 10km ride shouldn't cost more than 30zł. Taxi fares are higher at night (10pm to 6am), on Sunday and outside the city limits. The number of passengers (usually up to four)

and the amount of luggage doesn't affect the fare.

There are plenty of taxi companies, including the once monopolistic, state-run **Radio Taxi** (☑191 91), which is the largest and operates in most cities.

» Avoid unmarked pirate taxis (called 'mafia' taxis by Poles), which usually have just a small 'taxi' sign on the roof with no name or phone number.

» You can flag down cabs on the street or order them by phone. There's no extra charge for this and many firms employ dispatchers who can speak at least some English.

» When you get into a taxi, make sure the driver turns on the meter. Also check whether the meter has been switched to the proper rate: '1' identifies the daytime rate, and '2' is the night rate. A typical scam is to drop the flag to the higher night rate during the day.

» Remember to carry small bills, so you'll be able to pay the exact fare. If you don't, it's hard to get change from a driver who's intent on charging you more.

## Tours

The following Polish agencies offer organised tours in Poland:

**Fabricum** (☑42 636 2825; www.fabricum.pl; ul Drewnowska 58, Łódź) Specialises in tours of Poland's Unesco sights and following in the footsteps of the country's beloved John Paul II.

**Jarden Tourist Agency** (☑12 421 7166; www.jarden .pl; ul Szeroka 2, Kraków) Specialises in Jewish-heritage tours.

**Mazurkas Travel** (☑22 389 4183; www.mazurkas .com.pl; Al Wojska Polskiego 27, Warsaw) Major tour operator with tours of Warsaw plus trips to Kraków, Gdańsk and Białowieża.

Our Roots (☎22 620 0556; http://our-roots.jewish.org .pl) Specialises in tours of Jewish sites, including trips around Warsaw and sites throughout the country. Based in Warsaw.

**PTTK Mazury** (☎89 527 4059; www.mazurypttk.pl, in Polish; ul Staromiejska 1, Olsztyn) Runs kayak tours along the country's best rivers in and around the Great Masurian Lakes.

# Train

Poland's train network is extensive, easy to use and reasonably priced. It's likely to be your main means of transport for covering long distances.

That said, service has been cut back in recent years to many smaller cities, such as Zamość and Sandomierz, as competition with the bus network has intensified. For these cities and many other similarly sized places, you may find yourself relying more on buses or a combination of bus and train.

## Types of Trains

Poland's rail network has several different types of trains that differ primarily by speed, cost and level of comfort.

**ExpressInterCity/EuroCity** (EIC/EC) At the top of the heap, EIC/EC trains run only between major cities, like Warsaw–Kraków and Warsaw–Gdańsk (EuroCity trains are international versions of the ExpressInter City trains). They offer the highest comfort levels, including air-conditioned cars, as well as the fewest stops and fastest speeds. They are also the most expensive. Seat reservations are mandatory and cost 16.50/12.50zł (EIC/EC), regardless of the distance travelled.

**Express** (*Pociąg ekspresowy;* Ex) Express trains are similar to EIC/EC trains and

offer comfortable seating with only six-person compartments, as well as faster speeds and fewer stops. Ex trains require a mandatory seat reservation (12.50zł).

**TLK** (*Pociąg Twoje Linie Kolejowe;* TLK) TLK trains are low-cost express trains that run between major cities at speeds approaching Ex trains, but at fares that are around 60% of Ex and EIC trains. They can be very crowded. Seat reservations are mandatory in 1st class only (6zł); 2nd-class seating is unreserved and often fills up. Bicycle access on TLK trains may be limited.

**InterRegio** (*Pociąg InterRegio;* IR) Inter-regional, or IR, trains are the standard Polish 'fast' trains running between regions, with stops at most medium-sized cities along the route. IR trains normally don't offer 1st-class seating and no seat reservations are required.

**Regio** (*Pociąg Regio;* Regio/Osob) These trains, sometimes noted on timetables as *osob,* are much slower than other trains as they stop at all stations along the way. They mostly cover shorter distances but also run on longer routes. They are less comfortable than express or fast trains and don't require reservations. They're OK for short distances, but a longer journey can be tiring.

## Train Companies

For years, the trains were administered by the state monopoly **Polskie Koleje Państwowe** (PKP; Polish State Railways; www.pkp.pl, in Polish). PKP still runs a useful website with an online timetable, but in the past decade the network has been broken up into two different operators that manage different routes and trains. The two operators are **PKP InterCity** (PKP IC; www .intercity.pl), which runs all of Poland's express trains,

including the ExpressInterCity, EuroCity and TLK trains, and **Przewozy Regionalne** (www.przewozyregionalne.pl, in Polish), which takes care of most of the other trains, including what are called 'fast' trains (usually slower than express trains). These include the popular and reasonably quick inter-regional trains and the super-slow regional trains (Regio or Osob).

Both networks cover the country and work in conjunction with each other. In many cases, you'll buy tickets for both at the same station ticket windows. The only difference is that they do not honour each other's tickets – so buyer beware.

## Timetables & Information

*Rozkład jazdy* (train timetables) are displayed in most stations, with *odjazdy* (departures) on yellow boards and *przyjazdy* (arrivals) on white.

These timetables provide a lot of useful information in addition to what times trains arrive and depart, including the type of train. EIC, EC and Ex trains are sometimes highlighted in blue print. IR trains are marked in red and the very slowest regional trains in black.

Additionally, the letter 'R' in a square indicates a train with compulsory seat reservations. There will also be some letters and/or numbers following the departure time; always check them in the key below. They usually say that the train *kursuje* (runs) or *nie kursuje* (doesn't run) at particular times. The timetables also usually indicate which *peron* (platform) the train departs from.

### ONLINE TIMETABLES

There's a useful online timetable available at http:// rozklad-pkp.pl that shows the schedule for all Polish trains. It's relatively straightforward, but

# Polish Railways

remember when inputting city names to use Polish spellings (Polish diacritical marks are not necessary). Input your desired times and dates, and whether you want to see options for express trains (in blue), fast trains (in red) and slower trains (orange).

Hitting return pulls up a range of possible trains, showing departure and arrival times as well as the duration of the journey and any train changes you might have to make.

At this stage you can check the box by the train you want to take and retrieve further information on 1st- and 2nd-class fares, along with comments such as whether bicycles can be taken onboard, whether seat reservations are mandatory etc.

## Tickets

There are several options for buying tickets. Most of the time you'll purchase them at train station ticket windows. Expect long lines at busy stations, though they tend to move quickly. Still, plan to be at the station at least half an hour before the departure time of your train and make sure you are queuing at the right ticket window.

Most ticket windows can now accept payment with a credit card, but look for the credit card sign on windows to make sure. Otherwise, it's cash only.

As cashiers – especially in smaller cities and towns – rarely speak English, the easiest way of buying a ticket is to have all the relevant details written down on a piece of paper.

If a seat reservation is compulsory on your train, you'll automatically be sold a *miejscówka* (reserved-seat ticket).

You can also board a train without a ticket if the ticket line's not moving and the departure is imminent. If you are forced to get on a train without a ticket, approach the conductor to pay a small supplement – 4zł on ordinary and fast trains, 6zł on EIC and Ex trains.

Couchettes and sleepers can be booked at most station ticket windows; it's advisable to reserve them in advance.

You can buy tickets online for PKP InterCity trains on its website (www.intercity.pl), though as of this writing the website was difficult to navigate. Alternatively, private travel companies can help book tickets online. One of the best is **Polrail Service** (www.polrail.com).

## Costs

Costs for Polish trains vary greatly depending on the type of train and the distance travelled. First class is around 50% more expensive than 2nd class.

The most expensive trains are the EIC/EC/Ex trains. Prices for these trains typically include the basic ticket price, as well as a mandatory seat reservation, and in some cases a supplement.

As a guideline, the approximate fare (including compulsory seat reservation) on an EIC train from Warsaw to Kraków is 115/153zł in 2nd/1st class for the three-hour journey. The trip from Warsaw to Gdańsk costs 123/165zł in 2nd/1st class for around six hours.

Going down the chain of train classifications, TLK trains offer express speeds at prices that are typically around a third less. The journey from Warsaw to Kraków on a TLK train costs 52/80zł in 2nd/1st class and takes around three hours. The journey from Warsaw to Gdańsk costs 59/90zł in 2nd/1st class and takes six hours.

IR trains cost about the same as TLK trains and

usually run about as quickly, though sometimes they are much slower. An IR train makes the trip from Warsaw to Kraków in around 3½ hours and costs around 45zł in 2nd class; from Warsaw to Gdańsk it's nine hours/49zł.

The following table shows a rough approximation of fares by distance for TLK and IR trains.

| DISTANCE | COST |
| --- | --- |
| 50km | 17zł |
| 100km | 25zł |
| 150km | 35zł |
| 200km | 37zł |
| 250km | 42zł |
| 300km | 48zł |
| 350km | 49zł |
| 400km | 52zł |
| 450km | 55zł |
| 500km | 60zł |

Additionally, a 2nd-class couchette sleeping four/six people costs 71/60zł, while a sleeper for two is 141zł. A 1st-class compartment on an overnight train costs an additional 270zł.

## Discounts

Students and seniors are usually entitled to some form of discount on Polish trains, but the system is complicated and seems to change year by year. Your best bet is to ask whether you qualify for a cheaper fare when you buy your ticket.

Young people under 26 can save 26% on EIC and Ex trains with a valid identity card. Note that the discount is not valid on all routes nor at all times.

People over 60 can purchase a *karta seniora* (senior concession) card for 75zł that provides a 50% discount on 1st- and 2nd-class seats on most Polish trains except PKP Express InterCity trains. A separate card costing 150zł is needed for these trains, but obviously this only makes sense if you're going to be doing a lot of rail travel.

## Train Passes

If you're planning on a lot of travel around Poland, consider buying an InterRail pass. Passes are only available to those resident in Europe for at least six months and are priced in three bands: youth (under 26), adult 2nd class, and adult 1st class. Tickets cover five/eight/10/12 day's travel within a month and range from €65 to €185. See www .interrail.net for more information.

## Train Stations

Most larger train stations have a range of facilities, including waiting rooms, snack bars, newsagents, left-luggage and toilets. The biggest stations in the major cities may also have a restaurant, a *kantor* (currency-exchange office) and a post office.

# Language

## WANT MORE?

For in-depth language information and handy phrases, check out Lonely Planet's *Polish Phrasebook*. You'll find it at **shop.lonelyplanet.com**, or you can buy Lonely Planet's iPhone phrasebooks at the Apple App Store.

Poland is linguistically one of the most homogeneous countries in Europe – more than 95% of the population has Polish as their first language. Polish belongs to the Slavic language family, with Czech and Slovak as close relatives. It has about 45 million speakers.

Polish pronunciation is pretty straightforward, as each Polish letter is generally pronounced the same way wherever it occurs.

Vowels are generally pronounced short, giving them a 'clipped' quality. Note that a is pronounced as the 'u' in 'cut', ai as in 'aisle' and ow as in 'cow'. Polish also has nasal vowels (pronounced as though you're trying to force the air through your nose), which are indicated in writing by the letters ą and ę. Depending on the letters following these vowels, they're pronounced either as an m or an n sound following the vowel, ie ą as om or on and ę as em or en.

Most Polish consonant sounds are also found in English. Note that kh is pronounced as in the Scottish *loch*, r is rolled and zh is pronounced as the 's' in 'leisure'. Consonants are sometimes grouped together without vowels between them, eg in *pszczoła* pshcho·wa – with a bit of practice they will roll off your tongue with ease. In our pronunciation guides the apostrophe (eg in *kwiecień* kfye·chen') indicates that the preceding consonant is pronounced with a soft y sound.

If you read the coloured pronunciation guides in this chapter as if they were English – and not worry too much about the intricacies of Polish pronunciation – you'll be understood just fine. Note that stressed syllables are indicated with italics.

In the following phrases the masculine/feminine, polite and informal options are included where necessary and indicated with 'm/f', 'pol' and 'inf' respectively.

## BASICS

| Hello. | *Cześć.* | cheshch |
| Goodbye. | *Do widzenia.* | do vee·dze·nya |
| Yes./No. | *Tak./Nie.* | tak/nye |
| Please. | *Proszę.* | *pro*·she |
| Thank you. | *Dziękuję.* | jyen·*koo*·ye |
| You're welcome. | *Proszę.* | *pro*·she |
| Excuse me./ Sorry. | *Przepraszam.* | pshe·*pra*·sham |

**How are you?**
| *Jak pan/pani* | yak pan/*pa*·nee |
| *się miewa?* (m/f pol) | shye *mye*·va |
| *Jak się masz?* (inf) | yak shye mash |

**Fine. And you?**
| *Dobrze.* | *dob*·zhe |
| *A pan/pani?* (m/f pol) | a pan/*pa*·nee |
| *Dobrze. A ty?* (inf) | *dob*·zhe a ti |

**What's your name?**
| *Jak się pan/pani* | yak shye *pa*·na/*pa*·nee |
| *nazywa?* (m/f pol) | na·*zi*·va |
| *Jakie się nazywasz?* (inf) | yak shye na·*zi*·vash |

**My name is ...**
| *Nazywam się ...* | na·*zi*·vam shye ... |

**Do you speak English?**
| *Czy pan/pani mówi* | chi pan/*pa*·nee *moo*·vee |
| *po angielsku?* (m/f pol) | po an·*gyel*·skoo |
| *Czy mówisz* | chi *moo*·veesh |
| *po angielsku?* (inf) | po an·*gyel*·skoo |

**I don't understand.**
| *Nie rozumiem.* | nye ro·*zoo*·myem |

## KEY PATTERNS

To get by in Polish, mix and match these simple patterns with words of your choice:

**When's (the next bus)?**
Kiedy jest (następny    kye·di yest (nas·temp·ni
autobus)?    ow·to·boos)

**Where's (the market)?**
Gdzie jest (targ)?    gjye yest (tark)

**Do you have (something cheaper)?**
Czy jest (coś    chi yest (tsosh
tańszego)?    tan'·she·go)

**I have (a reservation).**
Mam (rezerwację).    mam (re·zer·va·tsye)

**I'd like (the menu), please.**
Proszę    pro·she
(o jadłospis).    (o ya·dwo·spees)

**I'd like (to hire a car).**
Chcę (wypożyczyć    khtse (vi·po·zhi·chich
samochód).    sa·mo·khoot)

**Can I (take a photo)?**
Czy mogę (zrobić    chi mo·ge (zro·beech
zdjęcie)?    zdyen·chye)

**Could you please (write it down)?**
Proszę (to    pro·she (to
napisać).    na·pee·sach)

**Do I need (a guide)?**
Czy potrzebuję    chi po·tshe·boo·ye
(przewodnika)?    (pshe·vod·nee·ka)

**I need (assistance).**
Potrzebuję    po·tshe·boo·ye
(pomoc).    (po·mots)

## ACCOMMODATION

| Where's a ...? | Gdzie jest ...? | gjye yest ... |
|---|---|---|
| campsite | kamping | kam·peeng |
| guesthouse | pokoje gościnne | po·ko·ye gosh·chee·ne |
| hotel | hotel | ho·tel |
| youth hostel | schronisko młodzieżowe | skhro·nees·ko mwo·jye·zho·ve |

| Do you have a ... room? | Czy jest pokój ...? | chi yest po·kooy ... |
|---|---|---|
| single | jedno-osobowy | yed·no·o·so·bo·vi |
| double | z podwójnym łóżkiem | z pod·vooy·nim woozh·kyem |

| How much is it per ...? | Ile kosztuje za ...? | ee·le kosh·too·ye za ... |
|---|---|---|
| night | noc | nots |
| person | osobę | o·so·be |

| air-con | klimatyzator | klee·ma·ti·za·tor |
|---|---|---|
| bathroom | łazienka | wa·zhyen·ka |
| window | okno | ok·no |

## DIRECTIONS

**Where's a/the ...?**
Gdzie jest ...?    gjye yest ...

**What's the address?**
Jaki jest adres?    ya·kee yest ad·res

**Could you please write it down?**
Proszę to napisać.    pro·she to na·pee·sach

**Can you show me (on the map)?**
Czy może pan/pani    chi mo·zhe pan/pa·nee
mi pokazać    mee po·ka·zach
(na mapie)? (m/f)    (na ma·pye)

| at the corner/ traffic lights | na rogu/ światłach | na ro·goo/ shfyat·wakh |
|---|---|---|
| behind ... | za ... | za ... |
| in front of ... | przed ... | pshet ... |
| left | lewo | le·vo |
| near ... | koło ... | ko·wo ... |
| next to ... | obok ... | o·bok ... |
| opposite ... | naprze-ciwko ... | nap·she-cheef·ko ... |
| straight ahead | na wprost | na fprost |
| right | prawo | pra·vo |

## EATING & DRINKING

| I'd like to reserve a table for ... | Chciałem/am zarezerwować stolik ... (m/f) | khchow·em/am za·re·zer·vo·vach sto·leek ... |
|---|---|---|
| (two) people | dla (dwóch) osób | dla (dvookh) o·soob |
| (eight) o'clock | na (ósmą) | na (oos·mom) |

| I don't eat ... | Nie jadam ... | nye ya·dam ... |
|---|---|---|
| eggs | jajek | yai·ek |
| fish | ryb | rib |
| (red) meat | (czerwonego) mięsa | (cher·vo·ne·go) myen·sa |
| poultry | drobiu | dro·byoo |

**What would you recommend?**
Co by pan/pani    tso bi pan/pa·nee
polecił/poleciła? (m/f)    po·le·cheew/po·le·chee·wa

**What's in that dish?**
Co jest w tym daniu?    tso yest v tim da·nyoo

**I'd like the menu, please.**
Proszę o jadłospis.    pro·she o ya·dwo·spees

**That was delicious!**
To było pyszne.    to bi·wo pish·ne

**Cheers!**
*Na zdrowie!* na zdro·vye

**Please bring the bill.**
*Proszę o rachunek.* pro·she o ra·khoo·nek

## Key Words

| | | |
|---|---|---|
| bottle | *butelka* | boo·*tel*·ka |
| bowl | *miska* | mee·ska |
| breakfast | *śniadanie* | shnya·*da*·nye |
| cold | *zimny* | *zheem*·ni |
| cup | *filiżanka* | fee·lee·*zhan*·ka |
| dinner | *kolacja* | ko·*la*·tsya |
| fork | *widelec* | vee·de·lets |
| glass | *szklanka* | *shklan*·ka |
| grocery | *sklep spożywczy* | sklep spo·*zhiv*·chi |
| hot | *gorący* | go·*ron*·tsi |
| knife | *nóż* | noosh |
| lunch | *obiad* | o·byad |
| market | *rynek* | *ri*·nek |
| menu | *jadłospis* | ya·*dwo*·spees |
| plate | *talerz* | ta·lesh |
| restaurant | *restauracja* | res·tow·*rats*·ya |
| spoon | *łyżka* | *wish*·ka |
| vegetarian | *wegetariański* | ve·ge·ta·*ryan*'·skee |
| with ... | *z ...* | z ... |
| without ... | *bez ...* | bes ... |

## Meat & Fish

| | | |
|---|---|---|
| beef | *wołowina* | vo·wo·*vee*·na |
| chicken | *kurczak* | *koor*·chak |
| cod | *dorsz* | dorsh |
| duck | *kaczka* | *kach*·ka |
| fish | *ryba* | *ri*·ba |
| herring | *śledź* | shlej |
| lamb | *jagnięcina* | yag·nyen·*chee*·na |
| lobster | *homar* | *ho*·mar |
| mackerel | *makrela* | ma·*kre*·la |
| meat | *mięso* | *myen*·so |
| mussels | *małże* | *mow*·zhe |
| oysters | *ostrygi* | os·*tri*·gee |
| prawns | *krewetki* | kre·*vet*·kee |
| pork | *wieprzowina* | vyep·sho·*vee*·na |
| salmon | *łosoś* | *wo*·sosh |
| seafood | *owoce morza* | o·*vo*·tse mo·zha |
| trout | *pstrąg* | pstrong |
| tuna | *tuńczyk* | *toon*'·chik |
| turkey | *indyk* | *een*·dik |
| veal | *cielęcina* | chye·len·*chee*·na |

## Fruit & Vegetables

| | | |
|---|---|---|
| apple | *jabłko* | *yabw*·ko |
| apricot | *morela* | mo·*re*·la |
| bean | *fasola* | fa·*so*·la |
| cabbage | *kapusta* | ka·*poos*·ta |
| carrot | *marchewka* | mar·*khef*·ka |
| cauliflower | *kalafior* | ka·*la*·fyor |
| cherry | *czereśnia* | che·*resh*·nya |
| cucumber | *ogórek* | o·*goo*·rek |
| fruit | *owoc* | o·vots |
| grapes | *winogrona* | vee·no·*gro*·na |
| lemon | *cytryna* | tsi·*tri*·na |
| lentil | *soczewica* | so·che·*vee*·tsa |
| mushroom | *grzyb* | gzhib |
| nut | *orzech* | o·zhekh |
| onion | *cebula* | tse·*boo*·la |
| orange | *pomarańcza* | po·ma·*ran*'·cha |
| peach | *brzoskwinia* | bzhosk·*fee*·nya |
| pear | *gruszka* | *groosh*·ka |
| pepper (bell) | *papryka* | pa·*pri*·ka |
| plum | *śliwka* | *shleef*·ka |
| potato | *ziemniak* | *zhyem*·nyak |
| strawberry | *truskawka* | troos·*kaf*·ka |
| tomato | *pomidor* | po·*mee*·dor |
| vegetable | *warzywo* | va·*zhi*·vo |
| watermelon | *arbuz* | *ar*·boos |

## Other

| | | |
|---|---|---|
| bread | *chleb* | khlep |
| cheese | *ser* | ser |
| egg | *jajko* | *yai*·ko |
| honey | *miód* | myood |
| noodles | *makaron* | ma·*ka*·ron |
| oil | *olej* | *o*·ley |
| pasta | *makaron* | ma·*ka*·ron |

| Signs | |
|---|---|
| **Wejście** | Entrance |
| **Wyjście** | Exit |
| **Otwarte** | Open |
| **Zamknięte** | Closed |
| **Informacja** | Information |
| **Wzbroniony** | Prohibited |
| **Toalety** | Toilets |
| **Panowie** | Men |
| **Panie** | Women |

| pepper | pieprz | pyepsh |
|--------|--------|--------|
| rice | ryż | rizh |
| salt | sól | sool |
| sugar | cukier | tsoo·kyer |
| vinegar | ocet | o·tset |

## Drinks

| beer | piwo | pee·vo |
|------|------|--------|
| coffee | kawa | ka·va |
| (orange) juice | sok (pomarańczowy) | sok (po·ma·ran'·cho·vi) |
| milk | mleko | mle·ko |
| red wine | wino czerwone | vee·no cher·vo·ne |
| soft drink | napój | na·pooy |
| tea | herbata | her·ba·ta |
| (mineral) water | woda (mineralna) | vo·da (mee·ne·ral·na) |
| white wine | wino białe | vee·no bya·we |

## EMERGENCIES

| Help! | Na pomoc! | na po·mots |
|-------|-----------|-----------|
| Go away! | Odejdź! | o·deyj |

**Call the police!**
Zadzwoń po policję!　　zad·zvon' po po·lee·tsye

**Call a doctor!**
Zadzwoń po lekarza!　　zad·zvon' po le·ka·zha

**There's been an accident.**
Tam był wypadek.　　tam biw vi·pa·dek

**I'm lost.**
Zgubiłem/am się. (m/f)　　zgoo·bee·wem/wam shye

**Where are the toilets?**
Gdzie są toalety?　　gjye som to·a·le·ti

**I'm ill.**
Jestem chory/a. (m/f)　　yes·tem kho·ri/ra

**It hurts here.**
Tutaj boli.　　too·tai bo·lee

**I'm allergic to (antibiotics).**
Mam alergię na (antybiotyki).　　mam a·ler·gye na (an·ti·byo·ti·kee)

### Question Words

| What? | Co? | tso |
|-------|-----|-----|
| When? | Kiedy? | kye·di |
| Where? | Gdzie? | gjye |
| Which? | Który/a/e? (m/f/n) | ktoo·ri/ra/re |
| Who? | Kto? | kto |
| Why? | Dlaczego? | dla·che·go |

## SHOPPING & SERVICES

**I'd like to buy ...**
Chcę kupić ...　　khtse koo·peech ...

**I'm just looking.**
Tylko oglądam.　　til·ko o·glon·dam

**Can I look at it?**
Czy mogę to zobaczyć?　　chi mo·ge to zo·ba·chich

**How much is it?**
Ile to kosztuje?　　ee·le to kosh·too·ye

**That's too expensive.**
To jest za drogie.　　to yest za dro·gye

**Can you lower the price?**
Czy może pan/pani obniżyć cenę? (m/f)　　chi mo·zhe pan/pa·nee ob·nee·zhich tse·ne

**There's a mistake in the bill.**
Na czeku jest pomyłka.　　na che·koo yest po·miw·ka

| ATM | bankomat | ban·ko·mat |
|-----|----------|-----------|
| credit card | karta kredytowa | kar·ta kre·di·to·va |
| internet cafe | kawiarnia internetowa | ka·vyar·nya een·ter·ne·to·va |
| mobile/cell phone | telefon komórkowy | te·le·fon ko·moor·ko·vi |
| post office | urząd pocztowy | oo·zhond poch·to·vi |
| tourist office | biuro turystyczne | byoo·ro too·ris·tich·ne |

## TIME & DATES

**What time is it?**
Która jest godzina?　　ktoo·ra yest go·jee·na

**It's one o'clock.**
Pierwsza.　　pyerf·sha

**Half past (10).**
Wpół do (jedenastej). (lit: half to 11)　　fpoow do (ye·de·nas·tey)

| morning | rano | ra·no |
|---------|------|-------|
| afternoon | popołudnie | po·po·wood·nye |
| evening | wieczór | vye·choor |
| yesterday | wczoraj | fcho·rai |
| today | dziś/dzisiaj | jeesh/jee·shai |
| tomorrow | jutro | yoo·tro |
| Monday | poniedziałek | po·nye·jya·wek |
| Tuesday | wtorek | fto·rek |
| Wednesday | środa | shro·da |
| Thursday | czwartek | chfar·tek |
| Friday | piątek | pyon·tek |
| Saturday | sobota | so·bo·ta |
| Sunday | niedziela | nye·jye·la |

| January | styczeń | sti·chen' |
| February | luty | loo·ti |
| March | marzec | ma·zhets |
| April | kwiecień | kfye·chyen' |
| May | maj | mai |
| June | czerwiec | cher·vyets |
| July | lipiec | lee·pyets |
| August | sierpień | shyer·pyen' |
| September | wrzesień | vzhe·shyen' |
| October | październik | pazh·jyer·neek |
| November | listopad | lees·to·pat |
| December | grudzień | groo·jyen' |

## TRANSPORT

### Public Transport

| When's the ... (bus)? | Kiedy jest ... (autobus)? | kye·di yest ... (ow·to·boos) |
| first | pierwszy | pyerf·shi |
| last | ostatni | os·tat·nee |
| next | następny | nas·temp·ni |

| boat | statek | sta·tek |
| bus | autobus | ow·to·boos |
| plane | samolot | sa·mo·lot |
| taxi | taksówka | tak·soof·ka |
| ticket office | kasa biletowa | ka·sa bee·le·to·va |
| timetable | rozkład jazdy | ros·kwad yaz·di |
| train | pociąg | po·chonk |

| A ... ticket (to Katowice). | Proszę bilet ... (do Katowic). | pro·she bee·let ... (do ka·to·veets) |
| one-way | w jedną stronę | v yed·nom stro·ne |
| return | powrotny | po·vro·tni |

**What time does it get to ...?**
*O której godzinie przyjeżdża do ...?*  o ktoo·rey go·jee·nye pshi·yezh·ja do ...

**Does it stop at ...?**
*Czy się zatrzymuje w...?*  chi shye za·tshi·moo·ye v ...

**Please tell me when we get to ...**
*Proszę mi powiedzieć gdy dojedziemy do ...*  pro·she mee po·vye·jyech gdi do·ye·jye·mi do ...

**Please take me to (this address).**
*Proszę mnie zawieźć pod (ten adres).*  pro·she mnye za·vyeshch pod (ten ad·res)

**Please stop here.**
*Proszę się tu zatrzymać.*  pro·she shye too za·tshi·mach

#### Numbers

| 1 | jeden | ye·den |
| 2 | dwa | dva |
| 3 | trzy | tshi |
| 4 | cztery | chte·ri |
| 5 | pięć | pyench |
| 6 | sześć | sheshch |
| 7 | siedem | shye·dem |
| 8 | osiem | o·shyem |
| 9 | dziewięć | jye·vyench |
| 10 | dziesięć | jye·shench |
| 20 | dwadzieścia | dva·jyesh·chya |
| 30 | trzydzieści | tshi·jyesh·chee |
| 40 | czterdzieści | chter·jyesh·chee |
| 50 | pięćdziesiąt | pyen·jye·shont |
| 60 | sześćdziesiąt | shesh·jye·shont |
| 70 | siedemdziesiąt | shye·dem·jye·shont |
| 80 | osiemdziesiąt | o·shem·jye·shont |
| 90 | dziewięćdziesiąt | jye·vyen·jye·shont |
| 100 | sto | sto |
| 1000 | tysiąc | ti·shonts |

### Driving & Cycling

| I'd like to hire a ... | Chcę wypożyczyć ... | khtse vi·po·zhi·chich ... |
| 4WD | samochód terenowy | sa·mo·khoot te·re·no·vi |
| bicycle | rower | ro·ver |
| car | samochód | sa·mo·khoot |
| motorbike | motocykl | mo·to·tsikl |

**Is this the road to ...?**
*Czy to jest droga do ...?*  chi to yest dro·ga do ...

**Where's a service station?**
*Gdzie jest stacja benzynowa?*  gjye yest sta·tsya ben·zi·no·va

**How long can I park here?**
*Jak długo można tu parkować?*  yak dwoo·go mozh·na too par·ko·vach

**I need a mechanic.**
*Potrzebuję mechanika.*  po·tshe·boo·ye me·kha·nee·ka

**I've had an accident.**
*Miałem/am wypadek. (m/f)*  myow·em/am vi·pa·dek

| diesel | diesel | dee·zel |
| leaded | ołowiowa | o·wo·vyo·va |
| petrol/gas | benzyna | ben·zi·na |
| unleaded | bezołowiowa | bes·o·wo·vyo·va |

The following is a list of terms and abbreviations you're likely to come across in your travels through Poland. For other food and drink terms, see p36.

**aleja or Aleje** – avenue, main city street; abbreviated to al in addresses and on maps
**apteka** – pharmacy

**bankomat** – ATM
**bar mleczny** – milk bar; a sort of basic self-service soup kitchen that serves very cheap, mostly vegetarian dishes
**bazylika** – basilica
**bez łazienki** – room without bathroom
**biblioteka** – library
**bilet** – ticket
**biuro turystyki** – travel agency
**biuro zakwaterowania** – office that arranges private accommodation
**brama** – gate
**britzka** – horse-drawn cart

**Cepelia** – a network of shops that sell artefacts made by local artisans
**cerkiew (cerkwie)** – Orthodox or Uniat church(es)
**cukiernia** – cake shop

**Desa** – chain of old art and antique sellers
**dom kultury** – cultural centre
**dom wycieczkowy** – term applied to PTTK-run hostels; also called *dom turysty*
**domy wczasowe** – workers' holiday homes
**dwór** – mansion

**góra** – mountain
**gospoda** – inn, tavern, restaurant
**grosz** – unit of Polish currency, abbreviated to gr; plural groszy; see also *złoty*

**jaskinia** – cave

**kancelaria kościelna** – church office
**kantor(s)** – private currency-exchange office(s)
**kawiarnia** – cafe
**kemping** – camping
**kino** – cinema
**kolegiata** – collegiate church
**komórka** – literally, 'cell'; commonly used for cellular (mobile) phone
**kościół** – church
**księgarnia** – bookshop
**kwatery agroturystyczne** – agrotourist accommodation
**kwatery prywatne** – rooms for rent in private houses

**miejscówka** – reserved-seat ticket
**muzeum** – museum

**na zdrowie!** – cheers!; literally, 'to the health'
**noclegi** – accommodation

**odjazdy** – departures (on transport timetables)
**ostrów** – island
**otwarte** – open

**park narodowy** – national park
**parking strzeżony** – guarded car park
**pchać** – pull (on door)
**pensjonat(y)** – pension or private guesthouse(s)
**peron** – railway platform
**piekarnia** – bakery
**PKS** – Państwowa Komunikacja Samochodowa; former state-run company that runs most of Poland's bus transport
**Plac** – Sq
**poczta** – post office
**poczta główna** – main post office
**pokój 1-osobowy** – single room
**pokój 2-osobowy** – double room
**przechowalnia bagażu** – left-luggage room

**przez** – via, en route (on transport timetables)
**przyjazdy** – arrivals (on transport timetables)
**PTSM** – Polskie Towarzystwo Schronisk Młodzieżowych; Polish Youth Hostel Association
**PTTK** – Polskie Towarzystwo Turystyczno-Krajoznawcze; Polish Tourist & Countryside Association

**rachunek** – bill or check
**riksza** – bicycle rickshaws
**rozkład jazdy** – transport timetable
**Rynek** – Town/Market Sq

**sanktuarium** – church (usually pilgrimage site)
**schronisko górskie** – mountain hostel, providing basic accommodation and meals, usually run by the PTTK
**schronisko młodzieżowe** – youth hostel
**Sejm** – the lower house of parliament
**skansen** – open-air ethnographic museum
**sklep** – shop
**stanica wodna** – waterside hostel, usually with boats, kayaks and other water-related facilities
**stare miasto** – old town/city
**Stary Rynek** – Old Town/Market Sq
**stołówka** – canteen; restaurant or cafeteria of a holiday home, workplace, hostel etc
**święty/a (m/f)** – saint; abbreviated to Św
**szopka** – Nativity scene

**teatr** – theatre
**toalety** – toilets

**ulica** – street; abbreviated to ul in addresses (and placed before the street name); usually omitted on maps
**Uniat** – Eastern-rite Catholics

**wódka** – vodka; the number one Polish spirit

**z łazienką** – room with bathroom
**zajazd** – inn (sometimes restaurant)
**zamek** – castle
**zdrój** – spa
**złoty** – unit of Polish currency; abbreviated to zł; divided into 100 units called grosz

## Food Glossary

**bażant** – pheasant
**befsztyk** – beef steak
**befsztyk tatarski** – raw minced beef accompanied by chopped onion, raw egg yolk and often chopped dill, cucumber and anchovies
**botwinka** – soup made from the stems and leaves of baby beetroots; often includes a hard-boiled egg
**bryzol** – grilled beef (loin) steak
**budyń** – milk pudding

**chłodnik** – chilled beetroot soup with sour cream and fresh vegetables; served in summer only
**ciastko** – pastry, cake
**ćwikła z chrzanem** – boiled and grated beetroot with horseradish

**dorsz** – cod
**dzik** – wild boar

**gęś** – goose
**gołąbki** – cabbage leaves stuffed with minced beef and rice, sometimes also with mushrooms
**grochówka** – pea soup, sometimes served *z grzankami* (with croutons)

**indyk** – turkey

**kaczka** – duck
**kapuśniak** – sauerkraut

and cabbage soup with potatoes
**karp** – carp
**knedle ze śliwkami** – dumplings stuffed with plums
**kopytka** – Polish 'gnocchi'; noodles made from flour and boiled potatoes
**kotlet schabowy** – a fried pork cutlet coated in breadcrumbs, flour and egg, found on nearly every Polish menu
**krupnik** – thick barley soup containing a variety of vegetables and small chunks of meat
**kurczak** – chicken

**leniwe pierogi** – boiled noodles served with cottage cheese
**łosoś wędzony** – smoked salmon

**melba** – ice cream with fruit and whipped cream
**mizeria ze śmietaną** – sliced fresh cucumber in sour cream

**naleśniki** – crepes; fried pancakes, most commonly *z serem* (with cottage cheese), *z owocami* (with fruit) or *z dżemem* (with jam), and served with sour cream and sugar

**pieczeń cielęca** – roast veal
**pieczeń wieprzowa** – roast pork
**pieczeń wołowa** – roast beef
**pieczeń z dzika** – roast wild boar
**placki ziemniaczane** – fried pancakes made from grated raw potato, egg and flour; served *ze śmietaną* (with sour cream) or *z cukrem* (with sugar)
**polędwica po angielsku** – English-style beef; roast fillet of beef
**pstrąg** – trout
**pyzy** – ball-shaped steamed

dumplings made of potato flour

**rosół** – beef or chicken (*z wołowiny/z kury*) bouillon, usually served *z makaronem* (with noodles)
**rumsztyk** – rump steak
**ryż z jabłkami** – rice with apples

**sałatka jarzynowa** – 'vegetable salad'; cooked vegetables in mayonnaise, commonly known as Russian salad
**sałatka z pomidorów** – tomato salad, often served with onion
**sarna** – deer, venison
**schab pieczony** – roast loin of pork seasoned with prunes and herbs
**serem i z makiem** – dumplings with cottage cheese/poppy seeds
**śledź w oleju** – herring in oil with chopped onion
**śledź w śmietanie** – herring in sour cream
**stek** – steak
**surówka z kapusty kiszonej** – sauerkraut, sometimes served with apple and onion
**sztuka mięsa** – boiled beef with horseradish

**zając** – hare
**zrazy zawijane** – stewed beef rolls stuffed with mushrooms and/or bacon and served in a sour-cream sauce
**zupa grzybowa** – mushroom soup
**zupa jarzynowa** – vegetable soup
**zupa ogórkowa** – cucumber soup, usually with potatoes and other vegetables
**zupa pomidorowa** – tomato soup, usually served either *z makaronem* (with noodles) or *z ryżem* (with rice)
**zupa szczawiowa** – sorrel soup, usually served with hard-boiled egg

# behind the scenes

## SEND US YOUR FEEDBACK

We love to hear from travellers – your comments keep us on our toes and help make our books better. Our well-travelled team reads every word on what you loved or loathed about this book. Although we cannot reply individually to postal submissions, we always guarantee that your feedback goes straight to the appropriate authors, in time for the next edition. Each person who sends us information is thanked in the next edition – and the most useful submissions are rewarded with a free book.

Visit **lonelyplanet.com/contact** to submit your updates and suggestions or to ask for help. Our award-winning website also features inspirational travel stories, news and discussions.

Note: We may edit, reproduce and incorporate your comments in Lonely Planet products such as guidebooks, websites and digital products, so let us know if you don't want your comments reproduced or your name acknowledged. For a copy of our privacy policy visit lonelyplanet.com/privacy.

## OUR READERS

**Many thanks to the travellers who used the last edition and wrote to us with helpful hints, useful advice and interesting anecdotes:**

**A** Frederick Abrams, Aitor Alejos, Phil & Hilary André **B** Reinier Bakels, Duncan Bell, Hans Bendz, Alain Bojarski, Adrian Borowiec, Marta Borowski, Andreas Boström, Beeleke Bredero **C** Adam Carr **D** Kasha Dubinska, Jon Durham **F** Katy Ferrar, Robyn Floyd, **G** K Gaultois, Giorgio Genova, Godfried Geudens **H** Benjamin Himmler, Julie Hirschler, Hadrian Howarth **J** Geert Jennes, Ralf Jeutter, Hannah Jones, Andrew Joseph **K** Bart Komorowski, Peter Kosmider-Jones, Andreas Krone, Ela Kuczmarski, Pawel Kwiatek **L** Pauline Lockstone **M** Jan McKeogh, Thomas Merrett, Mrs Mott **N** Adam Nicoll, Jason Ning **O** Marcia Orlowski **P** Andrew Page, Kim Prince **R** Michael Raffaele, Jackie Reddy, Joanna Rosinska, David Ross, Barbara Rowe **S** Marcin Sadurski, Valerie Schnee, Monica Shelley, Lisel Sjögren, Steven Spayd, John Stabb, Wilbert Staring **T** Mario Toups **U** Joanna Urbanek **V** Marieke Van Autreve, Maurits Van Der Hoofd, Ines Vermont, Meg Viezbicke, Ross Vincent **W** Clare Walker, Igor Winiarczyk, Szymon Wisniewski **Z** Cheri Zangmeister, Jacek Zoch.

## AUTHOR THANKS

### Mark Baker

My thanks go out to the friendly people at Poland's tourist information offices, particularly the very helpful folks in the Warsaw Old Town office. My friend Letitia Rydjeski, of Polish origin and an unabashed fan of all things Poland, is always willing to read over my notes and suggest corrections. Thanks too to my co-authors, Tim Richards and Marc Di Duca, for making this edition a smooth ride.

### Marc Di Duca

A huge *dziękuję* to my Kiev parents-in-law, Mykola and Vira, for taking care of my son Taras while I was travelling. Huge thanks to tourist information staff, including Szimon in Toruń, Aneta in Sopot, Włodzimierz in Ustka, Joanna in Kołobrzeg, Szimon in Szczecin, Michał in Grudziądz, Kinga in Malbork and Sylvia in Kętrzyn. Thanks to Maciej for helping me in Łeba. Lastly, to my wife Tanya – thank you for your support during my travels and write-up. You were great.

### Tim Richards

As always, I'm indebted to the helpful staff at Poland's tourist offices. I also appreciate the national train company PKP, whose services save me from having to travel too often by the dreaded PKS bus. Fond regards to my Polish friends – particularly Ewa, Magda and Andrzej – for their companionship and insights into their mother country. Thanks also to the members of the English Language Club in Kraków, who supplied both friendly conversation and hot tips on good new restaurants.

Cover photograph: Statues at Książ Castle near Wałbrzych, Witold Skrypczak/Lonely Planet Images

Many of the images in this guide are available for licensing from Lonely Planet Images: www.lonelyplanetimages.com.

## ACKNOWLEDGMENTS

Climate map data adapted from Peel MC, Finlayson BL & McMahon TA (2007) 'Updated World Map of the Köppen-Geiger Climate Classification', *Hydrology and Earth System Sciences*, 11, 163344.

## THIS BOOK

This is the 7th edition of Lonely Planet's *Poland* guidebook and was researched and written by Mark Baker, Marc Di Duca and Tim Richards. The 6th edition was written by Tim Richards, Neal Bedford, Steve Fallon and Marika McAdam and the 5th edition by Neil Wilson, Tom Parkinson and Richard Watkins. The first four editions were written by Krzysztof Dydyński. This guidebook was commissioned in Lonely Planet's London office, laid out by Cambridge Publishing Management, UK, and produced by the following:

**Commissioning Editor** Dora Whitaker

**Coordinating Editors** Michelle Bennett, Catherine Burch

**Coordinating Cartographers** Karusha Ganga, Andy Rojas, Peter Shields

**Coordinating Layout Designer** Paul Queripel

**Managing Editors** Kirsten Rawlings, Tasmin Waby McNaughtan

**Senior Editors** Susan Paterson, Angela Tinson

**Managing Cartographers** Anita Banh, Amanda Sierp

**Managing Layout Designer** Jane Hart

**Assisting Editors** Elisa Arduca, Carolyn Bain, Hazel Bosworth, Adrienne Costanzo, Andrea Dobbin, Michala Green, Kathryn Glendenning, Anne Mulvaney, Ceinwen Sinclair

**Assisting Cartographers** Karen Grant, Alex Leung

**Assisting Layout Designer** Julie Crane

**Cover Research** Louise Byrnes

**Internal Image Research** Rebecca Skinner

**Indexer** Amanda Jones

**Language Content** Annelies Mertens, Branislava Vladisavljevic

**Thanks to** Shahara Ahmed, Helen Christinis, Erin Corrigan, Ryan Evans, Victoria Harrison, Paul Iacono, Yvonne Kirk, Catherine Naghten, Trent Paton, Gerard Walker

**449**

# how to use this book

**These symbols will help you find the listings you want:**

| | | |
|---|---|---|
| ⊙ Sights | ☞ Tours | 🍷 Drinking |
| 🏄 Beaches | ✹ Festivals & Events | ☆ Entertainment |
| 🏃 Activities | 🛏 Sleeping | 🛍 Shopping |
| 🍴 Courses | ✕ Eating | ⓘ Information/Transport |

**These symbols give you the vital information for each listing:**

| | | |
|---|---|---|
| ☎ Telephone Numbers | 📶 Wi-Fi Access | 🚌 Bus |
| ⊙ Opening Hours | 🏊 Swimming Pool | ⛴ Ferry |
| Ⓟ Parking | 🌿 Vegetarian Selection | Ⓜ Metro |
| ⊖ Nonsmoking | 📖 English-Language Menu | Ⓢ Subway |
| ❄ Air-Conditioning | 👪 Family-Friendly | 🚊 Tram |
| @ Internet Access | 🐾 Pet-Friendly | 🚆 Train |

**Look out for these icons:**

| TOP CHOICE | Our author's recommendation |
| FREE | No payment required |
| 🌿 | A green or sustainable option |

*Our authors have nominated these places as demonstrating a strong commitment to sustainability – for example by supporting local communities and producers, operating in an environmentally friendly way, or supporting conservation projects.*

**Reviews are organised by author preference.**

---

## Map Legend

### Sights
- 🏖 Beach
- 🛕 Buddhist
- 🏰 Castle
- ✝ Christian
- 🕉 Hindu
- ☪ Islamic
- ✡ Jewish
- 🗽 Monument
- 🏛 Museum/Gallery
- 🏚 Ruin
- 🍷 Winery/Vineyard
- 🐘 Zoo
- ⊙ Other Sight

### Activities, Courses & Tours
- 🤿 Diving/Snorkelling
- 🛶 Canoeing/Kayaking
- ⛷ Skiing
- 🏄 Surfing
- 🏊 Swimming/Pool
- 🚶 Walking
- 🏄 Windsurfing
- ⊕ Other Activity/Course/Tour

### Sleeping
- 🛏 Sleeping
- ⛺ Camping

### Eating
- ✕ Eating

### Drinking
- ☕ Drinking
- ☕ Cafe

### Entertainment
- 🎭 Entertainment

### Shopping
- 🛍 Shopping

### Information
- ✉ Post Office
- ⓘ Tourist Information

### Transport
- ✈ Airport
- ⊗ Border Crossing
- 🚌 Bus
- ⊕ Cable Car/Funicular
- 🚲 Cycling
- ⛴ Ferry
- Ⓜ Metro
- 🚝 Monorail
- Ⓟ Parking
- Ⓢ S-Bahn
- 🚕 Taxi
- 🚆 Train/Railway
- 🚊 Tram
- ⊖ Tube Station
- Ⓤ U-Bahn
- • Other Transport

### Routes
- Tollway
- Freeway
- Primary
- Secondary
- Tertiary
- Lane
- Unsealed Road
- Plaza/Mall
- Steps
- )=( Tunnel
- Pedestrian Overpass
- Walking Tour
- Walking Tour Detour
- Path

### Boundaries
- International
- State/Province
- Disputed
- Regional/Suburb
- Marine Park
- Cliff
- Wall

### Population
- ✪ Capital (National)
- ◉ Capital (State/Province)
- ● City/Large Town
- ● Town/Village

### Geographic
- 🏠 Hut/Shelter
- 🗼 Lighthouse
- 🔭 Lookout
- ▲ Mountain/Volcano
- 🌴 Oasis
- 🌳 Park
- )( Pass
- 🏕 Picnic Area
- 💧 Waterfall

### Hydrography
- River/Creek
- Intermittent River
- Swamp/Mangrove
- Reef
- Canal
- Water
- Dry/Salt/Intermittent Lake
- Glacier

### Areas
- Beach/Desert
- +++ Cemetery (Christian)
- ××× Cemetery (Other)
- Park/Forest
- Sportsground
- Sight (Building)
- Top Sight (Building)

## OUR STORY

NOV 2 6 2012

A beat-up old car, a few dollars in the pocket and a sense of adventure. In 1972 that's all Tony and Maureen Wheeler needed for the trip of a lifetime – across Europe and Asia overland to Australia. It took several months, and at the end – broke but inspired – they sat at their kitchen table writing and stapling together their first travel guide, *Across Asia on the Cheap*. Within a week they'd sold 1500 copies. Lonely Planet was born.

Today, Lonely Planet has offices in Melbourne, London and Oakland, with more than 600 staff and writers. We share Tony's belief that 'a great guidebook should do three things: inform, educate and amuse'.

# OUR WRITERS

### Mark Baker

Coordinating Author; Warsaw, Mazovia & Podlasie, Malopolska, Carpathian Mountains Mark first visited Poland in the mid-1980s. At the time he was a grad student in Eastern European studies at Columbia University in New York, and he was smitten by the friendliness of the people, the bizarre politics, the history and the vodka. Now permanently based in Prague and working as a freelance travel writer, he remains enchanted with the country and has the chance to visit and write about Poland frequently. In addition to Lonely Planet *Poland*, Mark is co-author of the Lonely Planet's *Prague* and *Romania* guides. When he's not on the road writing, he teaches Central European History at Anglo-American University in Prague.

Read more about Mark at:
lonelyplanet.com/members/markbaker

### Marc Di Duca

Gdańsk & Pomerania, Warmia & Masuria Marc has spent nigh on 20 years criss-crossing the former communist world, the last seven of them as a travel guide author. A respected writer on Central and Eastern Europe, Marc has penned two guides to Poland for major UK publishers and a pocket guide to Gdańsk, a city that remains one of his favourite European stop-offs. Research for this edition of Lonely Planet's *Poland* involved munching through perilous amounts of *zapiekanki* ('Polish pizza') in dodgy milk bars, stalking Copernicus 500km along the Baltic coast and successfully buying a train ticket to Szczecin. *Poland* is Marc's 16th Lonely Planet guide.

Read more about Marc at:
lonelyplanet.com/members/madidu

### Tim Richards

Kraków, Silesia, Wielkopolska Tim taught English in Kraków in the 1990s and was fascinated by the massive post-communism transition affecting every aspect of Polish life, and by remnants of the communist era. He's returned to Poland repeatedly for Lonely Planet, deepening his relationship with this beautiful complex country. When he's not on the road for Lonely Planet, Tim is a freelance journalist in Melbourne, Australia, writing mostly about travel and the arts. In 2011 he released an e-book collection of his newspaper and magazine articles about Poland, titled *We Have Here the Homicide*. You can see more of his writing at www.iwriter.com.au.

Read more about Tim at:
lonelyplanet.com/members/parallax42

**Published by Lonely Planet Publications Pty Ltd**
ABN 36 005 607 983
7th edition – April 2012
ISBN 978 1 74179 322 2
© Lonely Planet 2012  Photographs © as indicated 2012
10 9 8 7 6 5 4 3 2 1
Printed in China